MORNING STAR OVER AMERICA

The New Millennium
AD 2000-2002

Anthology of Messages
The Blessed Virgin Mary

William L. Roth, Jr.
Timothy Parsons-Heather

The Morning Star of Our Lord, Inc. is a nonprofit, tax-exempt, 501(c)(3) religious and charitable organization which is incorporated under the Laws of the State of Illinois. It has been established for the dissemination of various apologetic works in defense of the Truth of the Holy Gospel of Christianity. It is the intrinsic role of this Corporation to provide pastoral consolation to those lacking in faith, the infirm, homebound, incarcerated, deprived, dejected and those who are otherwise suffering-humanity for the sake of the Glory of the Kingdom of Jesus Christ. All proceeds from this book are being donated to other charitable causes to help feed, clothe and house the poor, and for the reproduction of various spiritual manuscripts for distribution on every continent of the world. If anyone would like to contribute to this worthy cause, you may do so through the following website address.

The Morning Star of Our Lord, Inc.
Springfield, Illinois
www.ImmaculateMary.org

Published by The Morning Star of Our Lord, Incorporated
Used with permission.
Copyright © 2007
William L. Roth, Jr. & Timothy Parsons-Heather
All rights reserved.

Publish date: August 15, 2007
                Feast of the Assumption of Our Lady

ISBN: 0-9671587-5-3
Printed in the United States of America

The Morning Star of Our Lord, Inc. has published nine works to date by William L. Roth Jr. and Timothy Parsons-Heather, the initial being their sixteen hundred page, two volume diary which meticulously chronicles the opening days of the miraculous intercession of the Most Blessed Virgin Mary in their lives. These men are under ecclesial obedience to His Excellency, Bishop George J. Lucas, of the Diocese of Springfield in Illinois who reserves final judgement concerning their disposition.

*Dedicated
to
America's Unborn Innocents*

Morning Star Over America

The New Millennium
AD 2000-2002

Table of Contents

Prologue   By William L. Roth Jr.

AD 2000 1

AD 2001 115

AD 2002 265

The Lord said to Moses, "How long will these people treat me with contempt? How long will they refuse to believe in me, in spite of all the miraculous signs I have performed among them?"

                                        Numbers 14:11

Prologue
by
William L. Roth, Jr.

When compiling these beatific message-texts from the Most Blessed Virgin Mary during the dawning hours of this new millennium, I pondered what additional information might be needed to explain their context, answer individual curiosities, benign and otherwise, and provide better perspective for each reader as to how the divine intercession of the Queen of Heaven occurs to my brother and me, as opposed to simply allowing each person to imagine its dynamics, however inaccurate that speculation may be. Many facts and allusions describing the divine relationship we share with our Heavenly Mother are contained in our initial two-volume Diary, *Morning Star Over America*. It is a composition wherein we have meticulously chronicled the opening days of this miraculous charism from 1991-1996. Although there has never been an intentional effort to date where we have attempted to delineate any deeper nuances of these experiences, it is imperative for all to realize that any further descriptions that may be given only pertain to our present circumstances, as many alterations of our ongoing spiritual relationship with the Holy Virgin Mother have occurred throughout the years, and subsequent amendments or modifications to this spiritual gift could well take place at any next series of moments. Despite this flexibility, the orthodox substance of Her conversations with us has never changed since the first instant of Her miraculous appearance in our lives over sixteen years ago. The consistency of Her desires remains evidentiary in their holiness and truth; and Her instructions, parables, and teachings have never once opposed the Gospel Truth or Salvific Dogma proclaimed by the Roman Catholic Church for the last 2000 years. The only noticeable variations in the scope, mechanics, timing, and environment related to the reception of Her intercession have been in response to the deepening of our Catholic faith, much like a door would open wider each passing day revealing more that is behind it, along with amendments accommodating the responsibilities thrust upon anyone through the normal functioning of their lives. Our Lady said in the beginning that She did not come to commandeer our lives, but to assist in bringing them to perfection in Her Son Jesus. Truly, this encompasses a definition whose magnitude and variations are without limit in the possibilities of Her expanding role in humanity's conversion to Christianity.

While this book contains the prudently-abridged dialogue that the Most Blessed Virgin engaged with us at the opening of the third millennium, it would be beneficial to preface any conscientious examination of its contents by considering Her miraculous intercession to be more than simply "messages" a courier might deliver from a superior. No courier has ever had a relationship with his ministerial principal that remotely replicates the loving bond that the Virgin Mary maintains with Her children in Her Immaculate Heart. Worthy of note is the interior dissonance one feels while speaking in terms of "messages." Although I use this terminology as does the Immaculate Virgin, Her interaction with us flourishes in unseeable parameters far beyond linguistics in an authentic multi-dimensional relationship, a living rapport that is as real as any relationship with a friend or family member one may have. For example, we never say to others, "In my mother's message yesterday, she said…" Rather, we relate, "When I spoke with mother yesterday, she said…" The personal aura of the "relationship" is made manifest and evident in the latter description. Hence, the word "message" is inadequate, as it allows for the amputation of the words from the relationship. This is why She repeatedly asks humanity to "live" Her messages, for by doing so we transcend into the superscopic arena of the heart, where we encounter panoramic mystical dimensions and sense spectacular wonderments far greater than the mundane lucidity that finite combinations of twenty-six letters can dispense. There is a word, "kenosis," which refers to the "sacrifice" or "suppression" of the outward manifestation of Jesus' Divine attributes as God upon His entry into the world in human flesh. Likewise, there is a kenotic effect in the transmission of the glory of Our Lady's words as they assume their earthly framework as linguistic messages. During the transposition of Her indomitable Grace into the syntax of discernable human communication, Her Divine Eminence is obscured by the limited terminology of being merely a "message." Alas, for pragmatic sake, I use the phraseology while realizing it is impossible to circumscribe the infinite depth of Her presence and intentions in mere human words. The thematic works resting beneath the mantle of *Morning Star Over America* are more an artful revelation of Her exemplary maternal relationship with Her children than a simplistic dictation of the dialogue of certain events. Many of Her children should be reminded that a relationship with the Queen of Heaven cannot be embraced by simply perusing a generic codex of messages, looking for prophecies of Armageddon, and then discarding them as some private revelation only of relevance to the recipients. The Holy Gospel of Christianity is about the restoration of our "relationship" with God the Father as His disciples whom He originally created in His own image and likeness. Jesus Christ is the Messiah who reestablished our pristine union with the Most Holy Trinity through His Passion and Death on the Cross atop Mount Calvary twenty centuries ago. This familial bond with the heavens is initiated by our Baptism, convalesced in the penitential confession of our sins to a Roman Catholic priest, fulfilled in the subsequent reception of the Bread of Life from the Catholic Altar, and sustained in our sacrificial emulation of the virtuous life that Jesus Christ exemplifies through the power of the Holy Spirit beneath the maternal guidance of His Virgin Mother. The life of Christian faith to which we witness is then accentuated by our filial and fraternal relationship with the triumphant Communion of Saints and our earth-weary brothers and sisters whom we serve in humble love. Therefore, the grammatical messages are of a finite temporal scope, but they reflect, highlight and reveal the larger reality of our ethereal interrelationship with the Most Blessed Trinity and the Heavenly Hosts who circumscribe our existence with infinite Love. Those who see the text of the messages as the only matter of importance while discarding the miraculous relationship to which they witness will be making the same misjudgment as those who believe that Sacred Scripture is the only medium for Divine Truth, omitting the spectacular "relationship" that Jesus has maintained with His Catholic Church throughout its twenty centuries of Divine Tradition, including the miraculous intercession of hosts of Saints and Angels. *Hear me now! Those who are dismissive of the gift of the Blessed Virgin Mary's presence are not in communion with the Holy Spirit of Jesus Christ.* Faith is composed of both our awareness of and compliance with "how" the Lord chooses to close-out the ages. The appearance of the Woman Clothed with the Sun is the centerpiece of His apocalyptic will.

The world is awash with pseudo-authorities piping one illegitimate characterization after another of God's messengers, oftentimes relegating them to being nothing more than insignificant telephone lines in the reception of intercession from the personages of Paradise. While some seers may have served in this capacity or personally described their mystical responsibility in these humblest of terms, it is shortsighted, and perhaps sinful, for theological fear-mongers and other faithless autocrats to require recipients of miraculous intercession to be spiritually martyred before offering any conciliatory respect to the very people who are secretly enduring unimaginable suffering and grief so these detractors can be delivered from the flames of Hell, not to mention allowing them the opportunity to become beneficiaries of direct guidance from the Heavenly Hosts themselves. Authentic messages pronounce the power and authority of the person who generated them, no less now than in ancient days when a king would send his courier with a decree from his throne. Abusing the courier and maligning the message is to abuse and malign the intentions of the king; and he will always respond to such affronts to his dignity according to his own prevailing will. Many times we have heard of those who refuse to believe because the messengers never quite seemed humble enough. This is simply a way of saying that the seers have yet to grovel low enough beneath the egos of the doubters to be worthy of belief. This has been the same theme of faithless mortals since God began courting the attention of humanity. Jesus did not show subservience before the arrogance of human beings, and neither did most of the Saints; that is why many of them were killed. Many a bold Saint has been martyred in the lineage of the Crucified Lamb for thundering the Truth of the Almighty Father that no one wanted to hear. One of the reasons most mystics throughout history have been called to embrace such oblation, many doing so in solitary, is because humankind refuses to tender any faithful allegiance unless they see the unimaginable power and grace of the Crucifixion staring them in the face, a revelation which dawns long after they have imitated the conduct of those who crucified Our Lord. These things are related not through any self-aggrandizement or fear of suffering for the good of this cause, for I understand my place amongst the contingent of sinners who have walked this planet. But, God does not require spiritual perfection before someone is allowed to speak the Truth. In fact, the articulation of Christian responsibility is a vital element required for our elevation into perfection. It is the water that cleanses us, while too many are shrieking how dare we get wet. Our Lady wishes that we accept our dignity and responsibilities as the children of Truth, and allow the divine purposes of the Almighty Father to be delegated according to His good pleasure. Therefore, I boldly proclaim my relationship with His Divine Queen for the purpose of forcing into the light all the attitudes that impede the progress of Her success. Sadly, the bantering onslaught of rampant human pride has thus far squelched mankind's response to the seismic intercession of the Most Blessed Virgin throughout the world in our time. The source of this dampening, aggressive indifference can be found in those who are instructing others to ignore Her help because they wish to popularize a priority of faithless pursuits that have nothing to do with the deliverance of the souls of men into the paramount rafters of Paradise. The Matriarch of Heaven is calling humankind to holiness as if there may be no tomorrow. Her miraculous appearances around the globe are to the benefit of every person given the breath of life, and are one of the final gifts of The Divine Mercy of Jesus Christ. She is the prophetic Woman Clothed with the Sun who is depicted in the Book of Revelation, and is being manifested before the shivering soul of this final age so in need of conversion. Creation is rapidly taking the mystical shape it will compose for the Second Coming of the Son of Man. I have been told that time is very short; humanity en masse must quickly and deliberately transcend any prideful requirements, humbly listen to this Lady of Grace, and obey Her sanctifying directives so that we may assume the "relationship" that demands our obedient faithfulness. She wants the Holy Gospel of Her Messianic Son to come to the full brightness of Pentecost. She pleads with us to retreat from the edge of the infernal Abyss and prepare for the Judgement of the Ages. Come into the Light and be seen by God among His faithful ones! Our Lady said on one of the first days of Her visitation, *"There is no doubt or question in faith."* While some may scoff at this total abandonment, believing that it is naive or irresponsible, contingent upon some reticent, half-hearted discernment of spirits and events, we must instead revel in our loving affection for our Virgin Mother while holding Her guiding hand. Jesus Christ commands no less. She is more than a biblical personage of Christian history or a dogmatic principle to which we must give assent. She is a living, breathing Peacemaker for humanity with the Savior of the world who is interceding with each of us at this moment; interacting, nurturing, and guiding us, as well as every person who has ever been conceived. She is the Mother of all those who will ultimately be redeemed. Hence, there must be an invocation of faith in the reality of Her miraculous presence. Away with the tussle of egos and the constipation of theologies; let there be no speculation; banish the fear, silence the debate, crush the disobedience, and forever exile the doubt. It is imperative that we believe everything that issues from Her sacred lips, knowing that the Queen who appears to this age articulates, possesses, and embodies the Universal Truth, applicable and authoritative to every person ever given the breath of life. We must wish to know the Truth of Her Son Jesus to the fullness of Her Immaculate Heart, living-out our years in unison with the highest measures of Her Grace. Our Lady is the embodiment of our future, the premonition of our resurrected beings in the flesh. She is the fulfillment of the rewards of the Gospel, assumed into Heaven, mortal humanity fully arrayed in immortal glory. Our abandonment relieves us of unfounded questions and flushes consternation from our discernment. It extinguishes fear because it is the blazing manifestation of our true faith. Freedom is a realm liberated from antagonistic debate and its destructive forces against our common bond. Unity is a gift of sacrificial love that we offer for the transformation of our hopes into celestial certainty at the Altars of the Roman Catholic Church. Our Lady said, *"Faith becomes knowledge to those who serve."*

    The simple content of this book was delivered through a spectrum of mystical intercessions ranging from interior locutions initiated through the Immaculate Virgin's grace to Her spectacular appearance in a raiment of Glory. No official historical record has been created regarding which messages were received through which order of intercessory magnitude because it is irrelevant. The recognition had to be made that this minute bit of information would have been inappropriately inflated into an abject oppression by some to personally decide for everyone else which messages carry more weight than others, thereby distracting many people with absurd conjecture, and scandalizing the innocuous abandonment by which Our Lady hopes we will all engage Her intercession. Although our Holy Mother's words have infinite mystical dimensions that will be revealed over the course of individual lives, She wishes us to receive them simply and obediently in our day, within our own personal circumstances, and according to a little child's understanding, while leaving Her to accomplish the macro-dimensions of conversion and the flourishing of God's Love in each of Her children's hearts. The Holy Spirit has dispensed many gifts or "charisms" throughout the centuries to people of faith for the elevation, articulation, and strengthening of our relationship with God and one another. For those who may be curious and cautious as to what an interior locution really is and how it manifests itself, the following description is offered for our particular case. "Interior locution" is a generic term having diverse, yet specific contexts and manifestations for each individual due to differing degrees of openness and the unique composure of someone's spiritual constitution. Its simplest definition is "interior communication." Everyone can remember certain times when they have carried on a wholesale conversation with themselves without uttering an audible syllable. An authentic dialogue occurs within the consciousness during these occasions. At other times, multitudes of thoughts flash through our minds, inspiring choices and directions in our lives. Further, there are natural processes of deduction and intuition as each person seeks to arrive at answers to questions and the satiation of curiosities. All of these instances possess the characteristics of language that make-up the corpus of interior communication that we engage with ourselves. Amidst this whirlpool of awareness, we must realize that not all thoughts flowing through our minds are self-generated as if it were a closed system lacking influence from the outside. The Holy Spirit also communicates with everyone, even though God's voice is often overwhelmed by the babbling of our own conscience, the aggressiveness of our egos, and the dialogue we are engaging with ourselves interiorly, much like trying to hear one person amongst the din of hundreds. This interior noise is part of the normal operation of our identity because it broadly reflects what we have consistently experienced within our uncultivated interior life in the absence of prayer since our youth. Our personal ruminations are a pandemonium that is excited by our passions, and which is nearly always turned on with the volume cranked up. The natural trait of human beings is to assume that every thought that occurs in our psyche originates exclusively within our own mind because we do not understand how something we are thinking could actually come from outside the boundaries of who we believe ourselves to be. For instance, consider if we were about to be the victim of a horrible accident, but moments before the incident, the thought of our forgotten responsibilities suddenly comes to mind, beckoning us to change course to a different destination. Was that thought the insight of the Holy Spirit through a communication of divine origin, or a mere coincidence? Would it require a humble heart submissive to our responsibilities to choose the change in direction when we actually wanted to do something altogether different? The answers are obvious to those with faith. Another example is the often mentioned "mother's intuition," an inherent sense of the unseen, defying logic and reasonable deduction. These types of guidance by the Holy Paraclete are occurring through the lives of God's children just beyond our self-awareness, constrained and measured by Heaven within a bounded context where our capacity for faith is preserved. Thoughts such as these could be considered "locutions of inspiration," and are within the natural boundaries of our normal awareness and subject to our discernment. It behooves anyone to mention that Satan exists just as Sacred Scripture declares, no matter what any human being believes to the contrary. Evil is not just some metaphorical image created by people wanting to reduce the presence of outright wickedness to symbolism. Satan is a spiritual personage of malevolent demonism who can inject thoughts in the same manner; such are called "temptations." One of the powers of prayer is the cultivation of our discernment so that we recognize the temptations of evil for what they are, and so that our ego is diminished in order that we may fluently and gracefully respond to those locutions of inspiration with which God blesses us, often through our Guardian Angel.

For those who disbelieve that anyone having passed beyond the boundaries of death actually has the ability to influence our lives, the truth can be rather astonishing. Everyone must realize that the Blessed Virgin Mary has a providential role in the universal Redemption of humanity as our Heavenly Mother with all the powers and prerogatives reserved for Her as the Queen of Heaven and Matriarch of Creation. The Savior of the world uttered titanic declarations of consequential Truth from the Cross when He said to the Immaculate Virgin, "Woman, behold your son," and to St. John, "Behold your Mother." The Mother of Jesus Christ is still alive, assumed into Heaven just as the Catholic Church confirms, and is spiritually present in this world after 2000 years, as is Her Son. They are influencing and teaching humanity with unimpeded determination toward the Kingdom that every living creature will ultimately come to know. There is not an authentic Christian who would deny that there have been multitudes of paranormal occurrences where departed loved ones, angels, and even Jesus Himself have either appeared or spoken to people on the Earth over the previous two millennia. Everyone has heard of inexplicable stories of divine intercession from small children who do not know enough about the subject of miraculous appearances to make them up. Our culture has been inundated with the phenomenon of "angel mania" in recent years where people have openly professed their belief in angels and how they assist us. Even if someone chooses not to believe such things without the concurrence of Sacred Scripture, ponder Matthew 27:53 which speaks directly to the scope of what God will deign to save us. We are a Resurrection people; the tombs are open! Therefore, why would it be difficult to accept that Jesus allows His Immaculate Virgin Mother to interact with His brothers and sisters here and now in order to awaken us to the realms of Heaven and help us love as He loves? The Truth which God asks us to accept is that He has sent the Most Blessed Virgin of Christianity, the Queen of Calvary, to certain children of faith to be extraordinary recipients of explicit, miraculous communication from His Throne for the dispensation of divine guidance in unquestionable and unmistakable forms that are beyond the casually consistent parameters of our human constitution. Consequently, we see the apparency of these messages and apparitions, and others like them in many venues and times throughout the history of the world since Jesus' Resurrection. Through these special charisms, God has allowed the Immaculate Virgin to elevate the intensity of the locution (communication) beyond natural inspiration and the nebulous limitations of our discerning faith into a substantive, authentic, motivational, and goal-oriented dialogue that cannot be mistaken as merely a figment of one's creative interior poise. When this Lady of Grace engages the "transcension" from Heaven into the recognizable parameters of our mortal exile, it is inappropriate to downplay the mystical experience as being a product of one's imagination because each recipient knows that it is the presence of another person "appearing" within the circumference of their private awareness. Hence, one can properly discern the contrast between delusion and deificly inspired communication. Progressing further, the locutions can increase in power and revelation where other more complex manifestations of miraculous interaction become prevalent, such as sensing the emotions of Our Lady, recognizing Her demeanor, even the manifestation of the apparition of Her entire person, and the composition of interior contemplative visions expressive of the topics of Her conversations. The mystical occurrence of infused knowledge, or "afflatus," whereby the seer is miraculously instilled with a comprehensive understanding of a previously unknown body of information in an instant, can also become a component of this elevation of the locution. While I mention only these few manifestations, there are as many more that can be generated within the creativity of God's omnipotent genius in His desire to redeem His children. This is why ecclesial discernment has been taken aback on many occasions, leaving the miraculous intercession of the Holy Spirit in relative obscurity as if it is some delusional aberration instead of the flourishing power of deliverance and Light needed to amend the course of a lost humanity in the present. Our faith must be deep enough to embrace what God wishes to accomplish in this moment, not simply recognize what He may have already accomplished for the benefit of previous generations. He is trying to save ours by addressing us in the here and now in supernaturally profound ways! Nothing is impossible once He breaches the parameters of our exile and finds our souls lifted to Him in heartfelt faith. He can take us anywhere, show us anything, shear us away from any fault, guide us around any obstacle, strengthen us during any trial, elevate us to share in His omnipotent reign, and unilaterally bend history into the shape of the Cross for the moment of His Second Coming. Our Holy Mother wishes us to concede our part by embracing Her contemporary intercession and living by the most vibrant faith that we can muster in the fulfillment of our commission to Her service because the Most Blessed Trinity is poised at every second of time to dispense robust allotments of His mystical Love. As a result of humankind's differing measures of faith over time, God is gauging the extraordinary power of His revelatory Spirit for the preservation of our greatest display of faith and the extreme measures of His Divine Mercy. He pines to reveal Himself to us entirely, but demands that His revelations be met with the complete concession of our trust in Him. He is preserving us from rejecting Him in the full light of understanding, a spiritually condemning offense that many at present would no doubt perpetrate against themselves. We are seeing incremental hints of His invincible presence because our collective faith is too half-hearted to meet Him at His fullest Glory. Yet, His compassionate Will still allows His Immaculate Mother access to our worldly station through Her mystical appearances to make-up the distance lacking in our faith.

The messages contained in this book were received during the course of our prayers on the specified dates and times shown. As we begin the Most Holy Rosary, my interior constitution assumes a shape as if it is righting itself, like the prioritization of my sense of awareness aligning with the purposes of the Most Blessed Virgin Mary. I have often thought that this same orientation should occur with anyone else who prays from the heart. The temporal world relocates laterally into my peripheral awareness; its dimensions recede as my interior vision becomes more dominant and focused upon Heaven and the Infinite Love that Our Lady possesses. This moves my former sense of reality to the margin of my consciousness as if it were a two-dimensional photograph. Although there have been times when the ringing of the telephone distracted me from this focus, and for which I was subsequently admonished for not turning off the ringer, I do not consider what takes place in the temporal world during the time I am speaking with Our Lady as of any notable significance. I don't suppose that this is an altogether unfamiliar state with anyone who has passionately focused their attention, but it is of note that it is extremely easy to focus on the intercession of the Blessed Virgin because the supernal attraction of Her presence is so compelling. One could imagine holding a gun, and while looking at its detailed contours, someone suddenly grabs it from your hands, cocks the hammer, and points the loaded barrel between your eyes at a six-inch distance with their finger trembling on the trigger. The depth of focus on the gun is immediately changed, and an elephant could walk past without your realizing it. While fear can psychologically paralyze someone, Infinite Love is overwhelming in captivating and maintaining your attention. As we begin the Sacred Mysteries of the Holy Rosary, our Holy Mother makes Herself present to my soul before She begins speaking in much the same way. Her words are not what initially signify Her presence, rather the magnified extensions of Her Grace impact my heart initially, imparting knowledge of Her presence and an enlightenment of peaceful joy before She speaks. In these moments, Our Lady acknowledges my attendance as Her special son much like a renowned orator would look down at those of whom they are most fond before turning their gaze to the masses to deliver an eloquent oration. Many times my preliminary sensation is as if She nods and says with holy pride, "Watch what your Mother does now!," bearing sparkling eyes and a generous smile that could melt the aggression of a beast; then She metaphorically turns to the lectern. When She begins with a salutation such as "My dear children..." or another triumphant exclamation, Her presence becomes fully manifest, and I begin to experience the extensions of grace and the magnification of Heaven with which humanity will be blessed on that particular day. In other words, the locution is magnified to the beatific dimensions of Her particular intentions. She speaks personally to my brother and me, but I also experience the timeless reverberation of Her words, where all ages join us in the events of the moment. Every person who will ever hear that message is timelessly brought into our company during Her intercession. I realize that She is speaking to all of us in unison, although each other person will not experience these moments for themselves until some special day in the future when their eyes fall upon the words of the message, and they embrace their relationship with Our Lady with an open heart and an abundance of faith. I have always hoped that each person who reads the words in this book will mystically sense this original moment when we were together with the Queen of Heaven, because it becomes that "now" as you read Her messages. Just as I am here at this moment speaking to you, Our Lady is even more present in each of Her offerings. She transcends boundaries in heavenly fact that I as yet only pass with Her assistance through my faith. Our Lady has demonstrated to me on several occasions the timeless parameters in which She reigns. There have been moments when She called me to review past messages years in the future from when we originally spoke. These conversations of the past were the actual dialogue verbatim of Her present discourse, relevant to the issues of the present day and the thoughts of the current occasion. In other words, when Our Lady spoke to me initially years before, She was outside of time speaking to me in both the present and the future simultaneously. I could hear Her voice outside of time where my past and present became one with the veil of my human exile almost removed. Many biblical scholars are oblivious to this timeless quality of the Bible. To them, it is nothing more than a history book to be dissected according to the ancients who wrote it. They even believe that the Book of Revelation is nothing more than a symbolic writing pertaining only to the era in which it was written, describing only the contemporary events surrounding the original author and the persecutions of that time, discounting its prophetic warning to our day and the final destiny of man.

    The first part of Her message nearly always possesses the intention of being both a universal and public revelation of Her miraculous intercession, not to be confused with the Public Revelation of Jesus Christ and the Deposit of Faith in the custodial care of the Magisterium of the Roman Catholic Church. I am always silent during this time, waiting for our personal conversation after the initial portion of Her message. It is easy to notice that the structure of the majority of Her messages in this book comprises an initial portion of the text directed to the entire world, particularly the United States of America, and a latter section composing the portion of our personal conversation that I am allowed to release. I see Our Lady's demeanor arrayed as the peerless Queen during the first part of most of Her messages and feel somewhat distant from Her in these moments as if She were standing on a podium concentrating on God's larger Kingdom. Her vocabulary and poetic artistry have ranged from simple conversations that would be directed toward a child to sky-rocketing orations whose command I have never heard in my life. The tone of Her voice has become pleading, appealing, earnest, sorrowful, pitiful, sympathetic, joyful, gentle, ominous, authoritative, commanding, but never dejected or hopeless.

There have been moments when Satan has approached and thrust unimaginable thoughts of dejection, despair, and hopelessness upon my soul prior to Our Lady's appearances, whereupon the Queen of Heaven clothed in majesty rose up around me in defense with a beatific power that would make planets quake, obliterating the smallest shadow of Satan's presence from every corner of my existence in the flash of an instant. The devil runs from Her like a coward from a fight. Humankind has truly not begun to fathom the power enshrined in Her Immaculate Heart. She can reduce the most hardened barbarians in history to repentant tears with the crucified Love that Her Heart possesses. She speaks in Modern English with a melodious accent that is gentleness itself, yet She has perfect command of every language, and has used vocabulary that is beyond my knowledge. Since She knows that I sometimes do not explicitly understand Her discussions, She will often ask me whether I comprehend all that She is saying. Although She already knows whether I understand, She queries in order to make me sure of myself. If I am confused, She paraphrases particular parts of Her instructions, but She will not function as a dictionary. On occasion, if there is a word with which I am unfamiliar, instead of telling me what it means, She will instruct me to collect my dictionary and research the meaning while She waits. I believe this to be another example of how Our Lady wishes me to live as anyone else would live.

In regards to the literary substance of Her messages, there are many people who have grown bored, and upon reading them now say, "Here we go again, the same old platitudes, more of the same drumbeat. More promises without results." These statements are a symptom of seeing only the messages and failing to live the relationship that She offers through them. For me, Our Lady fills all moments of my life, making them unique, enlightening, precious, timely and uplifting. Her messages are but a faint representation of the true life that I experience with Her because I know of no other way to fully explain our relationship by the designs of the human language. I offer the best picture that I am able to reveal, and ask everyone to accept and imitate it because the Queen of Heaven is waiting to embrace anybody who kneels to pray with Her. While Our Lady's intercession could never preclude my need to receive the Sacrament of Penance, She offers the requisite strength and holiness for the completion of anyone's vocation. I realize that my personal sanctification in Jesus is a work in progress, and it would be beyond my imagination to attempt such meticulous cultivation without Her kind guidance and understanding. She knows how to resolve interior conflicts and remove obstacles to my spiritual enlightenment with the precision of a surgeon, although I think with levity that She should use more anesthesia before engaging Her work, to which She would respond with a charming giggle. She can clarify our perception with a simple sentence, much like encouraging a child to look through the correct end of a pair of binoculars. One can easily imagine that the messages, parables, and lessons that have been released through our published books are not an exposition of the entire scope of our personal relationship, nor a complete record of the information that She has given, or an all-encompassing narrative of the depths of Her Grace that we have witnessed. The Scripture passage, "…the world could not contain the books…" is an appropriate description of how I feel. There has been much more shared between our Heavenly Mother, Timothy and myself than will ever be published. It is reserved for the private archives of Heaven. The unreleased components will remain concealed in perpetuity in the same way a penitent's sacramental confession is sealed within the bonds of the confessional during mortal time. I must say that most of our confidential relationship is composed of the spiritual intimacy shared between the Mother and Her sons, where She spent painstaking hours clarifying our vision, teaching us holier conduct, freeing us from the detraction of others, strengthening us in our spiritual trials, guiding our compassionate works, qualifying collateral events, protecting us from our missteps and the subterfuge of our enemies, lending us patience, encouraging human valor, wiping away heresy, commending us to Jesus' Divine Mercy, and instilling in us an impenetrable sureness to know that the powers and prowess of Heaven are beside us. The door of our relationship seems to be completely ajar from my perspective; and I am humbled, delighted and forever thankful. However, I am not foolish enough to think that God lacks the power to reveal more demonstrative visions of Heaven, Hell, or Purgatory that would reduce my simple wisdom to little more than the babblement of a baby. Indeed, let it be understood that there is a price for the Lord's mystical gifts. Our Lady once said that *"Mystical gifts only come through the diminishment of the flesh "* in all ways one might imagine that suffering and discomfort can be endured.

My heart is united with the Immaculate Virgin on a more permeating plane than with anyone else I have ever known. The gift of witnessing Her thoughts and sentiments firsthand, along with those of Her Son, implores due diligence from any observant soul. Numerous worldly reflections, attitudes, and biases become unequivocally concretized as being either in harmony with the intentions of the Almighty Father or glaringly discordant with His will. In many instances, gray is dichotomized into black and white. The Truth reveals clearly how many concoctions of human pride are rooted in sin and spawned from nothing but selfish ingratiation. These are none other than clandestine retreats from the front lines of the holy sacrifice of love. We live in the mortal world where what had previously been known as definitive aspects of morality and truth have become subject to leisure examination, scandalous scrutiny, and infantile derision by relativists who do not have the clout before God to make such pseudo-prophetic encroachments against the realms of His Beatific Reign. Centuries of noble traditions and dogmatic truth are being publicly desecrated by godless men and feminists who declare without authority what God's genius ought to be, and that it is undecided, vague, debatable and subject to the lowest denominator of their prejudice, all the while intimidating those who are weak in faith with the robes of false victimhood that they stripped from the Lamb of God, Himself. Far too many who bear the responsibility of propagating the Holy Gospel are lost, blind or afraid to speak truth to power, choosing instead to negotiate with diabolical darkness, coerced by the devil into thinking that it is nothing more than ecumenicism. An ominous contrast exists between the unholy hubris that has been cultivated through the manifestoes of pluralists and the beatific vision that Our Lady espouses. She will not ignore their repugnant falsehoods and unmitigated evil, no matter how benign She is. She will rebuke anything that was responsible for the Crucifixion of Her Son or that continues to malign the holiness of Her children. She is the greatest defender of those who possess the simple desire to become the best and most noble part of humanity, and the unrepentant remainder She will submit to the onslaught of the Most Blessed Trinity and Saint Michael's avenging saber. There is a wholly obscured reality that epitomizes the life and legacy of Jesus Christ on the Earth as His Mystical Body that is being overwhelmed by people who are motivated by power, prestige, financial gain, corruption of the flesh, and the satiation of their egos while they weep crocodile tears in order to evoke sympathetic license for their impious pursuits. Entire theologies and paradigms of thought have been generated, developed and regurgitated upon the Church of Christendom while the gun of secularism with its hammer cocked is held to its sacred temple with deranged throngs screaming for the trigger to be pulled. We are in an age that remains unconvinced of the demands and inevitabilities of the Holy Gospel, uneducated as to where Creation has traveled, unsure where humanity is going, and terrified to repudiate those who betray twenty centuries of virtue that have been carved into history by untold battalions of heroic Saints who sacrificially gave their lives to Christianity so we may see its Truth in our day. We are afraid that we may offend the offenders if we strip them of the fleece they have draped around their pretentious shoulders. The extinction of human pride is closing-in on their unsuspecting consciences with an abundance of miracles being dealt by God just beyond the awareness of these pungent reprobates who will soon be laid low by the unraveling of their audacity. Our Lady's intercession is their providential wake-up call. What can be said of any civilization that mocks and censors the righteous genius of ages upon ages of Christian Saints? How many dogmas of salvific virtue must be spate upon before everyone realizes that these tenets of humane decency were compiled and articulated through the wisdom of our forebears amidst the wake of their enemies' bloodiest misdeeds? These early Christians were the Lord's sentinels marking the paths of sorrow that they wished their progeny never to tread. As the Light of righteousness is being dimmed in our age, at what shade of darkness do we begin to call evil what it really is? That dungeon of Hell has already been divulged! The Almighty Father is not negotiating with humanity.

While cultural secularists believe that they have succeeded in flushing religion from the shores of our homeland, that they have sullied the Roman Catholic priesthood beyond respectability; and while the values of everyone of good character are oppressively slandered, the Queen of Heaven is declaring that those who willfully generate, suborn, and harbor vice and sin do not have a leg to stand on before the God they reject. They have no authority, license, influence, or future before His Universal Throne. Indeed, above every atrocity, *Woe to those who are responsible for the murderous lie of abortion!* Remaining obstinate and unrepentant, they are doomed to endure the everlasting fire! We, as children of Light, should not fear being accused of not loving those we are required to admonish for their attacks against the Church because our rebuke may be the grace that rescues them from damnation. We must be courageous enough to wrest the reigns of God's Kingdom from the death-grip of evil. The Age of Merciful Admonishment has breached the Earth's horizon, and Our Lady insists that Her Roman Catholic children must never take another step backward in uncertainty. Our will must be invincible in order to suppress the decadence of this world and extract our brothers and sisters' souls from its hedonist wreckage. It is not too late for the end to be beautiful. From this vantage point, we are all dispatched to engage Creation, seeking strength and foresight in the maternal Wisdom of the Queen of Paradise through Her supernatural intercession. And, this is what the messages in this Anthology are about; preserving humanity from the bloodbaths of oblivion.

    I have found nothing to which the Blessed Virgin will not respond, yet I discipline my material curiosities so as to honor our relationship by living the faith that She has taught. She has petitioned my brother and me on numerous occasions to live our reparative vocation in exile with a vibrant faith, no matter what circumstances revolve around us or what is inflicted in return. With this confidence, I know that if there is something that She feels I should know, She will broach the subject. I concede that there are places in my being that have been scoured by Her Wisdom when I would have sooner left them in obscurity. There also have been hundreds of times when She addressed my conduct and responded to questions in my thoughts, but I have declined to burden Her for answers during Her messages. It makes me giggle that She never misses a word spoken by Her children during any time of day or night. Things that we consider trivial in the course of the day are the very subjects She often elevates as worthy of attention. Conversely, there have been others that She considered irrelevant in the grander scheme of human Redemption which She urged me to dismiss from my thoughts. She has asked me to anticipate the answers to my questions on several occasions, implying that we must live with good faith, no matter how detailed the Lord wishes to be in revealing the future. The way in which I know the Immaculate Virgin is integrated into my thoughts and being, although it is not so simple to describe Her. This is not caused by any lack of knowledge or clarity about Her attributes, but the restrictions of my vocabulary as a medium for transmitting the facts. It is difficult to use language because people have presumed interpretations for certain words that are inadequate for what others wish to convey. Each of us has preconceived understandings of the usage of our words. And, causing even further distortion, the connotation of these words changes over the course of the years. For example, the term "fast" generates a different perspective in the mind of a teenager compared to an octogenarian. This phenomenon exists with each word in every language, multiplied by the number of people using them. And, to further complicate matters, the cognitive psyche of people constantly manipulates their sensory impulses as they try to reach interior consonance with their "preferred" beliefs. The latter concept was extinguished in me by Our Lady's eminence. I have never tried to interpret Her sentiments to be more aligned with my druthers, nor do I attempt to reconcile Her words with those clamoring from the world. I defer to Her in all ways by allowing Her conversation to dominate my mental capacity without question, which is oftentimes a uniquely humbling experience. In instances where I took a moment to ponder another perspective that I might have preferred, Our Lady quickly made clear that my thinking was not in union with Hers. Hence, what words best describe the Love that I know the Holy Mother has for Her children? I understand why Our Lord asks us to be of one heart and one mind with Him. The answer lies in the communication of Love that we are able to share. Consider living a lifetime with someone, growing in unison where your hearts, minds, languages, devotions, and goals become entirely one and complementary. Then, imagine suffering unimaginably for the salvation and survival of your loved-one out of complete love for them. What do they see and comprehend that could never be put into words? This is the beauty of human life where all words make sense. When we pass through the veil of exile into the Eternal Light of God, our lives will be the definition of the scope of what we perceived His Love to be. The Earth is the forum where meaning is assigned to the words we hear and say. Our lives will one day be the vocabulary we will draw from to speak with God and describe how we loved Him in return. Our sufferings will be our great oratory; our sacrifices, the masterpiece we courageously arrayed on this earthen canvas, lifted before Him like a tiny child proudly displaying his first crayon-scribbled page. Can you contemplate such a mystery? Our Lady has been speaking through the vocabulary of Her life whereby the scope of Her words has the spectacular dimensions of the immeasurable Grace that She manifests on Earth. What does this mean? Her life, and therefore Her words, are infinite Love; they are the voice of Her Son, the Word of God. They may be English, Japanese, French, Arabic or others, but She transforms, elevates, magnifies and bolsters them with power that is greater than all conceivable tongues. She has never failed to communicate Her Love to humanity. When She says the words, "I love you," the Crucifixion resounds in Her sacred voice, while the Triumph of

Resurrection reigns in Her eternal blessing. She has expanded the intensity, meaning, and significance of my syllables and prayers so that they more closely imitate the vernacular of Heaven. Their circumference of impact transcends any constrictions that mortals could place on them. This is how we speak to God. It is the work of trust that we must engage with a vibrant and courageous heart. How does someone pen his thoughts in poetic gratitude for his religious faith? Perhaps the remainder of this Prologue will suffice.

How imploring is Christ's Divine Love, with mountains high and steeples tall, that propels humanity into the presence of bygone kings and hailed Archangels; sufficiently reveling their eternal tranquility, and whose legacies are assured by dreams and prophecies still left ajar, much too adroit for mortality to impede or peerless objectivity to cease God's eloquence in burnishing us finely with the fair-faced constellations of stars. Heaven can open new doors like gunfire that we never knew was there, stunning our brilliance before the dwelling echoes have heard their last run or the ages passed very far from the luster of modern machines, shadowed meadows, memories lost, and much too wrinkled brows. We have laughed and wept in consanguine hope that all last acts will be fashioned by the ultimatums of men; where currents, concourses, galaxies, and lights suspend their awe to see what has become of Truth. Not too surprising though, it shall always be there, defying space and time, inducing and beseeching the world, pushing the universe beyond the limits of exiled humanity refined. We cling to parched lips like sparkling tears, waiting to be issued to Creation in resounding accession through the ranks of the Saints, like credos engraved in stone, transforming our souls from gnomes into giants with the prefigured Crucifixion of Mary's Messianic Son. Our age of diffusion, equation, and change is not a furlong too far or so elusive to our thoughts that we cannot grasp it like the cusp of a tiger's jaw poised to devour its prey. We are enlightened by such opening doors, ripened and reaped from fathoms and heights like weeds in our fathers' fields, given a new sense of purpose that breaches our bonds from the wily element of time. We are living in our finest and most majestic moments, and they are all about scaling mountains engorged with our Christian heritage and the expiating expressions of life. We journey through a faith with which we complement the indices of Nature and the archives of world history, depositing the remnants of our ingenuity into the supernatural foresight that keeps our existence running smoothly everyday. We make such brilliant exclamations about the meaning of human life that it seems almost too surreal to the senses the way we neutralize long-held conjectures and cast mathematical certainties into inexplicable doubt. All the intelligence in the world cannot reproach our trust in God, for it is in Him that we mortify our enemies and destroy their exploitation of our innocence, effectively annihilating them so God can visit upon us Christ's favored good fortune. Henceforth, what we believe about Heaven is buttressed by its flourishing Wisdom, eternal leverage, infusion of the heart, fraternal literacy, spiritual indoctrination, theological diplomacy, exculpating receptivity, and beatific culture, making it the universe's waterfall of Truth and the epitome of our personal satisfaction. Our best instincts are exercised in welcoming, achieving, sustaining, and deferring to the inevitability of Divine Love to conquer everything antithetical to its power, knowing ourselves that the Glory of eternal existence eventually pulls rank and makes its indelible mark on everything we say and do, and anything we shall ever become, so that our finality is ratified and capitalized in the realms of the panoramic unseen. Every fiber of human holiness becomes the offspring of our berth in time, our shelter of protection, and everything else about us that speaks to God's deific dreams. We bow before the floodgates of knowledge that remind us who we are and where we are going, hemming us to the unbridled genius of sovereignty Incarnate, touching our pursed lips with the healing balm of heroism refined. Why should we not crave the emphatic perfectionism that we learn and hold from the imperial magnetism emanating from Jesus Christ, issued to the world by the Dominion of Paradise in yet untold heights of Glory? His presence through the Holy Spirit makes our lives gentler, authentic, irrevocable, concise, and indomitable to the heart. Our own perpetuity is hewn from the anchorage and artworks of His Holy Sacrifice, standing unique in principle, commanding of human obedience, born akin to unimaginable suffering, transcending by His own right; vibrant, ameliorative, envisioning, prescient, deductive, and commending.

There is nothing more powerful in Creation than His purifying Cross. No envy of humankind can depose it, no burden of years can suspend it, no sleight-of-hand can deceive it, and nothing by ritual or happenstance can encroach upon its jurisdiction to redeem us or sap its perseverance from leading us back to the origin of the Saints and Feasts. His Sacred Gospel is a premonition that shall be forever relevant, consistent, and always brisk and shining to the Earth's four corners amidst any winds of change. By architecture and affiliation, the Kingdom of God is unprecedented and superior to the acts of all the ancients, and to this very day still induces the human spirit to pursue the pathways to Heaven by every means devotional and prefigured in the destinies of the heart. This is what Love plans for us, that we tender our lives to a flawless excellence and summit of moral scrutiny that only the Angels can surpass, realizing that we often descend from vaulted heights to servitude to see our future eye to eye. We blaze fresh trails and make new inroads by hungering for the cynosures of this Love, and everything to which we have ever belonged or ever hoped to see alive during these modern times of humanity's boldest resolve and our Lord's evocative decision of availing Paradise to be regained. We dare to explore the steepest heights of wonderment and stand at the precipice of Virtue, culling from our infinite thoughts the proper words to say that will bestow our blessings upon God, debating what He must have been thinking when He extrapolated His own creative intuition and fashioned us into being. And, now we know. He gave us life because He couldn't help it. He could not resist the curiosity that He often observes in us to make something out of nothing that is more beautiful than the stars, a species that speaks, sings, and writes volumes about the eloquence of His designs, who bemoans nothing by accident, and who moves in swaths across Creation to discover everything unknown in our path. Indeed, we were begotten so God would not feel so alone; that He might live, breathe, and have His own being through His little creatures; and this is why we must shed every tear for Him and imbibe every precious drop of Blood that spewed from Jesus' veins to absolve the Earth of sin. God's solitary oneness is why He came to save us in the folds of human flesh, and to spite the devil and the netherworld, and to prove that no poverty, illusion, misgiving or regret could ever survive the awesome prevalence of His stubbornness to succeed. Therefore, let us not be too quick to judge the Earth or repeal the synopsis of the galaxies the way it was supposed to unfurl, but ratify and bless the whole of it all, to exalt Christ's Love within us, and nurture and imitate His Divine Grace; for it is the irresistible sanctification of our brief sojourn through time and space at the heels and within the Most Sacred Heart of our extraordinary God, against whom no adversary could prevail, and no calumny can impugn.

"Because there is one loaf, we, who are many, are one body, for we all partake of the one loaf."

1 Corinthians 10:17

"Receive this Truth that I bear unto you, that I offer and dispense for your life's work. It is My gift beyond the far-flung ages and the long-hailed reckoning of your childhood years, for trust and living, the retrieval of your innocence to comfort and awaken you, and for the heart of your hearts from which our unity flows. The Truth I give you will embolden you, make you whole and sanctify you, and give you peace. Receive this Truth from deep within My body as your spiritual food, and consume it for your soul's sake. This is our best moment, for the future of humanity is at hand. My Truth is your pious compulsion and beatific excellence that suffers you in the ways of the Cross beyond the realms of the netherworld. Fear not the Earth's remaining days, for I am potent and reverent, and I will accompany you during your mourning hours, bolstering and fashioning a courage for you that cannot be deposed. I will comfort you like the Angels kiss the lilies, and lift you into God's transcendent Grace through the presence of His divine affections. I will bless you with eternal passion and cast your enemies aside, rendering you proficient in all things perpetual, and altruistic too. Know with every ounce of Wisdom that your trials are borne in Me, that your endurance is a gift from Heaven, creating life anew from the marrow of your bones. In this is your hope that flourishes tall and wide despite the shadows of the past or the darkness of your fears."

—Jesus speaking to William and Timothy

Easter Sunday, 2002

Morning Star Over America

The New Millennium

In the Year of Our Lord

AD 2000

Sunday, January 2, 2000
4:26 p.m.

"Yes, My beautiful children; yes is all that the many peoples of the world need to proclaim to the living Son of God, and there will be no more need for time. To you and to the many millions who have given their souls to the Blood of Jesus, I offer My grateful and profound appreciation, for you are the light, the salt, and the converting warriors who have given Jesus reason to take into His arms a new humanity, clothed in the Grace that He has bestowed upon you, and prepared to greet and conquer any enemy that would dare to snatch you from Salvation. Only your hearts can know this because the Christ of all Creation resounds bountifully from there in peace, Wisdom, guidance, goodness, and true nobility. You have entered a new year with hope because you know that I speak only the Truth—the Fruit of My Womb and the meditations from My Holy and Immaculate Heart. Now, you can feel the power and sense the victory greater than ever before! But, I must warn you, dear children, that this victory will continue to be revealed to you one day at a time. Your collective prayers are the dawn's early light with which you will soon begin to see the miraculous lines of the Face of God, to understand His mighty temperament, to bask in the glow of His expression of approval for you, and to dance happily beneath the glistening sparkles of His grateful eyes. This new year will bring you the same hope and joy of the Resurrection morning that has conquered your death if the world will only take to its knees and say 'yes' to the reasons why Jesus died on the Cross. My children, there can be no mistake in recognizing this Truth. For many years, I have described the beauty of the Redemption of humankind in this very room. A word at a time, I have told you that a moment is in the offing when the entire world will know what we have done here together. Please also accept this as a prophecy that will be fulfilled, and let there be no speculation or apprehension about it. The absence of your confidence in this matter has created an unjustified atmosphere of doubt and discontentment. These are the times of favor for which the collective universes have been waiting for 2,000 years. Therein lies your happiness and fulfillment.

Today, I have come to share My Love for you in a way that is in reflection of My first moments in this room. I see you as simply and humbly as I did before, although you are a much more wise and patient people. You know better how to pray in hopeful anticipation for the Return of the Son of God in Glory. Indeed, you have learned to allow the Holy Spirit to guide you in every way. I wish I could fully explain in comprehensible terms that you are a holy people in the sight of God, filled with converting Wisdom for your fellow men, and destined for a humble Triumph that only your Savior can effect in you. This is indeed a time to reflect upon the bountiful knowledge that you have gained, in communion with your capacity to take the Gospel message to the entire world. I will help you if you will be patient. While you have tried to be patient by your manual actions, you are still not patient in your hearts. My special little children, this is because you are very anxious for the King of Creation to succeed. My message to you is that He has succeeded already! Time itself is not your enemy. You must learn to see time as a peaceful contemplation of the joy that all hearts will soon know. While My Son is announcing His presence to the ages, be pleased that you have already heard and accepted His Word! This should always be a source of great joy in your hearts that transcends the ticking clock and the repetition of days. I have brought you to understand with clarity the things that will give you great peace and power. I have taught you not to fear the things that have haunted you in the past. This is a celebration of the Great Jubilee! It is a period of reparation, cultivation, and renewal! I have told you that God has taken your weaknesses and transformed them into great weapons of righteousness! The things that you have feared most have become the power which has defeated your enemies. You are no longer repulsed or made ashamed by your sacrifices of Love because your souls reveal what your eyes refuse to see. This is the essence of your trust, faith, and victorious memorial.

    My Special one, your heart is telling you about the power of God, and not binding you to the terrible errors of the world. You have been awarded a great accolade for hard work well done. You have the power to remain one in Jesus, regardless of what the world may show or tell you, and regardless of what may be your fears from the past. I promise you that the accolades that you receive for wielding the power of Love is more glorious than your soul has ever imagined. This takes courage for you to believe. You have great faith! And, this is why you are so happy! How happy am I that you have said 'yes' to all that Jesus has asked of you. My Special son, it is now time for Me to present to you a litany of praises that I wish you to remember. I ask you to hear and ponder them individually and collectively, as they are a portion of the great Light that is bathing the faithful with renewed hope.

> *The Mercy who saves has come.*
> *The Spirit who shines is alive.*
> *The Angels who bless have arrived.*
> *The Wisdom that glows is true.*
> *The Light of Heaven is forever.*
> *The soul of mankind is saved.*
> *The Son of God is resurrected.*
> *The Blood of the Lamb still flows.*
> *The Saints in Heaven intercede.*
> *The Holy Eucharist is Jesus.*
> *A penitent heart will know Salvation.*

The Mother of God is your Advocate.
The streams of Heaven quench your thirst.
The Glory of God is your food.
A Confession today will bring you rest.
The Day of Reconciliation is here.
The Deposit of Faith is true.
The Sacred Heart is invincible.
The Immaculate Heart is compassionate.
The Gospel of Jesus is your future.
The Grace of the ages is forgiveness.
The Divinity of hearts is conversion.
The Knowledge of God is service to the poor.
The Kingdom of God is at hand.
The Beauty of Love has arrived.
The King of kings is now reigning.
The Fruition of Eternity has begun.
The Purity of mankind is in prayer.
The Miracle of Redemption now lives.
The God of your fathers has forgiven you.
The Celestial Court is prepared.
The Cross of Salvation tastes sweet.
The time for Eternal Glory is now.

My little child, will you record these important petitionary litany-phrases in a safe place? You shall fully realize their power when you stand to announce them before the throngs and masses who will come seeking your counsel and prayers. Thank you for consenting to participate in the continuing conversion of the world. I am happy that you are enjoying My messages. You will see the progress that AD 2000 will bring. This is a time for reflection and jubilation!...."

Sunday, January 9, 2000
4:45 p.m.

"To My little springtime buds of Light, I know that wherever there is suffering, pain, sorrow, agony, or indifference, you will be there in good deed and holy prayers to bring the hope that feeds the heart and compassion which warms the soul. I have returned to you on this Midwestern day in America to seek your continuing prayers for all who are burdened and afflicted throughout the world. This is the Januarius during which you can ponder what the newness is all about, that of reconciliation and understanding, solace, peace, and conversion. Can you not see the fruits of the work that My holy ones are offering, feeding those who know not how to pray? Can you not feel the radiance that is only now breaking the horizon of your future? My little children, blessed are you who continue with perseverance toward the perfection that Jesus seeks in all. It is a lonely world to those who do not yet know Him, and to those who refuse to let Him in. I ask you to remember them in your humble petitions because not many will pray for them. It is an act of high piety to pray for the lost. Perhaps you know that it will make all the difference in the world to these lost ones at the end of time. The height of piety is found in the humility of the heart, the reaching-out in servitude and Grace to lift the oppressive yokes from the little ones who are so helpless amongst the rest. Desolation is abhorrent before the eyes of those who are holy enough to care, who are living in Love, and Love in them. The world reeks of indifference during this modern time when the prayers of collective humanity are needed the most. Through our prayers and these hours which we spend together, reparation is being made for many inequities, comfort is brought to those who suffer in Purgatory, and jubilation is planted in the hearts of the Saints who are eager to intercede. Why then, My children, will not the entire world cry-out for Jesus, for Justice, for Salvation? I will be seeking the answer to this question until the last child of Mine on the Earth hears My plea. There can be no proper reconciliation of Heaven and Earth as long as a singular soul holds-out in obstinance against the Love of God which binds all humanity as one. There is no Hell which can hold the converted, and no reason to wonder why the healing of the Earth cannot come today. We hold deep in our hearts the Truth because the Almighty Father has placed it there. Your Heavenly Mother is with you to help you destroy every facade that should attempt to distract My children from knowing perfect Love. Therein rests the reason that we pray together and ask all continents in every hemisphere to hear the voice of their Redemption, the Holy Spirit of My Son, Jesus Christ. There are no more reasons for My children to decline because every alternative has been buried beneath the ages by the Blood of the Cross. We rest in the comfort that the union of the highest Heaven and the most forsaken soul is found in the recitation of just one 'Our Father.' That is more than a simple wish or whim, it is the holy invitation to Jesus to reach well below the tabletops of the affluent to claim the souls who truly love Him with power. And, this Man of giant Divinity stoops to conquer the sorrow of anyone who is so humble to call-out His Name! This Gallant Star will shine with rays of Love so profound that the dungeons beneath the Earth are blindingly bright to the conquerors being held there. Yes, these holy men and women are the sunken vessels who await their resurrection from beneath the crest of the teeming seas! These little ones who cry in loneliness are causing the Angels on High to come running to their aid, and bringing the singing Saints to cup their ears in hope that they can hear the most faint of uttered words. My children, these are our people! These are the pious hearts who sparkle at the brim of Jesus' drink of consolation, waiting to be consumed by one who cares to the death that they again become whole and dignified in the likeness of Eden. When will they come to where the fruits are harvested every month? When God turns to you and tells you that you can stop praying now, time is done. Oh, what a glorious day that will be! The Son I call Jesus is on His feet now and is shuffling His vestments around His shoulders, looking across all the heavens in the joy and anticipation that the approaching moment has nearly come. He has trained His eyes on the inclement world and has told Me that it is time for Me to accompany Him on the journey of Life, of Everlasting Life for all who live and have died in His grace. My children, I cannot tell you the hour that He will come, but I can tell you that He was still seated before Pope John Paul II opened the Jubilee Door. And, now, He is standing to bring us all to the realization and reconciliation that His every prophecy is about to be fulfilled. How He shines in this Glory! How He knows that this victory is real and as new at this moment as twenty centuries before! How I come now in new anticipation because I see the new glow in His eyes! We wait for the word, the single most important utterance ever to come-forth in Creation, that of the Almighty Father: *My Son and My Mother, Bring Me My People*! These lofty truths are real and alive. This is factual Salvation and everlasting Glory! And, it is all for you! The parables are correct and the Gospel still breathes! This, My children, is why I come to you donned in happiness and peace. I come to implore you to pray for the weak, for those millions with crippling disease, for the millions begging to be born, and for the wretched lot who do not care why. This is the dawn of the new hour, and I have come to celebrate it with you..."

Sunday, January 16, 2000
4:14 p.m.

"To My very loving children who so seek the justice of your Divine Lord, I come again not because you do not understand the Love of Jesus, but because you know Him full well. You have accepted My Son for all that is good in humanity, for the ease of all your sadness, for the Light of Truth where there is darkness, and for the eradication of your most errant impressions of what Salvation is all about. Have I not told you that perfection and justice have already laid waste to evil and indifference? How many Saints before you have poured-out their lives seeking not the motivations of God, but ways through which they can alleviate the suffering of people for His sake? Humanity is crying-out from the depths of all that is malignant, and you are answering with kindness and service. If I were to reveal to you the outcome of the genius of Love in the world today, as I have told you before, you would lay down your hands in assurance that the Son of Man can do it alone. But, the Holy Spirit needs you as I need you, not to question and complain, but to continue in faith. If there is a scoreboard to this last century of the Earth, you would not be able to see it over the shoulders of the jubilant Saints jumping in ecstasy before you.

You are the Christian witnesses for the Holy Gospel of My Son on the Earth. Love in your hearts tells you that you have chosen the long and difficult path, one on which you will not always be able to see for the buffeting of hatred against you. It is not a lack of cooperation from the Kingdom on High that is causing anyone frustration, but the lack of Love of those around you. They have been given a will to employ as they choose. If that collective will has not yet been transformed into the perfect unity of all humankind under the Cross, then war and dissension will continue, division will linger, and human suffering will proceed. As long as there is one soul on the Earth whom God knows will convert at the last who is still giving-in to a renegade spirit, He will dispense the gift of asking the most noble in the world to suffer for his conversion. My children, you are listening and speaking to the Mother of that singular God, present in Three Divine Persons and Sacramentally-blessed on the Earth. I am the reflection of the Wisdom you need to grow to be like the Angels and Saints in Paradise. When you acknowledge an inequity or heresy on the Earth, that in itself is a prayer to God to change it and make the world more holy. Living for Jesus is not winning a game whose parameters will end before the mortal Earth comes to a close and then going on to something else. Seeking the Kingdom of Heaven to live as wholly on the Earth as it is in Heaven is an ongoing and perpetual process that will lead you all to everlasting Life from where you stand, sit, or kneel. Humanity will always need the grace-filled Sacraments; and God will always need you to defend them until the end of time, at which these Sacraments will be revealed in their true Light, their most clear Revelation. But, until the time when the Sacraments are exchanged, until they are transformed and transposed into perpetual fact, they will be opposed by the enemies of the Church and the rogue atheists who are determined to see Her fail. That is why you must not surrender to them, and why you must continue to pray and hope, awaiting in joyful fulfillment for the Coming of your Redeemer. The skies are not always blue because the Earth needs the showers that quench the thirst of the parched life below. Hence, there will be human suffering as long as there are spiritually-famished souls on the Earth who need the fruits of that Love to transform them into perfect Light.

My children, it is obvious that the Crucifixion of Jesus has already eliminated the stench of evil and indifference from the face of the Earth. But, not everyone on the Earth has accepted that Sacrifice as reparation for the fall of humanity from Paradise. It is not a lacking in compassion by God that makes the world an awful place, it is the blatant refusal of lost souls to wield His power and dignity that inhibits the Earth from being the perfect reflection of Heaven. I ask you to not allow the ensuing days to diminish your belief in all that you have written and prayed-for. You are wielding the power you wish to extend over the blasphemous forces in the world. Human suffering is already being diminished. Hundreds-of-thousands are already coming to Salvation in Jesus by your prayers and holy works. Do you believe the words

'It is finished (?)' Those whom you believe are being left-behind are already included in the Divine, benevolent, and healing plan of God. Was the Crucifixion an event that occurred during the mortal time of humankind? Yes. And, that suffering is still alive because it is the reparative balm for a tawdry and sordid world of people who are still running from that same Crucifixion. My son, you are asking the same questions that tried to frustrate My Immaculate Heart as I stood beneath the Cross on Good Friday. I asked God in Heaven—How can this horrible suffering and tragedy bring the restoration of Redemption for My adopted children? And, His answer was in the Blood being poured-out on the ground a few feet in front of My sorrowful eyes. He calls that 'Love in unbounded Beauty!' Can you not see, then, that these are truly the End Times? And, for that, you should be happy! How can My Triumph be seen by all humankind if My children run about the Earth saying that it is too dark to see it? That makes no sense either spiritually or physically. You must remember that the work that we have done together has already borne fruits upon which many are already feasting. If God had not dispatched Me to seek your assistance, how would you have gone on? My son, your brothers and sisters will come running for the holy confection of conversion once they have first savored the sweetness of Love inside their hearts, and not before. If you will continue to pray with Me and all the children of Light, that day will come. Considering how you feel while looking at this world, how do you suppose the Savior of the world feels, He who hung on the Cross and died for the Salvation of every soul? Do you believe that He is frustrated? The answer is no! He is patient, and that is one of the greatest fruits of His Divine Love. He is waiting for everyone to stumble upon the Truth and accept its overpowering beauty and perseverance. Many people will profess to follow Jesus in all ways until it comes their time for sacrifice, suffering, sorrow for the suffering of others, and their patience. Please remember that being with Me also means sharing My service as the Lady of Sorrows until God, Himself, says enough! These are the days which are transforming the face of Creation. You are living them now. Frustration and anger toward the Throne of God are the fruits of error and lack of peace. Prayer is the solution. I am assured that you will live only the happiness of the Holy Spirit in all of time to come. Please be accepting in all which God provides, wills, and allows. Your Master's decisions are most infallible in every way. At the end of time, you will see this very clearly. You will slap your forehead with your palm and say 'Oh, I get it!' Thank you for praying with Me today. You call with 'Hail Mary' and I have come! This is your holy blessing to help you continue through the ages. + I will speak to you again very soon. I will always love you. Goodnight!"

Sunday, January 23, 2000
2:00 p.m.

"It is for the cause of your great joy that your Mother Immaculate has come to pray with you. My children, you rest in the arms of the great Love of your Savior, and sweet is His compassion and comfort. You shall never know any greater joy than this, nor should you ever be tempted to seek a more noble berth from which to envision the unfolding of everlasting Life. The world is not at ease because it battles daily over the right to bear the name: Impressor of the universe. My children, the impact and impression that collective humankind has made in the history of the ages is pelted by periods of darkness and outright evil works. These are not just the shadows that are revealed by the children of Light, but are malignant forces that are on the move. The darkness is brought by the dormancy of millions upon millions of dead consciences. We have set-out to awaken them, and succeed we must! Those dark corridors will be flooded by Light upon the reveille of My children, My army of holy people who will soon rise-up like a mighty skyscraper and shed the scales of the Earth that bind them to indifference. My children, I have often told you about the difference between the knowledge of God and the resilient willingness to work for God. We are still transferring the Wisdom that the body of humanity needs to make this transformation, allowing the Holy Spirit to work in and through the children of Light so as to expunge all pales of darkness from the face of the Earth. This is why you are praying, and is also why your work is still an effort in progress rather than a finished work on a pedestal. If you choose to remain in union with this great prophecy, you will recall the reason why I gave you a word such as *accourse*. In the end and at the last, all of your hopes will be realized. But, I tell you and ask you to continue to be patient while you are laying those individual bricks. You do not yet know what God will do or allow. You are contemplating the completion of your labors, the additions and betterments that will augment your capacity to succeed, and the time-frame you wish to pursue. I tell you again that God will glorify your work, that your mission has already succeeded, and My messages have been given to the world. Whatever you achieve in addition to this is Grace atop of blessing, the extra garnish, dressing, and gravy for a Feast which already tastes sweet to many thousands of hungry hearts. Please do not walk in wonder of whether you will be successful anymore. Contemplate instead on the steady progress of watching the continuing victory unfold before your eyes. This is My perpetual wish for you from your Lady of Perpetual Help.

My children, the world about you is in its last turmoil because its energy of offensiveness is at its peak. I have told My children through recent decades that the Cup is full and running over. *'What does this mean?'* is what many of My children ask. It means that Love is being violated today as much as on the Day when the Savior of the World was crucified. It means that sin and deprivation are still pungent to the senses of those who desire the holiness of Jesus. You must remember that the Saints in Heaven were once mortals on the Earth like you, and so much in fact that they were lured and tempted in many of the ways of modern men. But, My children, you should always remember that twenty centuries of sin have never stopped the power of the Cross. Temptations of the flesh are no more powerful today than in the first century, but also is the forgiveness of God just as powerful today as it was then. Millions of souls have bequeathed lofty sonnets and poems to Creation about their desires to conquer the flesh. And, through The Divine Mercy, absolution, and ordination of the Plan of God, they indeed reached the plateau for which they could previously only hope to achieve. My children, those sonnets and poems are the memories that were penned by a people who knew to be holy, but yet did not know how to remake themselves into the image of Jesus of the Gospels. The Holy Spirit, My children, is He who is this catalyst and discipline. If not for the Divine Grace who is the Holy Spirit, there can be no righteousness of the heart or purity which is a prayer to the heights of Paradise for a better world to come.

Yes, when Jesus says that cleanliness is next to Godliness, He is speaking of the spotless heart, free from the encumbrances of hatred and deceit. No soul who has ever gone to Heaven claimed any remnant of the repulsive obstinance that divides men on Earth and causes shameless indifference to grow. The heart which is fed by the Holy Spirit willingly incinerates every scintilla of offensive nature that could cause a speck of dust to infiltrate the glossy perfection of saintliness. At the last, even through all I have told you about coming to see Jesus the best you know how, perfection is still perfection. Your soul will be rendered like the Divinity of Jesus at the last, or you will never set foot on the lofty streets of gold. My children, Salvation is this simple, but Mercy is also this real. Can you go outside your door today and greet very many souls who bear this perfection already? The answer is yes, but they will not keep it nurtured through simplicity and humility. Their perfection slips from their grasp because they have hands made slippery by arrogance, impatience, greed, and cynicism. My little ones, none of these traits is inherent in any soul, but are progressively learned through the passing of time. Remember that it is the 'God-side' of man that keeps mortals humble and holy. This is the wish of My Son for the Earth, and is what He asks of everyone who has been given the Breath of Life. Jesus knows full-well that this is a difficult process. Life is not easy because goodness is opposed in all quarters of the Earth. Men are apt to fail because sometimes their vision is clouded by distraction and temptation. Remember that bishops and Popes alike have had to go to confession too! This gives great venue for those farthest from Jesus to begin the journey of faith back to Him. Mercy is a long-distance runner, not just a sprinter in the darkness. And, for all the lost people you see who are wandering in hopelessness and ignorance, your prayers and the Holy Spirit are their compass and Light.

The friction which is generated within the spirit of a suffering soul provides the brilliance for all the world to see, not a searing heat that will melt it into oblivion. I ask all of My children to pray for the end of the *need* for suffering, as well as for the cessation of suffering itself. It is this lack of prayer that makes little children run in fear, expectant mothers to have their unborn babies killed, and mentally-afflicted saints-to-be to sit in corners with their faces in their hands, tears streaming down their cheeks while crying 'Please, just leave me alone.' It is wholly and exactly a lack of prayer that causes this pain and brings agony to a world which seems to be going nowhere but deeper into the pit of despair. My Special One, what I am doing with you is a salve for the suffering that I have described here today. Although it seems that much is still yet to do, God will never turn to you and say, 'It is not enough.' Always remember that one 'Hail, full of Grace!' began the downfall and defeat of every form of evil that Satan could possibly conceive. Jesus effected it physically through His Passion and Death, and Crowned it with His Rising from the Tomb. We still glow in the aftermath of His Resurrection! It is the Light by which noble men walk, the Wisdom through which wise men preach, the vision that allows young men to prophesy, the courage with which persecuted men prevail, and the perseverance through which humble men serve. That Light of Jesus will never let you down! He will always say 'yes' to Love again and again. He cannot wane because He is invincible and immeasurable. In Him, you cannot fail because you are heroes and conquerors. Nothing shall prevail against the power that you own in Him. This is His Promise, and this is what He has asked Me to tell you today. I ask you to always remember that I will never abandon you. You are My children for whom I have lived and loved. Thank you for your prayers... I will be with you always and everywhere. Please be careful when you travel..."

Sunday, January 30, 2000
3:31 p.m.

"What a beautiful snowy day you have been given on this blessed Sunday! Your Lady, Queen of the Snows is with you to pray alongside your petitions so that God will be moved to alter the face of the Earth. I hope that you remember to pray for all who have no heat in their homes, and for those who have no homes at all. We remember everyone who cannot seem to compete in the capitalist West, along with those in Eastern nations who have nothing to share at all. And, let us always pray for the deliverance of the unborn to birth, not just because it is a politically conservative thing to do, but because it is the Will of God that all life be brought to fruition. My children, as uncomfortable as it might seem to try to avoid in your country, just as eight years ago and four years ago, I ask that you not get caught-up in the hyperactive hustings of politics and elections that distract you from your prayers and our work. I am happy that you allowed Me to come to speak to you..."

Sunday, February 6, 2000
3:44 p.m.

"I come today to speak to My dear little children whose redeemed souls are the sweet fruits from the salvific Cross of Mount Calvary. My children, not only do I come to speak to you, but by calling you to action, I know that you will lead My other children to the singular Sacrifice which is the doorway to Heaven. You have begun this year 2000 in earnest, and time is so swift that it will be springtime where you live. This must be a renewed day, a fresh beginning for your hopes and expectations which always seem to become frozen beneath the stillness of winter. You do not yield well to the Plan of God because your consciousness is shaped by the environment around you. The atmosphere about you must continue to be one of prayer. I cannot tell you too many times that the people of the world are not praying enough, and those who do pray have all but extinguished their own light of patience, wondering when God is going to answer their call. My little children, love for Jesus means that you will live in faith that the unfolding of His Kingdom is on course. All who claim to be My children are searching for supernatural signs and miracles whose time has not yet come. The Resurrected Savior of the world is calling you to live this faith, this Love. He knows how your hearts yearn for change, for solace, Justice, and reconciliation. I implore you to continue to rest assured that the Holy Spirit is guiding you, is leading your way so that you can know already that you have succeeded.

My Special son, I travel the world-over and find it to be the same. My messengers to whom I have come know the Truth which I have revealed. They know the Gospel because their hearts are united in this New Advent. But, to My great sorrow, they will not exercise the patience that is required for other hearts to finally learn this Truth. My own little children are that hypocritically selfish! This gives Me great sorrow beyond all that falls before My eyes. My very own little children race throughout the world trumpeting that they know God better than the lost, and then say, *I want My Salvation now! I want My reward today*! So I ask, what do we do, leave the lost behind? Do we allow them to drown in their own sins and indifference, or do we teach them to swim the ocean of Divine Love? And, as we teach them, this takes time; time that is unfolding in this very age. You can see this in every direction you look. Why are not My children more patient? This is the question I continue to ask. I have yet to receive an answer. It is such an irony to Me that Jesus has thus far been 1,967 years patient, and I cannot urge My modern-day children past another rising sun without having to beg for another day's peace, patience, and understanding. Of course you should continue to pray *Thy Kingdom come*! Of course, you should pray that Jesus' Light will be the true dawn tomorrow. But, we should all pray that He will arrive to the cheers of believers, and not the wails of hundreds of millions who are unprepared. Thank God that the Reign of Justice did not fall upon the Earth today! Thank Him that He did not close the door on those who still have a chance to pass through! These are My grave concerns which keep Me moving about the world, seeking a more noble persistence in My children's hearts to know that Jesus will come in the fullness of time, and not before. And, what is that fullness of time? It is when every message that I have given you for nearly nine years is heard by every ear. It means that all on the Earth will eventually have the opportunity to turn a humble spirit toward their Lord instead of a defiant one. It means the time when the newborn cries of all the wholly innocent ones who have been aborted can be heard above the collective roar which ushered-in the 21st century around the world. I am telling you all of these things because all of this can happen in one day, one hour, or one moment! God knows when that instant will occur, and we yet do not. Would this miracle for which My children pray truly be believed to the depths of all hearts, the moment would be seized by the Savior of all Glory and the world would be ended at last. I will give you a better description. The world requires greater patience because Jesus is waiting for the likes of obstinate ones who pray the Rosary and claim to be My children, and then spit in the face of true warriors. He is waiting for people to deliver the gifts of bread and wine to the Altar who do not believe that radio hosts are the solution to western social problems. He is waiting for all priests to rise-up and say that abortion is murder and marital infidelity and divorce are mortal sins. He is waiting to see His priests on Earth who do not drive Lincoln Continentals. He is waiting for humanity to help My little messengers to an audience with the Pope because they are believed, and not being pushed aside by millionaires who purchase their way into the Vatican with the wealth they have pilfered from others. He is waiting for national leaders who will guide them in the conscience of the Christian Gospel, rather than rallying around the most distracting product of the day. The design of modern culture is deplorable because all of these things are still in the way of Thy Kingdom come! Does this answer your question?

    My Special son, it is only a sparse few people on the Earth who are willing to change this, and you are one. God will soon bring you the miracles you need to succeed if you will only be more patient. Of all the words I have told you in nearly nine years, *patience* is the one that I have uttered the most. It is the same all around the world. And yet, patience is the single virtue that is lacking in My messengers most of all. Why? Why will My children not listen? Because they do not yet truly trust God to get it right. Your impatience is portrayed subtly. The biggest lie that you are living is this incessant drumbeat from your inner-self that you are somehow not doing enough. It is the exact and sole cause of your lack of peace, even greater than your own disdain for the evil that others do and your recognition that good people will not employ their venues to change the world and alter the course of human destiny through their

Christian conversion. My messages to you will not cease. They will even increase in number as the world comes to a close. Nothing is definite when the outcome has been left to human discretion. I am happy that you are My children."

Sunday, February 13, 2000
3:33 p.m.

"My dear children, the Truth is clearly seen in time that everything I have thus far told you will indeed come to pass. With your work, you are about to forever change the lives of wholly unsuspecting people, souls like you who will be forever Mine to place inside the Sacred Heart of Jesus. I do not envy those who would attempt in vain to steal them from His embrace. I pity anyone who would even try at all, for the wrath of God has yet to come like He will rain on those who approach the Savior of the world and say, *give me back that soul!* They would be better to try to swallow the millstone around their necks with the bitter tears they will weep forever to come. I have seen those who have been finally united in My Jesus like a child in the womb. My children, your dear Savior is the same. He does not believe in or condone abortion after death! Today is, as you say, a signal of many auspicious things to come. I have shown you the power of patience, just as I addressed it in My last message."

(Our Lady gave me a text to read that had been written by the Angels. It was a celestial oration that was beyond any ever heard to this modern day. My heart was taken aback by its beauty and vision. The Blessed Virgin continued.)

"The reason I asked you to read this piece is because it is very similar to the statement of vindication that Jesus will offer to the Almighty Father at the Final Judgment of every redeemed soul. His words are of this majestic oratory. He will repeat it for every single soul ever given birth who has been granted Eternal Life, just before the God of your Fathers moves the tassel on your caps to the other side and transfers your souls in commencement onto the streets of Glory. My children, imagine what an assembly has gathered for this final celebration! Yes, the one called Abraham, your Father in faith, and Abraham the Emancipator of the servile will sit in adjacent seats to savor the joy! The Abraham of old was spared his son, while the Abraham of the nineteenth century was slain to make men free. God has always been the same; the victory of Justice is always in Him, and wonder, perfection, goodness, propriety, prophecy, and conclusion. I know that you can already sense the joy of the new springtime of Christianity which is pouring from future time. You could sense it in the openness, kindness, and nobility of your Bishop on

February 9th. There is a signature of imminence in the air that is becoming more apparent to many. My children, this is the greatest sign of My work in dispensing the graces of the Holy Spirit through My loving intercession. If the world will come to Me, all will be led to their Savior. If the proud will give their strength to Me, I will make them the most profound witnesses for the Gospel in the world. I know that I am preaching to the choir who already sings for Me, but I do not tell you often enough that your Salvation and that of the lost is the reason I have come. The Kingdom of God for which your hearts have yearned cannot slip from your hands during this new period of the harvest of souls. You can find no reason to defer your joy to any worldly sensations because the New Advent is growing more perceptible by the day. One day very soon, you will be like the little child who lay in a heap on the ground with his shoes jolted from his feet and stars above his head, saying with joy and satisfaction, *Life gets no better than this*! My children, I promise that everything I tell you is true. I cannot make it too clear that the day of endless sun is about to break. I sufficed this point with the words, *Your prayers are the Light of His dawn (February 23, 1991)*. You can see precisely what I mean. My Special son, your Mother is very happy with your work and pleased that you continue to pray the Rosary everyday. Thank you and your brother for being obedient and staying away from the stench of political rhetoric in the air. How nasty, snarly, and quarrelsome they are! It is alright to see it on the civility of the public airwaves. You see many more kind people when there are not millions of dollars in advertising at stake... Please remember to pray for the unborn, for those suffering in Purgatory, and for those who do not know God..."

Sunday, February 20, 2000
3:01 p.m.

"Oh, My dear joyful children, I beckon you to remember in your hearts that My Love is more overpowering than any force which might try to distract you from the Divinity of God. Wolves may try to break down your door, but My sweet lessons of Love will guide you in the way of righteousness and peace. I call you to hold fast to the teachings of the Holy Cross and remain beneath the safety and comfort of My golden Mantle. Today, I have come only to bid you peace and joy, and to remind you that the prayers of the faithful are keeping the hopes alive of many destitute souls. It is in this great anticipation that millions of My children live, and it is because of My intercession that God is asking you to respond. My little children, can you continue to realize this holy line of communication? Can you see in your hearts that the Light of Jesus is getting brighter by the day? And so, My Love ushers-in this great time of awakening, conviction, and conversion. I live in Heaven and on Earth because your souls are the saints of My Immaculate Heart. All that is of God resides with you there, and the Kingdom which He offers springs from that great Font. The Divine Blood which has saved your souls from perdition has flooded the world and become the reason for your lives. My Jesus is the great Lover of humankind. And, I offer Him to you from My Womb. Today is one of acclimation because it is the transformation of many lost souls into the Sacred Heart of Jesus. It is a process of change because the Spirit must grow in you to make you perfect. I have seen the invaluable fruits of this Grace by which you are eternally saved. When you pray, always remember that this same Grace places your holy supplications in your hearts. All that is of God is good, and all that is good He gives to you."

(I have been suffering from a terrible cold during this past week. Our Holy Mother responded to my condition in a very compassionate way.)

"My Special son, I see that you are presently not feeling well. These viruses have a particular function on the Earth, but they can cause great discomfort when they take residence in the human body. Some viruses consume other horrible strains that would be more deadly. They keep agents away from parts of Nature that would render your springtime absent of flowers and leaves. And, as you will soon see, the common cold virus is about to be cited as a tremendous ally in the fight against some inner maladies of the brain and spinal cord. I know that this information does very little to make you feel better today. You will find that your own system of human antibodies will be even stronger in the future by virtue of this experience. I do not wish to keep you very long today so you can rest. I have simply come because you are praying and to let you know that I am praying with you. We will pray together that your works bear fruit."

Sunday, February 27, 2000
3:43 p.m.

(Before I began to pray my Rosary this afternoon, I had taken my clothes which were left in the dryer from the day before and tossed them in a pile on my bed in the upper part of the house for later folding in preparation for the coming week. But, Our Lady began by addressing them.)

"Thank you for praying, but My holy messages will not come to those who refuse to properly fold their laundry. I will wait."

(I quickly went about organizing and placing the clothes in the appropriate drawers. Then, I returned to my prayers and was greeted again.)

"Thank you. Now I can continue to speak to you about the Glory of Heaven and the continuation of the unfolding of God's Plan for humanity. My dear children, you are seeing many false attempts by man to unite himself with God. Unless a soul is led by the Holy Spirit, it will not find everlasting Life or true meaning in mortality on the Earth. You, My little ones, have been one in the Holy Spirit for many years, especially the most recent eleven. You know that I own the reason for the only success that you can achieve, and He is the Child of Bethlehem who also owns you. Can you see how the human mind has taken many ponderers down many stagnant and errant paths? The Holy Spirit of Jesus will guide and teach you always. His Light is the Wisdom by which you walk. Take comfort in knowing that you are one with Him and traveling the road to everlasting Salvation. In that knowledge, nothing can discourage you."

(Our Lady went on to describe more poignantly the errors of false philosophies by saying the following.)

"Existentialism can be described as a dungeon. One is quite correct in describing such darkness and captivity. Only Jesus is the Light, and only Jesus can save your soul. The so-called peace that others feel who follow existentialism is not the peace of the living Spirit, but the stillness in the wake of their dead souls. That is why there are no choices in Christianity. There is no alternative to perfect Love and seamless obedience to the Truth of the Holy Gospel. If a man decides to choose, he must choose God, wherein any further choices are rendered obsolete. By choosing God, the decisions are already made which affect the purity, dignity, and destiny of the soul. The decision is already made to bow in deference to the King of all Creation and to relinquish your will and sovereignty to Him. There is no autonomy in this righteous state because the human soul cannot claim Salvation without Him. Hence, you are one in God through Jesus, and this is both your freedom and reward. No one should wish to exist anywhere separate from Him. Do you see how such philosophies as existentialism come to be? People will not accept the Cross of Mount Calvary or the Trinity of God. No wonder they are blind! Jesus saw their blindness during His Agony in the Garden that you are praying right now. His wish of 'Come to Me and see, and be seen' was being ignored by the barrage of self-interest by those who fell asleep! I ask what else He could have done before that Maundy Thursday to prove His role as The Christ! His miracles, prayers, and teachings seemed much too frail that fateful evening. And, I have told you that modern-day life is an image of the Passion of this noble Man! The world is again that garden on that sedentary night. But, the Son of Man has risen! This time, those who sleep are being awakened by the horrific Truth that they cannot fail this Master again! The twenty-first century has opened to be the night in the garden where no eye can fall asleep! This time, millions are awakening and crawling prostrate to the Altar to say 'I am here to serve You, I will not rest until my soul sleeps in Thee!' This is why there is great hope in the modern-day world. I am pleased to announce that rather than sweating droplets of Blood, the Savior of the world is shedding tears of joy that so many are following Him. Rather than looking into the sky and saying 'Let this cup pass Me by,' He is now saying 'Let Me drown in this chalice of Love from My people!' Oh, how prophetic was that night that has brought this living day! How you will remember on March 8th *(Ash Wednesday)* as you recall your destiny before Him. You may be marked with ashes, but your spirit will soar anew with the joy that all you have come to be is made perfect in His Grace. You will remember that human suffering is not inevitable because the God of Israel will take it away. All you need to do is ask the Messiah, My living Jesus and Manna of the Altar, and human suffering will be no more. My children, the world suffers not at the hands of Love, but because humanity will not take the Hand of Love. This is a collective manifestation composed of individuals who suffer alone. But, their collective agony is the Light of the Cross still glowing in the darkness of the world, and will continue until the last lost soul can see his way Home. I ask you to continue to pray for those whose lives have been given to join the power of the Cross. Indeed, they have not lost their dignity. They have found it there! They are claiming it for those who still refuse to know! They rest in grief over the pits through which many would fall into the fiery abyss, laying in wait for souls who could not find God without them. Remember that each time you see a soul on his deathbed, he is blocking a place in Creation through which other souls might fall into perdition. These saints are proud inside to fill this role. Just ask any one of them, and they will tell you. They are too noble to complain, too loving to say no, and often unaware as to the reasons why. Jesus has spoken to their spirits and asked them to join Him in the Redemption of man. In their own holy subconsciousness, they say in reply 'Our Lord, to whom else could we turn?' My Special son, that is the essence of what I have come to tell you today. I am very happy about your plans. Whatever you give to God in His Name, He will use for the conversion of souls. I know that your heart keeps asking when? Perhaps the answer will come when you prove that you accept the timing of His Will. The ark is not fully loaded yet. Allow Him to proceed without living in anxiety. Waiting in joyful hope is a fruit of your patience. Thank you for your prayers. This is My holy blessing for you. ✝ I will speak to you again very soon! Please remember to pray for those who have nothing to eat! I love you. Goodnight!"

Sunday, March 5, 2000
5:40 p.m.

"To My two beautiful sons with whom I am very pleased, I come to bring My everlasting guidance and prayerfulness. My children, I visit you today to remind you that the Holy Gospel is continuing to bring conversion to many lost souls. As this process unfolds, I ask for your patience and peace in the knowledge that the victory of Justice is nigh at hand. Can you not see its arrival just-past the horizon in your hearts? This patience for which I call is the inherent and spiritual slamming of your book upon the coffee table tops all across the world stage! The silence is deafening to those who are about to awaken to a new sense of Truth, just as your friend has portioned that the priesthood and the Holy Eucharist are rooted in the Old Testament because they are Sacraments of the New Covenant. I cannot make it too clear that the Holy Spirit is working in many ways that you fully comprehend, but yet do not completely see. This is why your prayers are so important; they feed this converting transformation through which the world is now going. I must tell you, My little children, about the caution that I wish you to take in reading and listening to lengthy dissertations from such intellectuals as social theologians and journal-artists. Words come very easily for these people because their vocabulary is so large. This allows them to draw many mental images that are oftentimes not contextual in the sense of sacrificial Christianity or of the Traditions and Dogmas of the Original Apostolic Church. Jesus is never difficult to perceive where He is present because Love cannot be concealed by intellectual architecture. Therefore, please continue to seek-out the simplicity in the writings and expressions of others, lest you find yourself grappling for the understanding of all the Doctors of the Church combined, including the holy works of Saint Thomas Aquinas. The metaphors, mental images, and poetic works must never make you have to decipher an equation or examine a corollary in order to discover the intrinsic Gospel message in a particular work. Had it been the decision of God, for example, your book could have been 1,600 pages of text with such difficult terms and expressions that only the most highly intellectual could have translated its message. But, in that sense, how could we have reached those who are still lost in pragmatism and the superstructure of grammatical quandaries? I again ask the world for the same simplicity that is apparent in your Diary, not for a course in quantitative analysis or arithmetic methods. The simple Truth is just that—easy for the little hearts to recognize. I am not impressed by high-flying theologies that try to render the understanding of Love, of God, nearly unattainable to those who need to understand the most. Remember that My answer was not a rhetorical qualitative affirmation, it was a loving 'Yes,' unconditional Love that still lives to this day. My affirmation is a simple Fiat—Let it be done! My children, the rest is a matter of prayer, contemplation, good works, and public example of the service, teachings, and Wisdom of Jesus. Thank you for allowing Me to record this contemplation, as I know that you have understood its content prior to this message. I wished you to have it in your collection of messages for the record."

(I recently placed a picture of a miraculous rose petal on my website that I had personally taken so everyone could share it. I know it is an authentic picture. Although this is an amazing gift that Our Lord wishes us to dispense to the world, a certain man chided me by saying that I should not advance such things because there are so many people who could duplicate a facsimile and perpetrate a religious fraud. His words put me into a state of uncertainty, to which Our Lady responded.)

"I also am quite pleased that you have placed the photograph of the rose petal on your website. You have done well. For those who call for the removal of this picture because someone else may have falsely reproduced it, would they also wish for you to discard these authentic messages because someone in another location might have reproduced them and called them their own? Someday, you will have to understand that you are never alone. Then, you will be most like the Savior of the world. You also have Me. There is no difference. Your faith makes it the same. Can you ponder what it is like for the millions who travel through life not knowing Jesus as their Savior and Me as their Mother? You are a fortunate little boy! But, we have not conceded the loss of any heart to despair! In time, we will fully succeed, just you wait and see!"

Sunday, March 12, 2000
4:44 p.m.

"My little children, I have come again to pray and re-pray the holy sonnets of Love which are so dear to the Sacred Heart of Jesus. You inquire whether the Love of God can overcome your sorrows, defeat your enemies, and destroy the obstacles to your faith. Yes is the answer! The Cross is your living evidence that you are victors and conquerors on the Earth for the Kingdom of Heaven. If you wonder what to call this joy, name it Peace! You have set-out on another journey of Lent, like the many you have observed before! You ask—what can I surrender to God; what is something new and special I can offer? You ask how this Lent can be a greater sacrifice and period of penance than any that have gone before. The answer is that God sees your patient conviction through the procession of time as this greater sacrifice. Not losing hope is your gift to Jesus! Continuing to sing the praises of Redemption when it seems farthest from your hands is your acclamation that man's unity in My Son is near at hand. I have told you about the graces and gifts that lead you always to new beginnings. Each Lenten season is a new beginning because it is your compliant affirmation to your Heavenly Father of your love for Him. I ask you to remember that the Holy Gospel is timeless, and that your Lenten gift to Jesus is as enduring as your joy in sharing His Eternal Resurrection. I bid you to beseech your Creator to bestow the awareness upon you that each sunrise and sunset is a unique and individual parcel of the greater reign of Dominion that He holds over His people. Then, you will be humble and holy, and your faithful intentions which seem like mere subtleties to the world will be seen anew as deafening clarions, ringing-in the calling of the Heavenly Hosts to every heart, into every land and all the nations.

My dear children, I ask you to look at all you have given to Jesus over the past decade and more! My Son does not forget, and He sees where you yet cannot see. He will grow your gifts of generosity with blessings of His own. Jesus knows and lives all mortal life with you, even from beyond the Grave from which He has risen. Your prayers have changed the world, and My Son answered them on Good Friday. He knew on that day what I would be saying to you on March 12, 2000 at 4:44 p.m. All of My messages are one, and you have been lifted beyond time to receive them because I have never taken a pause since I first uttered the words, *My forceful one!* It is you who have suffered the endurance of time and rejection, of sorrow and dissension, and of agony and disappointment. The Son of Man is incapable of allowing your lives in Him to be in vain. He cannot say *no*; it is not a word that even God Himself can muster to those who love Him. Whether you choose to believe it or not, the end of Creation is pouring-forth in front of your unsuspecting eyes. Your consciousness cannot see it, but your hearts and souls know it full-well. The lives you have given to Jesus are your momentum toward Salvation, a gravitating force and power that will instantaneously take thousands of souls to conversion with you. And, what is the origin of this divinity? Your imitation of Jesus and reciprocation of His Sorrowful Sacrifice on the Cross by your reception of the Holy Eucharist. The Son of God has married your souls to Eternity by the rings of His Precious Blood that flooded the Earth beneath the Cross. Go forth and enter these rings! With these rings does He wed you to the perfection and everlasting life of glorified Redemption! No mortal has the power to break these bonds! My Special son, do you remember the ring of gold that your brother left at the feet of Jesus on Good Friday many years ago? This is an intention of humanity, for humanity. Jesus seeks all of His children to reach-out to Him in similar ways. Many precious souls give their entire lives to Him as representatives of that ring of gold, an unending circle of sacrifice and suffering for the conversion of men. Jesus is sitting at the right hand of the Father as a much happier King because of such lives of love and faith. He sees your life, one with your brother, in much the same way. Just as the Holy Trinity is one singular Truth, the many faithful Christians who have bonded their lives for Jesus are His one Body on the Earth. My children, I come to you today as a very happy Mother. I have joy in My Immaculate Heart because of children like yourselves who are continuing to pray for the Arrival-in-Glory of the Messiah of God. His Return to the Earth is imminent, and your own patience is a portion of the Passion which He suffered to save you. Your anticipation is the Light which keeps other hearts warm. Your faith is the compass for the journey of all. Your joyful acceptance of your own participation in the Cross is the reason why the Body of Christ on Earth will remain whole, come what may. My children, as though many might see the conversion of humankind as a mass or function, let them know therefore that the system is in place and the catalyst is the Love of Jesus Christ. The spark which has set the flame ablaze occurred when the Son of the Most High rose from the Tomb and again declared with profundity, *I AM!* This is the essence of your hope and the reason you shall never desist in your humble service for Him. It is the purpose for your living, because I AM made it so. You owe all of this to Him in return. Your account to God is paid in full by the Blood of the Cross, but to the Lamb who paid it, you owe honor, praise, glory, and dignity. Every single Alleluia is the sound of your faithful voice piercing His eardrums in jubilation. He is with you in the desert of life, for He brings the Angels to comfort you and the Holy Spirit to convince you that He is the Truth. No night, no matter how long, can conquer the Living Day of the Son of God, My Son, the Prince of Peace and King of Creation! No spot on a baptismal gown is a permanent stain! No strife can outlive the Love who has destroyed it! No error can approach the Truth of Love and ever live to tell it! And, no grave can hold a grasp upon a soul who has been bathed in the Blood of My Jesus, for He has rendered the human soul unable to be bound by mortality or the Abyss that succeeds it! My children, your souls now have wings with which to fly in Eternal Paradise! You are free to know peace and beauty! You cannot be detained by despair because the jubilation of the Easter Mysteries gives you reason for joy! There is no longer sadness or wailing, and no more gnashing of teeth for those who are united under the Cross of Jesus. This is the anticipation with which you tread through Lent and walk through life. You are a good and noble people, and your inheritance is great. Give your hearts to this joy, and your trials will be few and your blessings many. My very Special son, this is My message for you today. Do you understand all I have told you?"

(I was nearly in tears while listening to all She was telling me. I asked Her to make it possible for everyone to hear what She said today.)

"My Son hears your prayers, and He will make this come-to-pass before your presence on Earth moves to a close. You are transforming their lives at this very moment. Does this day of Jesus not tell you that this is true? It is those who refuse to share who cause such deprivation, those who say that they will offer a pittance more only if they are given relief from the public mandate of taxation in return. I promise that Jesus hears your prayers and will respond to your pleas. You will see Him at your side when you hand the keys to those westside estates to the poor for which you pray. I will speak to you again soon to help you celebrate your new joy!"

Sunday, March 19, 2000
3:10 p.m.

"My sweet children, you bear the sheen of holiness, possess the nobility of princes, and emit the Light of Love which can come only through the Divinity of God. I come to you today on the happy occasion of the Feast of your foster father, Saint Joseph, although the Church has set aside his celebration for tomorrow. Please remember My spouse on Earth as the power of all the Saints in Heaven, and equaled with My new Spouse of all Eternity, the Holy Spirit of Wisdom, Love, Grace, and peace. Why do you wonder, My children, whether God will ever glorify your work and fulfill your intentions when He already has and will continue to do so? Your timing is not that of the Almighty Father, but your time itself has come to be His in this age and all to follow. I come again to remind you that prayer is the reason for your life, as well as your tangible works of servitude. Not all of your brothers and sisters know, and too many others will not comply. Your lives are making-up for them, and setting the stage for their conversion. This has been the case since the first followers of Jesus were called Christians at a place known as Antioch. You are the worthy descendants of the Holy City Jerusalem, and are the stepchildren of the first family of Nazareth. You travel inwardly and outwardly for God at the guidance of Angels and the Holy Paraclete. You search for shelter to bear your good news to the world and ask all who will hear you to respond to the admonitions you teach them. I am the Morning Star above your journey of this Second Advent, and the Lamb of God lives within you. Therefore, know our dear Saint Joseph as the contemporary power of sainthood incarnate who has tread the Earth before you to honor, protect, and serve your Savior and this Mother, all for the conversion and Salvation of humanity. Would that all My children be like Saint Joseph, the world would end in an instant with a flash of righteousness so bright that even God Himself would blink with astonishment. We are all one because our Baby Jesus brought the Earth more than conversion, and much more than piety. He has singlehandedly bestowed upon every soul who will accept Him the transformation from moving away from the Light of Glory to a celestial path back to God and the original Divinity who has created the universe. By no means is this simply a casual alteration! This is the actual re-creating of an existing humanity, side-stepping mortality and corruption by exterminating sin with the Blood of Universal Love! Yes, Jesus has reversed the flow of the death of mankind away from the Abyss, and has replaced it with New Life which flows irrevocably toward the mountains of invincible Paradise. The parting of the Red Sea was only a scratch in a marble surface compared to the canyon of hope that Jesus has restored in the hearts of men. The Deluge for which Noah prepared was a single tear of joy that God shed in knowing that His lost people would be saved by the Sacrifice of His Son. His casting of the stars across the dark velvet night was a sprinkling of seed that has now given birth to a new dawn of joy! The harvest is sweet and will begin as the King and Champion of the Cross ushers-in the permanent Dawn! I have told you that flowers have a soul called Love which makes them grow before your very eyes. My children, all Salvation is a flower, and you are the Love inside whose growth brings the Kingdom of God to bloom on the Earth. Your love and prayers nourish that Kingdom, each of you like a star in the night, resting, waiting, working, and praying while God the gardener watches you sprout to within His grasp. Your righteousness makes-up the Heavenly trellises where the Saints before you still bow to pray. The Father of Creation waters you with the rains of compassion which keep you aglow in the hands of His glistening Son. My children, not only is this a parable, it is the undeniable Truth! This is the Resurrection for which you are yearning; you are living it now! So, there is no connotation to a number of boxes or an allotment of days. Heaven and Earth are one, and everything *is*. The last chapter which was written by the Son of God has a postscript that many are still waiting to see. It is the pot of gold at the end of the rainbow, the view from the summit of Grace, the first fresh breath of Heavenly air, the best that has been saved for last. Yes, it is *Morning Star Over America*. And, it is sweet and kind, wise and prudent, and the reason two obedient little boys in a humble village called Ashland were given the Breath of Life. Please be patient, I am telling you the Truth."

(Within the past few days, my brother was again given the opportunity to appear before a public board for the purpose of advancing the message of the Gospel, especially with respect to caring for the poor. And, as is often the case, this group of individuals was immersed in self-aggrandizement and partisan bigotry. Timothy offered them great Light in the gentle way that Our Lady has taught him, but they scowled in defiance as if his words had no place within their thinking whatsoever. The Blessed Virgin was pleased with his witness to these people.)

"Your brother can bring a crowded room to its knees with commanding authority. He has done so with stately kindness, and with the power that cannot be denied: The Truth! You must be quite pleased by your own conclusions about men in positions of power. They deny this Truth; they deny any responsibility, and they dodge the finger of culpability and become quite obstinate in the face of moral courage..."

Sunday, March 26, 2000
2:19 p.m.

"Through the kindness of your prayers of holiness, I have gladly responded by coming to ask God to aid the world in its deliverance to conversion. Why do we do this? Because humanity is collectively meant to accept the Salvation which Jesus has won for you. My dear children, I ask you to recall the many purposes that were served as My beautiful Son spent forty days in the desert. This was more than a physical journey through a barren and dry place. Like the Cross itself, the penitential period in the desert proclaimed the spiritual cleansing of all humankind. His temptations portended your own power to overcome them in this day and age. His persistence in piety, humility, and self-denial is the tripod upon which He has placed His inner-vision of your future as the world comes to a surprising culmination. How can such flowers of Grace which include your own Redemption bloom from such a desolate place? Because Jesus' Blood on the Cross can grow righteousness and eternal life in the most devastated souls, those who are farthest from God, and those who have yet to realize that the Crucifixion is the reason for Life. Jesus' Blood is the genius of all the Heavens which makes humankind whole once again. The Passion of your Savior is the Wisdom that teaches you to follow the narrow path of Truth and Light. This river of Love is a laser to happiness and peace because all darkness is dispelled in its wake. Yes, this is the season of Lent, and you grow more aware by the day that God is with and in you to guide and lead you to perfection. I have revealed to you through many ways how this period of revelation takes you to a singular consciousness in God by the day Good Friday comes to pass. It is often asked, 'Where were the first Apostles during Jesus' forty days in the desert?' My little children, they were where you are now. They were living amidst the wicked, fighting for the Truth. They were preparing for the agony of their own forty days, praying that the Son of Man would remember them in the suffering of His own. Yes, He never forgot a soul; He never relinquished His power of perfection and divinity to the wares of the world. The spiritual journey which you now travel is a ratification of your unity with Jesus, and is your forward commitment that you will walk in His steps. Please recall what Jesus was asked to accept; the wealth of the Earth, the power of all kings combined, and a feast befitting of any emperor. Jesus did not refuse these temptations because He already owned the world or because He knew that He could turn stone into bread at the blink of an eye. It was not because He had already known Glory that He declined a view from the highest perches on Earth. No, it was all more simple than that. He refused these temptations because He is Love, and Love is sacrificial, caring, exemplary, and unable to be bribed. And most of all, Love knows that anything which is not a Sacrament from the hands of the Father is not worthy of pursuit by any mortal man. Your service in His Name is your Lenten gift to both the Godhead in Heaven and humanity alike. This Christian life is more than an assemblage of virtues, it is the reason why God has deemed you worthy to be called His children. It is the reason why babies laugh and flowers grow. This pious life is the existence of all goodness and divine essence in one body of man, awaiting the Groom to re-enter the cloud-shaped vestibule. It is the reason why suffering souls thank God for the opportunity to be united in His Son for the purification of those who despise them with outright hatred. This Lenten season which you have embraced is the flickering ember that will ignite the flame to incinerate all anti-Catholic universities in one gigantic flash of expulsion. My dear little children, you have chosen to join the ranks of the legacy of the Saints because you are united in that Love, and your soul cannot help but live in this bright peace. Somewhere in your most remote psyche lives a seed of loyalty to Jesus that refuses to be kept hidden. It calls and scratches and gnaws until your human will allows it to fly freely, just like you released the bird from your down-spout today. This is the seed of Divine Truth which has already bloomed into petals of beauty, witnessed by the twinkles in your eyes and the glow on your face. This is the Holy Spirit at His best in you, ready and willing to take-on any opposition because this same psyche knows that you cannot lose. I ask you to remember during the remaining days of Lent that this period of self-denial is more than forty consecutive days in mortal time. It is your recollection of the sinless peace that lives inside your hearts, a gift to those whose suffering persists for all 365 days of the year. It is your prayer to God to remake the face of the Earth in your time so that you can physically see what your spirit already knows to be soon on its way. I do not challenge My children to do many things because it gives the connotation that God requires you to compete with Him. My call instead is an invitation to become like Him in every way by living-out the words of the Gospel and imitating My Son. This cannot be easy because so many souls are divided from you. They cling to their own possessions like pacifiers, not knowing that at the last, they will choke to death on them.

Therefore, My pretty ones, I ask you to recall what I have said, and employ its Wisdom in the proper time and place. I realize that this seemingly contradicts the patience I have asked you to employ. But, in union with the Holy Spirit, you will see the timelessness of it all. Your Lenten prayers are beautiful. I promise that Jesus will answer them all. He does so because He is Love, and He will not betray the trust that you have placed in His power. It is your faith that is making the world a better place for everyone on Earth. My Special son, one of the key aspects of your behavior that pleases Me most is when you display your capacity to be happy. This consoles Me most of all. Your Mother sees you the same way that you see little Kolby! *(young nephew)* I am pleased that you will welcome Me to return soon. Always remember that I shall forever love you!"

Sunday, April 2, 2000
2:58 p.m.

"My joyful little children, I wish for you to remember that only by giving your complete selves to My Son will you know the true source of Divinity. He has called everyone in the world to be His apostles and disciples because there are souls who are lost in dark corners where only hermits would hide. He calls you to be His apostles, which is an early term in Greek that means, *one who seeks*. My children, it is important that you remember what it is that you are searching for. Are you searching for righteousness? Yes, this you must find in yourselves. Is it the material for which you seek? Only to incinerate it in a fire to warm your spirits and light your journey. At the last, is it a high public stature or social posture that is the basis for your apostolic commission? Not at all; this world is not the holy City of God. My children, God is calling you into an apostleship for the purpose of living as souls where the confluence of the acts of Mercy and the Beatitudes become one in your hearts! God does not only reveal Salvation to you by the miracle of faith and the Divine Sacraments before your eyes, but also by knitting your own share of the Cross with the singular one that has redeemed you. God gives you the cloak of holiness from His sacrificed Son, portended when the soldiers stripped His from Him on the day He was crucified. The banner, the torch, the sword, and the mantle were all passed to you on that day! Jesus said nothing to His executioners because He knew that you would defend Him today! When you stand and affirm your sacrificial love for His sake, your words resound from the backdrop of the Good Friday skies, echoing throughout all Creation for every last soul to hear. Your cries of loyalty and acclamation were the thunder that was heard from above! And yes, the soiled hearts that still roam the Earth are as silent today as the sinners who denied the Son of Man when they had only hours to join Him. This humble God-Man of just thirty-three years has already forgiven them all! They were ignorant, He pleaded to His Father; and many are still ignorant who walk in contemptuousness and haughty disdain away from the Most Blessed Sacrament that this mortal world shall ever know!

My Special son, these are the images of Lent that continue as your days pass quickly by. You have the advantage of biblical history on your side that was not written before we lived those monumental days. You know that the Lamb of God was slain in a bloodbath so repulsive that only a mere parcel of humanity bothered to observe! Little did they realize that the Father would transform this tragedy into the Salvation of their souls! Make no mistake, this great catastrophe is no Titanic laying somewhere beneath the North Atlantic seas! This is still the Life-giving Blood for generations to come, two-thousand years and counting, and all which preceded them too! This living Crucifixion cannot be expunged by the dusty shelves of centuries past. It cannot lay under the rubble of the bin of human inequity that is still attempting to put it behind them! I assure you that this is true because the Resurrection of Jesus gives Life to all that is good. And, the death of Jesus on the Cross, wiping the world and its humanity clean of sin, is the greatest act of redeeming Mercy ever to be dispensed from the Bosom of God. This, My children, is why we celebrate your faith, why we hope through prayer, why we see more clearly in your suffering, and wait with joyful anticipation for the Return of Jesus to take His people to Heaven."

(Yesterday, I was in the process of emptying my small garage so it could be demolished. I was removing truckloads of old materials that had been laid above the ceiling braces many decades ago. As I neared completion of the task, I lifted some old pieces of wood, and beneath them was a picture frame laying face-down on the rafters. It was covered with a thick layer of dust that had accumulated over the many years it had been there. I grabbed it as another item of junk and was ready to throw it into the bed of my truck, but as I turned it over, I saw that the frame contained one of the most beautiful images I had ever seen—Jesus elevating His Eucharistic Body as He did at the Last Supper. His countenance was majestically somber, yet emanated a peaceful power. The black-and-white picture was a framed First Communion gift that belonged to the previous resident of my home that dated back to June 1, 1919. I sat for a moment in wonderment about how something so beautiful came to be placed in the attic of a garage, and remained there unharmed for so many years, only to be discovered on this day. I considered it a great gift from God that had waited there for me to find it. During Her words, Our Lady referred to the picture.)

"I am happy that you discovered the First Communion relic from 1919. Do you know what night the picture celebrates? Yes, the Last Supper. I ask you to keep this relic as a gift from the Saint who used to live in this house. My Special son, of all the depictions of the Face of Jesus which have been made in the world, this one is the most accurate. I thank you for cherishing it so well. Someday, Jesus will allow you to see this in color, just as the transformation was made in the basement of the Springfield Marian Center in 1991..."

Sunday, April 9, 2000
3:20 p.m.

"Can it be possible that a humanity which is so unprepared to meet its Maker is about to see Him Face-to-face? Yes, indeed, is the answer to that query of holy revelation! I have come again to pray with you because there still lives the arrogant among the humble, the proud who oppress the simple, and the wicked who persecute the faithful. The world is yet fraught with peril and greed, and tart in the very quarters where it must become the most sanctified and sweet. My little children, your brothers and sisters must become like you, knowledgeable in the ways of the Holy Spirit, and willing to relinquish their lives to the advancement of the Kingdom of God on the Earth. The peril resides in the corners of Creation where the Blood of Salvation is rejected outright. My little ones, if I were to ask you to select a number that exists between 1 and 58,000, can you tell Me the number that would be the least among those selected? The number is, indeed, two. Do you know why? Not only is it the least obvious, those who respond would have an entire spectrum of 57,998 numbers from which to ponder, not knowing that the answer that God has provided is resting the closest to their soul, the reason for His inquisition of 'Will you come back to Me?' You may try this every day for the rest of your life, but you will rarely be given the answer of two. To many, God seems that ambiguous in a body of undetermined creation, a small contingency in an endless pool, and an anonymous spirit among all those who seek their allegiance. My children, the vision of the world must be better defined. The criteria for the judgment of righteousness must be so focused upon Love, that the consciousness of man must wish to stray no further than the singular God who has put the question, present in the Trinity, which is concurrently and omnipresently the Deity of Divine Purpose. Can you see that the multiplication of words of which Jesus speaks is a product of this propensity of mankind to be so undefining? Yours is a God of the particulars of goodness, service, holiness, and peace! Your Salvation is the explicit and concise fruit of the Blood of the Cross, not the many errant theologies which try to explain it away! Your ever-knowable Creator is concealed in the grace you cannot see because of the blinding Light of the Love you can see! Dare any soul to turn a disavowing shoulder to this redeeming Truth, and he will be simultaneously saying 'no' to Everlasting Life! Would there be one who would refuse to taste of the cup of suffering, and I will show you the same one who shall never set foot on the streets of perfect gold! My children, if there is a soul in the universe who bears the audacity to scoff at Mercy, that same soul will grieve forever in the charred remains of the creation which he has burned. There is no solace in rejecting the forgiveness of Jesus because that is where only Life can be found. So, those who will scan the continuum for any number but two cannot see the Hands of Divinity in front of their face. My pretty ones, I will not rest in My prayers and intercession until all of My children look directly where I point them, undistracted by the glittering world, whether it be material wealth, physical satisfaction, or promises from other mortals that have no chance of being kept. There is a charter of hope which hangs on the doorway of Salvation which reads 'Enter if your soul is well prepared!' That means only your soul, wrapped in the stately cleanliness of your baptismal gown and saturated in the Blood of My Son. The Angels who will escort you to His Throne will never approach someone who still holds fast to their wares or the stench of egoism, or the burdens of impurity. They will stand aside and allow these souls to see themselves as they really are, tethered to a weight so unbearable that they cannot escape their own fall. My children, Jesus is your profound release from these bonds! His Resurrection is the reason that Salvation will not let go! I am telling you today that there is hope for them all, there is perfection where there once lived corruption, there is sainthood where once stood sinfulness, and there is freedom to conquer any constraint which might snag your gown on your flight to your Celestial Home! This is the Truth that has conquered the bewilderment that keeps humankind asking the question 'Why?' This is the backdrop of all your dreams, the pedestal upon which the future rests, the pool from which the parched may drink, and the ultimate Eternity in which the wretched may finally escape the perils of time to once again take their heavenly seat of humility beside Forgiveness, Himself. All of this is inscribed upon that plaque which is posted at the doorway where the human conscience finally awakens to God. It is held there by the cohesion among men and crafted by hands of unity who have all come at last to understand what is written in the Gospels for the whole world to see. It is a phonics of service and love, pronounced with a deafening roar of 'We win, because Jesus has set us all free!'

My little children, I speak of this consciousness because it is coming of age. All of the kittens are finally realizing that they belong in the box because it is their deliverance Home *(ref. message of May 22, 1992)*. Your Mother has the joy of telling you today that these last days are meaningful to the point that My Son is about to bestow a blessing upon His people that is unprecedented since century number One. It is the Two, the Second Coming of this Valiant Warrior who is gleaming with joy that His followers are clearing His path. But this time, My children, He will not come alone! He will not warble in a Nativity cloth, but will roar with the power of the Cross! He will be accompanied by nobles and princes from every former age who dared to stand firm for His sake! He will usher-in servants and queens from under their habits which kept them in prayer in convents. This God of all Creation will shower upon the world the happy souls who have preceded you in death and have been raised from their graves!—your loved ones and leaders, fathers and Martyrs, and brothers and sisters of Light! All of them will come sailing into the land of New Liberty that you will know as Redemption! So, whenever someone asks you to pick a number, allow your heart to make the choice, and you will never, ever be wrong! Let Jesus be your Judge because He now holds your Judgment at bay! Let the Angels rejoice around you because I have ultimate victory beneath My Mantle, and I have already dispensed it to you. I give you Jesus! I give you peace and patience and love and pardon and Light! Thank you for allowing your Mother to love you this way! My Special son, I have given you My message for today, one that I know the faithful will love. I trust that you will be able to give it to them for Me in time!"

(I asked Our Lady a question about the opposition of those who reject the Truth of our living God and His mystical presence on Earth.)

"Let us allow Jesus to explain to others why they oppose the good works of the Original Apostolic Church. The answer to your question is to not allow their opposition to offend you because it is only transient in nature. Say what you have to say, allowing your prayers to do the rest. You should be pleased to be able to make your position clear. Remember My words from before, 'If you are not opposed, you will not be successful.' I wish to close with another thought about the tearful weeping of Jesus at the Tomb of Lazarus."

(This was in response to my recent contemplations. I had been praying to better understand Jesus' Heart in the moments when He raised Lazarus from the dead.)

"Do you remember that I told you about the irony of the agony and ecstasy of Jesus on the Cross? These tears that rolled down Jesus' Face were a product of His inner joy of what He was about to do, making a dead man walk again before the witness of the mortal world. Yes, He was sorrowful for all the reasons you already know, but He was also simultaneously overjoyed because He bore the power to overcome the wage that caused the death of Lazarus. This too preceded His joy in that His Crucifixion and Resurrection would redeem every soul who had faith in Him, even to this day. His weeping is for sinners, but His ecstasy is for those who are saved. They both roll from the same eyes which have seen the beginning and end of every universe and even time itself. This also is the source of your everlasting joy, knowing that your own tears are for the people of your day and for generations past, and for those yet to come. I will go now to shower more blessings upon the larger world, to teach and admonish, and to lead and intercede. Please continue to pray the Rosary for those who do not know God!"

Sunday, April 16, 2000
4:21 p.m.

"From the Divine Light of Heaven, I come into your midst in all ways to console, bless, and encourage you. My holy ones, not even the ages themselves can divide you from eternal happiness. Indeed, they give way and accede to the inevitable joy that you know in God. You are born as infant children to the Earth so that in your full maturity, you will know your own precious offspring as God Himself sees you now. This is the era in time during which you are to know Him best because you are at the very brink of His Return. Those who pass before you harbor no regret for having died. Those who once lived in faith are now savoring the reward of the promises for which they hoped. You cannot be denied Salvation when you take-up your cross in the Name of Jesus because God would never allow it. My children, I have seen God. I have seen the source of your everlasting joy. And, like the countless Saints before you, I know that human life on the Earth is no easy task. But, the reward is most assuredly worth the struggle. What mortal man could have known the Divine Mercy which would sprout from My Womb? How could anyone have imagined a Light so bright that it could be seen from the beginning of Creation to the last day of the mortal world and beyond? What soul could have fathomed a Divine Love so deep that the very Blood of Life would be extracted from His veins to destroy the Fall of Humankind? My children, I speak to you in dimensions about an infinite Deity. I call you to prayer outside the confines of your most private quarters. While you believe that you are kneeling alone in your humble rooms, Creation-Divine sees you perched on your knees, plucking a flower from beside the still waters of peace somewhere near a meadow in Paradise. You cannot be left alone in the Holy Spirit because this humble Paraclete clings to your soul for life in an otherwise lifeless world. Yes, I have seen God. He is indeed a Man, a Spirit, a King, and a majestic Ruler. I have seen this miraculous Love in every way, interceding to Him through My Son Jesus on your behalf. Dear children, in the dimensions through which I speak, I have not the phraseology to accurately describe Him. He cannot be confined to the echoes of My voice in this room or to words inscribed on a page. The Holy Scriptures are The Word which will take your soul to Him, but even they are like the mortal God-Man who had yet to reveal His Transfiguration. You must live this Gospel because the Commandments are the body who stands with you at the well! You must take this Love in hand as deeply as the spikes pierced His Flesh! Be impaled by Christian righteousness, and there will be nothing left in you for evil to skewer! My little ones, I come again today in peace, and I hold two of My precious children in My company. I bring with Me sweet Bernadette and dear Alta of your youth. *(Alta is Timothy's mother.)* This is the 79th birthday of little Alta, had she not been freed from the burdens of the Earth. Like all souls who have gone before, hers is now a land of perpetual birth and endless rest, dancing in the peaceful valleys and delighting in the highest peaks. Hence, My sincere little children of hope, please remember that this is your time which you are employing well, wise in the ways of God, preparing for the grand intercession of exile and Eternity, poised to receive the victory that was meant from the start, and expectant in all ways promised to you by the Savior of the world. You have been given many signal graces and miraculous wonders. Today is again Palm Sunday, reflective of the 1991 miracle in the skies, a reminder that God still loves you through the passing of this world, and a reward for the power you wield even today. My dear little ones, when that final day of Earth arrives, you will turn to your Maker and thank Him for the way the world eventually unfolded. You will see *reason* with a new vision because genius will finally be one in you. This is why you should always cast away your doubts and anticipate the fulfillment of the Covenant anew, pleased that you are participants in the uniting of Heaven and Earth, grasping only for more of the jubilation you will soon know with open palms of greeting from the Mighty Court which now awaits that day. These cannot be sad times because they are overflowing with this Truth. The images you saw in the Palm Sunday skies nine years ago are a signature of this opening fruit. I beg you to remember its scent that you savored then, to keep in your hearts the intentions of God on that quiet afternoon amidst the columns of graves. What better place for Him to reveal before you the ripening of this promise in your time! What a hallowed place to remind you of the Life which resides in Jesus, to which those souls finally were commended! This too is the solemnity and peace that you know when kneeling before the living Redeemer of the world in the Eucharistic Host; His Body, Blood, Soul, and Divinity in the Monstrance of the Altar where your Savior answers your prayers. The breath of God bellows through your pulmonary spirit as you seek His Divine Grace, knowing that there is nothing He cannot see, no prayer that will not reach His palate, no sorrow that will escape His comforting embrace. I beseech you, dear children, to continue to call upon Him today as you did nine years removed, knowing this time that all who hear your testimony will believe; millions will follow your lead, and great societies will embrace the messages I have given in this secret place, unbeknownst to even the most pious followers of Christ. I have told you the same as I once did Saints Bernadette and Alta on Earth; you will be despised and rejected among men, but the world will become a holier place. Not one pen-stroke or tiny petition will be ignored by the Messiah to whom you pray. Like the stitches in a garment or links in a chain, you are forever united in the fabric of Salvation and linked to the Kingdom above by the prayers you recite. Your soul is forever recognizable to God because you are laboring for His sake, seeing that the vine workers can always see the brightness in the sky, wiping their sweat with the soft brush of your love, and soothing their parched emotions with the counsel of your tears, shed for their own transforming sake. This is the journey which you have been traveling for many years on end. This is the mission which Jesus sees you fulfilling in the Glory of His Divine Resurrection. This too, My children, is why your very own souls will help make next week one of the most reverent in the Christian liturgical year. God's humble priests offer the Holy Sacrifice of the Mass to bring you the Manna of Life. And, they simultaneously bestow upon you the gratitude of a thankful God in Heaven without even knowing it. The Eucharist is your thanksgiving to God, but equally His gift of good standing upon you. My very dear little children, I have told you many things today about hope, joy, fulfillment, Redemption, and peace. I have an endless storehouse of Love to continue, but you have nearly expended the day. I will come back again, just as I told you I would before. I appear in response to your offerings and sacrifices. I come because I love you, and because the world so needs the Fruit of My Womb. Please have a pleasant Holy Week. Thank you for being My obedient children! I will be with you always. I will never leave you."

Good Friday, April 21, 2000

"If you tender the virgin reams of your impressionable heart to Jesus, where He might stoop to inscribe the future of the Redeemed, the Angels of Heaven will enshrine your holy goodness in an eternal framework of golden spires for all Creation to adore. But, should your spirit become the sordid leaflets of a saddened story bound only for the lost, your hopes will assuredly be cast into the leaping flames of the ever forgotten."

Saturday, April 22, 2000
6:10 p.m.

"Here amidst the mystery of this green Earth, sometimes dormant, often cold, occasionally barren, frequently frozen, but always blessed, will soon come the Eternal Messiah who has conquered the Grave by His invincible Love! My beautiful children, I have come to you tonight on this holy feast of the Easter Vigil to pray to God in Heaven that He will soon remake the face of the Earth by painting it delicately with the Resurrection of all sinners. These are the times during which the world must wait with high anticipation and wonderment, a humanity who must assuredly awaken at last to know with Divine Wisdom that Salvation is at hand. With all the power and Grace of the Church, My Son has conferred upon you the preparedness that you need to greet Him in confidence and peace. What is the celebration of this night? It is the expectation of the Kingdom of Glory at its best, a precursor for the final moment in time when Jesus will spring like the dawn before the eyes, hearts, and consciences of all men; when every soul will know who they are, why they are, and where they are going. The dispensation of this new beginning begs from the foyer of My Immaculate Heart to begin to pierce the world and all Creation, to consecrate the redeemed into the silent hours of thanksgiving Salvation and bring Light to savor all that yet cannot be seen by those whose faith is still keeping their love alive. I ask you to sit in that thanksgiving silence as you pray the reproaches which Jesus will ask of those who continue to reject Him. Kneel quietly before the Altars and apses of God's holy churches, and you will begin to hear the singular prophets of Divine Grace fall amidst your tears like raindrops on a metal roof, picking-up their pace as Jesus' Return comes ever closer, until the monsoons of Everlasting Life wash you all into the bays of Paradise. This can only be a celebratory night upon which Jesus will take you all into His arms and bid you to greet the preceding ages with gentleness and joy, and hold the hands of those who had to bear them in the night like your most prolific dreams wake you from your earthly sleep. Give yourselves finally to the King whose profile cannot be confined to the face of a coin.* *(See footnote.)* Admire and adore your Savior whose cloak has already wrapped you in 2,000 years of jubilation, whose Sacred Heart has long-since forgiven your sins, and whose Mercy speaks more profoundly than any oratory that might dare you to take any other road than humility. Acceptance is the face of the newborn foal who will soon carry your hearts to victory like a mighty steed. Prayer is the rapture that you have come to know in realizing that every one will be answered. The End of Time is near at hand, and your soul can barely withstand the joy. If only the faith of the multitudes would be transformed into this truthful awareness, you would see the Prince of Peace standing over you now. No grave, no mortality, no tomb, no torture, no Crucifixion, and no evil could cause the Son of God to spend Eternity in death. He has been raised from the Grave because Love is perpetually alive. God cannot be expunged; He cannot be lost; He will never be forsaken, and neither will He forsake those who believe in these things. I ask you to bow in deference to the little Prince from Bethlehem who has shown Creation what the title of 'King' really means. Grant Him the most stately of mansions in your heart, and He will reciprocally deliver your soul to His. Tonight, your inner-being knows the full vision that your faith can only imagine. The very essence of your spirit is glowing now because the Holy Spirit has set you afire. On this happy vigil of the high Holy Day of Christianity, your trust in the Man-God is giving you the radiance of a Heavenly Court, and you have yet to die to see it! Your embers are now zeniths and your flickers are now paling the lightning in the skies! These hours of bliss are your opportunity to realize what will soon happen when God the Paraclete finally announces at last: Jesus Christ has come! It is time for us to go out and meet our Lord and Savior!

    My children, just as this is the vigil that precedes the Easter Dawn, know in your hearts that you are preparing now! Know that My Child in the

Manger is unaffected by time; He pays no worship to the inclement shores of indifference which keep trying to wash Him away! He has no patience for obstinance from those who will not accept Him at all. Like the goats in the stench of their own illness, He will take only the savory souls who have been happily simmering in the warmth of His Blood to where the beginning of Creation rests. I tell you tonight, dear children, that you are a favored lot; you are a chosen and royal flock; you are blessed mightily, those who honor the forgiveness of the Father by running back into His arms to receive it. There are no callouses on His Heart because your conversion has made this world again soft and sweet! There are only scars of Love that have remained throughout the many centuries since He saved your souls! This is why the Easter Vigil is a new beginning for those who are lost, for those who disdain their very selves. The Kingdom of Salvation is approaching the horizon! So, lift-up your hearts to receive the Shepherd of the Heavenly Gates! Let this be your finest hour of paying homage to the Great Healer who has paid your passage back to the Kingdom once lost. If you can draw the conclusion that all things are possible with God, then there is hope for every soul. If you judge others, judge in their favor and grant them pardon in reflection of the Prince of Peace. Implore your brothers and sisters to imitate the kindness of Jesus, to walk arm-in-arm with simple love, and to absolve everyone who has ever offended you in the Name of the Morning Star. These are the prayers that I wish for you to hold in your hearts tonight, My children. This is the reason I have come. The world in stillness waits as in days of old. Join in that joy, and you will forever be glad that you have given your souls to My Son.

My Special son, this is the story of happiness that I wished for you to hear today. My son, I promise that mortality will not end until you have told of every word I have ever uttered in this house, every image, every parable, every lesson, and every promise. These are not just simply days that are spent in passing time, but a collective moment of perpetual preparation for the Return of the Savior of all humankind. Now, for the next weeks, we will celebrate this Easter joy! Thank you for your holy prayers on this anniversary day of your messages, the 22nd of the month."

* *Footnote.*
Although Our Lady delivered these words on April 22, 2000, I did not digitize them into a computerized format until October 14, 2001. On the morning of the 14th as I was dressing in my bedroom, I noticed an American half-dollar laying on my dresser. When I saw the impressed profile of President John F. Kennedy on the coin, I began to spontaneously think about what it would be like if all the coins had Jesus' image on them instead. I was carried away into a rather lengthy contemplation regarding the many dimensions that would be effected. I considered how some people might have difficulty distinguishing which coins were of what value, having only their size as a measure. I thought of the parable that Our Lord offered in Sacred Scripture about rendering unto Caesar what was Caesar's

when asked about the Roman emperor's image on the coin. *I thought about these particular things, and many others before I sat down to record this message which I had not seen since the Easter Octave of 2000. With this as a backdrop, can you imagine the Grace that was present when I reviewed the words, "Give yourselves finally to the King whose profile cannot be confined to the face of a coin." There was a complete timelessness present in that moment in a particular way, a signal grace and a proof of omnipresent divinity.*

Sunday, April 30, 2000
Feast of The Divine Mercy
3:00 p.m.

"Many hours of The Divine Mercy of Jesus have you prayed, beseeched, sought, invoked, implored, and been given. My little children, it is upon this Sunday, this Feast of The Divine Mercy of your Savior, that you realize that forgiveness is real, that Salvation is a breathing clemency, and that Eternal Life is an irrevocable gift to humanity. This great absolution flows from Love, from the Sacred Body of My Son, and is your essential delivery from the bonds of exile into the freedom of Paradise. Therefore, My little ones, you know at the last that Redemption is the confirmation and conferment of your own divinity. It is the deliverance of unending Grace upon your soul and those for whom you pray. You must not cower from the tenuous preparation which generates your conversion, neither should your faith become a tepid attempt at mortal goodness. Instead, My children, your Christian lives must be your authentic conviction to prayer, service, humility, and purity. God has given you His masterpiece in His Son. He has asked you to bask in the glow of His Countenance, to imitate His timeless perfection, to seek the wise counsel of His Spirit, and to take the hand of His Immaculate Mother. All of this is found beneath the Mantle of My Immaculate Heart. I will give you to My Son because I know this to be where you belong. I realize that you cannot get to Heaven unless you accept the Crucifixion and Resurrection of Jesus as just compensation for your sins. I commend you all to His Divine Mercy through one universal power. It is the Love of God! He dispenses Love to all peoples in as many ways as He chooses. His admiration for His children blooms from this creative Love. Everything you do in His Name resounds back to this unique and unparalleled perfection. You can never be shorn of divinity when you convey your soul, your heart, your singular mind, and your very life to this King of Creation.

My children, His response is always: *I AM He who has chosen the more compassionate course. I am the Love who has brought you Home, now at the brink of that Heavenly reunion of Creator and man. I have judged; I have sentenced, and now I have forgiven.* This is what drives the Saints and their pious successors on Earth to ecstasy in righteousness. This is the joy of the heart and the delight of your expectations. My dear children, the words that I choose to help you into a clearer understanding of Love will reflect it only if your heart is ajar and your spirit is in unity with the Gospel Covenant. Therein rest both the reason and purpose for the observance of The Divine Mercy of Jesus. You will recall that He has become all things to all peoples so that many will be saved. It is the purpose of the Hour of Divine Mercy to increase that number, to multiply the ocean of those who rest in the canyons of God's pardon by billions of souls. This is what we are doing together today. This is why we pray, why I seek your intentions in consortium with My own, and why you lay your souls bare before the Cross, the Vision of the Throne of God before you on the Earth. My children, with these noble petitions before your Father in Heaven, please remember all who will not pray and those who have no one to pray for them. Remember the power that My Son has given to you for the transformation of the world into the image of Heaven. Yes, there are intentions in your hearts that will not come to mind. Your Savior hears them anyway. There are countless souls whom you have never met who are in need of your prayerful petitions. God will respond to them as though they were pleading for your help before you now. I assure you that neither time nor space can prohibit your love from eradicating suffering and disease. No constraints can impede your King in Paradise from altering even history itself if you ask it in prayer. My children, when you turn to Jesus and tell Him that there is no more wine with which to dress wounded-humanity, He will flood the Earth with the savory juices of the grapes of Mercy in which every sorrow will drown, every breach of peace will be dissolved, every heart will be consoled, and every last whimper of any sad child will be expunged by the jubilation of the opportunity to begin again, to regain the virginity of their innocence once lost and a light once dimmed by mortal error. There is no wrong that cannot be made right, no death that cannot be made into life again, no insult which cannot be taken back, and not a single drop of human dignity that cannot be returned to the flask of happiness and joy. I have come today to tell you about Divine Mercy because Jesus seeks for you as much as you desire His Love. He knows that His very Being is a Divine gift to humanity, and one that must be accepted in order to be enjoyed. So, My little children, I bring that joy, that peace, that pardon, and that Grace. I am your Notre Immaculata who lives still to take you to your Advocate before God, My Jesus, for whom you now live and He in you. This is My message, My Special son. I have told you that My messages would be as pretty as those in times past. I give them to you because I am that same Love which encompasses your spirit. I am the Matron of the Deity to whom you pray. Today is a special honor for Me because I am allowed to see the wide dispensation of Mercy that Jesus is bestowing upon His loving children as you hear these words. I see that you are about to make your prayerful contribution to this blessed day. I hope that you will enjoy this prayer, to recognize how your love is in union with Jesus! I will never stop loving you!"

Sunday, May 7, 2000
1:46 p.m.

"My children, be pleased with your own hearts in that you have given your souls to Jesus! Celebrate the honor of knowing that your conscience is now guided by the Holy Spirit. There are many hours and countless days to come during which you will be happy to know that you have chosen the wiser course. My little ones, Wisdom is in knowing that the years to come are circumscribed by the everlasting Eternity which Jesus has promised before any of them ever begin. His Second Coming is imminent, as the testimony of your own lives truly reveals. There are too many signs and wonders for you to ignore the impending revelation of the last days of mortality. These hours can teach you more than any of the previous centuries if only you will continue to prevail in determination to seek the Truth. This is why Jesus is so deeply consoled by your service, sacrifices, prayers, and holiness. The world is changing now because you are transforming the inner essence of your fellow humanity. You are causing the expression of mortal purpose to be a manifestation of Divine ordination. How are you doing this? I will tell you simply in three words: You are love. In this, you can be of no greater power. Your nobility can perceive the Deity from no higher perch. Your humility can be of no sweeter origin. And, your future can be no more perfect than the destiny that you have chosen. You must realize how valuable your soul is. He has revealed many important facets of endless time to you through My Immaculate Heart. However, the importance of your soul to My Son is the most significant. Because you are a Catholic Christian, you belong to the throng which knows Jesus best. At the price of seeming redundant, you must know that your achievements through His Resurrection are the goodness through which many others are becoming His own. Indeed, the love that you share is the source of great comfort and refreshment to your Savior. Your prayers set His Sacred Heart aglow with justified admiration for all the lost, all who deny Him, all who refuse to come back into the fold. Your sacrifices are the delight of the Trinity, the jubilation of the Angels, and the pleasure of the Saints. You give new birth and dignified life to the Grace of obedience. You ignite flames of compassion for the poor and counsel for the wicked. You make amends for error and reparation for outright apostasy. You are a reflection of the Annunciation, the Nativity, the Passion, Death, and Resurrection of Jesus, all in one glorified moment. You are the feast to the Eyes and Heart of Jesus so that He may no longer look with a forlorn gaze at the people He has come to save. His joy reflects the happiness that your brother extolled as he wept while seeing the little children receive their First Communion at Saint Frances Xavier Cabrini Church today, and as they each carried a flower to be envased at the foot of My statue. Please do not wonder about the origin of this joy because you already know it. It is simply that God is pleased by what you offer, your creative obedience that makes the Earth a better place. Of course, you have been told that selfish pride is a terrible scourge. I am calling you to a humbler proudness to know that you are making your Redeemer so happy. This should give you both desire and the willingness to seek opportunity for many months to come. The principle is that the work that you have set-out to do will be effected by the miracles you are returning to God. You are the consecration of humanity back to Him, the devotion that He seeks in all His children, and the Light that flashes the Gospel message throughout the world like watching an ordnance detonate on the surface of the Earth from the highest of altitudes in the darkest of night. This is what your happy Savior sees as you commit your inner-self with joy to His purposes in His Name. I have spent a great deal of time expressing this to you because it is very important. You play a vital role in the dissemination of My messages to a barren world. You know that My words are true because your writings have grown from a sapling to a universal arbor. You did this by employing the power that God gave you to wield, transforming your greatest fear into your most prolific force for the goodness of men."

Sunday, May 14, 2000
3:50 p.m.

"How pleased I am to return to this very holy place to pray with you and to offer you words of encouragement during your meditations. My special children, even though your hearts and consciences rank among the most developed on the Earth, even though you are the senior elect, the varsity, and the emeriti who teach the world through your friendship with the Holy Spirit, you are still My wee little ones, the infant souls who shall always reside within the care and shelter of My Immaculate Grace. I am humbled to know that you have remembered to call upon Me on this celebration of Mother's Day. I am indeed your Matriarch and Advocate before Jesus to the Throne of the Almighty Father. To Him, your pain is the substance of miracles, your tears flush the world free from error, and your prayers are the proclamations through which the Angels make music before the Deity. They repeat your petitions to Jesus to the sounds of joy and gladness while the Saints of old cry-out 'Amen.' My dear little children, you have been told that the Third Secret of Fatima is being revealed. Many are missing the point. The emphasis is not upon the particular substance of the Secret, but that the Secret itself is finally being revealed. This is the focus which they should address. *Why is now the time for the Third Secret to be revealed? Why us? Why our generation?* My children, the answer is rather simple. The Reign of God is at hand. You can see this more apparently everyday. And, the world should also ponder the reason why it was *this* Pope who has been identified from the 1917 manifestations and miracles.

This should give civilization pause to realize that this must be a very apocalyptic time in mortal history. Please remember your reading today. There is no other Savior of mankind than Jesus Christ. The unfolding of His Plan and the advancement of His Kingdom has come. You will see this more clearly in the ensuing months.

My dear children, this also speaks to the skepticism that many have about the Holy Gospel. Many have said that the Word of God is contradictory. The Scriptures state that the Son of Man may return at any given hour, any day, and that neither He nor Myself know that time. Their complaint is that, *how can this be true and yet the Mother of God can give a secret in Fatima in 1917 without knowing that it would be revealed to have occurred in 1981 and exposed to the world in 2000?* The answer is that the Secret was to have occurred contingent upon whether Jesus returned before then. You must know that the substance of the Secret was given by the Father, and only He knows the day and the hour. If Jesus would have returned the very next day after the Third Secret of Fatima was given to the little child who still lives in a convent, Creation would have had no memory of it having been given. There are no secrets in Heaven, no prophesies of disasters and doom, and no unfulfilled promises. This, My Special son, is true genius. I must say, however, that the secrets and promises of Medjugorje will physically occur because they deal specifically with the consummate conversion of humankind and the dispensation of signal graces for holy works accomplished. Those who are skeptical about the Third Fatima Secret need only to employ faith that it was given exactly as it is now being revealed. One final point is necessary in this discussion. If the Third Fatima Secret had been an issue for the future and not one of the past, all humanity would have laid their souls along the line of one mortal event and not the immortal Resurrection of Jesus from the Grave. The Holy Sacrifice of the Mass would be placed second in many minds of good faithful Catholics because they would have finally had that first bite of something that would not require faith upon which to base their Salvation. I have not been sent to destroy faith, but to strengthen it. The Sacraments of the Mother Church are graces that enhance Wisdom, trust in the Holy Spirit, true goodness, and light. These are living organisms of the Kingdom of God on Earth now, not a prospect that will only be fulfilled in the future. At the last, all will know that the Gospel is accurate; it is the faith of humankind that will finally heal you. Soon, all who follow Jesus will collectively rise and walk together arm-in-arm into the hallowed halls of Redemption, the outstretched Arms of My Son, Jesus. At the end of that corridor is invincible Light, the center of all Mercy, the Sacred Heart which has purified everything that was corrupt in those who are bound for Everlasting Life. My Special son, I have given you the words I came to express today. I come in response to your love for God, and because you are My little children. Thank you. Please pray for the purity of poor sinners!"

Sunday, May 21, 2000
Canonization
St. Cristóbal Magallanes and Companions
2:59 p.m.

"I am your Love forever, My children. And, I am your Immaculate Advocate before the Wonderful Counselor. Concealed in your hearts, I have implanted the Wisdom through which your souls know the Truth. And, for this reason, you are now partakers in the Communion of Salvation and My austere children of Light. This is a special day because of the new Saints of the Latin Americas. I assure you that their holy intercession will flood the Earth with newborn hope. Let us continue together to revel the guiding help of all the Saints to assist the sorely bruised world. In you now lives the Holy Spirit of Resurrection, and the flame of God is still burning brightly there. It has been said that no one can know the secrets which reside deep in the hearts of those who meditate in fondness for Jesus. But, they are mistaken! The aura of righteousness is unmistakably curious to the world! The banner of Love that sails across the lofty skies of Christianity is as clear as the clapping of the noonday chimes. No one can misinterpret the true works of the Paraclete from On High, that pious Dove which gives your lives charm and new meaning. My dear ones, Paradise feeds upon the fruits of your conversion as you reciprocally receive the Eucharistic Jesus. No one can divide your singular presence before the Throne of God; no one can impugn your hungry spirit as you open-wide the doorways for Christ. No thief can steal you from the comforting embrace of your Father at the center of Everlasting Life, the great and Divine Dayspring of meaning for those who humbly seek it in His Name. My children, there are millions of words which can express the multi-faceted Glory you are about to receive. However, there is only one to describe the reason you will inherit it. The word is *Love*. I have spoken to you on many occasions, and will fulfill the spanning of a decade come next February. The singular thread of cohesion throughout all is the magnitude of the power with which Jesus loves you. There is no such thing as a parable of truth if that parable is not based upon the Life and Teachings of the Son of God. There is no suffering that is worth the pain if it is not offered to Jesus in honor of His own on the Cross. You must give your entire being, your very lives, your hopes, and your every encounter with human existence to the Man-God who has preserved your souls for Redemption. Where then, I ask you, is your most frightful thought? Where is the fear that has been taunting you since you so carefully took your first steps? Where is your anxiety and trepidation that causes you to be reticent in your faith in God? They are all exhausted and extinguished in your Divine share of the Cross on Earth. They are lost in the great expressions of inner-courage that you raise every time you tell someone who hates you that you love them. They are incinerated in the flames of your affirmation of faith that you profess to be like Jesus in all ways, including the avoidance of sin. Therein this Christian conviction you may not boast of mere pride, but you may assuredly boast of victory at every moment and happiness upon any avenue. You may tell your detractors that you are pleased that they will join you in Paradise someday because you have already seen their souls in the shadow of the Cross, despite their present errors and contemporary wretchedness. Yes, in your love for Jesus, you may already make plans to savor the riches which are now only a few more sunrises away from your hungry lips. You may look into the eyes of those who scold you for being fanatical in the cause of Christ and thank them for seeing Him in you. I am telling all the world that there is no other Salvation from the throes of Eternal damnation than the Blood of Jesus Christ! This should make the world leap with joyful anticipation because you have to look nowhere else. You need not search in forest glens or around the boulders of night. You need not fight the world for wealth and fame, because Jesus will not be found there. My Jesus is not concealed in skyscrapers or movie stars, or in fashions or pearls. No, My children, the Messiah of God is inside you, and an ever-present Grace in the pitiable lives, minds, bodies, and souls of the poor, the suffering, the despondent, and the oppressed. He is in the hearts of tiny newborn babies, and those who wished to be but were killed before they were ever given a chance. The Holy Spirit of Love is in the kindness between neighbors, in reparation for the bloodshed of war, and in the reconciliation between peoples too long estranged by greed, hatred, and visible bias. These cannot be concealed because they have been flushed into the open by the Blood of My Son. Now, the day in court for all who hope for the sharing of the fruits of the Deity has come. Justice has finally arrived in the fulness of Grace, not upon a horse or sheltered by armor, not sailing the calmer waves by some distant shore, but impaled to the Crux where two limbs of a tree mark the spot on the map of the Earth where God says, *'The treasure is located here!'* This is where you should dig to discover the goodness of your own hearts. This is where you will find the war chest to pay for your passage back Home. My children, what you will find there is a receipt for your journey already paid! You will find your own vestments to dress your souls in defiance of death, and a stone once rolled away from the face of a Tomb used as a paperweight to hold you fast to Salvation as the winds of corruption try to blow you away. These are the images which the Holy Spirit brings to your days. These are the parables of brightness and peace, of Love and forgiveness, of the future and beyond. All Creation can see as you progress toward that inevitable Port City of Light. You are like the little ants at a picnic, inexorably marching across the carefully-strewn fabric of Life, seeing the Feast that is your Host at the end of your journey. My Special son, I have so much more to say. I promise that I will fill these pages before the end of the summer with more words of Love for you."

(I told Our Lady that I was joyful. My brother and I had just completed some very difficult repairs on my home, which went very well.)

"I am also happy, but I was given reason to weep when you bumped your head. Please be more careful. I like the new back door! But, you are absolutely correct about sealing it against the rains. You and your brother work very well together, like two little children at play. Please be assured that if not for My lessons, the two of you would be fighting by now. But, what fruit could be borne from that?"

(At that moment my thoughts wandered to the seeming lack of acceptance of my first Diary. Our Lady responded.)

"What makes you believe that your work has not been successful? Please recall that it was thirty years before Sister Faustina's Diary prospered. This will not happen to you; there is insufficient time. Thank you, My children, for sharing your love and memories past."

Sunday, May 28, 2000
4:51 p.m.

"There have been blessings abound in your lives of Love, My children, but none the likes of those which are yet to come. Your Lord and Savior is factually and spiritually one with you because you are in His likeness, daring with courage to take-on the world that is numbed by corruption, eager to live for that which you cannot yet see, and invincible in the Light with which you blind others to the errors that they would otherwise never allow themselves to overcome. My dear ones, we have gathered again in this very holy place, this shrine to prayer and obedience, for the purpose of God. Hence, Jesus is also with us to hear our voices beseech His omnipotent power. This is not an oath that we have taken lightly since the days of February 1991. This is the continuance of our unity for all the definitions of 'goodness' that your consciences can apply. You will someday see the world as it fully exists at this hour, made more whole and sweet by the Angelic Salutation which you have so carefully and lovingly uttered. Now, I come to tell you of even more blessings because God will not desist in responding to your supplications. Many have said in centuries past, *'How many ways can Jesus show His Love for us?'* The answer to this inquisition is, *as many ways as humanity will allow*. My children, you will soon see the completion of another great essay which the Angels are dispensing to help guide the world to the Son of God. They will speak of the future that is already bleeding, but one that flows incessantly toward the Grace of Absolution. What is the barter; what is the cost? There is none because all accounts have been reconciled by the Holy Cross. The essential substance of mortal inequity has been avoided and disbanded, dissolved and destroyed. Now, Love not only can grow past any obstacle, but on a truer course made clear by the straightening of the crooked and finding of the lost. My children, you are busy these days with the details of the world and the changes you effect before you. It is good to concentrate on the work at hand. But, I continue to ask you to bask in the spiritual victory that you are winning. Do not forget the reclamation of decency that you have captured for Jesus. Never ignore the distance you have already traveled toward Heaven and the millions you are leading behind you. Yes, you have a tendency to forget your far-reaching triumph through the Grace of My Holy and Immaculate Heart. This is why you must be thankful to God for even having the ability to muster the Spirit of gratitude that He places in your hearts. Your compliance and joy have been the source of your success. You have banished wickedness through the mere circumference of your souls. Those who oppose you are stunned by the stature of your Divine piety. All of this is a gift that you now hold in your hands. This is real peace and true prosperity; this is Eternal profit and Everlasting Life. You lay yourselves in your beds inside the arms of your Mother and wake each day to the righteous approval of God. His Love is soft and warm to the touch of your invocations. The texture of His blessings is like silk against your face, like a running brook across your fingers, like the dove who flutters just overhead. The future holds great promise. These days are the continuing preparation for the acknowledgment by the world that your work is of God. You have accomplished everything that He has asked you to achieve, and much more will come. The Heavens are happy today because of the imminent observation of the Ascension of Jesus. This annual anniversary is the cause that made way for the Pentecostal miracle, the Power that lives on the Earth today."

(In this moment, my mind recounted the words I heard from a priest at the pulpit who continuously discounts and waters-down the explosive miraculous nature of the Holy Spirit during each great Feast of Christianity that he preaches. It is as though he does not really believe in the miraculous power of God in our day, so he rationalizes and discounts the Father's work so no one else will believe in these graces either. Our Lady responded.)

"What an infinite blessing for those who believe! And, it is by this same Wisdom that you so correctly assess the words of the priest from the pulpit. Your soul knows the Truth; your spirit knows when the counsel it hears grates against God's Kingdom within you. Never be frightened to acknowledge that the veil is always clearer to you, that Jesus is one whom *you* know the best, that the Grace in which you are vested allows you to stand on the right side of the room with the sheep and not the goats, amongst the wheat and never the chaff, humbly upright against the heretics who are still trying to bring you down, still trying to modernize the most genius of all powers that are, the Love of God that will never yield to such error and will never change to please those without the faith required to remain in the First-Century Church. My son, this is why God is so pleased by your life. You are a pleasant aberration from those who have surrendered to contemporary cynicism and lust. I will continue to repeat that the gratitude is from your Creator to you. May I charitably tell you why your opponents will not yield to you now? Because you are 'Christ,' but in Him you will conquer over all in the time He has allotted, on the day that He has assigned. Can you imagine how patient He had to be for so many years on the Earth? And, how patient He must be with humanity now? This is why you please Him so. You give Him jubilation by your own poise, by sitting compliantly by until the Father lowers His palm. This is why He takes such joy today, because He so loves perceiving His creative Love at work. He watches with the eagerness of a parched laborer who is satisfied for a drink, like a bird loosed from a cage, like a lamp being removed from under a basket. It is most literally Jesus who physically grows in you; it is His Love that pours over the Earth. You are His worker, His instrument, His prophet, and His friend. You and your brother are humanity at its best, waiting eagerly to know that the Deity is pleased. My son, I have given you many wonderful concepts to ponder today. I hope you accept them with love. Please remember to be gentle."

Sunday, June 4, 2000
4:38 p.m

"It is your own communion with Divine Truth, My children, and only your committed communion with the Truth that will lead humanity into the Light of a better world. Your spiritual enlightenment is the catalyst for your temporal well-being and beyond. None of the distractions which social and political activists put-forth in the name of so-called public interest can lead the Earth to peace, unity, or justice. Love is the reason for the amelioration of every wound, every inequity, and every form and scent of corruption. Hence, this Truth is Love, and Love is an origin only of God, available to every man, and prepared to intercede when summoned. My little children, lest all the good works of humankind be in vain, please always remember that the essence and precedent to any righteous act is a heart bursting-forth with the Divine Power of the Holy Spirit, the real and true Presence of Jesus inside you, the final outcome of a world which has now been led to the brink of perfection in victory! It is not whether you have suffered or have been disappointed in the past. Whether you have failed before is never an issue. No, the most important aspect of mortal life is that you place your very being within the parameters of saintliness while you live, so that on the last day, you will recognize Jesus, and He will take you to His Father's Throne. Therefore, what is the greatest gift which a mentor and friend can leave to His people? That he ushered them heart, mind, body, and soul to the undeniable and inexorable Truth of the Gospel of Christianity. There, every need is met and all which has been broken is mended; all that is deficient is nourished, and everything that has been neglected is embraced and made whole again. The Trinity of God; Father, Son, and Holy Spirit is the Thrice-Blessed Deity who is calling you to the Wisdom required to adhere to the fruits and principles of creative Love. Inner-peace and prosperity are the profits of the final union between Heaven and Earth. These are the tangible reparations that any offended society should pursue, not material wealth or vengeful restitution. You have been told many times before that justice lives in a man *who knoweth how to forgive*. Your Mother in Heaven is telling you today that the ultimate genius of the human race is the exercise of that justice, by reaching forward in the Name of Jesus Christ toward the noble goal of uniting all the Earth beneath the Cross of Mount Calvary. This is not solely a passing yule or temporary restraint, but an all-out commitment to immortal perfection for everyone who lives. This is Love at its best, living totally to achieve oneness in the Messiah from Nazareth for every last generation. It will not be cordiality for today and war again tomorrow, but a free and everlasting peace beyond the end of time, a time whose years have already come, a slice of Eternity which you can realize in your day, and a peek into the forever that no one thought would ever come. I say to you again, the element of this great coalition of mortal peoples is Love that is personified by Jesus Christ. And, among many things that it is not, it is most assuredly not pride in societal achievements that do not include the least in the world or those who are hurting the most. Jesus did not come to crown the successful, but to show that true power lives in humble service and peacefulness. And too, among the many things that Love truly is, it is wholly encompassing of those who are committed to correcting their own mortal errors and misgivings. If one is penitent and comes forward for pardon, those who openly receive him are the Saints of the day. The obstinate ones who continue to reject them will eventually be cast into Hell. The Holy Gospel is this simple to understand. These are the principles that make diminutive works look like mountains in the grand survey of human existence. Little prayers are entire literary works which God enjoys at the midday Feast of the Angels to the light of the simmering sun. What does He ask of His people? What are the works which He requests? That every form of mortal inertia be directed to Him, and He will do the rest. When you tell Him that His people are suffering, He will dispatch you as His emissaries to assist them. When you bring poverty to His attention, He will give them your wealth. And, if you ask Him to save you, He will place your Redemption in a Cup of Blood and a Communion Host, and ask you to partake of His Son. In the end, My children, you will understand why there are beggars on the street and scraps from grand galas being thrown to the dogs to eat. You will know why limousines drive past ghettos and the occupants never stop to ask if they can feed the poor or heal the sick. Yes, what you will eventually know is that the Son of God never attended a gala or rode in a limousine because Love does not originate there. He came to Earth as a pauper, His people at their suffering best, to tell all the world that His Kingdom is not of this world at all. The Home of the Resurrected has no shades of evil or rancid physical quests. It bears no fancy marquee, propped-up like a facade where merchants peddle fake pendants to those who do not know the value of a stone. No, My Son is true, recognizable, and definitive Love, almighty and Divine power and supernatural Grace, given to the Earth by God in Heaven so that He might look someday in the corner of one of His mansions and see those who once most feared Him residing comfortably there. This is all He asks, that humankind will give itself a chance, an opportunity to be healed and blessed, to be blinded to the world and given the vision of invincible warriors, happy to be at Home in the Sacred Heart of Jesus, and aware that final justice belongs to Him who has created the universe, and to those who were persecuted for defending His Name. All of this, My children, is the blossom of Love and the definition of hope. It is the cause for real joy, not an election or institution, not a fancy or whim of fashion, but the transcending happiness that is God, like your fondest childhood memories happening again, like the taste you yearn to savor once more, like the dream you wish to finally come true. This is your Love that lives in your hearts, which knows God and cannot yet see Him that seeks-out the best in every man, and recognizes a rainbow as your marriage with Nature. This is the ambience of your union with Heaven, the one you will soon know with the precision of a razor, with the fulness of Light, and the ultimate blessing of your souls' Redemption. No goodness will ever die, but it might be temporarily concealed by the clamoring world. No act of ill will can be part of the afterlife, although the actors would like for you to believe that they do. The sunshine in your hearts is God residing there, and He shall not be overcast by the darkness of despair or clouds of aggression. He will not yield to vipers or allow any injustice to pursue you. Jesus will always be Life in you and taunt death to dare cross the line of His Crucifixion to make a pass at your soul. He waves His Resurrection from the Grave through Eternity like a flag in the air, letting all would-be encroachers know that no corruption can be found near the strength of this Standard Bearer. The virility of His Blood is the front-line against sin and poor judgment. It is the high-tide of success in a world bent on keeping you down. The King of all Creation is a just Master who knows His parliament well, those who work to achieve the appointments set-forth by the Father, whose objectives complement the good works of Heaven, and whose final speeches in office resound with, *Amen, Jesus Christ is My Magistrate and Leader, My Counsel and Maker, My Providence and Friend.* Now must humankind move forward in this evidential Truth, in this Love, united with this Justice, and embraced by the Pentecostal Power you will celebrate again in the passing of only seven days. My Special son, these are My words of Love for you today. I hope the world will enjoy them in the fulness of time. I know that I have kept you longer today, but I believe this lesson of harmony to be one worth expressing. At the End of Time, you will see the awesome refreshment that was granted by your intercessory prayers. I truly hope that you realize in what state of Grace you are living. It is because you pray the Rosary everyday and attend Daily Mass. Your messages for your second book are pretty to behold."

Sunday, June 11, 2000
Feast of Pentecost
3:38 p.m.

"So much happiness and peace I bring to this holy place because you too are My children of peace. You are the makers of joy and reflectors of Light. Why? Because you have accepted Jesus as the Savior of your souls and have invited the Holy Spirit to inhabit your hearts. My children, this is the celebration of the Birth of the Church-of-Faith on the Earth. God sent the Third of the Divine Persons of the Trinity to reside in and amongst the Apostles, Myself, and everyone thereafter through this day who would give Him room to live at the depths of the human spirit. This is the celebration of the day upon which the Paraclete descended from Heaven with the raging winds and tongues of fire. This is the 50th day after the Resurrection of Jesus from the Tomb at Easter. Thus, Pentecost is the 50th day, or five, ten times over. Therein you celebrate the pentagram of the Morning Star and the five Wounds of the Crucified Redeemer, captured as joyfully, sorrowfully, and gloriously Divine in the five Mysteries of each meditation. You celebrate too the Pentecost of Jesus ten days past Ascension Thursday, ten Hail Marys of the Mystery which has redeemed your souls. My dear children, I need not recount the immortal history of the Descent of the Holy Spirit for those who believe because the Paraclete is already defining Himself in these hearts. But, together we must pray for millions more to let Him in, those many lost sheep who have never truly known the satisfaction of living in perfect Grace and perpetual accord with God. We must do our designated part to lead the blind to the waters of forgiveness and those who will not listen to the sound of enlightenment. I have told you that to accept My Son is a conscious decision of Wisdom of the heart and a stroke of intellectual genius. The world must also know that the Son of Man will not bow to any errant excuses as to why He has been rejected by those who fail to believe. Every soul will eventually see that the acceptance of Love, forgiveness, and Mercy is the key to human absolution. It is offered by God, and must be imitated by His people on Earth toward one another. Complete faith in the one Messiah is based upon this premise. No one can be saved who harbors a sliver of malice or hatred in their heart for another man. This too is the simple structure and foundation of the Gospel of Jesus Christ. Left alone, no amount of mental guidance can lead the human psyche to understand this Truth. This is why the wise counsel of the Holy Spirit must be allowed to marry the mortal soul and become the nucleus of its existence on the Earth. The Holy Paraclete is not only the Advocate, but also the Leader of Righteousness, the epicenter of Divine action, and the Healer of inner-brokenness and seclusion in the lives of those bound to master the art of human mortality. I must tell you, My little ones, that the Holy Spirit is the magnetism to which all redeemed souls are attracted. Like the pathway is also the destiny, the Holy Spirit brings all who know Him unto Himself, a prophecy that begins the moment when Christianity is implanted in the lost. This is where the fruits begin to blossom. I tell you that I have seen the fulfillment of this angelic prophecy in billions of souls, from their moment of Baptism and conversion until their passage into immortality, for twenty centuries. It is a pleasurable sight because I know the power of the Divinity of God. I am the Mother of this same Holy Spirit. I am concurrently His Spouse, and joyfully disseminate the message of Love to all who will listen throughout the world. I dispense the Dove of Peace from the tips of My fingers like honey dripping to the palates of the famished. This is why you have seen My statues dripping honey from My fingertips, My message of Love for all to see. This is in remembrance of the bees who know not that they are building a perfect world by doing only the simple task assigned to them by God. This, therefore, is the celebration of the day upon which the helpless have become over-achievers, when the lost have become beacons themselves, when those who suffer finally know why, and when those who walk in darkness can see by the dawn of Light radiating from inside their own hearts. The expanse of human existence in which mortal history is only a part will bear-out the Truth that no power is greater than the Love who is the Holy Spirit. Nothing can compare to the enlightenment that comes from within; no warfare has procured greater freedom, and no multiple collection of good works can compare to the singular Descent of the Holy Spirit from the mighty Throne of God. Hence, My children, you know at the last that the essence of your very own Salvation is that the Paraclete in your hearts has persuaded you to accept My Son as your Redeemer. The Paraclete of which I speak is forming the words of the message you are receiving this very moment. And, your kind acts of faith and courage on the Earth toward the growth of the Kingdom of Paradise are prescribed to you by the Spirit from within. This is from where all blessings flow, from where you muster the valor to proceed at Jesus' side, where you procure the strength to stand in the face of rejection and ridicule, and from where you generate the words and phrases to convince your detractors that you are telling the Truth. To close My words for today, I repeat to you that this pretty Dove is also a hungry one. He seeks-out hearts who will allow Him to feast upon their loneliness and swallow-up their death in His victory. He wishes to bring the song of dignity to those who have long lost their own voice, drowned-out by the battles waging before them that are sprung by deceit and outright evil. I assure you that the home of this hungry Bird is where He is needed the most, where members of families are cast-out for following Him, where little children lay in filth and waste, where the stench of impurity will not allow Him a small cliff upon which to plant His feet. The Holy Spirit of God is hungry to heal those who cannot stand because of the wretched constantly knocking them down. And, He is prepared to admonish and forgive those who torture them. The aggrieved are a noble and perfect race on the streets of Paradise because the Holy Advocate on Earth will elevate them there. I tell you today that this Divine Healer has united enemies who have spent centuries apart in war and bitter anger onto the highest perches of everlasting Life, now looking down at the world and saying, *'Let that never happen to humankind again.'* And, one day at a time, God is listening to them. He is changing the face of the Earth, altering the very ground upon which sinners now walk, renewing the Spirit of unity that has been lost by centuries of corruption and cold indifference. I pray that you will soon come to realize that the Holy Spirit is not unlike your own Guardian Angel, that He is your friend and benefactor, your messenger, and your mentor too! My Special son, I have seen your happy death on the Earth. The Holy Spirit will never leave you alone; He will give you strength for each day; He will always allow you to know the Will of the Father in Heaven. There is no true sadness for you, perhaps occasions of sorrow that will pass, but you will forever rest peacefully in the arms of My Grace. Everyone who has accepted Me as their Mother enjoys the benefits of life in this state of blessing. I tell you again that you have not even seen the surface of the success you will know if you continue to live My messages, pray the Mysteries of the Holy Rosary, and attend daily Mass. Soon, you will be accompanied by such great numbers that you will be barely able to pass through the doors. I assure you that the Holy Spirit has been fused together with you in your heart, that you are melded as one by the flame in the Sacred Heart of Jesus."

Sunday, June 18, 2000
3:50 p.m.

"All Creation will know where you have been by the time your journey of the Earth is ended. For Eternity, all that is of God will shine in your reflection of His Grace. Those who would not know Salvation because of their own blindness will most assuredly be led to the Cross because the revelation of your life will give them the Truth. This is why, My dear children, you must proceed faithfully and dutifully in Jesus, for the good of yourselves and your unwary peers. The destiny of millions of souls is dependent upon your labors of today. You will know rest at the end of mortal time as the respite you gain in the Holy Spirit now. This same heritage has been vested in the genuine divinity of the Saints and the high perfection of the Angels around you. These are the days which will determine the moral temperature of man as God places His palm to the collective forehead of His children on Earth. Will He know you are sharing the goodness of peace, or will you be of hyper-intemperate rejection when the time comes for your day in the sun? Hence, I come calling you today to remember your prayers for achieving the fruits of Love in your time. Please be the beacons that you have been destined to become since the foundation of the world was first laid. Prescribe to others the good knowledge of Redemption that swells from your own hearts. Be makers of peace because your conscience dictates your conduct, not just because it inhibits the progression of war. I have come today to tell you that your immortal fortune rests in your willingness to imitate Jesus because you love Him, not just because it is what your predecessors told you to do. This is the true honor of human life. This is nobility, character, and humility. If you would only perceive the Earth as your Creator now sees its end, you would not only pray without ceasing, your petitions and intentions would always conclude, *Not my will, but Thine be done!* My dear little children, you have been given the vision to recognize a world which has rejected Love, but you have also been given the power to restore it to Love. This is why we are praying together here, and why you will not desist in hoping for righteous change around the globe. You are the true believers in the Gospel of Jesus because you will not concede to the false ideologies that oppose Him. You will not stray from the careful course that has been laid-out for you centuries ago, one you have been tempted to abandon, one upon which few will ever tread, one that will call you to question your own resignation before the most ruthless of men. My children, I tell you that there is a three-tiered powerhouse of Divinity which will conquer your failings at every mortal passage. While wholly perfect in union and each one unique, the Trinity of God is a singular blessing for all souls, a bastion of support and forgiveness, a founding legend upon which you may stand upright again. No mortal man has ever failed in any cause who has invoked the Holy

Trinity for support, strength, and Grace. My dear children, you already realize the Father, Son, and Holy Spirit as being your reason for life, your Creator, and your source of Everlasting Truth. The Almighty Father is He who has always been the Creator blessed. The Son of Man is the Messiah whose Passion, Death, and Resurrection has redeemed your souls for all the ages to come. And, when you ask yourself and all the peoples of Earth what to do about it, the Holy Spirit is your definitive answer. The Paraclete came to the world not just to live among those who know their Redeemer, but as the power of sound persuasion for the dissemination of the Gospel of Jesus to all nations, every race, and across all the continents. The Holy Spirit is the same Deity in your heart who resides in Heaven. He is your Wisdom and transcending ability to teach and lead. He is Emmanuel at the center of your being, to be employed as your Christian attributes among those who will soon celebrate them before all Creation. I have borne the Son who has saved you, and I have become betrothed to the Wisdom who teaches you why. As you continue to walk in faith until the end of your days, know that the brightest is yet to come, the one that will never end, where no one will ever die, when all joy will be one heart under the Cross and in the miracle of a singular Messiah who had the audacity to tell the evil of the Earth that sin can never live where the children of God remain. This is the legacy of His bloodshed on Good Friday and the New Life that was created there. This is not simply a restoration of your own livelihood, but the re-creating of your souls into a timeless divinity beyond the stars, past the collection of universes that bow as you pass them by, beyond the bleak darkness where the novas gather to sing for your good fortune, all the way to the top of the ladder of righteousness, to the front row beside the delegates and Hosts, amongst the royalty who have forever stood for Jesus since the first time He uttered the words, *I love My people most.* Yes, your soul rises like a balloon on a sunny day. It will never stop ascending, always elevated by the loyalty of God for those who accept Him, pausing only a moment to see what a rainbow looks like from the convex side. If you can imagine how God loves you, you will forever extol the Divine Wisdom of this same elevation. You will always recognize human Salvation as a natural mandate from the Throne of Almighty God. Your absolution is not some exception to an ordinary rule, but the Will of God for His chosen race, the reason He is Abba! Father!—the reason I am His Immaculate Mother who is so filled with Grace, and the purpose of the Nativity, Life, Crucifixion, and Resurrection of the Son whom I still hold in My embrace. You see, My children, there is a fire burning inside God like the fruit in a hearth whose embers are the graces which surround you, whose Light is the Love of your souls, whose whispers are the answers to your prayers. Even though Jesus died a horrible death of suffering and pain, He never once lost His sovereignty over those who brought it. He has procured for humanity a new dignity that could never have been granted to the cold hearts that still reject Him. And this, My children, is the warmth from that Eternal hearth which is still melting the frozen indifference that causes hatred between men and the inequities of an imperfect world. I assure you that every word I have ever uttered to you is true, the bold facts from the King of all Creation who is poised to bestow upon you the Kingdom of all kingdoms, the Paradise for which you have longed since before you ever knew it existed. Your Master pines for you to know Him. He yearns for you to seek-out His blessings. He waits just beyond the horizon to show you His Face. I wish for you to be happy in knowing that your mortality is nearly through. Take solace in the Wisdom that yours is the course of God, and that you will be quickly rewarded for all that you do. This, My Special son, is the context in which I ask you to continue in your holy meditations. It is good that you reach-out to others to show that you are not the face of irrational fanaticism. Each day that passes-by, more and more will realize that you are telling the Truth. I assure you that many of My messengers before you have suffered far more profoundly than what you have been asked to endure. Please know that your sacrifices are equally as blessed! Greater suffering does not imply that My messages of Love spread more fluently. Your own prayers and those of the faithful do that. Additional suffering fosters the conversion of lost souls. At the last, the more My messages are heard throughout the world, the less need for suffering there will be."

Sunday, June 25, 2000
Feast of Corpus Christi
4:45 p.m.

"Love. There is no other calling, no greater mandate, no more invincible power, and nothing else of any origin that can offer the Absolution of the souls of humankind. My dear children, you have heard the lyrics of the melody that Jesus is calling you softly and tenderly. While this is true, I tell you today that He is also summoning you physically, spiritually, and divinely. He fully realizes that you are hungry and that He is your only Bread of Life. Of course, many know that the imprisoned are absolved of their crimes through confession, but most are not aware that they are also simultaneously rehabilitated, paying their debt to society by the words, *Dear Jesus, I am heartily sorry for having offended you, your Body on Earth.* And yet, even in the wake of this confession, other mortals hold them bound to mortal penalty and outright vengeance. Can one who governs a state in which hundreds have been executed stand to take an oath which concludes, ...*so help me God*, as he is elevated as presider of a nation? Yes, because most of the people of that nation are equally as ruthless, uncaring, and unforgiving. And, when he says, *so help me God* on that day, let everyone who hears it call upon the Almighty Father to have mercy on his soul come Judgment Day. My little ones, this is the day that celebrates the single-most powerful grace which God has bestowed upon mankind since Jesus woke from among the dead. The Eucharist is that which mends everything that is broken. In another tongue, you know the Most Blessed Sacrament as the Corpus Christi, the Body of Christ. Perhaps if there were a different Creation in which humanity did not exist, that would not mean much. But, in real Creation, the one which God has chosen to create, the Body, Blood, Soul, and Divinity of His Son is the difference between Life and death, between sickness and health, and between Salvation and condemnation. The Holy Eucharist is your life, health, and Salvation. I am pleased to know that you have accepted the call of the Holy Spirit to join the ranks of the vindicated, and to bring as many lost souls to Jesus as you possibly can. That is what makes you true warriors and heroes, not whether you can succeed in public office or win a great sports contest. My children, I have told you repeatedly about the Kingdom of God, and that He wishes the Earth to be transposed into that eternal joy. The Blessed Sacrament is your Food for that journey, your vision and enlightenment, your strength, compassion, humility, and wisdom. That is why it is imperative that you continue to attend Daily Mass and live constantly in the Light of Christian charity. If there is to be hope in the human heart, let it be founded upon that holy order. I wish you could know how deeply I pray for all of My little children. I wish each of you could see through eyes of faith that Jesus is perpetually with you. If you muster thoughts of fondness for God, it is His Spirit guiding you there. Should you choose to help your neighbor in any benevolent way, know that it is the Son of the Most High working through you. And, if this land of America ever brings itself to again proclaim the dignity of life for those yet to be born, it will finally have opened the door of Grace given it from the hand of the Almighty Father wide enough for His Son to walk-in and say 'You are truly worthy to be blessed!' This, too, is a gift from the Eucharistic Sacrament, if only the citizens of these western hills and rolling lands will humble themselves to receive. All over the world today, many were reveling the power of the Holy Eucharist. They were stating the words of Truth that God wishes His people to hear every day. But, they were not taking this important message into the streets, the casinos, the brothels, or the houses where evildoers go. The words were comforting the ears of parishioners, servers, cantors, and lectors, but were not piercing the obstinance of the 485 billionaires whose souls are dead, or those who hold the keys to prisons, or those by whose command millions could be set free from political corruption and social oppression. These are the ones who need to hear and heed the admonishment of the Gospel of Jesus, to inherit, avow, and live-out the legacy of the Martyrs and Saints, and to shed their spiritual darkness by living in the Light. Again, the Body, Blood, Soul, and Divinity of Christ is their miracle cure. It is their transference into the jurisdiction of the King and Monarch of God, Jesus of the Cross, from whom they will never flee and will defend to their death. In Him, they will make themselves naked of the Earth so He will dress them in the nobility of Salvation. In this Jesus, they will void their own commissions of dictatorial selfishness and fall to their knees at the sight of the first pauper who happens to glance their way. Yes, through the Blessed Sacrament, they will proclaim that they are rich in Everlasting Life instead of steeped in the vast junkyard of temporary wealth. I come on this anniversary day of the Medjugorje messages, nineteen years advanced in time, to tell you again that your journeys there were not in vain. You are still the disciples that you learned there to be. You still reflect the Truth of the messages I have offered the world from such a diminutive spot on the Earth. I am truly grateful that you have remained at My side and inside the Sacred Heart of Jesus. I truly wish you could know how grateful God is that you are still saying Yes.

My dear children, I ask you to continue to remain at peace. I call you to be forever reminded that the days are passing very quickly for you now, but you must not be captured by the acceleration of their pace. Live slowly and simply, and God will do the rest. There are many people who have not had the benefit of My guidance in the same way as you, those who have lived for years on blind faith alone. You can see how some have views that are partially skewed. If only they would pray the Rosary everyday, they would have an elevated vision and holiness, even though I may still never utter a word to them in the way I have spoken to you. In time, all will know that I am their Advocate because the Angels who accompany you at your death bring your soul originally to Me, then I present you to Jesus, just as I presented Him at the Temple in the age of His youth. If you continue to pray everyday for the selfish, Jesus will hear you. He will not allow time on this mortal Earth to conclude without answering every prayer. Someday, you will see a beautiful Earth that already exists in Eternity which is living in peace, Justice, Love, and dignity. This world is a portion of Heaven, and its inhabitants include the billion little children whose lives were aborted while they were still in their mothers' wombs. I have much more to tell you in the years to come, but Jesus may return before then!"

Sunday, July 2, 2000
3:38 p.m.

"You who are My holy ones on the Earth, who reach for new opportunities placed before you in teaching the Truth of the Gospel; how can you be perceived as any less than Divine? You too are situated only a little lower than the Angels, and Jesus calls you to summon the strength and piety of your hearts to be His right guard, the warriors in His army who defeat the factions that would otherwise divide humanity, The Church. Today, I come calling to thank you for standing with those Angels and alongside the Saints so entire Creation will become a more sanctified place. You know that your prayers bring the power of God in you, and that you are all mighty conquerors in Him. There is no other station where you should forthrightly wish to be. There are many changes that are now occurring because of your humble supplications to God, the very petitions that are altering the course which human history might have otherwise taken. This itself is a principle legacy of the Third Fatima Secret. Why should you beseech God if you would believe that human existence and the destiny of humanity is set in stone, regardless of your living atonement in the Gospel? Therein rests the fulfillment of one of the secrets of your own. Creation is finished, just as Jesus proclaimed from the Cross. And, the Wisdom and prophecy that passed His lips account for the prayers, sacrifices, and amendments that His people would make thereafter in remembrance of that same Cross. You will find at the end of time that all of My messages to you over the years will culminate in one singular Truth, at one eternal moment. The days during which you rise and rest now are the precursor to that endless summit because your actions portend the separation of the goats from among the blessed sheep. You once contemplated a visual image of each of your holy thoughts as a graphic on a transparent page. And, when all of these pages are stacked in a pile, you will see the complete portraiture of human destiny. This image is accurate, and you are only now completing the templates that will allow even the most wretched among you to see their first glimpses of God. Salvation cannot be confined to a page any more than a mere sinner can save himself from eternal perdition. But, through the Grace of the Wisdom gained through the Holy Spirit and the Blood of the Cross, both the sinner and the page from which he reads become set aside into another dimension, one that moves the mortal soul in union with Divine Glory, one in which nothing of corrupt origin can enter, one through which the complete awakening of the human conscience becomes alive. The world is at the brink of this spiritually enlightening daybreak. The spirit of humankind will wish to scurry to the end of time, even before God declares it to be over. My children, this is why it is imperative that you be patient, and it is of great importance that you allow others to trip themselves over the miracles and supernatural facts now unfolding before them. If you are to fully succeed as messengers and representatives of My Marian army, you must realize that every conscience will awaken of its own accord. You cannot shake someone awake who is laying in material drunkenness. They must be brought to consciousness by the Light. The sound of your voice suffices to remind them, but they must willingly respond with 'yes.' This is what your prayers have been about over the past eleven years. When you speak to God on others' behalf, He will take your message to them. This is yet another of the invisible pages that you learned to know in My first thirty messages. If you tell Jesus that you love His people, He will make sure they know that you do. This is why I have told you that everything that concerns the conversion of men which has been spoken in this room, and in the lower level floor, will eventually be seen by all. It was on the lower level that you received My messages about the tall peaks of human holiness. Does this seem ironic to you? There is a pattern which has accompanied all of My lessons and teachings. I have incorporated them into your life as you know it. I have not removed you from participation in the trials of human existence with your fellow mortals. It is here that your most grand impact is being played-out. This is where you will recognize where the goalposts and scoreboard were located, where your brothers and sisters wore their patriotic colors, and where you stood amongst them to say that the real competition is to see who can lift the next one higher toward the Throne of God by accompanying them to the Altar. This is a period of unprecedented Grace for the world and an opportune moment in history. While the relationships between men cannot be wholly shed of governance and the distribution of material wealth, I continue to ask you to avoid the temptations that would draw you into politics or certain partisan gain. These things are only for the worldly, only for those who would be afraid to enter an Adoration Chapel for fear of discovering their internal self. I have known every corridor of human life and how men have struggled against temptation. I am not unmindful of the impulses that try like a ticking bomb to lead you away from the Table of Grace. I have trust in poor sinners who are trying their best to convert to purity and peace. And, I will soon usher-in an admonishment that will unequivocally convince the rest. My Special son, for all these reasons, I implore you to go on. I ask you to continue like you have never conceived before. While you will not be requested to give any more, the amount you will give by the end of time will be praised more than the billions* to be given in the months and years to come. Yours is the two-cents mite given by the poor widow compared to what the newly converted are about to provide. As I have told you before, you must accept these things in faith, and watch what the future brings. This leaves little left to interpretation because I have told you what God expects from those He has chosen and called. Please be sure to protect yourself from over-exposure to the heat outdoors!"

* *'Billions' simply connotes a measure of something. It does not necessarily refer to an amount of money. Our Lady used this word in order to draw a contrast and connection to the parable of the mite of the widow, not to prophesy great financial outpouring toward charitable works, although God's eminence reserves the right of fulfilling such an interpretation.*

Sunday, July 9, 2000
3:33 p.m.

"Where are the omissions which are keeping righteousness and justice from overtaking the world?—In the empty arms of humanity who collectively refuses to take up their holy arms, whose material obstinance has left their consciences numb, and whose rampant impurity is the manifestation of deadly disease through all the continents. My dear children, if the people and races of the Earth wish to eradicate the suffering which engulfs every shore, they must rid themselves of the sins and corruption of the flesh. These corporeal errors have been the origin of carnal lust, infidelity, and reprobation since mankind first walked the surface of the globe. But, it does not have to be this way. Jesus wishes His people to be whole, healthy, and pure in Him. The diminishment of the flesh should come through the spiritual uprising of Grace in His Holy and Sacred Heart. I ask My children to take heed of the teachings of the Epistles, and teach the world about the spirit by leading in the Holy Spirit. These are days of great terror and fear for many, like shadowy palms in the night which lurk so closely. No wonder so many lie in such reckless fright, they will not gain their strength and insight by approaching the Savior of the world. They will not repent, confess, and amend their lives. They refuse to accept the Thanksgiving Feast from the Throne of God and His Altar in Heaven, the Eucharistic Body, Blood, Soul, and Divinity of Jesus Christ. Why is their depression and disgust so profound? Because they will not avail themselves to receive these Sacraments and blessings. They will not submit their errors to the absolution of God. They will not allow their fractured mortality to be healed by the graces of the Church, whose power and unequivocal Wisdom can cure any malady and redeem any soul. In short, humankind only needs to give their hearts to the Messiah of Nazareth, their Emancipator on the Cross, and say—*Heaven help me, God hear me, Jesus have mercy on my soul.* Then will all that has perverted the lives of mortal men be expunged from Creation. Then will happiness reign over grief. Yes, only then will your land be healed. My dear little ones, too many have forgotten and many others never heard that I gently walked the pathways of the Earth. I have seen the same fear and indignation which still plagues the societies and ghettos that were apparent 2,000 years ago. Time has done little to ameliorate the horrors of human life because there is no compassion that time has to offer. Only the efforts of man, the complete conversion of the heart and soul of the inhabitants of the globe to Jesus Christ can bring that new beginning, despite the deafening passage of years which roars past like a thunderous herd in the night. Only the living testament of the Holy Gospel can restore humankind into the likeness of Paradise. It is in that New Covenant where every sickness is healed and all wars will cease. I have been bringing this same message of peace to every nation on

Earth for endless generations. I have offered the reason why humanity must invoke faith, and that reason is the Salvation of man. The Almighty Father dispenses miracles and cures, but He also requires His Creation on the Earth to read the signs, to live by faith, and to recognize His Divine Presence in the visual world about you. Living without this trust in Him is like continuously working against the grain of His lofty woods and trying with dubious failure to reverse the movement of the universe. Mankind will hold that power only when he becomes the likeness of Jesus. This process begins the moment you receive the Most Blessed Sacrament. As soon as the Eucharist makes contact with your tongue, the ground beneath you rests in peace because you are the new life in Christ standing upon it. The angels weep in happiness because they know that you will thereafter recognize them. And, the Saints in Heaven swell with happiness because you are living-out the faith that God dispensed to their own fathers many centuries before. The power and majesty of the Eucharist is much more than the union of your soul with Heaven on a given day. Your Holy Communion is your commitment to God that you will commence your efforts in assisting Him to close-out the ages with courage and love amidst an awful world of people who would rather destroy the world than hand it back to God in one united piece. I cannot tell you sufficiently today how My Son yearns for your unity in Him under the Cross when He Returns to redeem you. He requires the participation of everyone who will eventually arrive in the miracle of Redemption in the arms of peace beneath My Immaculate Mantle. You may be both weary and scarred by the journey, but I assure you that, by the time you have a Rosary in your hand, you will be like the fortunate gladiator who has won the favor of the King, the one who will be crowned with a champion's nobility once the battle is through. My children, this is the race to which Saint Paul has referred. It is not one for which he who finishes first will be crowned, but for he who finishes best. That authentic achievement is claimed by the collective body of humankind whom Jesus will marry and claim as His Body at the end of time. This is the mystical matrimony between the Woman of the Earth—the Holy Church of faith—and the Bridegroom who now awaits in the paradisial chamber. I give you My assurance that you will understand these things with spotless distinction as the future continues to unfold. Collective humanity is filled with the Holy Spirit, and Jesus is coming to reclaim humanity in Himself. The fruit which He seeks is the souls of mankind. You are seeing firsthand why human redemption and purification are called the Sacred Mysteries. They are difficult to place into words because they are confined to linear time for those who have yet to pass across the threshold of death, back into life. I am pleased that you understand. How happy with you is the Son of God! This is why these are such special times. Thank you for your endless efforts to receive My messages, to have your Diary published and made available, and for building the system that is in place which makes the spirit of people come alive. Do you see the domino effect which has begun in

Medjugorje? Thank you very sincerely from your very pleased Savior. My Special son, you help Me cry many tears of happiness and joy, like you shed in watching the 46 year-old see for the first time since he was only three. The principle is the same. You are seeing the Kingdom of Heaven now because I have been remaking your vision through the power of the Holy Spirit. I am unsure whether you are capable of realizing how happy that makes Me feel. You have said 'yes,' and the Kingdom of God on the Earth will long be the better advanced for your goodness. This is My holy blessing for you. + You have My Immaculate Heart in which you may always take solace. Therein rests My perfect gratitude for your life of Love! I will speak to you again very soon. I love you. Goodnight!"

Sunday, July 16, 2000
3:20 p.m.

"To continue feeding and rewarding your honesty and faith, I have come again to tell you the stories of Jesus and the Salvation of humankind in His Blood. I am the Blessed Virgin Mary, the Immaculate Conception, who bore Him in My Womb and gave Him birth in Bethlehem. When you cry-out for help, I hear you as I heard His plea back then. And, I will act in swift consolation for you, just as I tended to the needs of the Only Son of the God who has created us all. My dear children, the world still sleeps in moribund indifference, but we are making the awakening call that is heard by multiple millions. Yes, it is not enough simply to hear, because this same world must rise and wipe its eyes of centuries of collective doubt. My Son requires your own compassion, an imitation of His Love toward His suffering side. It is concealed inside the lives of the poor, the outcast, the oppressed, imprisoned, and persecuted. If the children of God will awaken and tend to their pleas, this world and all who inhabit it will be set free. Everyone must recall that the evolution of humankind has never been about His Creation, but rather about spiritual enlightenment. Physical growth has nothing to do with the conversion of the heart. Witness is borne in many adolescent saints who weep for ninety-year-old atheists who are about to meet the Face of their Maker in whom they never believed. If there is a time for listening to the Holy Spirit in the faith of young traditional Christians, that time is now. I once gave you a parable about the weight of human sins being carried upon a wagon passing over a bridge. The purpose is to teach you that time cannot destroy sin; only the Blood of Jesus on the Cross can do that. So it is with the transformation of the human heart from callous indifference into faithful belief in the Son of God. This must be done by every soul on the Earth now, no matter what their age may be. Death knows no threshold and comes to people of every age, so every soul must come to conversion now! As we pray together, you continue to recognize what makes a Christian complete. You know the Fruits of the Holy Spirit, and have seen them flourish in the young and the aged alike. This is what gives you the power and authority to teach and reprimand anyone who refuses to live-out their commission in the Holy Gospel. The Paraclete can live abundantly anywhere He is invited. There is no gradation in years that supposedly gives those who are advanced in age any right to reject the Wisdom that God places in the hearts of His youngest disciples. Indeed, some of the worst heresy on the Earth has been the product of elders and philosophers who believe that they have the meaning of life tucked neatly beneath their prejudices. Remember, it was the holiness and courage of a twelve-year-old Genius that caused the wicked to scatter inside His Temple. I will always tell you how to gain this same Wisdom because I know where He is found. He is also the Holy Spirit, and He is in you and all the faithful. He is alive in the Sacraments of the Catholic Church and present in every action that you take on His behalf. Spirit, Body, Divinity, Truth, and Love are all living and well in you, the Mystical incarnation of your Savior who so freely and abundantly walks the crests of everyday life, seeking to redirect the lost by the power of your encompassing Light. So, it is absolutely not your own fear of God that causes you to help your neighbor, but the charity of God living in you. It is not so much the awareness that you must serve which causes you to act, but the desire of your Almighty Father to remake the face of the Earth by the faith of His Church. If you walk through life believing that you must be a Christian because you are afraid to be otherwise, you have not yielded to the entire purpose of the Life of Jesus. *Do not be afraid, for I am with you*, are His words. Therefore, you walk forward in conviction, confidence, and peace. You would be selfish if you refused to do these things, not because you nobly advance them. Look at the healing and good will that grow in the wake of your footsteps! Your love knows no bounds because your labors flow into the lives of the neighbor next door and the travelers whose carriage has broken before they can complete their journey back home. Every day and every hour is another that builds that ladder to perfection which Jesus requires in you. At the end of time, He will collate them in their order of Grace, and the lost and weak will ascend them into His arms because of you. If there is pride to be taken, find it in your obedience and submission to God, not in what you do for others that sinners would also do. Allow My Son to continue to utilize your lives in Him because you are the fingerprints of His hands upon the world. If any inquisitor would search for any evidence of the Messiah's work there, he would find your lives under his scope. He would find the Body, Blood, Soul, and Divinity of Jesus in the Tabernacle, and the imprints of His fingertips where you have laid your own hearts and hands.

    My children, I have spoken to you for many years, openly and consistently. I will tell you the same for Myself as I am teaching you about others. I visit your home to pray with you and guide you to Salvation because

I love you. I wish for you to be in Heaven with Me someday amidst the happy Communion of Saints and the jubilant Angels. I cannot leave here because My Heart is here, wherein rests your Savior for consolation. This is why there is no mortal dust amidst the purity of your hearts. There is none to be shaken from anyone's sandals. All who come here in the Name of Jesus will never leave, lest they deny the very God who sends them. Hence, I am happy and pleased to be your Intercessor before Jesus. He has sent Me again today to reaffirm His Love for everything you do. This, My children, is the substance of the message I offer you today. I sincerely hope you like it. My Special son, you are adept in recognizing the political motivations of those around you. Thank you for continuing to stay away from the quadrennial politics of America. While I am impressed that you read the daily newspaper, please refrain from becoming caught by the details beneath the headlines of those articles about such politics. You see, there are millions who have yet to learn and accept the peace of the Holy Spirit. But, they will! They assuredly will!"

Tuesday, July 18, 2000

"This work represents a quantum deviation from the utter findings of men. We are fulfilling the Prophecy of Saint Louis DeMontfort and wielding the Sword of Saint Michael the Archangel."

Sunday, July 23, 2000
4:14 p.m.

With blessings abundant surrounding us, there is no doubt that we are presently living the ongoing romance between Heaven and Earth, the perpetual engagement of human life that is leading us ever more closely to the Divine Nuptials of God and man.

"My children, I come to this place because it is the precise location on the Earth where God placed you on May 31, 1989, this miraculous site of My Marian Visitation, so that I could bring you love, teach you to love, and share your love. It is your Blessed Mother whose joy is elevated by My messages because I know that you are living them. Therefore, I have given you protection under My stately Mantle where you shall forever bask in finished Creation, remade and redeemed in the Blood of My Son. Today, we pray again together and reflect in gratitude for one another in thanksgiving that God has made this miracle possible through your equally supernatural faith. All gifts from the Almighty Father are dispensed through His realization that you respond because you love Him in return. My children, there is hatred in the material world because others will not live-out the profession of Christianity as exemplified by the Church, the Son of God, the Holy Spirit, and the Angels and Saints. Hatred is much more than simple 'not Love.' It is a voluntary exercise to flee from the Truth and to pursue paths that have no value in the Kingdom of Paradise. The lack of vision that causes this error is the hardness of hearts which the Gospels have described. That error is the source of hatred and corruption throughout the world. I am telling you that the Love of Jesus is the healing salve for the rash of outright disdain that men hold against other men. Our reflection today is that we understand this to be a correctable circumstance. Every heart can change if only given the motivation. This is what conversion is all about. However, billions in the world have not yet drawn the correlation between atheism and hatred, between sin and corruption, and between indifference and suffering. Millions upon millions of these souls are otherwise good people who work hard and live independently; their callousness and shallow interaction are products of their defiance against the duties that are outlined for them by the Son of God, My Jesus of Nazareth. Therefore, He has told the world that the road to Salvation is a narrow one, both by the qualities of righteousness which His people must espouse and the sacrifices required to employ them. You know from the Holy Scriptures that all benevolence is found in Him, and that every act of goodness is accomplished in His Name. There is no other goodness to be grasped on the Earth because it cannot be fed through any other benefactor. Let us rejoice and be glad that God has made His Creation this way! Only He is the Power of Justice because only He is Almighty God; forever bold, present, and persistent in the Most Holy Trinity.

  My Special son, I ask you to employ these sentiments when you see others who do not reflect the Love of God in the ways I have taught. Pity them and know that your own life serves as mitigation for their ruthless error. Believe Me, Jesus knows what He is doing. He provides signal graces through the bellows of time. I ask you to be jubilant when you hear of acts committed by people that displease you. Their latter service to humankind through My Immaculate Heart will rival the conversion of Saint Paul. I ask you to remember that your life's work has mitigated such things. None of it will be remembered in Heaven. Oh, what a joy to see it unfold because you know that it has already been defeated and destroyed! Remember what I told you about the highest moments of life residing in ordinary time. Jesus is living your life alongside you now. He is the salt. You cannot even ponder your questions without His Spirit in you. The change that you desire in others is a process of growth, reparation, prayer, and time. If this were not so, what use would I have in speaking to you for nearly ten years. The miracle of the coming of the Kingdom of God has taken twenty centuries to unfold. You are at the last ages before Jesus comes in Glory. Why not savor this prospect instead of dwelling upon the impiety or impatience you see in others? All of this has been reconciled in the Holy Cross. Now you see the need for additional prayer and the conversion of humanity. Indeed, you see the reason why My Jesus has not yet returned in Glory. The world is not ready. You blame time, your daily labors, the eccentricity and indifference of others, violence, greed, division, and human miscommunication as the reasons why you have difficulty feeling elevated. The elevation still lives in you, now more than ever. All the ills that you see are much lesser in severity than they were ten years ago. The miracles are still alive! If you continue in faith, you will not allow these days to bring you any dismay. I have taught you about human emotions, intelligence, piety, the inner-psyche, Love, and sacrifice. Let Me tell you about a 2000-year-old agony that the Savior of the world is still suffering. Only your stouthearted faith will help, only your desire to succeed without knowing how many hours are remaining in the night, only your commitment to rise-up and stay the course without complaining that no one else will help you! Only by looking into the teeth of darkness and saying, 'I dare you to try to shroud my happiness with a negative thought!' I have seen the perfect Child of God grow into a Man who gave His entire Being—Soul, Body, Limb, and Sacrifice for you to be happy. He capitalized this joy by rising from the dead and taking you with Him. Since that first Easter sunrise, He has seen His legacy and Divinity spate-upon, abandoned, desecrated, and perverted. He has seen twenty centuries of heresy and bloodshed, and His little children embracing the very evil that He destroyed. Millions upon millions of souls have died for no other reason than whether they have rights to a parcel of land, a bar of gold, or another's hand in marriage. Countless others have perished because someone else simply did not want them to live, including those yet to be born, little souls who were made by the very hands of this Prince of Peace! All of this, and the sun still rises, the Earth still turns on its axis, the stars still shine, and a rainbow follows the rains. All of this, and your Blessed Mother dispenses a word at a time to anyone who will hear about the reconciliation that is just-over the top of the next moment. This is the story of patience; patience from the Divine power who can change it in an instant, but whose Mercy and compassion for humanity has kept His Wrath and Justice at bay for 2,000 years. Let Me finish with this point: The moment when the first Martyr laid-down his life for the cause of human Salvation, Jesus promised that his death would not be in vain, that all humanity would come to know Love before the last day of Earth clicked by. Since then, many Martyrs have followed and the days are still passing. Be thankful that they are. Be humble in the knowledge that only time separates you from Paradise, a time that is governed by the Will of the Father. While praying for His Kingdom to come, also pray for it to be at the right moment, that all humankind will be enlightened and prepared, that all will know Salvation by the Living Messiah within them. That is what this time is about, and this is the difference that the world needs to realize. I pray for the day when I can hold you in My arms as you stand redeemed in your glorified body. I am elated at the prospect that you will see the One who has been speaking to you Face-to-face in the Light of God's Divinity, fully revealed before your soul. I am pleased that you are willing to continue in faith until God calls you Home. When you see Jesus, you will finally know that your questions about patience were ultimately in vain. The reign of God is at hand! Be gratified that His Love is yours, and that you are one in Dominion with God already, prepared for the day when you first set your feet in Paradise."

Monday, July 31, 2000
Feast of Saint Ignatius of Loyola
7:01 p.m.

"My beloved little children, the world does not yet realize the Glory which has been revealed inside this sacred home. Jesus is still protecting you from the pursuit of others' publicity and corrupt intentions. This is still your home of peace, and all who enter know Love full-well by the time they have departed. You are entering August, the fair month which has brought so many proceedings and changes during years past, times of transition and preparation, and especially of revelation, as it was eleven Augusts ago when you came to know Me more fully. I have blessed both of you from the cradle because I have always known of your love for Me, revealed to Me as the Almighty Father placed the Queenly Crown of Wisdom upon My graceful head. It is Jesus for whom you live, and it is for this reason you have become My children. When you extol and advance the Kingdom of Heaven on Earth, it is My Son in you who lives and reigns. Please remember that Jesus told His disciples to enter a town and individual homes and to 'stay until you leave.' To some, this seems rhetorical because it would be impossible to do otherwise. The words seem too simple. Of course one would stay no longer after he has left a place. But, there is a message inherent in Jesus' words. Those who heard them would ask, 'How do I know when it is time to leave?' Jesus was shedding Light upon the trust of those who would listen, pray, and learn through the power of the impending Paraclete. He was telling them that it was Himself who would define the parameters of 'when you leave.' This precise Wisdom is still relevant today because the Son of Man lives in your hearts to guide and comfort your ways. I have seen yet to this day many miracles which are far too great to translate into words. They can only be seen with the power of the heart. This is why I ask you to continuously pray from the heart! Therein, you will see miracles abundant in a world which has been blanched into unsalted indifference by raw materialism and secular ideologies. Indeed, you are living such a miracle at this moment because of the advancement of your faith. You see because you love in the same way Jesus has asked. You hear the sonnets of Divine ingenuity because you are disposed to receiving the charitable gifts from God in peace, hope, and enlightenment. This is henceforth the cause of your own genius, the reason why you are participants in the conversion and Salvation of many. My children, I have come not only to elevate you in appreciation for you holy lives, but to dispel any myths that would cause you to believe that God would want you to somberly hang your heads in a very ugly world. This is a time of great thanksgiving because you offer your love to humanity with forthright participation, just as you did through your appropriate visit yesterday. You see hope in the eyes of your humble friends when you travel to be with them. You also gain the knowledge that your legacy of friendship, holiness, and peace precedes your arrival. I am pleased that you reach-out to the simple-of-heart with such happiness and joy. Two weeks from now will be the anniversary of the Vigil upon the mountaintop in Medjugorje. How happy I was to see you among the many pilgrims there. 1989 seems so long ago to you, but it was a mere moment in time for Me. I have seen the full fruits of your new beginning as they have been savored by Jesus, while you are only now starting to see them grow. If you will remain under My maternal care, you will always be able to see beyond the end of time and know that the joy that you will receive then is forever present now. If you did not believe Me, I know that you would not have stayed together with your brother so long. While others tend to make a mockery of My miracles, you are employing them as an advantage toward your continuing faith in God and an arsenal for the conversion of multitudes of nonbelievers in the ages to come. I cannot express with adequacy how your faith grows even more miracles from the ones you have already seen. Someday soon, the world will know that a rainbow is only an individual slice of a larger spherical rule of hues that are blended together by the threads of Love from Paradise, stitched by the wary Angels who know that mankind is much in need of God and hungry for the food of healing. Please allow your hearts to continue to be open to accept what the future brings. There will be many reasons for sadness, but do not give-in to such despair. Of course there will be deaths and suffering, but your happiness in the Holy Spirit will keep your joy afloat. When you read the Sacred Scriptures, you see the summation of your approach toward every new day and your agenda in fulfilling it. Please always know that My Divine Son is your Savior and Master. Nothing will be cast upon you that will so weigh you down that you will not be able to stand and humbly receive the dispensation of graces that give you strength to go on. God's benedictions are many; they are real, and are forever.

    I have said what I planned today in honor of Saint Ignatius. Let your hearts never be sorrowful. Let your hopes always be new. Look forever into the bright sunrise that Jesus has planned for you! May your souls be comforted in prayer, may your hearts be enlightened with joy. May you see peace through every heartbeat, let nothing become your annoy! Divine is the reason you are converted, redeemed is the reason you pray. May you bask in the Paradise which awaits you on that vast Resurrection Day! Thank you, My loving children, for allowing the Mother of God to share these holy moments with you, the dear babes of Mine whom I love as all others."

Sunday, August 6, 2000
Transfiguration of Our Lord
4:15 p.m.

"Now, dear children, I approach you again with hope and anticipation because your lives are their fulfillment and your prayers bring holy constancy, the peace of genuine Love, and the light of Divine Grace into the darkness where lost souls are squandering their valuable time in mortality. This is indeed a day of the celebration of the transfiguration of man because, in Jesus, you are sent to be Wisdom to the peoples. Every day is the remembrance of an earth-moving event in history, whether it be the awful blast of an atomic weapon or the passing of a Holy Pontiff into the Light of Paradise. Yes, Pope Paul VI is twenty-two years the happier today to see the fruits of his life on Earth to have so nobly advanced the Church of Faith in the revelation of God. Dear children, please know that I continue to bask in the knowledge that little Jesus is as anticipatory as you. He provides many signal graces and holy blessings so that every day of your lives is connected to the previous multitude by the continuing awareness of your Salvation. Please always remember that the Son of Man requires the enlistment of your faith to recognize these things. That is why you can know that the rainbow of last week was a reflection of your previous message. It is why you understand that each Hail Mary and Our Father and Glory Be you pray sets the wheels into motion that carry the poor souls in Purgatory into the happiness of Heaven, simultaneously compounding the number of Saints who intercede for you at the Throne of God. We have made the world a place of many gifts because we love in the same Holy Spirit who dwells with Me in Glory and in your hearts. Can you not see this interwoven majesty of supernatural unity? Can you not see how the days truly belong to Christ the King? That is why these special moments of messages are an intrinsic and unique part of the unfolding of the Plan of God for the Redemption of the human race. Jesus intended for these days to come from the Miracle of the Cross. These messages began there, and will culminate upon your arrival at the right hand of the Father who ordains them. Your Creator loves justice and right! It is He who collects the days into one immortal basket of plenty. He makes them to be connected by the universal intentions of the Church Triumphant, reflected by the petitions of His faithful in the world. Why else would your Bishop first see your brother's letter of request for a vocation on the Feast of the Saint of Vocations, Saint John Vianney? What is perpetually occurring just beyond your immediate comprehension is an orchestrated plan of cultivation, conversion, and deliverance. You are in attendance at the great dance of human history that has been unfolding in many ballrooms since the beginning of the ages. You march in step to the same song of victory as the Apostles who first saw the Risen Christ. The tone, cadence, and melody of Love have not changed since Thomas uttered the words of piety and admission 'My Lord and My God!'

Dear children, the world is a replication of Thomas, and all in it will soon raise their voices in the song of unity, 'It is true! There is no doubt!' The celebration has been brought from that first Easter, all the way to sunrise this morning and beyond. This is the truth above all things, over the passing fashionable products of capitalism, beyond the obstinance of those who are too encapsulated by karmas, high and away from a cerebral meditation which transcends the psyche, and overpoweringly destructive to any political locomotion that may pass through the city in the name of enhancing the lives and fortunes of the rich! Do not believe their false claims that they are pro-life when their chosen representative single-handedly refuses to stop the execution of scores of sinners whom he declines to forgive in the name of state-sponsored justice. Do not believe their lies! It is all for fame, money, power, and egoism to the exclusion of aid to the poor and pity upon those whose parents never taught them any better or left them with a pittance of opportunity during their formative years. These are among the reasons that I tell you that politics is as dark as Free Masonry. Neither of them will lead you to see the cold, hard facts of human misery or the mitigation of a horde of sins. Only the graces of the Roman Catholic Church will deliver all who call themselves human; only the Sacraments of repentance, reparation, and renewal can bring humanity to Light. The Tabernacles contain the Candidate who has already won the Victory, and it is He who has been elected King by the unanimous and popular vote of the singular God of all Creation. There is no democracy in that because there is no dissension! There is no question to put before the people because God has already selected the Master who reigns over all in the world. It is Jesus! It is Love! Now, the referendum is whether the societies of the world will accept their own fate and follow Him to Salvation. My children of the Earth, your own souls are on the ballot! It is you who must be the elect! I wish for your fortunes to be great indeed, but a wealth of knowledge and power deigned by Jesus for those who love Him! That is why you know that My words are not just hypothetical images of what might have been if the world were more perfect, but accurate descriptions of the entire universe as it will soon come to be! I do not rely on your dreams to make you happy, but upon the factual existence of Divine Grace which has awakened you from mortal sleep! So, feel the skies shake with the ballroom dances which those before you are enjoying! Someday, you will again think that it is thunder, but it will finally be your soul piercing the veil into everlasting Life! The flashes you see will not be lightning, but the countless camera bulbs being held in the hands of the Saints as they encapsulate your passage into their midst! And, the many thousands of moist droplets will no longer be the rains, but the happy tears of your Heavenly Father whose Heart is so touched that you have finally arrived back Home again. When you feel this gladness land softly upon your cheeks, know that they have just fallen from His. It is My high honor to watch this Glory unfold each time another soul sails gleefully back to Paradise upon the tears of which you spoke in your Diary, those of the faithful on Earth whose suffering made the image of the Cross perfect for every last sinner to see.

My dear Special one, it is part of that fulfillment that calls Me to this place every day and every week, to ratify your lives in My Son, to thank you for your holiness, and to pray with you so no one will be left behind when Jesus reclaims every last inch of the Kingdom He owns. I hope that you continue to be happy that I have loved you so, and that nothing can take My Immaculate Grace away from you. No amount of time can carry you away because, quite the contrary, you are traveling closer to Salvation every day. Always remember that Christianity means that time is on your side; it is not your enemy because it stands for your passage into Eternal Life. Those who grieve growing older do not truly envision the victory at the end. You have an exception to many of the circumstances—those who hold the dignity of Jesus Christ in their hearts. There is no grief or hopelessness in the heart of My dear MJ! Look at the majesty that is residing there! The Truth, the light, the piety, and the faith! Before the mortal world has ended, I promise that your Diary will have drawn millions to be like her, and I promise that you will have seen many of your enemies at your door. This is My blessing for you now. ✛ Thank you both in an everlasting peace for your faithfulness, service, and prayers. I will speak to you again very soon. I love you. Goodnight!"

Sunday, August 13, 2000
4:08 p.m.

"We pray again together, My little children, to combat the evil indifference of the secular void with the Kingdom and power of Almighty God, who is your righteousness, freedom, purity, and Eternal Salvation. It is natural for you to seek Redemption because you have accepted the Holy Spirit in your hearts. My holy ones, I will offer you a rather simple analogy. When you speak to someone else in your natural voice, you do not wittingly or consciously set the tone of its sound. Your voice is a product of your physical composition. Not very many people have a voice that sounds like any other, so this attribute is particular to you without even trying to effect it. When you meet someone, your mind is more concerned about what you are going to say, rather than with what particular tone of voice you will employ. This means that your sound is inherent to you, and your demeanor and attitude can affect this sound. For example, you can whisper so as to be more quiet, and shout to someone across the room. Such actions are directly motivated by your intentions and result in a different tenor of voice. What is the metaphor? Consider that your faith and love make-up your vibrating vocal chords. Every human on the Earth is capable of faith and love. If they do not employ them, they are not saying anything worthy of being heard in Heaven. Only the mortal Earth and the Abyss below can hear. But, when you live according to the Holy Gospel, your voice is no longer silent. Those who reject Jesus have no voice and cannot speak at all, while they who love Him are His great orators and representatives throughout all Creation. This is your natural voice as you compare what others hear when you speak to them in an everyday tone. If you live in faith and love strongly enough, your most simple act is a shout heard throughout the universe. When you pursue a mission of exemplary charity, the whole globe can hear the singing of your voice. And, when every heart lives the Holy Gospel of Jesus, the Almighty Father in Heaven can hear the choirs of mortal followers shouting a vibrant song in acclamation of His Glory. Yes, when you listen with the proper generosity-of-heart, you can still hear the deafening whispers of those lonely little nuns who sit alone in their chambers with a Rosary in their hands, having no one else to pray with them in the solemn hours of night. Therefore, My children, your faith and love compose the voice with which you cry-out to God for help. He hears the resonance of your pleas amidst the clamoring world. Those who have *not* faith and love are mute! This analogy helps you understand that anyone can speak to Jesus without physically uttering a word. The voice you hear in return is the sound of Mercy and Redemption as the Son of Man replies—*Let it be!* If any man will silence the secular discriminations of the world before him, he will hear the voice of God in the background beauty. If only the people of the Earth will listen to the Wisdom of the Holy Spirit rather than the bombs bursting in air, they will know the road which is most worthy of travel. My children, there are millions who proclaim to be silent so God can speak to them, but they still cannot hear. Their problem is that what they believe to be silence is still their muted voice reverberating in their ears because they refuse to speak to Heaven with charity and love. God listens for sincerity and submission, those who are predisposed to receive His Grace. Those who command His response or stand in indignation, demanding their share of miracles, are only speaking to the ghostly winds. I have told you on more than one occasion that God will be God, even if certain quarters of the mortal world demand additional proof. They are like the ruling parliament whose house is situated upon the deck of a sinking ship. They can promulgate regulations all they might, but they will never be placed into law because their authority is about to perish. I tell you today that their resolutions were not spoken in faith and love, but in self-ingratiation and the pursuit of power. The God of Abraham will let them sink! If only humanity and their chosen governors would follow the Holy Gospel of Jesus Christ as the Law of the land, every intention of the human heart would be hailed as the first order of business in the heights of Paradise. Jesus would place the Angels in treble-step with the words, *'Please hurry! We have more blessings to dispense! Please do not fall behind!'* This is the true voice that God is waiting to hear. It is the simple utterance of His Kingdom, absolute on the Earth, with no dissenters and no objectors to stand in the way. He wishes to hear every heart calling-out for provisions from above, a deluge of goodness and healing to bathe the world in newness and Light. Yes, the voice you use and the one you hear are one and the same communion song, composed and orchestrated by a singular King on His Throne. The swirling multitudes of heroic hearts are the echoing choirs that resound the victory that has shattered the glass wall dividing Heaven and Earth. If you will only listen and speak in the tone of Life, yours will be one in the endless rows of petitioners whom Jesus sees both singularly and collectively. Remember, what you wish for yourselves in exile is simultaneously what He desires for the Mystical Body that He is about to redeem as His own! So, please speak soundly of only good things; call upon God to make you pure and strong, wholesome and ready for the journey through the mortality-ending fight that will lead you to the foyer where you will be clad in the vestments of Absolution. Sing the songs of Love and Charity that will make everyone else join-in with you. What a day it will be when I turn to My Champion Son and say, *'Look, the whole world is singing! They are waiting for you!'* Yes, that day will come very soon!

My Special son, I realize that I am constantly telling you of what *will* come, instead of you seeing what is already here. It is with your faith that you speak in an everyday voice of hope and gladness. Ignore the utterings of naysayers who are holding-out until the final moment in time to convert. Heaven cannot hear them because they have no voice! If they do not convert and repent by the End of Time, their own indignance will be their condemnation. You know that Jesus prefers that their faith be their Salvation! It is His Love which accompanies their faith that allows them to tell Him so. Hence, at the last, is Eternal Salvation easy? The answer is no, but the commitment of Christian conversion is only a heartbeat away. It is the fruit of a prayer called 'perfect submission.' I hope that you fully understand My analogy; I have enjoyed presenting it to you. What I am seeking from humanity is that supernatural Love be the common voice among men. One cannot shout it out if its origin is not the heart. Thanks to your prayers and holy life, you have given Jesus many timeless eternities of happy songs to which to listen, ones He has called the Saints to hear. I know that you will recognize them when you come to Paradise because they have been composed by your heart. He is listening to them now. Thank you for heeding My voice of hope and Love, and thank you for praying with Me!"

Sunday, August 20, 2000
4:22 p.m.

"My dear children, I know that your faithfulness to Jesus is surpassed only by your loving desire that He succeed in repatriating every living soul back to the *terra firma* of everlasting Life. Your words proclaim it; your deeds reflect it, and your hearts prove it. This is the meaning of living-out your profession of faith through the Wisdom and Light of the Holy Spirit. I come again today to pray for humankind with you so the Earth will regain the dignity it lost when so many Saints before you died, before pride was the reason why children were educated, and quite long before materiality and luxury replaced sincerity and hard work. If you were to place the world that now prevails next to the one which will come to be, you will indeed see the measure of an eye completely open to the one that is now nearly closed. But, humanity is profoundly more decent and aware of their Creator now that Jesus has come to reside among you, a liberation which was effected twenty centuries ago. It is with a mighty joy that My visits to you are filled with renewed hope. The upswing of the eyelid of human understanding is now in motion. Soon, and very soon, every eye will see the Glory of the Coming of the Lord! This very happy and anticipatory time would not be possible without people like yourselves and the living witness that you are now expressing through every medium you can find. Of course, you are going to ask Me what I think, but please anticipate My answer with greater confidence than that. It would be an exercise in redundancy for you to pose such an inquisition because your heart has already seen My response. I look to the greater Earth toward finding those who know not to seek Jesus at all, notwithstanding that the thought of Redemption has never entered their minds. You are a found people because you are Christians who live-out your faith. The lost are those who are ignorant of the Truth; and the severely endangered are they who reject it outright, the atheists and thugs who persecute the representatives of Love around the world, and assert their false authority over those who have nothing to eat and nowhere to sleep. These are the ones who are persecuting Christ, and I am waiting for the day to come, and it will, when they seek-out My Immaculate Heart in the Name of Jesus and say, '*Did I do enough for God today?*' My children, that is when I will be most happy to respond, '*If you are for Him, you assuredly cannot be on the other side.*' The purpose you must understand is that all of your work will lead them and stir them into action. Thousands upon thousands are already moving toward Salvation by the diminutive number of books that are swirling about the world. I tell you again what I have told you all along, millions will come to Redemption because of the work that has been done here in this place. I am not making a promise about something that might come, but a prophecy of a fact that is already being fulfilled. Let Me state it more clearly. There is nothing that could destroy the cultivation that is ongoing; nothing, nowhere, no time, and of no consequence. Please, there is nothing of the highest scandalous nature that could reverse what you have already done. Dare to imagine what that may be, and nothing will be there to inhibit your work. How can anyone explain the profundity of your Diary? You see, the power of your protection rests not in your hands, but in Mine and the Savior of the world. I know that you believe everything I tell you. I realize that your trust transcends any fear because you are wise in the Omnipotence of the Almighty Father in Heaven. You have learned that Jesus requires more than just casual faith. He commands your unfettered commitment. Commitment! This is how you see Him now. Your new commitment encompasses all you submit to Me today and your continued participation in His Holy Grace for the rest of your life. This is what He seeks in every man, not just those to whom I speak and the millions who are otherwise moved by the Holy Spirit to seek the righteous path. This is why My happiness is more than simply knowing that the followers of the Gospel are alive in the world. I am elated in the fact that new converts are being won with the passing of every day. You see, tomorrow is the anniversary of that 234th day in 1984 which so profoundly opened your eyes in the reflection of Jesus' Name. Sixteen times over, you and your brother have unwittingly celebrated the procession of an age of sound Wisdom, of maturity, trust, and peace. The grain of wheat fell to the ground and has indeed become new life as Saint Alta of the Heights. Remember that the same applies to all who sleep in Christ and awaken to the bells of the Resurrection that ring throughout Creation from the very first moment of Easter. You travel throughout the darkness, but your faith is still impeccably bright. You see and hear the testimonials of those who claim to know freedom, but you can still see the chains of their mortality which their own blindness refuses to reveal to them. This does not make you any better or make God any closer to you. However, it very much means that your soul is much more available to Him! He can reach you as the next planet in the series, but theirs is yet light-years away. Again, it is a distance they must travel because God can come to anyone with equidistant ease. Do you understand? The lost must come closer to the Son in order to be more warm and better reflect His Light. Now, we continue to pray for the world and look forward to the day when all humanity will be one in the Holy Cross."

Sunday, August 27, 2000
4:09 p.m.

"Our prayers together are of such urgency that they make the difference whether many people of no faith come to complete conversion through the Holy Spirit of Jesus! My little children, I have affirmed to you before that faith is truly a gift from God and can be procured or ordained in no other way. Hence, let us beseech the Heavenly Father to bestow this soul-saving gift upon everyone so the entire body of humankind can walk together on the thoroughfares and boulevards of Everlasting Life. My desire also is that compoundingly more people will wish for Salvation of their own accord, that every heart will be a witness to the Grace that has redeemed humanity. God speaks of a tall order that will be the righteous awakening of every conscience still sweltering in the melting-pot of the world's population. All in all, it is yet a single Earth which is inhabited by the people of many walks, created to be blessed and embraced by the confident hands of Jesus Christ. He already knows that He can reach them all. I would not be here at this hour if this were not so; I would not be speaking to you; I would not continue to hope for the collection of every nation under the Holy Cross if this were not so. Therefore, it is the alliance of all souls through the miracle of Jesus' Crucifixion that we seek because only in that consortium can all peoples receive the benison of the singular Crown from the singular King of kings. My children, compliance with the Gospel is not mandatory for mortal existence to reach its culmination in death. Sinners do as much. But, Jesus calls you out of sin, to be sinless again both through the Wisdom of the Gospel and the genius of His Sacrifice. He does not offer a *quid pro quo* approach to human absolution because He has nothing to gain should any man or woman accept or reject Him. His Glory will still be as Omnipotent. However, the gain is by humanity at large and the wholesomeness of the integrity that Jesus' Mystical Body will inherit at the end of time. What a delightful prospect that Jesus would return to the Earth in Glory and see that His vineyard is an expanse of fresh flowers without a single weed! What a bountiful blessing it would be if the Son of Man came back to redeem the mortal in the ravines and valleys of the globe and see these landscapes inhabited completely with humble sheep, and not a goat within grasp! This is not beyond your prayers and His power to achieve. The Earth is already turning so as to grind the finest wheat of human contrition for the tables in the Kingdom of Paradise, the making of a recipe for complete success. Can you imagine a world in which the chaff is reserved for a labor no longer required? These things are not only probable, but are within the reach of human achievement. To everything there is a season. Let us espouse the possibilities that the time for war has passed, that the time of division is over, that the time for binding-up the wounds of broken humanity has permanently begun in the name of perpetual peace. I offer My Immaculate Heart and My stately Mantle as a new beginning for the world, that all peoples will come to Me for introduction to the Prince of Reconciliation and Absolution. Please allow Me to bring you unending joy in the Person of the Son of God! Oh, how happy I would be to see every soul bask in such Divine Grace and healing. There is no error He cannot erase, no sorrow He cannot mend, and no enemy He cannot defeat. Jesus knows what your heart savors when your soul is hungry and you know not what to eat. He is this satisfying Meal! He is the portion who has been allotted to you by God, the wealth that you have always treasured, the sun you wished would always shine, and the sunrise that you never wanted to fade. My children know Me! The people of the Earth are My little ones, and not one will see the Face of their Savior without knowing Me first! My children, this is why the Earth is peppered with apparitions of My Immaculate image like lightning strikes in the darkness. There is no gloom that can keep Me away! I do not fear the hollow scowls of the everyday world because I know how it will end. There are reflexes just waiting to be unleashed if only the haughty will humble themselves to pray. God has planned a great new dayspring of hope for those who finally call upon Him. I tell you, dear children, that He is still aghast by the hypocrisy He sees in the world. He sees giant paved overpasses upon which limousines travel, while the neglected sleep sorrowfully in poverty below. He knows the intentions of those who live in wealth, and He will finally see them gasping for air in the containment of their own greed. We can still reach them! We are doing it now! We are transforming huge magnates into servants for Justice during each minute that passes! Yes, inequality between men is being mended because the hoarders are dying in their beds. When all is said and done, My children, all that will be left is flowers. This is My promise to you and My oath to the Father in Heaven. Just as Jesus walked with Me through the fine sands of His youth, He shall walk with Me amidst the mountaintops of Glory that He will soon bestow upon the hearts who proclaim Him. Soon, you too will see Angels instead of camels, and the Face of Almighty God in place of the Star above the Nativity. I know that the faithful can already sense these things because your belief is your bearer of Light. My children do not yet need to see from the summit of success to know what is on the other side. Yours is a prophecy of enlightenment which has already come true. It is an age of sustained hope that is now here to stay. This is the peace which is forever lasting, that which the Ecclesiastes could only tell of to come, but now has finally arrived. It lives now in your hearts, and will be ratified in physical fact once you have perceived the glorious Second Coming of the Messiah to the Earth. The presence of the miracle of your own resurrection is now inside you, nurtured like a seed at the center of your being. God is growing it like a daffodil preparing to breach the soil to take-in the full light of day. This is the beauty to which you are called, to be forever pretty for the Son of God. It may become inclement and dark where you now tread, but remember that flowers do not sleep just because it is night. Maintain your beauty and the fragrance of Divinity, for you know not when the Savior of humanity might stoop to take-in your scent! I give you the promise that your fragrance will be sweet if you tender your hearts to the Holy Gospel and live what I am teaching. I am forever grateful that you are so kind to allow Me to speak to you!"

Sunday, September 3, 2000
3:43 p.m.

"Set humanity free! Show God the courage that died with mortal weaklings long ago! Lift-up this vessel of greatness by your own rising tide of willingness to succeed in Christ! Be His pageant of earthly valor, and glorify His Kingdom while you live! You truly do not yet understand what healing you are being asked to deliver to the world. Please prayerfully try to imagine it. Consider a father who is hungry for the food of obedience, love and discipline, and see it in the context of how you console Him. His is the joy you feel, the same expulsion of wrong, the very same flourishing of goodness, peace, warmth, and security. This beautiful day is remarkably more blessed because the Holy Spirit has descended upon your hearts, inside the chamber of Truth where, through your lives, He can convert and transform the Earth into the Kingdom He will redeem. My dear little children, I have come again to speak to you in His Love. I wish to do so; I pray that you will always respond, and I know that you will. Indeed, I will join in your prayers no matter what they may be because I realize that your desire is to see the world of Justice about which I have spoken finally come to pass. By all means, its passage has already begun. The Almighty Father is aware of the world as the work of your hands shape it to be. He feels the same emotion in which you partake of your relationships with others, and knows equally well what dispositions cause you to have grave concern for the well-being and Salvation of other souls. Why should it be, My children, that such mutual participation be taken for granted by those who do not desire to know God in return? It is their lack of faith and absence of spiritual direction. Each soul must ask to be guided by the Light of Everlasting Life. Where there is confusion and doubt, there is greater the reason to pray! No discernment is either effective or complete without invoking the Wisdom of the Spirit of Christ. Even you must do this as you respond to My messages. God the Father cannot lead you astray, nor will He allow one of His own chosen ones of the mortal Earth to do so. This is why prayer is so powerful, My children. It is the elimination of doubt and also the answer to all your questions of faith. Your commission in the world is to deliver the Gospel message to all who will hear. This is a tangible service, a physical sign of the presence of Jesus in the body of humankind. There are more beautiful facets to the perfect jewel of Christianity than there are forces that are still trying to depose it. The Light of Love shines in more directions than there are enemies who would try to conceal it. This is why witnesses for Jesus always win. They perpetually have a lifeline with the Eternal Divine. When the foes of righteousness step forward to object, the friends of the Messiah respond, *'Overruled!'* When brutal forces threaten persecution, the allies of Redemptive Love say, *'Thank you!'* This is why you cannot lose, My children. There is no weapon in Creation that can harm you now. This is true because you make it so by standing beside Jesus. When you are united in Him, no one can approach you and say, *'Who is that standing next to you?'* All in the world, even those who claim no faith or any spiritual benefactor, know yourself and the Cross that extols your goodness when you place your very life in the Most Sacred Heart of the King of all Creation..."

(I asked Our Lady how we could help our Bishop become more courageous in his call to conversion. She responded in a very revealing way.)

"If you fire a weapon a day for a year instead of 365 weapons in one day, which would you choose? This is what will happen. Hence, do not try to deplete your arsenal approaching one bishop at a time. Soon, they will all be moved at once! Can you not see the genius of Jesus in this?"

Saturday, September 9, 2000

Hallelujah! Now, by your love, compassion, daring, and delight, Jesus has a new reason to hope again! You are indeed the valedictory obedience that He has been seeking, the giant faith He summons from little men. By what He sees through your eyes, you have whet His appetite to pour out His Grace over all the world! You are the opening of the new springtime because you dare to define His courage before an indefinite world! Now there is fresh venue through which the Saints can muster the sleeping righteousness of the mortal Earth! The birthday of the Immaculate Virgin has never been so sweetly observed! With each new embarking mystery of your compliance, the world succeeds again in overcoming complacency and denial. With every stroke of your heart, the immortal being of the human conscience grows wider, flows more rapidly, and senses more deeply the purpose of God in the universe. It is Love and Creation! It is consolation, peace, transformation, and absolution! The God of Abraham is called to holy arms because you are allowing Him reason to fight! You are His strength and vigor for a new campaign of composure, His stature of high command and distinction, and the level heights He will seek before His Sacred Heart crests in satisfaction that the soul of humankind is finally His to keep!

So please, keep striving by virtue of your valor! Tear down the remaining walls of obstinance and the obese reticence that keeps the holy from marching onward, ever forward to the last remaining bulwark that is yet to be discovered.

Continue to hone God's blade of satisfaction by shining in the pit of the night! He goes with you as you take Him there, back to the fires of your youth which still kindle in the darkness, back to the places you yearned to conquer as an adolescent child. Let your new Wisdom of Salvation be your rear guard as you retreat no more! Make this moment in history more than an archaic happenstance! This is now your time to bridle the forces which diminish the most noble of men, and unleash the captive ingenuity that is the driving force behind the reconciliation of the lost, lame, captive, and indifferent. Only by reaching into far-off places have you done this! Only by severing the isolation of insolent hearts have you regained the power and direction to lead them to Christ! That is your challenge to proceed in confidence. It is proof that the Spirit of God is alive in you, is revealed through you, and succeeds with you! You have already berthed the commission of a new age of change! You have propelled dignity into the forefront of genuine consideration because you stand for the very reason to have hope! The world can never go back to inhibition because you have conquered its shame! Crossing the horizon of commitment, you have brought humankind and all her allies to a newer corridor of awareness, closer to the center of Creation, toward the origin of Light, and within the perimeter of all immortal possibility. Keep going, we say! Let the drudgery of the past expire in your new Light! These are your days, your years in the sun of Justice. Be stately there in presence, and never shun the mightiness that is your own to wield!

...your Dominion Angels

Sunday, September 10, 2000
12:57 p.m.

"Yes, you do well always and everywhere to give the Lord thanks and praise! You are the princes of exemplary Grace because, by your concessions to Jesus in obedience, you allow the Kingdom of Heaven to supplant the mortal world below. My children, I thank you for the many times in which you have said 'yes' to God when it would otherwise have been easier to decline His call for greater sacrifice. But, you are a loving people who know that the world must change for the better. Your prayers and good works bring this change because God wishes to reward your faith in Him. You, My Special son, are continuing to receive the benisons that may have been delayed, waiting for a future time when you might have been more open of heart. But, you did not desist in your humble service, and you have the intercessions of the Angels to prove it. Just when it seems apparent that the only sound coming from humanity is a death knell for their future, you rise again with courage to conquer the evil forces and indifference that makes them blind. You will be richly rewarded in Paradise for the life you have given to Jesus toward the conversion of humanity and the making of reparation for their errors. Sin is conquered by your living in the same Passion which Jesus endured to absolve mankind entire. Thank you! Thank you for caring and for not surrendering to the influences of time and material. God knows to call upon you now, at a moment in history when others have let Him down. There are thousands whose lives have been blessed who do not hold a whit of thankfulness for the Messiah who has made it possible. The true blessedness that these people will soon know is when their perishables finally do perish and all that remains is their nakedness before the Truth of the Gospel. Along with many other faithful, you are the reason why My Son keeps trying. How could He concede to those who despise Him when He sees you fighting so courageously for His sake? I tell you again that you do not realize the goodness you are effecting. The small message from the Angels of yesterday is trivial compared to what they will eventually reveal to you if only you keep going. Many are the signs that you are receiving for the offerings you have made. They are part of the Eternal Light in which you live and the Divine prescience that guides you ever forward in time. These are small blessings which help you to see the larger Grace that has become your life! It is true that God takes refuge in your enjoyment of His Love. The more you let yourself go in His power, the greater indulgence in pardon you will see for the world. Have you yet been able to intelligibly grasp why this is so? It is you, His loving creation, whom He is watching with eyes of pleasance and comfort. You should be thankful that you are pleasing Him so well. It is the victory over the mortal Earth that you are professing. I have come today to again tell you how pleased is Jesus that you are still working for Him. Can you not sense the powerful influence you are having on the Earth? If only you could see it from the immortal side! Someday you will! You will be thanking Jesus for a great deal more from your Bishop before time is done. You are learning that what makes great people humble is that they already recognize the scope of their power. They will wield it in the best way to execute the circumstances at hand. This is something that you should always remember. The same holds true of the prayerfulness you inspire by virtue of your Diary. You are humbled because you know the invincible nature of its content; the miracle cannot be dismissed. There is no need for you to be other than humble; the Diary is the aggressive Truth which speaks in your place. Do not be afraid to wield your power."

Sunday, September 17, 2000
3:17 p.m.

"My compassionate children, you wonder how sorrow, grief, obedience, and suffering can be transformed into the fruits of peace and Salvation because the time seems long for their endurance. I tell you, My little ones, that these are the timeless gifts of Divinity that you offer to the Almighty Father in exchange for the conversion of the world. The indifference of outcast hearts is a luxury they cannot long afford. It is your lives in union with the Passion of Jesus that sets their sights upon the authentic riches of

Everlasting Life. I know that those of righteous heart are offended by heresy and the criticism of the Mother Church. Please allow your awareness to be a cause for your continued prayerfulness rather than contempt. The Almighty Father accepts your courageous offerings that you tender in honor of His Son. Your replication of His patience and Wisdom will be your victory at the last. My Special son, I need not remind you of the miracles you have seen. You know that you have brought to completion the Sacrifice which made them possible. You have been instructed about how to continue, but you have not been told why. If you share in your mind's eye the world as you have come to know it, you will recognize the signs that reveal the effect of your work. There are tens-of-thousands who have already seen your Diary, most of whom are now awed into prayerful silence and personal contemplation. The words of divinity which I have given them through your work are culturing their consciences with a multitude of ways in which they will soon respond and reach-out. Your Father in Heaven and your Savior at His Right Hand have depended immensely upon your many contributions. The common factor in your faithful years of service, especially the past five, is that you have truly enjoyed them! But, the most important treasure is that God has even more enjoyed watching you love Him! He is not given much delight upon the Earth, but those like yourself excite and console His Sacred Heart in the same series of beatific events. You do not realize at this moment what all of this actually means. You are a great deal like the mind of God because you hold a salvific purpose, a righteous motivation for what you do. Do you know the generation of joyful expectation that you undergo? This is the same feeling that God generates when anyone calls-out His Name to change the world for the better. This is His ecstasy that prayer brings to Him, and the most powerful is the Holy Sacrifice of the Mass. There, His Son is committing Himself upon the Earth prayerfully, just like you do when you are called. This is how you make the Earth a better place. God is moved by your kind obedience, and knows that you understand when souls are redeemed because you have said 'yes' to Him. If only you could know His invincible joy every time you say 'yes.' He is ecstatic because you soothe His horrible disappointment when Adam and Eve said 'no.' While Jesus' Crucifixion reversed the terrible tide of human condemnation, your own sacrifices move mortal hearts on the Earth and those in Purgatory to the fully-revealed Light of the Glory that has saved them. This is what is meant by your sharing in the Divinity of Christ and, although many do not yet understand, how you make-up for what is lacking in the Cross. What is lacking is not anything that Jesus failed to do or did not suffer, but the portion which God has reserved for His people to be accomplished through the centuries of time. This is why it is so essential that you attend daily Mass and participate in the Sacraments. The Holy Mass is not only the revelation of Jesus' Last Supper, Passion, and Death, but also His sending forth of entire humanity to reflect the Crucifixion they have just witnessed. It is your own participation in the holy Thanksgiving of the Eucharist. What good is food if it is never eaten? Therefore, you make-up for the lacking of which Saint Paul spoke by being the sacred vessels upon the Earth of the Divine Body and Blood of Jesus into the world. This is all that is lacking in Jesus' suffering, more people to receive His Sacrificed Body from His Altar in Heaven. When all of your brothers and sisters come to the Table of Everlasting Life, the suffering of the Son of God will be complete. Please be clear about one thing. Every sin known to man has been washed away and flushed beyond all existence in time and Eternity by Jesus' Blood on the Cross. There is nothing lacking in the expungement of sin from Creation, but there is not yet total unity of humankind in the suffering which will bring the lost to a seat at the Table of Grace. This is why Jesus has told the world to 'take up your cross and follow Me.' He means your share of the one Cross upon which He was crucified. When you do the kind and obedient things that God asks of you, you are not only carrying your own share, but you are simultaneously bearing the weight that others refuse to carry. Can you see why He is so pleased with you? What you do in the Name of Jesus, you do very well! You know why you have been asked. You know how and why, and the when is now! This is your time!"

(Recently, a newspaper article was run depicting a Lutheran minister offering his service to his congregation before the Altar of a Roman Catholic Church. It has been a practice in some locales to allow certain Protestant services to be conducted in Catholic cathedrals because the size of these churches better accommodates the robust crowds at such gatherings. Our Lady responded to the one I saw.)

"I have seen the coverage of the newspaper of the Lutheran committing a horrible aberration at the Altar of Sacrifice. Yes, it is an unacceptable event. And, if not for your love, God would be offended into punishing those who are responsible. The Church is having to fight against social pressures and political expediency. The Holy Father refuses to embrace this fallacy, and has spoken the Truth for which he will long be remembered after he is gone. What he has stated about the Original Apostolic Church and Catholicism will unite Catholics around the world like never before in history once this Pope has died. Do you recognize the genius in his words and deeds? Please do not be awfully concerned about who is ordained where, but keep your eyes peeled on the glorious recognition by all humanity of the Triumph of My Immaculate Heart soon to come. I would be remiss if I did not mention your birthday coming in three more days. I have spoken to you for many of them! While your body is growing older, your joy and faithful spirit are forever new, young, and decisive in the Truth. I have told you before that you are moving ever more closely to the newness of Everlasting Life each day that passes. Remember that it is your loving sacrifices that bring God to answer your prayers."

Sunday, September 24, 2000
4:52 p.m.

"Today, My children, I come to remind you of the awesome favor in which you rest in the eyes of your Creator God. You continue to allow the Holy Spirit to find sanctuary inside your hearts, the depositories of your faith and reservoirs of compassion on the Earth. It is through this favor that conversion is taking place. Again I ask you, how could the Son of Man turn His Divine Face away from such genuine loyalty? How could He deny the petitions of such a chosen race? It is herebeyond His pleasure and joy to see you to success, not solely for your own sake, but for the betterment of human life for those whom you desire to succeed in holiness, health, peace, joy, and prosperity. Indeed, your faith in the Salvation of others will be their transference to the Dawn of supernatural enlightenment. Please let Me be clear, I have brought you the promise today that for every person who rejects your Diary, another hundred will be given the gift of knowing it as well as you do. Your words are correct. I have not come into this holy place and dispensed ten years of lessons and messages to see them fail. So today, My little ones, is a day of reflection because the work you have already offered is a sweet tree of Divine fruit. Why do I tell you this? Do I desire to build your self-esteem or elevate you before the multitudes of the uncertain? The answer is a resounding 'no.' I tell you this because God Himself wishes to hear it. Finally, someone will listen; someone will respond, pray, sacrifice, and live-out the Gospel of Jesus with such allegiance and longevity. You are dear to My Immaculate Heart, and this simultaneously places you in a high state of Grace before My Son. I wish you could know the times during which many others have desired to lead your lives. Through your own compliance, they are finally beginning to do so. You can only imagine the shock and jubilation on the faces and in the consciences of the happy 100 people who have laid eyes on the books you mailed to them over the past ten days. There are insufficient words to describe their newfound revelation through the power of the Holy Spirit. Many of them have said that they were lost, but now are found because of My intercession through your Diary. Now, upon the report of the Trumpets to close-out the mortal ages, many more will know and accept the Redemption that has come to them. As I have told you in years past, if only one soul is won to Salvation by the work we have done here together, not a speck will have been in vain. You can see by now that your Divine messages are a large portion of the role that many will play in the Triumph of My Immaculate Heart. This day of reflection is more than a barometer of the status of your labors, it is a turning-point in your service for God. This 24th day of September AD 2000 is the very essential day by which you will later come to recognize this Jubilee Year as a fulcrum for the transformation of humanity. You can sense this

Truth as I am speaking to you now. You are willing to be led and taught, willing to surrender your lives to the goal of Christian unity at the Altar of Sacrifice around the entire world. So, I call you to renew your hope. I have many more beautiful messages to offer, well beyond the tenth anniversary of their beginning in 1991. It is a rare occasion when any earthly mortal is allowed to hear these words. You are not chosen because you are good, you are good because you are chosen. Jesus is alive in you, and He intends to succeed in making your own lives an instrument of His Peace."

Monday, October 2, 2000
6:47 p.m.

"My dear little children, I see and hear many things which please My soul, so blessed that it is. How could a mother be more pleased than I am with you? I have taken you under My Holy Mantle since before you were born. Together, our quest is for the lost, to bring the children of God to the forefront of the public debate, and especially during the ensuing nine days, to reveal to the world the fulfillment of the Saint Louis de Montfort prophecy of who the Children of Mary truly are. You are counted in that number. You are those who are like brine in the drink of the rich. You will continue to be despised for stating the Truth, and will be described as being arrogant for not compromising what I have taught you to live. All of these are good things because they speak to the contemporary fulfillment of the Sacred Scriptures. You will learn that those last times according to Saint Louis have passed-over the eastern horizon, and morning will be broken in the hearts of millions. All of this is because My children pray and obey. You lead the world to Jesus because you are inclined to know Him by the Divine order of the Holy Spirit. I am asking My messengers to pour-out their best prayers in a chain of invocations around the globe to concur with the celebrations in Rome in the next nine days. I know what pleases God most in each of His little ones. Would it be possible for Me to beseech of you and your brother to invoke your most powerful prayers for the next seven days? You should take great humility in this because of the impending pronouncement for the Feast of the Most Holy Rosary! I will raise My hand in triplicate each of those days of prayer of the next week to bless you. Your prayers are beautiful in the sight of the Angels, and are a perpetual source of direct intervention to impede the terror of evil in the lives of the oppressed and others who are wretched. Please be proud of your service to the Almighty Father! Thank you very much for giving your entire self to the Glory of God."

(Over the course of two recent days, Timothy and I have assisted a very poor couple rebuild a kitchen in their home. It was very dilapidated, to a point that even the floor had rotted-away, leaving it in need of complete replacement. We

worked for two extremely long days, and even into the night, moving appliances, laying flooring, rebuilding stairways, installing paneling, reworking the plumbing, setting cabinets, and even moving laundry facilities from the basement. I felt an intense sense of accomplishment and relief at the completion of our project. I would have never dreamed that so many things could have been repaired in such a short time. Our work was worth every moment of the effort upon seeing the happiness beaming from the young wife's face as she looked upon her new kitchen late that night. She acted as if she had never owned something so nice. I was very glad at that moment that I was able to assist them. Our Lady referred to our work.)

"Jesus wept in love for your goodness and kindness. How well you have served these poor ones! The feeling you hold in your heart is the same affirmation that Jesus felt on the Cross. How you were tired and weary! How you did not desist until you accomplished what you set-out to do! Always remember that Love is Divine, transforming pain into joy at the utterance of one grateful heart. This is the Glory into which the Earth has been reborn because of the Sorrowful Passion and Crucifixion of My Son. You share in that Deity every time you reach forward in Jesus' Name to improve the lives of those to whom He is so close, and in whom He is so present; the broken, poor, and disadvantaged, the crippled, the incarcerated, and those who are persecuted for lauding His Holy Name. Can you not sense in your heart by now that you are of the chosen people who participate directly in the Redemption of the world? This is why you continue to be called. You will one-day see the bountiful Heaven you have shaped by your life on Earth. I will succeed only because of My children, especially through the Novena which you have chosen to offer. Remember My triplicate blessing, a treble means of assuring your confidence in succeeding through the power of My Son, knowing that praying the Rosary is sheer goodness on sight! Thank you for loving Me! Thank you for loving Jesus and for lifting-up the wounded human family. I give you a special blessing because the next nine days will truly change the world!"

Sunday, October 8, 2000
3:50 p.m.

"That the world may be blessed, purified, converted, mortified, and redeemed, I am the Mediatrix of all Divine Graces from the heavenly Throne of God. These moments in human history are greater than the ability of any historian to record them. Kept in a unique pocket of this mortal time, I have come to announce with renewal the purpose of prayer from the heart and the enlightenment of the conscience of man. There is no wealth which can purchase the Wisdom that I bring and no dissension that can drive Me away. My dear children, through the power of My Beloved Christ-Child, I hereby lay claim to the humanity who belongs to Me. I assert My authority to reign as Queen of the Saints and Intercessor to Jesus on behalf of all the faithful. It is the Holy Rosary which you must hoist to your shoulders of righteousness to serve as your shield against all evil and the spearhead of your petitions to the Father. Now, all of those who claim to be Christians must awaken and live-out the profession of their faith. Indeed, My children who profess to be Catholic must elevate the Original Apostolic Church before every soul on the Earth, like it or not. The graces dispensed through the Catholic Church are a blessing for all humankind. That is why the world must be educated both in the Holy Gospel and the Divine Traditions of the Church, the Priesthood, and the very prayerful service of all the Clergy, the religious, and the laity. No one is exempt from service to God and His people if they expect to proceed toward the highest seat of absolution. The Angels and Saints are not just a complementary group of holy spirits who watch the world go by. They are powerful participants in the transformation of the Earth into the Kingdom of Divine Royalty through the one Paraclete of Jesus. I seek anyone who will listen to believe in bold faith that the lessons in *Morning Star Over America* are true. And, you are seeing the fruit of this now. Today is the continuing culmination of a princely Papacy which is growing the awareness of mankind in the role of their Mother! I gave you Jesus 2000 years ago, and soon I will give Him to you again in Glory which He has foretold the universe. Please pay Me no worship and pay Me no homage! It is the King in My arms who rightfully deserves this praise! Mankind would do well to remember every word I have said! There is no time for doubting, despair, rejection, and procrastination. You, O' humanity, are the heirs of the Passion which has been so despised by the indifferent ages before you! You are the beneficiaries of the patience of God and the Mercy which still feeds the lost! I beseech you to not turn your back on Redemption now! The climax has finally drawn near! The plot has unfolded and you remain to see the world inverted for the cast of all generations! Nowhere else can your heart be brought nearer to God, and at no other place can you see firsthand the closure of the ages. The thousand years in the sight of the Almighty Father is but a single dawn away! This is the millennium which will heave the haughty over the cliff of perdition and raise the humble to new heights of joy! It is not a rebuke of humanity to try to be in the number who will fly freely amongst the winds of Paradise. Indeed, bring them all with you! Shout-out your jubilation because you have known the Truth all along! Remember the wretched who really never listened to anyone. I promise that they will hear you loudly and clearly now! I give you the consolation of My Immaculate Heart in which to savor your hopes and capture your dreams. God would never allow them if they were not meant to come true! This is the hope in which you must live and the reason that you should anticipate anew the answer to your petitions. Just as sure as the candles flicker on the Altar, I bear an angel on My right and one on My left whose scent will forever tell of the knowledge I bring.

My Special son, the events in Rome have been everything you wished them to be. Thanks to the pious and powerful prayers of My faithful ones, many noble manifestations are now underway. I hope I have given you reason to continue in faith that God's Will is being done and that you and your brother are playing a living part in the conversion of mankind. I ask you most of all to continue to be happy. Thank you for the generosity and charitable actions which your work is affording the world!"

Sunday, October 15, 2000
3:45 p.m.

"If you try, My little children, you will be able to personify the hope which is embraced through your prayers because God is indeed the Love described by the Dominion Angels in your affirmation from them. When your confidence is assured in your trust in the Mercy of Jesus, you are able to see the motivations more clearly in your heart that God wants you to perceive. And, what are these righteous causes? The most imperative is the continuing growth in divinity of the moral conscience of mankind toward a purity that no dissension can impede. The recitation of the Holy Rosary takes you there. Next, as you continue to become physically one in the heated battle for human Redemption, you must partake of the nourishment that only Jesus can provide. The Holy Eucharist is your source of strength. The Blessed Sacrament is the union of your spirit with the Savior of the world. The Sacrament of Reconciliation is also your motivation, also a Grace from the Almighty Father to continue to shower you in absolution. Confession of the soul is where God declares that the Blood of His Son has prepared you for the perches of Paradise. These are the multi-dimensional and interfacial motivations for which you must pray, and in which you should participate. My children, the Sacraments of the Church are your collective cooperation with the God of the universe to prepare you for Eternal Salvation and bless your soul for holding the desire to come back Home. They are God's ways of giving you the sweet fruits of perfection before your heart stops beating on Earth. You have noticed by now that Jesus accepts your petitions and sacrifices because He desires you to live in His omnipotent Light without being shamed by your own inequities. He has borne them for you so that you may see His reflection in your own Eternal being. Please know that He has done this both lovingly and wilfully because He has already seen the people whom you will eventually become, like Him in all ways, including the absence of sin. It may be difficult for you to imagine a life in which you will never be able to muster a sorrowful thought, but that time is now coming. Your Heavenly Mother will be the most grateful for that day! It may be equally as difficult to imagine a time when one-hundred percent of the people grow as fluently in prosperity as the wealthy ten percent are now, but this too is only a new dawn away. And yes, who could imagine a man who despises My description of an airplane crash in Pittsburgh also falling to the Earth in an airplane in Pittsburgh? Those two occurrences fell on the birthdays of your Blessed Virgin Mother and your biological mother. It is a disunion with the graces of God to disparage His work in this new time of righteous atonement. My children, it is not necessarily an indication of your own victory when your enemies fall, but a signal that the Triumph of My Immaculate Heart is marching forward, despite the clattering of mortal opposition that surrounds you.

Today, you have been resting again from your labors to help the poor. These are special times because you are effecting the generosity and charity that My Son calls you to achieve. Those who are His people live like you; they pray and serve in love and obedience, and will reap the reward that is due them at the end of time. You are storing your wealth in Heaven, and your riches there will be profound. You cannot find such a return on Earth. I have come today to reaffirm that Jesus is glorified by your holiness, and humanity is the greater because you have complied. My Special son, I have also come to ask you to continue to lift your prayers for the unborn and for the poor souls in Purgatory. What innocent and helpless ones are those who are yet to be born! How pitiable are those who suffer in Purgatory! We pray for them because Jesus hears our pleas to come swiftly to their aid. When anyone calls upon Him, He will hear and respond. The problem with those whose hearts are not afire for Jesus is not only whether they choose to believe in the miracles He brings, but that every new one they see makes them realize how useless their possessions have become, for which they have worked their lives to attain. They fight with all their fervor to conquer the feelings that they have not instead been serving stout-heartedly for Jesus. It is similar to the feeling one would have to discover that their new home has burned to the ground after all they have endured to procure it, after all the laboring by so many. How could they accept a word from anyone who told them that it is gone? The majority of Christians, especially some Catholics, see miraculous revelations as being somehow foreign to the faith of the Mother Church. These miracles are not only to build upon the faith of God's people, they are also the product of the faithfulness of holy people! Pray that Jesus will do what is required to conquer the mortal will of those disbelievers who are arrogant and brash. I assure you that there will be no such thing as rejection when the time is finally ripe. Oh, how I can foresee every soul treating you with true kindness in the years to come! You must realize how happy your work has made the Lord! This is the reciprocity of servitude, prayer and revelation, the reason why people must approach the goal of conversion and Redemption with the acceptance of little children. I will bless humanity in many more ways, and those you place under My protection... There is a period of unprecedented peace about to come to the Earth. Millions will take time for My messages. As you can see by looking at the globe, there is still terror, heartbreak, poverty, and aggression. I tell you with definitive assurance that the Glory of Jesus will strike them down. Thank you again for praying with Me for so many years, and for your devoted love. Together, we continue to change the world while bringing Creation to Grace!"

Sunday, October 22, 2000
3:19 p.m.

"To the elation of the Almighty Father, apparent in the profundity through which the Angels speak, you continue to console the Sacred Heart of Jesus, whose perpetual rhythm is the acclamation of Love for humankind in its entirety. My dear little children, you are told of the passage that reads, *Lord, where else could we go?* Our Divine Lord reciprocally poses the same question to His faithful ones on Earth. Proof-at-hand is that I have come again to pray with you and to invoke your ongoing discipleship so every soul can know the conversion and Salvation you have claimed. What joy! What a certifiable peace that has become your lives! Therein resides the best of all human dispositions! Thank you for choosing the pathway of Christian confirmation. It is your only unambiguous means to true absolution. It is the only profession that will lead your soul into complete union with the Creator of the universes. My dear ones, these previous nine years and eight months are the high privilege of your Immaculate Mother because I have seen you yield to the justice of Heaven which often seems so incomprehensible to mortal men. All the Saints have joined Me as the desires of Paradise are being fulfilled on the Earth. How can a single crucified Messiah lead to the Salvation of every man? How can death create Life? These are the Sacred Mysteries that compose the miracle of Jesus' Resurrection. This is the basis of your faith and the reason you are so blessed when you live by it. If you observe Creation through the eyes of Everlasting Life, you will see beyond the mountaintops of your highest hopes to the certain realization that these are likewise prayers of the heart, your aspirations of achieving an absolution which takes you beyond any lack of mortal understanding. If you attempt to imagine the justice of God by employing the thematic reasoning of the world, you will fail to attain an accurate perception of the Truth. This is why Jesus said that His Kingdom is not of this world. He knew that He is the Truth in perfect Flesh, and this is why the people of the Earth chose to reject Him. Indeed, if the world had been the reflection of that singular Truth 2,000 years ago, there would have been no need for humanity to hear the teachings He brought. Sadly, the Earth was an imperfect place, and the faithless proved it when they brought the Son of Man to trial and crucified Him. Now, through the embracing of His Victory over the Grave, the universe has been perfected by His Grace. The problem is that the mortal-living refuse to accept it. And, those who understand it are reluctant to proclaim it. Still further, those who proclaim it are victims of some of the most vile ridicule, mockery, and persecution ever known to Creation. This too is a facet of the Sacred Mysteries because the Holy Spirit in faithful hearts is the true enemy of the assailants who punish the faithful when they stand upright for human Redemption in Christ Jesus. Whatever you do, My children, please do not dignify the false argument that your faith in the Gospel is a circle of errors and contradictions. God knows precisely what He is doing when He dispatches the Holy Spirit to strengthen and enlighten you. He endorses the prophetic messages that His Holy Angels deposit at your doors. He admires your obedience and accepts your offerings as very serious petitions. These things you also may not understand, but you will completely know as the table of time fulfills its course. There is no crudeness in the wait if you will only receive the Wisdom that God brings. You have been told before that your greatest fears have now become your most powerful weapons. This, above many other things, is your own personal participation in the Sacred Mysteries of human absolution. Since each lash of the Passion of Jesus was in reparation for the sins of man, each offering you make to God at this moment in time is a high thanksgiving gift to praise the Messiah who has saved you. Every time you say 'yes' to Him, you are making a supplication for which He has already dispensed your blessing. Please remember what I have told you about the deception of the element of time. As you unfold your life as one great moment in Eternity, you will have no regrets from which to hide and no confession that will cause you fear. True confession of the soul is to know that God accepts your being as you are in light of your compliance with the Gospel. You will be perfect when He says you have been perfected. This is the power of His Divine Mercy and a blessing from His storehouse of Love. There is no bounty that is more benevolent or kind. I ask you to ponder these wishes as you continue to pray for the world. My Special son, today is again the 22nd. You are correct, they seem to pass-by more quickly now. This is because you are living the dignity and divinity of forgiveness. It means that Jesus has hold of your heart, and He will never let go. His gifts are timeless, and you are accepting them well. I have said what I came to relate for today. I know that you can see the signal graces I am bestowing upon you as the days continue to pass. Your hopes will be fulfilled. I have told you they will occur. You are My children whom I love dearly! Thank you kindly for reciting your prayers. I will reecho them to Jesus for you!"

Sunday, October 29, 2000
4:02 p.m.

"Good afternoon, My dear little children! What happy warriors you are in the victory that has ensured the Triumph of My Immaculate Heart! The sweet taste of Divine joy that you savor so urgently is only a few more sunrises away. When you look upon the deplorable world, do not cringe in disdain at all you see. Remember the Truth I have brought. There is more Glory in the world than there is drudgery to pull it down. I ask you to remember that the naked eye cannot yet see the return of your Salvation because it is still cloaked in God's anticipation for humanity to change. Blessed is the world who yet cannot see! I tell you again that the harbor of your hope is justifiably filled because the promises of God are at hand. I have carried in My Womb the reason for your happiness, and I confirm by My words that these are the moments you shall remember as the growing of your awareness that humanity has been drawn to the warmth of His Love. My children, you address the battlefields of the twentieth century being strewn with corpses in your first book. This is one of the main subjects that most readers are remembering because, if not for war, they would not have died. Human souls hunger for peace and a renewed reason to believe that it will be lasting. This is what I am teaching through you and the encouragement you have been offering others on My behalf. You are disseminating My messages of Love throughout the Earth. You have never had greater reason to have high optimism for your lives. You are the new prophets of the latter ages, and the Holy Spirit has employed you to spread the message of Good News. The clock of mortal time is slowly running-out on the world, and all Creation is moving to the corridor to listen to everything you have to say. Hence, the miracle still continues! The countless new pages that you are now receiving through the miraculous intercession of the Holy Dominion Angels are a delight to behold. They are revealing the Truth to humanity about the condition of your hearts, the blessings in the Church, and the plainly-stated reasons why everyone should begin to pray. I am telling you that it is *you* who are making this miracle come forth. Imagine what a new book you will have that will be filled from cover to cover with the spiritual admonishments you are recording here! Through them, you are learning more about your hearts, about the conversion of the lost, and the condition of the souls of your brothers and sisters. There is so much distraction in the happenings before you, but I assure you that your messages of Redemption will have the last word. They cannot help but be the echoing of the final utterances of man; it is inevitable before the exultation of Jesus!

My Special son, I ask that you continue to receive the new pages from the Angels with joy! They are the advisory counsel that the wicked need to hear and the consolation that holy hearts have been seeking for generations past. You can detect by their tone that they are derived directly from the hand of Truth. The words that you are hearing each night are your continued reflection that all is truly well amongst the living, while the enemies of Love are on their way out. I am so pleased by My little Angels because they so gleefully deposit their sweet Wisdom at your doorway and go on. The passing hours only bring them back again when those hours are filled with prayer. Again, regarding these new pages which are being so profoundly brought into the world by the projection of your love, you and your brother must remember not to concede to the competition that abounds in the secular world. The public elections are one such distraction. This work that the Angels are delivering is too important to have either of you distracted by that process. With all the duplicity, lying, and wasting millions of dollars on the media that could be feeding the poor, you do not need to get caught-up in such a damaging process. You have your love and the Heavens to support you. Your prayers and the Sacraments secure and lead you. You do not need politics to stain it. Thank you for obeying your Mother; and most of all, thank you for accepting the reasons why. My Special one, I have concluded My wise counsel for this day. The fortune in your humble prayers will soon come to pass. I offer you My high commendation for staying the course in your fight for the conversion of the world. Your Father in Heaven is pleased! He is spatting in Satan's face by asking you to teach proudly what you know of this life. It is a mockery what evil has done to so many that it is almost surreal to comprehend. This time, it is a glorification of the Divine obedience that has destroyed him! Do you feel the power of Jesus? This week, the Dominion Angels will make your eyes tearful with joy!"

Sunday, November 5, 2000
3:47 p.m.

"To My dear little children, this is how I love you and express the miraculous intercessory Grace that our Father in Heaven is allowing Me to dispense. Please remember that I am your Immaculate Mother who has been speaking to you so profoundly for nearly ten years. The essence of the Divine Love I bring is the simple, age-old, yet new rising sun of Love to whom I gave birth in the stark surroundings of Bethlehem. We have come to another week which has opened with the Sunday message of *'Love your God with all your might, all your strength, and all your heart!'* Please be My grateful children as we continue to help your brothers and sisters find the pathway back to God through the comfort of My arms where the Blood of Jesus is awaiting their souls. Today, My little ones, I would like to speak about the ongoing messages you are proceeding to record through the intercession of the Dominion Angels. I would like to tell you how they interact with you, and how your exchanges determine what they tell you any given day. First and foremost, it is the Love that you share in Jesus that makes the Divine intercession you are experiencing possible. If not for the strength of your faith in God, none of My intentions for the world through your mortal hands would have been feasible from the outset. I am surrounded by an entire Heavenly Court of Angels, each group of which has their own role in the formation of humankind for your position of Grace before the Throne of God. The Sacred Heart of Jesus is both the crest upon which each of you stands and the center of your nourishment in comprehending what the Angels come to say. The fact that you can understand what they are saying is due to the power of the Holy Spirit in you. Yes, I have said that the Holy Spirit in your hearts is the reason you are able to comprehend the same Paraclete who speaks to you. This is a function of the reciprocity of Heaven and Earth. These Angels live with you and among you; they permeate the veil of tears between Heaven and Earth on an intermittent basis. This is unlike your Guardian Angels who never leave your side. You are each aware that your Guardian Angel is juxtaposed such that you avail yourselves to their Grace any time of day. The Dominion Angels and Myself interchange our loveliness when you are predisposed to receive us. There are moments during the lives of many when we are shielded from some aspects of human behavior. We never fail to see the misery or the offerings of Love and sacrifice that each person on Earth provides in the Name of Jesus, but we do not always see everything for which confession would be necessitated. Do you understand? In other words, we know that there may be a lacking of peace in the world, and Jesus tells us that this is oftentimes the case. The fact is not that we are never interested in whether My children on Earth are less than perfected in Love, but the matter of how this may occur is between yourselves, God, Jesus, and the Holy Spirit. Indeed, as I am asked to intercede for you to Jesus during every moment of your lives, especially when you ask for absolution for your sins, I oftentimes do so without the specific knowledge of the particular transgression about which you are speaking. My role as intercessor is to take your case specifically to Jesus, that you have called upon My Grace for help in your conversion, purity, and refinement. The specificity of your particular sins is between your soul and the Blood of My Son. I did not die for you on the Cross, Jesus did with immense strength and courage, and because He is Divine Love to the infinite degree! While I have made this point regarding your confessions, it is toward the purpose of telling you that I remain loyal to you during every awkward moment, your momentary bouts with anger, and your falls to the wiles of the world. If you tell Me about them; if you call on My intercession to help you avoid them, I will ask Jesus to hear your prayers with the ratification of all the Love in the Kingdom of Heaven over which I reign as Queen.

The Angels are more than a rudimentary or part-time gift to you. As I have said, we see every good act that you pour-forth for Jesus, every prayer, every sacrifice, and every petition you offer in spirit or material gift. It is our pleasure to recognize the conception of new life at the hands of the Almighty Father. Yes, we know about the darkness of the temporal world, but just as you cannot see the black pit of the Abyss below you, we choose not to dwell on that same horror that moves across the world at an awful pace. The point is that should any soul on Earth expect or anticipate the intercession of the Angels, the Saints, or Myself for that matter, you must make that higher calling to live in the Light! This is why I once asked you to run where the sun is breaking through the clouds and shining on the mortality of the Earth. When you effect the love you have been pouring-forth, the Angels see it and are moved to seek My counsel in what they offer. They are like little children leaping up and down all at once upon seeing their Father at the end of a long day. The response from Heaven to them is, *Go and speak to them! Go share the Wisdom of the ages with their aching hearts!* Therefore, you have pages to record every night. This, not coincidentally, is why *Morning Star Over America* is so prophetic to behold. The Angels have accompanied Me to make it possible. This has been the same all over the world since the start of My direct intercession to those who have become Saints upon their deaths since the first century. Yes, it will continue until the Son of Man comes again to redeem the Earth. You will also find that the tone of these Angels fits the urgency of the times, and is in no way tepid in nature. Why should they apologize to sinners on the Earth who have the audacity to deny that they even exist? But, you are My little children, My Chosen and Special ones; you are the humility that springs forth from My Immaculate Heart because you have already rejected the pride that would make you ignore the Gospel message that the Dominion Angels have deigned to give you. Thank you for continuing to employ the special prayers that make this possible.

My Special one, gone is the day when I want you to be overly concerned by what other people appear to think about our work here together. I realize that everyone on the Earth wishes to be liked, even yourself, and this is a natural case. When you are persecuted and despised for the sake of Jesus, you are continuing to stockpile your riches in Heaven. Remember that you are proceeding to live-out your obedience and love before humankind. The Divine purpose that you are espousing would not be fitting for the sacrifice you are making if everyone in the world came to pat you on the back. And, I know that you and your brother grow weary doing the work I have asked you to accomplish, alongside the other improvements you are making to your home.

However, you are still succeeding in extraordinary fashion. I can only ask you both to remember Love! Remember that Love is greater than fortune, material, process, and proceeds! This is a very unique time in history, not only for the venue through which you are receiving My messages, but the way the world is able to procure them. Can you imagine what the Earth would be like if the Apostles of the first century had your technology? And, what of the globular Internet upon which to disseminate the message of Jesus as the Messiah? I will tell you the reason why it did not unfold that way. It is simple. Everyone who had the capacity to write, and the technology to do so, would have written their *own* Bible for the world to perceive. In other words, the Scriptures would not have been able to be brought from the one Holy Land, but all nations would have tried to lay claim to the place where Jesus Christ laid His head, and where He taught, suffered, and died. Likewise, no one has the interest, patience, or resources to attempt to somehow redefine *Morning Star Over America* to be anything other than what it is. My Special son, if in February 1991, I would have told you what would have caused the continuation of your messages and what gives them the power they have, what would you have said? Therein rests the reason why you are one of the princes of Divine Love in the world, one of Jesus' most holy ones, and heir to one of the highest perches that the loftiness of Heaven has to offer. I will seat you next to Me! Please remember the poor in your prayers, and prepare for more beautiful messages."

Sunday, November 12, 2000
3:15 p.m.

"Yes, My dear little children, today I have come to continue the message of Redemption that I was destined to provide since the day My Son was crucified for the Salvation of every soul! I remember that My Immaculate Heart was so pierced on that day, but I can still hear the clear reverberation of Jesus' words to intercede in communion with the Holy Spirit for those whose kind innocence has led them to recite the Sacred Mysteries of the Most Holy Rosary. Therefore, My children, you can be assured that I will continue until the hour when Jesus returns to judge the living and the dead because I will draw no dying breath. It is with great joy that I have come to speak to you again today because I realize that it was only two short years ago when you allowed the Angels to dictate to you the poem which so elevates My role in your conversion and Salvation. Should you choose to receive it, they will return to offer you another one soon. Please understand that there is no limit to the sincere codices of exultation that the Heavenly Court has already compiled in honor of My Son. All you need to do is continue praying, and the world will proceed to be inundated with sweet blessings from this holy place. No one really knows what revelations are being exalted from within these walls. Neither does anyone know the power you are wielding through the gifts you are giving to God in return. Today, I would like to tell you that the very pretty pages that you have been receiving will continue to flow into Creation. The outer realms of joy that Jesus holds in His Sacred Heart are pouring into the world like springs from a fount because of your love for Him. It is true that no likeness of beauty has ever been given to the Earth as the ones you are recording everyday. Yes, it is because God sees with eyes of affection that you are employing every resource at your disposal to make Him happy. This is the reciprocity of Heaven because your prayerful actions translate into His continuing blessings upon humanity. The two coins I am offering God at His Throne in Heaven are your very lives, My Special and Chosen ones. With them, He is enriching the Earth with consolation and Grace. Please be confident that there is nary a soul who has passed beyond the bonds of death who is not comforted by the way you and your brother are humbly serving the Almighty Father who has created, Redeemed, and summoned them into the Celestial Court of Paradise.

When My children kneel and obey Me at the sight of My requisitions, it is a signature of predestination. When Jesus said that Creation is finished from the Cross, He took special care to connect the hearts of the faithful who have passed onward with Him into the Light of Salvation and those yet to be born. This is a portion of the intention of My message here today. Many around the globe are praying for the answer to the question, *Where was I before I was born?* I would like to offer you their answer as you pray the Sacred Mysteries of the Holy Rosary. Before I do so, My Special son, I would like to respond to your acclamation of *Bring it!* This is a kind and courageous proposition! It represents the dedication that My Jesus seeks from all His people. Even though I am giving you the substance of His words, I am lost for a language that you can understand to express how happy He is with you. For all the multitudes of ways that twenty-six alphabetic letters can be conjoined and combined, there is insufficient means to provide an accurate description of the consolation you are giving to His Most Sacred Heart. I am depending upon your deep faith to recognize how happy He is. You are being given many signal graces so that you can see how your lives are elevating the world within reach of many gifts that are bringing great healing to humanity. There is new hope because My messengers have yet to surrender the charge that I have urged them to make, save some who will not live for Jesus instead of themselves. Yes, you have prevailed in the Mind and Sacred Heart of God since long before anyone on Earth might ever possibly conceive. The origin of humanity is a manifestation of Love itself, which has no beginning. Many have questioned, *Did God create Himself?* The answer is that He did not need to be created because there was never a moment when He did not already exist. God has no beginning, and He shall never cease to be. Now, that is powerful Love! God is the omnipotent Father of everything that is seen and unseen, and anything you might imagine in-between. Others have asked whether He created those whose souls will reside forever in the fires of Hell. Of course He created them, just as He created Adam and Eve and the Orders of the Angels, one of which fell to pride and deceit and is called Satan of the wretched and the damned. I have told you before that these souls own no station in Heaven because they reject Divine Love. They are guilty of hatred and blasphemy against the Holy Spirit. You know from your faith that such mortal sin is the reason for the condemnation of the soul. The point I am making is that Love has always existed, not just in the natural spirit of creative power, but to the contemporary being of all that is righteous, good, blessed, and absolved. The Blood which Jesus shed on the Cross not only expunged the sins of mankind, but the moment when sin was effected at the Fall of Adam and Eve. There will be no retribution against Adam for the exile of mortal men because those who are saved will see no record of such error. Certainly you will recognize the Scars on the Body of your Savior, but you will be elated with joy to the depths of your being when He tells you how He got them! My children, I am asked to see that you will wish to wait until the moment when you see His Holy Face to hear this response. The silence of these momentary intercessions is the calm softening of the voices of those who have approached the stage of Creation for the opening of the New Jerusalem about to begin before your eyes. All the attention that humanity has to offer is about to be captured by My Son because His Presence is so commanding and Divine that all other directions on the Earth will disappear. I tell you these things knowing that such images might seem foreign to you in nature, but they are absolutely true. I first hinted them when I assured the world that every little child who is given to Redemption will be able to hear the sound of the Light of Christ. This is how your souls recognize the taste of Heaven in the Holy Eucharist, because you are consuming God's Native Son. It is through these exemplary images that Jesus told the world long ago that His Kingdom is greater than its physical constraints. And, the spiritual perfection of His Love can only be resolved from within the human heart. This is why Salvation is wrought by the diminishment of the flesh. My Special son, do you understand?

This is a time of continuing opportunity for you. I have noticed the excitement in your heart of the prospect of having three or four-hundred pages like the ones My Dominion Angels are giving you for deployment against the indifference of the world in the months to come. They are ever so much more powerful for many reasons. First, your spiritual faith is more mature than it was at the beginning of My intercession. Second, you understand better what pleases the Lord. Third, you have cast away any interior reservations about the ways you intend to serve Him. Your prayers have been ongoing for more than ten years, and this gives you a tenure of seniority that cannot be ignored in Heaven. You have said 'yes' to Jesus, and He is effecting the love in your heart for all that it is worth! I tell you again that there is no other way your life could have been more purposeful for the conversion of humanity. I know that you also realized it before I ever repeated it to you. You are humbled by these words because you are a child of Light. Everything you do must be a product of Light, both spiritually in your heart and by the physical things you do. Even when you are offering great prayers that are bringing more pages from the Heavens, you must always be in the Light. There is a certain consistency in Love that cannot be overcome, and this is your personal will. There should never be a time when you bow or concede to the temptation of believing that you are not doing enough for Jesus. Never should you believe that the blessings upon the world will be less if you choose not to offer a particular sacrifice. Always remember that the Passion and Crucifixion of Jesus is sufficient to redeem any and all lost souls on the Earth. What you are asked to do is pleasing to Him; you are effecting the continuation of the blessings that He dispenses to the world and the deliverance of the Poor Souls in Purgatory to the bounty of Paradise. All of My children must realize that mankind was created by God in accordance with the Sacred Scriptures because the book in your hands had to start somewhere. It is the genesis of your creation in the Garden of Eden that is recorded there. This means that you are the product and effect of God's Eternal Love. I see no reason why this same divinity cannot be brought to humanity at large to this day. The collective conscience of the world must be restored to decency and purity for all. The time is not too late, but the moments of opportune Grace are passing, even as we speak. There will be sufficient longevity to the mortal world to allow for all your hard work to have an efficacious effect on bringing countless souls to the foot of the Cross. Now, I must go to bless other parts of the globe. I have not addressed the ongoing political struggles in America because they are negligible in the higher order to which Almighty God is summoning man to participate. Please pray for the end of capital punishment, euthanasia, and the sinful scourge of abortion. The window display that you have procured of the Pieta is another example of why your Savior is so happy with you. I know that you understand the sorrow in My Immaculate Heart which has been captured by Michelangelo and others in the depiction of the moment when My Sacrificed Son was laid in My arms. No greater mourning could any Mother have suffered, but no greater joy in Truth could any have for the future of the souls who have given themselves to Him. There is truly no such bitter-sweetness that is more worth the tasting."

Sunday, November 19, 2000
12:58 p.m.

"Now, another beautiful time has arrived during which the Glory of Heaven has come in complete union with your souls in this special house of prayer! Dear children, I love you with an everlasting fervor that you yet cannot fully understand. There is no other way you can comprehend this Divine affection that God has for you except through your prayers; prayer from the heart! For many years, you have known this Truth and have not relinquished your desire to succeed under the Cross of Salvation. My dear ones, it is not sufficient for the followers of Jesus just to acknowledge His presence. You must engage the living faith that you have been given as a gift from Heaven, a special dispensation which you gain through your Baptism and the Invocation of the Holy Spirit. After all, this is what prayer is about. When you continue the fight for Justice, your case is heard by God, and He will answer your petitions with the armaments you need to win the battle. This is not limited to simple and tangible facets of the everyday world, but of the bestowing of miraculous gifts to you by the bundles! Today, I am asked to help you better understand the motivations in the Mind of God by clarifying and strengthening the purposes He often has to complement. There are no words to accurately describe the ecstasy that God feels as He watches your lives unfold to the return of your blessings and gifts back to Him. It is your prayer and your love of compassion that stirs His Mercy for the rest of the world. Your work will be the catalyst for the spiritual conversion of those still lost in the darkness of the industrial western hemisphere. Only you know what sacrifices you have had to endure to accomplish this great blessing for your fellow humankind. I am happy that you recognize that the many thousands of pages of your holy work are not only effecting the conversion of many and the release of an equal amount from their suffering in Purgatory, but please know that each one of your books which you complete has been conceived by God through you. This is a holy matrimony that no one can dispel, and a new freedom that captives have wished to savor for 2,000 years. You are living the Resurrected Jesus, and the tables are turned so that you have no fear of anything that might cause you to be reticent in your service to Him. It is enough for this day if you will bring yourself to live in the jubilation of everything God is seeking in you. He is pleased and elated by you and your brother, a part of the Body of Christ of which every portion will make Him as happy as you both are now. God knows that you have been specifically chosen for the task to which you have been assigned. He knew that you would not allow the Holy Cup to pass-by without your having taken a drink. He has known this since before you were born because He created you this way. You and your brother have been 'sent' just as Jesus has been sent. Of course, you were given a free-will with which you could have taken another path, but God created you with advanced knowledge of the road you have chosen to accept. Do you understand the extraordinary miracle of your consent, that you gave God your heart long before He gave you life? This is the case with everyone who will eventually spend the rest of Eternity in Heaven. I can read the question that is now being brought into the sphere of thoughts in the back of your mind. *Why would God ever create a soul whom He already knows would go to Hell?* His decision is to dwell on the free-will of that person and the Mercy of Jesus, which can reverse the effects of time and sin, and alter the Judgment of God. When a soul is washed clean in the Blood of Jesus, this transformation also amends the thoughts of God and transforms His Eternal Spirit to envision a soul who had been bound for Hell into a simple dream. Jesus awakens Him and tells Him that His thoughts about those who were destined for condemnation were only a nightmare that will never come true. This is the power of the Blood of the Cross which has the Divine Creativity to redesign what the world and the entire universe are all about. This is a portion of the 'New Heaven and New Earth' about which the Holy Gospel speaks. Jesus returns to the first moment of time, back to the origination of Genesis and the most profound nature of creative Love, and remakes what was placed there in the first six days. Your prayers are extremely powerful because they complement the intentions of God as He watches Creation unfold. This is why prayer is the power of God in you, and is why Jesus is one with the Father where His power to create is just as intense. Indeed, this is why you will become Saints and inherit the power that Adam and Eve could never conceive. Through the intense vision of the Holy Spirit, you are already able to perceive the jewels of Heaven from where you sit today. This is what we are doing at this very moment in time. Hence, you also understand that the great courage you wield is the genius that has made your faith more than a living sign, but a facet of the Creative Love that first shaped the universe. There is great joy in this because it is what you have been seeking all your life. I am joyful that you rest in assurance that you are always loved, and that God is never unmindful of the sacrifices you offer Him in return for the Salvation you have inherited from the Cross. Indeed, was it the accidental work of your hands that made the piece of wood appear before your eyes yesterday? Not at all! You are living-out the perfect distinction of being synchronized to the Will of the Almighty Father by your passage through time. I will take My leave now to attend My other children who are in need of My intercessory prayers and holy words. I hope you have a happy Thanksgiving, and enjoy the pages you are writing."

Sunday, November 26, 2000
12:29 p.m.

"Now, let our blessed communication between Heaven and Earth resume! Let all humankind know that there is no more to be grieved, for the Son of Man has been raised from the Grave! My dear little children, this is among the many Divine reasons why Jesus Christ is King! Let this Feast Day be a new beginning for your hearts! I promise the oath of My Love for you that the Savior of the world will remember your souls on the day of Judgment. There is plentiful Redemption for the humble and contrite, and much to be discerned by those whose faith is still very weak. Please lift-up your hearts to acknowledge the inexorable march of time toward the end of the ages when everyone will see and know His Light perfectly. For now, we pray that all will be brought to the spiritual renewal which is found in penitential confession and the Most Blessed Sacrament! I always remember you in My prayers because I love you as God Himself loves you! My little ones, today you can feel the Triumph of Jesus, as He is the King of the New Jerusalem. I am keeping a watchful eye upon the world while He prepares to enter it again in Glory! Many of My children have asked whether I have gone to other worlds to proclaim the Reign of My Queenship in Heaven. My answer is that the Earth is the only frontier that has yet to fully accept Salvation in the Cross. This is ironic because it was on this same globe 2,000 years ago when Jesus died to redeem all sinners in Creation on that very Cross! Yes, His own people indicted, convicted, condemned, and Crucified Him. Now, the entire Earth which has been saved by His Passion and Death is rejecting Him as a whole. I am telling you that not everyone has done so, but like the many who called for His execution on Good Friday while others writhed in pain knowing who He was, the majority of people on Earth outrightly reject their Eternal Salvation in the Blood of My Son. I have come today to continue our quest to convert these billions of lost souls so their residence in Heaven can be assured. We cannot do this in only an hour, a year, or a decade. Our prayers must be very lengthy and from the heart. I thank you for continuing to pray with Me so the joy of God can be fulfilled as He sees every last one of His children arrive at His side in Paradise. My Special son, it should be rather obvious to you by now that you and your brother are playing a special role in this ongoing transformation of man... Let us turn our attention to your state of heart. You must not assume that every dream that you have is a premonition, but you have had one in the recent past that was precisely that. You were praying in advance for the success of many, and not even God would allow your mind to sleep until you prayed-away the sorrow that might have come to those involved. It is true that the Almighty Father uses you like a fine instrument in His hands. You sometimes become a quasi-inanimate subject in the process, but your human will must continue to be tendered to Him for His Holy Works to succeed. This is now much more clear to you! And, I am pleased to announce the favor in which you are found with the Dominion Angels who spoke to you yesterday. Thank you for allowing Me to pray with you on this Feast of Christ the King! It is always a greater portion of My pleasure to join My supplications with yours for the conversion of sinners, for the poor souls suffering so pitiably in Purgatory, and the many other intentions of our hearts. Please remember to pray for the unborn during the coming Season of Advent."

Sunday, December 3, 2000
12:53 p.m.

"To My holy children, I come again for the benediction of the greater world! Thank you for offering your prayers to God the Father on High, as you know that He hears you well. Now, we have begun the Advent Season together for the year 2000. The celebration is indeed a part of the greater Advent which you celebrate during your entire lives. The Christmas Season is the Advent of your present-day world, a parenthetic period of prayer and transformation for the entire body of humankind. My children, it is during the Holy Season of Advent when most souls are released from Purgatory into the Everlasting Light of Paradise. I have told you in times past that this is a reflection of more mortals in the world turning their eyes and hearts to the Nativity of Baby Jesus. Now, more than ever, He wishes you to know that His Return in Glory is ever so much nearer than it has ever been, not simply because of the passage of time, but because His faithful people on the Earth are praising Him to a much greater degree... I wish to remind all the world that the simplicity of Christmas is of the greatest importance in the Sacred Heart of Jesus. He does not wish for volumes of highly proprietary words when listening for your prayers from the heart. Jesus desires everyone to approach Him with a single mind and open heart. Please bring your holiness to Him as a special gift and offering of homage! As simple as this may seem to many, it is still extremely difficult for people who are far from the Truth. Those of My children who pour-out their lives in prayer and peace know full-well that Salvation is a gift which must be received with unconditional love and a penitent heart. God does not command that you match His Love, but He most assuredly requests that you embrace the Holy Spirit so your soul can be perfected by it. Once you have tasted the sweetness of purity and Truth, you will never revert to the groveling world that is still trying to hold you down in grief, sorrow, guilt, and anger. Prayer from the heart is your source of strength! Often have been the times when I have reminded you that a simple collection of words or thoughts about your Christian faith is not sufficient. Your love for Redemption must be a living presence of the Divine Light that flourishes from deep within your own conscience. This is the love to which your Savior responds! He does not wish for you to offer your love as though you are handing Him a dusty rendition from a library bookshelf. He asks to receive your actual living, moving, breathing conviction as though you are a star on the stage of Creation, playing-out your desire to be saved as though it may be the last words and actions you might ever utter! But, always remember, this cannot be a facade or ruse! It must be your truest state of piety and littleness before the King of Heaven and Earth who savors your freedom into the bliss of His Kingdom even more than you desire it yourself!

You will be praying for twenty-one more days prior to the Eve on which the Divine Light of the universe began to shine brightly like the sun from within a tiny Manger. This is the Glory who has seen fit to live among you, and lives in your hearts today. No one can come unto the Father unless he turns for Salvation through His Crucified Son. The entire destiny of your souls is dependent upon your allegiance to Him and your movement toward the highest state of spiritual perfection you can achieve. Yes, this is a very difficult task if you will not pray to understand what the Glorious Deity has to say to the waiting world below. I have come to help you be the best people you can be, and to advance your love toward accomplishing that task with honor and loyalty to God. Thank you for allowing Me to bring My loving Grace into your midst, to help show you the way, to ask for your prayers, to teach you how to enlist the intercession of the Angels and Saints, and to make you more peaceful in knowing one another in the world. This is My call, and you are My beautiful children. Let us pray together during this Season of Advent so all the world can be converted to pardon in the Child of Bethlehem. My Special one, I greet you personally and thank you for all you have done for Jesus during the past eleven years. The gifts which you continue to offer Heaven have made the release of your book possible. Tens-of-thousands will soon disperse them to millions of people around the globe. My messages will be read aloud during the homilies of priests, during My Marian Cenacles, during Rosary prayer groups, to the dying on their sick beds, to those who are in prisons and nursing homes, and countless suffering souls everywhere. This is the legacy of your work for Jesus. I am happy with you, and He is thumping His chest knowing that you belong to Him! You are indeed a blessed little boy! The Angels in Heaven are gleeful when they come to visit you everyday. Sometimes, they pause at your feet at night while you are sleeping because they are fond of the purring you do when you rest. There is no way you could ever conceive at this moment how much you and your brother are loved! The thankfulness that is held springs forth from My Immaculate Heart to your awaiting ears! We have loved each other in the ways that God fully intends!"

Sunday, December 10, 2000
1:29 p.m.

"Now comes your loving Mother to greet you once again on this Second Sunday of Advent. We are 'Love' together because we are the creatures of God who will live as one in Heaven someday. I know this to be true because I am the Queen of the Almighty. I have come again to seek your prayers for the living and the dead, and to ask you to remember everyone in your petitions who has called upon you in their hour of need. My little children, today I would like to implore you to consider the proposition that has been placed before you so many times before. I have told My Medjugorje children that they must become like their Mother so as to understand the Will of God. What does this mean? It means that you should invite Jesus to live in your hearts in the same way that I invited Him to take residence in the care of My Immaculate Womb. I am your teacher and the Mother who loves you like no other. Hence, when someone approaches you and asks for you to be merry for Christmas, you may reply to them that everyone on Earth must be like Mary for Christmas and always. I said 'yes' so you can also say 'yes.' My message is the same as it was in 1991. Having passed nearly ten years more, you have a clearer understanding than ever before what I was saying to you then. It means to concede to the Will of God not because you fear the consequences, but because you love Him so dearly in your hearts that you cannot help but say 'yes.' This type of devotional love for God is more than your words and actions, it is your internal commitment that you will be like Jesus in every way. Please remember that the Holy Paraclete who lives in your heart is likewise Jesus, the same Jesus who died on the Cross to save you. When you accept the Holy Spirit, you are simultaneously professing your acceptance of the Crucifixion of Jesus as expiation for your sins. This may seem to be an ordinary matter when you repeat it so often during the passing days, but your conscience will always redirect your attention to the very first time you ever uttered it, if your prayers are from the heart. I will help you when you pray the Most Holy Rosary. My Special little son, I come to you today with teary eyes of gratitude for your acceptance of the Love of Jesus. Yes, you may write as many letters to your Bishop as you wish, or anyone else of your choosing. My Son will lead and guide your thoughts and hands so you will never decline the urgency that stands before humankind to move forward in faith and trust. There is little time for those who reject even the beginning of faith. It must be known that there is very little time remaining. The Cup that was once full is now running over! This is why your actions and efforts are needed, now and in the long term, so belligerent hearts can become mellowed, and so those who refuse to pray will turn to God for pardon, strength, Wisdom, and forgiveness. I am not asking you to speed-up the process of your work, but simply to remember it earnestly while you are engaged in the matters of life. I tell you again, the Holy Spirit will never abandon you or leave you alone in your holy contemplations.

I am ushering your understanding of the power of God to new heights that only few mortals on Earth can comprehend. Thank you for listening! I am happy that you are willing to allow Me to teach you to love. There is truly nothing else in Creation worth learning. We can do nothing together without the Holy Spirit firmly situated inside your heart. I am speaking directly to, and through, My Son to your soul when you pray with Me. I must go now to visit My other children who are reciting the Holy Rosary. Of course, I speak to all of you simultaneously, but I still have many lost children who are in need of conversion, and you are helping Me reach them. I have found that you are living the greatest joys of your life. You serve with compassion and appreciation for the gifts God has given you."

Sunday, December 17, 2000
1:08 p.m.

"This is our day of happiness together, My little children! We pray as one heart because the world demands it. Hereafter, all mankind shall be transformed into the Light of Eternal Peace. Please accept My humble gratitude for the lofty intentions you lift in the Name of My Holy Son everyday. Thank you for caring about the conversion and Salvation of every soul who resides in the mortal world. I have come again today to join steadfastly in those prayers because I know the hearts who have yet to be stilled in Jesus. You have moved sincerely in the Love of the Advent Season to another celebration of His Infant Birth. We remember the many previous observations which you have celebrated, even from whence you were once little children. It is imperative for you to remember that while you are learning so much more about your Salvation in Jesus, you are also learning a great deal about yourselves! You are far stronger than you ever had the capacity to believe. Your desire to be obediently holy in the eyes of God is more genuine than ever before in your lives. I realize that many people are frustrated because they seemingly do not possess the means to the future in their hands. This is a catalyst for great distress and worrisome hearts. My children, you have always known that the key to life is the Love of My Sacrificed Son, so beautifully Resurrected from the Sepulcher to effect your everlasting Salvation. With this knowledge already poised in your deposit of faith, how could one be so impatient? How can you be unsatisfied presciently knowing the sum of the integers in the vertical column of life? I bring you joy because it is very difficult in the modern-day world for you to silence your hearts sufficiently to listen to the peace of the Holy Spirit living in you. I promise My continuation in an effort to help you understand. Now, you can see all around the globe that the

Jubilee Year 2000 is nearing its end in less than thirty days. What does this mean to you? Where are the signs that humanity has been seeking? I tell you today that the Triumph is in the hearts of the silent children of God. When will My children begin to lead the procession of Victory into the mall-ways of the world at large? Have I not told you for generations that I cannot succeed on the Earth without the prayerful efforts of My dear children? Indeed, who shall these ...*Children of Mary* be? Throughout all the centuries, you are they who harbor the Holy Spirit in your hearts, the Love who guides your consciences and calls you to have greater compassion for the suffering poor. My Special son, if the citizens of the Earth would know Love as you hold Love in your humble heart, the Triumph of My Immaculate Heart would have previously come. It is obvious what distracts humanity from understanding their mandatory role in the transformation of the globe to righteousness, peace, and Divine accord. If this Love is not shared throughout, how can Jesus force the trauma that is about to ensue? There will be no need for chastisements to be brought upon the world because humankind is making itself suffer enough! The sorrowful aspect of this Truth is that only few know the reasons why. Far too many people are attempting to disguise their hatred for others beneath the mantle of righteousness, and too many are likewise living in mortal sin without conscience, while labeling anyone who might dare teach them the Gospel Truth as being hate-mongers and fanatics. What an ironic and ineffective approach to human life!

My dear son, this is not only the case in your country, but is rampant all over the world. Take a brief journey in your thoughts around the globe, and you will see the deprivation of heart, spirit, conscience, and goodness that exists. Just as your little Angels have been helping you understand, all inequity exists because humanity would rather sin than live the propriety of holiness through Jesus. Why? Is it because they do not wish to make the sacrifices? Of course, but there is more than that. There is a high economy that prevails in the world with regard to what people will expend to sustain the progression of their sins! The inequality among men is more than simple isolationism, it is an outright competition to see who can reap the greatest wealth and material goods from another society first! Millions of people have the false perception that manifest power exists in the physical traits of the Earth. Such is no power at all, but is a continuation of the same corruption which first felled Adam and Eve from Paradise. True power, raw power, is in the Wisdom of Truth, no matter where that Truth may lead! Hence, we come within two weeks of ending the year in which so many people thought human life would be different. There was to be blissful harmony around the globe, sharing all that is good amongst those who are most in need, a new generation of purity, and an enlightenment of the human heart that is rivaled by no other age. I tell you that humankind must do its part for these things to come true. Please know that the Triumph of My Immaculate Heart is underway, simply and benignly as was the Birth of Jesus in the Manger of Bethlehem. Please do not be concerned whether My Immaculate Triumph may be without fanfare. The shock of the coming future will prove that a wholesome awakening of humanity is about to take place. This is not a long-term prophecy on which many should stake the nature of their faith; it is the solemn Truth about which the whole world must revolve in order to come to their enlightenment in Love. There are miracles which abound in the world, and your discernment about them must be wise. My Special son, I have told you that God will ratify the works that are completed in Him. However, only one-half of those who indicate that they are speaking with Me are actually doing so. Now, you must wonder about the signs of discernment of which you speak. Foremost, you must know that the allegations against Father Jozo (*Medjugorje*) are absolutely false! It is the work of Satan, against whom the very people who claim to be defending God's Truth refuse to pray! There are other, more subtle, indications that are prevalent in the world.

This is the sadness that has befallen so many of My miraculous messages and those of My Son. You now have another example at your hands. I am not announcing these things to disappoint you or to raise doubts about the Holy Will of God. I am only telling you to further substantiate My earlier statements that humanity has an agendum of its own that many people are refusing to relinquish in their quest for true Wisdom and the Will of the Father as the future continues to unfold. Please be wary about such things. Your discernment is your knowledge of the Truth of Love as I have taught you to know it. You and your brother have experienced My lessons for nearly ten years. There are unequivocal attributes and characteristics accompanying My messages that are apparent and unmistakably clear. Can you tell Me some of them? They are Love, Love, Love! And, they are sacrifice, penance, humility, civility, and prayer. Most of all, My purpose has never been to hang a cloud of fear, doubt, or apprehension above the heads of My children. A mother's role is to comfort, encourage, nourish, and prepare. These are the things that I have attempted to do with you and My other children all over the world. Of course, the ominous speech of Jesus is to warn humanity about the Justice of God, just as He did when speaking to Saints Bernadette and Faustina. The Mercy of Jesus' Blood is always the better determiner of human destiny. Fear is a generation of humankind. Jesus is not attempting to evoke anxiety in you, rather the capacity to know His Wisdom as the peaceful alternative to the writhing material world. You may discard the two pages I presented to you today. There has been no lasting damage done by them, nor will there be. It is simply an example I have employed to make My point. Can you not see the extent to which Satan will go to end the brightness that the miraculous manifestations of Heaven are bringing? If everyone had your faith, there is no way that the devil could succeed. Indeed, your faith is the faith of a warrior. You must know that your brother is capable of finding such error, not because he is a skeptic, but because he understands what I have taught him quite well. When anyone looks at *Morning Star Over America*, they do not find these exterior prophesies of oncoming events that portend issues requiring a blind faith to perceive. Your miraculous work is a textbook about why humanity must love, how to love God and man alike, and the potential of beauty in which the world can end if only everyone heeds the Wisdom of the Holy Spirit. I have enjoyed speaking with you today! Now, what can I say to urge your safety while traveling this week for your work? Please be adamant about the protection of all! I have a different relationship with each of My children. It is a concept of disposition. And, I speak to My messengers in ways that best befit their abilities to comprehend, and this reflects the way you have listened your whole life to the impulses around you. You are seeing the effects of the sensationalism of which I have spoken today. Pray. Do nothing more, simply pray. You will receive a uniquely special Christmas Eve message next week."

Sunday, December 24, 2000
1:01 p.m.

"There is peace on the Earth because Emmanuel is with you! Gone are the days of despair and the hours of fear! No more shall the wicked lay waste to the good will that has been so long in arriving in the hearts of the blessed! This, My children, is the holiness of the Celebration of the Feast of Christmas. The next thirty-five hours will take you on a journey of new hope and vigor in the Lord! The Fruit of My Womb was laid in the Manger so that all humanity can know that God has become Flesh and lives to this day as Love on the Earth. Let no person from this day forward ever coerce you into believing that there is reason to be sad anymore. God has deigned it fit to return His people to His side through the Birth of Baby Jesus. Now, the Archangel Gabriel is truly singing from on High that the Child of His Holy Inquisition has been born. Now, all Creation is made new, every heart has a reason to open-wide and receive the Divine affection of the Almighty Father; those who could never before know dignity can finally raise their heads, and the Poor Souls in Purgatory can enter the Light of Everlasting Life by the sudden flocks! At no other time in mortal history, save the Paschal Mystery of Easter Morning, has humankind been so blessed to receive God again in their midst. We who reside in Heaven and on the Earth are connected forever through the Christ-Child, for He is the Mediator between God and man. The Celebration which begins this evening is much more than the Light of the world, but the sunrise in your hearts and the conquering of the last horizon before you can know the end of the ages as they have already unfolded from the Cross. My children, if any one of you ever held-out reasonable hope that God would bless you upon the very path of life where you walk, the Birth of Jesus is that blessing! The faith which you have placed in the Holy Gospel, so specially detailed by Saint Luke, is forever consummated in the little place called Bethlehem. The songs you sing to this day are the echoes of the homage which has been paid to the King of kings. I too am happy and blessed to be the Mother of your kind Savior! Now is the time for you to survey your lives with the intention of knowing this Child from My Immaculate Womb to perfection! Had there ever before been a day so bright in history as this one? Had the flicker of the Love of God been so evident? These interrogatories are answered in the sinless Flesh of the Child who has come to deliver you to Paradise because He is the fulfilment of the Old Covenant in the Person of the New Messiah! All ages became one on the evening when Jesus was born in the same way that the entire world became the Cross at the hour He was Crucified. So, now everyone who has ever lived in hopelessness can cast it away for the new beginning in the Word Among You. Now, the ailments of the mind, spirit, and body are healed in the Child whom so many came to see! The first pilgrimage on the Earth was the massive crowds who came so humbly to greet their newborn Salvation. What faith! What Love! This is the same conviction which Jesus seeks in the hearts of humankind today!

Let us join our voices in prayer to Jesus that everyone who lives will come to His Nativity with the great anticipation of their innocent faith! Let all come with the expectation that Redemption is born to everyone who accepts the Will of God. There is reason for humanity to know anew that God has not left you in exile for long! Remember the faith of your fathers! Embrace the encouragement from your mothers! Theirs is the last age which has now gone to greet the Truth face-to-face! What they would tell you now! This is the generation whose time has come for both remembrance and the advancement of the modern world to the faith of old! All of My children must abandon their transgressions in favor of the new Confession of the soul before the Baby Jesus, the little One who waves His Hand and the world is again made new. With the innocent smile on His Holy Face, He takes you under the Arc of His Mercy! In the timelessness of the Holy Trinity, His Birth is your initiation into the solemnity of the Christian faith, for the Holy Spirit has been planted in your hearts to see this Revelation in joy. Now, the world moves from flock to Host because every soul seeks a new beginning, an opportunity to advance toward life everlasting, and a reason to see beyond the cataclysm of death. With the prayers of all the Saints who continue to adore Him, your souls are already walking the skyline of Eternity, well before the passing of your mortal flesh. If you feel confined by the temporal world, if you know that the Spirit is the whole Truth, if you can see Heaven better by closing your eyes to your physical environment, and if you yearn for the impending culmination of the reunion between God and man, then Christmas is your reason to leap with joy in recognition of your Salvation at hand, much the same as the child John leapt in the Womb of Elizabeth! Yes, it is very cold outside your homes today, and the darkness will come at early eve. But, you recognize the contrast with the endless Light of the Love of Jesus and the present hour which He has asked you to accept Him as the Redemption for all who seek to live beyond the grave.

My children, there are so many means by which Christmas can be defined, and you have already heard many of them throughout the years. Please do not allow your tardiness-of-heart or your repetitive hymns from so many Christmases past to cause you to perceive the Celebration of the Birth of Jesus in a mundane or ordinary way! I have told you before that there is no Sacrament which exposes you to the Nativity other than your reception of Jesus' Crucified Body at the Holy Sacrifice of the Mass. However, Jesus' Body, Blood, Soul and Divinity is the same God-Man in the Eucharistic Host as He is upon His Birth in Bethlehem and His Crucifixion on the Holy Cross! He still requires your homage today during the Exposition of the Most Blessed Sacrament as He did of those who came to adore Him while He lay in the Manger as a newborn Child. This is the same Son of Man who blesses you with Wisdom as He did those who came in great faith to the High Feast of His Nativity. Can you feel this new joy springing in your hearts as I speak? Do you realize that Christmas is the Birth of Jesus, celebrated through the element of time? Indeed, as you have said so profoundly in the past, this is the Eve of Joy! Please remember all those prophetic meditations that have come from your heart in years past as you again see another one come and go. Now, My Special son, I turn My Heart and eyes to you and your brother for a special Christmas blessing. You can tell by definitive terms that God is still with you, that Jesus is the Love of your lives, and that My miraculous intercession is continuing to the good of the conversion of the human race to Salvation in the Cross. As you have hoped in your heart, these are your words of blessing:

This is I AM who is come into your midst in the presence of My Mother to return to you My great commendation in the Love and Mercy of My Sacred Heart. To My Dear Fathom, your soul has already been forthrightly saved! You are a Saint from Heaven already whom I am asking to continue your work in the vineyard of the world. Thank you for echoing the Fiat of My Mother, and your Mother, for I could not have converted the world to the Cross on My own without your help, lest I brought great suffering and chastisement to many. You are a rivulet of My Great Ocean of Mercy on the Earth. I thank you, I bless you, I love you, and I support you! I Am Truth! What I am telling you today will come to pass very soon, in your mortal lifetime! Be Happy! Be Well! Be Faithful, My Dear Fathom! Your Jesus, your Love...

Now, My special little children, I wish for you to know that this same Jesus who has just spoken to you is in the process of celebrating His birthday! You may afford Him proper homage as you attend the Vigil of Christmas and Christmas Day Mass in the next hours. Please always remember the Love that everyone in Heaven holds for you. My Special one, you may speak to Me! Please remember to offer the Masses of this weekend for the Poor Souls in Purgatory. This is their greatest time of comfort, blessing, and release! Thank you for giving strength and encouragement to your brother for the things that God is asking him to do. You will both clearly see the reasons why someday. You will find that 2001 will bring you even greater blessings and honor from God which you would have no previous way to anticipate! Always remember that the element of time is on your side to the end of the mortal world! And, your pretty pages will resume the day after tomorrow. I know that you will like what you see and hear. As the Spring 2001 grows nearer, I will remind you what to do with them, how to uniquely afford the publication of a second book, and exactly to whom it should be distributed. You will never have reason to sit and wonder what the world will bring you next. Please be happy in whatever God allows you to experience. I will finish today with My great Christmas blessing. I will speak to you on the final day of 2000 and give you a special message for the solemnity of the first day of the year, the Feast in honor of My Immaculate Motherhood. Please seek from God the Christian conversion of lost sinners."

Sunday, December 31, 2000
12:42 p.m.

"Now, My dear little children, our prayerful intercession together has come at last to the end of another year! Yes, at the break of this new morning, we have completed precisely 3600 consecutive days on our spiritual journey in the process of teaching the world about the virtues of Love, charity, hope, and prayer. We have only yet begun the greatest of our relationship in My Son because the time is coming when you will greet Him, Myself, and the entire Court of Heavenly Hosts face-to-face. For now, we begin anew in 2001 which will fall upon your part of the world in less than twelve hours from this moment. I can assure you from inside the reverential confines of this holy place that the new year will continue to be a period of ultimate enlightenment for the mortal world; your prayers will continue, My fond blessings will be poured into your lives as they have been so graciously dispensed to you in the past, and all the world will know Salvation better because of your faith. I ask you to remember your service to God not only as your prayerful life, but that your impassioned work for Me is a portion of God's admonishment to His people that the Kingdom of Everlasting Peace is at hand. I have reminded you both periodically and perpetually that the depths of your spirit is where true goodness is found, not in the materials of the world or the fashions that serve only to distract sinners from knowing My Son in unconditional peace. If someone were to describe your works in the form of a parable, they might accurately recite the quotation from the pauper who became a prince by happenstance and said to one of his subjects, 'Go home and confine yourself in your closet, and pray to God that He turns that stone inside your chest into a human heart!' This is the essential thesis of what you have been doing for God for over a decade and counting, especially the 3600 days to the hour during which you have never once declined My urgent invitation to prayer, penance, sacrifice, humility, Love, fasting, and peace. There is nothing to inhibit the remainder of My children from gaining the same blessings which I have dispensed to you if only they will utter that prayer which was so profoundly counseled by the pauper-become-prince. Therefore, My children, the world continues to unfold, time is still at hand, and you are yet moving through it at the pace of the Grace of God. As you have now aged ten years older, your faith has grown by an immeasurable amount. The love you hold for the suffering and weak is now at a zenith in your mortal lives, and the prayers you are offering for the mitigation of sins have the power of the mightiest Saints. There is no reason for you not to be elated at the onset of this ensuing new year. You will look upon this message which has been given to you in the dead of winter on a warm summer's day in the future and realize at last that all time is truly one. God has reformed your consciousness and granted you a new Wisdom of freedom and dignity because you have served Him well. My Special son, there is an insufficient number of ways by which I can offer My gratitude for your decade of service by nurturing My messages, maintaining the purity of your prayers, conferring your compliance to the Will of the Father, and agreeing to endure the burdens and sacrifices He has asked you to bear. You might believe that you have done very little on the road of prayerfulness in attempting to convert the exiled world to the Most Sacred Heart of My Jesus, but many others would have heretofore surrendered themselves to the physical Earth long ago. You have not because you are able to Fathom the mystery of the Love of God for His Creation and His full intention of delivering the souls of the lost back to His side. Some may wonder what would be in the closet which that pauper-prince referred to so profoundly in his holy command. I can tell you that the closet to which he has referred is the outward Love which Christians hold for the body of humanity, but shutting-out all other distractions and temptations, dwelling instead on the Grace of the Sacraments of the Church.

    You will recall several points of interest that My little Dominions have discussed with you in recent weeks; some of the main issues have been addressed either directly or implicitly in My messages and in your Diary. Remember that the rest of the world does not see as I have taught you and your brother to see. What is of the ordinary to you is quite alien in nature to those who do not yet know God. This type of patience and understanding will be required of you as the future continues to unfold. There is no magic potion which can be rubbed on sinners' souls to make them holy again. It is an act of their free will to accept the Blood of Jesus in reparation for their sins. Only the Blood of the Cross has the power to absolve a mortal soul of their transgressions against God and to grant any sinner the Wisdom to accept the Holy Spirit as their guide back to the Land of Salvation. While I know that you are aware of these things, please remind yourself on a regular basis that most of the people who are still trying to grow their faith from the smallest of beginnings will find it very difficult to forego the impulses of the material world. Now, your life with your brother is continuing into yet another springtime of prosperity, peace, good health, and holiness. You should be grateful to God for these blessings. Please be aware in the process that He knows full-well that your service to Him has never been tarnished by a hint of doubt in your heart as to whether you are engaging His Holy Will in completing the charge and commission He has asked you to accept. There are written signs all over this house which prove that you are in compliance with the Church, with the miraculous revelations that have accompanied Her, and the transition which you and your brother have made to become united with the Angels under the guidance of My protective Mantle. There will most assuredly be greater signs of sorrow in the years to come, and you will be forced to battle anxiety again. But, you will succeed because you are My precious little children. The desires of your hearts are always greater than the pressures of the day or the offenses which seem to pelt your heart with agony during the passing hours ahead. Please do not ever surrender your joy to any despair, and always turn your face to the skies for the consolation you need from the gentle Hand of God.

The rest of the world is still bubbling and brawling in materialism, greed, faithlessness, and impurity, but you are not a portion of it anymore. I have told you on a number of occasions that every single word I have dispensed to you is toward the purification of another soul on the Earth. This is an ongoing process which will never cease, even through the day upon which you deliver your soul to Jesus for deliverance into His Kingdom of Heaven. I am confident that you are learning about your inner-self to a much greater degree by what the Dominions are placing in your pretty pages everyday. These great spiritual works are coming directly from the substance of your Christian conscience through the power of the Holy Spirit. You have extremely powerful works that will bring your recognition as a public visionary for Jesus to a peak. Your Diary is still in the process of reaching thousands of unconverted hearts. However, the additional angles through which you can teach humanity will bring an equal amount of enlightenment to their souls. You will see all of this unfold as this age passes before your eyes one day at a time. As I have admonished you before, I will tell you again. If you are not patient in this process, you will not succeed. If your spirit is not at peace while Jesus is utilizing your life for the greater good of His Kingdom, you will turn and run from Him to a place which knows no peace. Knowing in advance that you would never do this, patience is now your only alternative. My Special son, your thoughts must not be of the nature as if to say to God, 'Hurry up!' The Son of Man cares very little about such sentiments because He knows the condition of the rest of the hearts in the world...

None of the words I have said today have anything to do with lessening My Love for you, only to assure you that I am your Mother in every way! I am pleased that you accept My Love in all its Divine aspects. There is a stark difference between discipline and advice, and I am happy to know that you are accepting My recommendations as being sound advice and not a form of spiritual punishment, let alone a corporal one. Thank you for remembering Me on My special Feast Day tomorrow. There is no greater way to begin another year than to stand at the side of your Holy Mother as I walk you through the trials of time with the Holy Spirit as your guide.

Morning Star Over America

The New Millennium

In the Year of Our Lord

AD 2001

Sunday, January 7, 2001
3:00 p.m.

"My obedient children, you know from the deepest fathoms of your hearts that God would do nothing to bring harshness into your lives or lead you down a path that is devoid of His sanctifying of Grace. Therefore, I ask you to realize that everything for which you have been urged to pray will surely come to pass. The power of your petitions is strong, and the strength of your faith in knowing that you are in compliance with the wishes of Jesus is even more masterful. I know that this is why you have persisted in prayer, and it is why I have appeared today to accompany you in them. It is not only holiness you are called to pursue, but your knowledge of the reasons why you are to be sanctified. There is a purpose and origin behind every spiritual impulse which is pleated within God's Beatific Light for the propagation of supernatural Love, piety, penitence, forgiveness, and the acquisition of Wisdom. Hence, it is good that we join in beseeching the Lord to continue healing humanity through the benevolence of His mighty hands and in the Most Sacred Heart of Jesus. The epiphany of which the Holy Spirit speaks relates directly to the revelation of the Kingdom of God appearing at the center of your souls through the actions and intentions in your daily lives, and through the glorious Moment of Truth that is coming to you all, the auspicious occasion when your spirits are delivered by Jesus to the Firmament of Heaven as your gift for the perpetual ages. I know that your capacity to pay homage to Jesus as the King of Creation is as much integrated into your lives as it was of the Magi so long ago. Not only are your holy intentions of like accord, your travels are through much the same difficult terrain. There are many around you who would wish that you not embark upon your journey to present yourselves to the Anointed Son of God. You often walk haphazardly and are intentionally misled by God's enemies who tempt you to do otherwise, so you must always remember that Jesus is concurrently your Pathway and Destiny. He guides your steps toward righteousness, and He is the Truth you will embrace with fealty and dedication at the end of time. When His motivations are clearly understood, the human soul will eventually begin to sense its own value or risk lurching into sudden infamy by the cruel misdeeds of the evil influences of the Earth. You must be wary of the latter because Satan is the father of lies who lures you into sin by merchandising his heinous demagoguery of fame and fortune to distract you from reaching for Heaven, employing every means at his disposal to appeal to your unkempt emotions.

So swiftly flow the years from beyond your capacity to comprehend them! How happy is Jesus that you continue to recite the Sacred Mysteries of the Most Holy Rosary, for they are your constant in such an unstable world; they are your rock when the shifting sands of time surrender underneath you, and they fully compose the integrity of your faith to know that human Salvation is true, that Jesus is Truth. How honored and humbled I am to participate so profoundly in the Redemption of humankind! Of course, I am pleased that so many hundreds-of-thousands have taken the road of prayer, fasting, and penance. But, I can only ask! The miracle of My intercession is a benefit to many, and Heaven is quite the greater for it. I am the Queen of Love who has come into this place seeking more of My children so that the number of souls beneath My Reign can be increased! This is how the good will of men becomes replete, and the Creator of the Universe can recline gladly on His Throne with the comfort in His grasp that the Sacrifice of His Son has restored the equity of His Kingdom on the Earth, which has for so long been broiling under the heat of uncompassionate greediness and haughty dispositions. Therefore, My little children, I have arrived today to pray with you, near the conclusion of ten years' intercession. This may not seem like an invested sacrifice for you, but Jesus is standing on the cusps of His toes and pumping His fists in the air with joy that you are clinging to your faith, that you have not let go, and that tens-of-thousands are His by your generous servitude. Yes, it is not so much what you think about human extroversion, it is the petitions of your hearts that matter the most. If your mind aches during the tide of days, such pain will subside. But, the love in your heart for Jesus and humankind must remain of the same tenacious royalty and holy prowess. My children, there is no indication that your faith will ever wane, nothing in the proceeding history of the Earth that will preclude you from finishing the tasks that My Son has implored you to perform. Now, you sense the necessity for the events which have transpired during the past ten years. You realize the essential nature of the sacrifices you have made, and your inner-beings are comfortable with the standard of living which has become simultaneous to your mortal existence. That standard is God's Holy Love! You are forever Mine through this Love, and forever will your benisons be of the Grace of Paradise for your acceptance of Him.

    Now, I shall address My Special one to whom I owe great thanksgiving for allowing My Son to work through your life, and for Me as the Intercessor who has taught you the meaning of Christian faith in terms that you had heretofore never known. Mine has been a complement to the knowledge that you have garnered through the Sacred Scriptures, and now the entire world can bask in the higher radiance of your Wisdom. Knowing the Lord the way you have pined for Him for nearly forty years, you have realized all along that He would never leave you out in the cold. As the future provides and unfolds, I ask you to become ever more embraced by His Holy Will for the completion of the Earth. There are assuredly many things ongoing that you do not fully understand, that there are prophesies through other messengers that have yet to be fulfilled, secrets which have yet to be revealed, signs to be exposed, and promises of miracles redeemed. I ask you to remember that as long as you proceed in anticipating them, they will eventually come to pass. No other person on the surface of the globe knows better than you that God knows what He is doing. There will be another new springtime coming to where you live in the passing of several more weeks, and another season of jubilation will have sprung again. Why the reason for such joy? Because you are still united in the Truth, and nothing can ever take it away. You know from where your temptations are derived, and you realize how to succeed in conquering them. I have seen countless other men who have been as blessed as you who have asked, *But, where are the crosses that I bear?* My response to them, as well as to you, is in your awareness that Love is the antidote to the world's gruesome torment, and you must be patient while Jesus allows His Kingdom to unfurl. This is one of the greatest crosses of all. When someone agonizes from a physical ailment, they can pinpoint the reasons why. If there is mental anguish which is bringing darkness to someone's heart, they often know the source of their lack of peace. However, those whose saintly professions of faith are poised like relics in reliquaries in the Sacred Heart of Jesus grieve an interior suffering that will pass only after the world is brought upright! This is where the luxury of your trust must be the strongest because few on Earth know the feelings inside your heart! You should not tread through life in lethargy and depression simply because the Holy Gospel has not been fulfilled by humanity en masse. I am not suggesting that you are, but many before you have, and others are doing so as I speak.

This is the depth of your crosses for now. You wonder when the hundreds and thousands will pray the Rosary with you, and fight to procure a copy of your book before someone else gets a chance, before their number quickly runs-out. There is no reason for you to believe that this will not happen, but imagine the sense of peace that you are living while being more anonymous for now. You have indeed fulfilled the wishes of Jesus in allowing His Holy Work to be the greeter to the world, for now you have much more to do for Him, and the placid tenor around this place is still very much required. There is a temperament of peace which continues to surround the holiness of these walls, where the Angels appear almost everyday to impart newer courses of Wisdom for the rest of the world. You are able to write-down the loftiness of their impressions of human Salvation so that, in time, everyone alive will come to know the bounty which has bloomed from your lives, your hearts, your actions, and your undefiled sacrificial love. Today, therefore, I continue to commend you for accepting the Holy Spirit when the Earth is in such an hour of great need. The holiness of the years is multiplied because you are the sons of God's Love; your lives supply His purposes, and everyone who has ever been given the breath of life will be more gentle for it. Yes, this is a time of epiphany for Creation because humble children like you continue to reveal the preeminence of Jesus to a body of humankind who must be perfected in His Love. I have reminded you of this Truth during the past ten years more times than you desire to count. And, you are succeeding in your goals; you are keeping your promises; you are living the Spirit of charity, chastity, hope, and faith. I place the oath of My Immaculate Heart upon the deliverance of your souls to Heaven as My Sacred Pledge. And, it is not so much that God's modern prophesies are not being fulfilled, it is that the perception of humanity to know that they are genuine is skewed by their curiosity for their fulfillment, that their faith has been supplanted by their cultural demands. The elevation of the Earth by the graces which have become an integral portion of the contemporary world are almost too intense to be grasped by the faint of heart! Because of the Jubilee 2000, not only will the future be increasingly filled by the revelations of the Holy Gospel by your Diary, but will be followed by *At the Water's Edge* to deliver humanity to the Grace of your original work. Can you see how these things are intertwined? Time is not so much a factor as is the sureness of human faith! But, you will see many who refuse to accept the things I have told you today about My intercession. My honorable son, there is some sort of inherent anxiety that accompanies other men when they cannot run into the woods and ram their heads directly into a tree. They require that the Divine Truth kiss their feet, as though they are kings seated on imaginary thrones who have clapped their hands together, demanding that the Lord prostrate Himself in their presence. You and I realize that the God of Abraham, our Almighty Father in Heaven, expects humankind to participate in honest faith toward reshaping His earthly Kingdom, including the espousing of certain prophesies, which as of this date in time most mortal men are declining to do. This is among the reasons why they search for the slightest flaws in the Sacred Mysteries of Salvation as a means for them to renege from fulfilling their part of the mission of the spiritual conversion of men. My message today is Jesus' gift to you. This is not even a grain of sand on a shore compared to the graces that are still to come because of the Jubilee 2000 and for your faith and love for God. I commend your souls to finding the lost, but this does not imply that every day will bring suffering. You will make it through the night. Do not be concerned with the distractions that abound. Please keep your eyes trained on the Glory emanating from My Immaculate Heart, and your success will be assured. It is the Light of Jesus radiating there! I love you with the power of the Cross and the Resurrection of My Crucified Son!"

Sunday, January 14, 2001
1:03 p.m.

"The Love of Jesus who has forever come to dwell in your midst has waged through the fires of Holy Passion to greet you again on this day! We are praying so that His Five Wounds will be consoled, that His Sacred Heart will be granted the presence of the souls of humankind—converted, pledged, and redeemed. My children, your Blessed Mother comes to you again today with the joy and elation of this manifest miracle in My sights. Where does a Mother who is so pleased by Her children begin the task of thanking you? How can you properly know how effective your work is for My Son, even as profound as the linguistics of My words can be? This is our time together, a prelude to your own passage into Everlasting Life in which you will become the intercessors for your lost brothers and sisters. You invoke the Mercy of Jesus to deliver the souls from Purgatory into the heights of Glory. My children, this is why I am so pleased, and this is why I have returned today to thank you, to bless your lives, and to seek your continuing participation in the transfer of all mortal creatures into Paradise. Yes, the chore does seem to be a nighly impossible prospect at times because not all of My children have come to My feet and to the Cross as you have so willingly done. Please remember that you would not know Me if not for your faith, and this is the foundation which we are still trying to promulgate inside the hearts of other men. There is no end to the happiness that comes with this Wisdom of Truth, the Love that no mortal man can defeat. I daresay, My little children, that your successes will be far greater in magnitude than you could possibly preconceive, and the blessings which you seek for them will come much sooner than you ever imagined. Let us be thankful to God for His goodness in bringing your faith in Him to perfection through the Sacraments of the Church, through your simplicity, and the relinquishing of your hearts to Him. Can you not see the Holy Light breaking ever more closely at the dawn? I told you nearly a decade ago that your prayers are of this Light, and you have offered your compliance and love graciously. Today, I have come to pray with you for the changing of the leader in your country, that he will submit to the Truth in a way in which he has heretofore refused. He has been a solicitor in the Culture of Death by allowing the execution of lost sinners. Now, he is given the opportunity to preserve lives instead of destroying them. God is handing him the reigns to declare to the unborn, 'You may live.' At this time, his closest advisers are saying to him that this is not a compelling issue. This is why I am urging you to promise to pray for him so that abortion in all ways will be ended. He will have the rostrum in six days to tell all mothers that they must choose life with his help and through the power of God. One president cannot stop abortion because new life begins in the womb. It is the mothers who must be convinced that the little children they bear are worthy of the freedom of breath and life. I have told you before that no government can grant the false liberty to anyone to take the life of unborn children; and appointed and elected officials must refuse to provide the funding for causing the abortion of God's littlest ones. Before I speak to you next week, this leader will have taken an oath to a secular Constitution that is far from the essence of the Truth. By upholding its covenants, he will not necessarily be concurrently living in accordance with the Will of God. Please remember that the rule of the majority can oftentimes be corruptible and displeasing to Christ Jesus. This is the case with regard to abortion and capital punishment. If anything, such money should be used to feed the poor and safeguard their health, not to take the lives of the Holy Innocents who have yet to be given their longevity in the physical world. I know that you understand, and that you will pray for all Americans so people everywhere will uphold the dignity of human life. You are led by the Holy Father in Rome who calls for all egregious offenses against the Dominion of God to discontinue. I am pleased that those practicing their religious vocations are devout in maintaining their promises to fasting, prayer, penance, chastity, and Love. However, one does not have to be cast into the Holy Orders to live in Peace and Grace. I call all My children to maintain their lives in union with the divinity of the Holy Spirit, to commit to offering more prayers and Litanies, especially the Rosary and the Chaplet of the Divine Mercy. Even if someone takes time only for Seven Our Fathers, Hail Mary's, and Glory Be's in the headiness of their daily life, the Earth will become a holier place. God hears the sounds of your voices, even if your prayers are said silently in your hearts. Whether you are laboring at your workplace, or homebound, traveling to another city, or sitting quietly alone, Jesus waits in patience for humanity to speak to Him. I wish for My children to live in the assurance that the purpose for your waking hours is to strive to become more like Him, to offer yourselves unselfishly toward greater service to the poor, and to imitate the lives of the Saints whose kind intercession you invoke. Your ongoing connection to the higher graces of life depends upon the consecration of your lives to My Immaculate Heart and the Most Sacred Heart of Jesus. We are the gentler ones who have come to your aid with the help of Saint Joseph so every family will become more like ours.

Now, My Special son, I have turned My attention toward you, toward the affection in My Heart for you and your brother which knows no end, and toward the continuing graces that I lay before your altar. I always know that your love for Me is immense and that you wish to be obedient to the Will of God through Me in all ways. Today, I bear no lesson or particular mission or teaching. Your lives reflect holiness, peace, and progress. The work that My Angels are accomplishing here is nothing less than miraculous. Heaven is a realm in which you shall reside when you pass from this life, and you will eventually know that it is being defined by the work you are allowing to proceed in this house. Are you learning from the Angels many things that you had never known? Yes, they are capable of placing the thoughts that you have previously had into providential rhymes so the rest of Creation can see the love in your heart. I must tell you that your gifts of yesterday before the altar in your home delivered many poor souls from Purgatory into the Light of Everlasting Life. Jesus is grateful, and His newest Saints are interceding on your behalf. Your questions about how to dispense your work more prolifically are rather rhetorical. You are participants in the purification of Heaven on Earth by the surrender of your will to God; that is, your creative labors are always products of the Holy Spirit working both in and through you. Be careful to never throw your pearls to the swine! The Lord hears you; what are the specific prayers you are saying for the victims of the earthquakes? Pray that they will be found alive and in good health! Yes, this is the mandate of prayer. I concur, and I am also asking Jesus to assist those who are innocent victims of every kind of disaster, both natural and otherwise. This is the petition that is most important; that people will help other people. It is what the life and teachings of Jesus are about. No greater Love is there than to offer your life for your friends. This is why He is so overwhelmingly pleased by the physicians who travel to secluded locations where there are deadly diseases to cure the sick and destroy viruses that are killing so many thousands everyday. There are many reasons to continue your prayers, and the Hosts of Heaven are grateful that you are remembering the 'least of these' in the dailiness of your lives. Remember that the greatest prayer you can offer is your attendance at the Holy Sacrifice of the Mass. You should remember that the more you share the blessings that you and your brother have been accorded in thanksgiving to God, the more perfect the Earth will become."

Sunday, January 21, 2001
1:38 p.m.

"My blessed little children who are the happiness of My Immaculate Heart, I have come in Love to where I am welcome, to the place where My intercession is not cast aside as cultish foolishness. Please remember how grateful I am that you are dedicated to prayer, receiving the Divine gifts that make you both happy. Today, you are also given the Grace to recall that your sanctity is in your love for God, and the Holy Spirit always gives you the proper words to say. Thank you for wielding them so well. Today is another day of prayer for the unborn who reside alive inside the wombs of their mothers. I have asked you to pray for the end of abortion many times. Let there be no question about it; abortion is an egregious sin for which remitting reparation is made through the persecution of My Marian messengers. When My locutionists are cast-aside and thrown into the dungeons of contempt, it is a prayer for those little souls who are yet to be born and for the mothers who have committed the grievous sin of abortion. Let not your hearts be troubled because you are plying Truth as a weapon for the end of infanticide every time someone offends you in the Name of My Son. Little children, I am happy when you travel the avenues down which you discover the diaries, opinions, and contemplations of My other seers. Indeed, the questions are always, 'How can I bring them to listen; why will they not understand?' The generations have been filled to effervescence with witnesses for Christ Jesus who have asked this question, and many who have gone before you know the answer in the fulness of Light. There is reason and purpose, both of which you will know when God the Father says that it is time. Please be elevated unto joy in realizing that your faith requires you to ask '...why will not the world understand the messages which I am dispensing to humanity?' Was not the same sorrow and agony suffered by My Son in the Garden of Gethsemane? Can you now understand the questions that He posed to those who fell asleep around Him, even those in whom He had bestowed the fondest reasons to have faith in Him? So, this is not a time during which you should be asking why the rest of humanity will not listen, it is a time for you to be grateful that they actually have something miraculous from Heaven to subscribe to. All will know and realize the intentions of My messages in due time, and not a moment will be wasted for the purpose of My offering them. The fact that many are not responding does not mean they never will. Remember that just because a field has never been seeded does not imply that it is barren. Through all your faithful works, your prayers, and the effort you are placing at the feet of Jesus, you are changing the world in ways that you do not yet realize. Of course, it would be a special benison for you to see it now. But, I assure you that your efforts would be diminished if you could see the outcome. You might become complacent and overconfident. This is the reason why Jesus walked the Earth in the likeness of other men. The faith of the rest of humanity was key in their recognition of Him as the Son of God. Are not My messages to you the same Love and the identical Holy Spirit? Are they not also veiled in the gauntness of human life in that other people see them with an almost casual indifference? Does this not mimic the treatment of My Glorious Son? So, now you know that God is not only persistent in requiring the good faith of humankind, He is also consistent in concealing His identity beneath the coarseness of the poor, in the Holy Sacraments, and through the pastoral episcopates of those who have been chosen to disseminate His words. And, hereon you have discovered the prescription of your mission by participating in His supernal works. Again, your faith is enhanced in this process because you are required to love our God whom you cannot see by accepting His intercession that you can perceive. How do you know that I have come from the Kingdom of Salvation? Because the Holy Spirit of God in your hearts has revealed this Truth. Let Me be clear! The Son of Man wishes for the restoration of peace and decency in the material world, not a catastrophic protraction of duplicity and deceit. He wishes likewise for the conversion of lost souls, not for you to concede to the illicit and ungainly impelling of the flesh. He loves those who receive the Most Blessed Sacrament everyday so intensely that He will not allow corruption to befall you. Therefore, you are correct in defending what you know to be true, and you are commissioned to admonish those who attempt to violate it. The sorrowful words of My humble messenger Christina are rather prophetic, 'What more can I do?' Her answer from Heaven is to simply continue living-out her allegiance to God in the ways He has summoned. All who are participating in this Holy Plan must accept the same response as their strength to go on.

My Special son, you are a fortunate one because you and your brother have suffered only little. You have not been hauled in chains before public councils or Church inquiries and condemned as rogues or heretics. I have shielded you from this because your commission is such a long and arduous process. Just look at the pretty pages that you are writing everyday! And, the best of them are still forthcoming to compile the text of your second book. You will be pleased, elated, happy, and fulfilled to know that all of this is to the greater Glory of God. Let Me be clear again. When you are looked upon scornfully by others, it is not only a rejection of your testament as to what is happening, it is a defiant rejection by others who disbelieve that God loves them sufficiently to allow such miracles to occur in their midst. Their conduct is not only a repudiation of you, it is their own concession that they do not fully accept that Jesus loves them through any means He chooses to employ! I ask you not to be disturbed in your inner-soul by these things because they are a natural failing of humanity, and everyone will be blessed by your inevitable strength. There is much more to do; please be affable in the process of ushering the Kingdom of God to the Earth. It is also an aspect of your nature to replay an incident in your thoughts a dozen times over, as if to question whether what you have said and done is an appropriate means to reveal the Truth you are bringing forth. Such second-doubts are the workings of Satan! When you spoke to the person at the restaurant today, you were united with the Child Jesus in the Temple. The crass hypocrisy of those who attend Holy Mass and receive the Body and Blood of My Son who treat your brother the way they do is too grotesque to be true. They would do better to oppose his work with you without ever knowing God from the start! There will be repercussions that you will hear, but do not allow them to fester into any worry on your part. Again, all this is to the fulfillment of the Sacred Scriptures. You have never before been allowed to see them unfold so clearly before your eyes as you have in the past ten years. Families have been sorely divided; they have called you and your brother evildoers as if to be defenders of the Faith, and their rejection of you has equaled that of the Saints and Martyrs who lived generations ago. Consider yourselves fortunate that these days are happening with the Grace of earlier times!

I am grateful that you dispensed a copy of your first Diary to the professor at the college yesterday. Indeed, he remembers your meeting before, but never has he heard such a recounting from His Holy Mother in Heaven. This is a new beginning for him. Soon, he will be pleased that he discarded 800 of his secular books, and he will now be prone to throw the rest away. Your lives are a perpetual process of timeless Grace that you are only now becoming capable of recognizing. Surely ten more years will come and go, but never will you stop learning how to love to an infinite degree, and never shall you lose your desire to see God's Face. I remind you with unparalleled certainty that you will see Him soon, and you will behold Divine Love with the vision of your souls, not through the lenses of faith. If you continue patiently, that time will arrive. I urge you to understand that you bear the continuing blessings of Jesus upon your souls because your good offices are wrought through your trust in His Love. Where else could you turn to procure such peaceful lives of happiness? So, I ask you to be encouraged by the works of your days; know in advance that you have already succeeded; and never, ever look upon the rest of your friends with disdain. It is quite acceptable to be sorrowful for what they do and fail to do, but never look at them through eyes of scorn. This is a prospect that is given to God, and God alone. Jesus is Heaven's Mercy, and God the Father is infinite Justice. Together through the Holy Paraclete, they have completed the Absolution of humankind. Your eyes may be filled with pity and your hearts moved by regret, but the new hope by which you live is the Cross of Love at the center of your being. The Crucifixion is your conscience and goal; it is your confidence and Wisdom, and it is your pardon and deliverance. You are speaking to a Mother who knows you well and who understands your needs. I am beseeching God on your behalf to satisfy them with great dispatch in the Plan that is in communion with His Will. I assure you that every good blessing you have proposed on Earth will be bound in Heaven at the Throne of the Almighty Father. You are such a beautifully innocent child! You are pretty and prayerful, pure and holy, and serving and peaceful. You love your Savior with the power of the Cross, and would go to your death defending Him. Your station amongst the Saints is immense, and the Light that shines upon you is blinding to the rest of the Earth."

Sunday, January 28, 2001
2:20 p.m.

"Now, to the sweet darlings of My Immaculate Heart, I come praying with you, beside you, and for you! The Mother of your Salvation is your Protectress of the destiny of your souls into Heaven, not only because it is the Will of the Father and the intention of Jesus, but because you are My children, and I wish for all of you to come back home! Had the Love of God been anything other than Divine, you must believe that it would not have existed at all. This is the perfection which calls you blessed, who gives you abundance and courage, and who resides inside His Holy Kingdom on the Earth because you have said 'yes' to the summoning of His Spirit. What a blessed station in which you live! These are the reasons why I have not lost hope for the spiritual conversion of all peoples, that the strength of Truth in those who accept the Cross will become so powerful that all Creation will follow. You must always remember that God's goodness and the world's evil will never peacefully coexist. The concepts of parameters and tolerances do not apply in the victories for pure hearts because the principles by which you live are either right or wrong. Therefore, I have come to this place to grant you assurance anew that these holy days shall yield to the new springtime of hope, and you will again be busied in the fields of harvest. The labors you are pouring-forth for My Son are resonating with the profits of a much higher accord so the conversion of many will result from your beatific works. There is a stark, blustery realism that fosters the whimsies of indignant men, and this is why I invited you on March 28, 1999 to be mindful of the prayers you wield to alter the fortunes of hundreds-of-thousands, and even millions of desperate souls. These months henceforth proceeding are proof that you accepted the challenge that I laid before you nearly a decade ago in time. My children, do you not sense this power growing to a proper proportion in your lives as the weeks and months continue to expire? The righteousness of which I have spoken is of the self-sacrifices that you offer God in the likeness of Jesus whom you are emulating, and in the scores of lives that are being amended through the dispensation of your works. I am asking you to become fasted in the Church's orthodoxy by accepting the Lord's wonders and miracles. This is how you overcome the stature deficit between your weaknesses in sin and the Saints you wish to become. Please remember that no one suffers wholly unto himself, and that you are the singular Mystical Body of the Christ in whom your souls have been mortified. I summon you to the pinnacle of Jesus' perfection through your sense of community in Him. It is entirely appropriate for you to be deftly partisan in your desires to claim your share of His Sorrowful Sacrifice. After all, you are Christians, and you own that right in Him. When the enemies of the Church say that atheists can be rather territorial, they have not even seen the beginning of the Crusades for Jesus Christ that will ensue before the ending ages arrive. This is not a prospect that God takes lightly! It is a manifestation of the Salvation you have already been guaranteed! Your inner-absolution is a product of the love from your spirit amidst the temporal world! Never again will it be quite the same because of your faith and loyalty to humanity, especially to the tender-of-heart and those who wish to know their Redeemer better. Now, the task upon you has become a burden of joy and gladness! Your labors are the nectar to which the forsaken of the Earth have been drawn to be purified by the Passion of Jesus. They trust you to know who He is and why you have been granted so much access to the visions of Saint John the Divine that have been revealed to you. Surely the most prolific phenomenon is that you have never surrendered your willingness to believe! Your trust that the prophecy I dispensed to you about the Chandler Cenotaph awaiting your arrival to offer an eloquent oration of liberation and Justice to the rest of the world is rightfully preserved! I assure you that every theme of final conquest and jubilation of which I have spoken shall prevail. Should it be the Will of the Father, it may be some years in the offing, perhaps at the moment when He arrives at last, but the days about which I have spoken that overlap one another like permeable sheathes will occur! Your life on Earth is not a venomous phantom or a function of strange happenstance, drudgery, or God's outright audacity in punishing you. It is your prefigured preparedness to be repatriated into the Kingdom of Love that most of your nobler ancestors foretold.

My children, your minds may wander and your thoughts sometimes stray, but your hearts will never tell you a lie! They cannot bear untruth; it is impossible for your hearts to betray you! The sentiments you feel may change from time to time, but the awareness of Salvation as you have come to understand it will always be the center of your actions. This is why your perception of Heaven must always be founded in the Holy Cross! So endearingly you pray everyday! You begin each morning with the recitation of the Mysteries of the Most Holy Rosary, and are still praying them when you rehearse for dying by falling asleep at night. I assure you that this is a great sign of predestination, not only for yourselves, but for everyone for whom you pray! Please remember the scenes from 119 months ago when your brother proclaimed, 'More Hail Mary's! She loves it when you say the Hail Mary!' His assertion was true during those days, and they are equally as accurate now. As you have entered the 21st century, you have uttered hundreds-of-thousands of Hail Mary's, and the world is a much holier place. How do you know this to be true? By simply looking at yourselves, the sanctity which has been brought-forth in your own hearts, and how your peers are amending their perception of your role on the Earth. This has led thousands to take another view of themselves and ask how anyone could stand by the Truth with such bold, unwavering faith. While the reasons might be sometimes difficult for them to ascertain, they are redundant for us who believe in the promises of God. It is your faith, your love, and your desire to see Heaven someday in the fullness of Day. These are the gifts which Jesus has given you from the Cross, into your birth into the temporal world, and far-beyond the constraints of any cold mortal grave. My children, your flesh will know death someday, but I promise that your souls shall not die! They will never be plunged into the darkness that befalls the future of ungodly men; they will never reek of the stench of temptation, and they certainly will never be situated within a scintilla of the reach of the leaping fires of condemnation. The reason for your higher station is found in the Blood of My Son and your Wisdom to accept Him as your Savior. How many times have I articulated this over the past ten years? Never enough! My messages of conversion are as constant as the timeless Cross, itself. I am like you in many ways! I also espouse the desire to see mortal men exalted before the Throne of the Almighty Father! I beseech Him to provide His all-powerful Grace! And, I am still imploring the Divine Mercy for those who yet do not accede to His Dominion over the races and nations. Although I never knew sin, I am much like yourselves. It is the avoidance of sin that I implore you to pursue. This is not too much to seek from such a beautiful species, those who are the descendants of the Apostles, Disciples, Martyrs, and the Saints! You realize what it means to yield only to God and the service of His people on Earth, and not to material wealth or forces of the flesh that can lead you to another course.

My Special son, today is the anniversary of the marriage of Thomas and Alta Heather. They have chosen to renew their vows in the purview of Heaven. Their wishes on Earth, their prayers, included their matrimony that would transcend their graves. When in Heaven, God allows you to live whatever blessings you wish. They have joyfully attended the countless birthdays of their three children whom they lost to death at very young ages. They have taken a bow on their graduation days, and held their children in their arms. I promise that your secret wishes will be granted to you in Paradise. This is why every soul must yearn to seek the Light of Heaven! Seek only Heaven! Seek only Heaven! I harbor many stories in My Immaculate Heart about those who have '....lived the sweetest moment again,' and others who have been granted the Grace of transforming those that were not as sweet into occasions that are delectable to the taste. Whatever sorrows are burdening you now will be taken away, but you will thank Almighty God in Eternity for allowing you to suffer them. I have stood in the foyer of Paradise, preparing to make My entrance into your blessed home today, and I turned to the Angels who always accompany Me, the same ones who are beside you during every moment of the day; and I told them to watch carefully the Wisdom of Jesus in motion. Only a few moments later, you spoke to your colleague about the dismal condition of the weather, and that you would not be able to drive to a meeting to avoid endangering your life. This was a great prayer to Jesus, a way to thank Him for protecting you, and a source of gratitude to the Angels and Saints who are cheering for you. Thank you for remembering Me as you live. Now, I know that you are reading the final fifty pages of your new book. I am pleased that you are recognizing the beauty in their words and the intentions they hold for the conversion of humankind. Yes, there is no doubt that their tone is a rare reprimand against the hypocrisy in this new age, but there are plentiful blessings for humanity in them too. It is true that you must tear-down the world's old kingdom of disgrace in order to prepare room for the New Kingdom of God's Love, peace, piety, and rest. Without your having allowed the Holy Spirit such a comfortable place to lay His head, none of this would have occurred. You will reap a reward to a degree which you do not yet have the capacity to comprehend! There is no limit to what Jesus will do for you at the end of time. If your heart can muster any image, you can be assured that it will be given to you. Of course, the world in the meantime is a far more horrific place. We are again praying for those who have lost their lives in the earthquake half-way around the globe. It is their poverty which is to blame; and yes, it is the greed of the so-called corporate beasts in America that is to blame. The writings of the Dominion Angels in *At the Water's Edge* are making this quite clear. Please continue to pray for them, and for your own country that legalized abortion, so that it will finally come to an end. I will also ask you to watch in prayerful contemplation as to the outcome of the 'capital punishment' that is to be inflicted on the one who is convicted of igniting a bomb in Oklahoma in which 168 people were killed. This will be a watermark for the so-called 'new compassion' of the one who has proclaimed that he has accepted Christ in His heart; yes, the new President who has already been responsible for so many other deaths by state-sponsored vengeance.

    Can you see why I weep with such agony in My Immaculate Heart when My children turn their faces away from My invitation to a higher station of Grace? Please let Me tell you; your work, faith, and love restore the smiles which I hold for all who come to Jesus for Salvation. You can see why it was so difficult for Him to perform miracles when He walked the Earth in sinless Flesh. People these days are closing their hearts to the continuing gifts of the Holy Spirit and relying mainly on past manifestations as their source of inspiration. These people are the sinners who have yet to fully understand the power of Living Salvation in the Most Blessed Sacrament. The Holy Eucharist is the key to the Eternal future. Without full acceptance of the Divinity of Jesus in the Most Holy Sacrifice, human hearts cannot open to the continuing gifts from Heaven that help keep your faith alive. The people who place little value in the miracles around them usually never sense the power of the Body of Christ in the conversion of humankind to the Cross. Thankfully, their error has no adverse effect on the Plan of God to absolve the world."

Saturday, February 3, 2001
1:42 p.m.

"Now, My little children, you are aware that God wishes you to concentrate upon the substance of your prayers rather than how long they last because you see the benefits He deigns to you quite readily. I have appeared today to speak to you because you pine for Him from the heart, and this is the reason for the uprising of those who oppose the Church. I love you so much that I can scarcely keep My tongue as I see you lift the praises of Jesus before so many others. Therefore, you are allowed to share My thoughts in a comprehensible way. I speak to you about My cherished Jesus because He so strongly commissions your trust in the surety of God's Providence. How painfully was He Crucified! It is widely known that His enemies esteemed Him not, that He was rent and tortured only because He spoke the Truth. I implore you to remember that His Spirit still lingers where His Apostles were slain, and His Covenant is your legacy on God's behalf before the enduring years. I witnessed My Son being sorely misjudged and condemned to death on the Cross, and all I could do was stand in horror and trust His Word that He would rise again in Paschal Glory at daybreak on the Third Day. When He commended His Soul to the Father, the world became His coffin, and My tear-drenched lap was His makeshift catafalque. And, when He was carried away by His bearers, I knew that the Son of Man had finally found a Sepulcher. It seems only yesterday when He was raised, just as He said, and time has spent quickly to this age and the anniversary of your messages from Heaven. What a righteous people you have become, open to all the possibilities that God has placed at your hands! If not for your servitude here in this place, His miracles would never have succeeded from whence they first began. Please offer Him thanksgiving at every opportunity because He is your source of strength and all graces from Heaven. Can you now contemplate the dimensions in which you are loved, still knowing that you do not comprehend them all? Can you also see that the Crucifixion of Jesus was brought through the same Sovereignty that is trying to teach humanity about Christian sacrifice to this day? I am aware that you are doing your best to effect the conversion of many because you have yet to surrender your embrace of the future and the Will that the Father holds for you. All the Heavens are grateful for your compliance and desire to prosper in peace. My children, there are many souls who are in need of your prayers as the days and months continue to expire. There is evidence that the intentions in your hearts are reaching the heights of Glory because God is answering you in many different ways. The revelations that are breaking before you by the hour give you pause and reason to proceed! I am confident that you will soon come to know the intentions behind every holy action that the Almighty Father ushers before men; it is just that some people are not as open to receive them as you have become. Please remember in prayer those who have been stricken by disease and are victims of the disasters of Nature. I have told you several times before that they are the result of the transformation of humanity into a higher state of Grace. Please do not be mistaken; anything that contradicts the Will of the Father is not Love, and His Dominion often unfolds in mysterious ways because only He knows the purposes behind the evolving of the Earth. God is the Creator of every universe and owns the right to rearrange them as He pleases. There is no doubt that Jerusalem is the centerpiece where He has wrested from the underworld the Redemption of humankind because it is on this solemn soil that His Divine Son surrendered His Life. Can you share with Me the memory of His Passion and Crucifixion, knowing all along that such meditation is the petition that lifts the hearts of the faithful to do more in this age? Indeed, even those who maintain no spirituality at all are startled to recognize their new conscience when we pray for them to be awakened from their spiritual slumber. Every error in Creation was first wrought by the hands of exiled humanity, but all expungement of error is a Fruit of the Passion, Death, and Resurrection of My Son. How many thoroughfares have I traveled to tell you that such atonement can be found only in Him? Not enough! We must continue praying together because the Communion of Saints in Heaven is growing larger by the day, and because those who live on Earth are returning their hearts to the piety that the Lord seeks in them. Thank you for responding to My call for prayer, holiness, fasting, peace, and conversion. You are learning your lessons well. Your Creator is grateful; His Kingdom is blessed, and your lives are filled with joy as a result of your labors in His Holy Name. My Special son, you are working sufficiently to record My previous messages for transference into other manuscripts in the timely future. Thank you for your obedience! Do not be unduly concerned about what to write because, when the time arrives, the Holy Spirit will give you what to say. If you continue to strive for success without surrender, you will be victorious in all ways righteous through the Triumph of My Immaculate Heart. I will be with you and praying for you now and beyond the time when you join Me in Heaven. This has been a good day for you; there were walls that came crumbling down, and you realized it. Please become accustomed to this feeling; it will manifest itself again in the future as you greet at the water's edge those who have opposed you for so long. Jesus will lead everyone to partake of a drink of reconciliation at God's behest in honor of My Immaculate Heart. The Truth is so plain before everyone's face that this process cannot cease. I hope you are made happy by the Victory of the ages that is almost here. The reason why *Morning Star Over America* will prosper is because of your succeeding books. It has been this way all along. What if someone baking bread was insufficiently thorough in incorporating the ingredients, omitting the yeast from the dough? Everything would be complete except the one thing that makes it rise. People tend to lose hope in claiming victory because they have yet to live long enough to receive the blessing from God that will ensure their final wishes. This is why it is important for you to never concede defeat to any force or faction in the world. Depend on the Sacred Heart of Jesus for strength and the Holy Spirit for Wisdom, and you will never fail."

Saturday, February 10, 2001
2:43 p.m.

"From the heights of Glory and past the length and breadth of all Creation, I have come to pray with you today; on this day of high hope and deep Love for the children of God, for the oppressed and lonely, for those who do not yet know Love, and all who will be transformed and converted by our work here together today. This is the Grace for which you have longed and to which you have yielded your years. Thank you for remembering Heaven while you are postured on the Earth, for the Hosts above you are in communion with you in your faith. My dear little children, there is no other way by which you can come to the final realization of your destiny in God than through the Sacred Blood of My Sacrificed Son, and this is why it is so urgent that all peoples around the globe come to understand it. The Most Blessed Trinity is the precise awareness which your souls require to comprehend the Will of God for you, the Thrice-powerful Wisdom who is calling you to a newer state of enlightenment and peace. These are the days that will lead every man to the Light of knowledge because God is overwhelming the Earth with His infinite Mercy. You can see, My children, that the world is a much brighter globe on which you now live, made-so by the countless sacrifices that the children of Jesus are offering. Your espousal of the Virtues of Divine Truth are allowing many who are remaining in the darkness of their own making an opportunity to see precisely where their souls are stationed in time. They have no sense of what beatific Truth is about because they are too blinded by their bland indifference. They have deposed themselves within the boundaries of time, while the Love for which they should be seeking is of the elements of Eternity. Yes, we are praying because we are helping them to be transformed, remade into the likeness of the holiness which they must become. Please remember that My little children are scattered the world-over, and many of them do not yet comprehend the power that they wield from inside. When they pray and choose to accept Love, they will have been given the kingpin to topple every adversary, just as you have been given the Wisdom to seek Heaven and not the temporal world. This is not only a time for the searching of their renewal, but also a time for My children to be thankful that the venue of Love that Jesus has poured-out on the Cross is being offered to them. This is the ongoing cenacle of mutual charity that humanity needs to survive; your prayers of peace and Light, the Sacred Mysteries of the Most Holy Rosary, and the penance and reparation that you are offering Jesus as time continues to pass for those who offend Him to such intense degrees. Please remember that the Passion of My Son is a living balm to humanity, and that His Most Sacred Heart still lives, breathes, and suffers the sorrows that all of Heaven knows when the world will not commit itself to seek Love in all its Divine Bliss. Yes, you are the fortunate ones who have accepted the gift of righteousness which God has offered to everyone else. You have been told many times that you cannot do this alone, that even your own spirituality is an endowment from the Throne of the Almighty Father. Is humanity such a deserving race of royalty that this is true? Indeed, it is through the Eminent Love of God that He has chosen each of you to return to the fold of the blessed. You must decide to exercise your own will for the benefit of His Kingdom, and the Holy Paraclete will guide your every step. I ask that you continue to work and pray in the tranquility that has become yours from the Life, Death, and Resurrection of My Son. Hereafter, you always know that Love is the blossoming of the Heart of God, that He is the seed, the plantation, the harvester, and everything else Divine that sustains His Creation.

There are still many races of people on Earth who have not been accepted into the collective family of humankind because they seem overly backward and undeveloped for modern men. They might be less than knowledgeable about the things of this world, but most of them know God as the High and Omnipotent Father who has given them life. Such contemplation is much greater than what those who live in developed places are offering to the King of the Redeemed. Let us pray together that My children will recognize that Love is not a matter of the material Earth, and not an exercise of pleasure for the sensual physique, but the willed bestowing of the human spirit to God, to make a difference in what the rest of the nations see when compared to those that are addicted to the expendable aspects of the universe. Let us pray that this will be their time of conversion, this 21st century which has begun with such hope in the Return of Jesus in Glory to Judge the living and the dead. So many have asked how there can be souls who have gone to Heaven before the world has come to an end. The answer is because there is no such attribute as time in Heaven. This may be quite difficult for many mortals to understand, but it is now occurring that the Earth is already living in the suspended period between Jesus' Ascension and His Second-Coming. When someone delivers their soul over to death, all time is transcended and their unity with God is assured in the Bloodshed of My Son. I have told the world on several occasions about this matter, but many refuse to listen. The time for responding to this revelation is now because time itself is near an end. We hold in our prayers the destiny of many lives. God will answer Me, His Mother, and His children who wilfully pray for the Salvation of the lost souls of the Earth. This is the rationale behind My messages to you, as it was a decade ago. My Special son, this is the moment for you to acknowledge in humility that you are making a difference in the outcome of Creation. If not for your good service and open heart, we would not have succeeded at all. I ask you again, just take a look at your second book, and you will know why. Now, I must be assured that you will be extremely careful in your travels over the next few days. What confidence can you afford Me? If you do not return safely, our work will come to an end, and many souls will suffer. It is your own will that causes you to be either careful or reckless."

Sunday, February 18, 2001
4:17 p.m.

"Now, My special little children, your prayers are being augmented by the continuing strength of your good works through your concession to the power of the Holy Spirit! Yes, this is the additional blessing which you are offering to Creation by your good faith and loving efforts on behalf of the conversion of your brothers and sisters. You know that their lost souls must be touched, and you are indeed giving them the consolation and enlightenment they require by virtue of the new awakening that Jesus is bringing into the modern-day world. Let us pray then, dear children, that everyone will take heed of what you have come before them to say on God's behalf. Let us ask for the healing of every illness, for world peace, for the preservation of human life in every stage, and for the elevation of the dignity of the poor everywhere. My Special son, it is only by the love in your heart that you have dedicated your new book for such a pious cause. If only you could understand how pleased is God with your love for them, you would shed happy tears, just as He weeps in gratitude for your concern for their welfare. Your trust and hope are your strengths that have carried you through such staunch opposition during the past ten years. You realize that this week will mark the 120th month of My intercession to you. While this is a profound milestone, it is inappropriate for you to stop and celebrate the passing of time. There will be abundant hours for you to share the victories that are about to arrive when Jesus tells you so. For now, you have the loyalty, vigor, and venue to continue praising God in His Holy Name, and proceeding toward the inevitable Triumph that is now unfolding before your eyes. Can you not sense the peace and jubilation that is brought through the Angels? Therefore, awaken every morning with confidence that the race is still ongoing for which the souls of humanity are gently caressed in Glory. I offer you My humble appreciation for lifting Me up before humankind in such a powerful way. Everything you have said about the indifference of the theologians is true; and all the rest of the facts which you have defined will be equally as well received by the rest of the world. Please allow Me to provide you a short example of how the reaction will be. As with most anything else which touches the human conscience, many of those about whom you have spoken will respond with outright denial and anger at the outset. But, in an extremely short span of time, they will know that you have accurately described the world as it is. While you have given them a simple glass of water about the righteousness which they should be seeking, you are actually quenching their thirst for the Truth about life. As I say, they will cry 'foul' as being accused of being part of those who deny My Queenship over the Universe for a brief period of months. They will scatter all over the Earth, claiming that you are trying to poison them. They will use terms to misconstrue your intentions, claiming that you have given them a rancid mixture of dihydrogen oxide. And, what is that? H_2O. Yes, the very waters of holiness that they need to know their Lord and Savior in the way that He wishes them to know Him... Why will they describe your intentions in such a tone so that the lay-people of the Earth will not be able to understand them? Why will they accuse you of employing chemical warfare instead of humbling to their prepositions of what Love is all about? Because they are not in communion with Love when they refuse to manifest My presence throughout the world, and they know it. Do you understand what I have told you here today? You have nothing to fear, however. As a matter of fact, you have increased reason to feel reassured about everything unfolding in your midst these days. The future is bright because you are celebrating your love for Jesus in so many different ways. As you know, it is the valorous one of May 1995 that has brought the miracles you have sought. I hope you can see the workings of the Lord around the globe, that He requires patience atop of greater patience, that He provides ample time for lost hearts to be cultivated, and that He chooses certain souls to participate in the reparation which is being made for the sins of the modern world. There is no way I can place His gratitude into words. I only ask you to remember that He sees suffering-humanity in the same way you have described in the 'Dedication' of your book. Your character is as clean as crystal glass. That 'flapping' of which you speak is only their diversion which they will have to deploy because they will see a chasm between their position and the Truth of God's Divine Providence.

    It has only been a brief moment, a swift breeze through the airspace of time during which we have spoken when compared to the Eternity you shall enjoy in Heaven with Me. I must remind you that your soul will remain youthful and your intentions childlike, just as Jesus has asked. However, your physical body will soon age, and you will notice the signs. Please grow older with dignity and poise. It is imperative that you seek medical attention when you feel the need, and not believe that something will simply pass of its own accord. Your heart is suffering a phenomenon whereby its electrical impulses are becoming disarrayed. While it is mostly a nuisance, it can be serious if you leave it unattended, especially in later life. It is possible for you to calm yourself down while you are seeking treatment; there is no reason for you to enter into shock. I have explained this in lieu of other medical terminology that you do not understand. It consists of a dysfunctional breach of communication between the brain and the heart. There are sufficient medications for you to take that will restore your life to its normal course. The patients who die do not seek treatment. I have told you this because so many people needlessly pass into an early death because they are too obstinate to visit a doctor. I know that you are not one of them. You can visit your physician at any time and tell him the history of your problem, and that it is occurring more often. Please see a heart specialist, not a general practitioner or doctor of internal medicine. I certainly hope I have not frightened you. You are otherwise in excellent health. Walking will assist the healing of your condition. I will continue to provide your messages as long as God allows. I know that there is no immediate end in sight. Please pray for all the intentions I have placed before you over the past ten years. While there has been much mitigation of suffering, you know that there is still much more to do. I am confident that the entire world will eventually come to realize the power of a single Our Father, Hail Mary, and Glory Be. You are teaching them more about it everyday. Thank you from the center of My Immaculate Heart."

Sunday, February 25, 2001
4:33 p.m.

"Tell them all you desire about the Coming of the Lord because, in time, everyone will hasten to your every word! This is the season of great joy because it is the revival of the human heart. And, within the next few days, you will begin the celebration and observance of self-denial, servitude, almsgiving, and perpetual prayer. I am pondering once again the pious ways that the people of Love on the Earth are giving of themselves to those in need and to the many children of Jesus who are still deserving of a share in His great blessings in the world. It is you who share Him, My beloved ones, because His Divinity comes to the Earth from the center of your hearts. As Jesus was tempted in the desert to take another course, your greatest temptation is to turn away from those who are suffering for His Kingdom. Please remember those for whom you have dedicated your second book in all your prayers because this is particularly the Lenten Season when God will take notice of your caring hearts. This is no time for His lambs to be silent! Now that you are preparing to observe the Season of Reparation, remember the Stations of the Cross. I have told you ten years ago that Jesus is at His Station for you now, so please be there at His. Be attentive and prayerful in the Light of the concourse which connects Heaven and Earth in the Cross. If not for the kindness of the Man-God who has saved you, there would be no reason for you to look to the skies anymore for answers. My Immaculate Heart is filled with great hope because I know that the world will turn to Him at last, regardless of what you see before you today. The many distractions you encounter are the manifestations of a globe gone awry. I have been asked to tell you by the passing mortals who have been borne into Eternal Life that there is no martyrdom that is not done in the Name of Jesus Christ. It is often said that America 'holds these truths to be self-evident.' The definitions of those parenthetic principles come together inside the Cross of Mount Calvary because all freedom and goodness is justified there. The people of the Earth weep for their own individual causes because their hearts are telling you that there is something special occurring between the human spirit and the perfection of God. My dear little ones, it has also been said that you only weep for yourselves when the greatest Love falls before you for the sake of the souls of the world. Please always remember in the future that societies will hail men of great accord if their service is only to them. Once they kneel before the Cross of the Savior who has destroyed the evil that is blinding them, they will not wish to come back to their feet until they lay their souls inside His Salvation once again. Please be the Eternal optimists whom I have taught you to be! There are polemics being discussed and volumes written about the scandals of men. But, the story of righteousness is far too great for the universe to hold the number of books required to take it all in. When you pen your memories of the greatest days, let them be one of these books, one which serves to elevate the greatest of what mankind has to offer at his best, about the tremendous sacrifices that have been made for centuries by the humble followers of the Catholic Church of Christianity that have made Her the Bride whom Jesus will marry on the final day in time.

I have told you in most every quarter of the globe that the Resurrection of My Son is the Good News which has displaced the doubt that ignoble men will make it to the Land which has been Promised to the humble of heart. Jesus gave the Beatitudes so that they could listen to the sound of Love reverberating in their hearts, souls, and minds; not to make a scandal of the weakness which also comes from the sins of men. Why would anyone set-out to improve the lot of the poor and then partake in the effort to destroy the very system which has promised to assist them? Please be quick to ignore the rampages of those who only tell you what Love is not, but then refuse to live-out the Truth of whom Love really is. Charity in admonishment is the Wisdom which shall overcome the weaknesses that tarnish the sheen of perfection that God is seeking in humankind on the Earth. Where any two are gathered in the Name of His Son, there He is amongst them to guide, lead, bless, and deliver. Only Jesus is the Truth and power that is required to provide the manifestations that will enlighten other men. Therefore, be Jesus; and God will make you all healers of men. My little ones, never before have I been happier with the state of My Church. I know that She is led by people who are trying to the best of their ability to allow My Son His Divine Reign and Holy Providence over those who have been saved in the Blood of the Cross. I know that there are many benign intentions which have backfired in time because the intonation of their petitions lacked the charity which will humble other hearts. Then, they will employ the faith that will lead everyone to the Altar of Sacrifice, in Love for God and affection for His purpose. Hence, I speak to you today about Charity, Faith, Hope, and Love; and the greatest among these is Love. You, My children, are the witnesses of many errant actions of other men that they are effecting toward the explorations of new avenues through which to perceive human life. There is no such phenomenon as a New Age modernism of the Church because Jesus has not changed since He gave Her life at Pentecost. The philosophies of the ways in which God shall be worshiped and Jesus praised are not as comparably sound. The unwavering power of the Holy Sacrifice of the Mass can heal any illness in the ranks of those who call themselves Christian. There is no need for defecting factions to take to the airwaves in an attempt to point fingers toward those who are weak. Only the Holy Mass is the answer to their supplications. Remember that the world does not flow from flock to flock, but from flock to the Host. This is what I meant ten years ago; and the same is utterly true today. If there are imperfections inside the Holy Church, they can be eradicated through the same perfect Love which has redeemed the souls of humankind. The Most Blessed Sacrament is the power, but only few will turn there to receive it. As difficult as it seems to understand, the expulsion of conflict among any peoples rests at the center of the Sacred Heart of Jesus. This is where the Holy Eucharist takes you, and this is where I have been admonishing humankind to go for the past 2,000 years. I have done this happily and humbly because I know that My children are very stubborn; and this too has never changed since the founding of the Church. Know inside your hearts, little ones, that the reckoning of the ages is in the Fruits of Love which you savor so very sweetly at the Holy Sacrifice of the Mass. It is the greatest prayer that any human heart could ever utter.

  Now, My Special son, it is My pleasure to address your own humble little heart today. You know that My Love for you is immeasurable, and this is another gift which shall never be taken away. I have the honor of speaking through the power of the Holy Paraclete to tell you that God has come among you in a very unique way because you have invited Him here. I bear in My arms the Baby Jesus because He is My gift to the world and to the Love for Him that lives so profoundly in your loving heart. I ask that you contemplate how your loyalty to Heaven is very strong in an equally immeasurable way. The Hosts on High are likewise as dependent upon your service to God as you are for His every blessing in your life. This is a time during which your very days are unfolding the news which I told you would be forthcoming many years ago. Be pleased that you have known what you have lived in advance. You will know in the fullness of time that there is truly no other place that you would have rather been in 2001 than where you are right now. Your life has meaning and purpose because you have given it to Jesus, your every waking moment and slumbering ones too. Yes, this is your answer. I have so much Love for you that no miracle could possibly reveal it all. I know that you live inside the circumference of faith because your soul has already found its predestined home in the infinity of Paradise. I assure you that the element of time is very deceptive because you and I will be standing alongside the other Saints in Heaven someday, and you will refer to this February day and tell Me that it was only like a brief second on the clock of the contemporary world. This may be difficult for you to see at this moment in time, but your Eternity in the Light of Salvation will come to face you before you really ever knew it was that close at all. Indeed, your work for Jesus will have accomplished everything that I intended it to achieve. Souls by the ten-thousands will have come to the Cross because you have offered your life to convert them. There is no way that you can properly understand what this gift of life means to the God who has given you the power to comprehend Him. So, let this be the day when you finally accept in humility that you cannot escape His grasp, and that you would never wish to do so anyway. The Angels who love you have become your beacon and your signal that God is alive and well in your heart and love. Jesus has been watching your work since before you were born, and He has ordained your every action in His Name. To everything there is a season and a purpose under Heaven. For whatever reason that is yet inexplicable to you, His Love for you is reflected in the gifts which you return to Him. The greatest of all love you are giving to God, and His is offered to the remainder of the world in return. My thanksgiving is in offering My Love to you!"

Sunday, March 4, 2001
12:57 p.m.

"The compass of Love which Jesus has placed into your hearts through the power of the Holy Spirit is directing your souls toward the Cross! Dear children, too many lives are wasting away while Americans do not know to anticipate the piousness that is about to enter the mainstream of the globe's collective human conscience. I have prayed in fulfillment of many prophesies and promises to offer you the Wisdom to turn to the Lord for Salvation in His Son. Please remember that I am sent by the Almighty Father in Love, but I also come of My own free will because you are the offspring whom I shall present to Jesus when God says the time is ripe to close the world. Please never forget that dogmas and doctrines do not exist in a stark cosmic void. Christian sacrifice is the equator of a sanctified Earth; and not unlike gravity itself, your holiness prevents you from plummeting into the netherworld as though you were falling into the vacuum of outer space. Science has discovered that the world is not flat; and if diamonds have facets and sheens, your Christian piety has pristine dimensions and seeable authenticity. I realize that manifold generations have come and gone since Jesus first told the citizens of Earth that the Kingdom of God would be at hand before they passed into death. He was correct then, and His prophecy is true today. The Kingdom of Everlasting Life is nigh, and all within the sound of My voice should prepare to greet the imminent Glory that awaits those who are cleansed in the Blood of the Lamb. There is no time to satiate your cravings for carnal exploitation, colonial imperialism, and moral relativism. My children, it may seem as though this is a frequent theme of My messages, but it is even more than that. It is My perpetual prayer and admonition wrapped in the Truth that I have been dispensing to the world for centuries. I have longed for the hours when the conversion of millions at a time will occur, but so many are still steeped in the distractions of materialism and the flesh. While this is the case, it is also a problem that is abating with each passing day. Just when it seems like the impieties can grow no worse, there are some who lunge the dagger of indifference and outright rejection in deeper. The focus of many people's lives is no greater than their penchant for glamor, lust, fame, and wealth. These are only baneful illusions! And, if they speak out at all, most moral leaders equivocate at the podium about matters of faith and Truth for fear of losing their audience, effectively fleecing their flocks of the opportunity to repent. I come to remind you of the impermeable Love that has been living inside you since you first gave your hearts to Jesus. Nothing in Creation can destroy that seed of resurrected innocence growing there. You are protected by My Mantle of Motherhood, and cannot be harmed by the barbs surrounding you. Thanks be to God! I wish for you to continue to be steadfast in hope because the terrible things you see in the world cannot last much longer. The sacred mechanism of ethereal communion consists of fostering practical forbearance, the acquittal of debt, and irrevocable clemency. You have been told many times in the past that the Victory of Love is yours. The clock is not your enemy anymore because you have given your existence to God. These are the days that will bring you the joy of success in living-out your promises to Him. Your work is of a blessed accord when it is given to Jesus, and the next days and weeks will be no different. Can you see the jubilation that the Heavens are taking in the subsistence of your days? There are miracles around you, and your conscience allows you to receive them because your hearts are filled with love. It is not difficult to know God and to become His children when you are one with Jesus at the foundations of forgiveness. Please know that the strength that you hold in your hearts is His holiness living there, and your purity is the artwork of His Passion.

    I would never be one to overly boast, but I am deeply moved that you have remained faithful to the words I have spoken for so long. Again I acclaim, there is no other life that would be more inspiring, and no greater use of your resources than the gifts you are offering for the conversion of lost sinners. You are fortunate because the Holy Spirit knows you belong to God, and the tendering of your lives to His purposes has caused His decision to remain with you to be an easier one to make. When you survey the Earth with the prevalence of your prayers, it is not difficult to perceive where the pockets of hatred lie and what their effects are on the universe as a whole. My Special one, the strategic genius of your second book makes it clear that the corruptible nature of man does not allow him to move beyond the confines of mortality unless everyone who wishes to grow in perfection begins with the Holy Sacrifice of the Mass. The very intention of human life on the globe is to take everyone to their absolution and contrition in the Crucifixion of My Son. There are hundreds of additional ways that I could explain this to you, and I probably will. But, suffice it to say that you are listening to the wise counsel of the Angels, and you are obedient to the Truth of God that you know is coming from their mouths. This too is another miracle in itself. They speak because you have never given-in to the allurements that would have otherwise taken you down another course. We pause during these days of Lent to remember that Jesus' life was absolutely horrible during His forty days in the desert. Hence, I wish to tell you today that your observation of Lent is also a period of self-denial, and one of additions, rather than only subtractions. Your spirit must continue to grow in vividness as you anticipate the Paschal Mysteries that will culminate in the Easter Celebration. I suppose you are aware that your entire life is a time of giving, but particularly more during Lent because your heart turns inwardly quite more to see where your faith has taken you. While you must be satisfied that you belong to Jesus, you must also sense the commitment that He will fulfill your every need on the way to Golgotha which He asks you to accept on His behalf. 'Take up your cross....' is His way of saying that He wishes you to be equally as loving in peace as in times of war. Your noble fights against evil can sometimes make you more aware that humanity is in need of great Love, but times of peace can often make you complacent in knowing that Love is equally as powerful when there are no enemies to fight. Do you understand what I just told you? I am honored that you are continuing to pray the Rosary everyday and complete the work on your second book. God will forever be grateful for everything you have done for Him. Thank you for offering the Holy Rosary again today for the conversion of the lost!"

Sunday, March 11, 2001
3:53 p.m.

"Yes, My dear little children, I have come to pray with you for the conversion of humanity to the Sacred Heart of My Son! Let no one be confused about the nature of the Heavens to see this growth to its destined end. I hold the jubilation of human souls within My reach, for under My Motherly jurisdiction is the Child of Bethlehem, Christ the King, the Savior of humanity. How pleased I am that you are continuing the struggle, the effort, and the love which has brought you to conclude that God wishes you to attend to those who do not know Redemption. These are not idle hours because time is very short before the culmination of the mortality which you have overcome in the Blood of Jesus on the Cross. Can you see the Light of the City of Love shining in the night? This is your destination and the homeland for which you have been praying for so long. I assure you that not only will your Salvation greet you there, it is already in you through the Holy Spirit of Jesus in your hearts. Today, you offer the continuance of your affection for the Sacrifice of Jesus to rescue maniacal sinners from their own devices. There are countless ways to express your love for God, but none is greater than paying homage to the Messiah whose Lenten mission you are celebrating now. It is in preparation for Easter that you learn to be patient, how to disavow the artifices of the material world, and how to maintain your inner-strength, holiness, and purity in the face of unbridled temptation. If only you could sense the brightness which rests at the end of your journey, you would forge onward through the darkness of life with great joy. I offer My sincere intercession as you pass through the coming months and years, sharing in your prayers of loving Adoration for Jesus and your obedience to God. Wherein is your affection, this is also where your destiny shall rest. Please always give Me your hearts; give Me your very lives and deeds; place your petitions with Me for transference to Christ Jesus, and I will take them to the Throne of Omnipotence where they are answered in accordance with the Will of the Almighty Father. My obedient children, do you know by now that His Will is unconditional comfort for each of you? There is no time set aside for doubt or sadness on your journey back to the halls of Paradise because the Greatest News to ever fall upon the souls of the world is in the Sacrifice of My Son on the Cross and His Paschal Resurrection from the Tomb. Now, you see that your brothers and sisters carry forward through life and into the future with many questions on their minds because they are not seeking the reason for life in the Holy Sacrifice of the Mass. I have told you on numerous occasions that the Celebration of the Eucharist is the atonement of humankind with God through the Crucifixion of Jesus on the Cross. His Mercy is poured-out before you and upon you as you pray the Holy Mass as one people. The Most Blessed Sacrament is your thanksgiving prayer that God has forgiven your sins completely to the core of your inner-being. I am pleased that so many of My faithful ones have taken-up their crosses and followed Jesus in the way of self-denial and prayer during this Lenten Season of 2001. I am with you as you offer the Stations of the Cross. My children, this is not only a time for reconciliation with God, but also with your fellow man. You have been told about this in the Sacred Scriptures, that you should harbor no grudges or hatred against your brothers on your journey to the Altar of Sacrifice. Please know that if they refuse to accept your contrition and good will, God will bless you just the same for offering it to them from the depths of your heart. Please pray for your enemies, for those who hold themselves aloof before the Holy Gospel, and for those who utterly despise you for defending it.

Please always remember that no act of good will can go unattended forever. To whomever you show love, they are required to respond in-kind by God before they will be allowed entry into Heaven. I assure you that the Truth will blaze like fire in the faces of those who cast your love aside, and their sight will be restored by the flames of compassion which God has for them. Yes, His Mercy is brought through your prayers, your petitions of goodness that live at the center of your Christian faith. All you need to do is offer it, and Jesus will make sure that it is never misplaced. This is why the Angels have told you on more than one occasion to never give-up, never give-in, and never cower to those whose lack of faith in Jesus takes them on a completely different course than He wishes them to go. It is you who lead them, your love which enlivens their hearts, and the trust you hold in the Word of God that helps guide them home. Regardless of what anyone else might say, Jesus is worthy of all the worship, praise, glory, and honor that you may bestow upon His Sacred Heart. Anyone who states otherwise has closed his heart to the Wisdom that flows from the Throne of God in Heaven. My dear little Special one and Chosen one, I have come also today to bless you for the work you are continuing to do for My Son, your Lord and Almighty God. After the passing of so many years during which I have spoken to you, it is sometimes easy for you not to truly understand what I mean when I say that you cannot know in advance the Glory which is rushing into Creation through your work. Please remember to humble your hearts as the future continues to unfold. These are quite special times during your life because you have made it so. I can do nothing without your 'yes,' and you can see what this really means by now. I am happy to boast to the Saints and Angels, and to God Himself, that you are My children. How could any mother be more proud than to have two stately sons who have taken-on the burdens of praying incessantly, attending the Holy Mass everyday for many years, and sacrificing your private hours to finish the work of the Lord instead of fashioning your existence around what the secular world offers? So, please humbly accept My gratitude and Love for making such a difference in the shaping of the Kingdom of Heaven to be inclusive of many souls who would not otherwise own a share of its blessings. We are not finished, and it is obvious that you will be fighting to the last second of mortal time to receive the Flag of Victory from the hand of Almighty God.

As those who are reading *Morning Star Over America* are discovering, there are seemingly endless parables describing the Truth about Love. Anything in the world can be crafted into a lesson about where the Mystery of Salvation can be found in the hearts of the faithful living for Jesus. These are sacred oracles about conversion because, as you can see, conversion is not simply a matter of lifting the heart to the Father in Heaven, it is a linear continuum of human events, living in accourse with the Holy Spirit as your guide. More and more people are only now coming to understand that it is through the realization that life on the Earth is transitory does the heart look more toward the skies. Even the event that you just watched on television is an indication of this. Yes, there were tens-of-thousands of people holding three fingers in the air in honor of a deceased competitor whom they considered to be a secular martyr. This was their inadvertent parable of the Blessed Trinity, God's way of using them as instruments to implant His presence in their subconsciousness. What they did not have the benefit of knowing is that they were participating in it. If the collection of human souls on the Earth would take a step backward from the focus they hold on the tangible details of the globe, they would see these things clearly because they would not be so distracted. The Holy Spirit will light wherever there is the silence of peace to bring Peace. This is what the solitude of prayer is all about; it directs the concise focus of the human spirit totally on the Divinity of God. Therein, you can know the reason why I call so many to prayer, especially in large numbers, because the silence of holiness lives through the cohesion of multitudes of peoples who have assembled to hear the voice of Jesus. And, He will speak to them! He has done so for centuries, and He shall continue beyond the end of time. These are among the reasons why your labors over the past ten years have been so successful. Your heart is open to every possibility that Heaven affords because you have come to expect them. The key to your interaction with Jesus is no less than this. It is your anticipation that He will hear and respond to your every need that is in alignment with His Will. When it comes to remaking the Earth like Paradise above you, the definition of His Will has already been declared. This is the basis of Love around which you must fashion your prayers and force the night into dawning anew in His splendid Light of Resurrection. This is where your souls are going, and this is why your hearts are so touched when you see or hear anything that is obviously from the hands of the Heavenly Hosts.

Can you see that there are innumerable revelations that are now ongoing to indicate that your persistence in love is bearing new fruit? The future that God has planned for you is a bright one, if only you can withstand the wait that will take you there, and bear the griefs that He asks you to endure along the way. Let Me tell you in advance that there is no opponent ahead of you right now, and your friends and loved ones, even your enemies, are being drafted by your victory across the finish-line of Immortal Love. Everyone is cheering your success, not because you might overtake an enemy who has lost, but that you will complete the race with nothing near to impede the margin of Triumph that you have already extended over anything that may hold you back. This is how Jesus is watching you, sitting on the edge of His seat with His fists in the air as you fly in the face of every opposition toward the New Kingdom that knows no parting or sorrow. Every team is of the color of Divine Love beneath the Holy Cross. Yes, you envision yourself taking every turn with caution and courage, just like the competitors on the racetrack today. You are passing those who are mired in the treadways of the Earth, those looking in other directions, and whose arrogance has left them twisting in the wind. You have already won, and there is no reason for you to suffer anxiety. Please enjoy the ride as the Most High King cheers your life into the land of joy where the Saints will welcome you home. Thank you for trying your best, for loving Him, for embracing the cause of righteousness and Redemption, and for allowing God to be as touched of heart as you are at this moment. In time, every good thing for which you pray will come to pass. It is only your impatience that can spin your hopes beyond control. Life is a matter of warmth, and this is your hour to fan the fires of righteousness while the rest of the Saints fall into place. They are there, I promise, even though you may not be able to see them. They detect your rear guard, and they know you will lead them to the epicenter of prosperity and peace in your love for the Savior of the world. Countless lost souls are depending on your abilities because Jesus has anointed you a leader among men. Please remember that no victory can be won without your participation, a labor you are giving with unconditional love. Thank you for taking such good care of your brother."

Friday, March 16, 2001
From Rev. Father Joseph Timothy Murray (1913-1991)

"You are every bit the nourishment that any soul shall ever require, short of God Himself. So, let no cold wintery insolence ever embitter your heart, no wolf in disguise ever devour your joy, and no stubborn obstinance ever stand in the way of your reaching-out to every man, woman, and child with the Good News of human Redemption in the Firmament of the Cross; the Wisdom of God, His Angels, His Saints, and the Divine Splendor of Perfection He has given to us all through Jesus Christ Incarnate, Crucified, Entombed, and Resurrected."

Sunday, March 18, 2001
3:31 p.m.

"You can hear the Angels calling you in love from the Holies of Paradise for your continuing affection for God and for the conversion of every sinner on Earth. And, it is true, My children! Let this age open for the arrival of the righteousness which is yours because God wishes for the crescendo of the Earth to be this way. I offer you My greatest Peace on this day because you have come to the eve of the Feast of a visionary man, the stepfather of Jesus, Saint Joseph. Please call on him during times of trouble, when you feel alone, and when your enemies are pursuing you like hounds in the chase. Saint Joseph bears in his arms the Wisdom that is at the heart of everyone who belongs to the Father. This serene man who never departed My side wields the gentleness of a lamb, the docility of a dove, and yet, the mighty command of all the Martyrs combined and the strength and power to wield the Wrath of God wherever his service is summoned. My children, it is with this hope that you march onwardly through the weeks and months which are only now forthcoming because greater revelations will come to you. Yes, your hearts are clear and strong, and they are also about to be filled to overflowing with the joy that Jesus gives you to know success like no other mortal has seen. I offer you this as a rite of My promises because I know that you have the faith to believe My every word. The prayers you are saying now, the humble petitions that you lift as you prepare for sleep at night, your meditations prior to the Holy Sacrifice of the Mass, and the passing thoughts of piety you offer on the street everyday are the shaping of your hopes into reality. You have many friends who walk the Earth with you, but only one Divine Savior who is My Son, the Almighty Redeemer of humanity. As you continue to live in the Light of this Truth, your soul is warmed by the peerless satisfaction that all is well in time and Eternity. The commission you have been given in the Holy Gospel is fulfilled by your adherence to the call of the heart. Please remember always that I have come to touch your hearts, and it is according to you how well My work is done. When you answer My invitation with obedience and humility, the world changes into the image and likeness of Paradise. I bring thanks for you today because every day is another step on that sacred journey. This is why you can hear the Angels calling, because you praise God in all you do. You answer His call to soothe His Sacred Heart by living the Love through which Creation was made, and through which His Only Son was begotten. I am the lowly Handmaid of God who is the blesser of everyone, and I am also the Queen who knows Him best. Through this Wisdom, I speak to you in confident assurance that you are pleasing in His sight. Oh! Make no mistake; when you are found to be in error, I certainly will remind you! But, your lives are made increasingly more perfect by the Crucifixion and Resurrection of My Son. This is also why I am humbled by your progress in becoming the saints who will someday pass like the multitudes before you beyond the veil of mortal tears into the endless ecstasy of Salvation. It is why we are praying together, and what we wish to come to pass for all humanity on Earth.

    Please pray with Me for this American nation as we seek the cessation of abortion and capital punishment. The days are continuing to expire before the leaders of America will vengefully put a criminal to death who is claimed to have killed 168 people in Oklahoma. It is not his gruesome sins that they are trying to exterminate, it is his pitiable soul. He is in need of our prayers, but they who will soon execute him will have an equal amount of blood on their hands. This is the perpetuation of an agendum of revenge that keeps America in such turmoil. There is such a lack of prayer that only few seem to care what happens to the weak and unstable. I submit prayers aplenty for those who are affected, and I ask that you join Me in beseeching Jesus to spread His Divine Mercy over everyone involved. Yes, a deficit of prayer and austere living has led to the gross tragedies around the globe. As we extol the Gospel of Jesus before the rest of humanity, please join Me as your Mother to seek and touch the simplest hearts who are suffering in remote places. My Special son, I ask you to remain tethered to My Immaculate Heart at all costs because many people harbor bane attempts to destroy the intentions of your newest book. They have known you since you were a child, and will claim that you are not a prophet of God. They are absolutely wrong, and will eventually come to realize it. However, the nation the future brings will be sullied by sinners who despise you. I know that you will sustain your peace because you have come of age; you are mature in your faith; you are confident of who you are, and realize what the Son of Man requires. There is obviously a relentless barrage of naysayers who would rather destroy their enemies than pray for them. Prayer is what their souls require. My message here today will not be extensive because I plan to offer lengthy ones in the future. I came to pray with you, to tell you that I love you, and to thank you for taking care of your brother. I was happy that your heart was touched by reading portions of your Diary last evening. You are the only reason why it has been possible. Again, I have told you about this in times past. God is pleased by your obedience in all things that make Him happy. It is with this loyalty that you continue to ponder your frontier and whatever innovations you need to enhance the beauty of your third book. Yes, you are a valorous and courageous man. I thank you for responding to whatever exalts the Lord through your life."

Sunday, March 25, 2001
3:49 p.m.

YES!

"Jesus is yearning to see your souls reach beyond the stars where Heaven can embrace you! I am the Immaculate Queen of the Salvation of humankind, and I have come to remind you that the world is blessed in, by and through the Love of God who will ensure your victory over death. Please tender your hearts to Me and I will lift the prayers that are still lacking in your daily petitions that will bring the culmination of your joy. I am of God's spiritual cohesion, keeping you close to the hearth of Love at the center of My Son's Most Sacred Heart. You will know no fonder peace because only Jesus is the happiness that comes from the Right Hand of the Father. I assure you that you do not realize the power in My words and the intentions Jesus holds to deliver you to the arms of His Holy Redemption. It is for these reasons, My dear ones, that you must say 'yes' to Love. Your own compliance must mirror the Fiat that I offered to the Archangel Gabriel on the Feast of the Annunciation. I wish the entire of Creation to know that I have never regretted that day, for My Immaculate Heart still beats with the simple affection through which I saw the Sacred Mysteries unfold as mortal time evolved swiftly thereafter. These are your moments and sequences to give over your lives to Jesus because you will have no greater opportunity to convert. It is imperative that you answer My call to greater holiness, servitude, piety, prayer, penance, and Grace. These are the benefits of your acceptance of God's Love because, through them, humanity is healed and refurbished again. Since you are the Mystical Body of Jesus on the Earth, you are the reason for His Bloodshed on the Cross. He suffers still because of the millions who reject Him, but His Divine Mercy remains the same. I wish you could know from the perspective of immortality that all of this is true. My Son is your timeless Gatekeeper who wishes to absolve every soul of their errant ways. Now, you forge-on through the days and months that will take you to the foyer of death. There is no need for any hesitation anymore in giving yourselves to the Cross. I offer every single essence of My Divine Being to assist your conversion to the Holy Gospel. Please do not be dismayed by those who say that it will not matter in the end. Theirs are the souls who will be agonizing that they refused to accept the Truth. I ask you to remember the days when you were much younger and did not know to seek the greater power of righteousness inside your homes. How helpless and weak you knew you were. Now, you have come to recognize your strength in the Son of Man! You are helpless to the extent that you decline to acknowledge His Omnipotent Will to refashion the Earth into the image and likeness of Paradise! When I tell you that you will not realize your passage from this life into the next if only you will heed My call, I am saying that your lovingness and perfection will make you saints in these days. And, when I proclaim that you must refrain from sin because you wish to be like Jesus, this is the manifestation of the Holy Spirit in your hearts!

My children of Earth, too many centuries of goodness have passed beyond the chasm between your mortality and the everlasting ages for you to turn back now! Please do not forsake the pennings of your fathers and grandfathers before you who knew to seek God because His Spirit lived inside them! Indeed, this is not the moment for framing darker days of faithlessness and disbelief, this is the instant when the priceless revelation of sainthood is knocking on the door of your generation! Again, I ask you to respond with an affiant 'yes!' I urge all hearts to call to mind the Eternal Triumph that has been won in the Resurrection of Jesus from the Grave on Easter morning. This Season of Lent is a welcome reminder that you are the blossoming fruits of goodness on the Earth to be savored by God when your souls reach the Celestial City beyond your passing. These are times of great jubilation and assurance because you have been given the opportunity to participate in the indomitable power of the Cross! When you rise at morning's light and seek the world anew, your own newness thrives on the whispers of peace that bring your hearts to the solace of that first Easter Morning. Yes, your souls realize the Truth when knowledge fails to keep you apprised! Please raise your hearts and hands to the Wisdom of the Messiah! He is searching for you now; He is yearning to take you to Heaven, and His Love is keeping you warm in the cold. How blessed are they who love the Law of the Lord! Therefore, let no sorrow or grief befall you, let no suffering deter you from seeking the Love who lives behind the horizon, and let no flesh tempt you to surrender the purity that has created you again in the Lord's Immortal Grace. I seek your prayers for these things because I know everything that God wishes from you. I pray for you; I intercede for your intentions before the Throne of the Almighty Father, and I teach you through the nurturing Love that has become your bastion of hope. I can help make your faith more strong if you will give your lives to the inviolate protection of My Mantle of Motherhood. You search for rainbows when the storms have passed, and I am telling you today that your acceptance of Jesus is this happiness before the storms are ever through. Live not beyond the realms of His Divine Love!

My Special son, this is a holy day in your Lenten Season because so many ponder the Immaculate Conception that God has seen fit to place into Dogmatic Law. I ask you to remember that every soul has the potential in their heart to be just as sinless through the divinity of the Cross. Let us give them ample time and plentiful opportunities to turn their lives around and return to the fold of those who are bound for Paradise. Yes, it is true that Jesus is likewise the Immaculate Conception in that He was born without sin and never committed sin because He is incapable of being less than Divine in all ways seen and unseen. When the Scriptures say that He became sin for the Salvation of the world, it simply means that every transgression was foisted upon Him for expiation before the Court of His Father in Heaven. Now, you understand what this means. It is important for you to know that you are to reciprocally become the image of Jesus by allowing the Holy Paraclete to take-up residence in your heart. Therein, you are becoming sinless."

(I told Our Lady that I hoped I was becoming sinless for Jesus.)

"My little son, after all I have been telling you for the past ten years about the greatness of your progress toward becoming the likeness of Jesus, how could you doubt My words? Why would you allow the syllables to depart your lips that you are unsure whether you are becoming like Him? If you accept the power that God has given you to wield, you will no longer doubt your own resolve. I tell you again that there is no need for you to be concerned; I beseech you poignantly to not turn back now. You can see the mightiness that has led you to the Universal Love which has become your primordial nature. We shall not desist until the lives of you and your brother have harvested the conversion of millions of lost souls. This is the Day of the Lord! It is only through your faith that you have the willingness to believe. There is no one in the history of Creation who has had greater faith than yours; no one, nary another soul. I am not complimenting you, I am simply telling you a fact of Truth. This is a gift from the Heart of God for which you have offered your daily suppliance all your natural life. I ask you not to worry about the effects of your labors on those who oppose you or the retaliation they might exact. Remember to be cautious in protecting yourself, but do not allow this to lead you into any sense of discontent. There is nothing that Jesus will deny you in accordance with God's Will when you invoke My Maternal intercession. I am elated by your lifting of so many prayers! Please be at peace this week and get plentiful rest!"

Sunday, April 1, 2001
3:47 p.m.

"My dear children, please do not allow the ineloquence of the passing days to lead you to believe that there is no inherent beauty in human life. Through the love you share in the depths of your hearts, you are raised above and beyond the dismal toll that makes men cower at their own lack of dimension. I have watched for a seemingly ceaseless time while you have grown to be the children of Light, as your consciences have been awakened by the Holy Spirit, how great your works and deeds have become, and with what high expectation you greet the rising sun. This cannot be a time you will look back upon as being mundane because you help the Saints shape the sparkling bliss of Heaven. I am the Queen of Paradise, and I hold the station from which I know and see all things. If you will persist in believing the Promise that Jesus has given, there is nothing you cannot achieve as you continue to live. You are blessed and are making way for the celebration of the coming Palm Sunday in your march toward Easter. As this week passes and you prepare to greet the remembrance of Jesus' entrance into Jerusalem, remember that the New Jerusalem resonates with His Divine Salvation and never once betrays Him. I know that you are in the number of souls who continue to pray for success as the next months and years proceed to pass. My children, Jesus knew that to deny His brothers' Salvation would be tantamount to fratricide, and that even as infant children, you were born into this world already mortally wounded. My Son was aware of the sparse existence that your forbears scratched from the deserts of the decimated Earth, that He would discover your signature in marsh and glen, high above the netherworld where the falcons take to flight. And, He smelled in your presence the pungence of anger, fear, and jealousy, and the Seven Deadly Sins wrapped around your throats like garrotes, cutting you off from the living, breathing excellence of Paradise alive. But, even in this, He has already seen your most handsome hopes of nobility and faith that everything can change, and that the stench of this modern age will soon be no more than an onion or two in a bed of cascading flowers. Christ Jesus knew that you, among all species, would recognize how futile and fruitless life on Earth would be without His salvific Grace. Therefore, I have come today as an exercise in your blessedness to reaffirm My commitment to the completion of your work. I see that you are planning to travel tomorrow to see the miracle of your second book being printed. I tell you over and again that this is a gift which you, and only you, have brought into Creation. It is a fruit of your love for God and for the people who so need your petitions to improve the future of their fate in death and their conversion to the Holy Cross. The Lord sees your second book as a chastisement for humanity because the peoples of the Earth are in need of reprimand. Yes, it is a frank admonishment about the condition of life in these mortal times and how Jesus plans to bring a great reckoning soon to eliminate the error about which you have spoken. Not only should this give you pause to reflect about other ways that He wills to awaken those asleep in sin from their wanton arrogance, it should help you see that there need not be any physical punishment brought-down from Heaven upon those who deny Him. When their souls finally realize the distance they have lived from the Truth, they will pluck-out their eyes and cut off their hands that kept them from knowing their Salvation to the fullest and immeasurable extent. Now the month of April has come, and you will see the Earth bloom into Spring again. Does this mean that the hot summer days must be the casual passing of heated rhetoric and dogged days of despair for millions among you at home and abroad? Does it imply that My children should take a business per usual approach to the celebration of Ordinary Time in the Christian Liturgical Year? For many, this is exactly the pace into which they will fall, but not for the humble children who know their Savior well. The coming months will be a period of reflection and preparation because the hour is near when Jesus will end the ages, and those whose brows are dripping with the sweat of righteousness will be blessed with a Glorious Crown! I am happy that the news I bring is always good. Your lives are sad enough by the way you are mistreated by those lacking the faith that would lead them to be the image and likeness of Jesus' Divine Love. Please continue to raise your hearts in expectation that everything for which you pray will come to pass, so that you will not have to endure a wait that might tempt you to believe that your supplications are in vain. Every prayer matters in the Most Sacred Heart of Jesus! My little ones, our moments together are special to Me because you care about the culmination of the world to accept the Plan of God for the people He came to save. If not for your prayers of compliance, He might ask the reciprocal question of Creation, where else would He go?

The Almighty Father searches for people who seek not the Earth or the materials upon it, but for the Spirit of Love who has overcome the multiplication of profits by the dispensation of His Holy Grace. Yes, you are rich in Love, and are likewise the heirs of a fortune of Redemption at the end of time. Will that be today, tomorrow, or a few weeks from now? Will it be in another decade or two? God knows the answer, and has told you that time is now very short. Therefore, I continue to speak to you as a gift of His Love and ask you to not be deceived by the seemingly perpetual turning of the calendar years. Reach for God's endless Eternity instead, which is human Absolution in the power of the Cross. This is what your existence is about, and it is why you are observing the Season of Lent and the upcoming Paschal Mystery of the High Feast of Easter. My Special one, I know that you are tired, that your body aches, that your mind is weary, and you find it difficult to accept the repetitive nature of everyday life. But, please do not allow these things to impede your view of the larger picture of the endless Divinity which has become your most viable purpose. Too many of My messengers have laid-down their Rosaries and walked away because they became distraught by the slowly passing element of time. It is true that life seems endlessly daily, but you can see that it is forging toward the same Glorious Day on which Jesus will return. I have never sensed for a moment that you will ever resign, but when you become disdainful about your daily schedule and lack patience in what you see others do, it is the beginning of the hardening of your heart. I am telling you this to preempt any further deterioration of your happiness because My Love for you is so great. I ask you to seek the freshness in every new dawn because Jesus is always with you in its breadth and length, and I continue to hold you beneath the protection of My Holy Mantle. Can you recognize the sense of peace that keeps trying to make its way into the center of your heart? Please allow Jesus to reside there because your heart is the most comfortable place in Creation for Him to rest.

Indeed, He is alive and well in the Tabernacle, but too many leave Him there abandoned. While residing in your heart, the Holy Spirit accepts you as His companion of Love until you are welcomed into the heights of Heaven."

Palm Sunday, April 8, 2001
1:29 p.m.

"Dear little children, I wish to tell you today that I have repeatedly advised humanity throughout the centuries that it is necessary for ensuing generations to build upon your faith in the Holy Gospel, and to never subvert it. Celebrate the Truth about the mystical presence of Jesus in your hearts, but do not attempt to change the meaning of what He has said. Call on your brothers and sisters to join in the fight against hatred in the world, but never send them onto any battlefield on which you have not yourselves engaged. Admonish them to offer the charity of their lives and wares to those in need, but not until you have given everything at your disposal to utter exhaustion. I have seen many of these wise and generous virtues neglected as the body of humankind continues its march toward the end of mortal time. There is much ado about speaking to the needs of the Earth, but those who are the children of Light will transform their sentiments into tangible actions, sufficient to the juncture that suffering is mitigated and those who do not understand the Christian Gospel will repent on bended knees before the Cross. Now, you are celebrating the procession of Jesus into the Holy City of Jerusalem where His Passion and Crucifixion would occur. Can you see that the same will happen to you when those who reject His Salvation speak highly of you? This is something about which you should be wary. Today, I harken to Palm Sunday ten years ago, although on a date in March, during which your holy prayers brought additional miracles into your presence. This has not changed to this day because I am still here, still speaking, and still asking you for the confirmation of your lives for the conversion of the remainder of humanity. My Special son, there has been a question in your mind that you have been pondering for many years that I am prepared to address today. Do you remember wondering whether I would have called upon you to become a messenger and seer if you had not been summoned to Medjugorje? Your travels abroad were not the sole origin of your destiny to be a messenger, but part of it. All of this was placed into action when your family moved to the western street on which your brother lived and played on his porch in your little village. You can follow the history of these unchallengeable events since then. The reason I have brought this to your attention is so you can apply this same sense of destiny to the remainder of your life. You need not feel surprised when you see things unfold before you, while your heart and conscience tell you that they seem to be natural events. Through your praying of the Holy Rosary, you are lifted out of time and placed into the Eternal Will of God. This has also been the case with your brother since he was a helpless young child.

I know that you have brought these thoughts to mind. Do you know that the universe is unfolding as it should? Therein rests your happiness and assurance that your prayers have been answered, that your life has been and always will be an example to Creation regarding how anyone should build upon their relationship with Heaven. I will lead anyone who calls upon My intercession to the doorway of faith, but they must initiate that first step past the framework into the fullness of allegiance to the Blood of the Cross.

As you enter Holy Week, please remember to pray for the poor souls in Purgatory so they will be granted the Eternal Light of Heaven to the echoing of the bombs bursting in air on Easter Morning. They will be grateful, and will become intercessors for you as your earthly life evolves. All Love is one, and it is necessary for everyone to understand that this Divine Perfection is a function of the Will of the Father. Do you have a question about why so many people cast My intercession aside?"

(How can some who lead the Church and those who counsel them refuse to accept the work of the Holy Spirit within the children of their flock unless they witness a popular manifestation of supernaturalism on their own?)

"The answer is the same as it has been over the centuries. They would not heed the call of Jesus, and they Crucified Him. They spurned the teachings of the First Apostles, and they martyred them."

(Since they act like this, how is it possible to follow Church elders with any semblance of abandonment?)

"If you looked upon the leaders of the Church with such innocent abandonment of which you speak, would there be a need for Me to appear by private revelation? The Holy Spirit is doing God's work through those who are trying to do better one day at a time. You know that you would not have evoked these questions prior to February 22, 1991."

(I said, 'It is sorrowful that the vision of the power of faith in Christ is so diminished. The Church is woefully atrophied when those who are responsible for reaching-out in faith refuse to do so.')

"This is precisely the reason why Jesus dispatched Me to intercede as Mother of the Church. It might falter without My guidance. Remember the holy anthem refraining the fact that you are sent forth by God's blessings. I am heralding these blessings, whether those who oppose Me know it or not. Do not worry, nothing that will affect the absolution of humanity will be lost. This is why the Church is not just the collection of the faithful who have professed their belief in the Creed and Salvation in the Cross, it simultaneously exists in each and every heart. The Church prevails through both."

156   The New Millennium

(I asked whether there is an infallible element to this collection of the faithful. I mispronounced it the first time.)

"You said invallability. Do you mean infallibility? You must discern the application of the term. To be sure, you agree that the infallibility of the Holy Father in Rome rests in understanding God better than other men. Any ecclesial judgements through this are remnants of that arc of indomitable Wisdom. It is plausible for anyone to be infallible in the eyes of God. Why has only the Pope been so declared? Because his is the authority of Saint Peter from whose bindings all beatific encyclicals are derived. Without this centric nature of the Church, there would be any number of splintered sects claiming to be the Holy See. There can be no infallible souls on Earth who do not recognize the Holy Father as the Vicar of Christ. There is phenomenal potential here!"

(I remarked that it is disheartening to see others abuse the teachings of the Church and the writings of the Saints as an excuse for not having to listen to any other mortal human being, and by such activity, reject the messengers sent by the Almighty Father.)

"My son, the refusal of mankind to accept all this is the same sin that led to the fall of Adam and Eve, that of pride."

(I added, 'They do not wish to surrender the control that they think they possess.')

"Theirs is not a byproduct of fear! It is arrogance and obstinance against what the Lord wishes them to do. You see it everyday, nearly everywhere you turn. However, you also see the glistening stars of holiness and acceptance around you in such people as the priests you admire. Father Schmidt is one example, and some of the lay persons you have met who have taken your Diary on raw faith alone, ratifying your own faith, worrying that they might never blossom into the children of God that you have become, agonizing that they may be the ones to offend Him, and concerned that they might be those about whom you have written. I am saying that there are living saints around you, people who have yet to die, walking the Earth in organic flesh. They live in stark contrast to the indignance of others; and their prayers, humility, and love have made-up for the rejection of your enemies. You know who they are. Your heart is as great a messenger for human piety as anything I might say. Hence, you go forward in the knowledge that everyone who seems far from Jesus will come to know Him; for example, those who appear to be offensive to Him now. The world cannot end without the occurrence of this transformation because God will not permit it. Can you see why I ask you to be heartened? You must be able to draw a circle in your mind that is larger than the grief of a single day or given space in time. When you learn to do this well, you will never surrender to sadness or rejection again. Just wait! You will see that I am telling you the Truth! I hope you will recognize with impassioned openness during Holy Week and the Feast of Easter that Jesus loves you."

Easter Sunday, April 15, 2001
2:43 p.m.

"Now dear little children, your prayerful season of self-denial has blossomed into the sanctity of Eastertide again! Another celebration of the Paschal Mystery of My Son's Victory over Death has arrived, and you are continuing to pour-out your lives in earnest toward His Second Coming to Redeem you from exile. Yes, your Advent of the heart will bring your souls to the fount of Absolution as you pursue the servitude that allows you to lift-up the rest of humanity in dignity and poise. You may wonder what I might say that differs from other Easters during which I have appeared amidst your prayers to offer My intercession. Each is the remembrance of the Resurrection of Jesus from the Sepulcher, but it is you who are growing in holiness with each passing year. Hence, as I speak about Easter, My message is the same, although I am addressing much more understanding people on Earth. Your wisdom is in the fact that the righteousness in your hearts and your willingness to effect it have grown into larger blessings for the temporal world. The teachings that Jesus gave to you centuries ago are still being taught to new generations who come into their own as time continues to pass. Where are you among them? You are My dear children who have tendered your hearts to the transformation that only the maturity of the Holy Spirit can provide. In this, you are changed into children again, but quite advanced in the knowledge of God and worthy to be called His followers and disciples for this modern period of Christian works. Can you see that your comprehension of His Will is farther advanced than ten years ago? You are growing, advancing, developing, and marching onward to the end of the Earth when the Great Easter of Salvation will be bestowed upon those whose hearts and souls are tendered to Him. I ask you to ponder how your holiness makes Me feel as I see your righteousness take hold! I am the gracious Queen who is overjoyed with gratitude because you are praying and listening well. You are the seasoning of Justice in places where there has been only error and indifference. I come to you on another Easter Sunday to tell you that My Love has never waned from whence I offered My Fiat to the Archangel Gabriel, and neither has Jesus' Passion for your Eternal Redemption. We are both still the same. The seeable signs of spring are part of the revelation of this Sacred Mystery, while your spiritual advancements are a measure of how your understanding of His Love has been procured. If you reflect the affection for God that is living in you now for the rest of your days, your soul will know that Easter cannot die, no matter what the season of the year or the topic of the liturgical celebration. I have indicated to you on many occasions that your heart cannot deceive you into believing anything that it does not feel. When you nurture your heart with the Truth, only the Truth will prevail as your ballast for sustaining and recognizing the influences of every other facet of your being toward your brothers and sisters, and to you and your internal relationship with Heaven that awaits your arrival. This whole prospect rests in your desire to seek the Light of Love, and this is where your heart either convicts you or brings you closer to surrendering to the forces that will eventually take your soul toward Providence everlasting.

My children, your hearts will tell you on the last day whether your souls are worthy of the Divine Mercy that My Son offers. This is why I speak to your heart; it is why you must continue to pray from the heart, and this is also the reason why the heart is the residence of the Holy Spirit. When it comes to converting you to the Truth of Jesus' Word, the Almighty Father has solicited the core of your being, that of the intrinsic nature of your heart, because He created you in Love, and it is your return to that Love that He is seeking. Every person in Creation has been given a spiritual heart with which to sanctify and comprehend, to pray and relate, and to surrender and convert. I have asked every one of My children to concede to the Truth that Jesus places there and become a follower of the charity, hope, and Love that is explicated in the Holy Scriptures. Your essential understanding of the Profession of Faith rests in your acceptance of the Bible. Please know that the mandates and tenets of the New Covenant are enlivened by your compliance with them. My Special son, I have always made it a purpose of My intercession on behalf of the rest of the universe to speak specifically to your heart during My messages, and today I am pleased as pinnacles to do the same because of the new book that you are distributing to humanity. I remind you that I am the Mother of God, and I have advance knowledge of many things. The beauty of this book has taken Me by surprise. Please remember the occasions that ushered its beginning. I hope you understand the power of this work because you will see many things occur as a reaction to what you have said. I will speak to you in the future about the Morning Star books. What do you feel about them at this point? Do you remember how many years expired before Sister Faustina's Diary was distributed? I told you that such would not occur with your Diary; it will be when God deigns the time. I must remind you that everything that takes place for the conversion of humankind requires time for them to open their hearts to the Truth. Whenever I make this statement to My messengers, they immediately pose the question, '...why is it true that anything that is evil seems to propagate overnight?' My response is that evil is ultimately dead and cannot live long in anyone whose heart is being pressed into service for God. It is in the conversion of the lost that real greatness comes. This is the reason for the wait. Yes, it can occur overnight or in the flash of an instant, but mere mortals do not seem to be tendered to such emulation of the Divine perfection of Jesus with any semblance of immediacy. It is an arduous process of growth and development. People are far away from Love! If we can instill the desire for faith in Love in every human heart, the cycle of conversion will be complete. The process of the growth and development of love in the hearts of men begins with the acknowledgment that they are guilty of sins and omissions. Most have not gotten to this point! How can someone change for the better if they do not believe they are in need? For all these reasons, I continue to speak about enlightening them and revealing the Truth of the Gospel in their day, before it is too late. Can you sense the urgency of your manuscripts, and yet the patience required to dispense them? This is an irony and seeming contradiction. You will see many more awkward circumstances before your soul is delivered to Heaven. This is why you must pray and hope for the arrival of the Kingdom of God on Earth. And, this is how you know that My messages are always the same; I have addressed constantly changing circumstances in a rather indistinct world. If this seems like many different extremes, it is because you are able to compare the condition of the Earth with the better one you envision in your heart. Indeed, we are back to the heart again. Next week will bring Divine Mercy Sunday and the Hour of Grace. When you pray to Jesus for the amelioration of these things, He will respond in accordance with the Will of the Father. I will be praying along with you. His Will is His Will, and it is our commission to pray to discern it and ask Him to amend it in accordance with His Divine Love. You are growing in Wisdom, and are expected not to retreat from defeating your fiendish enemies. Can you see the fine line that makes people give up? They look into the skies with the gifts of righteousness in their hands and the power of the Cross in their hearts, asking God why He has forsaken them before a humanity with ulterior motives, allowing their aspirations to feel defunct. I pray for this to never happen to you, and I urge you to carry-on without cowering to your adversaries who try to soil the Grace of your recent ten years' work. Why was the Son of Man crucified on the Cross? Do you remember when God asked Abram to sacrifice his son? Can you see yourselves somewhere in the midst of this process? And, since the end of time is near, you may not know when Jesus might come and say '...enough, your work is finally finished.' Do you see more concisely that the Will of God is being extolled? You must trust and face fear at the same time, become a child and an elder statesman in the same hour, and be reticent and aggressive in one moment, according to the love in your heart. There is always danger before you that you must avoid while walking with valor in that florescent flowerbed. You are becoming a Saint because you understand these things better than when you first knelt to pray with Me today. This is your simultaneous trust and faith. Only by patiently enduring such trials can you teach your friends about Love, about giving their souls to the Cross that has saved them, and about never saying 'no' to whatever sacrifices they are summoned to make. You are a teacher of faith in the Holy Gospel because of the gifts you have given God in return. One of the best is that you are leading His humanity to the shore of the water to drink. If you cannot see the sweetness in this, you will do so before much more time spans the breach between your awareness and the Truth hitting you in the face. You have been so close to your work that you cannot know the shock other people experience. Why is this great gift coming to you? Because you are willing to thread the needle between security and danger, between wiling away the hours and charging the gate, and between praying from the heart and simply thinking about God. You are giving Him the gift of yourself in return for His blessings of life, consolation, genius, devotion, resourcefulness, and joy. You are becoming like Christ Jesus because you have come to the mountains willing to climb, rather than turn away, trying to circumvent them instead. It is on this Easter that you recognize the growth and development that I have seen in you and your brother. This is why today is not just another timely observation of My Son's Resurrection, but your conquest of your former selves. You have not asked God to let the Cup of Sacrifice pass you by because you honor Heaven and humanity. It is in pondering these things that you know why there seems to be such agony in what I ask you to do, which has led to the mystery of the Angels enlightening your lives and the rest of the world around you.

There is an entire volume of greatness in the Most Sacred Heart of My Son that He is about to jettison onto your souls while He hovers overhead. There are millions of blessings that you are continuing to obtain for the rest of humanity because you are 'Love' in ways that you have never before known. The passing of Easter and the suns and moons is more than the growth of your faith, they are the cadence of your compliance with the Will of the Father by means you have yet to comprehend. There are vows and sacred beauties glistening in the twilight of the morning that will soon descend upon humanity because you have come to your feet and said 'yes' in reflection of Me. The hundreds-of-thousands of Hail Mary's and Glory Be's you have said have been the liberation of equally as many sinners' souls who have been delivered from Purgatory into the prolific fullness of Heaven. The prophecies about which I have spoken are coming! However, the ones being brought to humanity now will be recognized by Creation at large, and the millions of sinners who have come back to Divine Love by the strength of your work will be the blooming wreathwork around the Sacred Heart of Jesus. Their voices and the fulfillment of their oaths will ratify, prescribe, and ensure that the prophesies about which you are speaking will come true. Their desire to be perfected in the Blood of the Cross will become the stillness of those who stand and oppose. The Kingdom of God is at hand because this is His Will for the universe He has made. Does the Almighty Father reserve the right to end it as He pleases and lift-up those who are groveling at His feet? The answer is an obvious yes, and He is utilizing the gifts and blessings of lives like yours to hoist them back to dignity and Grace. Hence, prayer and affection are more than just conquering evil and death, they provide the ability and capacity to see why in the end. It is the transformation of disdain into joy and the renewal of lost hearts that inexplicably do not seem to care. It is the release of prisoners from chains and the despondence that has broken them so low to the ground that they cannot muster the happiness to walk freely of their own accord. This, My child, is Easter! It is coming to the front of the class, clearing your throat, and telling the rest of those who thought they were so intelligent what you really saw from those back rows! You could see who was passing their notes to whom, where those noises and kicks came from that the teacher could not see that were mistakenly blamed on you. It is redressing the wrongs that have made the world a miserable place, and lifting Justice itself into the limelight of the Earth in the form of the Cross. You see, more than Jesus was raised from the Sepulcher on Easter 1,968 years ago. It was the elevation of the dignity of men, and your own capacity to know. It is your comprehension of how a group of faithful believers could have been so crushed by grief on a dark Friday afternoon, and yet so elated with jubilation at first light on the Third Day hence. These are the sources and origins of the ironies of God, the causal Truth that leads to the betterment of man in this day, not solely in the Final Judgement of Heaven. How can joy be lost to a human species who has an understanding of this? How can the everlasting Light not be blinding as the sun while the world continues to prepare for the unfurling of the perfection in which it shall be brought to an end? You will find the answers to these questions among the tears that countless people have shed throughout the centuries, My children. And, you can see it in the afterglow of their hearts, in hearing the echoing of those bombs bursting in midair above their hopes and dreams that they lifted in the Name of the Christ who has walked away from death and borne the Truth to the billions who have believed in Him.

My children, My holy and special ones, please never allow anyone from any walk of life to ever take away your Easter joy! Let no sadness or deceit from your friends coax you into surrendering your faith, because everything I am telling you is true. The Light that is shining upon you now is warm to the touch of the Love who is basking inside the Dominion and power that has been given to you. I am humbled that I can come to this place and know that the King in My arms is welcome, that His generous Spirit has a place to rest, and that perfect Salvation can repose His head in peace. Why not make this the best Easter you have ever known, not because of anything I might say or do, but because you are growing to understand the Love who has claimed you for the higher purposes of life? You are given to the Divinity of Paradise because it is there where you will eventually come. No matter what happens on the streets where you live, regardless of the suffering around the globe, it is all coming to a close because you care enough to know Love, to become the followers of the Messianic God, and to walk with Him as He has conquered the grave. When you rise in the morning, it will not be quite the same day, but you will be the equality of Love in the prayers you recite. Your souls will be of the same essence of Truth; your hearts will be much more aware; your desire to succeed will be even more enhanced, and your opportunities to do good will be nearer at hand. You have always known and remembered that God requires your conviction, and this is what He will demand from you as you pass from this land into the ended ages. When you look into the deep blue eyes of the Genius who has saved you, it is then that every one of these days will finally make sense. You will understand every word I have spoken with perfect distinction, and recognize how you responded in obedience to God's every design. I give you My promise that you will be pleased for many reasons aright. I have been teaching you because this is what I was asked to do from the Cross. Indeed, I would have done it even so. I urge you to continue to call upon the Saints and Angels for their help, attend the Holy Sacrifice of the Mass everyday, and remember the goodness you have offered in the process of amending the world. These are the real signs of the success of Easter and the reasons you observe it with joy. My Special son, I ask you to be very cautious and bold at the same time, and I will help you along the way. I have come because you are willing to pray, but mostly because I love you in ways that you cannot fully comprehend. Thank you for celebrating Easter with such faith!"

Sunday, April 22, 2001
Feast of The Divine Mercy
3:17 p.m.

"My dear little children, the real and tangible aspects of this Holy Feast are engulfed by the faith in which you have approached it because Jesus will bestow His forgiveness upon those who beseech His Divine Mercy from the depths of their hearts. This is a Grace that lives beyond all others in that lasting Absolution is the essential purpose of the Blood of the Cross. Without the Son of Man having shed His Blood on Good Friday, there would have been no pardon for the sins of men. Therefore, today is not only the observance of your faith in being prepared for the Glory of Heaven, it is your unabridged anticipation of being taken there. Please believe that your love for God warrants this disposition. Never allow any hint of doubt to enter your minds to the otherwise. I have come to pray with you because I realize the significance of this special time which was foretold by Sister Faustina seventy years ago. When we pray for the erasure of all that is ill in the world, My Son will make it true. Whatever you seek from Him not only today, but forever in accordance with the Truth you acknowledge in the Sacred Scriptures, please remember that it shall be yours, regardless of what the element of time may tempt you to believe. Children, the Divine Mercy has been preserved not only for those who accept Jesus with their entire soul, heart and mind, but also for you to petition for sinners who have not yet internalized their Salvation in Him. This is a particular day on which you can elevate those who do not know that their own penitence is necessary for the conversion of their souls to the Cross. While it may seem nearly impossible for the most wretched among you to fall to their knees in confession, they will do so at the reciting of your prayers. You need not fear your enemies who have not been exposed to Christianity; it is those who have already come to know Jesus and have rejected Him that you should ask God to dispense His influx upon, whether by miraculous manifestation, spiritual enlightenment, or clear and simple chastisement. Whatever it takes to resuscitate lost souls from the permanence of death is acceptable in His sight because He knows that the hour is near when Jesus shall return to take His people home. Remember that for the sake of His Sorrowful Passion, He will bestow Mercy upon your souls, and that of the whole world. This is a Divine Truth about the Providence of God that cannot be perverted. When you proffer your thanksgiving prayers in the future, remember to include your gratitude for this one. My little ones, of each hundred people who live on the globe, only five reside in America. And yet, this same percentage of five consumes over one-third of the resources of the Earth; they are committing horrid offenses against Nature that are unparalleled by any other country, and are murdering more children in the womb than any other republic in the league of nations. What does this say about the need for the transformation of the Americas to the Divine Mercy of My Son?

  I mention these things because I desire for you to pray for the souls who are responsible for such atrocities in an urgent way. They are apt to reject their own submission at the end of time if they are unaware of the Dominion of Christ Jesus beforehand. They must come with haste to the Blood of the Lamb to be cleansed and renewed in thought, spirit, and hope. As you pray the Sacred Mysteries of the Holy Rosary on this Feast, please remember that the enemies of righteousness are abundant among you, and they need your daily petitions on their behalf. There is nothing benign about their moral turpitude or the deceitful conduct they must shed. They live in error and contempt, and must be washed and purified. Please remember what I told you about how burned flesh must be scrubbed free of dead tissues. There is no need for Heaven to apologize for these truthful circumstances because under the Gospel of Jesus, this is the way humanity is converted. No one knows this better than the Saints. I also plead with you to be mindful of the souls suffering in Purgatory when you call upon the Divine Mercy of My Son. There are celebrations, cenacles, prayer groups, and public recitations all around the globe today for this noble cause. The Miserere is being said in multiple tongues as the faithful beseech Jesus to lend them an ear of forgiveness, and I assure you with all the trust in My Immaculate Heart that it shall be done. These are the promises of God for the modern-day world, and I offer you the honor of His

Kingdom that it will come to pass. My Special son, I am also particularly pleased that you have chosen to memorialize the kind souls who have been so good to you over the past ten years, as well as those who have impugned your work. Is it not possible on this High Feast Day for you to know the great power that you continue to bear toward the conversion of the Earth? Do you wish to continue this majestic procession so everyone can know their Savior? Are you spiritually and physically prepared? I have told you that your 'yes' from a decade ago would be a gift to humanity, and this is what is happening. I could have played no part without your agreeing to do all the work, make the sacrifices, face the objections, and feel so alone at times. It is true that Christians look with pity upon those who do not know the Lord, the sinners who feel it necessary to shun the sacred history of the Church that has led so many into Paradise. Somewhere among the shards of their despair and the shifting ages, they must find new hope. I only ask that My children never appease the appalling beast of secular humanism or offer encouragement to their unimaginable error."

Sunday, April 29, 2001
1:42 p.m.

Go Forth, All Ye Valiant Conquerors!

"Love, little children, is the reason for every hour and the Eternity you seek through the Cross of My Son! When you live in Love, believe for the sake of Love, and tender your hearts to God in Love, you are one in Him. Today, I come in the knowledge that you have given your lives and plans so that the entire world may be converted to Christianity. I proceed as a consecrated Mother because so many are responding to My call for sacrificial prayer and holiness. The ages that cleft for you are filled with the divinity of your making because you are being perfected in the Holy Gospel. Imagine what the centuries have wrought because millions before you were equally as blessed! Ponder how the errors of the Earth have been mitigated because so many followers of Jesus have said 'yes' to the self-denial that has made them holy and good. It is for this that I appear during the midst of your prayers, because I know that you care for all souls who have yet to know Salvation in the Redeemer you have claimed! My Special little son, I have deigned today to be one with you in the mainstream of joy because I hold you dearly within My Immaculate Heart, and I know you are Mine. How multiple are the hours when I greet the world knowing that it has been enhanced by your prayers and gifts. There is nothing that cannot be achieved when you beseech the Almighty Father because, like Me, He is in love with your generous heart. Therefore, I have come to be with you and ask you to persevere in remaining with Me in the

Wisdom that yields the conversion of the souls of exiled men. As we pray together, I hope you never forget that I love you beyond all imagining. My Love has been touched by the perfection of the Divine essence of God streaming from your heart. I cannot overstate the trust we share because of the expansion of your perceptive greatness before the Cross, in the Cross, and by the Cross. You offer a faith of such marvelous magnitude that there are no words to describe it. Your Mother is one with you in righteousness. My messages extol succinct images of peace, challenge, transition, and power. You should collect your thoughts and understand what goodness you have bestowed upon humanity. There is a joy in My Immaculate Heart that rivals the jubilation of Jesus' rising from the Tomb. Do you see that you have given hope to humanity, that I wish to urge every soul to nurture a refreshed sense of courage in their hearts? All of this is because you wish for Me to be a happy Mother. You have given Me much more than a pretty bouquet of flowers, you have offered Me an entire Earth in bloom. Let Me assure you that My response will be proportionate and massive. It is as though there are no barriers to impede our progress. This is among the auspicious surprises that God has given Me because of the prayers and novenas of My children. Tens-of-thousands have asked that My Immaculate Heart be consoled after the Feast of the Divine Mercy, and you have been the answer to their prayers! You have been My source of consolation, Love, peace, and comfort! I bid you to witness carefully what this Mother will do in response to your faith. I need not pose the rhetorical question of how I can repay your kindnesses because I have the authority to answer it. Watch and see what I do. I have been like a Mother sitting in a chair with My hands folded in My lap when one of My beautiful children approached and surprised Me with a gift of humble love. This is what you have done. I have seen your humility and Divine determination for the Lord, your Savior, and for your brothers and sisters who will be coming home in fruition of your service. Can you imagine My joy as I witness your faith in Jesus emanating with such intensity? I have not seen symbolic work, I have observed your Christological genius reshaping Creation. This, My Special son, is what I have been trying to evoke from every Christian on Earth. Thank you for being one of only a few seers to unconditionally say 'yes' to Me. I assure you that you will recognize the signs and miracles to come. I wish to tell you that the world is ongoing in love because the Holy Spirit is alive and well through every borough and precinct, in every city and hamlet, in all hearts who are given to God. There are thousands who are conceding that you have been telling the Truth for over ten years. Do you recall when I asked Bernadette to soil her face with moistened earth? Her obedience prophesied that many would be converted to the Sacred Heart of My Son by the humility she displayed. Such is the same fruit which has been born from your messages. I assure you that from this day forward, your experiences will have greater meaning, magnitude, authority, and urgency. You have been speaking openly with the

Mother of God since February 22, 1991. This gift is manifested by the intensity of your love. You offer it freely; you have allowed Christ Jesus to come closer to you, and we are unified in My Immaculate Heart. Therefore, be of joyful spirit in realizing that your faith has been the restoration of many souls into Grace. I ask only that you be humbled and willing to know that you are a Valiant Warrior for the Messiah of Almighty God. Thank you for having responded to My call. There is a timeless capacity in Creation called the intrinsic Nature of Divine Love. You have reached its epicenter because of the faith you have given to Jesus. Can you sense that you are only a mere micro-instant from touching the Face of Heaven? When your service on Earth has ended, you will be allowed passage into this Glory to the conveyance of untold numbers of Saints with streamers falling from the skies and tears rolling down the cheeks of those to whom you have been so faithful. You will love living in Heaven, and you are closer to it now. As you are aware, God laid a heavy burden on Padre Pio that he carried for 50 years. Do you recall the date when he received the Sacred Stigmata? On your birthday, and for good reason. Can you see how God's Divine Plan of Redemption unfolds in supernaturally precedent ways? Your vision is clear because you have tendered your heart to Him. Should you continue offering your loyalties to Me, you will witness the Providence of human Salvation unfold before your eyes. Hence, My message is one of thanksgiving. Please commit this day to memory for the remainder of your years because I will forever hold it dearly inside My Immaculate Heart. For the month of May, My messages will concentrate upon My gratitude for you rather than ecclesial lessons because I wish it to be the celebration of the far corners of the Earth dedicated to Me. My lessons will resume in June, the month given to the Most Sacred Heart of My Son. My spiritual easement to the broken hearts of suffering humanity is strengthened by the resolve of your faith."

Sunday, May 6, 2001
2:53 p.m.

"Welcome to the bastion of My Immaculate Heart. My Special one, I know that you live prayerfully filled with holiness to invoke My intercession before the Throne of God, and I appreciate your devotion to the Redemption of humankind. There is intense visionary prescience in people who receive the Holy Spirit. When your comrades boast of fond imaginings and unlikely feats, ask them to what they attribute their newfound expertise, and from what fate and immutable source is their sudden gift of prophecy procured. What could possibly be the genesis of their inexplicable empowerment? There can be no other way to describe it than the preeminent Love of God. How forever grateful I am that their love for Him transcends all parlours of Creation. We proceed through Heaven's Virtue and Divine Origin by continuing to speak about the future of humanity, more blessed than when you began your prayers, and increasingly more perfect than before you fully knew My Immaculate Heart. Today, I would like to speak about how fractured and particalized is the condition of the Earth to be reunited under the Cross, so we must pray and labor for stronger cohesion among the nations. It is important for everyone to approach the Cross with reciprocal love, and it is imperative for every heart to know that there is a renewed sense of decency that must be afforded. This is why the Holy Father in Rome, the Vicar of Christ, is traveling the continents issuing apologies for his flocks and predecessors who are no longer enduring their mortal years. Indeed, through his pontifical sanctity and pastoral bequests, he is asking for forgiveness from anyone whom the Roman Catholic Church has offended through history so no soul will bear grudge against it. The Greek Orthodox Church and other religions must acknowledge his apologies and carry-on in unity for God as one humanity. The Holy Spirit will unite all peoples through the humility of the Pope and the Chair of Saint Peter if others will tender their hearts. Yes, you see that he is likewise calling on the Muslim community to offer the sacred alliance of Christianity in their midst. Let us pray for his success! I have told you about the fractured nature of the world on many occasions, but never before has My call for unity been so strong. Why? Because the hours are exhausting while the Earth awaits the coming of your Savior. My son, My little Special one, there have been countless prayers that have been lifted for the sake of unity of peoples, and this is what mutual pardon is about. No Pontiff has traveled to so many places; no other has sought the forgiveness of so many, and none has understood the power of absolution better than Pope John Paul II. Yes, as you have appropriately said many times before, the world will not realize whom has been in their midst until his patriarchal mission has been completed. It is no coincidence that his Papacy has spanned so many years with so many sacrificial hours of goodness, peace, and Grace. As you continue praying for humanity, remember that Pope John Paul II is one of the greatest blessings that God ever bestowed upon the Earth. And, after lifting those prayers, place his humble service in the proper perspective within the context of the presence of Heaven through all the Saints, and move onward. The passing of this Pope portends the nigh end of the world, and it is one of the last passages of mortality that will unfold. God alone is the determiner of these things because He is the Master of time. I tell you this so you will persevere even as your own life comes to a conclusion. The Earth is growing older by the moment, while the hearts of its citizens are becoming a great deal more tender and young, like those little children whom Jesus bids you to imitate. Henceforth, the particalized nature of humanity is being alleviated by the Divine Love inside your hearts and through the foreboding gathering prayers that you peacefully offer in the shadow of the Holy Cross.

I am pleased that you have noticed a deeper presence of Jesus' power and revelation since we last spoke. This is the result of your love and devotion for your Mother. Jesus desires you to conceal yourself inside My Immaculate Heart when you seek a respite from the throes of the world. Therein, you will also be carefully caressed in His Most Sacred Heart, so benign in nature and the strength you need to endure in faith. We continue beyond the horrors that remain in the paths of so many errant lives; we lift our petitions to enlighten them, and to console and heal those who are offended and violated, and to grant Wisdom to everyone who has yet to learn of the genius of God. We seek not to destroy, but to gently admonish and teach; and to love, bless, purify, and convert. These urgent benisons are the purpose of the charity of the love that God wishes to procure from those He has created. The essential beauty of the piety by which you live is the same as it was in 1991, and you are still relating it perfectly. You understand what hundreds-of-millions are only now becoming aware, that the Love of My Immaculate Heart is the transformation of their temporal nature into the spiritual awareness that will take them to their Redemption in the Sacrifice of My Son. My Special one, I said many years ago that there can be no true conversion without sustaining your own suffering imposed by those opposing you. This prefigured office is not only yours to take, but theirs to freely grant themselves. Why such an apparent redoubling of discomfiture? Because all human hearts are united in the Passion, Death, and Resurrection of Jesus. When everyone suffers together, even at the hands of each other, perfect unity will be achieved. All the apologies in Creation are insufficient if those to whom they are offered do not amend their lives to effect the cohesion of humanity. As I state, at least the Catholic Church is doing its part through its Supreme Pontiff to make this unity flourish. He appears to be the only religious figure who is making this effort around the globe. This is because he knows the power of redemption over the other clergy since he is the Vicar of the Savior of the whole of humanity, and he is aware of his role. As he has said in the silence of his heart, 'where else shall humanity turn for the guidance and Wisdom to know their Salvation unless I lead them there?' My son, will you remember everything I have said and tell your brothers and sisters? As in the past, you and your brother have the capacity to write it down once with pencil and paper. I am grateful that you have come to Me for your knowledge of Heaven, and I am appreciative that you allow Me to share your life. Your long-suffering love for the Lord has been the granting of His miraculous gifts. It is your commitment that He is rewarding because He knows it to be a fruit of your faith."

Sunday, May 13, 2001
Mother's Day
2:13 p.m.

"My little children, thank you for the everlasting love that you have made My gift this Mother's Day. Let us share the Peace that is ours by the presence of God in our hearts. This is the meaning of your lives and the eternal design by which God has wrought your liberation from the mortal Earth into the berth of Salvation in His arms. We celebrate today because this is the destiny you have chosen as My children. Can you see the pristine royalty that has become yours in the Sacred Heart of My Son, that His purposes supercede the existence you share across the prairies and milestones of the globe? You are in more than a state of preparation for the jubilation of Heaven, your souls have begun experiencing it now. This is why your trust is well placed in the Father of Love. Your search for life's meaning is culminated in the Cross, and your souls are already aware that they have arrived at the doorstep of canonization. I pray with you not only for the conversion of the lost, but in thanksgiving for your having joined Myself and the Hosts of Heaven as practitioners of peace who belong to Christ Jesus, to have and to hold, never worrying about the darkness of death. My Special son, the Lord is thorough in His speech, and for the most part leaves hyperbole to forensic titans, but I do not speak in abstraction when I say that the barrage of error that is claiming so many innocent lives worldwide is a precursor to the horror of Armageddon. You live in the company of war-making men who are more concerned about lending earshot than maintaining foresight. Rather than custodians of Nature and propriety, they have become militants, scavengers, and pirates stirring the Earth's cauldron of contemptuousness and deceit. Most Americans lead lives of managed turmoil in a ribald culture of antisocial vulgarity and perverse innuendo. Make no mistake; their advancing age is no presumption of wisdom. Please tell your neighbors near and far that the Mother of God told you today that the moral fabric of the United States lay in shreds on a ground that is tattered by their indifference toward God's spiritual Truth. They are guilty of vast wrongdoings ranging from catastrophic indiscretion to capers and misdemeanors, and it all represents an undue taxation on the collective human spirit. Coping with this has become the history of your lives; and regardless of what men in black robes say, only the Good Lord affords you the presumption of innocence. However, you refuse to prescribe to such things, and are sent as Jesus' clarion to humanity, belling the arrival of a new age of reckoning. There are no expressions to describe the warmth in My Immaculate Heart for the trust you tender God's supernal Kingdom. His appreciation is explicated through these messages and My intercession on behalf of humanity at His Throne. While the latter is of crucial importance in the spiritual refinement of men, the former is My wholesome gratitude for your devotion, service, humility, and movement all the way from the foundation of the world to My Glorious Coronation. As the ages continue to toll, I remain confident that the Plan of God is clear to you, that He is utilizing your life with greater influence over the enlightenment of humanity about the Blood of Jesus on the Cross, how the suffering poor are a factor in the reconciliation between the sinful nature of man and the Divine perfection of Jesus, and how these intersect during the Holy Sacrifice of the Mass. Can you discern the simplicity of this as the days come and go? And yet, it stands before Creation as the awesome wonder that has moved the mystical conscience of humankind to action. God hears your prayers for His people, and He responds accordingly. I have promised that many things would occur more rapidly than before, and you see that they are. How could you turn to one of your brothers or sisters after this and not answer their questions with the swiftness of the Holy Spirit in your heart to reaffirm that the Holy Gospel is sufficed to the syllable? Every day that passes fosters the effecting of the promises that are still holding firm, those I made to you ten years ago. You are seeing the purpose in My first messages during which I had yet to begin speaking in sentences. It was you who were developing through your growing interaction with Heaven to the dialogue we are conducting now. Why? Because you have continued to say 'yes' to every word that God asked Me to convey. This is profoundly important for you to understand because you are one among only few in human history who have remained at My side. The rest have meandered away in disinterest, or grown impatient, or chose not to offer their whole hearts because the sacrifices to which they were called were repugnant in their sight.

But, not you! You have never yielded your determination to the boggling doubt of the netherworld, and are therefore gaining your communicative works as a benediction for the rest of humanity to prove it. I know that your future will never be the same as the life you led prior to 1989 because you have not only been captured by My Immaculate Heart, you have relocated the essence of your being there, and you are taking a large portion of contemporary humanity with you. You have not done this alone. Jesus has been your source of Wisdom and strength, and your human will has been the crux of reasoning that has made your spiritual judgements loyal to His power and the deliverance of lost souls to His Grace. Your prayers continue to amass a treasury in the heights of Paradise. Please do not dismay at the things you see in daily life that seem to depress your heart. Not one of them can distract you. As I have said, I wish to devote these messages to remind you how you are loved and the ways you are altering the knowledge of God that is held by the public around the globe. It is no coincidence that your brother was greeted by the US Congressional Representative last Thursday while you were in Chicago. I will allow you to proceed living with the happiness of what gifts Jesus will dispense because you help Him remember why He was so egregiously Crucified on the Calvarian Cross. This is the Father's joy even more than yours. The prayers that we are reciting together are the peace and healing for many who still suffer the throes of sickness, despondence, and poverty. There is a keen new enlightenment occurring in this American nation because you have consecrated every day to Me. I am gaining new warriors in the fight against evil because of your love. Every soul who has been given the breath of life will see this someday; and how will you be able to greet them all? Eternity will afford the timelessness to do so. Your days have garnered the sweetness of the peace in which Jesus was born in Bethlehem. Your soul is obedient to the Almighty Father, and especially to Me; and this is the message that has been delivered to the world. My words have been authenticated in your lifetime. I know that you wholeheartedly trust what God does and effects in the matter of mere instants. Thanks to your continuing prayers and good wishes, and especially the love you are wielding by the commodity of your universal acceptance of the Angels' advice, everything is unfolding according to the desires of your heart. I am saying that you are suppling lost sinners whose lives would otherwise have the rigidity of ancient stones. They have never pondered Christian apologetics as ground-swelling and heart-rending as the volumes you have written. And, many are seeing for the first time what you have known for the past ten years. This comports with the miraculous Truth because you have given your life to Heaven through the Mother to whom you were bequeathed on Good Friday."

I recently was sitting on the front porch with Timothy in the middle of the afternoon watching the luxurious tour buses pass which were filled with passengers who had traveled from all parts of the country to visit the tomb of the esteemed late President Abraham Lincoln. As they proceeded one after another, I thought what an opportunity it was to share Our Lady's messages with them. I did not specifically know how to accomplish this, so I pocketed it in my memory as just a holy intention, and left it at that. My brother and I went to the kitchen to get something to drink, and when we returned to the porch, one of the tour buses had stopped for no apparent reason directly in front of the house. All the high school students with their chaperones were walking toward it from a Lincoln souvenir shop where they had earlier been dropped-off about a block away. I knew Our Lady had heard my wish, so I rushed into the house and grabbed a couple books, thinking the students might share them while they traveled. As one young lady passed the porch, I told her that I was an author, and that I was offering a book if she desired to have one. She kindly accepted and thanked me, then asked me to autograph it for her. She boarded the vehicle as I returned to the porch. Suddenly, dozens more students began filing off the bus and running across the yard onto my porch, asking if they too could have copies. It was like putting a match to gasoline. I dispensed nearly a hundred copies, all needing signed, of course. The children were kind and grateful. It was a very pleasant exchange with people I may never see again until we are in Heaven. After they drove away, I sat in contented wonderment as to how many of them were about to have their vision completely transformed by the Grace of our Blessed Mother in the same way She awestruck me almost a dozen years ago. These truly are some of the most amazing days to be alive.

Saturday, May 19, 2001
7:19 p.m.

"We arrive at the hour when Heaven desires your presence again through the venue of prayer and the dedication of your souls to My Immaculate Heart. This is your endowment of messages from your Mother, from the Seat of Wisdom; and your holiness will be profoundly enhanced by your sacred obedience to My words. Thank you, My children. Thank you! Can you know the Divinity of Jesus as you live today? Of course you can! My pretty lambs, it is in your participation in the higher graces that allows you to transcend the morbidity of the years. It is your faith and petitions from the heart that bring you to the precipice over which you can see the grand and noble wholesomeness that has become the hallmark of your lives on Earth. No mother has ever been more in love with her children than that which I hold for all who were adopted by Me. While My intercession has played a role in the conversion of humanity, the prayers of the faithful have brought it to pass. I remain here because I have seen the fruits of our prayers, and because My Son is glorified by the solicitations that are fashioned by His elect. Please never forget that it is toward the enlightenment and perfection of humankind that My intercession takes form. My Special son, today I have hovered beneath the roof of your humble abode seeking the virtue of your allegiance to Jesus. While I know that it is as immeasurable as His to you, I realize that you will hold nothing back in giving yourself to Him on behalf of the lost. This has been a standing gift that you have offered Him for the whole duration of your adult life. And, thanks to your loyalty to your brother kneeling faithfully at your side, we are succeeding in the presence of the Angels to manifest the Will of the Father. Always remember the Biblical passage that says, 'As the Earth brings forth the plants, and a garden makes its growth spring up, so will the Lord God make Justice and praise spring up before all the nations.' *(Our Lady stated a passage from Isaiah, 61:11)* I will tell you something today that will help you understand a great deal more about the Mercy and kindnesses of Jesus. I wish to refer to the little one who visited you today. Here is a child who has been abandoned since he was a boy, left to roam in loneliness and fear when he needed his mother's love the most. As you can see, he was cast aside to fend for himself, and was torn apart inside and physically abused. He was given no spiritual direction, and not even a semblance of affection from his family and peers. This is a soul who has suffered the darkest torments of human life. He has been spiritually lambasted by the gross atrocities of his exile. I mention his presence because he is one of many hundreds-of-thousands who are in the same condition. If you look at the calamities that have afflicted many areas of the globe, you will see people who have been victimized at the hands of those who hate them. And, what is their reaction? They are confused because they cannot find anything to warrant such loathing, aversion, and abandonment. They convince themselves that if they are going to be despised for no reason, then they will give humanity reason to detest them. They effectively self-fulfill the fate that they fear the most and have tried to overcome since their early years. Does this make them children to whom God will not respond when they call His Holy Name? The Lord will answer them because He has borne the injustices of being rejected, discarded, punished, abused, bludgeoned, and laid in the Tomb.

    My Special son, I have shed copious tears for these broken children and the countless more who endure such neglect. It is providentially imperative for them to embrace the comfort of Jesus. There, they will find healing and a fuller future. Once they hear the Good News of the restoration of their dignity in His Most Sacred Heart, they will never recede to the bitterness that confounded them again. Sadly, most of them may never reveal this healing on the exterior because their memory still clings to their deprivations. But, their souls will always remember the rejuvenation they inherit through the Holy Spirit upon seeing Jesus' Face. I pray that they accept this peace even sooner so they can become messengers of the Gospel in their time. The eminence of peace is an ocean that runs throughout every land. Yes, it is only a matter of everyone taking to the edge of the water, and they will see its crest. This is the hope that many generations before have lived, those who were persecuted because of their faith in Jesus or the color of their skin. This is a time of contemplation for your Bishop and many thousands who are seeing your work the first time. If you look upon it yourself sometimes, you will perceive the depths of its beauty. You will enlist the moving of your heart all over again. I have deigned to pray with you today because you are an intrinsic portion of My Love for God and humankind. You are the faithfulness that I have sought on the Earth for 2,000 years. I hope that you will finally understand that I cannot succeed in My commission to convert humanity to the Cross of My Son without the fullness of your participation. I have no doubt that you will continue to be My obedient child, all the way past the moment when you come to Heaven. I have given you many parables about the spiritual cohesion between Heaven and Earth. I have also recently noticed that you are enjoying calling them to mind when you are speaking to other people in public. This is precisely what I wished for you to do. I also remind you today not to discard or misplace the pictures that you sketched for your Diary. These will be a valuable asset in teaching the world about the life of Jesus and the foretelling signature of His precious Love as His Will unfolds. I have not given you any thought or image that you will not employ. The universe is growing older by the hour, and yours is the Wisdom that many will seek before the Plan of God completes its course. It is striking to see so many unsuspecting people pick up your second book and wonder what could possibly have been the motivation for someone writing it. You know inside that the Lord is your purpose, and the conversion of your lost brothers and sisters to the Blood of Salvation is the goal you are seeking. Thank you, My child! Thank you for not surrendering. You differ from many others in that you implement My suggestions immediately upon hearing them. Some of My messengers are growing pale in their faith. It is as though the urgency to be holy has departed their hearts because they are having to wait-out the Will of the Father to cultivate the Earth through the element of time. I have asked them over and again to be more patient, as I have likewise summoned you. While you have complied, it has been difficult for them. Can you tell your Mother what keeps your faithfulness intact? My little one, you are making Jesus weep in thanksgiving for the value of your faith. Yes, Jesus is holy, patient, kind, persistent, consistent, merciful, and filled with Peace. These are the things He has instilled in you. Can you see that you are not the person whom you might have been if you would not have said 'yes' a decade ago?

God is the genius who birthed the children of your parents of five little girls and a son, so there would be one completely like Jesus to live amongst them and in their midst. You are that Special one! And, the world is more holy because of your abounding work, your acceptance, your compliance, and the genuine nature of your love for the Creation that God has blessed. There is no other nation in the world where your service has been so required. Indeed, you are not a product of your country, your countrymen are becoming a fruit of your love for their God! The slowness of this process is a testament to the patience of the Lord who has given us life. We seek to procure the best of all aspects in the souls for whom we pray, and God does the rest by the power of His Dominion. There are no barriers to remaking the Earth like Heaven because the Paschal Mystery of Easter has brought miracles to the world. Can you not see that your life is a product of Jesus having been raised from the dead? My Special son, this is more than the valuable time that you are investing for the prospering of Christ. These are the ages when you are one in Him and alongside Him to cover the vast acreage of the Americas with the cloak of His Grace. You are a believer and a doer, a servant and a prayer. I do not say these things to make you feel good about yourself, I tell you because it is the essence of Truth. Saint Paul was standing in your shoes many centuries ago as confident as you are now as to what is ongoing around you in the Kingdom of God. This is not haughtiness or a showing of pride, this is the Truth for which you have lived and thousands of others have already died. I come to speak to you to lift your heart into the Heavens with Mine, and to tell you that your life is an example in Eternal Good! You could not have gotten there without My Divine intercession and the Love of Jesus. But, the fact remains that you have listened and learned, and you believed and reacted. This is leaps and bounds beyond what I have been able to encourage others to do. There are innumerable millions who have questioned the timing of God. In the 21st century of communication and the readiness of the news, what would have happened if the Lord had postponed the Fatima miracle of the sun until now to reveal? I hope no one assumes that it will not happen again! I assure you that the miracles you are seeking will occur, but the Almighty Father is supplying plentiful time for the intentions of our prayers to transpire. When you read and hear about other religions on Earth, how does it make you feel? I have given you messages from ten years ago that affirm that most of them have never really been told. As soon as their flocks turn their lives over to Me, the Immaculate Mother of Jesus, there will be no opposing factions to the Roman Catholic Church. This, My son, is why the work you are accomplishing is so gravely important. And, whether you can see it or not, your efforts are succeeding one soul at a time. It is also why we pray together everyday, and why I have chosen to speak to you and your brother at least once a week. My trust in your faith tells Me that you are pleased by things as they are. You will feel ever more blessed once you have seen your third book that you are penning with the power of God. I urge you to remember to live safely as the future greets you at each passing dawn. Thank you for the depth of your prayers!"

Sunday, May 27, 2001
10:26 a.m.

"These are the endearing hours that sustain My hopes in the conversion of humanity because you are My holy children praying for it to come true. Yes, we live a lovingness that has no end, a trust that is of the Divine Nature of God, and a direction of good fortune toward those who have little to claim for themselves. Please remember that while the Feast of the Ascension is celebrated, your hearts must be aloft in the Holy Spirit, lest you fail to comprehend the reason why the power of Love is so piously revered. The Heavens are pouring-forth the Grace of righteousness so much that the Earth is flooded by the Omnipotent Light of the Justice of Providence. Can you see and hear the jubilation of the Ascension of Jesus to the Right Hand of the Father through the caroling of the Angels in your midst? Your lives are paralleling this beauty because you have given them to the Blood of the Cross. You might wish to know when all the words will be said that accurately describe the Godly blessings you are receiving. There is no stopping them because your hearts will always be able to generate another parable about the prudence that has taken your spirits to Jesus. Yes, Jesus is the Word, and He is without dimension, weight, or measure. My Special little son, I am pleased to greet you on this Feast because I know that you are obedient to My intentions and responsive to the call of My Immaculate Heart. Yes, it is true that I come to you in sorrow today, not only because of the things I see, but in the missing acts of holiness that I do not see. I am the Mother who can set the world aright in Justice and Peace if your brothers and sisters will listen to Me.

God has given Me this power because it is a reflection of His Love for Creation. Let Me be more concise. When My Little Child from the Manger turns to Me and says that He wishes to play with you in the meadows of Paradise someday, I take it seriously. I will make sure that you and Jesus stand in the rays of sunlight in the Glory of Heaven, and there is nothing anyone can do to stop it. Can you see how important it is for our work to succeed? You are an extremely charitable person who loves God more than you can ever describe. This is why I am helping you tell Him on your behalf. God adores you, He needs you, He cherishes you, and He implores you to never forget that His Love is greater than anything that might try to harm you, or cause a hope to slip from your memory that would comfort you, or drudge any mood that imprisons your spirit of relief. And, the obvious way to make lost souls come to such a comprehension of God is by their union with the Cross of suffering that has Redeemed them. Only by sharing in the Crucifixion can a human soul be freed and spared from the bonds of hatred, callousness, fear, and despair. All antagonism and arrogance are destroyed by the participation of the human soul in the Passion of Jesus. This is why you are so happy today; it is why you are not offended when I speak to you about being more understanding. The problem is that you are attempting to make an overwhelmingly lost humanity turn to righteousness overnight, when the Savior whom you love has been waiting for 2,000 years.

Even in times when I teach about Truth by speaking to humankind's subtle weaknesses, I remain the gentle Mother of the Nativity, especially when I am required to reprimand My earthbound children. Conversely, secular pagans expect you to submit to some form of blood punishment before they finally discover that you have done nothing wrong. The burden of the struggle for common decency seems to be prevalent these days. This is the effect of a humanity that knows only to fight for more wealth and to destroy their neighbors' dignity in the process. This is your capitalist nation functioning normally. My little child, do you see that you and your brother are together not only to assist humanity to learn about the Holy Gospel, but to confront secularism as well? There is no other time in either of your lives when your companionship and cohesion has been more important. You are working at the fulcrum of your spiritual mission, not the end. And, you have the proper authority to rebuke anyone who acts obstinately against other people. Thank you for observing the Ascension of Jesus with such a prayerful tone. Next week, we shall celebrate the birthday of the Catholic Church. The Feast of Pentecost is your reminder that the Holy Spirit is alive in your humble heart. This is why you are weeping tears of joy with Me today. Thank you very much for your prayers!"

Sunday, June 3, 2001
The Feast of Pentecost
4:30 p.m.

"May the Peace and joy of the Holy Spirit be with you always! These, dear children, are the words that have blossomed your faith into Eternity. The Earth has finally awakened from its morbid coma! I celebrate with you this high Feast of the birth of the Mother Church. This is a validating and advantageous time for you to be one with Jesus as His chosen loves because His Divine Mercy is at its fullest. I protect you as the Mediatrix in whom you place your trust to usher the Truth of Jesus into a fallacious world. In Him, you are united with the Almighty Father as the citizens of Heaven that you are about to claim. Please invest your well-guided anticipation in the ages of Glory you will inherit, and remember this Holy Day as one that helped you to be elevated into the arms of the Highest Love. My children, we have been praying together for what seems to be a long time for you, but only a brief interval for the likes of the Saints who are now beginning to intercede for you the strongest in your lives. I have told you that you are living toward the Holy Cross, not moving away from the Crucifixion as though it were fixed inside the element of time. This is your era of spiritual purification and the strengthening of your resolve so that you can partake of the Light of Day without squinting in fear from what your Judgement before Everlasting Truth will bring. When that time arrives, you will see that your mortality has been much as it was meant to be, that there have been signs on the pathway of existence to guide you everyday. There have been untold signal graces too, which have augmented your faith and given you increased courage to forge onward with assurance. None of your labors have been in vain because every prayer you have lifted has changed Creation for the better for someone, somewhere, and at some point in the ongoing struggles of humanity. I expect that you will not be surprised to see these things soon, and that you will finally realize that your death is the extension of your lives in Jesus. My Special son, there have been hundreds and thousands of graces that have kept your hopes intact. Your life with your brother has been saturated with joy because you have seen fit to complement the Truth living in your hearts. The eclipses that have bound you together are many. The timing of Jesus to keep you close has been of an accord that no human could possibly conceive. Now, you have been given an option for a title and subtitle for your next book. 'When Legends Rise Again' is a suggested name, but not one you are mandated to use. It speaks not only of the innumerable souls who have evolved to become great Saints, but of the heroism that lives in everyone today, and the countless acts of goodness that can be offered. It is a recollection of the missed opportunities that would have been clear signs to the Earth of God's miracles in the universe. If you wish, the Dominion Angels will help you write a supernatural manuscript that will define the world as it should be, leaving only tears of joy and hope in its wake. As you know, it is God's Love for you and His desire to transform humanity into piety that makes this possible. The fact that I am speaking to you is in itself a miraculous fruit of the Feast of Pentecost. Today, I am praying with you for the end of abortion, for peace the world over, especially in the Middle East, for the end of famine and disease, for the poor souls suffering in Purgatory, and for all other personal and private intentions that My children are lifting across the hemispheres. The Almighty Father is the Sacred King whom He has always been, and He understands the plight of His modern people as well as He did in the beginning. Your age is no different in this respect. He heaps fond affection upon you and your brother in this place because you not only pray for yourselves, but also that your success will harvest the conversion of the whole world for the Sacred Heart of His Son. You can envision the entire globe situated within the circumference of your hearts, and this is why He can hear your petitions so clearly as He presides there in comfort and peace. I have come also today to ask you to remember Jesus' Sacred Heart as the month of June arrives. We acknowledge that the signs about which I have spoken need to be multiplied in the awareness of hundreds-of-thousands of people. As you grow in years, you will see this occur."

Sunday, June 10, 2001
1:40 p.m.

111   333   777   1111

"My dear little children of faith, these are the signs and wonderful works of the Triune Deity in the mortal world today, where you see them complementing the Will of God wherever the Holy Spirit inspires. You have surveyed them; you have experienced them firsthand; you have seen the likes of such signatures in the temporal realms of daily life, in the archives and memoirs of the Saints, and as guideposts to keep your heartstrings tethered to Jesus. Yes, they are signs and wonders, and much more. However, they are not meant to be a distraction from the work you have set-out to do. All of them lead to the Infinitus, the beginning of the infinite New World that is about to come. Please remember that Heaven already lives in you, and therefore you are a viable element of Heaven from where you stand. No man can point away from his holiest spiritual self and parenthesize Heaven as a place about which someone else might refer to as 'at.' Saints do not live 'at' Heaven, they live 'in' Heaven. This is why I ask you to pray strongly to believe that Heaven can be achieved inside you as you walk this sacred ground. It is easy to observe that there is rampant hypocrisy and social injustice in certain quarters around the globe. And, tomorrow is to be a red-letter day in the

United States because of the national public execution of a condemned criminal. Those who will carry-out this vengeance are too blind to see that their own error is just as horrific in the eyes of God. Error is error by inherence. Sin is also sin, although committed in varying degrees of egregiousness. I hope that you can fully comprehend that the gravity of human sin is a measure by which each person on Earth should evaluate their own judgement of themselves. Again, sin is sin, regardless of the severity, and there are assuredly some sins that are greater in the eyes of the Almighty Father. However, the one I am addressing here is the only one which is unforgivable, that of blaspheming the Holy Spirit. Such is the reason why God dispatched Saint Joan of Arc to cleanse the Earth. This is also the basis of why so many fail to understand the temperament of Nature when they react to losing a two-million-dollar home to a mudslide by blaming it on God."

(I asked, does Nature have a soul that reacts to man's abuses against it?)

"No, Nature is an attribute of the physical Earth, and has no specific gender. It is prolific because of the life-sustaining organicism that God placed into being billions of years ago. However, humanity should perceive Nature as more than an allegorical aspect of Heaven because all seasons concurrently exist there. That was a thoughtful question you asked, and I am happy you posed it. God utilizes forces of Nature to interact with His earthly people. When you pray to cease storms, it is not the storms that hear and obey, it is Jesus who calms them."

(How did Jesus immediately calm the storm?)

"Love. There is no greater power in all the universe than Love. I am pleased that you discovered this before you turned 40 years old! This does not imply that you cannot honor and serve God by communicating with Him in treating Nature with gentleness, tenderness, care, and preservation. This is likewise a supplication to Him of high magnitude."

(I asked our Holy Mother about the magnitude of our opposition and the potential for their chastisement. I was afraid of the consequences they were calling upon themselves.)

"Saint Joan of Arc took her calling seriously and never once looked back or stopped to ask why. She never had time, and neither do you. Jesus will take care of your opposition. The way He does so is as you have said, to give them reason to pause and reflect upon the priorities of life as they are related to the Salvation of humanity. This is the same for societies everywhere; speed appears to be the essence of human existence because it is only through motion that they are able to procure material possessions at the cost of the plight and neglect of their fellow men. There are many who live too rapidly because they have had to spend their prior years fending-off their predators so as to procure the necessities to support their own dependents. The world is a spasm of competition when people refuse to share."

Saturday, June 16, 2001
6:20 p.m.

"Let this day be the one during which you become no longer surprised that the miracles being bestowed upon you are gifts for the spiritual genuflection that you have afforded Jesus, that His gratitude is expressed in the vast largesse of His Most Sacred Heart that He fully dispenses upon those who have yet to truly know Him, that the Love that pours-forth from the arms of the Almighty Father encases you in forgiveness, compassion, Divine Mercy, and Salvation. The Blood of the Cross that Jesus shed is the source of Grace, and this Grace is your deliverance to Absolution. I seek sincere hearts who will allow the Holy Spirit to enliven them. Blessed is the soul who comes forward before Creation and proclaims that Jesus is the conqueror of evil and wanton hatred. My children, please do not allow the passing days to lull you into complacency, wondering when the errors of the Earth will end. You are living the emboldened age of the Resurrection of Christ; you are ascending to the summit of the highest accolades before Him, and your faith is completely warranted for the best belief you can muster that He has set the world aright through the Crucifixion for the Salvation of the lost. The present day of this New Advent is more than a progression toward the enlightenment of humanity in Love, it is the arrival of a perfection that is yours for the taking; freedom from sin and tawdriness, rich with the banquets of life, and wholesome to the senses that the Holy Paraclete places in your being. Should this day and age pass-away without all men coming to this understanding, the Good Lord would never allow. Therefore, He is still advising, admonishing, healing, and delivering. His Faith Church on Earth is still teaching and uniting, cultivating and blessing. There is no stopping Her because there are no enemies in Her path who can withstand the march of righteousness to the Hill of Mount Calvary. I am pleased to tell you that sufficient is the determination of the Church that nothing will prevail against Her or charge Her gates to break-down Her dignity. Please live the awareness of this Truth, and remember that the past has been amended by the Holy Sacrifice of the Mass, the Sacrament of Reconciliation, and the humble petitions that are being lifted everyday from the hearts who have been gathered around the Altar. For all the reasons God has deigned, He wishes that all will follow Jesus back to Heaven. Together, we have labored mightily against the forces that have tried to diminish the happiness of the faithful who stand humbly before the Cross and beseech the help of My Son during their daily lives. Jesus is the fountain of Peace and Justice; and these are the gifts that are yours today, tomorrow, and forever. As we pray for the transition of the conscience of humanity to the Paradise of Absolution, please remember those whom you do not see everyday, even those whom you will never meet in the expanse of your mortal lives. Please recall that prayer is obedient, and that those who pray are the mindful children of God whom He shall remember when He comes into His Kingdom. The struggles and perils of the material world are manifold, but the strength that is wrought through the Holy Rosary is stronger than any force that may oppose you. Remember that the recitation of the Rosary is in itself a supernatural event. I am with you in all ways possible, knowing what you seek from Jesus through My Immaculate Heart as you rededicate your lives to evangelizing the Gospel Truth in His Holy Name.

How could Creation and humanity be better blessed? The transgressions that occurred in the Garden of Eden have been expunged by your Sacramental Baptism and the Blood of the Cross. I weep happy tears knowing that your souls are no longer forsaken! Of course, there is much error left in the world that must be alleviated by your prayers and sacrifices, by your reparation and the multitudes of novenas that you offer. I tell you that God sees and hears them; He knows that your love is with Him, as His is with you. As fully as I can explain it to you, this is the Day of the Lord that is filled to the collar with joy and decency, with the renewal of the face of the globe in ways that you might have only dreamed about. There may be sorrow within these days, but I beseech you to remember that there is no basis for sadness in the age of Glory coming to the fore. People who live this hope cannot fall to the despondence that overwhelms those who have little faith. I am standing with a Glorious Crown atop My head as the Queen of Heaven and Earth, the Queen of Peace, the Queen of Love, your Intercessor, Mother, and Benefactor before the Divine Mercy of My Son. I ask you to take My Love to your advantage because I am living proof of the determination of God to redeem the souls of men. We wish for the impoverished to have a place to lay their heads and something to eat; and the prayers that we are lifting are bringing this to fruition. We hear the faint cries of unborn children in the wombs of their mothers, asking God to allow them to be given the gift of longer life; and He hears them through the intentions you are raising to Him today. Those who are in their last agony on their deathbeds are witnesses to the Passion that has brought great healing to the rest of the world. So, My children, I ask you to never holdback the Love that you have accepted and come to know. Never yield to the fears that your enemies are trying to infect into your hearts. Be My little children for the lot of your lives, and Heaven will rejoice knowing that your pain is the deliverance of those who will not kneel before the Cross. Those who are locked in prisons are waiting for you to remember them to Jesus, and

He will set them free. The multitudes who are slaves to toxic substances and impurity are suddenly awakened when you tell the Son of Man that you wish for Him to make them whole again. These are among the reasons why you reach-out to the greater world from this humble place where you pray and listen to the Wisdom of your Mother! You gather at My feet and tell Me that you cannot see a difference being made before your eyes, but I remind you that your having gathered here *is* that difference. There can be no conversion of human souls to Salvation unless they allow the Holy Spirit to reign inside their hearts. I am pleased that I have given Him birth; I am humbled that the Lamb of God was born of My Virginal Womb as the Messianic Word, the Sinless Flesh, and the Wonderful Counselor of the Eternal Ages. We have worked tirelessly for hundreds of years since our arrival back in Heaven to intercede before the Lord, assuring Him that Creation is listening, that the people in whose custody He has placed the destiny of so many others throughout the generations are responding to His blessings. The sun above the Fatima skies has done more than warm the hearts and the Earth with the premonition of the final ages, it is a prophesy that the Justice of God will soon fall to the ground upon which you walk like a ball of fire. It is reason for everyone to have hope that nothing short of perfect affection for the King of the New Jerusalem will ever be allowed to escape from the lips of those who will be given the blessing of Eternal Life.

My children, there are scores of parables in the leaflets of your memoirs that you have penned for the world to see. I have come to you so that you may better know the Giver and Author of Life, that you will have life to the fullest in Him. May I say today that success is already here? What you do from this day forward is the continuation of that great service. Remember what the Sacred Scriptures tell you about the Living Bread of Life, about the Revelation of these final years, and about the stated purpose of your existence in the parameters of time. You understand these things because you have said 'yes' to God. You have learned because you have listened; you have changed because you have prayed; and your work is never in vain because you have loved. What a wonderful new beginning you have brought to yourselves and the fortunate people whom you have touched! I have watched and prayed while you have participated in the mitigation of much suffering around the globe. I have seen the reason why Jesus has not surrendered anyone to the bowels of the Abyss. He holds you fast to the faith that carried your fathers to His embrace. Yes, those great Saints are the poise, pose, and purpose that have kept you going. Their intercession has allowed you to remain aware of your capacity to amend the future and alter the course of human events. This is your time! I implore you to remember this with profound humility and authentic compassion in the likeness of the Lord. My Special son, you have recognized that the words I have spoken are meant for the greater world, and reflect the offices you are lending. It is true that I give you many compliments for the love that you are living, and it is also true that each of them is founded in the bounty of Heaven. You ask as the new days greet you, 'where do I go from here?' My response is as always, you are already arriving there! It is the Love who lives inside your heart, Christ Jesus who will never die again, the Divine Nature you have sought since your adolescent days, the reason why the world continues in the anticipation of its spiritual replenishment in the City of God when He commands that time be manifestly finished. We work and pray because I cannot succeed without you. I am forever beholden to you for having responded to My call and never turning back into the temporal world. If you continue in the patience you are offering, you will see everything that lives in your heart unfold in your lifetime. Indeed, you are already seeing the signs. I have many more lessons for you, and I know that you will accept them. Remember that Jesus is the source of holiness for all humankind. You will never do anything for Him that will ever be in vain. You will see countless times over that you will never outdo Him in generosity. There is a discipline to which you have given your heart, and that discipline is the source of the Victory you seek. I continuously ask you to remember in your daily prayers those who have displaced themselves far from God, especially during the Holy Sacrifice of the Mass."

Sunday, June 24, 2001
Twenty Years in Medjugorje
6:02 p.m.

"There, there, little children; be not afraid anymore of the Earth that is so vexatious to your spirit because your Immaculate Mother has embraced you and enveloped you in the Peace and Grace of the Savior of the world. Call yourselves to understand that the temporal environment of your exile is not as it seems; God is closer to your hearts than you realize; the hems of righteousness have bound you to the Love that can never forsake you, and this is the hour when humanity must realize that the Kingdom of God is at hand. I have come to you today as the Queen of Love, the Matriarch of the timeless Grace that has delivered you to the precipice of Everlasting Life. You can see with clearer hope and destiny in your eyes because the future has been prefigured by the Blood of My Son on the Cross. Wherever there are souls who are yearning to come home, there is My Son whose Crucifixion receives them. It is a miracle of the universe that this has occurred. It is a gift of Love from our God of Love, the omnipresent and generous Father of Creation. I speak to you today upon the occasion of the twentieth anniversary of the Angels who preceded My appearance in the hills of Medjugorje, where you were called to begin your transformation into the fold of Divinity and Love. These two decades have been the reshaping of your knowledge of prayer, penance, Love, sacrifice, conversion, fasting, and peace. Many have been the hours when the world has paused to reconsider the presence of the Father in the lives of humanity because of the faith that has been placed in My messages. Indeed, this is no time to cease the process of enlightening the consciences of those who are called by the Holy Spirit to become the children of Light. I would not be here speaking to you if our Divine Lord had not commanded it, if His Will had not been to utilize your lives in His Plan of conversion for your brothers and sisters. How special it has been that you have accepted this role! What an honor it is that you have said 'yes' in reflection of the Fiat that I offered the Angel Gabriel upon the occasion of the Annunciation. Millions of pilgrims have come to the Yugoslavian shrine to begin their lives anew, to assert their promise to God that they have accepted the Cross of Jesus as reparation for their sinfulness. It is the power of the Angelic Salutation that has brought so many millions to believe that Salvation in the Blood of Jesus is real. Now, for the next days, weeks, months and years, we will set-out to enlist millions more to offer the Good News to the world at large. If the greater body of humanity would come to believe in My Motherhood the way that My pilgrims of Medjugorje have accepted, our work would be strongly enhanced. Too many do not realize the special gifts and graces that I bring to the Earth at the behest of the Almighty Father. The dubious and curious have made a philosophy of studying the phenomenon of My role in the Salvation of God's children, rather than actually coming to Me in prayer for My powerful intercession. I am a loving Mother who is close to Her children, not one who has come only to reprimand and scold. This has been the same since before the present age was placed into being. My Special son, I am continuing to pray for your intentions. Jesus knows what they are because He is painfully in love with you. He sees how faithfully you attend the Holy Sacrifice of the Mass, even when you may sometimes be too tired to stand and walk. As you now realize, these are important months of Grace for you personally, as well as for the rest of the world."

Sunday, July 1, 2001
3:33 p.m.

"There has never been a time in history when the Mother of Jesus Christ has called upon Her children to pray with such intensity as I am during these passing years. Why? Because there has never been greater opportunity for the inhabitants of the Earth to learn about human Salvation with such dispatch. Sadly, this is also the untimely era when Satan employs all of the technological advancements at his disposal to distract you from the simplicities of life to which you are called by the Spirit of God. My children, I am not part of the material collusion by which many are spurning the sacrificial Love that will make the world a holier place. I am a simple Handmaid who has been pronounced your Queen by the Almighty Father who has seen fit to convey your souls to Everlasting Life. Please join My prayers for the restoration of compassion and morality on Earth so there will no longer be people suffering at the hands of the posh and arrogant. Help Me remember them to God so He will shine His Glorious Face in Peace onto the celebrated and the vanquished alike. I have come to this home to ask you to instill in humanity the need for turning again to the Holy Sacraments of the Church, and especially the Sacrament of Reconciliation; for without confession, there can be no repentance of the soul. The righteousness that Jesus brings to the human spirit is winning the souls of lost sinners by a vast margin over the indifference that is attempting to pull them down. The Triumph of Love is far and away a much more appealing destiny to those who yearn for Salvation because there can be no preservation of human life in anything dealing with the culture of death. Where else but in this western world should the leadership of industrial nations pursue the Cross? It is sorrowful that there is such selfishness in America, that there is so little reaching forward with healing hands and honest intentions to those who suffer. We must earnestly pray that the moral decency that is missing within the United States is restored. What kind of Patron Saint would I be if I did not implore you to turn to Jesus for Truth, healing, and Grace? Why would God give you My Immaculate Heart if He did not intend for you to seek His Peace and consolation there? I am here, My children, listening to your pleas for My intercession before the Cross and to the Almighty Father through Jesus! I turn My attention to you, My Special one, because I know that you will tell the rest of humanity what I have come to say, even on your own terms that they may better understand. You are a mortal being who has immortal vision and the desire to see your Savior succeed. The lineage of history has shown that you are one of the greatest contributors to the teaching of humanity about the Blood that Jesus shed on the Cross to redeem the world. Your devotion to My Most Immaculate Heart is unsurpassed."

(I told Our Lady that I wished that I had a miraculous gift to change people instantly from the inside.)

"My speaking to you is the miraculous gift you are seeking. I do not wish to diminish the sincerity of your statement, but you will in time see that My words have been your miracle all along. What makes you assume that you are not touching the hearts of people to whom you refer since they are not revealing how they are being changed? What appears to be their defiance is only a defense mechanism for the exhausting moments of time. It takes a grand amount of listening, praying, and discernment for many to realize the scope of what you are saying. Speed is not of the essence to them because most all you have written in your Diary and second book is new to them. Have you witnessed anything resembling your Christian moralizing anywhere else in Creation? I will offer you an example to speak to the point that I have made about the velocity at which you feel humanity should turn their attention to our work. Can you tell Me what the following numbers have in common?

12   34   56   78   90

How many people would guess that they are a sequential series of Arabic numbers grouped in twos if I had listed them backward or alternating? It would have been much more difficult if I had asked the same question if you would have seen them like this.

34   78   12   90   56

The vision of the world seems to be paralleled with the latter of these two examples, and you are trying to urge them to understand the proper sequence of the first example. Now, look again at the second series of numbers and tell Me how anyone could possibly recognize with ease that they are the first ten numerals in another order. They would have to cease looking for the value of each number and disregard the variances between them. In essence, they would have to ignore considering the amount of each, while instead turning to a search for evidence that would lead them to realize that the numbers are related only because they are random quantities of the first ten Arabic numerals. Do you understand? In other words, the quantity is of little consequence, just like you have previously written about looking for the connection between all the Crayons in your coloring box. The point I am making is that the Earth as you see it is still fixed in determining the differences between qualities that do not exist, measures that are in no way comparable, and variances that have no means for evaluation. Humankind is on a blind hunt for meaning in a system of meaningless norms that they themselves have created. You are trying to focus their attention upon the center of Love, the Cross upon which Jesus was Crucified, so they will know what is worth seeking. Therefore, all in all, it is apparent that you are having extraordinary success as of this point in the commencement of the world and the history of men. There is frustration not because you do not have the tools to change the face of the globe, but because other people are continuing to defy the Holy Spirit by refusing to take them in hand and begin studying what is ailing humanity these days. For this, you must pray. It is true, as you realize, that you cannot lance someone's heart or insert a syringe and pour the Holy Spirit of Love into their being. If this were possible, Jesus would have taken them into surgical operating rooms long ago. Indeed, it is a judgement of Wisdom that each should make on his own. You are still leading them to the water's edge, but it is they who must lower their pride and take a drink. My son, there are countless other ways that I could explain what I mean when I tell you that humanity is lacking in the spontaneity that will take them to expecting the unexpected in their relationship with God. You must also understand the nature of compassion in your little heart. You have been wounded deeply as a child, and you wish for no one else on the Earth to face the pain and sorrow you endured. It is true that no one who sees Redemption well should stop hoping for all those who succeed you to live free from the imprisonment of hatred, indifference, and agonizing fear. If the collective will of humanity followed the blueprints of your prayers, the Kingdom of Heaven would arrive from inside the body of humanity before Jesus ever took the opportunity to return. This, My son, is what He is waiting for. He knows that it will happen; He realizes that you are praying; He has not surrendered these little ones to anything less than His Life-giving Blood, and He wishes for you to see it in the annals of your years. Why has He not taken the Earth by surprise and overwhelmed it with more miraculous signs? Because He knows that the prescient Love in which He was born into the world will eventually prevail, with humanity's faith intact, over everything else that is still trying to distract you.

Jesus' Sacred Heart is a refuge of high hopes, even though He has already seen the end of time. He stands at the peak of the universe, calling His sheep to come seeking His embrace. Of course, He has dispatched the Holy Paraclete into every heart and conscience to do His bidding. He is speaking to Himself at the inner-being of every soul on Earth with the urgency in their heart to wish for a better world and a new beginning under the Domain of the Almighty Father in Heaven. My son, can you not sense that every day brings a greater venue for all men to respond? And, this is exactly what is occurring beyond the scope of your ability to perceive. I have told you this on another occasion once before. If you spend your time hoping for the transformation of the Earth into the Kingdom of God, and then fall into despair because you cannot see it with your eyes, then your hope is not of the fruits of good faith. If I offered you a litany of the achievements of righteousness on the Earth today, we would have no time to speak of anything else. There would be no hours for teaching the rest who have not yet achieved full holiness. You can see the signs of God in nearly every conceivable aspect of space and time, particularly the one in which you live. Humanity as a whole still yearns for the leadership of contemporary icons, heroes, and legends. They will follow the pathways of greatness wherever these children of God travel. When you have completed your description of this by the first of next year, even your own writing will help you comprehend. Thus, I have spoken to you today, hoping that your joy continues to be complete in the awareness you have gained during the past ten years that God is in control of His Creation."

Sunday, July 8, 2001
2:44 p.m.

"My prayerful little ones, if God had not chosen to fulfill His promise of Love at all, would there still be a Creation? So many philosophers and theologians have been so suspended in the midst of answering this question that they have refused to know the need for their own Divine existence inside the Providence of His Kingship. There is no other food for life than the perfection which is gained in knowing the Maker of all that is good! Toward this end, you and I are gathered today to pray for a greater comprehension of the family of man, that everyone who knows the Truth will turn to those who do not with the intention of helping them understand. The simplicity of the Most Blessed Trinity is a Mystery to behold, but one that is never a stumbling block to becoming one Love with our Singular God for they who are united in His Son. Indeed, just because there exists the Triune Deity to which all men are called, there is but one Love; and that Love is the essence of becoming immortal and being perfect again in the sight of the Omnipotent Father. I call you then, little children, to continue the march toward everlasting Salvation by never stopping the fight against those who refuse to believe, the many who are trying to hold you back, those who would rather destroy your faith.

These are the days of essential Being, the natural course of events which are revealing the destiny of Heaven to the children of Light, the many-faceted walkway of righteousness upon which God is by your side and within the strength of your hearts. Christians have professed the noble and sacrificial cause of Love because this is why you have been born! Life on the Earth is your acclamation that God has created you, that He has given you the breath to speak His praises throughout all the Universe! No enemy can defeat you because their opposition is burned in the flames of Holy Love inside your hearts! Yes, the Holy Paraclete has set your very power into motion in an otherwise quite sedentary world! I ask you to continue the journey back to Heaven, just as the Sacred Scriptures has commanded in the Liturgy today! There is no cowardice which can ever stop you from succeeding because, believe it or not, time is now on your side, where it has been since the Resurrection of Jesus from the Grave. All the stars in the Heavens are in alignment now, not for the purpose of predicting the future, but to sparkle in the midst of your own awareness that it has already come! The Kingdom of God is at hand!

These are the reasons why I have asked so profoundly in many places around the world that My children be both bold and beautiful in the midst of your piety and service to humanity at large. Indeed, the Angels have instructed that there is no fear in those who Love with the greatest power, except to realize that God is the Dominion and the Refuge over all with greater Wisdom.

When decent men rise from their sleeping quarters at the break of another day, their purpose is to seek the God of Abraham and beseech Him for blessings anew. I have told you over and again that the Valor of the Cross is the expungement of all the transgressions of human souls from the beginning of time until the end. Your profession of faith is concurrently your confession that you are helpless alone, that you can know no Life without the Savior of Mount Calvary! My plea today is that all mortals on the Earth will prepare the way by which your predecessors have gone, that you will let go of the material world and join them at the intersection where they have passed into the Eternal Ages. One need not yet die to know the Truth in the fullness of day! Be Love! Thereafter, your soul is united with Heaven by the invocation of your intentioned destiny and the eradication of suffering from the globe.

If this were not the case, the Holy Spirit would have told you long ago. God would have wasted no more of your precious mortality if His Eternal Word was not meant to be passed-down to every generation since the Birth of His Son! I am the Immaculate Mother of this Love! Please accept that I have brought many miraculous signs and graces from Heaven so that the present age will know, and so that anyone who is born in the flesh can walk upright in the fullness of peace, Grace, and Everlasting Life. I have spoken to you about Grace for many hours, indeed for a seeming Eternity, because it is only by the Grace of God that He has forgiven you! What does this truly mean? Is it possible that a debt so large as the one created by the sin of Adam could be erased by the Passion and Death of a single Man? Always remember that His Resurrection is the evidence! Eternal Redemption cannot lie in the grave, or it would be no new beginning at all! The First Fruit of the Holy Cross is the very One who bore it and died upon its horrible crux to save the world! Were He to have never walked again, what future would this have brought to those who were created in His image and likeness? Therefore, the Cross stands as the future of Life for all who accept it, for those who acknowledge its burden in their own lives, and then believe that it has absolved them! The Blood of Jesus which was let there is the acquisition of the forgiveness of every sinner who ever tread the face of the Earth.

Dear children, My being here is, in itself, a fruitful factor in your Salvation because I have come to assist in the conversion of the lost to the Son I bore to save you. And, I am brought by that same Love, that equal devotion which is now resting inside your hearts from the Right Hand of the Father in Paradise. You are manifested inside this same capacity of Love, this same portion of the higher order of Creation which has called you blessed! Be not dismayed by where you shall earn your next dollar or whether you will be entertained before the fall of the night; everything has been placed into Eternal order by the Son of the Most High God. The Mysteries about which you pray are revealed in your relationship with Him; and there is no other way to fully know God with this ultimate transformation of the human conscience and will.

Yes, your communion with perfection is found inside this order of Love. Why are the Saints in Heaven already there, notwithstanding that the Final Judgment has yet to come to the Earth below? Because God has given you all the advocates that you will ever need, beginning with Me! It is not simply a Catholic purpose to ask the Saints for help, it is a human involvement in the greater purpose of life for every soul who is still breathing the mortal air. I have come as the Mother of all humankind, not just those who belong to the Original Apostolic and Catholic Church. By all means, I am calling every soul to new Life in the Sacrament of the Eucharist, by conversion and prayer, and through the power of the instruction of the Holy Spirit in those who realize that it is useless to protest against the Divine Nature of the Church anymore. The example is perfectly true—for those who are clinging to their lives while hanging on the cliff of their own weight in sin and error, only the Holy Eucharist is their anchor, lest they fall into the Abyss and be forgotten forever past the end of time. When the human soul makes contact with the Most Blessed Sacrament, it takes flight and lets-go of the temporal world altogether, toward the greater purpose of Love. If life on the Earth is to be perceived as collective humanity clinging to a cliff, I ask you to hold on together! Never let a single one perish by allowing them to loosen their tether in the throes of temptation and error.

  This is an age during which the very perception of God by humankind will be made more keen to the eyes of the consciousness of all. Why? Because, as I have said, the Kingdom of God is at hand. One need not necessarily look to Nature for the answers or the signs, but around the Divine service of the Holy Father in Rome. He is your evidence that Jesus is about to enter His Reign on the face of the globe and put the past to rest. The Vicar of Christ is, himself, a Signal of the Revelation which has been revealed by the New Covenant for your age, for all the ages combined. His pious words and sacred acts are the essence of reconciliation; and he is proving the fortitude of God on the Earth very well. Why should brother take-up arms against his brother, when everyone knows quite well that Love is the ultimate unifier in a world which reeks with such division? Jesus Christ is the only Savior of the wounded souls of men, and the End of Time will bring the encapsulation of this Truth to everyone. How can this Holy Pontiff fail when the Almighty Father is on his side, when the Morning Star is in his sights, when all the Angels and Saints are supporting his every move from the City of Light? He cannot fail! He will not fail! I implore the societies and nations of the Earth to listen to his command, to follow in his sacred steps of forgiveness and asking for forgiveness! This is the sweet Pontiff who is so dear to My Immaculate Heart that nothing in Creation could ever drive him away!

  Many are the hours and days when man and woman, alike, lay on their beds to ponder the purpose of life. The Holy Father in Rome is proving to the nations that the purpose is Love! Anyone with a sliver of hope can see it in his eyes and know from his words that the End of Time is near, and the God of all Ages will come to take them Home! I spend the precious time which God has allowed for Me to speak to those who will listen, telling all that human life does not need to be lent to agony, sorrow, and disease. Ask God to alleviate them all, and He will do it! He is just waiting for the many who will call His Holy Name to dispense the Mercy and healing to the Earth that it so desperately needs! My prophecies and exclamations are not of some impending doom or inevitable chastisement from on High because God knows that His children have the ability to alter the unfolding of history and the curvature of the globe. I have told you this too, My children, that the answer is prayer! The Apostles who walked with Jesus on the Earth knew this with the greatest of intentions; and they are still praying for the world to this day in the company of the Holy Trinity to which their souls have been called. Can you not sense their yearning for the Salvation of the world, calling now through the ages for their millions of successors to accept the genius to which they have been drawn?

In all of this hope, My little ones, you still see a world of people who continue to say 'no.' But, that will not be the final response they will utter to God. Yes, the continuation of time will show you that each one will ultimately wield their own sense of responsible Love, because it is this Love who has given them life from the womb. I am a Mother who carries great joy today because I know these things to be true! There is no doubt that I am sorrowful for many who are oppressed during the wait, but I know that the final outcome of the world will be a return to the mountaintop of happiness again. Here, too, if this were not so, My voice would have dropped into silence long ago. I cannot tell you the hour when the last moment of the mortal Earth will come, but I can tell you that it will eventually arrive. This is enough to keep Me going around the many cities and hidden hamlets of the Earth, seeking those who will look up again in faith that the Father's Will shall be done. I come to this humble home in America because you are being guided by the Morning Star to which you have tendered your lives for so long. You will never stumble on your way because you can see the reflection of your path in its glassy seas! Great is the purpose for which you are living! Mighty is the strength that you have been given by the God who has placed it there!

My children, the key prevalence for all those who live is 'respond!' It is not enough just to see and to know, the world must respond to the Living Christ who has asked you to live once again! 'Bring Me your tired and your poor' indeed! This is no statue of a former god, this is the Living Life of Love who has said that *HE HAS COME FOR YOUR TIRED AND YOUR POOR*! He is walking, teaching, and breathing for the purpose of conquering the fathoms where sinners used to hide. He shall not wait for them to somehow wash upon His shores, or come sailing along in some accidental grace! This is Jesus! He is the Son of Justice who cannot be taken away, whose Light cannot grow dim in the face of rejection or disdain! This is your pro-active God who does not stand along the edge of an island and pretend to be freedom for all. He is the mainland shore who is already standing at the center of the Ocean of Love, in which He beckons all men to drown their sorrows and be lifted from the throes of despair. In My Arms rests the Light to which all humanity is drawn, from the perils of the globular seas, from the cities where they boast of their angels, to the rolling acres and towering peaks! I am asking you to hope again, dear children! I am asking for you to finally stand for once with a renewed strength upon your feet and turn your faces to the skies in relief and say 'My God, my God, I finally believe!'

This is the reason that I continue to hold My hands of blessings over your little heads and pray that God Almighty will shower the delights of His Sacred Heart over you. I can lift you to the heights of His peace if only you will hold on to Me, if only you will not quit the fight again, and never, ever let go! I can see your troubled hearts and trembling hands in the night, those who are shivering in the cold of disbelief and painful regret. All those who feel like they have offended God too much to ever be absolved are absolutely wrong! There is a new beginning for everyone who lives, those who are addicted to drugs, they who have given their past to the pleasures of the flesh, the many who cannot see because they choose to remain blind by their own callousness, hatred, and unmitigated arrogance and greed. Again, I say to you, the key to this change is 'response.' React to the intercession of God, and He will guide the lot of you to the peaceful ravines where you can be brave again, where you can draw a new breath, take a fresh drink, sit on your tired breeches and look into the skies with a wholly new arrival again! Respond! Respond! Is this not, too, the essence of prayer? There are no endings to the countless years during which a homily would continue that reveals the newness of Life in the Love of My Son. There is only the unrivaled destiny of wholeness anew, a way to escape, a means of protection, a model for flight, and a change for the best! If it is only one 'I am sorry' away for those who cannot bring themselves to accept, please get down on your knees at the feet of your brother and beg his pardon in advance! Tell him that Jesus is alive in you, that the Holy Spirit is prostrate at his side and begging him to consider your soul as having been refreshed, absolved, and enlightened, and that you wish for him to join with you there!

Where are My children to whom I am calling, asking them all to fall in joyful reunion in front of the Cross in this very same way so that the reconciliation between God and man can begin? I am a Mother who is wearing a Mantle of protection for the lost and forsaken, a living devotion to those I inherited on the Hill where My Son was killed for the sake of your souls. I do not stand with spikes jutting from My head and the salty seas eating away at My pleats. I am the Mother of Love with the Living Crown of Glory atop My head! I am wearing the Immaculate laces of Satin and Love to which all those who yearn for Salvation in God still cling! There are no stony tablets in My arms for a secular proclamation that has long passed into the annals of history. I bear the Savior of the world who is calling out from His humble Manger throughout the portals of time for His people to finally know Him! There has never been a generation that needed to pass any further than the Love which He offers from the Cross! Let there be no mistake! The Son of God has made it clear that graves are for cowards! Only those with the bravest faith who accept Him as the Redeemer of the world are fitful warriors to fight in His stead! No hollow chamber or pit in the night can kill those who Love in His likeness! There is no defeat awaiting those who are scurrying about the Earth in His Name!

So, let us go on together in peaceful accord; you, My children, the birds and the beasts, all who serve to the delight of the Lord! Be at rest in the knowledge that there is no stopping the Light of the World. Come to Me, all you who have chosen *NOT* to be weary anymore! Walk in the beam of Light who glows in My Arms, and never again shall you call yourselves poor! You will be rich in the Love of God! You will own the enemies who have finally been put down by the purpose of your faith! This, My children, is Love at its best. This is the Glorious Crown which has already circled the globe, taking the waiting to the deliverance for which they have longed! High, above, and away they all now fly freely in the space of Divine Joy, never again surrendering to the walls that choose to discriminate against their hopes for a better day to come! The soaring eagles are quite envious of those who are given to God! They sit on their lofty perches on high mountain ranges and look-out with generous glee while admiring the souls of the Saved. 'Where in the world did they come from?' they ask amongst themselves. 'We have never been able to fly like that!' And, these same eagles come from those towering peaks to join you in flight, all who have beckoned for My help. I will ensure that Jesus will take you back to your Heavenly reward. He will not say 'no' to Me, I promise you that! So, upon the occasion of the heated summer days in America, as you ponder the hours that pass, the seasons which come, and the fortunes which might slip away, please never stop hoping for your Salvation in Jesus. He is more than any address that a Saint might deliver from the plateaus of the globe, higher than any summit which the Angels might ascend, and more peaceful than the solace that your hearts always gain when you find that you have won the race! You can 'be' this victory in your hearts! You can know that Heaven has predestined your success, and your competitors will be the first to come to a stop, run in the path of your tracks, pull you from the charge in which you have been engaged, pat you on the back, smile as though the end of the world has come and *EVERYONE* has been crowned its king, and embrace you with a touch of Love so profound that no one will ever let go, never, ever, ever. If you will only stay with Me, pray with Me, be patient in the face of rejection, continue your search for the Truth, be peace amongst the ravages of war, bring decency where there is only the impure; all of this will be yours, soon enough, and plentiful enough. Indeed, not a million speeches could ever capture the joy that is yours for the taking in My Son on the Cross. No victory could ever catapult your jubilation to a greater degree. I ask you to 'respond.' This is the key.

    My Special son, I have spoken to you today because of the hope you bear in your humble heart. Yes, the ones who have left many courses in total despair because their hearts have been so aggrieved can return again and depart this time as the victors over all. God will make the world aright, if only the world will give Him the chance. I thank you for your love. I have told you in the past that Heaven is beautiful because the children of God are beautiful. Hence, you are the lilies of the fields!"

Sunday, July 15, 2001
6:47 p.m.

    "Somewhere amidst the cohesion of the thunderheads, you can see and hear the placidness of the more simple lives of Love to which you are called and the riddance of the callousness which has been the subdivision of humanity in too many places around the globe for seemingly endless ages in the past. This is a new day! My children, the broader scope of your spiritual awakening has taken you to a new land of happiness and opportunity, one which can bring the consolation that so many of My children are seeking from the rest of the world. There are so many who would ask 'why now? Why not heretofore or after this generation has passed away?' The answer to any such interrogatory is that the Will of God is the provision of Life for every man, that all may come to comprehend the unity of all peoples and nations under the Cross of Salvation which Jesus suffered for the Redemption of all. Is it a matter of redundancy for a child of God to stand aright every day of his life and proclaim that he is waiting in joyful hope for the coming of His Kingdom, even if that soul shall die before the Arrival of Jesus in Glory? The answer is no, there is no redundancy, because all life is one. The days are only an alliteration of a poetic existence of peace and joy in the faith to which you have been given, the faith that has been dispensed to your hearts from the Love of Almighty God!

    There are so many proximities and parameters to which humankind responds! But, God is never subject to such incarceration! His is immortal Life in an endless Kingdom of happiness, Love, fulfillment; a land where there is no death or threat of death, no danger or reason to fear, and nothing to ever set a soul's sights on anything other than the perfection of endless Glory! I ask you to always remember that I have come to be with you as a portion of God's Plan for the imminent sovereignty to which all who are blessed will bow! Yes, and this too will be done of the free will of man! So, today, we are together again in prayer for the restoration of the decency that humanity seeks. We are called to prayer inside the loveliness of My Immaculate Heart, where Jesus has placed the world for the preparation of His final Return. These days are suddenly now being transformed into your own portion of enlightenment, for the dispensation of knowledge which will lead you to the foyer in which you will continue to be wrapped in the Grace that will make you all saints!

My children, I ask you to remember that the maturity of the continents is never a function of time, but the process of understanding God in your own days. While the hills and meadows sing of their lofty stature in His sight, it is you that they truly envy! Theirs is the joy of knowing that their inhabitants are journeying toward a great reward, to the Land of Plentiful Peace! You have been told that there will be no more room for crying, no tears, no sorrow, and no grief in the Heaven you will soon possess. If you must cry, please do it now, My little children, for there is no reason to shed a tear beyond the breach which is the veil between Paradise and the mortal Earth! If there is weeping in your consciousness, weep with the power of the Cross in your hearts, both in sorrow for the sins of the world and in complete jubilation that they have been wiped from the face of Creation! If you must dance, step forward and take the Hands of the Christ who is your Groom, He who is so powerful and strong, He who is at last your deliverance over the threshold of death into the Life anew for which there is no parting. If you wish to stand upon the ground during your starry nights and hide the moon beneath your thumb, let that thumb point also to Heaven with the affirmation in your souls that you are alright, that you have accepted! * Yes, indeed, that you will soon be boarding that celestial ship of Godly Absolution which will rocket you to the shores of the New Jerusalem."

* *a parable of the movie Apollo 13 where Commander Jim Lovell was standing in his backyard obscuring the moon behind his thumb as he was contemplating his journey to the moon.*

"My children, I have given My oath and honor to this same God, answering to a humble little Angel asking Me whether I would bear His Son for the purpose of remaking the face of the Earth and filling Heaven with the souls He came to save. I have said 'yes' in the likeness of that same Angel Gabriel. When you are united in Love, there is only 'yes,' there is only the affirmation of your gratitude that you have been chosen by Jesus to accompany Him Home. Indeed, who am I that the Lord would call on such a simple Maiden to give birth to the Holy Christ-Child! I will tell you that it is God, Himself, who knew that My success would be ensured because He knew to give Me these children of the latter times—you! The prophecies of old are now coming to pass because you are all just like that little Angel and the Love inside My Immaculate Heart who met on that fateful Feast we now call the Annunciation. There are no litanies in the world which cannot be made real if only My children will recite them! There is no such thing as an unanswered prayer because there are no people of God who are unloved! Yes, I call you to the celebration which is about to ensue because so many of My children are reconsidering their role in the purpose of life. How happy I am that the greatest awakening of humankind is now unfolding before your eyes. And, just in time! Just in time!

Just like a little child who has wandered too close to an uncovered well-shaft, humanity has ventured so very close to losing all that was gained by the generations past! Too many transgressions are being ignored, too much suffering is being left unattended, too many prayers are being left unsaid; and, oh what a waste! But, I have come running to take your hands before you fall into the Abyss! I have come in the Name of the Lord to tell you to reverse course, to plead with you to pray, to beseech your understanding of the higher graces of life, and to implore you to allow God to lead you, and to leave your own errant courses behind. I wish to tell you very clearly today, My children, that in My Immaculate Heart, you cannot fall! You assuredly cannot fall! This is why I have come! No more will Heaven stand by and watch you weep without responding anymore! We can see the response which is coming from all corners of the globe, from those little children in the former Socialists Republic who are bound by ropes and wires to their beds. * Jesus hears their cries because you are praying for them! He sees the little babies in their mothers' wombs in the nations of Africa who have been stricken by fatal diseases, even before they have passed into the hands of those who will deliver them to birth in a hospital room. By your prayerful hopes and contributions, these little babies will finally have the chance to stand tall in Creation, once and for all, and proclaim that it was the supplications of the living that preserved them from so quickly joining the dead!"

* *referring to a recent news program documenting the conditions of orphanages in the former Soviet Union.*

"There is no shame in the dignity of being called a Christian; there is no cowering in the corners of the continents anymore! You are living the time which has been the blossoming of your new beginning in the Resurrection of My Son! Hereafter and beyond, you are now the strong ones, those who have humbled yourselves to lift high the Cross and tell the rest of the world that Jesus is the standard to be met for the measure of perfection! There is no inherent arrogance in telling the world that you will be saved and taken to the Mansion on High! Yes, be proud of your humility, even if this sounds like a contradiction in terms! When your Blessed Mother tells you that I am proud of you, it is wholly different from the pride which fell Adam from the Garden of Eden. This is a joyful acknowledgment of your Victory over the grave! No one knows better than I the sorrow which was brought onto the Earth to make this Triumph known. We weep now over the sorrows of those who do not yet understand, not because we have given-up on ever converting them! If ever there was a time when I need to assure you that the conquering of evil has been completed, this is the time, now is the moment; these are the days during which you should rise from your sleepy naps and say, 'Indeed, the world is one step closer to Salvation today because the Reign of God is at hand!' Although I continue to admonish you to get your rest, it is almost too bad that you require it because the fireworks of Victory are still ongoing all around the world and at every second that is ticking from the clock! You will see all of this someday!

If you speak of the alignment of the planets as being a sign of things to come, get ready for the awesome day when they are bobbled with joy as though they have fishes on their lines because the Son of Man is just around the turn of the distant Universe, waiting to usher His children to the City of Light, the Divine Station before which those celestial stars are only footlights in the sands. These are not solely some quaint poetic images of an imaginary world, they are the real Truth about the fruitful lineage of the Sacred Mysteries which you already observe! God is about to take you to live in Heaven, little ones! Do you really know what this means? Can you cease the motion of the tangible Earth for only the briefest of instants to understand that the world that you know is passing away? Should time continue to pass, you are only a short series of months away from 2002, a time that seemed like a miraculous temple to fear not so long ago, but is really only a skeleton in a closet to the millions of souls who can see it already from the other side of time. Humanity upon the Earth has come to an intersection and a fork in the road at the same unique moment; that is to say, you need not choose to turn away or decide for one over the other. Your only direction is upward, skyward toward the forgiveness that is continuing to fall from the skies like the showers which grow your fields.

It is midday and, simultaneously, the pit of the night for the world these days, but the Dawn of your Resurrection is only a breath of the Almighty Father away. If this seems urgent in nature, then your hearts have finally decided for Him. If your conscience is telling you to fear what you have done and failed to do, then the Holy Spirit is alive and well in your hearts. But, if your faith is strong and your Love is committed to Jesus, Wisdom will tell you that all is right from within. The stars are in alignment, indeed! And, why do they move? What makes them glitter in the yonder skies so that your eyes squint to see what they will eventually do next? Because the God who resides within you begs to see His own reflection in your lives. I have told you early and often that you cannot seek the Kingdom of Heaven on your own, that it is Jesus who is living within your heart that makes you yearn for the Light of Eternal Day. I am the Mother of this Light! You have been given to Me! This is the resplendent perfection to which you are called, to walk in the Truth of the Love who first came to ask Me for the Fiat which has given birth to the Savior of the world, the same Love which took Me to the bedside of Elizabeth, the very same Love which leapt her little boy in her womb, the same Love which has blossomed from a Trinity of Three, now waiting for your own Love to make your conversion complete. What is all of this that I am hearing about signs? With all due respect to the dignity of man, how many more signs do you need? How much more evidence of God do you need?

Cannot a perfect Child in a Manger be raised and persuade a world of people to accept that He is now seated at the Right Hand of the Father, but had to go through Hell to get there? Can the men, women, and children of the Earth not understand that He had to suffer a shame which is nearly beyond comprehension to set them all free from the bonds of their sins? Does not the world understand that He was impaled to a Cross and ridiculed before He surrendered His Spirit back to Heaven in order to remake the Creation that was set into place from the first? Is it too much to ask that you believe that this Holy Son, the Messiah of God, was raised from the Dead by His Father in Heaven to spite those who hated Him on Earth? I ask that none of you fall prey to the doubt that befell Saint Thomas! Believe all of this that I am telling you before it is too late! Believe without having seen! Pray like there is no tomorrow! Fall to your knees and pray to My Son for the strength to unite in His Cross by taking-up your own for His sake! I beg you to believe that what I am telling you is true! Then, there are those who continue to refuse to pass beyond the blessings of the Mosaic Law. These are the truly special people of God! They are His chosen race, those who held-on for so many centuries before. I ask you to be kind to them, to feed and nurture their faith, to accept the convictions to which they hold about the Psalms, the Proverbs, and the Ecclesiastical Truth! Do not cast them aside, for these are the pretty souls who have so consoled the Earth with their suffering and plight. Do not hold them at arms length because they are different from you. Before My work with the globe has been concluded, you may have to compete with them in the race for the blessings of the Cross! Peace is the answer, and Love has posed the question. What will you do with your days? There is an entire evangelism which lives in the power of your prayers! Please ask Jesus for whatever you desire, and He will respond in-kind.

My Special son, I trust that you will eventually deliver these words to the rest of the world. I will tell you when the time is most opportune. Can you not see with what Love your Mother is looking at the little ones who have been placed under My Mantle? Can you not see the patience with which you must live? I am thankful and grateful that you are continuing to pray with Me, and to pray for the world which is so in need of your petitions. I would hope to someday come to speak to you and begin a message with 'This will be My last, because Jesus will be returning before we have the chance to speak in faith once more.' As soon as I know that to be true, you will be amongst the first to know. I again implore you to believe that the power of your Victory need not wait until then. We will continue to work through the cluttered world so that everyone will come to understand what we have been doing for all of these years. You can, indeed, see many signs unfolding already... I say the things in My messages because I have such tremendous Love for you! This is My blessing for you now! + I will speak to you again very soon! I love you. Goodnight!"

Sunday, July 22, 2001
10:15 a.m.

"Now we come together again, little ones, to pray for the purification of the Earth and the conversion of every heart to the Truth that is gently offered in the Sacrament of the Holy Eucharist. We gather on another twenty-second of the month, whereupon you continue to know the revelations of God for the future, for the deposition of the conscience of humanity, and the justified adjudication of the Almighty Father of the response of the world. Why do we not simply pray on the final day and determine it to be sufficient? Because the graveness of the condition of humanity and the hours remaining before the Return of Jesus in Glory will not allow it. We are the only hope for many for whom no one is praying, the solace for the lonely who are searching for Jesus, and the counsel for those who espouse only the wickedness of their ways. It is this error that we are trying to rid from the societies whose leaders refuse to address it. Now, you are seeing summits around the globe where certain kings and princes have gathered to discuss the alleviation of the suffering. But, are they not truly only speaking about how to harvest more benefits inside their own borders? When there are prayer cenacles that outnumber the sands beside the seas, then there will be the redress of human grievances and the mitigation of wrong. It is only by faith that these things are done because all souls must call upon our God whom they cannot yet see for Divine intervention. My intercession is a fruit of this blessing. We shall not desist in succeeding to transform the entire conscience of man into the fullest understanding of the Light of Jesus. Then, they will know that there is peace and justice in sharing the Holy Gospel and living in obedience to Pope John Paul II in Rome. There have been many twenty-seconds of the month on which I have spoken about these things, and I am grateful that you are responding with love and affection for Jesus and for Me. The Holy Trinity lives in abundance where you go because you have invited your Savior to take-up residence inside your hearts. What is it you are thinking? My intercession seems as brief as only twenty seconds of the ticking of the clock? Yes, what a parable about the swift passage of time! My children, today brings many new opportunities to the world because I have arrived to speak to you and to listen. Why? Because the wishes of Jesus from the Holy Cross on Good Friday are still the same. What people would deny their Mother whom they respect and admire? Is not My Immaculate Heart as tender as a flower; are not My intentions as pure as the fields that bend in the breeze? Am I not the Lady of Perpetual Help who promises never to stop loving you, aiding your development in understanding the true nature of personal sacrifice, and leading you in prayer? Has not My Son told you from the beginning that My visitation to you is for the purpose of birthing your souls into the deific rays of forgiveness that are continuing to stream from His suffering on the Cross? I have told you on many occasions that real passion is the interior grief of a loving soul for the sins of the world. It is authentic Love, not something based on the tepid natures of time and infatuation. Therefore, the Passion of Jesus is reparation for the transgressions of Creation against its God. His Agony is genuine and true; His trust in your capacity to change is real, and His determination to take you to Heaven is unsurpassed by any other feeling ever generated inside the hearts and minds of men.

Please be aware of the reckoning of the ages about which we have spoken in other places of the world, in your own books, and that will never wane until it eventually occurs. This need not be a time of fear and trepidation, nor of anxiety. The Return of Jesus in Glory should set your hearts alight in inner-peace and anticipation! For all the joy and goodness of the Earth, this is the time for which Christians have been waiting since the Holy Spirit descended upon the Church at Pentecost. Lift up your hearts! My intense jubilation cannot be destroyed by the sorrows that otherwise bring Me to weep for those who have yet to choose the Cross of Victory. We have many more miles to travel on our journey of taking the Good News into the world, the Holy Gospel that lives long past and generations beyond the moment when the first century Apostles were taken into Heaven. My children, I wish not to dwell upon the art of inquiry, but can you not see that the universe as it has been created by God is unfolding in accordance with those same Sacred Scriptures? This is the age of the element of vindication for suffering men and women, for those who have little from which to choose, and for the ominous acts of they who do not know to ask their Savior for assistance in overcoming the forces of mortal life. My messages are not meant solely to be premonitions of the Judgement of God, they are intended to prepare you in happiness, to help you prosper in peace, to procure your pious offerings by giving yourselves to service, prayer, fasting, conversion, and understanding. Please believe Me once and for all that the Almighty Father is a God of Justice who has the capability to wield it wherever He chooses. Must Holy Wrath and chastisement be a portion of the end of the mortal world? The answer is a definitive 'no.' It is only the sinners on the Earth refusing to decide for Paradise who make these things happen. I call your attention to anyone whose beleaguered heart will turn to Me; remember that no village shall be destroyed should there be one righteous soul there to convert the community. This is what time is for, My children! This is why Jesus is waiting! I urge you to plead in His Name for Peace on Earth! There are some who refuse to turn away from the world, who wonder what may transpire when they shutter their eyes in sleep. There is no reason for such worrying. Place everything in the hands of Jesus and follow in innocuous faith to the Hill of Calvary. Did He not say that this would be a difficult path, but also that His burden is light and His yoke easy? When so many of the children I love read My messages, they wish to know the motivations of My words and thoughts. Each of these is to understand that it is God who sends Me because He loves you so much. He came to Me first; I have come to you now, and Jesus will soon come for you all one last time to take your souls to Heaven. This is the continuing march of your spiritual conversion, Christian Redemption, and transfer into the Light of Glory that is awaiting your arrival. So, please do not look for regret when you see your faces in the mirror. Remember the Sacraments that have been given as you receive them in faith! They are not symbolic signs or latent objects along the way. They are factual and real Graces that feed your souls the nourishment they require to remain firm in the tenacious Will of God.

If only you could know how the frozen peaks of those mountains that so many are risking their lives to ascend are telling humanity to 'go back down and pray, work hard, and seek peace amidst the valleys.' Those frostbitten summits are not the answer to the question as to whether humankind has courage. They do not stand as trophies for those who conquer them. They are the reason why you should not climb in subconscious numbness to see Creation from the top of the globe. They are beckoning you to seek it from the warmth inside your hearts. This is where true victory lives. It is in vanquishing the poverty of the ghettos and tending to the sick who lay in street gutters. The summits of the Earth are raised wherever you witness challenges to human dignity and realize that you have the faculties to hold it intact. When you stand for Jesus where there live the poorest of the poor, you are already at the top of the world. Where is human heroism when so many choose to scale the lofty peaks of global mountains when there is so much work to be done below? My precious ones, I have given this message in America on a warm summer's day where countless little children lay in their own poverty, where indignant partisans turn their backs on them in the belief that paupers are somehow a deficient society of souls. America has grown indifferent toward the rest of the developing world and those nations who have yet to begin any semblance of advancement at all. I am the Patron Saint of this America, and I call on you to never shun or spurn these poor people again! I beseech you with the power of love in your hearts to feed them; give them shelter and clothes upon their backs, and a warm place to lay their heads. I implore you to do this because I seek this consolation for My only Son. Please do not leave Him out in the cold as was done to Him on the night He was born. This is My request for you today, My children. I ask you to remember how you yourselves are blessed, and to share your inheritance with those who are very unfortunate among you. My Special son, I have come today to also thank you for keeping your faith so strong, for heeding the call of the giddy Angels, for standing upright in the battles for Justice, and for praying with Me for so long. Your attendance at Holy Mass is the source of your strength. I am quite aware of the sorrows that you bear because I carry them with you. Please remember that there is consolation in this message for the rest of the world, and for you and your brother, too. What are your comments and questions for today?"

I made mention that I do not think people are responding quickly enough to Her intercession.

"I will ask you a simple question. Do you believe that I am not wielding the influence of My Queenship sufficiently? You are much more impatient than you need to be. If ever there was a soul whose photograph could be placed next to the word 'impatient' in the dictionary of the English lexicon, that person is you. Have I not told you that the Triumph of My Immaculate Heart is nigh at hand? Wherein lies your complaint with the unfolding of the Plan of God as seen by Heaven? I can see in your mind a single word that takes us to My previous statement. The word is 'when?' I am so happy with you today! I am pleased that you love God so much that you would expedite the fashioning of His Holy Will. What makes you believe that this is not occurring? Because you cannot see it? You are living in a circle of about a hundred people whom you see, but your work is part of a capstone that is converting six-billion people and taking millions more out of suffering in Purgatory into the Light of Heaven. You are basing your wishes on a count of a few thousand peers. Do you understand the analogy I have made? Please believe that you are achieving your stated goals, lest you become the modern Saint Thomas the Apostle, disbelieving that you are championing the causes of righteousness without seeing them firsthand. I will tell you why I have given you these words. God considers it to be self-serving to require proof and evidence that your work for Him is being advanced in hearts into which you cannot yet see. I do not wish to leave you with the inference that I do not appreciate your concern for the conversion of the entire globe in the next instant. The transfer of the world's holiness into a more apparent light does not seem to come quickly enough for those who love God."

Sunday, July 29, 2001
4:02 p.m.

"The prayerful wishes that you offer Jesus as the hours continue to pass are being brought to you, as early do you seek His kind assistance and Divine Love. Should your hearts be broken and in need of the solace of His Grace, be not afraid anymore of the sorrow, for He shall take it all away. My children, I bear the happy news to you today that these are the days during which your deliverance is being assured, while you lay prostrate on the floor of the Earth languishing in pain. If your anxiety gives way to certain depression, allow Jesus to lift you to the dignity of Easter and bestow upon you the happiness that reigns in the miracle of His Resurrection. There is no need to fear the Will of God if you do all the things that He asks you to do. There is no trepidation in knowing Him, no way that you can fall from the holiness that keeps your spirits aloft. I have come again today to ask you to acknowledge that all good things come from God, and that your needs are met in the Blood of the Holy Altar of Sacrifice. When you partake of the Body of Jesus, you are wholly favored by Him, and He continues to dispense His healing and blessings upon you. Can there ever be a pain that He will not remit? No, there is no such thing as pain inside His Most Sacred Heart. No human guilt can survive the forgiveness you are afforded when you give your lives to the King of Absolution. Today, I have appeared to ask you to garner greater strength in the knowledge that Jesus will never forsake you, that He cares for His flock with the gentleness of a Shepherd, that He will never feed you from the bitter trough, and that you are always given His compassion when you rest your heads upon the consolation of His Breast. My Son will never place any burden upon you that you cannot carry with Him. I must ask you to accept that I have seen with My own eyes the awful carrying of the burdens of mortality by My own Sacred Son, and by the masses who have seen fit to follow His Holy Light through their own good consciences. There have been only winners in this sojourn through the forests of danger. There has been enlightenment in Wisdom, Truth, power, hope, courage, graciousness, and Love. Please maintain no grudge against your neighbors who would have you turn another way, or who would punish you; for they know not what they are doing. I beseech each of My children through the prudence in your hearts that you learn to recognize the wolves who prey under the pretense of being a nobler cadre of men. Through your prayers by the power of the Holy Spirit, you are made keenly aware of the perils of this world. It is not in fearing the passages of life that makes you weak inside, but the weakness of your faith that makes you cry in fear. Let no one be mistaken; your existence here in exile is not easy; it has never been easy, and it is likely not ever to become so if your brothers and sisters do not tender their hearts and souls to God. This also is what we are praying for. There is no need for suffering in a world where everyone belongs to Jesus. If all on the Earth would be a reflection of Jesus by becoming the Love which He has espoused through His Eternal Being, your future would be one of jubilation and fulfillment. Is this some synthetic existence to which you are called, one that can be made by the motions of your hands? No, love is natural to the human spirit, and cannot be manufactured or mistaken for temporal stimulation. Love is the incorruptible essence of your soul that manifests beyond your Baptism, and your participation in the Holy Sacraments of the Roman Catholic Church. While there are billions upon billions of decisions that are made everyday in the secular realm, why cannot one collective affirmation be offered to God that everyone will seek their Salvation in Jesus? Is this too much to ask the societies of people who have been so blessed with healing, prosperity, longevity, and Redemption? Is God being too forward by seeking your gratitude for giving you life and His plentiful pardon in the Blood of His Crucified Son?

There are too many moments that are cast aside during which you might otherwise be mitigating the suffering of the poor and those who lay ill in their rooms. Why not let these be among the decisions of the temporal world? When paupers turn their faces to the skies and ask, 'Why does God not bless me?' are they not placing the lives of the indignant directly before His eyes? Are they not asking Him to assess the dissemination of the goods of the Earth and wondering why they are held in so few hands? Indeed, are they not searching for Justice amongst the adversaries of peace who are hoarding resources for themselves? If there is poverty in the world, it is not because Jesus is not hearing and responding to the prayers of the poor, it is because those who should be feeding them have shut Jesus out of their lives. It is a Biblical prophecy that is about to be fulfilled; those who will not share will be among the last, if at all, to enter the Kingdom of Heaven. Your Holy Mother has come seeking the participation of those who are guilty of these transgressions to heed My call to be generous, to share the wealth that belongs to the entire body of humankind. Now, as this new century unfolds, do the citizens of America assume that they are mandated to be not unlike the improprieties of the last one, or that the way of progress toward dignified human development be remanded again to the citizens of the West? Dear children, it is time for a reversal of fortunes to finally come to men. This will arrive through the awakening of the hearts of merchants who continue hiding their wealth in their caches. They will be called to suffer much for the error they have wrought across the thousands of miles of the globe. If you will only wait, you will see that what I am telling you today is about to come true. Our God of Justice is forthrightly the God of the just; and the rest He will throw to the hounds! Humanity must always remember that His Holy Wrath is a carnivore and will prey upon the lives of the people who reject Him. He will devour those who carry hatred in their hearts and spate them into the cauldron of Hell. This is not an omen that must inevitably come to pass. However, it is a future that He will deploy if the millions who fight against the Holy Gospel persist in their ways. I am your Mother! I am asking you to see Jesus through the Light of Day and turn away from the darkness of Earth! Call upon the Lord to come to your aid, to teach and guide you, and to remake you into the princes and knights of the meadows of Paradise.

For all these reasons, we pray for the spiritual conversion of humanity to righteousness. There can be no such conversion unless you heed My messages as they have been given from My Heart. There will be no true peace on the Earth if My children continue to run and hide from the admonition which is found in Jesus. I am never unsure what will help remold the consciousness of the body of man because I have seen Creation from the utter summit of Holy Perfection. It is possible for everyone to make it there. Jesus has made way for this deliverance to be completed in the physical lifetime of everyone alive. Does it take the severe misunderstanding of mortal men to cross this bridge of hope? Does it require that the insolent continue to carry a grudge against those who have offended them for the end of time to arrive like a thief in the night? No, My children, no! Peace can begin anew on this day in time! The face of the Earth can be transformed like the flash of a solar spire if only the Holy Spirit is allowed to do His work. There is no need for the aggrieved to surrender their hope in the coming of this day. When you ponder the reshaping of humanity at large, can you not see the straightening of the passage which will lead you to Christ? Can you not see that the slaughter of innocent unborn souls is only one 's-curve' away from turning their plight into laughter again? Please bypass that road; delete it altogether, and make way for the straight invitation of God to heal you again. I urge you to walk forward with the anticipation that these happy things are arriving with the passing of every new day. This is the expectation in which you should live. If there is despondence or anxiety about your health or what the future may bring for those you hold dearly, hand it over to Jesus, and He will make things alright again. Yes, His Love is this profound; His Peace is this great; His power is this mighty, and His Holy Will is sculpted by the hands of the Almighty Father to make it all come true. There are many Marthas on the Earth, but there are also millions who are continuing to endure honest hardship and suffer interior pain. Let us never forsake them in the lifting of our prayers. Please see the Most Holy Trinity in them, that they pine for your petitions so as to reunite Heaven and Creation below. Now is the time in history when your participation in the Plan of God is most important by calling upon the Angels and Saints from above. Never before has there ever been more Saints to come to your aid than there is in your day. So many generations have come and gone; and there are Legions of Holy Angels here, too. They aspire to intercede for you because their love is One in Being with the Father as is Jesus, Himself. My dear Special son, how happy and filled with joy I am to have been allowed to speak to you again today. You can see that I have offered the greater world another message from My Heart that will continue to stir them into action for the cause of the conversion of themselves and those they will know before they tender their souls to Jesus in death. Thank you for holding to the Truth by the genuineness of your faith. God is highly glorified by the prevalence of your Trust in His Word. Is your skin condition abating by now? *(I contracted poison ivy working in the yard.)* You are a mortal human being. Be thankful that you are allowed to participate in the eradication of the sinfulness of the Earth and the reparation that God has been seeking from so many for so long. It is through this purpose that your condition has been wrought. I would ask, however, that you never touch another greenleaf outside the house unless you are wearing a pair of gloves. No other mortal on Earth loves you more than your brother Timmy, and his love is well placed because you are all-deserving of the loyalty that he is affording you. Please continue praying that the Good Lord keeps you side-by-side until the length and breadth of His Will is done. I shall be with you, too."

Sunday, August 5, 2001
Saint Mary Major
5:08 p.m.

"Being blessed by the Holy Paraclete means more than allowing God to take your soul to Redemption, it means living for Heaven now, that you will always yearn to be Love on the Earth. Does your heart sense the opening of this victory already? When you allow His Love to be the reason for your living, it does. Surely the Lord's goodness and Mercy shall follow you all the days of your life. There is no question that Jesus is this centuried origin of Triumph for you, in you, and with you. If your life seems mundane and lacking of the Divine and supernatural Pardon that you must accept before your entrance into Paradise, then you have not surrendered to everything He wishes to receive from you toward the evolving of His Kingdom in time. I ask affectionately that the world remember this day of the Feast of Saint Mary Major because it marks the beginning of many beginnings for hundreds and thousands who have lived. There is more to celebrate on this day than the laying of the cornerstone of the Statue of Liberty whose elegance I surpass, or even the birthday of the first human to set foot on the powdery Moon. This day is the remembrance of a parish and a church to which many have come to be converted in the Name of My Son. Today, we are filled to overflowing with thanksgiving for all who have devoted their lives to My Immaculate Heart. It is not just My 'day' because I am the inviolate Matriarch of all the days, months, and years. It is the day of the Lord to whom I am imploring every living soul to be devoted; it is the reason why this Feast Day is commissioned. Honor My Name and Queenly station if you will, but the best way to offer Me your heart and soul is to be one with God, for He is the Author of Life, even Mine; and it is He who has prescribed such an auspicious ending to its conclusion for all who believe in Him. My little children, the happiness of every new season is the knowledge and Wisdom that the Truth is always perpetual, and nothing in the physical world can prevail against it. I once had a messenger question Me whether the words 'always perpetual' were redundant when stated consecutively. My response was the same as it is now; there is no redundancy in Grace and Love because there is no linear time to supercede it. Every star is of its own essence in the darkness of night, and yet one with the constellations that compose the sprinkling beauty of the foothills of Heaven. Does it seem impossible that someone might see the stars at noon on a bright midsummer's day? Not in the Kingdom of Heaven. Whatever you wish to see, whatever period or moment of remembrance you desire to relive, whatever victories you choose to savor for the unending thousands of years, these things are yours in the Blood of the Cross and the Resurrection of Jesus from the Sepulcher. You can address your friends and say that you will likely not return in a moment's time to speak to them again, but that you will see them in a briefer ten-thousand millennia, which will seem like only seconds in the Everlasting Life of Paradise to which your souls are about to be delivered.

There are so many things that your predecessors are wishing to tell you that are only an instant away, a flash of the Return of Jesus in Glory before they will see you again. The Saints are the blessed ones who are equally as fortunate to have you pray with them in the Faith-Church on Earth, the Church-Militant, that is still fighting for the retrieval of everything good that will ever engulf the Earth and all humanity in the periods that are continuing to expire. This is the faith to which I have led you and taken you; these are the new heights that hold you in an almost suspended state, away from the darkness, fear, and travails of those who have already succumbed to the netherworld. I am continuing to pray with you during these special days because I know that many of those who have turned their backs to you will eventually be the same souls who will lay down their lives in the paths of those who oppose you and everything you stand for in Christ. It is in Jesus that you have your well-being and sustenance, and it is because He is in you that the world is powerful, not in a temporal way, but toward the arrival of the Eminent Rule of God the Father over all He has created in the effecting of His Will. When you ask if the withering hearts of the ashamed and alone are part of this Will, the answer is that His Will is to transform the whole of Creation by the acclimation of their suffering in compliance with that of His Crucified Son. There is no heart that is diminished by personal agony and grief. There is no life that is wasted by sharing in the Passion of Jesus because God has said that human existence shall unfold this way. Whereon would any mortal soul require any greater explanation for His Grace? So, these prayers that we lift together everyday for the continuing presence of holiness in the world are toward the evolvement of that purpose, so that noble men and women will indeed be called to their highest accord in the reason for their enlightenment, and that they will utilize this same righteousness for the conversion of millions more whose lives have turned some other way. This is the real meaning of leadership; it is acceptance in the great Virtues to which God is calling humble men, to prayer and love in the likeness of those who first walked with His Holy Son across the acreage of the globe. It is to concede that only Heaven is the reason why human life is blessed, and knowing that the two are inseparable for the purposes that are still maturing in the annals of history for people who are living on the Earth to grasp firsthand. Where do we allow our prayers to go? What is the reason why I ask My children for their petitions about things that they yet cannot see? Because I can see them, and I know that most of them are only one simple prayer away. I know God because I have seen Him. I have borne the Messiah into the Earth in sinless Flesh, and I have undeniable evidence that the Holy Gospel is word-for-word the Truth as it has been handed-down by those whose lives were dedicated to sharing it. Yes, it is oftentimes quite difficult to persuade some of My children to utter that one, singular prayer that will take them to a lifetime of fulfillment in their dreams. But, if My little children will turn to Him and say, 'Dear God, please let me win,' then He will declare you a victor on the spot, and the entirety of Creation will know it. Have I not told you that human prayer is of this power because it is to the inclusion of your faith in the mightiness of Heaven? Please do not surrender to doubt; know that we will hear that simple utterance of faith from everyone on the Earth before they die. It is for all these reasons that you are to be more happy, not just to be obedient to Me when I seek it from you, but because your hearts have learnt it on their own from the Holy Spirit who takes residence in them. If there is misunderstanding and misjudgement in the scores of societies around the globe, it is because not everyone has taken to the singular God in the Most Blessed Trinity; Father, Son and Holy Spirit. It is because too many are continuing to ask 'why' rather than 'why not.' I tell you that those who are the gravest detractors of Christianity will be your fondest admirers before the world is through. I just heard a loud 'amen' from Saint Paul amidst the background voices that are cheering in Heaven as I speak to you today.

Be not dismayed by the element of time or the forces within it and around you that are trying to diminish your faith. They cannot succeed; they never have, and they never will. Your fight is not really against them, but against your own impatience and lack of understanding in knowing that the Almighty Father has a sublime purpose for everything He does. The articles of your faith are greater than the smattering of promises you have made to Him; they are your very life and the innate nature of your Eternal Being to which I refer. When you were yet little children walking through the park in the small towns where you lived, each of you heard the hollow sound of the chains against the Maypoles when no one else was there. They seemed like the clamoring of a lonely bell that said to you that there is nothing on the Earth truly worth seeking if it is not in communion with the rest of Creation. It was your audible sign that what you have in common with other men should take you to the palaces where each one can live in peaceful stead. The breezes that you felt against your faces during those earliest days were God's kiss to tell you that everything would be alright if only you placed your entire trust in Him. None of this has changed to this very day. My children, you have tasted many contrasting things in your lives; victory, defeat, humiliation, shame, sorrow, antagonism, and misunderstanding. However, there is only one Divine Triumph that will eclipse the preeminent nature of time. The hours that pass are not your enemies, for they are the endless power which you should invoke to become the holiest followers of Jesus. Your bodies will continue to grow old and fade away, but there is no way that your souls will be cast-out from the inspiration that lives endlessly in your hearts to perceive the Face of God. This is the reason why time was given to you altogether, because there is hardly another way that you could have prepared for your grand entrance into Paradise without it. Time is not a curse, but your alliance with the Holy Scriptures and the perpetual nature of their message to those who will live with the Angels and Saints someday to the delight of every friend you will ever know. Yes, I approached that same messenger that day and posed a question in return, *do you not believe that the rising of the sun at each passing day is equally as redundant? Or, is not the setting of the sun also a mark of the same repeating term?* We agreed that each and every one is separate and different in its own right, that each serves a purpose under Heaven, and that one does not know when the next will be the last before the arrival of the Almighty Savior of humankind to culminate the Earth as it has been known and begin the everlasting essence of Eternity without end. The vision of the human heart is an awesome prospect to behold because all Creation can be seen from there. It is not just a physical organ that can be transplanted into someone else, but a Wisdom that belongs to the soul. It is graciousness and delight; and knowledge, affection, compassion, deliverance, perfection, and peace. No weary mind could ever think of extricating these things from beneath the shales of mortality, let alone hold the offices to do it. I ask you to continue to pray from the heart for these reasons, and because you know that it is the right thing to do. Be the Love that is of your faith and goodness; go where timid men fear to travel to make the most of your power, and be gentle in your evangelism and bold in your admonishments. When you do these things well, you will step from your own vehicles of Redemption and thank Almighty God that He gave you the principled invincibility, Truth, deliverance, and willingness to do it.

    My Special son, I have spoken to you about many reflections today. I have tried to lift your heart to realize that Heavenly Feasts are for those who have the faith to believe in them. Most of all, I have spoken to you because I continue to believe in you. I know that you are My child, and that with your brother, you will know no parting or failings in My Immaculate Heart to which you belong. Do you hold any comments in your heart for today? These are pretty days and will be a good week for your continuing work and the distribution of My messages to those for whom they are urgently intended. Thank you for participating in this so willingly! Thank you for being so charitable in your faith in Jesus! Millions will stand and weep at the stature of your work, even at the thought of trying to match the intensity of the way you have given your life to God."

Sunday, August 12, 2001
3:00 p.m.

"God's Love is patient, kind, dignified, indelible, compassionate, charitable, peaceful, responsible, and true. I hope that you anchor your hearts close to the Sacred Bounty of Jesus because He will feed you through all these virtues, bearing you the greatness which is fitting of our Omnipotent God, and humble for the span of the mortal ages and the Eternity that belongs to you. My children, I have spoken to you about Victory and Triumph; I have urged your spirits to be of the pureness of the Angels, and I have formed and shaped you as in My Womb to be worthy in the sight of God. Your compliance has placed you in the company of the highest Court of Grace because you have said 'yes' to this same Love that is your Redemption, your deliverance from poverty, and your elevation from the throes of the agonizing world. Please remember from this day forward that there is decency in the humbleness of exalting the Lord, that He is pleased to know and accept you because you have become His newly inspired people once again. My Immaculate Heart is touched as I speak to you today because many more are reading *Morning Star Over America*, and those who believe in My words and in your work number in the multitudes. These are the important moments during magnanimous days for which we have prayed, that all those whom Jesus would lead to your Diary are indeed feeding of its plenteous righteousness and peace. I hope that you continue to know that there are many more who will seek and find, those who only think that they are losers, but are truly winners who have yet to claim their crowns. It is difficult for them to approach the irreproachable Light of God and not take to their knees in acknowledgment, faith, love, and delight. I tell you that the Holy Spirit makes them open their hearts ever wider to receive Him, and to ultimately understand the purpose of human existence on the face of the Earth. I have again posed the question to the universe as to the fateful decision that must be made by each and every soul. Does any man on Earth have the misguidance in his mortal fabric to turn his back on the Truth? Only those whose hearts are closed cannot see through the eyes of faith. What then is the meaning of good will to them? Do they live by a moral code or a system of behavioral ethics at all? This is also why I am beseeching and encouraging everyone to turn to the Cross of My Son, for therein rests the fullness of understanding and the reason why every eye should be focused on Heaven. My children, we do not pray for empty promises! Jesus has told you that you will receive full-well that for which you ask in His Holy Name. There are no accidental graces that fall unto men, they are blessings from God the Father who knows you well. I am evidence of His Holy Will to urge you to comprehend the meaning of Love, to take you to the brink of personal sacrifice and beyond. My special priest-sons are speaking about this self-denial all around the globe, and that there are oftentimes feelings of repulsion that accompany the service of humanity in the likeness of your Savior. Those who have overcome such reluctance are the fortunate souls to have already been conscripted into the Army of Saints who are about to be taken into the highest ports of Paradise. You cannot yet know how pleased is Jesus that you accept the mighty commission to which you have been assigned, for there are throngs who still call themselves your enemies. I have told you in times past that their rejection of the Gospel message is a signature of your personal allegiance to and with the Holy Spirit of the Lord. We walk forward together in the assurance that your lives are one in Him because you have surrendered your material, time, and the essence of your beings to the New Life that you have engaged in your desire to seek the Kingdom of Paradise while it can still be found.

It is oftentimes during the summer season such as this one when you see the Earth so fully abloom. Can you not understand that there are no cold wintery nights during which you will shiver in the darkness when you reach the summit of Divine Love? There is the culmination of Spring and Autumn of the Paradisial beginning of the Eternity you have gained by upholding your Baptismal vows, by your confessions, and your participation in the other Holy Sacraments as they are made available to you, and are appropriate for your continued growth in Christian Truth. There are countless people in the world who cannot decipher why there is no more brightness before their spiritual eyes when they leave their homes in the morning to begin the day. If these pretty souls would only continue to be the advancement of the Love of Jesus in the most unsuspecting places, especially in the secular world, they would be nearly blinded in a pleasing way by the goodness they would see growing there. There are others who retreat from their doorways, hoping to greet nary a soul at all, just wanting to be left alone to pine and weep on their own because they find no defining purpose in the cohesion between men. They do this because they have yet to spiritualize the meaning of life to include Jesus Christ in their daily plans. I have told you that Christian faith is the true presence of God in the universe, but many have mistaken Jesus as being just another prophet who holds a certain venue through which to speak to the rest of the Earth. For goodness sake, He is the precise definition of human chastity and Salvation! He is the restoration of the ill and disabled, the lifting of the poor out of the violence of the ghettos, and He is the purity for whom so many who have fallen to transgressions of the flesh must look! Jesus will never turn His back on the sinners of the world, for it is for these that He came to be born, to live, to die, and to be Resurrected from the Tomb. His Crucifixion is evidence aplenty that God loves humanity to the death. When the deep-seated hatred is expelled from the Earth by the acceptance of every soul of the Love that Jesus has given, then His higher Kingdom will be understood; then He can stand alone as the King of Creation upon the stage of chronological time. He is the ushering of immortality to those who are still living backward by reading the entries in their history books! Love among human peoples is the future and the Life that cannot end anywhere imaginable. There is a profound beginning to be discovered by everyone who comprehends this, particularly those who practice the heathen way of life. Their spirits will never go hungry again because the Wisdom of God infiltrates the very first crack in their obstinance in turning away from Truth.

Today, My children, I ask you to reflect on these poor souls who have yet to understand. Remember that it is always a choice of the human will to say 'yes' to Jesus, just as you have said yes to Him. If those who oppose this Doctrine of Love are looking for a miracle, tell them in Jesus' Name that the miracle is that they have lived for so long and have not suffered being completely torn asunder by evil before now. They must know that God has been protecting them all along because He knew the day would come when they would say 'yes' to His Son and affirm their allegiance to the Cross. This is what makes every one of My children messengers, not just those to whom I speak in a discernable way. The visual and audible signs of the presence of the Love of God in the world come from your appearance, from your statements, and your actions of Truth which abound from the faithfulness in your hearts! How can they not respond to the Love for which they seek, especially when it is inside you as you stand before their weary faces? I tell you with great assurance that they will answer, and they are continuing to proceed in your footsteps that you have so boldly taken down the road to Mount Calvary in the image and likeness of Jesus. It is your adherence to the Sacred Scriptures that provides your direction in life. Jesus did not ask you to take-up your crosses and set out in any direction you please. He has asked you to take up your crosses and follow Him. So, when someone asks for forgiveness, you will not be walking in some other direction from them in accordance with your private destiny, you will be walking exactly upon the pathway that Jesus walked when He pardoned the entire human race! This Absolution is continually present and still ongoing in you by the actions you take to relieve your brothers of the guilt they inherited from their fathers and the errors they have made of their own accord. When you tell the rest of the world that the Mother of God has spoken to you, that She has come to teach you how to love, remember most prominently that I have come to ask every soul to forgive those who have trespassed against them. Again, this is in reflection of the Holy Gospel to which I refer. While I have asked you to pray for the conversion of sinners, remember to everyone you meet that I do not just mean those who live miles away that you may not yet know, I am referring to the same people whom you greet on the street everyday, in the marketplace, and those who contact you anonymously for the soliciting of capitalist gain. There are no barriers to the communication to which you are called because everyone you meet has been created by our Triune God who will judge the entirety of the Earth. Please remember the statement that I made beginning this message. These are not optional traits to be randomly employed whenever a situation warrants it, they are ripened fruits of the Holy Commandments to which each individual is called in perfecting the essence of the 'self.' We shall not desist in making these things a portion of our goals and objectives for the rest of the world as Jesus allows time to unfold in accordance with God's Plan. I have told you before that the Father has leaned to His Right Hand and whispered into Jesus' ear that the time for the Reconciliation is very near. When He did this, My Messianic Son had His hands laid on His lap. Today, however, Jesus has His arms commandingly folded across His Sacred Breast and is peering aside toward the Trumpeters of the Ages in anticipation of bidding them to intone their instruments with their final blast. And yet, humanity continues on as if not to realize that there is so brief a time remaining for them to get their affairs in order. The Christian Doctrine is the true fulfillment of the prefiguration of human life, and Jesus is about to make Himself known to every soul, the living and the dead. God is pleading for your patience because He is already awakening the sleeping on His way back to the exiled Earth. These are the feelings of anticipation that humankind must comprehend because the excitement of the Saints is about to burst at the seams.

    Now, My Special son, I hope you are pleased by the words I have offered for the benison of humanity. I come during this hour when there is so much hope outside this house these days because of the love which has been ongoing inside. Your petitions are heard because your wishes and those of Jesus are one. When you speak of the heroic faith for which you pray, there are countless heroes who are mustering strength by reading the things you have written for Jesus. Indeed, this is an heroic age when those who were once extremely timid are gaining even greater strength to stand for the Truth that springs from the Love of My Son. You can see that you do not have to be the winner of an earthly event to be a champion in the eyes of God, as you heard the words of the competitor today who fell from the race by his own mistakes and blamed nobody but himself. This is the human decency to which I have referred so many times in the past. There is no desire for blaming someone else when one's vision is in accordance with this basic decency within. Thank you for your prayers! Next Sunday morning will be seventeen years since your brother's mother came to Heaven, and I will speak to you then."

Sunday, August 19, 2001
3:25 p.m.

"With endless Divine Love, I rock you gently in the cradle of My Arms while assuring you passionately that Jesus is your King and Salvation. My message to you today is that yours is the Kingdom too, and the Power, and the Glory forever to come because you have been regained within the invincible beauty that is perfect Love at the Right Hand of the Father. Jesus has taken you there timelessly, although your voyage through the waters of the mortal Earth continues at the pace of His Will. I ask you humbly to accept all that He asks you to bear, to laud and praise His Holy Name without end, to strengthen the weak with the Wisdom of your faith, to pacify the wailing through the counsel of your allegiance to the Cross, and to be singularly one inside the Sacred Heart which has become your salvific Vessel. Kindness and Mercy assuredly await you during every day of your life. It is true that God will never fail you, the Heavens shall not forsake you, the winds of Truth will always prevail to be your ease of Grace back to the Land of the Birth of the Saints. I continue in their presence to call you to peace because there is no terror in knowing the King of Peace, that there shall no more be war inside the timeless parameters of Everlasting Life, and gone are those horrific memories that have too long made you weep in sorrow for your sins. There is more than a beatific Dawn to greet you in the Morning because God has placed an unending Day of Gladness at the shores to where you are being led, gleefully acrest of the Blood which Jesus so profoundly shed to Redeem you from the lost who, at the end of time, will have their own new plight to suffer. Can you not see this wonderful day in the offing?

I am happy to speak to you today because these are the continuing times during which the world is being cultivated—mortified to expunge even the slightest veniality from your breasts, and conditioned to be able to travel through the perils that still haunt you to this day. God has made it very clear that only perfection awaits you, and such is your goal during your lives on the Earth. He asks you to strive to achieve it in Love because all things are possible in Him. He moreover beseeches your prayers for your brothers and sisters who yet do not know Him. And, those who have already passed into the Light of the Pinnacle of Creation look back to the world they left behind with sincere affection for those who still struggle. As a blessing through the intercession of one who has passed there seventeen years ago on this Sunday morning, the following is a gift of Love for your faith, the voice and Wisdom of the Savior of the World."

(Jesus speaks)
"To My faithful lot of children whom I deem to call My Own, can you not see that My Love has forged the pathway that you are, indeed, continuing to blaze for those who still seek? Just like the world in your midst, that trail must also be pruned and sheared so as to keep it clear for all succeeding generations. This is what makes you continue to search and call, to manifest, to repeat and pray. The Glory that I own, I give to you! Please take it freely of your Will to the perfection of humankind! With this Love, Peace, and gladness at the Center of My Sacred Heart, I promise that these days and your lives shall never pass in vain. I bless you with the strength to carry forward at the behest of My Father, who is in Heaven. You are My Honor and Grace; you are My humility and joy; you are the reason I Live. Come unto Me!"

(Our Lady resumed speaking.)
"My children, it is with these holy words that I commission you to live-out the happiness that you have gained through the Resurrection of My Son, He who came to be and who Is because God has so loved the world. If you truly try to comprehend that which is His Love, you will come to know Him concisely. How do you know what this daily search is for, and where, and why? The Holy Spirit, the Third Person of the Blessed Trinity, is this same Divine Power in you to wield toward all understanding, knowledge, judicious temperament, and peace. If you seek these virtues in the Name of Jesus Christ, you shall become each of them and bear them to all the world. How could any soul be any more jubilant than this? I daresay that it would not be possible to be so on any other path. Outside the windows of this beautiful home is a world that is filled with error and regret, one that cannot yet know true peace because many who inhabit it have yet to accept the Cross as their reason for life. When many among you try to imagine what lies beyond the horizon, they are helpless to know because the weakness of their faith has yet to transcend the vision from their eyes. How can they imagine what lies just beyond the stars when their heads are hanging so low in despair from the ravages of their sins?

It is in the overcoming of sins, the transgressions against God, and the faults of the self that becoming holy is all about. This is not some unattainable mission that has been assigned to those who are somehow supernatural in essence, it is the struggle for everyday men to achieve. Indeed, it is the imperative charge that the Holy Gospel assigns to everyone who lives! Be now My good children of pious purpose and pursue all of this which is good! Take every step on the advancement of the righteousness of God to remake the face of the Earth! Remember to pray for the suffering who are making reparation for the wickedness you see! Whether you choose to accept it or not, there is always a greater purpose in the normalcy of your days than you can readily see with your eyes. These very messages of Mine are sufficient evidence of that!

The nations and continents of the world compose wholly more than a collection of capitals and states, they are the foundation from which many spiritual heroes have grown. Their lands have been the bounty to feed those who have traveled the globe for the purpose of evangelizing the Christian faith. These are the true warriors of Love, not those who have advanced the placement of a multi-colored banner on a political battlefield somewhere. You can engage this spiritual fight from where you reside, from inside the confines of your home and hearts, too! When I call you to prayer, especially for the conversion of all humankind, it is to the deliverance of the many who are held captive by all those vices which keep them from knowing their Savior at all.

So, when you see your brothers and sisters who ask you why God does not bless them, kindly remind them about Me! Implore them to stand upon the caption of faith and describe themselves to their friends and peers as belonging to the Handmaid of the Lord! Then, they will know what human life is for! Then, they will grasp that new beginning that they could never hold-to before, for I will lead and teach them about becoming great Saints! I will ask for their concession to Jesus and for the entire origin of their being to be placed inside the Cup of Eternal Redemption at the Holy Sacrifice of the Mass. There are no haughty protestors there! No mortal can place his lips to this suffering Cup and say that it is not of the Truth! Let Me tell you! I have been there! I have seen this compassionate beginning and the ultimate culmination of human life, itself. When the Crucifixion of the Son of Man rises inside the heart, there are no longer any roles for the liars and cheaters, no room for those who are addicted to the sins of the flesh, and no desire to seek any other pathway but the Spirit of God. No neighbor who is truly in search of God will ever fail to find Him because it is He who has searched for them first. If they say that they will try and refuse to persist in the fight, they have failed both themselves and Him, alike.

Time is wiling away, and there is no more room for trite excuses and lame expressions. The Kingdom of God is at hand! Let they who claim to own any higher dominion come to the fore and take their beating now! Let them fall at the feet of the Lamb of God who takes away the sins of the world and say with active submission in their hearts 'I had no way of knowing that the power of Your Truth was so profound!' Then, they will be glad that their suffering was the healing from their addictions, and the Love of the Almighty Father is the balm for the wounds they have inflicted upon themselves! Yes! All of this is in the near offing, just before they see with emblazoned embarrassment the pain and agony they have imposed upon those who loved them the most, who tried to get them to listen while they only wished to wander astray, those who cried in their beds at night because their loved ones would not listen to them! It is the same with those whose fathers have cast them aside because of their allegiance to God, and the sons who never took time to listen to the Christian witness of their God-given fathers. Jesus is assuredly setting the world aright, one relationship at a time. There is no need to worry anymore whether the faithful are on the straight course. The separation of the sheep from the goats is nigh, and I have the pleasure of telling Creation in advance. Yes! This is the reason for My appearance here today and for all the blessings that I bestow on My children everywhere, and why I have prayed in the sunlight of Heaven for 2,000 years to turn My children around once and for all to see the Brother, Savior, and Friend who is their Redeemer and God.

My Special son, I have spoken the words of Love that I have prepared for today. I hope you have enjoyed them, and that you shall remember with fondness Saint Alta who has been with Me today. She was a warrior on Earth, and is a great intercessor for you and your brother during these crucial years. You will see her again soon, and all the Saints whose intercession you rely on to soften the texture of your lives. Thank you for standing beside the youngest son of Alta, for taking him in, for holding his hand when he is weak, for caring for his timid heart when times seem too difficult to bear. I will continue working through your lives until every soul on Earth seeks you to tell you about your 1600-page Diary, 'I am reading it, and it is beautiful.' You have every reason to hope for the Triumph of My Immaculate Heart, and no reason to despair."

Sunday, August 26, 2001
3:28 p.m.

"Now comes another Sunday upon which we will pray for the convalescence of the conscience of humanity so everyone can awaken to the Glory and Light of Jesus and return to the fold of the Children of God. I carry inside My Immaculate Heart the mother lode of petitions and hopes from generations past, from those who are weeping at the foot of their beds and kneeling on priedieus in sanctuaries around the globe. My special ones, the world is not too large for Love to conquer, for it already has; and Jesus is the King who performed and captured this Victory. I am pleased to announce today, as I have said before, that evil is dead, and that humankind's disavowing of Satan will bring Justice to the Earth. Many hundreds-of-thousands offer their petitions within the brief expanse of a day, and I wish that millions more would turn to Me for guidance and the dispensation of the graces that I afford humanity through My Maternal intercession. Today, I would like to remind you that the Lord knows that faithful Christians suffer a mindless menace of negativity and a barrage of callous insults. In too many ways, these emotional traumas leave scars upon you much deeper than the sword. However, Jesus seeks your enduring courage because America is on the brink of collapse through the subsidence of its moral foundation. Too many Americans have yet to learn that the prerequisite for forgiveness is repentance, and the protocol for Salvation is sanctity. Hand on Heart, I am telling you with all the compassion I can muster that this much change. Make no mistake, there are villains on Earth who would see you lynched at the gallows for your faith in Jesus Christ, but the colloquial term that accurately describes what God will do with America's hedonism is to reduce it to smithereens. Be bold knowing that He will defend you! Do not fear to cantor the praises and recite the epitaphs of extraordinary Christian men. No one should confuse their apostolic zeal with inexplicable delirium or emotional fanaticism. The former is your spiritual birthright in joy, your inheritance from the inescapable protraction of religious Truth. This is why the Lord calls you to patience beneath the Cross. His prescription for inclusiveness declares that the conversion of humanity must be finished correctly rather than prematurely. This is peace and inner-strength, which is vastly different from the irreligious bigotry that is fomenting so much violence in your neighborhoods. I say to you, be noble of intention and sound of heart. Avoid the connotations of impurity on your way to the Altar because they prohibit your soul from witnessing Jesus' Sacrifice with untrammeled clarity. The Holy Paraclete incenses your conscience with Truth, allowing you to see deeply and clearly into the chambers of your heart. When you see the Kingdom of God there, do not be afraid to celebrate your Roman Catholic heritage in every way holy, humble, and reverent. Can you possibly imagine what human life would be if everyone approached Me as their Mother and came to the atoning Cross of Life? This is not beyond the realm of this age because prayer brings untold blessings from Heaven. Be more aware of this as you enter another month that leads to the fall, for the years are passing quickly as they have before; and the Reign of God is here. All Jesus asks is that you seek Him, that every soul embraces His Gospel to serve, pray, understand, and convert. These are the seeds of new life that Christians should be sowing.

All anyone needs to do is review My messages from 1991 and beyond. The simple words of Love and encouragement that are found there are the begetting of a vision for new life, a beatific prefiguration for comprehending the unbounded scope of God's Plan for the culmination of human events. I need not rephrase or repeat them now because time is short, and I have much more to say before the Son of Man returns in Glory to deign the finishing of your lives. Please comply with My persistent request for your authentic prayer, confession, fasting, penance, abstinence, Love, holiness, and peace to which I have been leading My children at Marian shrines since My Coronation as Queen of Heaven and Earth. These are not difficult virtues to attain since you are working diligently toward them now. Your convictions take you there because you have nowhere else to turn for the sustainment of your spirits and the gaining of everlasting Redemption. This is chief among the inferences you conclude about the meaning of life, that Love is the reason, the process, the pathway, and the final destiny. Broken hearts reap their healing inside the

Divine Love of Jesus because He has entered their depths and planted the Providence of Paradise at their core. Only perfection can bloom from them now. He is the Immaculate Patriot who has fought profoundly for your freedom from sin and error. You can fully renounce the material world and know why. There is no sorrow in removing the obstacles before you because you have new ambitions, those that are in alignment with the Will of the Father. If your obedience is strong in echoing His voice, you will stop wailing that the world is against you because you will no longer care. Let men ignore the goodness you lay in their path because those who reject you and your work will eventually stumble at your feet and grasp the seams of your breeches, asking you to pull them from the depths of despair. In Jesus, you are their health and advisory witnesses to the Gospel Acclamations you offer everyday. This should bring you joy in knowing that you are in complete communion with the Legions of Angels who ensure your protection as the months and years continue to pass. How do you know they are there? By the same faith which tells you that this is Me, the Mother of God, who is speaking to you now. You seek the destiny of millions of friends by responding to the call of Grace that I am whelming over the Earth from beneath the sanctuary of My Holy Mantle. When the world is through, you will hereafter know that you were not only born among men, but that you were called to become servants and sanctifiers of mankind in the way of your Savior. When Jesus speaks of taking-up your crosses, your yoke, and the burden which is placed upon you by the secular void, remember that you are a portion of His divinity wrapped in flesh, waiting to be transferred by your own passing and His Paschal Resurrection into the fullness of day. This, My children, is the meaning of anticipation. Your happiness begins now because you know that My Triumph has begun, and you accept in advance the outcome that God put into place. You have written and spoken that mortality is irrelevant regarding your hopes in the Promise of Salvation in the Blood of My Son. Therefore, know that time is on your side because it is the stream that is carrying you to the gulf of this joy. All whom you meet along the way are curious about the Holy Spirit in you, so I ask that you convey God's presence to them. This is an age when darkness no longer prevails in the face of His Light, unlike those of two and three thousand years earlier. The Sacred Mysteries of the Most Holy Rosary that you have prayed today are additional reasons for you to know because your hearts and souls confirm that they are the Truth. Can you not sense the happiness in My words, in the tenor of My voice, and in My expectations for the conversion of millions across the Earth in the future? They need to realize that it is their destiny because, for Me, the future has already arrived. Yes, it has opened for all who have crossed the sanctioned bar into the hands of Jesus. There are endless multi-cultural reasons why so many societies shy from the graces of Love, but there is only one reason for them to return. This is the Cross, and the Son of God who was Crucified there. I have urged you to remember that Jesus is all the seasons of the climate of God. He is the unifier of all cultures and the fount in which every soul bathes to take away the stains of the sleeping generations, and in which your own forefathers drowned. We realize that there is overt unity and goodness in the Cross, and that any soul who accepts the Blood of Jesus is one humanity with Him. I ask My children of every language, every way of life, and all vocations to follow this path by heeding the call of the Apostles and claiming a share of Heaven. If it is by the exchange of knowledge that this shall be done, let the process begin in earnest because every child under the sun will eventually arrive at the same Truth of the Most Blessed Trinity, or perish while rejecting it. I have spoken of the weeping that comes during the enlightenment of the soul, but it is a miraculous sign that the world has finally been conquered by those who have been silent for so long. There may be memories of torture and violation, but they have been incinerated in the flames of Justice that flare from the Sorrowful Crucifixion of My Son. The Lamb of God was commissioned to choose those who are His, and these are the ones who will be first among the succession of Saints. My Special one, I am pleased to speak to you on such a clement day when you are enjoying your life through the Wisdom of My Motherhood. You will be 40 years of age in a brief time, but only a little child in My arms for the Eternity to come. If only you knew how happy this makes Me, you would shed copious tears of joy! There are infinite reasons for you to be thankful to God, multitudes you have yet to see, and scores that lay just beyond your immediate comprehension. You are making this possible because you have said 'yes' to the Mother of every good thing."

Monday, September 3, 2001
Labor Day
3:13 p.m.

"There now, little ones, it has become increasingly apparent that there are no enemies of peace and good will who cannot be made to surrender to the desire for the love that you bear inside your hearts. With the Holy Gospel as your living guide, you are the leaders of a more bountiful age, the one during which every foe of Jesus will be laid bare. Will you continue in His Name to uphold the decency that you have chosen to embrace? Thank you for taking these special moments during your lives to remember Him, and to call your fellow men to seek the Cross upon which He commissioned your repatriation to the Garden of Paradise. My children, whether or not you recognize it, you are becoming the geniuses who are sanctifying human life upon the Earth because you have remained faithful to your Mother. Look and see that it has been many months and years during which you have prayed with Me! Heaven has been enhanced, emboldened, enriched, and underscored by your willingness to see beyond the elements and distractions that are imposed upon you by time; you continue to be focused upon the Redemption you are about to inherit. I have seen this during your entire mortal lives, and now you have given these same lives so you can see with the vision that has presented My Grace to you from the first. As I have told you repeatedly that the Angels and Saints savor the endless joy of your affections, so do the beasts of the wilderness, the fishes of the seas, and the birds of the air know that they are residing amongst the societies of God who, like His Son, wield dominion over them through the invocation of His Love. It is in this preservation that you are their protection, and they your companions. When you rise to greet the morning dew as the fall comes near, you see with assurance that the passage of time has become a component of your Wisdom to seek Jesus while He can be found. Hereafter, you realize that the Holy Spirit is seeking you too; and the singular Truth of the Almighty Father has been joyed by your reunion upon the Resurrection of Jesus from the Tomb. Is the meaning of life this simple, you ask? Perhaps the conducting of human affairs seems quite more complicated by the sinful nature of men, but the essence of your existence on Earth is as clear as seeking to find the Kingdom of Heaven. God has wrought this gift even before you shall die because the righteousness that you espouse is the reflection of Jesus within your hearts, threaded through your days. Let there be no mistake about this; you exalt the Paradisial Love of your Savior when you understand in fullness that your soul will live inside the beauty of Heaven someday. There is no greater fortune known to man than to anticipate this joy and confidence at the summit of your mortal years. Today, I have come during the hours when your nation is remembering the manual labors of those who strive to succeed in the marketplace, those who toil to feed themselves and their children, and those who have no sustenance of their own. It is the work of human hands that has made this a world in which many are living in amenable quarters. My call to America is to remember those who have no way to gainfully care for themselves by reason of sudden misfortune, ill health, or the oppression that is heaped upon them by the avarice of others. I know no more benevolent service than for you to defend them, often to the diminishment of your lot, and to uphold their dignity by the sacrifices in your lives. Your brothers and sisters are a benediction from God, and He asks you to nurture them when you might sooner pursue another course. You are called to clothe their nakedness and defend them against their predators, just as you do the animals in the woods and their offspring who are defenseless against those who live according to no morality whatsoever. You will be plentifully blessed to remember that there are multitudes of the meek and mild who are impugned and effaced by others' wickedness that springs from their refusal to accept the Beatitudes as they have been issued to humanity from the lips of the Messiah of God.

"Now, My Special son, I thank you from the center of My Immaculate Heart for offering your life to Me by accepting the challenge of undertaking still another book. I know that this is not easy for you because there are many other avenues of life that you might have chosen. I realize that you have been asked to see many things in your sight for more than they appear to be. In the process of completing your next book, the Angels will deploy a huge number of weapons of massive power against the heresy and greediness that have pervaded the American culture today. These are visually and physically capable of being humanly observed. While I ask you to understand with maximum faith, you know what these weapons are. I cannot urge you more plainly than this to go forward in the knowledge that the Almighty Father is pleased by the way you are saying 'yes' to everything He asks. We have been a conducive source of Grace for many who are weak, and there are untold more who will benefit by your love for Him if you continue to participate. Do you remember when Saint Bernadette rubbed the moistened soil onto her face? It was this that spilled the healing spring at the Grotto where I appeared. Now, you are being allowed to deem to your own obedience so the Lord will be satisfied that your heart belongs to Heaven and your life to Me. You and your brother have been joined for the purpose of being faithful hope for the conversion of lost souls. I only ask that you proceed with the priceless trust you have shared, in the unimpeachable bond that makes you My children, and with your bountiful hearts reflecting the perfect submission of Jesus during His Passion and Crucifixion. You have garnered vast blessings for humanity, a number that would make even your most modest expectations teem. As you attend the Holy Sacrifice of the Mass and witness the awesome presence of God, you are viewed from Heaven as paving the thoroughfares upon which millions will approach Him in due time. How has this been done? By the bravery of your faith and your thirst for Justice within the bellows of time, a thirst that is being quenched as we speak. When you stand upright for the perfecting of the human spirit in the Cross, other people will take notice and atone for their transgressions. They will seek pardon for their offenses and amend their lives. This is their response because they know you are close to God. Your piety will breathe; it will be the transformation of whole societies into the Light of Truth in accordance with the Commandments of the Lord. Indeed, monumental changes are born in small places. From this purview in Creation, in your present day, you are sowing the seeds of righteousness that will yield the freedom of multitudes by the Grace of Salvation. Please never lose sight of this hope because I promise that everything I am saying is true."

Sunday, September 9, 2001
3:22 p.m.

"That I would come speaking to you, My children, is called miraculous by some, but it is merely a manifestation of the eloquence of God's Peace that ushers Me here. Please rearrange your piety in accordance with the virtuousness of the Beatitudes about which you were caroling in the Holy Sacrifice of the Mass today because Jesus' intentions for humanity are those same principles that are setting Creation aright. Can the Almighty Father change the face of the Earth from the inside out? If everyone who lives there will accept His Holy Spirit, He can. My children, it is imperative for you to remember that Jesus is more than the Martyr and King who was Crucified by a world filled with hatred, He is the First Fruit of the Cross and the Resurrected Messiah who has remade your beings and cleansed your souls. This can be said of no other man! You become like Him when you accept the Holy Gospel He proclaimed, and be pleasing in His sight by living according to its statutes. I have come to pray with you because it is My mission as your Mother. I teach and guide you to know My Son because you are too blind to see for yourselves the things that hinder you from rising above the distractions of the globe. I energize your faith and goodness on solemn occasions, especially when you are summoned to suffer. Many of your brothers and sisters are asleep in sin, but they are soon to be awakened by the inundation of the universe with Glory. It is the commitment of those who have known for many years that will hold them by the hand and be their mentors. I am calling upon you to accept this professorial role. You are the forgers, teachers, and gladiators who have learned to endure and survive the struggles of righteousness; you have been disdained, ignored, vilified, and punished for your assertion that human life does not have to be this way. My message is clear regarding the self-denial that is your imitation of Jesus. When you surrender the material things that distract you from knowing Him better, you tender your consciousness to being more holy in defiance of your enemies. You become accepting of the sacrifices that made Saints and Doctors of the Church of your predecessors, the Christians who had the Wisdom to advise legions and societies to take the hand of God and never let go, no matter the cost. This is a pretty September day when the rains are bringing relief from the heat of the summer. I hope you see the healing balm of Jesus' Love this way because He is relief for the tongues of those who are parched by the wickedness of their ways. It is true, I am the only creature from the Kingdom of Heaven who never died, but My Immaculate Heart was crucified with Jesus. I appear today to tell you that there is no mother's pain that I have not felt; there is no sliver of torment I did not experience and continue to understand. It is for these reasons that I say that I know what ails humanity and what exacerbates the aching inside My children's hearts. If you call upon Me and follow in the footsteps of My Son, your ills will be alleviated and your plight overcome by the jubilation of your communion with the heights of Paradise. My Special son, I remind you that your strength surpasses any other power that you might imagine in your day. You know that I have been teaching you for over ten years about becoming 'Love' in the presence of a world that perpetrates its denial of Jesus at nearly every turn.

Even the things I have been teaching you by our limited encounters in My messages are more beatific than I can explain. I have accorded you parcels and plats of a much larger picture over which you have control, but you could never have internalized in a single hour or day, perhaps even in the recent decade while you were kneeling and listening to Me. Every day that passes, you enter more in the record book to expose the failings of humanity. You will move Creation far from being those little go-karts in the backyard of your neighbor in 1975 to the notorious Winston Cup extravaganzas that have captivated millions of people worldwide. Since you understand such parables, please always remember that your heart and soul are being groomed for the genuine Victory that is forthcoming with greater ferocity than you ever before imagined. I support you in your toils because I have brought you to harbor ominous weapons that you will someday unleash against the enemies of Jesus all at once, like a huge explosion, inducing every volcano on Earth to erupt in applause of your grand finale for the God who first made them heave. The universe will join in unison to the news that your forceful Triumph has begun as a child of the Mother of God! These things are unfolding before you, and it is the Holy Spirit in your heart that is telling you so. God, the Saints, the Angels, and every goodness that spires from Paradise see you seated humbly in your morning chair reciting your prayers in order to make this world a better place. Your Savior and King has raised His head and allowed tears of joy to trickle down His cheeks while He sees you offering the obedience that He has come to know in you. Indeed, when you see the transformation of the Earth at your hands and those of like heart around you, the description of their glorious revelations will not be in parables anymore, but of the subsistence of literary prose that will push your enemies so far into the oblivion of Creation that only their best contrition will lift them up again. Such is what I have sought from them, and is every bit the reaction I have come to demand. Hence, it is for these purposes that I speak to you, and why I assure you that your every move is a mark toward the goal of the conversion of humanity in this generation in time. I am the Mother of God, and I will succeed. Please remember the verity of My words; I will succeed! I insist that you walk into the future with fonder hope and happiness, knowing that your election as members of the lineage of Saints has been won, and your Resurrection from the dead will be your inauguration day. I am prone to say to you and the billions of souls who reside in the world to, '...place your palm upon the Word, raise your right hand, and repeat after Me.' I hold in My arms the Messianic Savior of the lost!

Yes, there are many things that are still ongoing on Earth that are repugnant to God, but they are being expunged from the minutes of history and the legacy of Eternity by our prayers. Never allow your knowledge of them to bring you lack of peace, for your prayers render them meaningless to the culmination of your lives. This does not imply that they are insignificant in the sight of Jesus, but He knows that your lives of reparation are taking care of them for Him. While the venial sins of men are brush fires to which your prayers are dispatched, your goodness and peace are the walls of flames that are keeping hundreds-of-thousands from descending into the mortal Abyss. This is what I always meant by preemptive contemplation, and is likewise the petitioning that has brought such solace to the Savior who reconciles everyone to Himself. I owe you a monumental debt of gratitude for listening to Me throughout the years, for welcoming Me into your home, for summoning the Saints and Angels to remain at your side, for requisitioning the Holy Spirit to guide you in every way, and for allowing the Father in Heaven to be your Lord. We walk in a veritable harmony of Divine Light that supercedes space and time. I know that you accept this as true because your heart belongs to Him. My goals have not only been enhanced by your holiness, God's Heaven to which you will be delivered has been glorified beyond description because you have given yourself to Me—your Mother, your Mentor, and your Matriarch. I thank you in a way that you will see when focusing upon the King placing your tassel of governance into a grander dominion than you have ever known from here. I hope you have enjoyed My words today. Can you discern the vision that you have wielded in a new and enlightening way? Can you see what it is for? Do you feel strong, powerful, and emboldened? This is the permeable signature of divinity to which you are being led. Your kindness is a gift for the world that your brothers and sisters should emulate for sustaining peace in their hearts. Thank you again! Please remember to pray for those who are living in their mothers' wombs to be given the gift of birth."

Sunday, September 16, 2001
3:56 p.m.

"My dearly beloved little children, I ask you to remember at this time in your nation's history that the conversion of humanity often comes at great cost, and is not so much in what God wills to happen, but rather in what He allows so that all races of people will realize how far they truly are away from the perfect transformation toward perfection which is discovered in the depths of the Holy Cross. All suffering, agony, desperation, and realization are profoundly placed in perspective from the purview of Mount Calvary. Therefore, it is only through the Love of the Almighty Father that you are placed inside the Being of Jesus, and He in you; and the Kingdom of Heaven is glorified not by your error, but in the Truth that you are all being slowly taken there on the wings of those who have been chosen to be His instruments of peace and destruction, alike. I am the Patron Saint of this great American nation, and I have seen the essence of suffering and horror from the highest pinnacle of human existence. It is you who are participating in it now, for it is you who are loved; and it is your Creator on High who has placed you in His favor, even to the point that you are worthy to be among those who are given an allotted portion to agonize for those who will only turn their backs and run.

If you wonder whether it is God who has wrought these terrible things upon your country, do not be tempted to blame Him for the error of sinful man. It is He who mitigates all that is yet ill in the mortal world, through His own mysterious ways. While there are so many ironies that surround the meaning of human existence upon the Earth, and so many other paradoxes that seem to take your hearts to despair, please remember that nothing in the material world is worthy of transfer across the chasm of the ages into the incorporeal universe and onward to the celestial heights. Why has Jesus ordained such a pathway where your steps are so intrepid and dark to the tone? Because it is He who has tread there before you; it is His Sacred Heart who is now providing you Light; and it is His liberty which is setting you free, not the flames and smouldering rubble that seem so poignant to your sight, not the rushing scenes and blaring sirens, and not the watery eyes of the New Colossus who stands so prettily in the harbor, helpless to do anything more than she has been capable of doing since her arm was first raised there so many generations ago.

Therefore, I tell My children and My country to rise again, to be lifted past the angst which is pulling your hearts aside, to remember those who have fought to their deaths for the righteousness which has set you free, and to call upon the Sacred Mysteries of the Trinity of God for consolation, renewal, resolve, and strength. This is not the time for war, there is no time for war between men when only their political sovereignty is at stake. The true battle that matters before God was begun twenty centuries ago when He asked you to be not unlike His only begotten Son, He who has been Crucified to take away the sins and the effects of the transgressions that you are seeing to this modern day, He who is still your Shield and Help in time of trouble. My children, the events of this past week did not begin in the hours, weeks, months, or years before they occurred; they began the moment that the Son of Man asked you to be perfect as He is perfect and proclaimed that anything short of that Divine perfection would result in certain devastation and annihilation. You are seeing history repeat itself inside a mortal parameter where good men continue to be silent about the Christian Gospel, and then call for the use of weapons of mass destruction in the wake of the awful effects of their own indifference.

There are no comprehensible words that can truly mend the hearts of My children who have been so afflicted by the loss of those they love, only to know that they are now in the presence of the Creator of the universe, and to move ever so swiftly toward the Sacraments which will again make them whole. There is nothing in human grief that is of a lateral accord, other than to share it with your brothers and sisters, because such grief is always of the vertical elevation that belongs to the Heavens. Hereafter, your nation will forever be closer to the Paradise which engulfs the entire globe and clothes you in its Grace. Millions of people will hear My words of this day only long after I have given them, and another war has been commenced, only beyond the terrible explosions of new conflagrations and the counting of increasing tolls of casualties who will be numbered as being among the dead. I again tell you that there is no war short of dying for the Son of God that is worth the waging; for anything less than this is only vengeance, or the lion who will chase the flea who has bitten him and left a swelling mark on his flesh. There is only a false nature in the unity which springs from patriotism because constitutions and waving banners cannot take you to the pinnacles of holiness; they are only distractions along the way to divert you from the true Will of God to remake the face of the Earth into the authentic likeness of the Holy Gospel through the Messiah who has redeemed you. Once the terrible years before you have passed into expiration, you will see that My words here today are the true orations which should have been lifted, along with the proper Requiem Masses which are already being offered in reflection of the commendation of the dead into the Holy Arms of God. Please seek your solace there, in your awareness that their battles are through, that their souls are now facing the Light, that they now number in the thousands among those who are praying for you from the other side of life.

List not those offenses that you will count among many for which you will seek justice, for Justice is a gift which only God can dispense, and you are a part of the Peace from which Justice is grown. Be the seeds of hope from which forgiveness may blossom; turn your other cheek and be the noble ones who must now have a newer sense of purpose in the Passion of Jesus Christ; and go not backward in revenge, but only forward to the meaningful reunion that all humankind will find in the Glory and compassion of His Sacred Heart someday. Thereupon, I pray for your consolation during these times of distress; I seek you to bask only in the happiness that you are all worthy in sharing the power of the Cross; and I call upon you to remember the meekness and determination of the Lamb of God Who has taken away the sins of the world by bowing in Grace before His persecutors and reminding them that, outside of time, they have already been defeated. This is not the moment for a shameless search delving into the portals of time-honored hatred or a reason to reclaim the limelight before the nations of the world. The American society, the sublime purposes of democracy, and your national pride have not been shamed by the events of this week, but only glorified and taken closer to the Throne of God. Let not your hearts be troubled by thoughts of retribution, lest you become equally as dark as the wretches who have brought you to tears. This is the age of the Resurrection of Jesus from the Grave, and it means for you to turn to Him instead of your arsenals of war. This is a testing moment when your hearts are shaking, rather than the underground where the detonation of other bombs would otherwise make the Earth to tremble by mistake. Wear your wounds of battle proudly for God, and know that He is your Peace. Come to Me, instead, all who are torn apart by the throes of human life, and I will truly take you to the Doorway of Heaven where the Prince of Peace will give you every sensation of Love for which you have yearned since you were only little children swinging on the playgrounds of your fathers' homes. Let this be your remembrance of this awful time! Call not upon your response to the hatred which has befallen you, for it has already been defeated by the Messiah on the Cross. Go forward in the confidence that Jesus is the Providence of God who has chosen you, too, as His worthy Nation of many races to be united in Him once again.

  My dear Special son, I hope that you will transfer these words of consolation to your suffering people someday. They will be consoled both retroactively and in absentia for, by then, they will all accept that I began speaking to you on February 22, 1991. Please know that all of your thoughts about the terrible destruction in America being a portion of the conversion of humankind are true. God does not wish for death and horror to befall His people, but you can also see how many are only now coming to know Him from the first. I will cease speaking to you now in reverence for those who have passed into Jesus through My intercession. This message is yours to use as you please. This is My holy blessing for you now, to be passed along to every soul who is alive in your country today. ✝ Thank you for saying these prayers today! I will speak to you again very soon. This has been a very good week! I Love you. Goodnight!"

Sunday, September 23, 2001
1:47 p.m.

"Every child of God who resides on the face of the Earth should consider it a grave dereliction of his spiritual duties to fail to remember the repose of the souls of the faithfully departed when attending the Holy Sacrifice of the Mass. When you are numbering your blessings, you should always count among them the Truth that your Savior listens to your petitions for the betterment of the station of all people everywhere, inclusive of the living and the dead. Yes, this is the universal consideration which makes humanity whole, beyond and past the mortality that always falls at the feet of your Divine Creator for His greater Judgment. I have come again to this home, where two of My very pretty children live, to bless and guide you, to teach, to pray with you, and to seek your participation in the enlightenment of all the world about the power of the Holy Spirit. If ever a home was blessed, My children, it is this one! Please remember that this is not a reward for your past contributions toward the conversion of the world, but God's recognition that His Son will always be welcome here. I wish for you to listen very carefully as I speak to you today, even more clearly than you may have in the past, because I know that the past weeks and ensuing months will try to be a great distraction from the work that we have set-out to do. If you are pulled into the ongoing discussions about the merits and demerits of international conflicts and political rhetoric, you will not fully understand Jesus' desires for you to remain at peace. Indeed, if the entire world had been admonished to this Wisdom long ago, there would be no such temporal discourse occurring in America today. Every soul on the face of the Earth should be concerned about the terrible words of the leader of the free world on September 20, 2001 as he and others were clamoring for a new global war to begin. This is no more than selfish vengeance at its best and the type of approach which will lead other nations into a global panic and worldwide anxiety. I have called more recently for all peoples of every race to return to prayer for consolation and not to arms for revenge. Sadly, however, My call is being ignored, and many millions are about to suffer the consequences as a result. Does the fate of the material world have to be this way? Of course not! The Almighty Father is a very merciful God of good will, and this is the response that He expects from those who profess to know Him. There is no such phenomenon as avenging an evil if those who seek it also employ the practices of outright evil themselves. This kind of duplicitous action will lead only to greater destablization for those who are innocent of any wrongdoing. My prayerful request is that everyone will turn to Jesus in contrition and peace so that intercontinental conflict can be avoided by all means.

You have entered a changing season now, where there will be that new autumn reminiscence about which you have often written and proclaimed. My call is for you to remember that you must be an innocent society of peaceful hearts. When there are losses that try to take you to despair, your response should always be of prayerful contemplation, always! All of this talk about readying armies for conflict and drawing battle lines has little to do with international accord, and nothing to do with justice! Therefore, My call is for more offerings of sacrificial Love in the face of personal loss, for actions of reconciliation over those of retribution, and for the entire world to gather under the Cross to see what true Dominion really is. There is no pain that My Jesus has not known! Call upon Him during times of disappointment and personal agony, and He shall make both of them take leave of your individual lives! Is it possible that the Mother of God could admonish every soul on the face of the globe for not seeking the reversal of the call to arms that the United States is now enlisting of its forces? My response is that those who are preparing for war are entering a grave condition of sin. Listen well to those who are asking for penance and forgiveness, those who have for so long been praying for peace, whose advice is now and already being thrown aside. I ask the peoples of the world to consider the plight and future of the innocent millions who have nothing to do with governmental struggles or international policies which affect only those who decide where the wealth of the world will reside. Think of those whose plight will only be worsened when the destructive reign of unleashed armaments beings to unfold. I have built a mighty army of souls who are the true children of God, those whose destiny is to live for the everlasting ages in Heaven with the King of all Creation. My army has amassed a force of goodness that no evil can affect or destroy, no matter what is deployed against it. No one who belongs in My army can visit or encamp the horror and terror that the faithless will see as the years continue to pass, because My legions of children have already been led to Victory in the Sacred Heart of My Son. I say to you today, if you wish to amass an invincible lot of souls who can destroy any evil in its path, take-up your Holy Rosary and get in line! There are many good souls who are working quite long and hard to help those who are afflicted these days, from infirmary to triage; and I must tell you that there are Saints in great numbers who are making the charge for peace where there are only the echoes of war. They know what suffering is like; they understand the hollow calls for bloodshed and violence anew! When you make peace instead of stooping to the ignorant bias of battle and knife, you move even closer to the nobility and humility that Jesus has asked of you. Therefore, find your peace in Him; enlist His command to be your guide, heed the lessons of the New Covenant Gospel, remember the sacrifices of the Saints, be faithful to the miracles of the Sacraments, place your futures along the lines of Grace, imitate the temperance of the Christ of all blessings, and take every concern in your lives to God in prayer. I tell you today, by the time you have done these things, there will be no momentary or present requirements for war, and no desire to prosecute a campaign of conflict against your neighbors. When you remember how great is the God of Abraham, you will remember the call to

Peace that His Son has placed before you in His Sermon on the Mount. When you stand high atop the mountain of absolution someday, He will ask you if you served His people by taking them to the foyer of pardon, rather than to the docks in defeat.

If only I could turn the attention of every soul alive to the Mystical experience of perfect Love, that you might stand and pray at the foot of the Cross until you fall to your knees in final understanding, you will tear-down the walls of your own skyscrapers and burn your stocks and bonds in the furnaces of your worst enemies to keep their spirits warm. Once the nations of the world realize that compromise is no substitute for absolute Love, even though it may temporarily resolve a boiling conflict, then you will know who God is. It is more important to eliminate the desire for hatred than it is to refrain from exercising it from the start. Hatred is evil; revenge is the work of Satan, and any nation that practices either of them for their own individual advancement has no place in the Kingdom of Paradise. There are chastisements that are in place to change the hearts of humankind, but I must tell you that the destruction which you have seen to date around the globe pales by comparison to those chastisements, should God decide to dispense them to His unwary people. The things you suffer now are no more than a mild breeze compared to the cyclone that Jesus is about to bring upon those who continue to cast His holiness aside. Please remember that My Motherhood is one of Love and compassion for all of My children, and this is the reason that I am telling you these things. Those who oppose the Sacred Mysteries of the Holy Roman Catholic Church are an impediment to human Salvation! Let there be no mistake; theirs is a bleak future if they do not enlist the faith required to understand what God wants from those who will live in Paradise with Him! A rejection of the Truth of the Holy Eucharist portends a horrible future for those who attempt to desecrate its purity! If you continue to ponder the reasons for the inexplicable violence in America today, it is because those who live across this blessed land are refusing to bow before the Most Holy Eucharist! My call for prayer, fasting, penance, confession, and conversion is being ignored by a nation of people who are being blinded by three colors of a banner with stars and stripes they are wrapping around their eyes. The victory you seek is not found therein! It is found inside your hearts! It is not the false unity of a government of people, it is the Truth and destiny in the Son of God! This is where you should place your sights, because it is upon your hearts that He has placed His own. I promise you with the authenticity of the Divine Nature of your Redemption, itself, that those who travel any other pathway than this which has been laid-out by Jesus are quite the errant ones; and such error will continue to yield untold suffering and injustice inside the borders of your continent and the world at large. I plead with you to understand and comply with all that I have told you here today, for there is no one who lives today in America who has seen the true Glory of the Coming of the Lord!

My Special son, I hope that you understand the need for Me to address the issues that I have today because there is great disharmony and fear ongoing in your land right now. Your brothers and sisters are weeping from grief and crying-out for revenge. The former is redressed by their faith and understanding, the latter must be expunged from occurring at all. I thank you mightily for taking time to pray with Me again today, that you have such foresight to know that only Jesus can bring the restoration and consolation that is so missing around you now. I ask you to remember that you and your brother are larger souls than to be shaken from your mission for Me, even if the battles arrive within inches of your front door... This is My blessing for you now. + Thank you for your prayers! You are My little ambassadors! I Love you. Goodnight!"

Sunday, September 30, 2001
4:26 p.m.

"Little children of Mine, you are the holy heralds who are speaking the Word of God to the masses so everyone alive will know of the sanctification that comes to humanity through Christ Jesus. Will you further acknowledge that the Earth has progressed well toward this holiness since we began praying together, more than a decade ago in time? We wish for the spreading of peace, one that the world can neither give nor take away; and this means more than just the absence of war. It fosters the evocative profusion of good will into places where there are those who study hatred and harbor ill will. As you look into the countrysides and cities across America and around the globe on this last day of September, a month of tremendous change, revelation, and tragedy for your country, you know that the human heart is the cynosure of spiritual cohesion. I have been summoning My children to this unity for centuries, but it seems that it is manifested only during the hard times when ferocity threatens the stability of ordinary days. My children, Jesus is searching for Christians of scrupulous discretion, steely candor, courtly poise, and transparent hearts. What can one conclude about an American nation whose Capital is a glaring contradiction of architectural beauty, Nature, history, and elegance situated alongside such corruption, poverty, crime, impurity, and inhumanity? To believe that the United States government is the closest thing to a model of democratic freedom is an outright disgrace. There is a pall of moral lethargy smothering your lifeblood that is unprecedented in the history of western civilization. Elected politicians play games against the rules with no cognitive sense of fairness. Scapegoating and lucrative partisanship have suborned grave scandal against America's innocence for the past 225 years, and the idea of ethics in the marketplace has become victimized by inconceivable greed. Those who sit in their leather armchairs on either side of the rotunda might refer to themselves as Christians, but such should not be seen as only a name; it must be their way of life and standard of conduct. I warn them to stop patronizing the enticements of the social elite and pay more heed to the suffering poor. Men who wear pinstripe suits, slouch in limousines, and drink cocktails for lunch with foreign dignitaries should take a more critical look at themselves and mute their inflated rhetoric of porcelain doll existentialism. They must magnify their loyalty to God's beatific mysticism and sacred designs, while discerning the benefits of spiritualism that bring sensitivity to the process of government by the chosen. Heaven is looking for new converts who will, in the Name of God, re-evaluate their contributions to humanity, men who realize that dilemmas and paradoxes are often about false choices having nothing to do with Eternal Truth. Is it any wonder why America finds it difficult to interest its children in living for the benefit of the whole? Even when the Holy Spirit invigorates the young, some neophytes undergo a period of shock, withdrawal, and decompression from the obsessive influences of reckless secularism, trying to recount their years in terms of supernal relevance while their whole perception of 'meaning' is changed. Even the adages of elderly men sitting on backdoor stoops proclaim that if you kick an animal long enough, it will stop following you. I call upon My children to cease manipulating other people's lives, timetables, and events; and loosen their grip from maneuvering machines at least while God is trying to infiltrate your hearts with His fondest blessings.

My darlings, you are entering the final course of 2001 during which the fall will turn into aesthetic beauty, the vision your soul has of the ending of mortal life, when you will live beyond the heat of the moment and bask in the appealing environment of autumn good wishes. I come today to pray and reflect with you, to offer My promise of intercession for you to Jesus and before God, that all that you wish for will occur in the immediate future. I have told you time and again that there are many souls who have yet to accept Jesus' Love and the Holy Gospel as their way of life. This is likewise changing as the seasons revolve. Thus, we work steadily in invoking the prayerful presence of the Saints, asking them for the recollection of the piety that the Almighty Father knows well, that they remind Him how good He has been to them, and that everyone who inhabits the Earth will emulate their spiritual presence in the unfolding of Creation. My Immaculate Heart is overflowing with peace today because I have witnessed the Lord effect the transition of humanity from indifference and error to faith and goodness in His own reverent way. It is a gladness for Me to see these things from the vantage point of My Queenly Station in Paradise. I offer you a portion of this vision when I take your hearts beneath My Mantle, pray with you, invoke the Divine Mercy of Jesus, and assure you that God is in control of His earthly Kingdom. Please do not be offended by your struggles, especially when you discover that they will bring the conversion of tens-of-thousands of souls to the Holy Cross. When you traverse the mighty nations of the Earth trying to decipher where might exist the secrets of human life and what is the purpose of the world, you are looking in the wrong place if you do not search deeply into the crevasses of the human heart. We hold the Truth that all peoples will eventually exhume them from beneath the rubble of their plight and suffering, that everyone who owns a conscience will be enlightened by what they know to be the Will of God, enlisting His Plan by those who trust Him. I also come to thank you, to say that people of good will around the globe would be remiss if they failed to incorporate your petitions into their own supplications before the Most Blessed Sacrament. There are many things for which we pray, and the most important is for the deliverance of every lost soul to Salvation. My Special son, how happy I am to have come to know such a grieving court of sinners who have turned to Me, not that they are weeping, but that they have accepted the Grace and righteousness to ask their Mother for aid in the reposition of human events. Now, I would like to address the pursuing of another manuscript that you are professing and authoring. It is developing to be another beautiful assemblage of words for lost sinners to see. We will continue because humanity, especially in the West, needs it so direly. It is only because of your goodness, honesty, and service to Jesus that this is being accomplished. Please do not worry whether your family members or strangers give you comfort or encouragement while your work proceeds in time. If only you could see how the Church is being defiled in other areas of the world, you would know that the indifference you encounter here is rather benign. Therefore, love more deeply and dearly. You are living days of high productivity for the Kingdom of God. The entirety of Creation is jubilant that you have given your years to Him, except those who despise Him. We will speak of the Feast of the Holy Rosary when I return to bless you again."

Sunday, October 7, 2001
Feast of the Most Holy Rosary
4:01 p.m.

"My children, as I address this message to you at this hour, the annihilation about which I spoke on September 16, 2001 has begun by the artillery belonging to the United States against innocent people of Arabian descent. This, as I have indicated, is a mindless act of vengeance that will bear nothing to alleviate the throes of terror against the developed peoples of the world. I urge you to pray for the end of war, from those in which such sophisticated ballistics are being used as you are seeing to the skirmishes where arrows and spears are the weapons of choice. Why do I ask for such prayers? Because those who are directly involved have already declined to do so. The future is one of bleakness for those who have turned their backs upon peace, and there are always many innocent souls who are wounded and killed in the exchange of such crossfire. You will watch the news through your various mediums as events evolve, and most Americans will take pride in knowing that revenge is being exacted at this moment. However, I must warn you that the counterstrike to occur will send people in the United States into further grief and mourning. This, as I have forewarned, is the escalation of the hatred, horror, and destruction that is the result of those who refuse to commend the masses to answering the call of the Holy Spirit to live in the presence of peace instead of conflict. It has been this way for endless millennia, as you know. Yes, this is the Feast of the Most Holy Rosary, and ironies abound in this country and around the world. Does our Divine Lord deign to shake your western shores with earthquakes at nearly the hour when the bombs of the United States are striking a foreign land? Such a question should seem somewhat rhetorical. My children, you have been faithfully reciting the Sacred Mysteries of the Holy Rosary for many years, and this is the anniversary of the baptism of My little Chosen messenger into the Church. Where could anyone's faith take him but to the reasoning that this is the Father's design? Do not all these signs manifest a grand awakening to those who are already looking on? Today, My Special son, I have come to speak specifically to you about how happy I am in your service to Jesus, to the Almighty Father in Heaven, and to Me through your acceptance of the Holy Spirit in your heart. Please know that you continue to be in great favor with Him, that your life is blessed because you have dedicated it to Love, Peace, Justice, and faith. I wish for you and your brother to lead your lives in seamless tranquility in hope that the Gospel of Jesus' Passion, Crucifixion, and Resurrection will be propagated to mortal humankind, regardless of the venue or the recognition you may receive. I know that you are a happy and holy child, and that you have turned the healthful age of 40 years. Please remember that you are comparatively young to the hundreds-of-thousands who live in America today. I attend My Marian cenacles around the globe with contentment and expectation because I know that they are mitigating much error in the world. You and your brother have been hosting your private prayers for years together, and the Angelic Courts and Saints have been here with you. Your friendship has spanned over 25 years. Thank you for trusting each other in knowing that you are striving toward the goal of Salvation for the creatures of God. I plan to continue offering many signal graces to encourage you because they preserve your peace and strength. It gives everyone in Heaven great joy to realize that you remain in this house of refuge and safely away from the turmoil outside. Do you have any comments or questions about anything I have said today?"

(Why do many people in the Church want to speak so often about 'justified war' instead of stating so clearly the message of the Gospel as you do?)

"The Church is comprised of sinners who are fallible in nature, save the Holy See in Rome. If the Pope's flock would follow his direction, there would be no war. When I speak to you, however, I have already perceived the fullest purpose and effect of the Lord's Beatific Light. I have never sinned, and I am not subject to the faulty judgments of sinners. When I tell you that there is no need for war, that there is no reason for justified war, I am speaking the essential Truth that has brought humankind through centuries of peril, with the Church still standing firm. Remember that the Fifth Commandment prohibits the wanton destruction of human life, and the Holy Spirit has said that the use of armaments must never yield evils that are more grave than those evils to be eradicated. Further destruction and carnage are inappropriate means for the restoration of stability and redressing international grievances. To prosecute wars to foster peace seems too much a contradiction in the mind of God. Thank you for speaking with this humble Handmaid of the Lord during your prayers, for remembering today's Feast, and acknowledging the need for holiness in every nation. Please enjoy the week to come. Thank you for elevating the poor souls in Purgatory by your petitions. I love you."

Sunday, October 14, 2001
12:58 p.m.

"The world speaks of a quintessential meaning to the progress of modern works, but there is nothing more contemporary than human love! I ask you to remember that the faith which you maintain for Jesus is the presence of God in you through His Holy Paraclete by whom you are led, and through whom you labor so profoundly for the healing of the nations. My children, ease is to know that there will be many more blessings to come; sacrifice is to know that you must overcome many terrible obstacles to reach them. It is through your petitions that you gain complete understanding of the interrelation of them both. I have come to assist you in actualizing this purpose because I am the Lady of Divine Love, the Mother of Jesus; and My wish is that His Kingdom shall come in your day and at this present hour. He has told you that it is already here in your hearts, in your lives, and in your pious recitations. My prayer is that lost sinners will discover Jesus as the Way, the Truth, and the Life toward their rescue from sin and their gaining of Everlasting Salvation. There are many among you who are continuing to struggle for a better understanding of God. They must accept the Holy Gospel as their credo and you as their breathing examples of His servitude on the Earth. Why? Because you are the disciples who have been chosen to manifest the faith of Christianity in the world today. It is true that there are many of My children who are being persecuted and threatened with the punishment of death for telling the Good News of Jesus in foreign lands. These are amongst the most noble of His followers because they will not reject their faith in order to gain freedom or spare their own lives. I have told you only a month ago that there would be more innocent blood spilled over the lands of the Earth because of war, and this is not the course that God wished for you to follow. The reaction of the western world for the taking of innocent lives a month ago is to ironically and hypocritically take more innocent lives in another region as a response. This is the blind ignorance of blatant sinners, not the reaction that is worthy of a nation that purports to be the likeness of Christ. When you elevate your prayers as time continues to pass, please remember those who are living through these political struggles. I tell you that they are the ones who are truly suffering. Those who are administering the marching orders to their troops in battle suffer very little, and life is quite easy for them. If they ask Jesus for intervention, His response is for them to cease and desist the violence, the bloodshed, the warfare, and the retribution. If their hearts are opened, they will listen to Him. The actions of the recent past are a definitive indicator that they are not adhering to His wishes at all. Many have stated that this has been the same problem through the course of human history. Again, the verdict from Heaven is that this would not have been the case if the entire of humanity had been converted to the Holy Cross of Jesus long ago. While this may seem to be a monumental task for some, it is only by virtue of their prayers for the Divine intercession of the Holy Spirit that it will come. This, in itself, is quite a simple and humbling matter. The meekness of human civility is a Beatitude that in no way implies weakness or a lack of righteous strength. If you recall the words of the Saints, you will recognize that every error, confinement, confrontation, and mystery is resolved and reconciled inside the Most Sacred Heart of My Son. This is why I come calling you to prayer and consolation in Him.

    My dear children, these days that are filled with such peril are as nothing compared to the former centuries when witnesses for Jesus were often beheaded, fed to the hungry lions, placed in public stocks, and given gall to drink. And yet, too many are still afraid to take to the streets with the Holy Gospel in a land where they are allowed to do so! Those who hail themselves as so-called 'reformed bible' churches are clearly archenemies of your faith, foes to the Holy Sacraments, and adversaries to the goodness that blooms from the Holy Roman Catholic Church. Indeed, participation in the Sacraments of Confession and Holy Communion are the only Graces that have converted and awakened hundreds-of-thousands of lost sinners throughout the centuries. I ask you to rebuke false apostles when you see them, and implore them to pray for their own conversion through the Truth of the Apostles' Creed. You need not embark on a search for them two-by-two or go knocking upon their doors because the Son of Man will root them out when the flames of His Justice begin crackling through their foyers. Then, they will see the error of their ways and come running to you for counsel and the ramparts of your love. The asylum they seek is your trust in the Word of Truth as it has been given through every Pope of the Roman Catholic Church who has been chosen by the Holy Spirit of God. I ask you to never be offended by those who oppose your faith because they do not know what they are doing. As I have said, the test of time is assuredly against them.

I wish for you to call on the great parishioners whom you have known for the last decades, especially those who have died, for they can see more clearly now the impact of their faith upon the living allegiance of your own. Indeed, if the Nobel Prize was to be awarded to anyone on this day in history in 1964, it should have been given to the great man *(Martin Luther King, Jr)* upon whom it was bestowed. He has been a living child of God ever since his death, knowing that his call to righteousness was a just one to share. If only more people upon the Earth would follow his peaceful demonstrations of the Truth of Jesus, there would be more debate and less warring. These are the times when you can look both backward with the advantage of lessons learned and forward with hope that you shall never repeat your mistakes again. With Jesus as your guide, you will know that you can never err, that Love is the plane upon which you will always travel, and that Truth is the eloquence by which you will forever speak, even to the moment of your passing into death. I have the fond vantage point of having seen the first words that millions of people have said to Jesus, once they have seen His Holy Face. Each and every one whose soul was taken to Heaven stated that they could not have known how beautiful He was or how horrible His Wounds, but they knew He was with them all along in their darkest hours and most intense suffering. This is how they recognized Him, as He bore these awful things in advance of their own. Woe to those who have lived their lives and have had no grief visited upon them by their greedy calculation, extravagant surroundings, and selfish motivations. I say, pity those who are about to see that they have lived in no way the likeness of Jesus upon the Earth, because their eternal future shall be very grim. Were it not for the ullage which is being sufficed from those who lay in infirmaries or at home while awaiting the surrendering of their flesh, any others who are indifferent toward the Holy Gospel of Christianity would perish in a flash.

My Special son, I have come again today to bless your life and tell you that you and your brother are continuing to be the presence of holiness where you live. Were it not for your obedience, faith and love, you would not have come this far in accomplishing everything to which you said 'yes' in 1991. I have told you that the Holy Spirit is within you, and that you would be the recipient of many signal graces. The one earlier today is another in that number. You must surely be able to see that these are the indications that you are living in accourse with the Lord, and that He is pleased by your work. I realize that you pray for everyone to come to know Me in the way you have. Your work will help them do so."

Wednesday, October 17, 2001

My four-year-old nephew Kolby recently experienced his little dog Buddy being struck and killed by a car. He loved his little pet deeply. They were inseparable. As I sat thinking about how devastated his little heart had become, I began to cry and Our Lady said the following: '...that your profound Christian goodness takes you so deeply inside the heart of a grieving child displays and confirms the kindness of your soul, the validity of your faith, and the authenticity of your love.'

Sunday, October 21, 2001
4:02 p.m.

"I appear here in the mortal world while never leaving the infinite beauty of Heaven and, on this day in your lives, to ask you to accept the everlasting ages which is the Divine Realm of Perfect Love in the Glory of God the Father. My call is for you to not only be holy, but to also become Sacred in the sight of Jesus, that your perfected souls will find a lasting home in His Sacred Heart, and so that your happiness may always be complete by your station at His side. There is no greater Light known to humankind or to the fullness of Creation than that which is the Love of the Almighty Father, manifested equally as Divine by His Son on the Cross. My children, can you not see that the generations in which you live are only a portion of the life which has been allotted to you, that death is not the end of life, but its transformation into your complete awakening? These October skies into which you peer are the solemnity of the harvest which your souls know to be imminent for all the world! The warring continues to be protracted around the Earth, and those who participate know not the day nor the hour when the Son of Man will call it all to a sudden end. Should He deem it to be in the next hours or days, will any wars that are waged not in His Name or toward the advancement of His Kingdom be of any circumstance? I plead with those who will listen to My words to heed the call of Jesus to be His evangelists for the entire globe, to take the message of Eternal Love to the streets and the mountaintops where every heart can see and all eyes will become trained upon the real purpose for human existence.

We pray together; all of the flock of Jesus works toward the goal of christening humankind into a new vestment of Justice inside the Sacred Mysteries of His loving purpose. I seek those who will utter the profound blessings that will make all mortals turn unto Love, who will beseech every man of conscience and good will to speak out loudly and clearly, to remold the morality of everyone alive about the inevitable conversion which must come to humanity before the expiration of time. Cannot the people of God agree that

Paradise contains this jubilation for everyone? Therefore, My appearance here today is His confirmation that this can still be accomplished in your day. The darkness of the world is contagious to those who refuse to escape its grasp, so much that a global pandemic of apathy and indifference has taken hold of the masses. My continuing summons is for this to end both swiftly and permanently, for My Son has plans for Creation that must be placed into being inside the hearts of those who will eventually go to Heaven. Yes, The Divine Mercy of God is Jesus; but every mind, heart, eye, and ear must be lent to the reason for Mercy; and this is a product of the allegiance of humankind to complete and infinite Love. If all the Heavens were to approach the Earth lower than any sinner could imagine, please know that I have brought them here now, to plead with you to finally understand that God is a Divine Creator of ultimate destiny, that there is no other way to the Redemption of your souls than through the Crucifixion of Jesus on the Cross. There are no substantive ointments that can remove your transgressions from existence; only the Blood of the Son of God can do so, a Blood that you must willingly accept in order to be saved! Is this a difficult decision to make or a defiant process? Only if you have not yet let go of the material world in favor of the transformation of your lives into Grace, which is the reason for your newborn righteousness. Whereabout can you travel to retrieve the expiation of your sins in this modern-day of deception and fear? It is not the Earth, dear children, where this journey must be taken, but rather the voyage toward goodness which begins at the center of your hearts! While you trek the many passageways on the land, seeking to uncover the secrets of human life, you shall not find them unless you accept Jesus Christ as the Loving Savior of your souls.

When you ponder the Paschal Mysteries of Holy Week, culminating in the Easter Resurrection of Jesus from the Tomb, this is your beginning to be earnest about the destiny of your own souls and the purpose of your lives. Did Jesus not tell you that the road would be perilous on the way back to Heaven? Has He not asked you to pray to His Father in the words that He has given you? Therefore, be the likeness of the Son, and you will please the Father. Give your entire lovingness to the service of His people, and you will be named as being among the Saints. Offer your bread to your brethren, and you will be fed the nourishment of everlasting Life. Carry the burdens of those who are weak, and the giant rewards you seek will be given unto you! My little ones, these are not just some hopeless musings of vitriol that you might read in the marketplace somewhere, this is the Truth as it has been dispensed by the King of the World through the lessons and teachings of His Life and by His Holy Spirit as He has been advising and admonishing throughout all the centuries since. Living as Jesus has asked you to live may not be a pretty sight because you will be assaulted and assailed by those who are His enemies. In this, however, is your joy complete and your mission anointed. Through the giving of your entire lives to the Kingdom of God, you will inherit what no man of material wealth can bestow upon you. Be not afraid that the foes of Love can destroy you because you have already been vested with the Triumph of human Salvation within the beauty of My Immaculate Heart. Despite those who continue to protest this, the Cross on which your Savior died can be reached most prolifically through My benevolent intercession. I have been provided the means to take your souls directly to the Mercy of God through My Holy Son, a Son to whom I would say 'yes' again and again. As He has asked Me to be your Mother, too, I am here today to establish the following which He has requested Me to seek, an entire Blue Army of holy people who know how to live in the image of Him.

Did He come to save the sinners? Indeed, He has come to save them and more; His purpose is to ask every sinner to take his brother by the hand and tell what he knows about the end of the world. I implore you to accept everything I am telling you as the Eternal Word because I have been commissioned by the Savior of your souls to effect the conversion of those who will live happily with Him in Heaven when the time is ripe. As I have reminded you before, I will not fail in this duty to which I have been assigned, the one that I have gladly accepted in Love for My children. I continue to call upon everyone to seek the holiness which is found in the storied sanctity that the Most Blessed Sacrament provides and reveals, indeed, by enlisting the noble causes of the many apostolates on the Earth such as the Eucharistic Fidellites. There is a destined purpose in every one of them, all to the advancement of the entire world to the Sacrifice of Jesus on the Cross.

My precious little Special son, I have offered the statements that I wish for the world to know today. They will receive them at the appointed time. Thank you for offering them to the entire world for Me! I come today not in brevity, but in profoundness that you will know that everything I have told you has unique, Eternal power! I continue to seek from you your trust that the world is unfolding according to the Plan of the Almighty Father, one through which millions are being changed by your participation. I am allowed to heap as many accolades upon you as I wish, for I am your loving Mother, and this is My purpose... You have had a very good week during the last seven days, and the forthcoming one will be a grace-filled one as well. I know that you are in a state of awe by the pages that My angels are giving to you. The ensuing chapters of your next book will be so profound that it will bring scores of people to their knees in thankfulness... I thank you for your humble service and sacrifices. Please know that they will live well-beyond the elements of time and space... Remember My words for you of October 17th, when your soul traveled so deeply into the heart of your little nephew... It was an awful moment for his little 'being.' Thank you for remembering to God what he endured... Thank you for all the work you have done! This is now My holy blessing for you and your brother. + I will pray especially for those whose identification was made in My message today. I Love you. Goodnight!"

Sunday, October 28, 2001
5:04 p.m.

"So that the Son of Man who was given birth in My Immaculate Womb can be glorified into these modern ages, I have come to you in Truth, for it is He who is the Master of your progress toward becoming new Saints. The King praised in Revelation 22:16 is pleased with you; His Dominion reigns with power over you; and today, the world is a much more holy place because of your faith. In the first decade of the 21st century, humanity is more pure because you are praying with Me. There are no gentle means to confront the world with the Fire through which Saint Paul spoke. It is by your valor and courage that you go on because, as you have already laid bare to God, you belong to Him and to humankind, and not to anything or anyone opposing Him. Wherever you go from here in the elements of time or space, you have become new creatures under Heaven. You have been molded and shaped into the likeness of the Christ about whom I speak, and the Eternal Father is equally grateful. My Immaculate Heart is filled with affection for you, that you would care so much to be one with Me in the magnitude of His Love, that you are among those through whom the Roman Catholic Church is accomplishing its mission. We have prayed together much in the same way that I have interceded for the emphatic generations before you. Indeed, your birth into the exiled world and your faithful ways have been God's response to the prayers of thousands of your predecessors who have gone into His hands in the Light of Paradise. Therefore, I ask you to never forget how special you are, that your lives have a transcendental purpose beyond the stars, and that the hope by which you live is being emulated by masses of people everywhere. When the night descends to bring rest to the nations, they often think that another existence has befallen them. There is a gloominess hovering in the darkness that is almost undefinable by the heart. However, when the sun rises from beyond the eastern horizon, those who see such helplessness believe anew that life must be right, for another day has begun. My children, this is the same transformation that you are helping Me spread; this is the deep erudition that your prayerful work is spilling onto the floor of Creation so that many who are forsaken can be found and know that they are walking toward Jesus by His Light at their feet. It is you, My dear children, who are drawing this Light from the Throne of God. Can you see that there are many doors upon which the Holy Spirit must knock? These are hearts, My children! And, they are brittle hearts! Even the presence of the Son of Man is enhanced in the mortal universe because you are His friends and helpers in the precincts of the Earth. You move swiftly to your brothers and sisters' homes in prayer to tell them that the Kingdom of God is at hand, and that they should expect to receive Him presently. With the whole Wisdom and Truth there is to bear upon the temporal world, God knows that you are His people. He is uniquely aware that you are His advocates and soldiers in the battles for peace and justice. Your reward is great because He loves those to whom He gives the Life, Death, and Resurrection of His Only Begotten Son. I have the distinct privilege and high honor of telling you that these people are you! How have you received and been granted this Grace? Because the Lord is the sustainer of your lives. Your reception and participation within Jesus' Most Sacred Heart is reason aplenty for you to be accepting because God knows that He will find you there searching for answers. While we pray and work forward with the interest of converting lost sinners, please remember that you own the right and destiny to proclaim that you are about to receive a Diadem of Salvation. It is not haughty or folly to boast of your Redemption because it is only through the power of the Holy Spirit that you confirm your eternal destiny before the offspring of your fathers.

My little children, some people believe that unseen Creation is inert, that it just lays there like a pall covering a tomb. On the contrary, it is in many ways more alive than they are. You should never desire to change the essential nature of your humanness; you cannot say that you have failed as a person and wish to become a bird or flower, or a piece of granite or a cloud in the sky. No matter what you think you have done, everything about you that lends to God's Kingdom is salvageable by Him. He has already instilled in you the loftiness of eagles, the beauty of roses, and the strength of cornerstones. You need only to comply with My messages; are you holy, pure, generous, approachable, and polite? Realizing that you may not be there should not cause you any anxiety, undue provocation, or sense of serial illegitimacy. Indeed, if you calculated all the unsung heroic acts of Christian men and women, you could fashion another world. Once the human heart is captured by the Holy Spirit, that person is remade into the image of the Lord because there is a private Pentecost that every convert experiences, opening doors previously unknown, and fostering a 'prologue effect' that regales the first innocence of that person all over again. This is the faith that dares the future to rescind it, and that challenges its enemies to match it. Therefore, I have come to make your faith more sensitive to God's supernaturalism and less dependent on the pharmaceutical mechanisms of the material Earth. Christianity is an ongoing exercise in spiritual sanctification and enlightenment, not a controlled laboratory experiment to be concluded before next Tuesday noon. My Special son, I have high hopes that you will convince your brothers and sisters that Jesus is pleased with everyone who has taken-up their cross and followed Him. Thank you for listening to My words. Please be assured that not only is the Kingdom of God here, the Triumph of My Immaculate Heart is at hand because you are the Light of His Dawn. Thank you for making the Cross the reason for the lives of many who have given themselves to Jesus! This ensures their Salvation, where they would have no other means to live."

Sunday, November 4, 2001
4:00 p.m.

"Dear children, the magnified abundance of your petitions for humanity is enlisting great graces for them and for yourselves, as hearts are changing by the droves toward embracing the Divine Love of Jesus. We pray together, and this is the pious gift that has made such a difference in America for more than the past decade. The work you have set out to do is splendid before the Almighty Father, especially the continuation of your new book about the imperatives of Christian Truth in the freest nation on Earth. Some will ask why it was of such urgency for you to inscribe it, and you may tell them that it was because the founders of your country declined to call the trust of its citizens to one Truth, but to a collection of so-called truths that were supposedly self-evident. This spawned the beginning of the pluralism which has been a gross blunder and the undoing of decency in America today. It opened the door for other influences in the faith and behavioral attributes of millions of people. However, you are working expeditiously toward returning them to the single Truth of the Love of God that is perpetually the Life of Jesus, borne inside their hearts. What a noble mission you are undertaking! Your work is not finished by any measure, for there are hundreds-of-thousands more whose souls will benefit in the immediate future because you are remaining faithful to Heaven and obedient to Me. Thank you! So many people ask whether there can be solace or true consonance in serving the Lord, and their response is in affirmative accord with the condition of their heart. Are they willing to sacrifice of themselves so their counterparts can be freed from anguish, physical suffering, and loneliness? If so, they will be pleased to say 'yes' to the sacrifices necessary to bring this to pass. Will they open themselves to their own suffering if God calls them to participate individually for the glorification of the Holy Cross? This is a determining factor for augmenting the conversion of lost sinners toward accepting the Passion of Christ in reparation for the sins of humanity. Just as God asks you to share the Easter Resurrection of Jesus, He seeks your acceptance of the darkest hours that led His Son to the summit of Mount Calvary. The essential nature of your compliance is in the authenticity of your allegiance to humankind, and to the Almighty Father, the Son, and the Holy Spirit. When you feel as though God is asking more from you than your spirit can bear, this is the moment when you are confident that you are closest to His Throne and accepting of the Divine Mercy of Jesus' Sacred Heart. My children, this is no loss of dignity, for it is assuredly your advancement upon the eternal reward that you will be given at the hour of your death. I am heartened that so many among you are pleading to God for the poor souls in Purgatory, those whose final cleansing is being effected so they can know the fullness of Paradise and preeminent Light.

Please remember to pray for them so you, in turn, will have many new intercessors to beseech the Heavens for your deliverance from Earth. It is not repugnant before God for you to ask Him to set them free, no matter what many who protest the Roman Catholic Church have proclaimed. Indeed, if not for their release from Purgatory, many of those who do not even believe in its existence might deny their final cleansing upon their mortal passing and cast themselves into the infernal Abyss. They should be grateful that those who are released from Purgatory remember their sorrowful souls from their stations in Heaven. Since this is a month for remembering the dead, not that any other is unimportant, please implore Jesus to bestow His Divine Absolution upon those who have been obstinate against believing and accepting the Grace of all Seven Sacraments. The entire expanse of Creation will soon know what a gift to humanity they have been. It is through your faith in them that your purification is granted, for it is by your trust in Jesus that you are saved. The Most Blessed Sacrament is your Food for Life, the Manna from Heaven, through which you are made strong, holy, and pure. This is a miraculous gift that must be accepted with contrition and joy. I am pleased that so many who once abandoned their faith have decided to regain it through their relinquishing of the paraphernalia of this world, and by their openness to the power of the Holy Spirit, your Advocate before the Throne of Heaven who corroborates your plea for clemency, especially chosen for you to be eloquent before God in the company of the Saints.

    Children, there are no villages or quarters in Heaven where you must seek refuge for the night as though the terrors of mortality might strike at your heels. Salvation is your perpetual gift of Light and an endless Mansion of peace, Love, security, holiness, and contentment. The parameters by which you think of your existence in mortality are superceded by your Resurrection with Jesus. After all, this is the destiny of your faith and the reason why you continue believing in Him. Saint Paul once spoke to a massive crowd of sinners and said that it is not in the making of war that is the battle, but ever thinking that it might be lost. There is no defeat in your march toward Christendom because you are sufficed true victory amidst the pain and grief of being rejected by those who oppose you. This is why the Passion, Crucifixion, and Resurrection of Jesus is such a Triumphant series of supernatural events. When you promise your participation in them, you are not to worry that you may fail. It is metaphysically and universally impossible for you to be defeated in the war against evil when you engage it in the Name of Jesus Christ. Moreover, there is no greater weapon at your disposal than the Holy Cross upon which He died, which is perfectly perceived through your recitation of the Sacred Mysteries of the Rosary. I have been pleased to announce that the Blood on the Tenth Decade of the Rosary of many of the Saints was not from their own fingers, but the Blood of Christ Jesus that He left in advance of their Consecration to His Most Sacred Heart. The emission of the scent of roses is not some random choice of Nature, it is the intentional signal of God that He is with you while you pray. The golden links between the beads do not mean that they are wearing thin, it is your auspicious omen that the Streets of Gold in Heaven are only a few more Hail Mary's away. I say to you that God has many reasons for leaving the legacy of His gifts to you in this modern day. Most of them are your signposts toward greater faith, but it is mainly an extension of the principled fact that He loves you. Where would He require any other reason to keep your hearts aflame? Have there not been stigmatists who have attested to this Truth, the one and only perfect Truth that is the sacred reason for the cohesion of societies of men? Please take comfort knowing that Saint Paul is standing in the wings alongside humankind with his index finger and thumb on his right hand almost touching, and his voice proclaiming to your awakening hearts that Heaven is 'this close' to reclaiming you for Almighty God and Christ the King. When you pray deeply and carefully with meditation from the heart, you can see and hear these things above the clamoring world. Those who ask you to discontinue attending daily Mass are part of the evil that Jesus came to destroy through the love in your hearts. Anyone who tells you that the Most Holy Rosary is simply an obsessive repetition of words is not even slightly in alignment with the Divine purposes that will keep their lives at peace. Therefore, thank you for praying the Sacred Mysteries, for many among you are lost and wandering about in a state of misery. Those who have held their faith in Jesus will be the envy of millions when He says that the end of the Earth as they have known it has arrived.

My Special son, I am sorry that you are suffering the symptoms of a virus. You will be feeling much better soon. Please understand that I am with you to safeguard your health before those who would try to make it worse, and I give you comfort through the night. You have been susceptible to such viruses all your life. You will return to the fullness of health very soon. I have been praying for all who have lost loved ones in the recent tragedies in America and in the upheaval of foreign wars that I told you would break in My message of September 16, 2001. However, the casualties have been lessened by the power and extension of your prayers. Thank you! God in Heaven and Jesus the Eucharist thank you for invoking the Holy Spirit. I am happy that you participate so joyfully in God's Plan for the conversion of His lost sheep. It is important that this be a sense of victory for you. After petitioning the way you have offered, you can retrieve whatever you need to make your journey of Redemption complete. In answer to the question you are pondering, please know that I foresee immense elation and jubilation by what you have chosen to achieve. I know that the strongest and clearest moments about which you speak are when you realize that your Mother is moved to supreme happiness by the things you accomplish for Jesus. Such prayers are the most endearing to My Immaculate Heart of any that have been offered for 2,000 years. Someday you will understand more clearly, for it is in the filial obedience and love that you are offering, and it is My desire to see you succeed. Your success is contingent upon whether you are convinced that your work makes the Earth more holy. You must feel this valiant Triumph to the depths of your heart and soul. I will circle the globe this week offering My blessings to the people who are calling Me. Thank you for your humble service by taking such good care of your brother. Your reward in Heaven will be great."

Sunday, November 11, 2001
3:44 p.m.

The Seven Triumphant Virtues of the Immaculate Heart of Mary

Darkness is Beheaded by the Marian Birth of Jesus Christ
Humankind is Purged through Jesus' Sorrowful Passion
Creation is Laid Bare by the Messianic Crucifixion
Humanity is Exposed by the Light of the Resurrection
Atheism is Destroyed by the Flames of Divine Truth
Converted Humanity is Newly Baptized
Redemptive Immortality is Spread Over Creation

"The God of Abraham is glorified that you, by your solemn volition, have chosen to carry your faith in Him to so many heights and through the years that you have given Him your souls. The prayers of the Saints have been answered by your lives, and Jesus dwells in your midst so that His Messianic mission can effect the joy of their tears. My children, through the service of your love for Him and for the Heaven He possesses, I have today dictated to you the Seven Triumphant Virtues of My Immaculate Heart. As in the days of old, their presence is the new beginning for millions who will come to know the reason for the Divine nature of humanity in Jesus, so that your hearts and souls are converted, purified, renewed, and redeemed through His Passion, Crucifixion, and Resurrection. I have never divulged these Virtues to humanity before now because the world has come to the age in which I am appearing the final times. Moreover, God has allowed Me to dispense them here because this place is the venue He has chosen for them to be revealed to complement the End Times. While this is in gratitude for your faithful service, it speaks to the dedication you hold for Me, the Mediatrix of all Graces from Heaven. My jubilation is in knowing that you are safe inside the Sacred Heart of My Son, that you wish for nowhere else to go to be christened by His Light; for there is no other Savior of mankind than Jesus Christ, and your hearts pine for His Truth, the Love of God that makes you wholly one in Him. Today, we are praying for every sinner to come to the fullest understanding of absolution, that it does not just imply a temporary reprieve from your daily mistakes, but that it is the expungement of the whole history of human transgression, down to the chaffy barnacles on your spirits. This is a permeating and righteous revelation of Everlasting Life to astrict you to Divine Truth when you before wondered what would be your fate. It is the dispensation of the unseen future inside your hearts. These are the transcending elements of the miracle of your faith and in the belief that you can be taken to the heights of Salvation, no matter what your error, in the Blood of Jesus' Cross. Too many people say they have never seen the Holy Cross, and that they cannot see it now; so how can they accept something they cannot physically touch? My children, your deliverance is much more sublime than this. Touching the Cross evolves from the sacrifices you make for the alleviation of suffering to the diminishment of the self. It is in loving everyone who has ever lived, even those you will not meet before you die. Seeing the Cross is accepting your portion of blame for the way Creation has deteriorated from the beatific goodness that Jesus calls it to be; and in that same realization, doing something through the Church to make it better. Seeing the Cross is knowing that there are inmates in prisons; and touching the Cross is visiting them there. Understanding that Jesus suffered a horrible scourging for the sins of humankind is to offer God your heart. Being pure and teaching others to be chaste is your response from Him that He has accepted it. These are the decisive acts you must acknowledge and undertake, and listen to Him so you will know how.

It is not through the eyes or with your fingertips that you see and touch the Cross, but through your love for the humanity that Jesus saved, by raising their level of awareness about His Kingdom at hand, and lifting their hearts enough through your own affection that they will desire to seek Him on their own. Then, after you have done these things, your soul will know its purpose, even before you have seen the pinnacle of perfection with your eyes aglow. Dear little ones, I have heard many peaceful prayers to this end because My faithful children know not how to begin to accept their crosses and live-out the meaning of their faith. I tell you today that human perfection is garnered by your intentions that bring you to see the Cross in the ways I have described. Jesus would have allowed no mortal man to depose Him from the Cross on Good Friday until He finished the world by His Death and completed the Salvation of the human race. He is telling you that He is the Messiah, and that you should work diligently to remove the crosses from the lives of everyone else, including those who declare themselves to be your enemies. The mission of the Church is caring for the people who cannot fend for themselves, to feed the hungry, clad the naked, set free the captive, and admonish those who walk errant paths; in effect, extracting their crosses from before them and within them that keep them from knowing that they are loved. This is the key to the New Covenant, My children! Do you love humanity, and does every single one of them know it? The latter, regardless of what some partisans say, is just as important as the first. Jesus mandates that you love one another publicly, that you prove your service to them within the purview of their hearts. These acts sustain the Litanies that you recite in the solitude of your rooms. Such is the way Jesus was Crucified before the world on the summit of a Hill.

Now, My Special son, I have gladly come to visit this home again because you are making Me monumentally happy. Your work has grown to be expansive, extensive and perpetual, and you are reaping untold benefits for the people of God. While I am humbled that you return a compliment to your Mother about teaching you how to pray, it is only your acceptance of the Holy Spirit that has made this true. I am speaking to the sanctity of My own Divine Son when I speak to you because it is He who responds from the depths of your heart. This is how He will deliver your soul to Heaven at the end of time when the Holy Paraclete returns to the side of the Father. For now, He is pleased to reside in you, and more happy because your faith allows Him to live in the temporal world through your welcoming life of trust and service."

Saturday, November 17, 2001
2:48 p.m.

"Having not suspended the gentleness of His Divine Mercy, Jesus continues to perceive the world through the gift of spiritual forgiveness that He has granted humanity from the Cross. I urge everyone who does not know His Sacrifice due to self-imposition or the omission of others to remember that there is no stopping the Love of God; He cannot forsake you or cause your heart to know any breach in the Messianic Absolution that belongs to you. Today, My Special son, I speak about this because I know that you and your brother are given unconditionally to being remade in the Sacred Heart of Jesus. Please believe that you are achieving this goal without exception and beyond hesitation, and this is why I am moved by your lives. Thank you for allowing Me to be in your presence again. We have a great deal of work to do, so please do not permit a single moment to detain your hopes from working together with My hopes to accomplish it. The power of good will cannot be put asunder by your adversaries who decline My intercession from Heaven. Is it not unconscionable for anti-Christian activists to attack a religious faith that refuses to compromise with evil, that addresses, condemns, and curtails the world's violence and the erosion of traditional family values? The loyalties of the heart to the sanctity of the Lord cannot be impugned. Even the illiterate and those with no sense of narrative have written poems and sonnets of their dreams; they are playwrights of the way Creation ought to be. Our weekly conversations are a deep reservoir of empathy for them. They realize where they were founded as children in the righteousness that engulfs the Earth in

Heavenly Light. Their radical reorientation to the Gospel can ofttimes be as simple as recognizing that it is there. Time alone may wither their memory, but it has no power to expunge the past. Things like physical beauty, acumen, and social popularity will always fade, but the invisible virtues that are harbored deep inside the heart will always remain. Anyone believing otherwise, those who hold like leeches to their hatred against their brothers, will find no amnesty in Heaven from their grudges on the Earth. Let us pray that unity overcomes whatever else lunges into being, and that the most solemn moments in history are farewelled by their newfound christening in the Lord's Paschal Supper. My dear children, you should never forget that the human conscience is a function of God's prolific orthodoxy, and your spirits are perfected by His paranormal Wisdom. Do not feel threatened by the rants of the Church's persecutors or feel indicted by modern skepticism, for you are living in an age that is pregnant with miraculous deliverance. Jesus looks for a sanctified Earth that has a sense of itself, that is dignified in Him in all things Divine. Your place inside Creation, both the present and future, and your legacy for that matter, must eventually make sense when laid parallel at the end of time alongside God's Omnipotent Truth. When the body, soul, and spiritual conscience are in perfect harmony, they are a veritable conclave of sound Christian doctrine, discretion, precision, and discernment. You will be victorious if you look at today's rabid secularism for what it really is; never mind that it treats the Catholic Church as though it is some sort of contraband. Beating back the enemies of morality is not a leisure or novelty, it is the reason you were baptized by water and the power of the Holy Spirit. This is the faith that has led to tearing down walls of oppression, bringing reconciliation between estranged family members and friends, changing monopolies into perestroika, and lending the whole Earth to the emission of good will from its farthest corners, never before seen in the history of man.

Conversely, your faith can be extremely fragile in a field of emotions, in an environment infested with the deep traumas of assault and exploitation, the scars of wars, and unattained personal goals. These things tend to lead your brothers and sisters away from the Sacraments of the Church. Some are so entrenched in mortal sin that they have become anaesthetized to its grotesque consequences, taking a devastating toll on such villains as pornographers, thieves, rapists, murderers, and blasphemers. As I told you a moment ago, the fact remains true that every man is responsible for the integrity of his own conscience; and trusting in the Providence of God is their surest way to repent. I wish for you to remember that God assures you that He will continue to accept your gifts to Him. I am embracing your humble heart with thanksgiving and hope because you are standing firm in the faith to which you have been led by the Holy Spirit. You cannot yet discern the joy that you are giving My Divine Son because your eyes still see the material world. As you know, the Kingdom of God is tucked neatly inside your awareness of what you cannot see, but know with affection in your heart. It is supernaturally imposed into Creation because of the sacrificial love that you have given My Son in compliance and servitude. Again, this is only the beginning of the means by which He plans to remold the Earth because of the offering of the gifts of your life and good faith in tandem with your brother. Humanity en masse must be reminded that you only deplete yourselves when you satisfy your basic needs without remembering that these same requirements are instinctive to all other life. If immorality in 21st century America had an ignition, it was not solely of long-festering biases, corrupt politics, corporate greed, illegitimate warfare, or racial discord. Indeed, these are symptoms and byproducts of the Edenic transgressions of Adam and Eve. Even America's social revolution and material excesses of a half-century ago did not foretell a different or unique degradation of the human soul, but were founded in the same disobedience that has stained humanity for thousands of years. Jesus wishes that you will not be shorn of the innocence by which you were conceived, but that you will turn to Him and escape the loop of unholiness that has pervaded these latter ages. I tell you that it is only by your submission and the relinquishing of your will that this shall be done."

Sunday, November 25, 2001
Feast of Christ the King
1:42 p.m.

"The angelic voices of the Children of God are heard with great urgency on this day of high Feast! The King and Master of Creation has opened His Sacred Heart to listen to the prayers of the faithful, and responds with the noble Love that has made Him your Savior and Judge. Jesus hears your every plea, and He wishes you to continue to enlist His aid toward the nourishment of your faith and the healing of every wound that hurts your hearts; for this is a King who is Almighty and forever, unlike those of the Earth who pale in time. I ask for your return of the reciprocal trust He places in you to know the Will of God through the Holy Gospel and the Paraclete of Wisdom who has taken refuge in your hearts. If there is any other prayer that should be lifted today, My children, it is for you to know that the Prince of Peace and Sovereign King will answer your petitions when you place them before the Throne of God in His Name. We pray together on this day, the last of the Church's Liturgical Year, before the Season of Advent begins. The preparation of the ensuing weeks should take your spirits to the remembrance of the simplicity in which Jesus was born. Never forget that it was the invitation of the Archangel Gabriel that brought the Grace into the world which has redeemed your souls, the Feast of the Annunciation, which you shall celebrate in exactly 120 days. Some quarters of the globe will observe it on

April 8, 2002. When you place the birth and living presence of Jesus into perspective, you can understand with greater sympathy how He suffered and was misunderstood by mortal men. While this is ongoing to this day, it is your humble prayerfulness that is leading many millions more to the Cross for the fateful drink of Absolution, allowing them to open for the Redemption that is found therein. My Special son, again I come to you in happiness and joy because of the grand works you are achieving through your love for Jesus and Me. It is a kind gesture for you to position all those brief biographies in your new book because many tens-of-thousands will identify them as their heroes and legends. Indeed, your kind words about My sweet Pope John XXIII are of great honor to a servant who was elevated by God. He was given to the Church through his birth to humanity on this day 120 years ago, as is recorded in history. Do you see how your days are a refraction of your entire life, as though you can pare the intentions of the Father down into the most specific intentions He holds for every month and year? You are a product of history, and yet you are also its maker. You can find the signature of God in your everyday lives; and His control over your station in time is revealing evidence. Therefore, we continue to pray together that you will always know His presence, and that you will never fear that you are left alone, even for the most brief of times. By all means, God has not ambly placed you into exile by reckless abandon or ever asked you to fend for yourselves. He is your strength in all ways, and your guidance and Wisdom to protect you through the darkest pits of night. He gladly shares the dignity you have garnered through your faith and trust in Him. As you have been foretold, there are countless signal graces surrounding you to remind you that you are so loved, and that codify the record of your days before the backdrop of Eternity. There are only few who recognize these things, and I am happy that you and your brother are among them. We have accomplished much toward the conversion of the Earth, and humanity and Heaven will be much the better for your consenting to respond to Me. I am listening attentively to the prettiness of the tenor of your prayers at this moment, and we shall never desist in our supplications for those who do not know God. Now, as you see the approaching season during which there is such exaggerated materialism in America, I pray that you will not allow anyone to refute your insistence that the world turn to higher spiritual values and away from collecting belongings that serve nothing except the greed of their owners. You will soon hear social economists challenge your new book who will say that you are espousing an ideology that will result in millions having no labors with which to earn a viable living if America turns away from the manufacture of many tangible goods. This is a pretense and untruth because owners and workers alike should be more spiritually focused toward Heaven, away from the physical world. There are children in the United States whose parents have had to construct large storage rooms inside their homes to hoard the toys they have accumulated over the years. What do these things have to do with prayer and the alignment of the human will with the intentions of God? This shall be a portion of your response to them. I have already seen the completion of your book, and it is a wonderful recounting of the reasons why the citizens of the western hemisphere should pursue more sacrificial lives of prayer and service to the poor. The evidence is hard and fast to make the case that America is a nation embroiled in synthetic surpluses and secular devices, neither of which does anything to further the Kingdom of Jesus to anyone. Your earlier writings state this point well. It was kind of you to place the ears of corn in a row outside the window where I am speaking to feed the impish little squirrels. Yes, they will eat it! And, they will bring along their friends. I simply wish you to remember that I am praying for you, and also with you. If I highlighted all the signal graces that abound in your life, I would have no hours remaining to say anything else. There is a certain charismatic sequence to the age in which you and your brother are living that was designed by God because He knew you as His children from the moment of your conception. There is no reason why this cannot be the same for every newborn child, if only their parents and guardians would heed My call to righteousness, servitude, and prayer, and accept the culture of life hailed by His Holiness, Pope John Paul II. I must depart to bless My other children. When you record this message and My message from last week for release to humanity, it is not necessary to include their numerical aspects, for they are signal graces for you and your brother to remind you that God knows precisely where you are located in time, and that He is forging your every step."

Sunday, December 2, 2001
2:44 p.m.

"Where there is found peace and blissfulness, where good men come to ask God for Divine intervention, where those among you are poor and despondent, this is where you will discover the compassion of Jesus Christ to bless and comfort humanity for Heaven's sake. I come today to speak in this holy dwelling where you have been inviting Creation to plead to Jesus for the conversion of sinners. I concur with your desires, and I ask My Son to respond to your petitions and to My auxiliary prayers. Please never desist in summoning Him as long as you live because there are too many errors yet to be amended; and sacrificial reparation for the multitudinous acts of desecration against the Mother Church is an urgent necessity. The lessons you have learned here, My children, are your memoirs of ways to live in the Light of service; not that you will be hailed as trailblazers in circles and societies, but that you may forge new ways for the Holy Spirit to enter the hearts of those you meet. Vested in you is the absolute authority of Jesus to teach humanity about His Sovereign Reign, and these are the most crucial times for you to lead. I have knelt praying beside you and for you, that you will succeed despite those who loathe you. It is true that you suffer despondence in your own right if you are not patient during the plight of the temporal Earth and remember that it takes time for humankind to change. Let this be your consistent charge as you pray for world peace and the vindication of every sinner in the Blood of Jesus. I have previously said that many people will not seek Him because they believe that their transgressions are beyond repair. The Blood of the Cross will expunge them so that no sinner should worry about his past. It is imperative to remember as well that a firm purpose of amendment must bloom from the heart for it to be sincere. Rhetorical promises do little to mitigate the wrongdoings that have been committed against the Kingdom of God and His humanity. It is important that everyone receive the Sacrament of Reconciliation when guilt befalls the innocent nature of mortal men, especially during the seasons of Advent and Easter. No one should presuppose that he is free from sin because the mind lapses into such complacency that it becomes difficult for the heart to know. If there are friends in your midst whom you have offended, or any who have transgressed against you, your reconciliation is within the Sacrament of Penance. There are too many who question the cleansing power of Confession, and much too large a number who protest against its sanctifying purpose. Once someone has opened their heart to God in the way Jesus prescribes, they will acknowledge the miraculous Grace of Sacramental Confession on the journey of purifying the soul. I plead with all My children to remember that Jesus is a forgiving Savior on behalf of our loving God. Whenever there is sorrow for sin, there resides His pardon. I ask the whole world to enter the Church for the spiritual vindication it requires through the virtues of peace, righteousness, and compassion. And, when you attend the Holy Sacrifice of the Mass, you better understand the Love through which Jesus surrendered His life so mankind can live theirs in immortality. These principles have been iterated over and again through the ages, and they bear repeating for those affected by the temptations of the Earth. Remember that goodness, faith, and humility are sown to the Spirit, not the corporeal flesh.

I ask My children on every continent to remember this Advent Season as the time for the elimination of war and the eradication of pestilence around the globe. Innocent people by the thousands are dying everyday from the perils of battle, and from dysentery, starvation and neglect. Why would this not be the appropriate moment for everyone to imitate the likeness of Mother Teresa and the devoted followers of her service to end the suffering of your friends? This holy woman left a legacy that is the reflection of Jesus on Earth! There is gross unfairness in the way the surpluses of your warehouses are shared, often to the point of distributing more to those already in possession of a great deal, and to the detriment of those falling further into abject poverty. This represents not only spiritual depravity and impropriety on the part of those in charge, it is an effect of the unchecked evil that is preying upon the mummified consciences of those who should do better by their brethren. We will pray these things away, and beseech the Lord not to heap retaliatory destruction upon those who are culpable for these crimes. There are plentiful gifts, goods, and wares for everyone alive to have a share of that which sustains them, delivers them from failing health, feeds them and their children, and teaches them to fend for themselves. If humankind refuses to redress these critical issues, it will foster the furtherance of the untimely destruction of their modern institutions and personal property. This is certainly not what God aspires to see happen, but He will allow it for the return of hundreds-of-thousands more to the Light of Revelation that is found in the Holy Cross. My Special son, I have turned My attention to you and your brother today. I remain happy that you are working on your present book, even more pleased than I was last week. Why? Because you are living through the days that will take you nearer its publication and release, and closer to the reception it will receive in the corners of the globe, indeed in all the regions of this American nation. I know that you recognize its message as a reminder to your peers that much is taken for granted where you live. I am grateful that you have accepted My commendation for trusting God to provide the resources you need to succeed in espousing the spiritual knowledge you are asked to pursue. There are approximately 130 pages remaining to complete in your present book which will be devoted to the evangelization of your Christian mission because this is why you are writing it for God. You are an author of profound spiritual Wisdom, courage, and humility. Thank you for every moment of your life that you are dedicating to His Holy Kingdom."

Sunday, December 9, 2001
3:03 p.m.

"Blessed are you who have chosen the path to holiness and peace, for yours is a future that cannot be impeded by the perils of time or suffering. My challenge to humanity is to never surrender to the despair that has made infidels out of so many agnostics before you. Sadness is a portion of mortal life that is overcome by the joy discovered in allowing the Holy Spirit to infiltrate and take permanent residence in your lives. My children, just as water flows naturally over the brink of a cliff, your future is to be as brightly pleasing in the bay of Jesus' Love, so that you will be unable to cease the jubilation by which you shall begin to live. This is peace and joy, and it is yours because God loves you to such an immeasurable degree. Today, I am happy to be here to exchange the gifts of affection and piety you offer for My complete and unconditional promise of continuous intercession for you before My Son. We are praying so He will extend every measure of Mercy for which you plead. Now, the season of Advent is moving quickly by, and the citizens of America are doing precisely the opposite of what I have requested; they are hoarding massive amounts of material goods to offer their friends and relatives instead of their love. It is naive to presume that Sacrificial Love can be offered to someone in the form of a physical object. What Jesus seeks during this season is more than this; Heaven asks for the offering of forgiveness where there has been offense, for reparation where there is transgression, and for reconciliation where there has been separation due to resentments and hardness of heart. If humanity will do these things, those material objects for which you seek will no longer have any meaning. You may remember in the older European nations that there were secular kings to whom their subordinates would say, '...would it please my lord that I should submit humbly into the slavery of your service?' There is a great deal in common with this query and what modern humanity expects from your neighbors, family members, and foes. No one should expect anyone to bow at their feet in subservience to win their favor. This kind of indentured servitude was destroyed by Jesus on Good Friday, and now there is no slavery inherent to men, and none to any unclean spirit. Jesus placed them into the Abyss where they can no longer harm the world's innocents. Sorrowfully for many, however, those who reject the Holy Gospel delude themselves by holding to the fashions of old; the dictators, autocrats, and rogue capitalists who believe that the Earth and everyone in it owe them their every last favor and currency. I speak of a lot of people whose future is destined for horror, regret, and condemnation. Why must this be true? Because they decline to enlist Christian faith, and they worry that their material fortunes will vanish, leaving them subject to the retribution of those they have persecuted for so long. This is the time of year when people everywhere should reconsider their priorities and those of greater society. How can it possibly be true that the most advanced republic in the western hemisphere has allowed itself to become so enthralled by the possessions in its hands, espousing the killing of unborn children, executing those who have been convicted by sinners of crimes that most anyone might be driven to commit, and disavowing ever knowing the Son of Man in nearly every public school across the land; thereafter throwing its collective hands in the air, bewailing that God's Messiah must have forsaken them by allowing them to be attacked by terrorists from afar?

    Does this blatant hypocrisy seem too obvious to ignore? Indeed, the poison of partisan politics is the chain by which many Americans cling to their massive amounts of wealth in the name of blind patriotism. Please make no mistake; I am the Mother of God, and I have witnessed His Wrath unleashed. Man has not seen what is about to be done in America to undo the egregious error that these people have wrought upon themselves. I feel sorrow in My Immaculate Heart because millions have refused to accept what I have been telling the United States since its inception. It is not solely a lack of faith that has caused this, but an outright rejection of the Truth I have been speaking. There is no need to allow any more innocent souls to die if only they who are guilty will recognize their own need for spiritual conversion and choose to embrace God's Christological virtues. There is too much crime in the streets and behind closed doors, but none is any greater than the organized crime of kneeling before the atheistic altars of materialism and greed, such as what many in the United States are doing. Our Lord God has a response prepared for them that will make the events of this past September pale by comparison. Why? Because the Truth of Love and Justice has been brushed aside for too long, and God is poised to react. If humanity will not pray, humanity shall suffer the inevitable result. Millions of Americans awoke on this morning sixty years ago trying to make sense of the events of two days prior in Hawaii. There was no sustainable justification in the actions of the aggressors, and none has been found to this day. Please do not attempt to blame the Almighty Father for allowing acts of destruction to occur, rather enlist the proper judgement which brought them into being from the first. Such events of six decades ago and three months heretofore are signs that the world is not situated upright before the Holy Cross upon which Christ Jesus was Crucified, and He is allowing you to draw the correlations that will help you understand. Let Me restate what I am saying; the Earth need not live in turmoil, terror and fear, from the borders of America to the streets of the Arabian republics, to the carnage in Northern Ireland, and the forty-three less celebrated wars that are ongoing around the globe today. Men make war because they refuse to practice Sacred Love, for their own purposes of mutual destruction, and to keep the remainder of humanity from gaining their rightful share in providing for their needs, nourishment, and peace. When will mankind awaken and see that these things are not aligned with the tranquility for which Jesus is calling? We can be thankful to God the Father that there has not been a destruction of the entire globe before this day by a nuclear holocaust. Were it not for My prayerful intercession, it would have already occurred. I love My children to the depths of My Being, and I ask you to accept Jesus for the Salvation of your souls and the restoration of harmony in the uncivilized world.

    My Special son, I hope you are not frightened by My words today, and I am confident that you understand the need for them. It is because of such sacrifices of the likes of Saint Thomas the Patriot that there has been great peace in the lives of those who obey the Law of My Son. His intercession has been profound and indispensable for your objectives with your brother and the mitigation of the arrogance of those who oppose what we are doing, what we have accomplished for eleven years last passed. Please do not be misled; these are crucial times for overdue changes, and they will continue with the recitation of your prayers and the contributions you are making through the writing of your books. You have worked hard; the Angels are pleased to be of assistance, and the world will be spiritually richer for your having allowed Me and Jesus to touch humanity through your humble love. Please do not be concerned about the inconvenience of your health problem, it will soon pass. It has been manifested because Jesus asks you to share in His redemptive Passion and Sacrifice on the Cross. Thank you for helping bring the Earth to His loving embrace."

Sunday, December 16, 2001
2:14 p.m.

"My children, in order for you to receive maximum benefit from your prayers, it is imperative that you pray from deep within the heart because this is where the truest intentions of your soul resides. When you make an assessment of your self-esteem before your conscience and one another, do not be concerned whether you prosper from your relationships, but that you live toward the enhancement of the dignity of humankind. Today, I have come to pray with you because every person on the globe is in peril, for the forces of evil are attempting to bring you to sadness and disbelief in the tender Love of Jesus that is showering from the Holy Cross. This is not only the time during which you are prepared to enter the final week of Advent, it is a moment for you to remember that only by choosing to be simple in Jesus' lineage will you avoid the snares of the scoundrels who are attempting to collude against your holiness. You are to be assured that you are surrounded by Heaven's domestic Angels, not unlike Jesus during the Nativity, who are your advocates and who ward-off those who would bring you harm. If you will call upon your Guardian Angels, you will be in a state of protection. I am hopeful that millions of Americans and others around the world will reassert their power in calling upon God for additional strength, and for Jesus to reverently extend His refuge where you place your childlike trust. My Special son, this is a particularly enlightening week because the Holy Spirit will continue to help you write in a forthcoming way about My Maternal role in human Salvation. You will find that the remaining pages of the chapter upon which you are working will reference the prominent issues you have encountered during the past ten years. I urge you to write them carefully under the guidance of the Angels because it is through this chapter that several tens-of-thousands will come to know Me the first time. Of all the lessons I have taught, the first they will recite is My call for the end of 'motion' that millions are still engaged in practicing. As the Holy Spirit has been assisting you with the inclusion of Latin terms in your book, God will help you paraphrase the concept of 'sistere,' meaning to stand still. Unless humanity fully understands this portion of My earlier messages that are part of your first Diary, they will never comprehend the rest. Such a term is used throughout My teaching, and is entirely pertinent in your day. Indeed, even the passing of the winter solstice is a product of this uniquely important issue; sol is the sun, and sistere means to stand still. Hence, the solstice of December is when the sun appears to stand still and reverse course so the Earth may work its way toward Spring. The cessation of human motion is much like this so the reversal of error can occur. Do you understand? I know that you are modestly pleased by the impression of your work because it is through your prayers that it is coming about. Only through your invocation of

Jesus' urgency to help you are you capable of producing the sublime images and phrases to persuade your prodigal brothers and sisters to accept the Cross, and to acknowledge the Father as their God. I promise that you are succeeding, whether you realize it or not. There are innumerable souls who are waiting patiently for the Lord to enter their lives, unaware that it is your servitude that will make it so. I say these things not to heighten your anticipation that you will see immediate results, but to seek your patience while the process unfolds. All of those who are in need of Jesus' inspiration will discover it in your books. This is the volume that will rescind the hesitant opposition of many who are unsure about the authenticity of your claims. My son, you are writing profound works because you have been obedient to your Mother. By such deference, you can be in no greater favor in the vision of God, for it is the culmination of your love for Him and His intentioned blessings upon humanity by the instrument of your life. This is no time for you to be timid or quiescent in defending the Truth. Stay close to your brother. I will not allow either of you to be laid before the villains who are casting My miraculous intercession aside. Being socially amenable at the expense of spiritual holiness for the sake of pretending to be at peace is an utter falsehood. This is the age of conscientious reflection that Jesus seeks from His people. I am pleased that you are writing with such intensity and Grace. I will speak to you next week, the birthday of your brother's eldest sibling. Christmas Day will arrive soon, and then 2002, and time will march in your favor."

Sunday, December 23, 2001
2:20 p.m.

"The melodies you will sing during the next fortnight are your reminder of what you should remember everyday; that Emmanuel is with you to bring you happiness, peace, and joy. I am the Mother of the Love that you share inside the sanctity of Christmas, and I have songs of My own that I sing for your souls, ones of opportunity and the immersion of your beings in The Divine Mercy which shall be yours upon your departure from this world and entrance into Heaven. There is an aura about Christmas that makes even the most hardened hearts step back in time, placing the events of the Earth into perspective at least for a moment, and wondering what next the Lord will usher into another year for your purification, enlightenment, and fulfillment. This is a commemoration that is like all others where Christmas blessings abound. I ask all Christians to remember that the poor souls in Purgatory are grateful for your intercessory prayers, even more than are you of Mine before the Throne of God, for this means their release into the Light of Eternal Salvation. Please never forsake them, even for a second, as you lift your Christmas petitions from your hearts! Be those who are aware of the intersecting nature of Heaven and

Earth, for it will someday be your opportunity to see the Face of God and the Glory for which all souls in Purgatory are pining. Humanity is departing a year that has brought stark revelations before you, the countless ways in which Heaven is communicating with you, God's signs and blessings, the fulfillment of Prophecy, and reasons aplenty for you to live-out your faith. There is no doubt that your vision of the Cross is clearer by now. Your eyes will see no greater benison than to train them upon the Blood of the Messianic Cross! Please move swiftly in your comprehension of the intentions of the Lord to bring you to Mount Calvary, and to the pinnacle of understanding His Will for you. Your share in the Resurrection of Jesus from the Sepulcher begins in your unimpeded and comprehensive acknowledgment of the reason He was Crucified. My children, your Mother is pleased as I come before you because I sense a different approach to the occasion of Christmas in many homes this year. Does it seem contradictory for My children in the United States to be more thankful to God for His blessings than in years past, when this is the same Creator whom so many were questioning in the middle of September? You are more grateful for one another now, for your relationships between mother, father, and children; and for the gifts of friendship, neighbor, and benefactor. I would never suggest that international tragedies are required to unite peoples, but the witness of those in communion with the Divine Love of God seems to be most apparent during such times. Grief and mourning do not preclude happiness in living on Earth; it is not inevitable that such things must come. But, our God who loves you is assuredly reminding you of the awful tragedy of the Passion and Crucifixion of Jesus during every moment of your lives, especially today, and the fruits His suffering has borne for the ages to come—the Redemption of your souls and your deliverance to His side in Paradise. For this, the misery of a billion ages is worth sustaining.

The Sacred Mysteries you celebrate during Christmas are a reminder that Jesus will return shortly; and when was the last time you heard the witness of a public official laud the praises of a charismatic High Mass of the Resurrection on the mainstream television medium like you did today? Are such things not the profitable repercussions of the faith of millions to whom these gentle people have turned for guidance and example for all centuries past? There can be no great leaders without the profound allegiance of those who follow. Henceforth, you are aware of the desires of Jesus for you to take up your crosses and follow Him to the Land of Promise; then you will realize your full reason for living, and will accept the bountiful burdens that are yours to endure. My Son is your vision and Glory, your strength in times of trouble, your friend and Redeemer, and the Holy One of Creation to whom you turn for miraculous direction every day of your earthly existence. By acknowledging these things during Christmas when the Earth is asleep in winter, you are saying that your souls are capable of understanding what it means to hope for Heaven's Light in the middle of the night. I ask everyone to read and recite the

Holy Gospel according to Saint Luke about Jesus' Nativity, to permit the Holy Spirit to expound upon what this means in your hearts, and to garner peace from your faith in the future and everything it fashions. When Jesus says He is with you, it does not only refer to this life and hereafter, but outside the parameters and passages of everything in your grasp. His Divine Love cannot be confined inside a prettily-wrapped package or suspended like an ornament atop an evergreen tree. The preeminence of His Sovereign Love is as resolute as the creative essence of the Deity who first made these things; and you will someday see that what I am saying is true. You need not wait until the moment you die, as you can tell by the infallible dispensation of the blessings of the Holy Father in Rome. His kind oration to the City and to the World is a presage of miraculous times to come, the passing-away of all that brings your hearts to despair, and the enlightenment of your minds that true Divinity is within your reach in the Seven Sacraments of the Catholic Church. I pray that you will never forget what I have told you today, world without end. My Special son, with these Christmas tidings, I offer My Motherly Love for humanity through your humble heart. I will speak to you again before this year is spent, but I wish for you to know that it has been one of the best you have offered to God. The innovative ways you have facilitated the conversion of your brothers and sisters by your writing is nearly too profound to put into words. The Dominion Angels are pushing onward in the completion of your book. And, I was touched to witness your compassion while watching the poignant television program this morning in reflection of the tragedies your country has suffered, and that those who were speaking were doing the best they knew how to express the sorrow in their hearts. There is great unity of faith in what they were saying, but none mentioned the Cross as the reason for the reconciliation between God and mankind. The future will allow them to state this more clearly. Thank you for your comprehension. I bless you from the center of My Immaculate Heart! You make Me encouraged by your consent!"

Sunday, December 30, 2001
2:59 p.m.

"If ever there was a time when any one society of people was blessed more in the history of mortal humanity, this is assuredly the moment. I have offered My consoling Immaculate Heart to My children of the Americas because you live in places where lauding the King of Justice is your right, responsibility, and honor. Today, I am pleased to tell you that all sovereignty is bestowed upon you to even a further degree through the Divine Mercy of the Sacred Heart of My Son. We are a Holy Family that espouses the virtues of Love, duty, servitude, and honor; and this is the moral excellence which we seek in Christians everywhere. As I have appeared in this place once again during the recorded year of 2001, I ask all who hear My messages to know that it has been a time of reckoning in many quarters and neighborhoods; the Truth of human conversion can be heard ringing all throughout your land, and the Cross on the Hill of Mount Calvary continues to be paramount to anything you will ever endure inside the parameters of time. I ask you never to be afraid of change because the constancy of the Passion, Crucifixion, and Resurrection of Jesus is always your Standard and Compass for your continuing journey through life. There are many weak members of the human family who need your attention, and I ask you to humbly focus upon their needs, as they are growing quickly older by the hour. Those who have the means to live in surplus should subject themselves to the tendering of those who have little means at all. Why in America is this so important? Because there is no mandate for sharing like there is in many other institutionally communal societies; those who are in need depend on the generosity of others who have plenty as their wares.

I have come today to speak to My little children, My Special one and My Chosen one, who have been quietly moving countless mountains of opposition from within the path of righteousness in your land. There are noblemen who are born into great fortune, and others who have inherited treasures untold, but theirs is nothing like the cache you are now building-up in Heaven. Jesus knows that you are not people who pursue material wealth or personal fame, but I assure you that the end of the mortal world is near and everything for which you ever dreamed is nigh at hand. Who could have prophesied the matter of only ten years ago that you would still be kneeling before My presence, listening to the Will of God for His world, eagerly savoring every morsel of My Wisdom, and working like little slaves to take the Word of God to the masses. Not only has your *Morning Star* already converted the hearts of tens-of-thousands, and *At the Water's Edge* has taken the souls of as many by great surprise, but now, your next tremendous work, *When Legends Rise Again*, is only a matter of ten days away from its completion. I ask you to believe Me when I tell you that those who are reading your works know that their origin is the center of My Immaculate Heart, that their strength is the power of the Cross, and their Divine nature is derived from the Holy Spirit. Please do not be ashamed to be proud of the work you are doing for My Son because He is quite pleased by the offering of your daily lives and mortal souls to His Kingdom; your minds, hearts, and every intention to the Love who has taken refuge in your spirits, and you in His. You live in a world of great imagining, and there are few dreamers who remain open to the powerful influences of God. Heaven seems like an unattainable place to many of them because they have not the faculties to seek it with an open attitude. These things have no bearing on the efforts of My children because your sights have been set anew on a Kingdom for which there is no comparing.

My little children, I have not the words to express the deep appreciation that Jesus holds for you as you enter another year of service to humanity in His Name. Yes, you are still running together through the element of time, hand-in-hand, with your vision trained keenly on the prospect that the rest of Creation will follow you to the Arms of God. This is a dream that will come true because the Almighty Father is Love, a Love that cannot fail, a Peace which cannot wane, and a future of Everlasting Life that will never end. You are the provocative children of the age of Christ's Dominion, 2,000 years strong and counting, like the many legends whom you have hailed so appropriately in your books. Someday, your names will be situated among them as having not only the profile of courageous Love, but an entire multi-dimensional genius by which you have altered the world and the course of human history forever to come. The Apostles and Disciples of the earliest days are pleased for you to be in their company, these who lead the Communion of Saints in prayer for the mortal world, for they know that you are aligned with the dignified Truth of service for which Jesus has called from the very first Word of the Sacred Scriptures to the very last. Saint Paul has been weeping tears of joy to the point that he is lost for words in describing the means by which you have joined in His message of freedom for the captives, food for the starving, shelter for the homeless, healing for the sick, and guidance for the wicked. He knows that all these things are found in the Son of Man, the Savior whom you praise today before a globe which is inhabited by no less than six-billion people strong. Each new soul you gain for Christianity is another candle lighted in the darkness. There is no doubt that, little by little, you are setting the entire world afire in the flames of righteousness. This, too, is what Jesus said would happen near the end of time.

My Special son, this is particularly a pleasing time for Me to speak to you because you have been the host to My intercession for nearly eleven years. I can see as you are reading your present manuscript that you can detect how momentous it really is. This is the power of your personal writing and the profound way that you have in moving humanity all together beneath the umbrella of God's Grace, one and the same as My Mantle. God will forever employ your works toward the advancement of His Kingdom. Every single sliver of manual effort will be pronounced as though it is being magnified a thousand-fold by the beaming light of the sun beneath a glass. No measure of time can contain the strength you are garnering to continue in your effort to assist the lost in regaining their identity again. Should all of your actions ever try to contain themselves in the confines of an hourglass, it would burst wide-open in a millisecond. You have power that has not been proffered to many other men because of your commitment to succeed in the Name of the Lord. There is no substituting the fact that you have never surrendered the mission that you accepted when I first came speaking to you. Your potency is in your faith, your Light is in your Love, and your Victory is in the Triumph of My Immaculate Heart, heretofore present and ongoing to this date, and to be capitalized very soon upon the Return of Jesus to take the redeemed souls who are given to Him to the Glory of their seeking. I ask you to be happy for them and pleased that you have afforded your Holy Savior the opportunity to remake the face of the Earth through the conviction from your heart.

I will be speaking to you again next week as the new year of 2002 ensues. It will be another period of great tribulation for many, spiritual progress for thousands more, and a time of great enlightenment for everyone alive. I ask for you to remember that those who live around you are getting inexorably older, and some of them who are close to you will be passing beyond the chasm of mortality into the hands of Jesus. When this occurs, it is a good thing. I am pleased that you joined your peers and made your presence known among your colleagues as a gesture of friendship. Your workplace is filled with good people; this is My gift to you. Saint Francis is elated that you have chosen to offer your labors under his name, and that he has been elevated in your new book! As I say, these are very special times for you, and you can even sense inside that they are in a new and remarkable way even more special than were the days in 1991 when I first came to speak to you. You are savoring many of the fruits of harvest now from the seeds that we planted back then. This is why Jesus is so happy with you; your life as a prophet is allowing many things for which millions are praying to come true in their lifetime. Without your service and dedication, this would never have come to pass. Thank you for an entire lifetime of saying 'yes' to God."

Morning Star Over America

The New Millennium

In the Year of Our Lord

AD 2002

Sunday, January 6, 2002
Epiphany of the Lord
2:55 p.m.

"My children, I have come to pray with you on this Feast of the Epiphany, the appearance of the Deity to the Magi, who were themselves bearing gifts that would portend the mortality and burial of Jesus. We remember that the prayerful souls all over the globe who hold to the Truth of the Cross feel in their hearts what giving to God in the Name of Jesus really means. It is through your faith that you can surmise what is beyond and beneath the Sacred Mysteries of His life. I have given you vital reasons to emulate His Divine Love, and I have shown you what occurs in Creation when obtuse human souls spurn Him. My special ones, it is imperative for you to remember that everyone around you learns about Jesus from the prevalence of your own holiness. Your friends understand more about Heaven when you offer your love through servitude and piety. I assure you that for clergy and laymen alike, the legitimacy of your faith in Christianity is fashioned by your intentions and measured by your conduct. In order for your purity to be flawlessly authentic, you must remain pure, and call upon others to accept this same purity through the Sacraments of the Church. There seems to be a growing consensus that something needs to be done to stop the hemorrhaging of the world's decency and civility, to stem the pandemic tide of violence and ill will that have become an atheist's dream and a Saint's nightmare. Some places have become stale with indifference, taking on the odor of battlefield morgues reeking with the stench of death. The Earth must be refreshed, reborn, and reclassified by the awakening of the collective human conscience. This is how wayward men avoid suffering the fate of the damned. Christians who pray for these souls wonder what it would be like to crawl into their minds with the extrasensory power to read their thoughts, but this would be of little consequence unless they could amend the motivations that generate those thoughts. Such would be an extraordinary expertise, although susceptible to the manipulation of corruptible human impulses. Hence, without a firm foundation in Christ Jesus, it does not matter how upright someone stands or earnestly they acclaim their desires; their feet must always be stationed on the solid ground of Divine Love. Most of My children assume that this is sufficiently expressed between biological siblings and companions in things like telephone conversations and greeting cards, and such quaintness is something that is rarely associated with the Church because of Christianity's intercontinental universality. The Sacred Scriptures always connect the small with the large, the simple and the difficult, and opaqueness with extrapolating Light. The unity of Christ's Mystical Body is found in your spiritual conviction to accept and proclaim the Holy Gospel as one humanity. You may look different from your neighbor in every conceivable way, and you may use your left hand to scribe your opinions instead of your right, but all men are oriented toward the single Truth of God. And, this is where Jesus has been so effective. He gave humanity all that He had, more than the Earth had ever received, and more than some people have been willing to accept. He offers a perpetual vindication that must be engaged and emulated, one that lives and breathes the brilliance of Heaven's Beatific Love. This is why lost sinners must approach Him personally, privately, and publicly. There are some who mistake the Epiphany as though it were some sort of transformation of Jesus into another kind of being after He was born. These are the same ones who also misinterpret His Transfiguration on Mount Tabor, believing that He somehow became more gloriously Divine than moments prior. Both of these assumptions are errant. The Epiphany is the realization by the Magi, and the entire world, that the appearance of the Deity had finally occurred, and these faith-filled people trekked to pay Him homage. Jesus had become Incarnate in mortal Flesh, and was just as Divine and Glorious as He was before His Virginal Conception inside My Womb. This is the same God who was veiled within the body of a Man, climbing to the summit of a mountain to further reveal the power of Love to Peter, James, and John. I ask you to always remember that the Child in the Bethlehem Manger and the Glorious Paschal King are one and the same Messiah.

    The Epiphany is January 6th as the Church has appropriately explained. You will recall that the Jubilee 2000 was also culminated on the same anniversary for higher reasons than can be expressed in the brief remainder of your lives. The etymology of the term epiphany is 'apparition.' This does not imply that the Magi envisioned the Son of Man as though He was not physically there, but their hearts were so impassioned by His sacred presence that they could scarcely take it in. God expects no less homage everyday from the humanity Jesus came to redeem. It is oftentimes difficult to maintain the intensity of your faith, but this is why I come; it is why I bring you ceaseless miracles and supernatural manifestations to buoy and strengthen your faith; and this is why there are diaries in Creation that comport with the hyper-extension of God's Truth and purposes beyond the Sacred Scriptures, to assure humankind that Jesus is as alive today as when He laid down His life on the Cross and was raised from the Sepulcher on Easter. The Almighty Father will thank His people for their gentle remembrance of His gifts which are manifold and multiplying by the hour. When your faithfulness becomes equally miraculous to the rest of humanity by your inherent proficiency in reflecting the Divinity of Jesus before the masses, then you will become the new epiphany for your lost brothers and sisters, the appearance of the Deity through the Holy Spirit living in you. This is made possible by virtue of your oneness with Jesus through everything He teaches, and especially through the Beatific Attitudes. My Special son, it is My pleasure to speak to you because I know that your work is bringing you nearer to providing another monumental gift to Creation, another book that will lift the spirits of tens-of-thousands. You have placed so many hours of labor into this opus that your brothers and sisters will be taken aback. 2002 is the year of reconciliation for which many are praying, and there are signal graces around you that offer ample evidence. All the Earth awaits the power of this great Love! Hence, please do not become distracted. You have another three books to compose in as many years, and I know that you wish to have as many moments in reserve to conclude them as you can. You will be proportionately pleased by your next book *Babes in the Woods* as you are with *When Legends Rise Again*. They are the substance of the love and Wisdom in your heart that are only now being spread into sentences. You have the faculties, the talent, the resources, the time, and the desire to complete the goals of your Marian apostolate because, like Jesus, you are God's child. I tell you plainly that the Heaven you will be given cannot be described in comprehensible terms; there are simply no words. I will continue praying that you will hold your trust in Jesus as He guides you through the events of the future. And, I ask you to pray for those who are unwittingly victimized by the greed about which you spoke earlier, where wealthy magnates and tycoons reap untold fortunes for themselves, leaving none for their poor laborers, and thereafter declaring themselves bankrupt. Yes, this is outright evil, the kind you have addressed in your book. You have learned a great deal about the Angels, and you are to know that their affections are as intense for you. They have aided you in ingenious ways in the past because they love you with the power, majesty, dignity, and strength of Almighty God."

Sunday, January 13, 2002
2:24 p.m.

"The simplest and most viable gift of flourishing goodness throughout the land begins at the center of the heart, for it is the mustard seed from which the great transformation of humankind must bloom and grow. I come seeking giants among peoples to accept the mission that Jesus places before you, that you might undergo and undertake the trials and efforts to garner a Creation of peace for the Kingdom of the Lord. My children, I realize that this implies no easy future, that it requires nothing less than your paramount faith. For these reasons, I continue speaking to you with urgency, emphasis, enlightenment, and compassion. If you are to remain the modern disciples of Christianity, there is no question that your burdens will be difficult to bear. For this, Jesus is your daily strength. You must be courageous so as not to stifle the progress that is already being made. It is true that there are Christians who are apprehensive about approaching other men and women with the Gospel strains on their tongues, but you must never allow such inhibitions to grow into discretion to a fault. There is nothing that can substitute your fortitude and hope for the conversion of anyone whom God places along your path. As I reminded My Marian priests a quarter-century ago to end another year, My speech is more compulsory than ever. It is timely because never has humanity walked so close to certain annihilation. My petition to the world eighty-five years after Fatima is for you to realize that God's Justice is unfolding according to His blueprint for the sanctification and Salvation of men. I was anguished twenty-five years ago before My priests, appealing them to implore humanity to turn back to God through prayer and repentance. Our supplications are in reflection of the Baptism of Jesus that the Church observes this week. While He obviously bore no stain of sin, His Baptism is the foretaste of the Sacraments of your purification that He has asked you to undergo. Has He not equally called you to take-up your crosses to propagate His final legacy? God deigns these things because through Jesus, He is your perfect singularity inside the gates of the mortality in which you serve. This can be a glorious summons if you live as Jesus requires. I have been accompanied by many Angels to visit you today, along with the Providential Dove of Peace who was so fairly hovering above Jesus' head when He was Baptized in the River Jordan. These loving creatures are increasingly more influential in the conversion of humanity because their role is as crucial as it was in the beginning. Modern hearts are in many ways more difficult to transfer to God's Grace because there are more temporal distractions keeping your spirituality from seeing as well. God is aware of this; Jesus knows it clearly; I have recognized it for centuries; the Saints of old have battled it before, and it is time for those who live in exile on the Earth to come to fuller compliance with the prayerfulness that will eliminate the barriers to purity and piety once and for all. My Special son, the Spirit of God and His Heavenly Court realize what obstacles are blocking the thruways to spiritual perfection for humanity. Through your assistance, they are more recognizable; they are being cleared by the trust of such Christians as you and your brother. I know that this process becomes consuming, and you are extremely anxious to see measurable results. Remember that God is in control of the element of time, and the Earth revolves upon its passage. I beseech you to accept that the Redemption of you and your brothers and sisters is on course. There are more objectives that need to be accomplished before the world is through, although Jesus will return in Glory soon. This is why it is increasingly important for My children to listen. The sacredness of the Holy Mysteries is as present today as when they were given to the world from their first century origin, and the exhaustion of the ages cannot take them away. Each and every person who has lived was forced to confront the inevitable conclusion of deciding for God, and nothing short of this could they do to be saved. Again, this has not changed since the Prince of Nazareth was raised from the Tomb, and it shall be this way until He comes again for you. The Lord has no tolerance for the sacrilegious onslaught of mankind's pride.

Will you consider praying with Me for the world's societies to understand the facts about which I am speaking? It is not easy and often extremely difficult to express the mandated actions by mankind that must take place, beginning with the amendment of the spirit of the human heart. Only prayer can do this because no physical force will suffice in the struggle of returning the Earth to Love. I seek your help because I know that this has been achieved beyond the bellows of time, which in itself is furthermore transcended by what we are doing. Your brothers and sisters are a much more benevolent people than they are portraying. Their engagement to Truth is wrought by their understanding of the Commandments that will transform the nations into the substance of Jesus' prayers. I beg you to pursue His Grace as pleadingly as the Saints pray for decency and community to return to the land of His birth. The order of Creation is fashioned by God's Will, and there is disarray because too many are rejecting it. As I have indicated to you before, this year has come with many new obstacles for My children to face, and they will never be cleared for victory if there are insufficient prayers. I know that they will be overcome; I can see their circumvention, and it shall be brought into reality through the petitions about which I have spoken to you for ten years and eleven months. We have a great deal of work to do because there are hardened human hearts to soften. There are sinners who are hoarding millions of dollars while their brethren lay in the streets with no food in their stomachs. Through the Angels surrounding Me now, you are inscribing the theses that will convert the wretched. Only few besides you have accepted the charge to pen their memories so the lost can be found. I have told you before that you are highly lauded in Heaven for this. Your sacred commission is not a matter of tiring, but of adjusting your perspective when you know you are weary. Did you ever hear of Jesus saying that He was tired? Do you know why? Because He often wondered what it might be like to become an elderly gentleman who could sanctify Creation by taking the hand of everyone on Earth. Knowing that He would be Crucified, Resurrected, and Ascended into Heaven, He bequeathed this work to you. There is insufficient time to commiserate about the effects of exhaustion. You have not seen what tired really means. Can you see why I love you? Can you not know that you are the holy one of God who is trying with such care to take every one of your brothers and sisters to Heaven when you go?

You realize that I must return often and listen to your voice. I desire to hold you. Come to your Mother who adores you, and rest in the Bosom who held your Crucified Savior! Come, let Me bless and caress you! You feel peaceful inside. You are pretty and Special to Me. Did not Jesus wield visionary Truth in the magnanimous nature of His Divine Love? Is this not what helped Him know that the Spirit is more powerful than the artifacts of the physical world? Therefore, He prevailed; and He does to this hour inside your heart. This should be a source of palpable consolation for you. What occurred after Jesus said to the Father that He allow 'this cup' to pass Him by, but would obey if it was His Will? You are spiritually amalgamated with Jesus for humanity; He allows you to drink from the cup of humiliation because you are loved. This is what thousands of others will do because of their sins of pride. You have never understood what you just stated any more clearly than you do at this moment. That, in itself, is the essence of My message today. You have been perfectly obedient since we began in February 1991. As far as your awareness, you are the likeness of many Saints by your knowledge of Heaven from your station on Earth because you have served without question or hesitation, and have never required an Angel to wake you in the night to tell you what to do. You can assuredly see that God did not spare the emotions of His Son to purify exiled humanity. You have inherited that legacy because you are equally as special to Him."

Sunday, January 20, 2002
2:56 p.m.

"The kindness with which you are praying is reflective of your commitment to Jesus, the Angels, the Saints, and humanity on the Earth. What a wonderful gift you are offering for the Grace of peace for which you have long sought! I also have come to pray with you because our tandem sentiments are powerful before the Most Sacred Heart of My Son. We beseech Him to remember the poor today, those who have no faith, the little ones who are offended by the brashness of the elite, and the unborn children whose birthdays are contingent upon our prayers for the cessation of abortion. When we ask God to shed His Light into the world, He will do it. The mere simplicity of your petitions is the seed of His tremendous pardoning for those who do not know to ask for the dispensation they require to take them appropriately to receive His living Absolution. I urge you to especially remember those who have made themselves your enemies because you are loyal to Heaven. There is plenteous forbearance for them because they are not aware of what they are doing, not that their ignorance is reason for their innocence, but that your love for them is setting them free. This is what the Son of Man has done for you, and He asks that you bestow it upon those who have shown you only their crueler side. My children, as you survey world circumstances on this Sunday, it is easy to see that there are many who require the compassion of those who hold great wealth. With the warring that is now ongoing, even greater than you could have imagined when I foretold it on September 16, 2001, and with the awful events prompted by the volcanoes many miles from you, there are tens-of-thousands of refugees who have no home or food, and no one to tend to their afflictions. We also pray today for the Catholic Church, that God will look over it and guide it toward the future. I ask everyone to honor the beauty of the Sacraments, and all who are ordained to administer them. It is imperative that we pray for those who are in their hours of discernment to enter religious vocations, for Jesus needs all the clergy to minister His flock that can be ordained. When you see a priest in a collar or nun wearing a habit in a secular crowd, you are observing the making of saints, those who are pining for holiness and reverence to be more prevalent in the world. It has always been the desire of God that His chosen people be obeyed, treated with respect, and incorporated in the prayers of the faithful earnestly and often. Let us remember them to Christ Jesus as we offer our petitions during your recitation of the Holy Rosary. Indeed, as you survey the condition of humankind, do not forget the infirm, the homebound, and those secluded in hospitals and the darkness of their rooms. All these people depend on us to pray for them, to seek the comfort of God to assist them in their plight. I ask you to pray outwardly for the rest of mortal Creation as you yearn for the purification of yourselves. Mighty are your hearts when you offer them sincerely for the consolation of your brothers and sisters. You have been told that the wind blows where it wills, but you must intentionally direct your love for those who suffer by recalling them to Jesus when you seek His aid. I have told you that He will respond to whatever you ask when you offer your intentions in His Name.

    I have seen miracles wrought through the power of prayer! It is important for you to remember that none of them is an occasion of happenstance. When you see a supernatural event reflecting the Will of God, it is a mandate for His higher visibility in the temporal world. Physical, mental, and spiritual healing can occur when you ask for His intervention. It is a measure of His good Will when you are capable of observing evidence of His response. Whatever the outcome, you can be assured that it is a promulgation of His Kingdom. My Special one, is this not what you prayed for when you were ascending to the summit of the Medjugorje mountains in August 1989? I ask you to remember how holy you were that day, with what hope you came to trust in Jesus on a more transcending level than you ever had before. Your faith is a gift from Him for which I had long prayed before that awesome summer night. To this day, I pray as well for the masses of sinners who walk the Earth, and for the poor souls who are agonizing in Purgatory. It is proper that you lend your petitions to them as well. I am pleased to report today that countless people whom you do not even know are benefitting from your daily prayers, your works, and the dimensions of goodness blooming from your humble heart. You are about to have another book printed that will persuade multitudes to decide for Jesus, to embrace His Love, to call on their Mother for guidance and intercession, and to ask the Lord to absolve them of their sins. I do not tell you this to heighten your self-esteem, I am only stating the facts. The obedience you have offered is reflected in the thoughts, words, and actions of millions of other human lives. For these meritorious things, you will judge worthily of yourself in the presence of God's perfection at the hour of your death. I have told you about the prospect of millions of people falling in ecstasy upon their reunion with Jesus, should He return in Glory before their existence on the Earth is through. Would this not be a fruitful way for you to remember how eminently beautiful is His Love upon sight? This is the vision I have been trying to impress upon you inside your heart. This can be achieved, and you can tell your brothers and sisters because you will wish everyone to know. If Paul Revere was a messenger of impending danger, William Roth is the clarion call of the Reign of God in a world that is only now awakening to the Truth. In this, the entire mass of humanity will discover the Fruits of the Holy Spirit, and peace and security will be the captions beneath your photogenic faith. No act of goodness will go unnoticed by the time history and mortality have expired. I assure you that the God of your fathers is recording your intentions for the Glory that you wish to savor someday. All the awakenings you have sought in other men will eventually come to pass; the healing which you have long beseeched Him to dispense will be brought into being; and you, along with your childhood friend who lay paralyzed on his back, will soon crisscross the nations telling about the Love of the Divine Savior who made it come true. The throngs of thousands will cling to your every syllable from the Chandler Cenotaph and mark their cadence by the rhythm of your bountiful heart. Why do I know that these things are true? Because I have implored God as the Mediatrix of all Graces from Heaven to bring them from His Seat of Divinity into the darkness of this world. Hence, the next time your heart seems to be despondent or you grow impatient once in awhile, I bid you to remember the future that is coming. Know with the fullness of the facts that I am telling you about the fulfillment that God has chosen for you and those for whom you are beckoning the indulgences of His power. When we pray together as we are at this moment, His Holy Will is lent to hear what His children and Immaculate Mother have to say. I am pleased to have been able to speak to you on this occasion. I hope that I have elevated your spirit and given you reason to know that everything we have been accomplishing for the past eleven years is on course. I remind you that you are gratified by complying with My wishes and the Will of the Father by being gentle with His Creation. It is your awareness that you are doing so that is making you happy. Please remember to pray for the unborn innocents."

Sunday, January 27, 2002
2:47 p.m.

"With Legions of Angels around Me, I come to pray with you today. My dear children, your Mother has arrived with a broadening smile because you are beautiful and loving to behold! I urge you to find your contentment in the solace of My Immaculate Heart as we embark on your newborn relationship with the Hosts of Paradise. Were it not for your obedience, this would not be possible; the people we are trying to reach would remain lost in the darkness of sin. Therefore, I hold you to My Sacred Bosom in thanksgiving for your willingness to witness for Jesus to many others whom you are beginning to know. Can you see this bright Light of revelation shining upon you and them? The sweet fruits of your servitude are feeding those who hunger for righteousness. My desire is that you will never stop praying for those who are distant from God, that you will persist in teaching them through your written works about the meaning of sacrificial Christian Love. After all the miraculous signs you have seen and the advancing of the prophesies that have been given to you, there is no doubt that you are still required to live by faith without having seen the pristine divineness of Heaven. I ask you always and everywhere to discover it in your hearts. My children, the Earth's metaphysical framework is comprised of billions of microscopic and ultrasonic waves of good intentions and diverse directions; bits and particles of reason, potential, artistry and reflection, with cameo appearances of visionary sacrifice and unprecedented valor. And, just as the pendulum on a timepiece takes you from the cradle to the rocking chair, there is equation and equilibrium to it all. The Lord commends you to interact with Him often; and while He is certainly authoritarian in spiritual Virtue and behavioral principle, He has never forsaken or been condescending to His creatures. He is overwhelmingly forthright, impeccable, and chivalrous. The Holy Spirit speaks distinctly, candidly, and concisely, while never impugning the dignity of those who are lacking in the good graces of Salvation. I remain deeply overwhelmed that you have complied with admirable tenacity in addressing the need for action against everything that contradicts the sacred discipline inherent in the lives of Christian men. Thank you for having responded to My call. What appears to be a random gauntlet of confusion to humanity is the overt process of evolvement and decision in matters of waging war and making peace. Indeed, as Saint Angela Merici explained, you have much more to do than worry about what comes next. You reside on Earth expecting to initiate your own new beginnings and the future of your offspring, unlike distraught ocean whitecaps waiting for the wake of the years to lay them to rest. When you ask the Lord to bring His healing graces to your broken brothers and sisters, it is His pleasure to reciprocate. Their umbrage and hurt feelings are like torn tissues;

they require ample time to mend. You surely cannot blame the Lord for wanting to intervene. Some might attempt to drive Him away because they feel patronized by a power over which they have no control, which is as ridiculous as accusing your neighbor of exposing secrets when the information he reveals is about himself. The overtures that Jesus has laid-out are coming in unfathomable dimensions because Heaven understands that they augment and strengthen your desire to be perfected through the Wisdom of the Holy Spirit. The entire globe is groveling in neglect, war, and impurity. It is these vices that we are trying to eradicate by beseeching God to hear us when we pray. I have told you that He will listen and respond because His Dominion is everlasting and reaches to the farthest depths of Creation. When I implore His consolation for you when you are lonely and afraid, He sends not only the Holy Paraclete and the Angels to comfort you, but His Immaculate Mother as well. I give My affirmation that I will intercede for you endlessly, until Eternity blossoms over the fullness of the Earth, because I am your Mother of Perpetual Help and your Queen of Peace for every age. My desires are a reflection of yours when you lift them to the tallest pinnacles of sanctity for humankind. The Will of God is for you to be granted the Salvation He offers through Jesus on the Holy Cross, and who was raised from the dead on Easter morning so you will reside in the Land of the Living forever. How could I not share this Glory with those who are loyal to Me? Hence, I ask that you never concede your present or future to the secular void that continues to lure you into its dungeons of despair. Your happiness is found in Jesus! You are walking deftly above and beyond the craggy surfaces of the physical world when you give yourselves to Him; only a little lower than the Angels do you venture on your sojourn to Paradise! With this jubilation in your consciousness, please remember everyone who has asked you to pray for them, and those who do not realize the infinitude of its power. You have launched your future in Jesus' palms, and He will deliver you to the Right Hand of the Father. I tell you that I have seen His mighty Throne. It is a Seat of Wisdom, Justice, and forgiveness. There is no need for anyone living or beyond the pall of death to be condemned because Jesus has forced Redemption through the shedding of His Blood. If I told you this repeatedly during every moment in time, it would never grow old, for the message of Salvation is true and everlasting. Please bring your cares to your Mother, and I will ensure that they are heard by the Almighty Father in Heaven. This is a wish that I hope you will fulfill on your behalf and those you love, even the millions you do not know, and the hundreds-of-millions with whom you will be joined in the fullness of Eternal Life in Paradise.

    My Special son, thank you for giving your gift of love to your brother on the occasion of his birthday. He will never be forty-eight years old again. And, it is important for you to remember that scores of famished souls are released from Purgatory into Heaven every time you offer your prayers. For them, this is all the meaning they will need for knowing why they were born and the reason our God of The Divine Mercy has taken them home. It is your love here on Earth and your daily prayers for them that make it possible because you are the likeness of the Savior who was Crucified for them when you offer your life, actions, words, and intents for their dedication to Heaven and their consecration to the Most Sacred Heart of My Son. Can you see that this reflection is happening as you offer your kindnesses in His Holy Name? You must surely discern the magnanimous arc of knowledge and Eternal Wisdom that has been encompassing humanity since Pentecost Sunday. You learn about spiritual absolution because you offer it to your enemies. And, you love your brothers and sisters because you are loved by the Lord. The hungry are fed and the weak are nourished because your actions reflect the generosity you have inherited from the Son of Man. These are among the fruits of the new beginnings about which I spoke in 1991. I tell you again that they are sweet to the taste of the suffering who have subsequently benefitted from your prayerfulness and sacrifices. Please do not desist because there are more eager hearts where they came from! It is kind of you to be in the company of your brother on his birthday because it has long been his prayer that he would spend it with no one else. I am elated to see that your next book is complete, and you are preparing to deliver it for printing in twenty-four hours. Yes, it is a beautiful rendition, and the next one will be so precious about the lives of innocent little children that it will bring humanity to tears. You once said that 'you can never go wrong with little kids and animals.' Indeed. Each of your books provides a different perspective of the same Sovereign Love. It is your legacy that everyone will remember, one as authentic as the messages you began receiving in February 1991."

Sunday, February 3, 2002
3:34 p.m.

"It is for the sanctification of humankind that I have come to pray with you today, little children. Would God not have it that we should hold them in such high esteem that we wish for all souls to reside in His Holy presence? Thank you for knowing His Love and spreading His Word beyond the seas and into the stark quarters of those who are hardened of heart against the spirituality that will take them to the Sacrifice of Absolution. I call upon humanity to give Jesus your heart, not symbolism over spiritual substance. We gather on this auspicious February afternoon to beseech the Almighty Father to dispense His forgiveness upon all who have sinned, and to rearrange their souls in alignment with His Will. There can be no nobler purpose for our prayers, and such is the emergence of our union and the way you must continue to pour-out your lives. Children, now that you have seen firsthand what the mistakes of men have wrought, can you garner the strength you require to proceed? Have the perils of the night made you more aware of the refuge of God's Immortal Day? Please let Me offer you advice that will enhance your wisdom about the furtherance of Christianity, and prevail upon the remainder of your years to evangelize it. It is true that most men search for secular institutions to grow their existence in an otherwise meaningless land, but America should stand for more than the logistics of survival on a hedonist plane. The failures of your country are not always so apparent because the materialism espoused by the rich has rendered them blind. God will purge the entire western hemisphere of this by trial and tribulation. The amount of suffering, agony, and loss that will lead prodigal souls into the clarity of spiritual vision has only begun. We must pray not only for America to convert to Divine Love, but that its citizens withstand the transformation. I ask you to remember that fear is not the purpose of the Lord, for He has never been a monger of anxiety or trepidation. Those who aspire to Truth realize that they have a distance to travel to be distinctly perfected in Jesus. Please be among the witnesses who shall see their spiritual conversion to culmination in the suffices of the suffering! I ask you to embrace the peaceful transition of accepting the Blood of the Cross from within, to take the message of Salvation to your brothers and sisters by emulating Jesus' Love and imitating His life. There are no strangers in Christianity, just friends and comrades whom you have yet to meet. Within the prefigured boundaries of daily time, God has placed plentiful ways to be reoriented in Him. It is unfortunate, therefore, that so many spend their last agony in abandoned places with no one willing to pray for them. Sorrowful are the occasions when the dying yearn to offer their last contrition, but no one is there to hear their parting words. One of the most pitiable situations is someone breathing his last with no one at his side to take his hand. I assure you that Jesus is with them, as am I, and also the Communion of Saints who welcome these citizens to their eternal rest to the caroling of the Angels. I know that it is improbable for everyone to be accompanied by their friends when they are about to deliver their spirit to God, so I ask My children to pray for their comfort in their hour of impending death.

This is a period of enlightenment for millions of Americans because the faults of deviate military aggression are being divulged before Creation. It is not difficult to ascertain the differences between war and peace because the former espouses no Truth or fairness over the deviltry of vengeance. I ask you to pray for your leaders, especially those who are spreading the errors of the West, which at this time are as malignant as those to which I referred when speaking of another empire in Fatima in 1917. While I desire to continue drawing correlations about them, I will wait until the future. Time is a crucial element in the renewal of the Earth. Gone are the days when people were seated on their hands in indifference while watching evil parade past their porticos because Satan is rapidly engaging all living souls during these times.

Everyone must choose to do good by refusing to practice malevolence. I have told you before that evil must be flushed-out and destroyed, but not by threatening words and vitriolic phrases. If you return to the righteousness that Jesus has taught, and pray the Holy Rosary will all your might, Satan will acknowledge the defeat he suffered on Good Friday and leave humanity alone. Indeed, call on Saint Michael the Archangel to drive Satan into the fires of Hell by His Sword of Love. His commission is more than that of bygone Biblical times, He lives in the contemporary world. This Archangel is your shield when you are tempted and under attack, and it is your Christian prerogative to invoke His intercession during your battles against evil. Wherever you ask Him to fight is where God will dispatch Him. This promise is as sacred as any prophecy you will ever know. There is not an instant when the Archangels are not with Me in the Heavenly Court, and with Jesus who is berthed comfortably in My arms and reigning powerfully at the Right Hand of the Father. It is for these revelations that I urge you to summon the mightiness of Paradise as your spiritual rampart. My Special son, no greater joy has been Mine than to speak with you. You are accomplishing the Will of Jesus with exalting measure. Without your goodness and willingness to proceed, the Lord's Kingdom would be poorer. You know that time is a deceptive prospect. All Divine Love is excelling, and the Father calls the generations to conjoin under the Cross to dispel the incongruities of the Earth. It seems only a moment ago that the photograph of your brother was taken the day after Christmas in 1961. How old were you? Yes, three months and counting! However, in Jesus you are both the same age. You are the maturity of pristine Truth because your souls have been restored to virginity in His Crucifixion and Resurrection. This is the reason I come to offer My counsel. My advice is that everything before you is unfolding as it should; you are living the present years precisely as Jesus planned. Your new book will be printed by those to whom the Holy Spirit leads you. Please do not be disheartened by the actions required to touch other lives. Your book *When Legends Rise Again* is so stately that God will not allow it to suffer any negligence in the temporal world."

Sunday, February 10, 2002
3:17 p.m.

"It is time for us to pray together, little children, because this is what we do for humanity. I have come, My Special son, to express My profound gratefulness that you have chosen to remain beside Me in the struggle to convert the world to the Cross. Should anyone ask what your Mother said on this date and time, you may tell them that I appeared and spoke to the advancement of your holiness and happiness. As a result of the compliance of your brother and his undying love for us, we maintain an especially grace-filled relationship that thrives because you believe in the miracle of My intercession. Your faith has been the transformation of entire segments of the human society to Jesus. This priceless contribution by you to those you do not know is as endearing as it could possibly be by a mortal man. It would be the envy of millions to see that they would receive the Heaven you are gaining. You are the sparkling facet of the gemstone who has captured the eye of our Creator. There is no substitute for the Truth, and this is what I am telling you. I told you long ago that there would be signs and wonders that would accompany your journey through life for saying 'yes' to Jesus. There are countless souls who are seeing evidence that you have been revealing this Truth since your affirmation in February 1991. Please do not be concerned that they might wish to dissect your life or that of your brother in search for flaws in your character. They will not find any. This is My promise. Therefore, I come to strengthen your faith, to counsel you during the propagation of your apostolic mission, and to support the observations and sentiments that you will offer before My message is through. First, please allow Me to give you another sign that your brothers and sisters will notice in the next years, then they will transfer their discovery to their friends. It has to do with whether I have given you expositions or messages that deal with prophecy, or anything I might have said that led to events to which I alluded that were completely uncontrollable by you. I refer to My message last week. Please bring the newspaper into the room, turn to page nineteen, look under the heading of Judaism, and read aloud the second sentence. Go get your message from last week. 'One of the most pitiable...' A week after My message, you see it inscribed in your newspaper. You may find it difficult to believe that people will notice this. Why? Because they have kept the published article and will recall it when they see your accounting of My messages in your diaries. They will see that I asked you about tending to the dying a week prior to their having read it in the press. They will know that this discussion was raised by a young Jewish maiden. Who might that individual be? Yes, it is Me. The point I have made is not only that dying persons should be comforted, but that I discuss matters with you before they are brought to the fore within a brief time thereafter.

And, what about the succession of days that are recorded from the death of your brother's mother until you were called to the mountains of Medjugorje? Can you see how prescient these things are? They are among the signs, graces, and wonders that I told you would be forthcoming because you have stood beside the Light of Truth in taking the Holy Gospel to the world. Now, you also see that the anticipation of the revelation of your next book is high among those who know that it is about to be released. It will seem like a short time before the next one is commenced. I urge you to be patient in their development, but be anticipatory about their efficacious results. The immediacy of the fruits of your labors may not come at the pace of your wishes. I will ask you to remember My advice when you read and hear the

Scriptural passage that has been selected for the Holy Sacrifice of the Mass for Ash Wednesday. This particular reading has been chosen for the Church for God's messengers like you. Will you remember to heed what is written there for Me? I know that you have been laboring long, and the hours have been oftentimes difficult to bear. However, you continue to seem strong and resilient over the course. You know that *Babes in the Woods* will tell the simple message that humanity must become like little children again, and will discuss the plight and suffering of many around the globe today. One of your dearest friends said that *Morning Star Over America* is helping her become like a little child, and she knows this is what Jesus desires. People who are fifty, sixty, and seventy years old are learning this for the first time from your writing, and this is only one of the multiple fruits of your compliance. I realize that you have become accustomed to My graces, but what will others think when they see such things as the 1933 days of you and your brother traveling inseparably to the Medjugorje shrine? This will be a tremendous boon for their faith. I am praying for the prisoners whom you saw on television last evening. This is one of the reasons why the chapter in your manuscript about setting free the captives is so relevant for Americans. Will you remember to reveal the issues I asked you to discuss with your brother? You are such an amiable and obedient child. This has been the home for the bourgeoning consolation of many tormented hearts! Please remember to dedicate your Lenten prayers for the intentions that you have in years past, and for the reasons I spoke about today, for the healing of broken souls in every way. This is what I ask you to remind your brother to do. Thank you!"

Sunday, February 17, 2002
4:23 p.m.

"The grand applause you hear from the depths of your souls is the sound of time culminating in the Triumph of My Immaculate Heart, the Victory of Life over death, and the elevation of the Passion of Salvation like the glorious colors of the freest nation on Earth from the summit of the Cross. I call you again today, My children, to share in the elation that belongs to the Saints and savored by the Angels. This is the Season of Lent during which you are reminded of the untold sacrifices that millions of souls before you have made so you can learn about the magnanimous gifts that are raining-down from Heaven. You are called to pray profoundly during these forty days, to assist your neighbors as Jesus asks, to heed the call of your Christian conversion, and to remember the Lamb of God who has taken away the sins of the world so that all who are reborn in Him can live anew. And, this year I urge you even more to realize that you are living in the shadow of the Resurrected Christ, and to remember that dignity is yours because My Son has remade you into the pristine likeness of Himself. Please do not fall victim to the wrongs that seem so unchangeable, for this is the Age of Enlightenment for every man and woman alive. My children, I know that you are given many burdens to bear, but you must enlist the vision of Divine perspective to help you through the darkness. A great deal of suffering is wrought by the vacuum in your brothers and sisters' faith, and your mission is to help them change where you can. As I have warned you before, atheism, agnosticism, and secular humanism are behemoth catastrophes meandering down a dark road to nowhere. Most of their followers feed only from radical discord, conflict, and social unrest; and they are determined to force humanity to sustain the hatred inside their hearts. They are desperate to find some meaning in their irrelevant views, conspiring to impede any connection between the pragmatic and the Divine. They are grossly emphatic in rejecting extraterrestrial Wisdom, and reluctant to see God's miracles as anything other than periodic intervals of coincidence and products of chance. They seem to be unaware of Heaven's sternly guided mandate to participate in the purification of the Earth; and some of them live in such detachment and seclusion that the only acts of daring they will ever see are their friends leaping from diving boards above their gated neighborhood swimming pools. Atheists are openly biased against God's Providence and resent any insinuation that their cruel vices are in any way responsible for corruption in the world. They tend to be empirical thinkers who rarely accept anything on its face unless it complies with their own preposterous prejudices against the Roman Catholic Church. What they must begin to realize is that anyone who rejects the Will of God offers very little in transcending values that is of any utility beyond their existence on Earth. Indeed, seeing Creation objectively is not about peerless eyes and disengagement, but allowing free reign for Heaven's sacred impressions to take root in barren consciences. Agnostics place little importance in hope, believing that too much disastrous history has already been recorded for the world to have a happy ending. However, as ironic as it seems, their ignorance is uniquely the reason why they have gained a reprieve from posthumous punishment, a reversal of fortune that lends in their favor. They will in due time see through clear eyes that purity is white, valor is crimson, and the Truth is crystal clear. I am speaking about their invocation of the Name of the Lord who gave birth to the mountains. Even those who are farthest from His Grace will feel encouraged to broach the subject of Christianity in an arena filled with thousands of heckling pagans.

My children, the lost sinners in your midst will someday arrive at such an awakening that they will look in hindsight at their present perceptions as being patently incredible, a context of societal ethos that is completely dysfunctional, wondering why they were so obtuse when the Lord was searching for no less than a world that is an epochal masterpiece of human love. They will realize that Jesus was born impoverished in Bethlehem because Heaven is looking deep into the universe for ethereal orbs to conscript. There is no denying the fact that humanity has been invaded by the same Creator who set them spinning in the dark of outer space. Irrespective of My past metaphoric speech, I assure you that you can take My description of Jesus' forging the Earth into the likeness of Paradise through the flames of Justice in quite literal terms. Differing times and circumstances can never alter or suspend the immutable Truth, and the Church's detractors cannot improvise their own gospel that contradicts the Christian New Covenant. This is why we shall address in the future the inexplicable malfeasances of God's foes and console the people who are victimized by their error. I intercede to neutralize the scathing barbs of cynicism against the soundness of your character by the enemies of your faith. I ask My children to dedicate your sanctity in obeisance to the Trinity, offering your persecution for the conversion of the lost. You will win at last because you are worthy of your fathers' hopes; and you will prevail because you are sanctioned by Eternal Truth. The exhaustion of your exile will not occur soon enough, it would seem, to preclude every tragedy from unfolding. But, when all is said and done, there must be something to give power to your movements and essentialize your trust. This is the manifestation of the self-sacrifice about which God has spoken for 2,000 years.

My children, the sun is moving closer to the center of the skies as the Spring will arrive in a few weeks' time. Look up at the newness of the world! Make your dailiness a happy beginning in the hope that God is bringing! Drink deeply from the Cup of Salvation and the Fount of Mercy because He knows that you thirst for His Love! From the Manger in which the Christ Child lay, to the perilous paths upon which He walked, on the road to Mount Calvary, and beyond the Sepulcher, Jesus has always been your beacon of hope and source of Eternal Light. I have told you that you are moving through time in union with this Victory, and His Mercy is shining more brightly upon you now. Take your parched spirits often to the Altar of Sacrifice, and you will know what it means to imbibe in His Peace. These are My wishes for humanity during this season of Lent; to serve My Son's flock, to feed His sheep, and to comfort the forsaken, all of this while holding your faces to the upward winds, allowing His rays of Beatific Dominion to shine upon your every dawn. We desire everyone to know this happiness because you have discovered what it means to beseech the Almighty Father for the favor of His Will. I assure you that He is pleased with you and Me because He spared not My Son to prove it. I am in alliance with the progress you are making in the successful conversion of your peers to the Truth of the Holy Gospel. And, My Special son, I know you would like to enjoy the day with your brother; and after this message, he is allowed to go outside. Thank you for keeping him in to avoid the dangers lurking nearby. I am happy that My Angels shower graces from My Immaculate Heart. The indications of the Lord's commanding Will are replete in everything you do, from the hills of Medjugorje, to the American plains, from those residing in Heaven, to you living on Earth. If only humankind realized the signs within your grasp, it would be awesome to behold. I will give you one in passing so you will know that they have no ceasing. Please look at the four digits on the form you completed in the bottom drawer to your right. Now, locate the same numbers on your brother's medicine bottle. Could anyone plan this? It is another gift to tell you that your life is on course."

(Even more strikingly, on October 17, 2002, I was reviewing this message when I received a telephone number from a young lady wishing to discuss Our Lady's messages. The four digits on the ticket on which she wrote her phone number are the same as referred to in this message—9988.)

"I know that your brother says arbitrary things, but there were four prints of your book-cover produced by the company before they sent the right one due to his kind persistence. The message of *When Legends Rise Again* is about to touch an entire nation. I hope you are pleased with your work; there is every reason for you to be encouraged by the literary pieces you have produced. The next volume will be degrees more beautiful and touching than this one. It will procure the effect of transferring the attention of humanity to your Morning Star messages. Thank you! If only you knew what it means to Me when you say that you love Me, you would leap with joy. Let Me assure you of a fact that you must always remember. I will have finally been able to show humanity how much I love each and every soul before the world is through because of the laboring you and your brother are doing; they will not have to wait until they go to Heaven. I promise that the hopes you are nurturing will come to pass."

Sunday, February 24, 2002
3:47 p.m.

"When you pray the Holy Rosary, little ones, you mitigate the horrible errors that make so many among you unhappy and impure. I ask that you continue to recite the Sacred Mysteries so that those who are in need of your petitions will turn to the Sacred Way of the Cross. I have been beseeching the Almighty Father on their behalf, and yours, that you might gain the strength and vision you need to see the journey of faith through its destined end. How happy I am that you have given over your lives to the beauty of Love, that you realize that only the Divine Perfection of Jesus should be your goal, and that you will indeed reside forever in Heaven as a result of your spiritual conversion. There are many souls who are still suffering, My children! Too many are poor and hungry, alone, naked, grieving, and abandoned. I have spoken most recently to you about those who have no one to call their friends. These are the poor children of God who often walk through life as though their entire mortality is a mission through the desert of despair. Please remember them to God, and ask Him to bless their hearts in a special way. I know full-well what it means to be rejected, and My Son knows the feelings which haunt His followers who are despised among men. This is a time of reconciliation between all peoples, especially those who have been cast aside by the lot of humanity. It is true that you cannot know where each of them resides, but it is imperative that you realize their existence in many places around the world. They are children who are hiding in the dark corners of orphanages and in caves to escape the explosion of rockets of war. These are the innocent ones who are suffering the plight of being threaded amidst the scourge of battle with no way to fight for themselves. The horrid aggression of the arsenals of the United States of America is causing the deaths of many of these innocent children and their mothers and fathers. This is a senseless and selfish infiltration of evil against poor indigenous peoples from foreign lands for the sole purpose of vengeance and public pride.

When you see placards in the hands of your foreign neighbors which call for the death of America, they are actually seeking the end of this horrible warfare which is causing such destruction in their homelands. They wish not to spread the error that is only to be blamed on a few thousand renegades. All they wish is to live in peace upon the soil where their ancestors gave their fathers birth. I am the Immaculate Mother of God and the Patroness Saint of the United States of America. I am ashamed of the government of your nation and the arsenals of war by which she is spreading her error. Please be assured that the justified Wrath of God will make the world a better place when such error is brought to conclusion... My children, I do not tell you these things as a matter of an idle warning; My words are the facts as they are being dispensed from the Throne of Our God! He wishes not for the destruction of America, but it seems that the United States continuously invites others to attack her by being so obstinate in the face of such global unrest. I ask My holy people in your homeland to pray for peace, and not make war! In the midst of the sacrificial season of Lent when Christians are called to reconcile between themselves and those of other faiths, the warring is only being escalated by those who so hypocritically received the imposition of Ashes upon their foreheads on Ash Wednesday. How can any public leader receive such a penitential rite and walk away harboring even greater plans to annihilate his enemies? I assure you that God is not going to allow this type of misconduct to go unchastised. I have told you that the Cup is filled and running-over, but now it is about to be pushed completely off its base!

It is for these reasons that I have come to speak to you today, and to pray that all of My children in the Americas will pray for the conversion of the western hemisphere to the Peace which is dispensed through the power of the Holy Spirit. You must remember how filled were the churches after the events of September 11, 2001; and now, most everyone has abandoned their faith again and forgotten what punishment this was for America. What else must God allow to ensure the permanent conversion of such a materialistic society? Does the awakening of the American people require the destruction of the entire continent of North America? I implore those who know Me as their Mother to warn the rest about the peril of the days to come. Is it wrong for those who believe in God to state that He is allowing the slow undoing of the United States because the American people have embraced such a culture of death as to allow the systematic abortion of 45 million little children in the wombs of their mothers? Indeed, anyone who might allow such a proclamation to pass their lips would be speaking through the power of the Holy Spirit, Himself! For those who are seeking omens and signs, for prophecies and premonitions, they should prepare to take cover. Of all the abominations for which the United States is going to have to pay a heavy price, and there are multitudes of them, the sin of abortion is the single one that will ensure the certain destruction of such a misguided nation of indifferent people. I assure you that this is coming, it is in the offing, it is imminent, and it is inevitable. Were it not for the suffering and sacrifices of so many who serve Jesus so well already during these days, it would have occurred forthrightly heretofore.

I do not bring you messages of doom and disaster, I bring you the Gospel Truth which has been given to you through the Holy Paraclete and the lives of the First Apostles. These are the modern times about which Saint Louis de Montfort spoke. I am traveling from nation to hamlet, calling 'Where are My children?' It is time for us to bring the rich and powerful to their knees, to force them into contrition by the smell of their own souls rotting before their eyes. The moment has come for them to see the flash of Eternity and be unable to find themselves anywhere in it! I know where My children are located. You are the quiet ones who have been standing-in-wait while those who are powerful and wealthy have had their day. My holy followers, the fulcrum of modern history has finally come! While the children of God have had to maintain the shoring of their strength by defensive measures for so long, the time has now come for the movement of the Army of the Children of Mary to take the field. You are now enlisted in the most noble ranks of souls who ever walked the face of the globe. You have now become the aggressors who are on the offensive! Your God in Paradise has finally given the command for you to take this world back from the wretches who have been trying to steal it from the grasp of His Son for the past thousand years! This Victory will come in your day! This Triumph will occur on your watch! When you assail those who have been lukewarm in the face of the righteousness of Jesus, please drive the dagger of their own death a little deeper for the Saints of old! Breathe the flames of Justice upon their arrogance and burn their heathen souls back into the fires of Hell! Speak the words of the Son of God, and they will go running back into the dark for cover, where the Christ of all has placed His garrison of back-up Saints to keep them from getting away. The flames that will consume the chaff are leaping for them now! Love is this power and might! Holiness is this giant movement! Yes! Those millions of legends from the past are just now rubbing their palms together for this day to have finally come! I ask everyone alive today to be a part of this culmination to the only Kingdom of Love that can withstand the final battle between good and evil—those who are the children of Light, warriors for the Cross, lenders of their sights and ears to the cause of Truth in a world that has been lying to God since the first dawn of its exile ever broke!

I ask you to place Creation on notice that the Queen of Heaven and Earth is claiming the Triumph of Her Immaculate Heart now! This is the 2,000th year that I told the humble Marian Movement of Priests to prepare for! It has finally arrived, and it is ongoing!... Let those who stand aside in pride and atheism prepare for their demise at the hands of the Lady with the Crown of Twelve Stars! Thank you! Thank you to the children I love, to the little souls of God who obey and understand, to the treasures of the Sacred Heart of My Son whom He is now placing into motion to conquer the wicked! The snarling despots who have been trying to pilfer the Victory of Love away from those who are helpless could never have anticipated the defeat they are about to suffer! They miscalculated the power of their enemies! They misjudged the Divine Omnipotence of the Cross! I say to them today 'You did not think that you would be caught and brought to Justice, but you are just as wrong now as you were when you first began.' My children on the Earth are as bright-shining as the sun overhead, and no darkness shall prevail over them anymore! I have given them the Resurrected Christ! With all the power of God and the strength of His Love, these are the Last Times; and those who oppose Him can already feel their demise creeping up their spines. Indeed! Fire and brimstone, indeed! This is a Mother who never once said 'no' to Her children, and She is not about to forsake them now! Why? Because I bear in My Arms the Son of the Almighty God who has created Heaven and Earth. No Hell can prevail against His Church, His Kingdom, His Justice, His Wrath, or His Divine Mercy! Prepare the enemies of Love for their defeat, for defeat is assuredly theirs! My Special son, thank you for providing the venue through which I am able to deliver My messages. One of the most powerful weapons in the war against evil is about to be transported to this humble home. All of Heaven is obliged that you have been willing to clandestinely prepare it, unbeknownst to the wretched souls who will be repudiated by it. If you had not said 'yes' eleven years ago, this would not have been possible. You shall see how this augments the unfolding of Creation in a means that will manifest intense jubilation. I hold you in My intercessory prayers, offering My Love for everything you do."

Sunday, March 3, 2002
11:07 a.m.

"My little children, I come from God's Paradisial Kingdom to speak to you, from a Land of Grace and Peace that no mortal is so prescient to describe and has not the foresight to anticipate with the precision of the Lord who created it. I pine for your souls to reach Salvation soon. My mission is to induce you to love Jesus and your brothers and sisters, and to make the Earth like the Kingdom of Heaven so you will say 'yes' to Redemption when He returns to take you home. We pray for humanity before the Cross because the Crucifixion is the eradication of human sinfulness, including the sins you learned from your forbears, and those you have conjured on your own. While My soul and every fiber of My Immaculate Being have never known sin, I realize how the transgressions of humankind make you unhappy. I offered My Fiat to the Archangel Gabriel so your integrity and divinity can be restored. Will you approach Jesus and receive this Eternal Blessing? We hope that the supplications of the Season of Lent will procure the conversion of humankind to Christianity. Only through the Sacred Blood that Jesus shed on the Cross are you delivered unto this, all whose hungry souls are deemed worthy by the Divine Mercy of His Love. My little children, your spiritual conversion must occur now because humanity is agonizing in such pain. You must participate in the Passion and Resurrection of My Son by dying to sin and rising as newborn creatures inside His Most Sacred Heart. Although your mortal passing will take you to the source of all that is unseen, you must live as though you have already laid eyes on the Face of God. You must refine, amend, and remake the globe to become the pristine Love that is growing inside you. Yes! You must become like Jesus, the Holy Spirit, and God's devotion for humanity while you serve in His vineyard. This focuses the awareness of lost sinners toward the enlightenment gained through His Wisdom. How must this be done? There is no other way to Salvation than the Crucifixion of Jesus, for He is the Way, the Truth, and the Life. Remember the sacrifices you have offered for those you love, and on behalf of sinners who do not know to make their own. Your gifts to Jesus will be repaid a hundredfold. Too many among you walk in darkness because there are only few who are willing to emit His Light of Love. I ask you to be the reflection of Jesus for them. Emulate His Grace and goodness for those who are not aware that His Peace is the culmination of their earthly sentence. I beseech your willingness to wield the inspiration of the Holy Paraclete where your brothers are lacking the knowledge of the Spirit of Truth. Enlighten the brazen throngs who are walking the pathways of life with nowhere to go. Guide them to Jesus, My lambs! You own the offices through the strength of the Wonderful Counselor to assist them in refashioning their lives on the foundation of faith. Only by doing this will they know that the wholesome realms of life for which they are searching can be found in their love for God. This, My children, is how you become instruments for Him. This is how you are able to live-out the prayers of the Saints!

I implore God's children to conduct themselves with the anticipation by which you expect the arrival of Easter. Could this be the year when Jesus returns to the Earth and closes the ages? Might this be the forty days that will separate the sheep from the goats? Who is to say that the Son of Man will not return as you hear the strains of the sanctity of Truth raining-down upon the Earth in the course of this night? I have asked you to live with this perpetual expectation because the end of time is near. Whosoever among you can provide evidence that this is untrue, let him come forward, for even his time is shorter than he earlier believed. The cycles and revolutions of the generations are about to be congealed by the stark, bold reality of the Final Judgement of Jesus Christ. Where will you discover yourselves? Will you be standing upright on the Rock of Salvation, or will you be plummeting through Creation to the Abyss like sand through an hourglass? Will the Light on your souls keep you from falling permanently asleep in death, or will the darkness of your sins conceal the Face of Absolution from your consciousness forever? If anyone should inquire why these things have been placed before men, remind them that the Mother of the God who willed Creation into being has posed them as the final questions before the veil of the ages is raised. This is not a cause for fear, it is a moment of Truth! To grow your faith, you must become one with the Divine Providence of Heaven's Eternal Love. As you survey human life from your mortal constraints, can you sense that there is no freedom in the chains of sin? This is a period of discovery when every soul must judge for himself whether he is in tune with the sanctity of God's Supernal Light. There is no other reason for your having been placed inside the element of time. Let not your hearts be troubled as to whether God has the power to save you, but will you allow Him to do so by turning your own lives over to Him? These questions must be answered immediately, not tomorrow or next week, but right now. Please be the obedient followers of the legacy of Heaven's citizens. You should realize that these are the most important hours for the exercise of your faith. The fulcrum of the history of men has arrived; the instant of making the most of your existence is here, and your compliance with the Gospel must be effected before you recline for another night's rest. You have spoken about the finest hours of Creation over an extended period of time, but it is humanity who must pray them into being. The course of contemporary events is shaped by your conscience. Will there be peace, or will there be war? The response to this is revealed once you decide. My prayer with you and for you is that you will choose for God to make your lives the emulation of His Peace, to look at yourselves honestly and wonder what aspects about His omnipotence moved Adam and Eve to yearn to be like Him. I tell you that your goals should never include the wielding of force over vulnerable men, but to serve them, to be their healers and teachers, their friends, their advisors and consolers. This is the most beatific amplification of your likeness of Jesus. This is the piety that He wishes every subject to see, to imitate the King! Should your hearts take a respite from their toils by summoning you to the fields of reflection to wonder how it would feel to be like God, the Holy Spirit will always prompt you to be like His Son. If you wish to imitate Him, reflect His Divine Love! This is how you are capable of creating new worlds through the essence of Divine Love that is sown inside your conscience once you accept Jesus on the Cross. These worlds will not be like the spheres you see suspended in distant galaxies because they will seem supernatural to you. It is not cosmic masses that you are asked to pursue, but a sustained and interpersonal community of Messianic Love. Hence, you will have transcended everything that is of physical nature, the call of the intellect, and the prospects of your broadest veins of conjecture. This is the Providential Love who nourishes you, who followed you from Eden, who was victimized to redeem your souls, and who will tender you to the Father inside the New Jerusalem. When He speaks about living in prayerful hope, this is what He means; this is the joy of rejuvenation, Wisdom, power of the heart, deliverance, fulfillment, exultation, and contentment. If you were able to drink these things from a flask, you should crave a potion of them now. When you partake of the Body and Blood of the Son of God who has taken away the sins of the world, you are remaking yourselves and inviting Creation to imbibe of your new perfection. My Special son, I wish for the sake of the millions to whom I have addressed My messages that I could speak for many more hours, but I want you to have your time. I will pair this message with another of its kind soon. You are listening to a Mother who is heartened by Her children, who is satisfied that My intercession is having the effect that God intends, and who is assured by Jesus that we are making the world a better place. There is much work to be done in your nation, around the globe, and beyond the stellar auras where the hearts of mankind aspire. Thank you, My son! Thank you for months, years, and a lifetime of devotion to the Deific Love about which I have spoken. Legends, ambassadors and doctors, those who bow and genuflect, and the mightiest souls who ever stood to proclaim their obedience to God are grateful to you for being the child of Heaven who is helping their dreams come true."

Saturday, March 9, 2002
10:33 a.m.

"Please remember, My children, that those who reject the spirituality that takes humanity closer to God are parasites feeding on His Divine Creation. They will be expunged by the righteousness that is overwhelming the Earth. I told you on this day eleven years ago that each Rosary bead is like the world in your hands. At that early morning hour, your brothers and sisters were far more steeped in sin and depression than today, but the number of people in your midst has grown since then, so your continued prayers are needed to a greater degree. You will find at the last that the human spirit must evolve to become completely united in the Holy Spirit Incarnate. These are special days of remembrance and revelation, and your work is far from being ended. Please remain with Me as we adhere to the Will of God for the furtherance of His lost children to the Cross. I come to you as a happy Mother, but one quite aware of the attacks that are ongoing against the Church. Should anyone who is without sin be among you, it is he who should speak, while others remain silent. We have prayed on a multitude of occasions for the purity of lost sinners. Let us proceed so that those who misunderstand the meaning of real repentance can arrive at the moment of dispensing forgiveness themselves. You are guided and protected by the Almighty Father who created us. I beseech you to understand from His Mother that His affectionate caress will envelope you wholly and entirely if you disavow your desires for false justice and vengeance. There is no need for denigrating others because their conscience will eventually allow them to judge themselves. The sequence of the vindication of humanity occurred during the Passion and Crucifixion of Jesus. He is the Son of Man who has promised to set the world aright. It is His Holy Paraclete who is shaping the just and the strong, molding them into citizens of peace. I implore everyone to become one in this number. It is in an entreating tone that I address the nations. Let not your anger turn its ugliness against the Sacraments that are purifying you before the Table of the Lord! What men seek most these days is the isolationism that is luring them away from suffering-humanity, causing them to turn their backs on the souls God has placed before them to nurture and heal. As it has been said on many occasions by a lot of Saints, this cannot be permitted to stand. If you engage the battle against evil in the Church, do such battle against Satan, and not the poor sinners he has influenced through time and temptation. I weep humbly for the transference of My children into the Bay of Absolution, the Blood of Jesus on the Cross. This is the rectification of error and the source of the Wisdom humankind requires to be made whole. Would it seem too much to ask if this Mother inquired Her children why the citizens of the Church would crucify their own spiritual austerity because of the weaknesses of a few? Those who do so are living the fallacy that they can seek greater purification for the Church than the Sacrament of Penance which it dispenses through its priests. I urge everyone to place these difficulties into perspective, and strive to preserve the dignity of the thousands who are serving their religious vocations with obedience.

What does the Mother of God ask of you? Pray! Pray profoundly! God is listening, and the Saints are communing before Him to advocate for the purity and faith of the Church Militant. Seek the gentle side of human nature instead of the vengeful one. Yes, it is true. There is one perfect Victim—Jesus on the Cross, consecrated into the Most Blessed Sacrament ever known to Creation on the altars of the Church. While humanity is called to participate in His suffering during your mortality, it is only by His Blood that you are made whole. Jesus has blessed those who are suffering in agony for the sinners among them who have rejected Salvation. I have explained the reciprocal nature of Heaven and Earth, and this is the most important time for you to recall that the Kingdom of God espouses self-denial, cultivation of the heart, stronger witness to Truth, and the realization that every man and woman must become united beneath the Cross to strengthen and unify the Mystical Body of Christ against the hellions of evil that are trying to conquer you. When you pray for this unity, you will understand what I said eleven years ago when I sought your compliance with the Sacred Scriptures, John three and three. I am the same Mother of Perpetual Help whom I was then. My message is as clear, My mission has not changed, and My purpose is as definitive. I have come to convert My children to Jesus! My Special son, I know that you understand the necessity of My words. They are timely, but it will be alright for you to deliver them after you finish your pending manuscripts. Above all things, and beyond the mysterious occurrences that are happening around you, you are maintaining the constancy of love that keeps your life from rocking to a tilt, away from the tranquility of Jesus. It is the execution of your duties as a Christian that is protecting you from surrendering to the attacks that are being made against the Church. God is pleased that you are willing to stand beside His flock. Indeed, it is the love you are professing, especially your testimonies in your prayer room, that is growing Jesus' patience and allowing His people time to prepare for His Justice and comprehend His Mercy. The American society is engaged in a great deal of criticism against the Roman Catholic Church, and it is your prayers for the purity of priests that is keeping this difficulty from becoming aggravated. You are appreciated for all you do in sustaining the Church during this period of turmoil. You are correct in your assessment. The secular media are sensationalizing the difficulties of the Church into a greater scandal to make themselves wealthy. It is true; before the Son of Man is through, their empire of wanton indiscretion will come crashing and burning to the ground with such ferocity that it will make the fallen World Trade Center towers look like houses of playing cards tumbling onto a tabletop. I promise with the Truth of Almighty God that this will occur. You know that the Lord asks you to proffer your spiritual love for the purpose of advancing His Kingdom, and realize that violence and destruction on the part of men is not the answer. However, Heaven will eventually strike back. This will require you and your brother not to be reticent about praying and seeking a peaceful future."

Sunday, March 17, 2002
3:38 p.m.

"Saint Patrick is not slightly honored by the carousing and gluttony that have become the trademark of his Feast across the earthly domain. I ask that My children admonish those who are desecrating the remembrance of his sacred life and dedication to the Church. Today, we honor the memory of those who have given their entire being to the spiritual conversion of their peers. Almighty God loves His people with affection and Truth, and He asks that all souls return this dedication in-kind. Will you join Me in prayer for the purification of humanity so the Earth will become the envy of Heaven? I offer My gratitude for everyone who is committed to remembering the sacrifices of love they are lending Jesus during this season of Lent. The next two weeks will be the committal of more intentions to Him; He will bless the participation of His Mystical Body to its mortification in repairing the damage inflicted on Creation by so many who have spurned Him in disgrace. It is imperative that we lift our urgent supplications for the cessation of abortion. Many millions of children whom God has placed inside the wombs of their mothers are yearning to be born, to inherit the call of righteousness when their time arrives to be baptized and receive their Christian awakening. Thank you for allowing the Son of Man to be your Truth. Without your obedience, the transformation of humanity to the dignified Virtues would be impossible. As the hours and days pass, it is important for everyone to remember that the Sacrament of Reconciliation awaits those who are separated from God by sin. This is not just a Sacrament that is efficacious to prepare you for Easter, but any juncture during the Liturgical Year when God's children require cleansing Grace and penitential forgiveness. Please bear witness to the masses that Jesus waits in the confessional to bestow forgiveness upon those who wish to be reunited with Him. In unseen Creation, you must know that there are multitudes who suffer in Purgatory, and they also request your prayers. There are countless hungry paupers on Earth who are living without shelter in squalid quarters, and I urge you to remember them too. I have returned so you will know that your sacrifices in faith have not ended, that your mortality is a period of readiness for the shining moment when you perceive the City of God above the atmospheres with the fullness of sight. This is not only the hope with which you turn-in for the night, but is the assurance you embrace when you awaken every morning. My Special son, I speak to you under the most pleasant circumstances because

I see that this home is about to be the center of another march of victory to hail the holiness of My priest-sons. Many people have wept tears of thankfulness upon seeing *When Legends Rise Again*. Their sentiment is that finally someone has stepped forward speaking the Truth with courage to raze the barriers that are prohibiting their children from achieving the purity they seek, to lift-up humanity around the globe, not just here in America; and to remember the debt that exiled mankind owes the hundreds-of-thousands who have passed into Glory who made life bearable for the afflicted. I come to remind you that you must not keep a tally or calculate a score about whether your works are being effective in your presence. God makes the most of your sacrifices in places you do not know.

My children, you must realize that modern humanity is for the most part an untapped gold mine of innovation, autonomy, zeal, discipline, and intrigue. You contain a veritable windfall of excellence waiting to be unleashed; and structured inside you is a capstan of heartstrings that can move entire solar systems you have never seen. All you have to do is trust in Jesus, and they will become like marbles in your hands. Before the witness of God, enamored by your genius, the listless skies dance with rainbows in reflection of your renown. The whole matter rests in your relationship with Him, knowing that you have the power in your prayers to transform your neighbors' porridge into family banquet feasts. However, you must embellish your faith! Some people think that the battles of human life are so rife with desperation, antagonism, controversy, and defeatism that the idea of winning is not worth the effort. Yet, with all the strength and majesty of the Earth and its stupendous attributes, even the relentless rocks and hills, most men do not appreciate how fragile it is compared to the auspiciously tenacious domination of love in the human heart. Most people are hesitant to accept this, but they come by it honestly because they have never really taken time to draw the connection between earthly life and Heaven. They have been suppressed by the pride of too many aristocrats who wield authority. What would they have the Lord do about the rotund arrogance of such public figures and their taught relationships with those whom they disagree? Have they already forgotten what happened in AD 33? Easter Morning came, and there was jubilation everywhere. I will tell you what I envisioned in My Heart. There were lines of crowds; masses and throngs marching in procession to the Sepulcher; banners, ribbons, and streamers filled the skies to both horizons to the singing of Angels' choirs; and thunder crashed and lightening flashed, but there was not a cloud overhead. Incense tinted the air, flowers bloomed on barren soil, there were starbursts of conversions, tears flowed like rivers, the valleys wept, the mountains rejoiced, grand symphonies played on sterling precipices; and one manifest King of Vindication stood high above it all. My children, Jesus' Resurrection was all about this, and this is how He recognizes the contrasts in your hearts. He knows that you would rather see candlelight than a funeral pyre, a deer drink than a jackal pounce, and an eagle fly than a crocodile lurk. You would rather see a child walk than a widow mourn, a parade ground than a cemetery, and a repatriation party than a call to arms. Heaven realizes that you would recant every pejorative syllable you ever uttered against your friends when tensions were running a little high, and that you pray for more opportunities to offer your congratulations than your condolences. You pine for wedding bells and jubilees, and puppy litters and apple trees. Jesus will not allow anything to douse your hopes or compromise your ambitions. If time will not tell you this, Eternity assuredly will. Henceforth, do your noblest to entertain pure thoughts; remember that temptation is a harlot who would do anything to steal you from the embrace of Chastity. Make peace with Creation through rustic images rather than urban madness; like croaking toads, not screeching tires; by benefitting Nature with a reflection of its own beauty wrapped in the serenity of your faith. These are the contemplations that will someday pass through the veil with you, surviving the Earth's last gasp, and living-on in Paradise.

Please be assured that your brothers and sisters are being changed, just as you have petitioned for them to convert for years. This is another time of intense apportionment for the Holy Spirit to require only the best from humanity, and the process is so grand that it is nearly impossible for you to comprehend its volume. Therefore, I ask that you trust My words when I tell you that your mission is on course. Your life has never been more productive than during these months and years. Thank you from the center of My Immaculate Heart for reflecting the Love of Jesus; for being a healer of nations, the Wisdom that is eradicating the shame of human oppression, and the exemplary elegance that the United States lacked before you were born. It is sufficient to say that you are Light, that you are loved, and you are embraced by the Providence of Love. This is My first message since you finished your latest book. I know that you are as pleased as the Lord and the Dominion Angels who helped inspire it from the core of your heart. It is a pretty monograph because of the great visions of genius that you have composed inside its text. You must remember this as a period of peace and revelation. Thank you for taking your presence to the village where you traveled Friday evening. The world is filled with people like you met, and your kindness is what allows them to reach-out in friendship. You became acquainted with hundreds more people who know your brother. At the end of time, you will both see the benisons that are yours for remaining My children of bold faith. And, you are anticipating the powers to which you can be given as your lives are dedicated to God. Your love is strong, your life is on course, your goals are within reach, and the Earth is much better for all of these."

Palm Sunday, March 24, 2002
4:02 a.m.

"My dear little children, the glistening skies above are overflowing with the Wisdom of the Lord, and are saturated with the signal graces of His Divine Love for which you have prayed. This is a robust period for Me as I appear before you early this morning because it represents a milestone of your faith where you are journeying to Heaven in the clemency of Jesus' Most Sacred Heart. I beseech you to remember that His Love is immeasurable in time and Eternity. To the good fortune that your souls are receptive to His Blood on the Cross in reparation for your sins, you are inevitably bound for rebirth in the lineage of the Saints. As you recite the Sacred Mysteries of the Holy Rosary, please remember to pray for the conversion of sinners, for the extraction of every ill influence from your midst, for the protection of unborn children, for the corporeal purity of those prone to lust, and for the eradication of the scourges of poverty and disease. Your work for God has been thus far overwhelmingly successful, and the lessons and teachings you are revealing about His Love are a balm for the millions who would not otherwise recognize His pardon for themselves. What shall be your just reward? Surely you know that it is your destination of endless peace and humble adulation! The past centuries and the ensuing future have become one Eternity in Jesus because His Kingdom yields to no disparate times. His goal is the divination of souls at the epicenter of His sublime protection. Can you see that every hour devoted to Him is a thousand more that your brothers and sisters will not be required to lament in anguish? It is in this way that your lives become a prayer and a commission of servitude before the Throne of the Lord. You will be entering Holy Week in a few hours, and this is a year of high importance to the Catholic Church. Errant influences are being purged from within its ranks as Lent gives way to the Paschal Mysteries of Easter. I ask everyone to heed the papal authority of the Holy Father in Rome for the purification of the Church, to be admonished should he issue reprimand, to pray at his behest, do penance according to his prescriptions, and offer your lives to sustain his strength during the years of his pontifical leadership. There are many opportunists who will come forward in the next few months in an effort to undermine and impugn the Hierarchy of the Church; and your prayers must be unfeigned, lest these wolves and marauders succeed in diminishing the pastoral role of My priests. There is a movement afoot to destroy the genuineness of your faith, to desecrate the sanctifying power of the Sacraments, and to dissolve your resolute intentions to stand beside the Mother Church during its period of struggle. This is a definitive moment in its history because all the faithful on the Earth are being tried and tested for their allegiance to its role in the Salvation of mankind. Please remember to obey the Holy Spirit who lives within your midst. Console the many who have been offended by the sins of the weak. Remain true to the Apostles' Creed by which you have professed your faith. And, by all means, attend the Holy Sacrifice of the Mass so as to assure Jesus that His Crucifixion is the centerpiece of your lives. Humankind is altogether too frail to succeed on the journey of mortality without seeking His strength and consolation. When He asks you to be refashioned in Him, this is the essence of what He means.

I am among you while you petition for the healing of humankind before the Cross. And, as you are aware, the week ahead is the principled celebration of your Absolution; that Jesus suffered an egregious Passion for your transgressions, that He was Crucified to take away your sins, and that He was raised by God from the Tomb on Easter morning to restore your life which, by the tunnage of Truth, you will surrender in time to death. When the Almighty Father completes His Holy Will for humankind, we shall share together the glories of Paradise, forging the new beginnings that seem so elusive to you, watching the opening of Heaven as the Deity of Truth is revealed at last, and praising God before His Sacred Throne for the endless ages to come. I have not only anticipated this day with prefigured joy, My soul has been vested with the honor of returning to Earth at this moment in history to apprise you in advance. Therefore, be hopeful that your excruciation is short lived compared to the Resurrection you will share in Heaven someday. Accept the crosses of suffering that the Lord dispenses with perfect submission. Remember the great achievements that humanity has made in making the world a better place because of your undying love for Jesus. I assure you that He listens and understands your pleadings amassed. Your Salvation is the anointing of the globe within His Grace. There can be no grander future for humanity than this! My Special son, I know that you and your brother have been sorely afflicted by the Spring viruses that are commonplace where you live. While I do not expect you to understand now, there is a purpose for it all. Thank you not only for suffering for the sake of the Kingdom of God, but for being patient while depositing your trust into the resilience of faith. I ask you to remember to keep your eyes focused on the goal of human contrition and not be concerned about the distractions that the Earth is heaping on those who are laboring for Jesus across the spectra of this age. I have great anticipation about the future because I know that souls like you and your brother will ultimately succeed as the 'Children of Mary' of these latter times. Daylight, sunset, midnight, and dawn are reasons aplenty to know that the protection of My Mantle hovers around you always. Please rest your spirits in the knowledge that your Immaculate Mother is with you through everything you must endure and sustain. I assure you that it was an intensely sorrowful time when I stood beneath the Cross to see My Son suffer and die to redeem the human race. However, no pain is worse than witnessing people turn away in insensitivity and disbelief to the condemnation of their souls. Thanks to your service and the pious societies of Christian people from generations passed, God's Creation is returning to Him wholly intact, absolved, cultivated, purified, and reborn. Thank you for giving lodge to the lofty Paraclete inside your heart! You may pray the Passionate Stations indoors this Friday afternoon. I will be with you, as I have been in the past."

Easter Sunday, March 31, 2002
5:15 p.m.

"If there is any immortal way that a Mother could touch your hearts in this world, My children, please let this be the day. Let these moments be those when you finally understand what it means to live through Eternal joy, to be the guiding dominions of peaceful accord upon an Earth that is still engulfed in war. I come to share the Good News of the Resurrection of Jesus from the grave, from which He has reclaimed your souls from death, and to the new beginnings which God had planned for you. You have seen the cinema production about legends of the fall, and those who have fallen; and I am the storied Lady of Wisdom who has the jubilation to tell you that all legends shall rise again! When you look in your midst and in the distance, you see the scourges that continue to plague the nations; the battles, diseases, social discord, religious conflicts, dying secular queens, rampant greed and immorality, and an almost inexplicable loss of hope in the fire which is the new direction of the human soul toward the Glory of God. Well, today is the celebration of the birth of the New Jerusalem, one that shall not be divided by battle lines, one who is destined to be complete in the hands of her Creator, and one that is only now breaking past the horizon of the Everlasting Dawn. Pray for her, My children, that she will not forsake herself amidst the awful warring and deprivation. Pray that this new world of hosts will accept the revitalized Spirit of Truth which has broken free from death on this day, so celebrated by the Church! If the words you hear to resound the miracle of this Easter Day are too frail to lift your hearts, then allow the Mother of God to tell you about Divine Resurrection, perfect acclamation, a sense of accord, and the power of God in the universe that no evil shall ever prevail upon again! My Immaculate Heart is aglow with hope today, even as the Holy Land lay under siege, notwithstanding the enemies of the Church who are trying to bring Her down, and despite the self-destructive forces who are trying to kill the gift of innocent human life. Easter is about more than victory because the Paschal Mystery lives past all the ages! The raising of Jesus from the Sepulcher is the living daylight that all Creation has pined to see since the fall of Adam. When your hearts see the reunion of the lost, the forsaken, the spurned, and the rejected, you are seeing the firelight of the Eastertide of Jesus! When you witness children being lowered in the healing waters of Lourdes and Guadalupe, your soul is seeing the boulder moved away from the Tomb and the Living Son of Man walk out with the power of Almighty God in His Holy Frame. As you forgive one another for past offenses, make reparation where there is harm, raise your heads in the middle of hopelessness, feed the meager, enlist the service of the able, tend to the infirm, and secure a new peace where there has been only the perils of war; you have forthrightly become seamlessly united in the Easter Resurrection. If the wincing eyes of an elderly man are weeping upon seeing the return of his prodigal son, your heart is tasting the Glory of your Salvation. You can witness these things in the mortal world if your hope and love are given to God. The flatlands and mountains that make-up America can be rejuvenated in communion and happiness if you accept that the Resurrection of Jesus has given your souls new flight. I urge you to believe this not only because it is a principle of your faith, but because only in this will you find your own reunion.

Today, we pray especially for those who are far from God, that they will become united in the family of the faithful who know they will be saved by Jesus when the time has arrived. I ask you to bless those who persecute you, give your provisions to the many who have none for themselves, seek the most noble course for all humankind to travel, and be the Love of God in the world today. All of this can be achieved by modern men because of the power of the celebration of this Easter Day! The night is not so long that you cannot find the morning; the pain you bear is as nothing when compared to the ecstasy you will know; the foregone heroes you have mourned are awaiting your conversion, and the commission you have been given by God to partake of each of these is located at the center of your hearts. If you wish to know the meaning of Easter better, come to Love. Should your conscience be awakened by the anticipation of your spirit, call on the power of the Resurrection, for the next flames you see may be those of the conflagration of the universe, and you must all survive them in the Name of Jesus! You must don the armor of humility to serve at the delight of the Angels, never-minding the arrows of hatred that try to pierce your divinity in this dangerous world. I seek in you the transformation of your enlightenment, to understand that all Creation is still groaning beneath your feet, across the broad hemispheres, and around the circular skies. Know well that you shall be the victors and champions of Immortal Love inside the Sacred Heart of Jesus. This is the true harmony that is playing in your heads, one that is taking your entire 'being' into the unity of Love that the Holy Trinity has given you to live. My perspective is unique to this world, and I wish to share it with you now. This is why I have come to implore you to pray, to kneel before the Altar of Sacrifice and receive the Blood of Salvation, and to accept within yourselves the pardon that is your Absolution. I beseech you to not allow your pride to keep you from taking to the floor of the Earth in humble submission. I beg you! I beg you! Let not the disciples of error who are surrounding you now convince you that it is infantile to ask God to save you. Come to His Easter! Call upon the Resurrection that is not only 1969 revolutions past, but that is completely timeless and immortal. Therefore, if you find that the meaning of life eludes you, discover it in Jesus. I stood beside the Cross of Mount Calvary with the same faith with which you are asked to live today. With what sorrow I grieved the loss of My innocent Son to the hatred of the secular world, but He was the Victor at last! Be now My children and My faithful people who can see through the experiences of Jesus that all Divine Love is one; you are the citizens of Truth who can proclaim for yourselves that you wholly refuse to be tread upon by the darkness of the world again. Accept the Passion and Sacrifice of Jesus as the amendment for your sins which has been required by God, and listen to His Spirit with your hearts during these last times. The God who loves us all has promised that My pleading before humanity would never be in vain. And, I am pleading to you now. Please accept the Crucifixion of My Son as your saving Grace, and His Resurrection from the Sepulcher as your final passage into Paradise. I offer this message for the world because this is Easter. It is the celebration of all goodness in Triumph over evil. This is the culmination of the Deposit of Peace which has remade the Earth into the likeness of Heaven. Just as the first Apostles did, stand with the firmness of Love in God, and He will dispense upon you the Triune Truth that you have been welcomed into His Kingdom. Let this become your message for the celebration of Easter and for your every new tomorrow. Allow this hope to supplant the tears of sadness that have heretofore strewn your faces with pain and your cheeks with the briny memories of the past. I usher the Messiah of the ages to make your lives complete, to cause your allegiance to God to be of the highest magnitude, and to shake the Earth to its core in jubilation that humankind is alive again. This time, My children, it is perpetual! Easter has brought you the last goodbye to everything you wished to hold forever and the expungement of all that would ever cause you to be divided again. With the faith that I am pleading you to enlist, your hearts will begin to live this joy.

I have already seen the Everlasting Dawn of Heaven. I know the mansions you seek by the passing of each new day. Please accept My pledge that they are assuredly there and prepared for your arrival. These distant shores of happiness are not so far away from you now because your voyage across the seas of mortality is nearly at an end. If you allow the Holy Spirit to be your vision and the Love of God to be your course, you shall disembark in the Land of Promise for which all the ages before you have pined. I say to the peoples of the nations; lay down your weapons! Stop the fighting over the politics of borders. Embrace one another for the purpose of defying the scourge of evil that is trying to destroy you. Humanity is yet young and vibrant, and hopeful too. This has been given to you by the Son of the Most High on the Easter that you acknowledge to be true. The litanies of poetics are assuredly the new rhythms of your hearts in the Psalms of God. Recite and invoke them! Yours is the youth of the new beginnings that can come when you accept the

Christian peace that God has given you in Jesus. Thereafter, rather than stalking one another for designs of deceit, you will ratify the co-redeeming Love that you are expected to share all the days of your life. God's parable for this Easter is in the person of the Pope, the Holy Father in Rome. He has an angelic heart of youthful faith. The vibrant posture of his vision is your message to begin anew. But, his poor face is God's signature of how He sees the groveling world. Would it be beyond any hope that you might give this Holy Pontiff reason to raise his eyes again in jubilation that humankind has finally chosen to follow him into the sanctification of all souls through the Providence of God? Is it too much to ask humanity to accept in faith what this giant of giants has been saying for nearly twenty-five years? *Be God's people*, is what he is urging. And, *be holy, too*! This is My Easter wish for the world in 2002. I ask as your Mother to take My hand, gather beneath My Mantle, pray in unity with My Immaculate Heart, and return to the blessings of God once again. My Special son, these are My hopes for you and your brothers and sisters on this day. I know that you are in agreement with the petitions that I place before God. Thank you for praying with Me. I hope you have enjoyed the words I have brought humanity today. You will begin a new month tomorrow, and I promise that it will be a blessed one for you."

Sunday, April 7, 2002
Feast of The Divine Mercy
1:42 p.m.

"To humanity who is waiting with such anticipation for the consoling peace of God inside their hearts, I have come to pray with you and to tell you that it can be found in the Divine Mercy of the Most Sacred Heart of Jesus Christ, the Only Begotten Son of God. There is no other amelioration for the ills of society, for the personal grief known only to those whose interior pain is their labor, and for the future of many with only little to their names who are anonymous to the wealthy. When the three-o'clock hour strikes upon every inch of soil on the globe today, this is the remembrance of the high moment of the Easter Octave, that My Son has rendered humanity worthy to walk freely into the Gates of Paradise. As I have told the world prior to this day and on many occasions, it is only through your acceptance of the Divine Mercy that you can forgive yourselves and deign your souls worthy of such a blessing. We pray today for those who do not know God, for the sinners who wittingly reject Him, for the millions who have accepted Jesus as their personal Savior and undergo the taunting of their atheistic peers, and especially for the alleviation of human suffering. When you celebrate Whitsunday in six more weeks, I ask that you remember that the power of your prayers is the Holy Paraclete, the Spirit of Love who remains in you as your souls are transferred to the Glory of

Paradise. Will you join His Immaculate Mother and remember to God the countless souls who are holding-out against the gift of faith which He so wishes to dispense to them? The Chaplet that you pray today is both reminiscent and prescient, for it allows you to recapture the best of your past inside the forging of your new beginnings in Jesus. My children, whatever would be the Will of God for humanity today is a manifestation of the surrender of the life of Sister Faustina to Jesus in a wholly sacrificial way for the glory of all the world. There is nothing corrupt in her being; her soul resides with the Saints in Heaven, and her legacy is the urging of all people to know that Jesus wishes to forgive every transgression against Almighty God through the shedding of His Blood. Therefore, as you lift your intentions to Heaven today, please invoke the powerful intercession of Sister Faustina to augment those petitions. Pretty are your souls when you ask God for forgiveness because your belief in Him transcends your simple acknowledgment that He lives, but also that He is the Divine power who can save you from eternal damnation. Were it not for this grand purpose that He holds in His Heart for you, I would not be speaking to you now. I implore you to pray for the Church, for all who are serving religious vocations, for the poor and elderly, the hungry, diseased, the dying, and those whose agony is hardening their hearts in their final hours on Earth. Please pray with Me that they shall understand the linking of their agonies with the Passion and Crucifixion of Christ Jesus. It is all to the purpose of uniting Heaven and Earth. I furthermore request that you pray that those who have been harboring grudges against their neighbors will release these emotions and take their brothers' hands in Christian Love. Only then will world wars cease and the deranged individuals who are plotting to take their own lives while killing others in the meantime will realize how disillusioned they are.

    Humanity is fighting more than the discernable divisions of religions and politics these days, for the peoples of the nations do not truly know themselves. Their self-identity has been put asunder by their lack of allegiance to Jesus. The forces of jealousy and competition for the affections of the masses are causing physical aggression and emotional strife in nearly every quarter of the globe; no region has been spared or left untouched by this horrible scourge. Only after the Earth recognizes as one that every race must unite against the evil forces of Satan will there be no more wars. A lack of human love is the common enemy of every region and sphere. Please recall that Jesus admonishes His exiled Creation to be perfected through His Sacrifice. This is why I continue speaking so profoundly about mutual forgiveness and the realization by every individual that there is nothing wrong with the world that cannot be corrected by the holiness which is appropriate for the world. Jesus has established this healing righteousness for this purpose alone. He asks for all to come to Him for faith, understanding, guidance, and Truth. No other in your midst can make this offering because He is the only Redeemer of your souls. Would it be your pleasure that He fall again at your feet and plead for your conversion? Is this what humankind would require from their Savior, Prophet, and King? His Sacred Heart is the largesse through which you are being invited to share in the Glory of the Father while still residing on the face of the globe. You need not yet die to accept the dignity of Heaven, if only you will love in its likeness now. Today, therefore, is about the Ocean of Mercy that Jesus has poured into Creation by His Sacrifice on the Cross. Why did He speak with such urgency to an ailing novice so many years ago, and why would the brief span of her years manifest the spiritual awakening of so many lost souls? Because it is true; God performs magnificent miracles in remote places. And, the graciously simple heart of Sister Faustina has been the birthing of the faith of millions of her brothers and sisters since. Our Divine Lord and Maker wishes that each of you will become her likeness. I once told you that your power for overcoming your faults and failures is prayer, the power of God in you. The Holy Spirit will not misguide you or lead you astray because He is the Truth of your factual existence and the transformation of your faith in the Almighty Father to your birthplace at His side. I beseech you to deploy the power that has been given freely to you for your own benevolence. Become the doves of peace who hover gently above the Earth below so as to ward-off the divisions which keep societies at war. Erase the battle lines where skirmishes are being undertaken by enlightening the ground between such foes and telling them the stories of Jesus. I tell you today that no soul who will eventually reside in Paradise will ever turn a deaf ear to your pleas. Yes, in effect, become the likeness of your Immaculate Mother to broker peace in these places where there has been only the remnants of war.

    If only you knew the empowering benefits of your prayers and the gratitude that Jesus holds for your saying them, you would pray without ceasing! Indeed, while the world has taken to its knees in supplication, there can be no time for the corrupt factions of warring and the untold atrocities that accompany them. Please peer across the vast oceans and within your borders and see that there is nothing on Earth worth fighting for more than Salvation! This is not a physical altercation between men and their captors, but the union of humanity as a single body of holy people against the horrors of demonism brought upon the world by Satan. The evil of Satan is your enemy, not those who are blindly influenced by him through the breaches in their own integrity. We must pray for the conversion of those who do evil so they will come out of the darkness and into the Light of Jesus. Whether they choose to believe it or not, every soul alive is capable of becoming a mighty warrior in the fight for Immortal Love. Therefore, follow Jesus in obedience and self-sacrifice by the Way of the Cross. My Special son, this is a day of high joy for Me because I realize that you remain true and steadfast in your commitment to Jesus, not wavering like so many who have professed to be much holier than you. Thank you! You are about to see that this week will be one that will alter the face of the Church, back to the holiness it has originally known. This is done because you teach the lessons to humanity that are needed for a better understanding of the Truth of Catholicism. Your book will not only eradicate and eliminate a great deal of misunderstanding by the societies inside your nation today, it will set the record straight for them to know that the American media are truly an evil empire and enemy of human Salvation."

Sunday, April 14, 2002
4:23 p.m.

"To the children who have been faithfully praying for the purification of the Earth for eleven years, I come to tell you that long will be the benefitting tenure of your petitions. Heaven is jubilant because I have been dispatched by Almighty God to assure you that the future is on course with the sanctifying presence of the Holy Spirit in millions of souls since your messages began. Do you know what this means for the culmination of humanity? Our God in Paradise is pleased by your service and gratified that you chose the holier virtues of piety, servitude, and respectfulness. Wherever you lay your hands and offer your hearts is a more holy place. Thank you! Today, you continue to bask in the remembrance of the Easter celebration. We have seen many come and go, and only you know the sacrifices you have made during your Lenten observations to make them amenable to your faith. I ask you to augment your lives with the concurrent service of self-sacrifice before suffering humanity while holding the Resurrection of Jesus from the Tomb in your permanent memory. This is how you live and serve in the lineage of the Apostles and the Communion of Saints who preceded you in death. As you have affirmed in many parts of this country, they are your reasons for joy and peace, and their intercession is the power you wield through the Holy Paraclete before God. My jubilation is knowing that they remain beside the Angels in surrounding Me in the haven that knows no sorrow. If there were any ways that you might be more fully blessed than to have been given such a compassionate assemblage of friends, God would have brought them to you by now. My children, the season of Spring has arrived with its brightly shining sun and blossoming buds on the greening plants everywhere. The winter has passed, and your hopes are lifted anew to the anticipation of what the midsummer's warmth will bring. I wish to tell you in advance that 2002 has evolved to be a blessed passage in time because of the work in which you are presently engaged. Allow the perpetual expectation about which I recently told you to be the reason for your happiness. I am unable to dispense to you the joy that will be like your deliverance to Heaven, but I own the capacity to instill that hope in you which will keep your spirits alive until Jesus takes you there. There are many changes about to occur around the globe that will serve to mitigate the horrors you are seeing. The sovereign states of America will be further stricken by mourning and grief because another egregious war will begin. Why? Because its citizens defy the converting messages of the Mother of God. Too many have yet to accept the intercession that I offer to bring humanity to the Easter life, so it is incumbent upon them to travel there by sharing in the Holy Cross. I do not tell you these things to bring you despondence or doom, but to reveal the reasons why everyone should increase the intensity of their prayers. The Messianic Cross of Mount Calvary is spread over immortality repletely, and with no means of retracting its power. The suffering of humankind, however, can be eliminated by the faith of God's people. You do this through your prayers, your emulation of Jesus, and treading in the footsteps of the Christological legends who have worked so painfully to bring His message of Salvation to you. Why not join their legacy and allow the finishing of Creation about which Jesus spoke from the Cross to become banns of Triumph, rather than the inexorable undoing of an unfaithful humanity? These are among the reasons why I plead dutifully for your hearts to remain open. Would it not serve the interest of Earth for its inhabitants to concede to the Sacred Dominion of the Father in Paradise whose Kingdom is not of this world?

The storyline of human existence may still be unfolding, but it is timelessly concluded in Paradise. It is one about the first created man betraying God while standing in His presence, then humanity inheriting that corruption in exile, and culminating with your return to obedience here and now, before you see His Holy Face. You must accept this pious summons with single-minded faith. If there is a discrepancy between your thoughts and actions while choosing the narrow path of righteousness, the missing link is found in the artwork of God's Mystical Truth and in the sacred lien that Christ Jesus placed on your future; for it is through His Sacrifice that you must pass to procure Everlasting Life. When you think about all the unfortunate souls who have been impoverished and imbedded with sorrow; from pasture, to terrace, to the Mount of Olives, you surely must be overwhelmed to realize that the Crucifixion of one Good Man has healed them all. I seek your patience whilst the universe takes its final bow. Do not rue the repercussions of your memory lapses as you grow older because they lead to the suspension of grief and anguish, and to your happiness. Like schooners canvassing the skies for new winds of change, your aspirations will eventually come true. Remember always that people must be prioritized over real property. Here in America, the Lord is searching for a nation that puts greater emphasis on hope than history so that your lives are marked with more than the pervading and often poignant images of the Enola Gay, the grassy knoll, the Eagle that landed, and thousands of coffins covered with star-strewn fields and red and white stripes. As contradictory as it seems, there is celebrity in holiness, but it comes with your sacrifices as much as faultless ideals. What does the psychology of greeting fate bravely really mean? It certainly implies the point in your lifetime when you cease living for yourselves and turn your attention to others. The Holy Spirit is utterly effusive with ginger impressions imposed upon humanity with some rather stark demands. America is supported and sustained by God in everything you accomplish on His behalf, quite properly earning you His deific benison *annuit coeptis*, meaning that He has favored your undertakings, which appears on the reverse of the Great Seal of the United States. God recognizes the driving impulses of His contemporary helping hands, that it is their penchant to be like Him that fosters their efforts. Hence, it is possible for an entire sovereign republic to be one collective Good Samaritan. When you reconcile with anyone, personally or internationally, you reconfigure the past by connecting the present and the future, effectively expunging the old and replacing it with the new. When you enrich the poor, nourish a hungry child, or heal a broken family, you are pouring new life into your nation's future. This, My Special son, is why I arrive in the joy through which I first appeared to greet you long ago. Can you sense, however, how brief this seems before the backdrop of your growing new perspectives? I come to seek your kind smile and compliant heart, which I know you gave to Me in 1989. I must remind you that My spouse on Earth, Saint Joseph, is sitting in his lofty place with a beaming smile because of the awesome carpentry you have done in your home. Now, you have not only an appealing place through which to enter, but one that is much safer, too. Your labors will result in the home that you wanted to create; functional, modernized, and safeguarded from the elements. The reason why the Lord is happy upon the passing of this week is the environment you shaped that allowed the visionary writing you penned to enter Creation on behalf of His thousands of priests. It is some of the most spiritually edifying, endearing, and remarkable writing you have ever scripted. I am jubilant that you understand that Jesus is working through your lives in ways that you may not comprehend, but to which you have offered your submission for the cultivation of the Church. As I have indicated before, I will be briefer throughout the period while you are compiling the body of your new book. I assure you that the end for which you are struggling will come with unprecedented accomplishment. Please do not allow the secular pageantry that you are going to see at Mass Tuesday to distract you from the simplicity that always accompanies your encounter with the Sacrifice of Jesus on the Cross."

Sunday, April 21, 2002
4:57 p.m.

"Now comes the Glory of Divine Love to speak to you through the power of the Holy Spirit. Please allow Me to resound the tone of enlightenment for My children on Earth, those to whom Salvation has been granted by the Crucifixion of My Son. These days demand the protraction of the great commission you are given by Jesus to persevere in the task of converting your lost brothers and sisters. Let there be no mistake, the Lord is pleased by your efforts and hears every prayer you utter from the center of your hearts. These are glad times because the prayers you offer are bringing the world to change. Even though you see such angst and fighting in your midst, they are decreasing by the hour. I call you to assist Me in urging humanity to enhance the prevalence of Heaven on Earth. My intention is to skewer the enemies of human Redemption and dirk Satan's hatred with the omnipotent power of Jesus' Holy Cross. I must make clear that where the Saints live, there is no such thing as dark energy, and this is what they wish to impress upon humanity in an attempt to erase the grave national scandal of unjustified pessimism in America. It begins with your effort to reach-out in faith because the basic instincts of a devoted Christian consists not solely of your own survival or that of the fittest, but of the protection and preservation of defenseless life; that of the innocent, maligned, and maltreated. This includes an outward expansion of spiritual sanctification to the diminishment of one's own environment of ease and comfort; the reduction of the mobility in which some people live, long enough to recognize that the less-fortunate are more than the inevitable consequence of a diverse society. You live at a tempo that you inherited and a future willed to you by your ancestors; and you are the extension of the prophesies they were unable to fulfill. Therefore, in their honor, be humane in your judgements, fair in your bartering, worthy of the trust of your acquaintances, and loyal to your Profession of Faith. Do not be facetious in your speech about such crucial matters as piety and revelation, and hope and change. Never forget that you were conceived in God's mind long before your mother and father were born. Do you suppose that you have the resiliency to look back and proclaim that these were the good old days? Do you swear oath to the solidarity required to complete your life's work while toeing the line of simple piety? Stay close to the Church! Your membership there proves that its mission of submersing the Earth in Christianity has never been a problem of courage, vision, or conviction, but of taking proper advantage of those not so rare opportunities to connect human suffering with the Crucifixion of Christ, coupling them inside the Will of God as partners in the sanctification of everything about humanity that tends to be corrupt. In a world that is crying-out for complementary thinking, how do you reconcile anticipation and patience, or personal tensions with spiritual warfare? Most important, what are the most scrupulous ways to fend against evil without resorting to revenge? In the interest of moral propriety, it is not enough to know that there are certain lines that you must never cross, but that you should not even desire to approach them. This is when discretion takes its finest form, where your spiritual vision becomes so clear and transcendent; fixated on the outcome of the universe, that wayward paths are not even considered as an option. This is how you live within the means of your conscience. It allows you to walk the narrow path instinctively with the breezes always at your back, lapping good will and peacefulness against the scruff of your neck like a butterfly instead of a bee. This is optimism, and is the unseen tide of your invisible faith. It is the reasoned conclusion that everything you sense about victory and Truth are factually ensured.

My children, Jesus realizes that your struggle for self-preservation has never really been so much about pride as it is creating a sustained sensation of prudence and dignity. This is a sure signature of the modern times in which you live, for the reorientation and reemphasis of your spiritual constitution for the good of all the ages and seasons. It leads to Salvation, and you will go there free; you will see anything that comes to mind without having to strain your eyes. In Heaven, the Lord will tell you who you are before you have the opportunity to state your name; and He will remind you that you are as beautiful as He hoped you would be. And, you will not say that I told you these things in AD 2002, but in the Year of Pope John Paul II, who will by then have resumed his role as ordinary citizen in the Church Triumphant. So, if it is true that most men go to their graves with their song still in them, remember to bring it with you to Paradise when you make your clear-throated proclamation before the Throne of the Father that you are beside yourself to finally see Him. I urge you to stand there in confidence and say, 'Lord, I brought a dream with me,' to which He will respond, 'Then come with Me, and we shall go live it.' This, My little children, is the substance of what I have to say today. To My Special and Chosen ones, I tell you that your consecration to Me is of imperative urgency in the finishing of the lives of men. Thank you for your efforts, and thank you for staying at each other's side for so long, precisely where God has placed you. This is a prefigured honor for you. My Special son, your writing is the fruit of your brother's presence here. There are many things you have done together that have made a charitable difference in taking the message of Salvation to God's people. There is good reason for every action that the Lord wills, fosters, and allows in the universe. And, there are more signs, miracles, and wonders to reveal as time passes-by. It is important that you remember the infiniteness in which I love you. I am pleased with the leaflets you are writing for your manuscript supporting the priests of the Roman Catholic Church. Please pray for the conversion of all souls for whom you are seeking Salvation in the weeks to come."

Sunday, April 28, 2002
11:04 a.m.

"My little children, you have gathered at My feet for the resourcefulness you require to comprehend the holiness of God in your hearts. This is the Divine Love to which you are being taken—the supernatural Being of Jesus, in whom you have placed your trust. I ask you to listen carefully because there are many distractions around you. Yes, I have come to share the Word of God with you as you recite the Sacred Mysteries of the Most Holy Rosary. The Sorrowful Mysteries upon which you are meditating at this moment allow you to deploy the power of the Cross against the adversaries of the Church. Please let the United States know that My response to the errors of the priests that have come to light in recent weeks is the one and the same body of work that has been penned by My Special one, the child who has perceived so many times the *Morning Star Over America*. I have not and hereafter shall not offer any other response to this unfortunate phenomenon, other than to request the multiplication of your petitions for those who are serving in priestly vocations. It is true that the devastation of corporeal impurity has affected certain people since they were small children. I ask you to pray, because in doing so, God will amend the circumstances that are prevalent in American secularism today. Humankind is composed of sinners who must do their best to leave their past behind and seek their renewal of chastity in the future of Love. My indulging messages are meant to take your hearts beyond the fray of human transgressions by enlisting your participation and constant communication with God. I seek this from you because the globe is groveling in warfare and grievous pangs of neglect. The spirituality you need to deliver you to newborn heights is found in your faith in Jesus. Can humanity see the wrongful ways that many societies are suffering at the hands of greedy tyrants? I ask not only that you remain the flock of God's Shepherd, but to seek His wandering lambs with an earnestness of submission, tenacity, leadership, courage, vision, humility, and perseverance. Now, there are additional plans for intensifying the battles against other nations. This does not imply that your prayers for peace are in vain. If you saw the circumstances in the world that might have been, shorn of the petitions you have already lifted, your spirits would lay flat across the Earth's spillways in sorrow. Hence, I urge you to keep offering your supplications to God. The Son of Man who was so painfully Crucified knows that you are in tremendous need of His power in your struggles against evil. So shall you share the Victory of Truth that He has won! The critical themes of supernatural history are alive in your hope for His Kingdom to come. Please remember that your prayers are always levied against the conditions about which you are praying, and the Will of the Father is divulged by the course of your intentions. I have told you in times past that there has never been a prayer that was left unheard. Please remember the bounty of this fact as you continue your lives because there will be many times when you might wish to desist. This, My children, would be a mistake. If you survey the entire Earth inside the parameters of your hearts in the way that I have asked, you would see that there is a cleansing that is ongoing around you. Should God be required to scour the Earth by some physical chastisement to reveal that not all souls on the ground are in communion with the Divine Truth? If ever there were decades when He has commended His Divine Mercy upon you, this is that series of years. Where you see moments when powerful forces relent from destroying their enemies, it is because the Almighty Father has intervened. Anything otherwise, My dear children, is when those same factions deny the Wisdom of the Holy Spirit. Even the most benevolent nations can be filled with error if they choose warfare over diplomatic coalescence. There is always a lacking of propriety when men choose battlefield bloodbaths over the Sacred Blood of Jesus on the Cross.

Now, the month of May will soon be opening to usher the hope of a fresh springtime, and along with it, Mother's Day. Will you remember Me when you need God's help and consolation during these awful days of the Earth? I am the Immaculate Conception, the Mother of Jesus Christ. Let no man who is living or deceased be confused about who is speaking to you. My plea is for peace over decimation, Love instead of hatred, nourishment and not deprivation, and Eternal Salvation instead of perpetual condemnation. Whereby any man shall hear and heed the call of the Mother of God, he is living the course of a blessed human life, onward to the supernatural designs of God for the resurrection of his soul on the last day in time. Christ Jesus is a fair and devoted Messiah, and He knows those who are His own. If it is a stern reprimand or forewarning that humanity requires to understand the sureness by which Jesus shall separate the wheat from the chaff, then consider My words as adequate premonition. It is true that time is short, and human indignation is rampant. When the culmination of the Earth arrives and the New Jerusalem supplants the verdicts of time, there will be nary a soul alive who will not perceive for themselves the way Jesus is seeing them now. He continues to ask of everyone, 'how will you judge yourselves?' If you believe you are worthy of His forgiveness, then ponder the question as to whether you have accorded the same to those who have offended you. This is the basis of the judgement of the soul. There is an absolute Truth of God's Divine Love to whom each of you must answer. Anything short of this in your unconfessed transgressions shall be held against you. Therefore, I continue calling all of My children to the Sacramental Rite of Reconciliation. The searching of the heart and the particular examens that will expose your hypocrisies should reveal any breaches in your compliance with the Commandments and Sacred Beatitudes. These are the provisions that help your conscience understand what is expected of the absolved human soul.

My Special son, thank you for allowing Me to speak to you and protract My intercession to humanity. I assure you that wherever you place My words, and through whatever venue, will be the proper place in time and history for the world to hear and read them. If ever there were a moment when I have been grateful to a child, now is My greatest gratitude to you for allowing My messages to proceed. The awesomeness of your book elevating My priests is one of the most sublimely unique ever to be penned by the hand of man. You can see that there are other volumes that are distracting Americans from reading yours, and this is why *When Legends Rise Again* received no more than a mere mention in your newspaper this week. I promise that it would have been anticlimactic for it to have been cited in any other way because yours is the work that will be hailed as among the codices that changed the course of human history. This is not some hollow patronage I am employing to offer consolation. I am speaking the Truth as articulately as the Lord has allowed it to be heard. It is relevant for you to recall that Sister Faustina was forced to wait beyond her death before her Diary was dispensed. God knows what He is doing, and I will tell you about the way that He is utilizing your faith and efforts as the future unfurls. The messages I have given you the past eleven years have been a revelation in themselves, and there is reason to believe that you have received only a fraction of them to date. Thank you for your promise of participation in the purification of the Mystical Body of Christ. There is a small sentiment that I wish to leave with you today. When people are living on the Earth, they display their love and affection by acts of charity, kindness and loyalty, and even mutual embrace. This seems to be the extent to which you are one. However, when you get to Heaven, your souls are allowed to be united in more transcending ways that are Divine and everlasting."

Sunday, May 5, 2002
4:16 p.m.

"My children, the Holy Spirit will always give you the words to say when the time arrives for your evangelistic professing of the Gospel before men, so please do not fret any encounter with your detractors or those who are otherwise opposed to Christianity. It is imperative that you remember to call upon the counsel of the Holy Paraclete during times of trouble or whenever you believe the appropriate expressions are eluding you that will help your brothers and sisters comprehend the divinity of the Love of God. As you are spiritually inebriated in the Blood of Jesus on the Cross, so are you enriched with Wisdom to state His Truth clearly to anyone who is begging to understand. Heaven is filled with bliss because there are so many thousands of Christian giants yet alive on the Earth who are willing to forge onward for the good of the Church. It is obvious that the enemies of the Holy Cross are attempting to minimize God's Third Millennium miracles as being products of chance, but their words are in vain and their entrance into the fold of believers is inevitable. I have told you on many occasions that the element of time is irrevocably on your side. Will you not hereafter take encouragement in these facts and endure your mortal exile with more ease? I repeat today with emphasis that God is in complete control of His Kingdom, and the effecting of your part to make its presence known to Creation has been a fruit that is sweet to His taste. On behalf of the Holy Trinity, the Communion of Saints, and all the little Angels, I offer My gratitude for pursuing your prayerful labors. This is the first week of the month of May, and next week will bring the occasion of Mother's Day. I ask everyone whose mother is still living on Earth to remember her with a small gift, a commemorative memo, or some other type of recognition. This is an important aspect of your familial existence beneath the stars. I am the Mother of Supreme Dominion, and I know what it is like to be embraced so appreciatively. Having a thankful collection of children is the greatest delight for any mother. And, Jesus extends His good wishes of Love, devotion, loyalty, and peace on this beautiful Spring day. There is a great deal of commotion that often accompanies the early months of a new year, and He realizes this. It is the best of all possible purposes for mankind to remember the source of the beauty of Nature, your God in Heaven who gives it breath. The Divine aspects of Creation that impact your hearts with such evocativeness are a product of His Love and desire that you be at peace with the elements of the Earth. I come to remind you that there are still many people being held against their will who are not permitted to sit near rolling streams or recline in open fields at night to enjoy the phases of the moon. Please pray for them; ask God to convert the hearts of their captors, and beseech Jesus to crush the human hatred that has placed them there. The worst of all prisons consists of the mortal sins that haunt the lives of the spiritually wicked, the impure, the wretched, and those who agonize over their past sins. We pray that they will open themselves to the healing presence of Jesus' Love so the Holy Spirit can lead them to the Sacraments of the Church, especially the Rite of Reconciliation. No soul will ever live in peace until he makes amends with God and returns to the fold of the blessed whose future is drawn toward the avenues of the Saints. As you pray for your intentions this week, I beg you to recall in your supplications those I have mentioned. The world is in overwhelming need of change because an insufficient number of people are praying, especially the pluralized West. However, those whom I know to be My faithful children will be pleased when the institutions that oppose My intercession are destroyed upon the command of God.

My Special and Chosen sons, I am heartened to be your advocate before My Jesus the Consolator because you have been His warriors for so long in the battle against human corruption. There are no expressions that allow Me to state how much He appreciates your participation in the End Times. I share these things with you, and make clear that I adore you beyond your capacity to understand, pleading for your patience. My Special one, I see the interior of your heart that seems so afflicted with pain. Will you share this with Me? Let us be clear; are you speaking about someone who has already seen your magnanimous work? Do you believe that this has affected your relationship with them? Does the matter come down to the fact that you, along with all the Saints, are rejected because your soul is in alignment with the Kingdom of Heaven? It is impossible for another person who is bound for Salvation to impugn your labors once they have witnessed your fealty to Jesus. I know the circumstances about which you are speaking. There are people who look at those around them as though they are no more than minuscule facets of Nature. Sadly, you are perceived this way at times. You have a princely heart, not unlike the writing you penned about Father Chester Fabisiak. You shall win at last! I know, however, that you grow weary wondering when the last will come. Finish your good works, recite your prayers, attend Holy Mass, produce your awesome writings, and God will take care of the rest. I realize that My attempts to comfort you are of little consequence because it is you who are suffering. I urge you to recall the darkness of the soul that Mother Teresa described, and many of the Saints and Doctors of the Church who endured the same. Your condition is nowhere like theirs. There will come a point in your life when you will look back upon these days and beg Jesus to allow you to live them again. I know that you understand; I truly know you do! Please live the judicial Wisdom that you are being given instead of anything else. Can you live a day at a time and sense the moments when danger might be building and foreboding, and choose wisely the better course? You are savvy and much more resilient than the evil that is trying to destroy you. As God's warrior, do not be afraid of going where you choose to travel, making sure that every avenue of righteous possibility has been exhausted, evaluating the extremities and circumstances, recognizing the fruits to be harvested, and most of all, knowing when to return to your billet for safety and protection. You must be cautious and optimistic at the same time, but never cavalier in the face of dark forces that you know will harm you. I am not telling you to cower before danger because your defense of God's Kingdom heightens your courage beyond any fear of death. I am simply asking you to be wary, perceptive, careful, scrupulous, and prudent."

Sunday, May 12, 2002
Mother's Day
2:58 p.m.

"Here rests your consolation, at the center of My Immaculate Heart! Please gather obediently at My feet so I may speak comfortingly to you, to nurture your souls in the Love of Heaven for which you are silently pining. I am elated that you have kneeled in veneration of the Mother of humankind. Will you not also pray for the millions of mothers whose infant children are in their wombs? Thank you! With the fidelity of God, I promise that I serve as your Divine Intercessor and the Mediatrix of all graces from Heaven. It inspires Me to see My children praying the Sacred Mysteries of the Holy Rosary because it is the beginning and captivation of living hope inside your hearts. It is entirely within the Passion, Crucifixion, and Resurrection that your intentions must reside, for these are the elements of your deliverance from death into Eternal Salvation. What would any mother say to her children today? There is no doubt that all appreciation and recognition should be accorded to the Almighty Father for sharing the gift of life. It is His Will to allow the passing generations to succeed on what would otherwise be an abandoned Earth. This is the posture of your exile, and also the foyer in which you are urged to prepare to meet your Creator. Jesus is confident that His Sacrifice is sufficient reparation for your sins and the benison that the family of man requires to become poised for their reposition in Glory. Now, the matter rests in the decision of sinners to return to the state of perfect Love through their espousal of Divine Truth. There is no means to measure your progress if you do not begin by remembering that your conversion is both a fruit and product of the Holy Spirit in your hearts. These are the moments of great importance in history because the collision of the mortal and Divine has never been more pronounced. There are countless wicked souls among you who are doing their worst to prohibit simple prayer, denigrate the Holy Sacraments, and distract you from knowing your Savior uniquely. The Holy Rosary that you are reciting is as deadly to their intentions as if God were to allow Saint Joan of Arc to return to Earth and cleanse it in the way she liberated France. Do not be confused; the Lord does not wish to bring this kind of suffering upon His people, but it seems that the nations will not convert to the Holy Cross through any other means. I pray that the message of the Holy Gospel will prosper by way of the intercession of Christians, the Saints in Heaven, and the prospect that evil will be destroyed in the exchange. While so many secular households are remembering their mothers today, it is a dire matter for them to end the scourge of abortion. How can the human species flourish if your unborn are not allowed to survive? There is no expediency in the horrors of abortion that is worth the price the guilty will pay before the Throne of God. The Sacred

Heart of Jesus is a Just source of absolution, but He is filled with the fires of Wrath for those who spurn the Commandments of His Kingdom. Wherever He wields His vengeance should be considered a pitiable location. If humanity is seeking a means by which *not* to live, you may ponder those places where His Divine Providence is being rejected with impunity. For every goodness that is brought by the lives of prayerful men, it is multiplied by five-thousand in the sight of God. I beseech you to pray deeply for the peacemakers among you, especially My little Jimmy Carter, whose love and mercy for the poor has taken him to Cuba. Why do I mention him? Why would the Mother of God be so specific to identify a single person on Earth? Because he is My son, a pious peacemaker, a healer of men, and a child of God. He is a brother of Jesus, filled with the same Holy Spirit who visited Me during the Annunciation. If humanity wishes to be like Jesus, I implore you to become like Jimmy Carter.

Pray that God clears the vision of your lost brothers and sisters by removing the matted deceit from their eyes, and try to comprehend the criteria that Jesus uses to define acquittal. Unlike the endeavors of worldly justice, it does not imply that there has never been guilt. With what compassion does the Lord look upon you! Many of you have seen the heart-rending sight of a lifeless, unfledged, thin-skinned baby robin having fallen from its nest, splayed limply across a sidewalk below the branch of a tree. It is in this vein that God perceives the helpless world. He has particular compassion for the *unhoused*, those who have not received the Holy Eucharist, because He knows that it will bring Salvation to them. Human life was never meant to be about frailty and depravity, but is designed to elevate you among the constellations as a species rendered strong, clean, pure, and well-read in themes of goodness, and dignified in the ways of Heaven's elite blessings. Never mind that you face a barrage of opposition on your journey to Redemption. You should internalize the idea that it is not temptation that separates you from God, but the committing of sin. When you recognize that all sin is condemnable, you will eradicate every potential to surrender to its specific kinds of weaknesses, some of which could later surface as other forms of corruption. While you must always be fair and gentle with yourself, it is your interpersonal transgressions that are the most offensive to God because they involve other parties whose innocence you have scarred, effectively creating collateral victims of your own Salvation to complement the Crucifixion of Jesus Christ. Never forget that God fashioned the universe and conceived you out of nothing, but has vested you with the power to leave a permanent mark on Creation through your will, as revocable as it is, so that your life renders either a positive imprint or a malevolent one. Therefore, you must ask yourselves the practical question of whether your earthly existence tends toward righteousness. Will you be memorialized as an ally of human Redemption or its enemy? Will the shadow you cast lead anyone closer to the center of Truth? Does your conception of Divine Love epitomize that of the Messiah who wields it? Remember that every human impulse that differs from His Truth is a function of your distance from God, whether intentional or not, and finds as its origin a specific pathology based on your psychological and environmental compulsions that grew within you as a child. Never underestimate the exculpating influence of the forces of acquired habit. When all is revealed, you will see that there are no miscellaneous sins that are attributable to nothing; each has been sprung from the same framework of delusion in a world gone wrong.

Now, My Special son, I have completed My message to you today. I know that you are still working like a bee on your book for My priests, and the fruits of your labors will be as sweet as honey. This process takes a good deal of extra time because of the intricate details about which you must write to capture the hearts and minds of your fellow Americans and people around the globe. What you are writing is worth the effort in explicating your love for Jesus. It will touch a large number of lives around the world."

Sunday, May 19, 2002
Feast of Pentecost
2:03 p.m.

"Here in the Divinity of Truth rests your hearts that have been claimed by God for transfer into the Kingdom of Heaven. You have also been chosen for life during these times so the souls of humanity will better know their Salvation in the Blood of the Cross. You will see that all the hidden aspects you ever knew about fairness, righteousness, faith, peace, Grace, Love, and Redemption have grown from the Cross; for the Crucifixion of Jesus is a manifestation of His willingness to die for your sins. Today, the homage of humanity belongs to Him because He has destroyed Satan. I ask you to never be afraid of the gruesome hatred which is the source of all unhappiness on Earth; and do not cower from the villainy that attempts to mock the faithful actions of men. You are victors in the campaign for goodness, and true warriors in the battles to teach your brothers and sisters the benefits of their compliance with the Dominion of God. My children, it is obvious that there are errant factions around you that have infiltrated the Church, who wish to scandalize the traditions of hope and faithfulness that your predecessors espoused and bequeathed to you, and who would stop the march of the world toward Heaven if they could. They will be devoured by the seas, not only because the righteous among you are too strong for them, but because God would never sustain them in the wake of the Sacrifice of His Son. We pray together that all the nations will understand that this invincible Plan of Heaven is the sole reason for the progressing life of men on the globe, that the conversion of all who inhabit it will bring the lasting peace that seems so elusive, and prepare every continent for the Second Coming of My Resurrected

Son. Hence, is this not a prophetic time for humankind? Do not the coming weeks and months foretell the greatness that is living in your midst through the power of the Holy Spirit? You are part of this power once you decide for God, embrace the Crucifixion, and give your soul to aid in the alleviation of the suffering of the poor. Children, whereby you are given in heart and soul to the excellence of this Love, the world is less infested with hatred. You cannot make this decision without the power of God within you, and this is why I ask you to open your hearts. Human action cannot manifest good works unless it is fashioned by and tendered to Heaven. Be one inside the Beatitudes; comply with Jesus' commands; be the ingenious lovers of His righteous accord; protect and sanctify human life; live in spiritual and corporeal purity; obey the laws of chastity; pray from your hearts for peace, and expect the coming of Jesus with high hope. These are the characteristics that warrant your identification as Christians. No evil can destroy your systematic works against sin when you filter your earthly existence through the Catechism. Not even those who fail to discover for themselves who and where they are stationed beneath the governance of God can control you. There is infinite spiritual superiority that is dispensed to those who accept the Holy Cross as the meaning of life, death, and Salvation. God the Father wishes you to share this Glory by working to ensure its propagation across the Earth. This is what I cultivate in His stead, and is why I accompany you. My Immaculate Heart is overflowing with Heaven's Light, and this is the brilliance by which you are guided, that you are asked to reflect. I have told you many times about the darkness of sin that has taken so many to sadness of heart and to lives of misery. Together, with your help, the Holy Spirit will guide them to the dignity of the Love of God. He wishes intensely that everyone will accept Him! He is the beauty of the silver springs to those who are thirsting, and the nourishment of the famished in every sense of the word.

    My children, it is imperative that you remember that many things about you that would lead you to temptation are derived from external origins, that you were not capable of concocting grandiose schemes on the day you were born. Now, as Christians, I urge you to shape your lives around your well-intentioned ideals and most benevolent tendencies. Exercise caution in your contractual affairs, and remember that even though your goodness may not always be acknowledged by mortal men, it is forever recognized by God. It has always been amazing to your ancestors in faith that invisible demons can inflict such conspicuous devastation, but I ask you to remember that your most righteous attributes also develop from within. And, they are permanent fixtures in those whose souls are bound for the Glory of Paradise. If you conduct a survey of all the stationary things in your lives, as few as they are, every one of them would be supernaturally connected to God's Beatific Grace. Once the Holy Paraclete takes residence in your heart, there is a dramatic retraction of the illusion that anything you pursue for simple satisfaction is important enough without doing it for the exaltation of the Lord. Once you are inspirited with deific Truth, all proneness to violence, licentiousness, temporality, and disorientation is displaced by the stated goal of rectifying the Earth through the supernal mandate of Christian propriety. Eternity becomes a prospect that seems not as far away as it did before. You begin to hear in color and see by tone and tenor. History and science begin to be perceived as secondary coincidentals behind the Sacred Scriptures and the anthologies of the Saints. Instead of seeing each new day as another brick in the wall to fortress you from life's unexpected changes, it becomes another piece of the puzzle that allows you to determine what is truly worthy of fear. My little ones, receiving the Holy Spirit means anticipating a future life that is wholly shed of sorrow, one where your sense of companionship with the unknowable universe becomes a reality that is forced by your own vision, and is independent of the evolvements of astronomy and the utility of time voids and space travel. Most of all, you finally see human pride for what it really is; an accomplice in the crime of disobedience that led to the downfall of man. It is a bright and beautiful daytime where you live, where I have deigned to appear this afternoon. Your laudatory prayers are comforting to the Sacred Heart of Jesus, whom I bear in My Bosom. He is encouraged by your labors because you offer them in remembrance of Him. Should you be called into deeper sacrifice for His Kingdom, He knows that you would submit. I assure you that there will be high praise for those sharing in His Passion in such an endearing way. My Special and Chosen ones, I implore you to hold fast to the Truth that the work you are doing for Jesus is destined for a much greater Glory than you can possibly conceive. If your patience is strong; if you anticipate seeing your contribution to the Victory of the Ages and the Triumph of My Immaculate Heart with the vision of little princes, you will see the essential sovereignty of Paradise in your midst inside the finished framework of the Earth. Thank you for knowing God, for choosing the noble courses in human life, and for accepting the Wisdom that has always taught you right from wrong, and goodness from error. I remind you, My Special son, that the discussion about your book for the priests will evolve more quickly than you might assume because humanity is predisposed to the debate. Its arrival is timely and will ensure that it is read by the appropriate eyes. After having spoken to you the past hour, I have completed My expressions to you today. Please know that the writing to complete your fourth book is appreciated in advance. Your memoirs are soothing to you because you inscribe them in accordance with the tenets of Truth. Yesterday, you and your brother prayed together profoundly here in this room and down the hall, and the Lord has been moved to offer you graces heretofore unknown to the most modest of men. I noticed that you highlighted the sentence in your manuscript about whether the Church Militant is perfect. The priest to whom you refer is theologically correct outside the element of time. He would find himself in the company of multiple detractors to whom you are addressing the thesis of your book. Should you not attest that the Church is nearing the summit of its perfected state? This acknowledges the passing element of time accordingly, and allows those who are adversaries of the Church to know that it is comprised of sinners."

Saturday, May 25, 2002
Vigil of the Most Holy Trinity
3:38 p.m.

"With the gentle Love by which you are consoled and healed, I have come again to seek your petitions for the purification of humanity, for strength for My humble priests, for understanding and forgiveness between peoples, and for world peace. Millions of souls are gathering this weekend for the American Memorial Day, a time of recollection and relaxation. The future is filled with consternation for many because their lives are meaningless in their rejection of the Holy Cross. They have become wayfarers across the acreage of wasted opportunities to know God better. To My Special and Chosen ones, you realize by now that Satan's evil hounds are frothing at the mouth because you are their nemesis on the Earth, especially since you completed your book supporting the Roman Catholic priests. You shall be elated by its effects, but there is no reason for you to presuppose its success if you do not pray! I advocate for the Church as its Mother in beseeching God to stay His Wrath against the enemies of Truth because thousands of them, nay multitudes, will eventually be converted to the Cross. I come today to remind you that the Most Blessed Trinity is praised by your efforts and given the offices of the entire world in which to magnify the Grace of God through My Immaculate Heart. Would it be improper for Me to recite each time I appear how much the Lord appreciates the gift of your lives? As each day passes through its motivated momentum of your spiritual obedience, humanity moves closer to Salvation. We shall finish the course of events that we began eleven years ago and usher-in the rites of the conviction of the blessed to the Most Sacred Heart of My Son. I assure you that whereby you are living for Him, your years are given to the powerful and invincible Wisdom of the Holy Spirit. Let Me tell you that you are so much in love with God that there is no turning back! He has taken hold of your souls and will never let go. Redemption requires your hearts! As we are altering the face of the globe in the procession of your works, I confirm that I would have failed if not for your faith. You are playing a key role in the Triumph of My Immaculate Heart. My children, it is obvious that you are in the bridal room of a grace-filled moment because your brothers and sisters will become so much enlightened by your book about the priests. This is why you are considered to be enemies of secularists, as they are foes of the Church. Please do not be dismayed by their insolence because they compose only passing phases of an American colonialism that is convulsing its last as we speak. Your elation is in the Child of Joy whom I hold in My arms. Jesus is filled with confidence because you have not surrendered to the hindrances of the world; you will not cede an inch of His Kingdom to the malevolent forces that are aligned against the Church, and your participation in the finishing of the ages cannot be deterred. Your strength is a source of comfort for suffering people surrounding you, and your holiness is the example that Jesus wishes everyone to place before men. Thank you! I have been telling you how your lives are forever changed when you receive the Holy Spirit as the deciding factor for your earthly priorities. In doing so, you become capable of deciphering fact from fiction based upon centuries-old dogmatic Truth, and how the Earth's systems of assumption and measurement serve only to exemplify the misjudgements of already debunked human theories.

My children, the presence of the Lord inside your hearts prompts such ideas as justice and fairness to adopt new meanings that are as prominent as the welfare of your personal families, and they become larger than life in instances involving sustenance and freedom. Is this not what diplomacy and treaties are all about? And, you inherit the Wisdom to stop chasing phantoms that only serve to benefit the motivations of your enemies. Indeed, you become capable of identifying them based upon what they stand to profit from your association. Becoming one with Jesus opens the door for you to recognize an entire side of you about which you have never been self-aware. All the potentials you did not know were there; your talents, capabilities, and relationship with everything previously unseen allow you to observe Creation in the context of why it was fashioned, rather than how; thus permitting you to concentrate more on reason than manipulation, and action than observation. Jesus wishes for you to fulfill the journey that He has asked you to undertake, and I know that this is never a source of displeasure for you. The impact and tandem beauty of *When Legends Rise Again* and *White Collar Witch Hunt* will be of colossal benefit for the faithful because they will lead everyone to the magnum opus, *Morning Star Over America,* at which time they will peruse the eloquent *At the Water's Edge* to complement their understanding of the need to turn to Me for guidance in their commitment to Christianity. You see that each of your books plays a unique role in your Apostolate, and most people will wait with bated breath for the release of the messages I have dispensed since February of 1997. Please enjoy what you are accomplishing because you are tightening the last bolts on another warship of Heaven's righteousness to be commissioned for My Armada of Love against the enemies of the Church, of My Immaculate Heart, and Jesus' Mystical Body. Yes indeed, savor the harvest into which you have placed your tremendous dedication. Satan is helpless against you because you are serving beneath the protection of My Mantle. There has never been another book in Creation that supports the vocation of the priesthood like you are doing because the vocation has never been pummeled by this sort of spurious attack. This makes your service in the history of the Catholic Church a crucial one. God will glorify your work if you never surrender to the persecution that follows. Show humanity that you belong to Me, and there is nothing in this world that can cause you to stumble and fall. Magnify the loyalty of your brother, your co-seer, as evidence to God that you are willing to offer yourselves in the way He desires for the conversion of the Earth. You should remember to weigh these things against your physical strength, and examine the parameters of the circumstances as well. My Dominion Angels will give you suggestions during the ensuing week to halt the taunting of Satan. I am sure you know in what frame of reference they will be."

Sunday, June 2, 2002
Feast of Corpus Christi
4:16 p.m.

"To the prayerful children of the Mother of Love, I have come to bring you gratitude and support for your trust in Jesus and to the Most Holy Eucharist by Whom you are fed the nourishment of your souls toward Eternal Life. Indeed, you have such life in you now because you welcome the Body and Blood of Jesus into your hearts, souls, and beings. Can you see how fruitful your Christian lives have become through the gift of the Most Blessed Sacrament? I assure you that the Eternity of Heaven has begun in you, and will be fulfilled by the Salvation for which you have pined through the years. This is a time of celebration and accord for humankind because of this. Please be My obedient children and remember to adore the Most Blessed Sacrament as long as you live on Earth. Yes, this is a day for recollection and reflection because of the power of Wisdom that the Holy Eucharist places inside you. Although you may be lame or infirm in many ways, the Body and Blood of Jesus sustains you. I am the Mother of the Corpus Christi who has been hailing you for generations to come to the Table of God's Love; and the moment has arrived for all souls to know why. The time for protesting and procrastination has ended because the Son of Man will return soon and seek signs of His Sacred Presence in those He has reclaimed for God. The Eucharistic Host is His guide for those who receive Him, and is the predestined Sacrament that signals the reunion of the mortal and the sublime. Thank you for allowing God to determine the effectiveness of your love for Him by being mortified worthily to receive Him. These are moments that encourage and engender the greatest trust humanity has to offer, even more than your survival through the worst world wars, pestilence, and diseases, because the Earth is shunning the Dominion of God in unprecedented ways. I assure you that He will never allow His Creation to escape His grasp, no matter what it takes to open the eyes of those who reject His Truth with reckless abandon. My Special one, I wish to tell you in this message that all the Heavens are grateful for this date in history when you have again afforded My Son the opportunity to speak with candor to the humanity He so loves. Where are the phrases that can express His ceaseless gratitude? Perhaps they are located in the action of His Mother, in the aspects of the life of blessings you are living, and in the future He has plotted for you. Would it be difficult for you to recognize His thankfulness by the evidence that you are living in the presence of the Angels and Saints in a miraculous way? By all means, His happiness is expressed through the gift of spiritual faith by which you have come to believe in Him! You are wielding the power and genius that is rare among men. Your words, actions, and deeds are the signatures of miraculous valor in this contemporary age. The sacrifices you are making are to the commitment of millions of lost sinners to the Glory of the Cross. The vision you are providing the spiritually sightless is of such great Light that Creation is being emboldened as well. These are not altruistic aspirations for some mortal man of a futuristic age, they are your accomplishments as you enter the month of June AD 2002. If only you will understand the measures by which you are being led by the kindness of the Holy Spirit, you will prevail through your knowledge of the secrets of the universe and the unseen Kingdom of God. I tell you that the rest of your life will be many times more blessed than that which you have seen during the past eleven years. Your writings, artworks, books, oratories, and canticles will be featured before humanity as great masterpieces for the Lord, and this shall be your legacy to humankind. Do not heap any undue praise upon your brother, for the credit is yours.

I call both of you to look with discernment upon America and see that the freedom you enjoy is truly worthy of protection. However, you must never forget about the disproportionate distribution of wealth that Jesus has condemned so many times before because it weighs heavily on the stability of your entire nation. Millions of skeptics of democracy are standing idly by while western capitalism is slowly cannibalizing itself. Your brothers and sisters are much in need of the edification that comes through the Holy Spirit, and humanity is susceptible to the self-effacing pressures of sloth and social disrespect. Please never worry that the Earth will end this way because Jesus will suppress into extinction everything that runs contrary to the enlightenment of His people. Avoid those who would hold themselves up as examples of mainstream American spiritualism because such are false apostles, and they often deny the tenets of the Catholic Church for their own political expedience. But, when they repent, the Hosts of Heaven will come running for them with the gallantry of a stately fleet of horses vying for the roses. God will evacuate the catacombs and labyrinths of every stretch of the Earth in search of anyone still yearning to see His Holy Face. It is only now that they are beginning to emerge from the subtle darkness, and to realize that the animating principle of sound spiritual persuasion is in their focus on the miraculous. Every form of ritual, theater, karma, and secular paganism reeks of illegitimacy before the backdrop of Eternal Truth. I urge you to remember that politics is little more than a haven for radical infidels and wolves dressed like sheep. Most of them are prevaricators and illusionists who practice deception, conspiracy, fact deprivation, and embezzlement. People in the highest offices often feast on cronyism, elitism, secret sororities, and separatism. Some of them are a greater threat to America's sense of security than any foreign enemy. Their lying, cheating, and stealing have become casual conduct in their affairs. I implore you to not resort to fanaticism in admonishing these people, but to neutralize their effects through your sense of community with the victims of their greed. Remember that I have given the world Incarnate Truth by simultaneously birthing God the Father and the Son from My Womb; not twins, but integrally One Deity with the Holy Spirit. Any person who denies a relationship with them is committing spiritual suicide, analogous to the deforestation of the soul and taking away the moral oxygen they need to survive the wreck of this world. The only way to prevail is their oneness with Jesus in the Holy Gospel. Despite what many Americans maintain, you will not discover the spiritualism that the Lord is dispensing in the institutional academe. Having said that, it is to your codices that I am leading your friends, and I have seen that you have begun writing *Babes in the Woods*. How humanity will be touched by this example of Christian Love! During the few moments remaining before I depart for My worldwide blessing on this Feast, I shall listen to you and respond to your sentiments. Yes, it would be appropriate for you to record in your next book the details of the Eucharistic Procession that was held today at the Cathedral. You have accomplished a great victory, but are unaware what it is. I would like for you to ponder it until next week because you will come to the correct conclusions before then. I have surveyed your thoughts and seen the reasoning that will help you understand your friends to whom you have recently spoken. Do they have something in common? Are they falling to the tenderness of your heart and discovering the peace of Jesus inside? Do your eyes not shine with the Truth of His goodness, and your words lavish the Truth of His Grace upon them? This is why you are His human likeness, and is what His religious teachings are all about. You are emitting the fragrance of His Messianic Grace. The influence of *White Collar Witch Hunt* on the American conscience is too profound to place into words. Thank you for writing it. The creative way that you inscribed the first chapters of your next manuscript in the prayer room yesterday at the table is the most effective of all. Please remember that this month is dedicated to the Most Sacred Heart of Jesus!"

Sunday, June 9, 2002
4:32 p.m.

"My little children, you shall never grow so old that you will stop learning about the Sacred Mysteries of the Eternal Salvation of humankind. Therefore, I have deigned to speak to you for the conversion of all. Please remember to pray for the tormented who have no one to care for them; the helpless and dying, those about to fall into mortal sin, mothers contemplating aborting the children in their wombs, and the millions who are sick and infirm for the Glory of the Cross. Even in the midst of these, I am hopeful in the progress of humanity to comprehend the role of self-denial. I remind the world through My Medjugorje messengers often that it is necessary for Christians to pray from the heart for this to occur. Will you emulate these messengers, too? There are many weakened souls who have been battered by the bitterness of their enemies, and fear is overcoming them. Be their justification to embrace the virtue of courage. I will teach everyone to wield the faith that brings peace to the Earth if My children will respond. If it is necessary before the ending of the ages, I will appear to each and every mortal alive to share the Gospel of Jesus. I know not the day nor hour when the Son of Man will return in Glory, but I assure you that it is soon, so soon that many will be slumbering and caught by surprise. Jesus will arrive as the Prince of God's Light to an earthly planet that remains embroiled in its own blinding darkness. Your prayers are the Light of His Dawn! I wish to speak to you about the mission of taking your love to those who despise you. The Holy Scriptures make clear that Jesus has asked the Father to forgive those who persecute you because they know not what they are doing. When you say that you are not as inclined to forgive your adversaries as is the Son of Man, you deny the Grace by which you have been absolved. It is notable that countless hypocrites seek the pardon of their transgressions from Jesus, but will not do the same for those who offend them. It is unequivocal that if you do not offer forgiveness to everyone who has trespassed against you, your supplications to the Almighty Father will ring hollow. The entire disintegration of good will in America is the product of the personal indictment of individual members of its society. As this is meted-out by those who are capable of inflicting punishment in the name of retribution, so shall Heaven rebuke these same ones who refuse to forgive their transgressors. My message is about forgiveness. How many times? Seven? Seventy-seven? Seventy-times-seven? The point is that your forgiveness of others should extend beyond any number of times that you may be offended. I bring the promise of God that He will bear no hardship against you if you will accept the penitence of your neighbors and walk with clasped hands to the foot of the Cross. Were it not for your capacity to understand and the venues that are accorded by Jesus numerous times throughout your lives, you would not be inspired to do this. I assure you that the greatest blessing known to mankind is the expungement of death and the sin by which it is manifested. Those lacking forgiveness in their hearts are spiritually dead, and they will suffer a permanent parting, never to rise again. This is of paramount importance to the relationships between nations. Forgiveness is the origin of friendships, the begetting of mutual trust, and the avoidance of offensive warfare.

As we pray together for such forgiveness, we remember the quarters of the globe where factions are still taking one another's lives because of racial discord, discrimination, hatred and disdain, and the struggle for food and material goods. We pray for people who have no homeland of their own and are unwelcomed by others where they might claim a place to lay their heads. God has implemented a plan of action to rid the Earth of such rife disagreement, but it will come at the cost of lives. Certainly the Mother of Jesus Christ would not say that an inevitable chastisement might be in the offing or that the sweetness of My words portend the suffering of millions of innocent souls! Therefore, it is humanity who shall decide this course. Please return to the sanctuarial Sacred Heart of My Son Jesus for the Wisdom that is still lacking in the consciences of your brothers. We must pray for this to come soon because time is short! Look not to the temporal Earth for signs, or toward continents that are set ablaze by bombs, but see inwardly at the center of your hearts! This is where the mode of Grace is found. The fate of humankind is discovered and enlisted by seeking the faithful hearts of those who honor God, for such are the prophets of these times. I ask for more than your courage in this regard, I am seeking your compliance with the Commandments and Beatitudes that Jesus described in the Sermon on the Mount. If humanity wishes the exile of mortals to end with grief and pain, this is the conclusion that God will allow. However, if you turn your hearts from stone into the tenderness of His Love, your transfer into Eternal Life will be of peaceful joy. Can you see from the past what the human will has done, can do, and is fostering at present? Your prayers for the intervention of the Lord, for My Maternal intercession, and the advocacy of the Angels and Saints rests on your willingness to call upon us. There is little time for delay. One need not be a modern soothsayer or stand to make fortunes in hoaxes by declaring that he is 'crossing over' to reunite the living and the dead. All you need to do is inherit and avow the Truth of God, and the miracle of coalescence will rest in your hands. If you desire to converse with your departed loved ones, offer a Holy Hour before the Most Blessed Sacrament, and your heart will touch them. If the impoverished wish to know from where they will procure their next meal, they should ask Christ Jesus to strike-down the avarice of the wretched, and they will be filled with feasts aplenty.

The exchange of Christian knowledge rests in the spiritual communication between humanity and Heaven through the Wisdom of the heart, put there by the Holy Paraclete. You need not behold these things with your eyes to believe them because Jesus places His Truth in you. By all means, your visual capacity cannot capture the bounty that Heaven extols. The senses that you own have parameters that are unable to grasp the beauty that embraces you in the Sacrifice of the Cross. These things are Mysteries because you lack the faculties to comprehend them from the mortal side of life. This is why you have faith. The way you perceive the omnipotence of God is not constrained by your thoughts because the power of the heart is as inexplicably vast as the endlessness of Creation. This is why I call you to seek Jesus from the heart, from where your prayers are lifted. Then, and only then, will you know how to grow your love outwardly into the world to eradicate the ills, errors, and wrongdoings that I spoke about today. I ask this because I know that you have the means to accomplish the tasks that the Lord places before you. My Special son, how wonderful it is to spend this time with you in prayer, to seek your kind assistance, and to tell you that you are loved beyond all telling. Everyone who is intended to hear this message will do so because of the Will of the Father. I noticed that you worked extremely hard digging around the house the past two days. You must be careful not to allow these labors to diminish your feelings of joy. If you work too quickly and to a toilsome degree, your chores will seem like corporal punishment."

Sunday, June 16, 2002
3:26 p.m.

"For all the blessings you are given from Heaven, dear children, the reason is Divine Love. Mine is the privilege of bestowing upon you the benison of being your Mother, and Mother of our God who gave us life. Would it be impossible to instill unto your souls the goodness He is seeking for the entire of Creation? The answer rests in your response to Heaven through your acceptance of the Cross, by embracing the Sacred Heart of Jesus as your source of being, and conducting your lives and affairs according to His Will. There is no question that Saints are being canonized by the Catholic Church, more in the past twenty-four years than in prior generations. I beseech humanity to realize that this is *reason*, the purpose of God in reminding you of your goals. Seeking the Salvation that is yours, with all its prescient dignity and happiness, is what the Lord deigns for you. Were it not for His supremacy, and the Sacrifice that has won your Redemption, and the intercession of the Holy Spirit, you might well have serious matters about which to be concerned. Now, however, your destiny is assured in the Holy Sacraments because through them your souls are purified, cleansed, and cultivated so that you comprehend the Eternal Light of Truth during your earthly tenure. There have been millions who learned the lessons of conversion before you who have left their trademark on history. These are the Saints about whom I speak many times, and I urge you to call upon them for help in the transformation and perfection of your souls. Christianity allows humankind to recognize the redeeming relationships between friendship and sacrifice, sovereignty and dependence, stalwartness and compromise, and discipline and love. By imitating the Saints, Heaven becomes a bastion you not only hope to see, but where you have already staked your claim. You receive these things in Jesus; you whisper a reverence that is deafening to the physical Earth; you free the arms of a world bound by sin and place the keys to righteousness in the palm of its hand. You are able to calculate with transparency the emotional extremes of elation and despair, judging what touches nerves and evokes reaction, and foreseeing the effectiveness of your designs for lasting peace. You finally observe through God's eyes what is worth loosening and binding, what should be encouraged or discredited, and how to discuss the sensitive subject of what He does with those who betray His trust. My children, all of these things compose the vital signs of your inorganic faith, reminding you that your birth and death are conjoined by the virtues of what you accomplish in between. I am not speaking about magic or symbolism, but of Providence; of the Light of Truth who stowed quietly into the night through the protection of My Womb. This is simple Salvation. It has nothing to do with such complicated matters as ballistic physics, forensic research, or medicinal biologies. Your Christian atonement is an urgency that supercedes all other great issues of your time, and you must pursue it with strong emphasis on the spirituality from whence you were begotten. It is unrelated to ratios and quotas, but fosters with relevance the blessings of civilized order and the preservation of life and limb. Remember that you come to Salvation by way of excruciation, by the Cross and sword, and by incense, affinity, persecution, and prayer. God issues life for His own Glory. There is no such thing as spontaneous generation; the Lord has created all things according to His Will. I pray that you will believe what I am saying. As crucial as it is to rid the world of evil and all its effects, it is equally imperative that you eradicate all forms of human skepticism, for the latter is responsible for lukewarmness, minuscule tithing, recidivism into the dungeon of mortal sin, hooking wires and sensors to the heads and body parts of seers and visionaries to determine if they are telling the absolute truth, and the reprehensible phenomenon of empty church sanctuaries.

My Special son, I urge you to remember everyday that you are loved beyond description, and now you are awaiting the arrival of a book for My priests that will awaken America about their role in the Salvation of humanity. It is appropriate that you chose to cite the words of Helen Keller because her life and teachings are part of the miracle of human love, an indication that everyone can communicate with God from the center of the heart. And, as you write *Babes in the Woods,* I concur that it is proper to refer to another mentor of little children, Annie Sullivan *(Anne Mansfield Sullivan Macy)* who was the miracle worker who taught little Helen how to interact with the world in ways that led her to be such a great author in her own right. You see that the Holy Spirit reigns in this, and such will be the impact that you and your brother will have on the annals of history. As you reflect about children, the depths of your hearts will be touched by your own experiences, and this will be the power of the innocence that your next book will draw from other men. Indeed, this childlike abandonment is what you have been summoning for thirteen years. I assure you that your labors will accomplish their goals; you will be successful in your mission. It is absolutely inevitable. I have come to urge you to remember the orphaned and the multitudes left to fend for themselves. Three-quarters of the inmates in prisons became estranged from their fathers at a tender age. Their Heavenly Father has adopted them through the Crucifixion of Jesus, but many of them have yet to accept their relationship through the Cross. This is what your spiritual works implore. Other kinds of incarceration exist through sinful habits such as impurities of the flesh. Can you see how important the role of My messengers is in enlightening humanity about deferring to the Holy Spirit? How rewarded you feel knowing that you are succeeding in supernatural ways. We pray for the eradication of every vice that suppresses humanity's future onto the seabeds of the Earth. It is a pretty day where you live, and I wish for you to enjoy it. Let Me assure you that there are few souls on Earth with whom Jesus is more pleased than your brother and you. I beseech you to cling tightly to your faith and love because you need each other, and I am your Immaculate Mother who needs you both! You must be strong, united, peaceful, and committed to the Lord. Someday, you will see the tears of joy that Jesus shed when your brother knelt and kissed the hand of the priest from Kentucky. It was a special Father's Day after all."

Sunday, June 23, 2002
11:11 a.m.

"While thanking you for remembering to pray for all the poor souls who are suffering the perils of danger, I join your hope that the Lord delivers them. There are isolated quarters around the globe where poverty and neglect are causing lives to be unbearable, and it is our prayers that lift them to the dignity of God's Love. My children, I find it pleasant to pray with you because you are open to receiving the Divine intercession of Heaven, and in this you will discover the elevation to hold you inside the center of Jesus' Most Sacred Heart. His plans for you include the incorporation of your petitions with the benign Truth by which He still reigns as the King of Heaven and Earth. I look apprehensively today upon an American nation whose citizens are about to enter another pagan ritual of secular, political sovereignty rather than espousing spiritual holiness. There is no doubt that this causes God to look upon this land with disdain, but He has not surrendered the mission of Jesus to transform your constitution into the righteous accord that is lacking here now. I wish to remind you that His imploring is forever of the heart, that you must turn toward Jesus from within, that the human soul is nourished by enlivening your faith. It is for this purpose that I have come to speak to you today as you recite the Sacred Mysteries of the Holy Rosary. It is true that kindness and Mercy shall follow you all the days of your lives, if only you will open-wide your hearts to receive and exude them. Your Christian conscience is centered upon Truth, a Divine Love that you are given from the moment of your conception in your mother's womb, when you are born, when you are baptized, throughout your lives, and posthumously. God witnesses and knows everything about you. There is no concealing your motivations from Him, be they benevolent or malicious. I ask everyone to remember that there is nothing hidden that shall not be revealed at the conclusion of time. My hope is that all souls will be receptive to His Mercy, and that only goodness will prevail here and hereafter. The Saints call you from Heaven to enlist them for your battles. The Angels are eager to be your spiritual advocates, helpers, and representatives before the Throne of the Father. I beseech you to call upon the Archangel Michael in your struggles against evil because by His Sword, they are cast into the fires of Hell. It is written in the Scriptures that this is true, and it is imperative that you remember to call on this holy warrior in your efforts to conquer sin. Whenever you are in danger or are afraid, the Angels come to your side. But, you must invoke their power by inviting them through the Name of Jesus! They are His ambassadors of the Cross who hold the essence of goodness in their grasp to rescue you from the snares of the devil. Therefore, it is suitable, proper, and prefigured that you enlist their aid.

My Special and Chosen sons, it is with jubilation that I address you because of the works you are affording the Savior of the world. There is peace and comfort in your lives because you have allowed the Holy Paraclete to take residence within you. Can you sense this when you see the rest of humanity groaning in so much pain? Do you know that the love you share is their lacking because they refuse to join you in allowing theirs to flourish? My children, the reason is because they are distracted by material things, travel, sins of the flesh, indifference, arrogance, and the plague of chemical addiction. If only they would fall more deeply in love with Jesus, they would bask in the peaceful accord in which you are conducting your lives. You are the fortunate sons who have decided to live by faith, and your faith is reciprocally fed by Jesus as His thanksgiving for the devotion you are proffering His Kingdom. He will bestow untold blessings upon you during this Liturgical Year, especially on November 24. Please pray in hopeful anticipation because all that you have ever needed to transform the Earth into the Kingdom you wish to acquire will come to pass soon thereafter. My Special one, I know that you have been spending hours categorizing My previous messages. My prescription for the healing of lost sinners is located there; all who wish to know Jesus will discover the origin of their desires in what I have said. This must give you pause to ponder how important your work for Jesus is. The Heavens are grateful that you accepted this challenge, that your heart is with the Son of Man in such a predestined way. Your reward will be of intense magnitude! Can you not see that you stand in the lineage of the first Apostles and disciples? God wishes your brothers and sisters to prosper in the peace of the Holy Spirit, and to make atonement with Jesus through the conviction by which He has expunged the sins of the world on the Cross. Wherever they can best satisfy these things, especially when they pray for the guidance of the Son of Man, is where He will ratify their existence in His Grace. Therefore, we shall pray that such conversion will come to all nonbelievers so they can share in Eternal Salvation when the Almighty Father reveals that the time has come. I desire to tell you that there is no peace that cannot be captured because the world, the future, and the conclusion of life are contingent upon how earnestly you pray for the changes that the Earth needs to be brought to dignity, Light, and the holiness of Paradise. Even many things I have told you are subject to this sacred amendment. This is why the prayers of the faithful are so important. Your books will lead millions to prayer! Thank you! It is alright for you to remember with appreciation the anniversary that tomorrow will bring. Thank you for praying so kindly for the Kingdom of God to come to humanity through the Cross of Jesus!"

Sunday, June 30, 2002
11:18 a.m.

"The courage that you muster to fight against the enemies of Christianity is a gift of the Holy Spirit from the Throne of God. Therein, your every sacrifice is blessed as a portion of the suffering of Jesus on the Cross because your souls have become one in union with perfection like Him. And, if you wish to continue to be like Him, you must worry not what your adversaries can do to your reputations or the health and safety of your physical bodies. I am not asking you to walk headlong into intentional danger, but fear not when such moments arise that you are threatened by the scalded dogs of evil who surround you now. It is true that the Catholic Church is both pure and being purified, and you are a force for good in this transformation. Is the Church to be crucified as the Son of God was nailed to the Cross? Let Me assure you that He, too, is suffering the agony of the ongoing sins of an errant humanity because His Love for humankind did not cease when He was raised from the dead. My children, the future of Catholicism is not like a piece of driftwood wandering about the oceans' crests. My Church is stationed high and away from the corruption that will fall every other mortal institution on the Earth. Therefore, remain very close to the Sacraments, and trust in the Church Hierarchy because Jesus is guiding them with all the power of God, Himself.

You will be accosted for defending your faith, even though your detractors will know that you are in agreement with them about the sins of some of your brothers and sisters. If anyone would wish to castigate the Catholic Church in its entirety as a result of the weakness of a few, such critics are under the influence of Satan. Anyone who is an enemy of the Roman Catholic Church when Jesus calls the world to completion will be cast into Hell. It is just as simple as this.

I wish not to speak brashly or abruptly about those who have yet to be converted to the Holy Eucharist, but I belong to the irreproachable Light of Heaven. I cannot be despised by those whose souls will eventually reside in Paradise. As it has been said before, sinners who bear hatred against the Mother of God belong to the Antichrist. Please deliver this message to the world-entire for Me, knowing in advance that the level of danger in which you might be entering will be elevated. I ask you not to dwell on this matter, or even write any of your opinion about it. It is not something you need to do in an extraordinary way. Simply place it in your other writings on the schedule you have already planned. My children, your God is filled to the brim with contempt for those who are assailing the Holy Roman Catholic Church... The angels decline to hover over those who harbor hatred against the Most Blessed Sacrament. The Living Wrath of Jesus awaits those who scoff at the Sacrament of Confession. I tell you these things not as doomsday prophesies, but as promises that My Son will cleanse this world of all heresy before His final mission is through. It is only through His Divine Mercy and the prayers of the Catholic faithful that those who belong to other religions and denominations are allowed admittance into Heaven at all. Hospitals and nursing homes are filled to near capacity because God has requested such holy souls to join Jesus on the Cross to defeat the enemies of the descendants of Saint Peter. My children, these are the facts, they are not portions of flowery orations or dimly-lit predictions.

Should not the Mother of God reserve the right to admonish humanity about its position against My Church? Do I not have the authority to speak with such Truth in rebuking those who refuse to believe in all Seven of the Sacraments? Let Me assure you—I am beautiful and Heaven is beyond description. But, those who declare themselves to be in diametrical opposition to the teachings of the Roman Catholic Church are ugly, unsightly, living outside the state of grace, and in a gravely sinful condition. This is how serious it is for anyone from any walk of life to defame the beauty of the Church, whether it be the media, public leaders, private journalists, other religions, or an anonymous man standing on a curb alongside a darkened street. Now, I must tell you that I have spoken these things from the depths of the Love in My Immaculate Heart for those who are guilty. I pray deeply for their conversion, understanding, humility, and prayers; but most of all, I seek a change of heart in them, that they may come to the Altar of Sacrifice to receive the Eucharistic Species of My Son. I ask them to come not out of fear, but because they believe! Indeed, I seek their Sacramental Confession based not only upon My admonition, but because they realize that their souls are otherwise separated from God by their unconfessed sins! There are many wakes to come for the dying who will have gone past the chasm of mortality without laying their lives bare before a Roman Catholic priest. Woe be unto them! Please pray for them now! This is the seriousness by which Jesus is approaching these latter times, and I am the Mother whom He has dispatched to speak on His behalf. I have said to humanity before that it is better for you to hear this from Me at this point in time than for Jesus to bring the backlash of your own obstinance to bear against you on the last day of the world.

My Special son, I assure you that I wish not to frighten you in My words today or cause you to lose any hope for the conversion of your fellow men. There are statements in this message that absolutely were required to be made. When you relate them to your brothers and sisters in a couple of years, I ask that you are sure to be clear to also say that neither you, nor I, are judging the worth of their souls. It is imperative that you assure anyone who inquires that 'The Divine Mercy of Jesus' is the reason that all non-Catholics are saved and allowed to enter into Heaven. In the end, the entire of humanity will know that it has been the Catholic Church, her priests, parishioners, and every semblance of prayer, servitude, and suffering that will have brought the Mystical Body of Christ to the Altar to be wedded with the Sacrificed Son of God. It must be a good feeling inside for you to know that you are on the inside of Grace, looking outwardly at the multiple millions who are about to come running to you as your friends and for leadership in joining you at the center of the Truth.

You wrote a very good book in *White Collar Witch Hunt...* For now, He (the God of your fathers) is happy to know that you have begun yet another book to be published early next year. Can you not see that you will have so many someday that your work, and Mine, cannot be cast-off and ignored? This is why your patience is required now, more than during any other time in your life. You will win sooner rather than later in accordance with how patient you are willing to become... I ask that you never surrender your hope that all the world is better for the acceptance you garnered to your God in February 1991... I give you My holy blessing for today. + I will speak to you again very soon. I Love you. Good day!"

Sunday, July 7, 2002
2:31 p.m.

"You are friends, brothers, and children of the Son of God. Please join Him at My Bosom for rest and consolation when your hearts are sorrowful and when dark thoughts unnerve you because I am the Queen and Matriarch of the Divine Love who has given energy and good measure to the Earth. You will discover in My Immaculate Heart the comfort that will help your spirits remain aloft in the Peace and Grace of God. Will everyone come to this rampart of refuge? This is My prayer for humanity, and it is the Will of God the Father. My children, you are witnessing the undoing of the enemies of the Church in your day. Your new book on behalf of the priests is a catastrophic manifestation to vanquish the adversaries of Catholicism. It is doing so as we speak. Some who received it are perceiving themselves to be living on the wrong side of immortal history, and they know not how to confess it without admitting their errors of the past 400 years. I ask that you be patient and allow your work to move throughout the Earth as God wills, to the point that millions more come to the Catholic Church for the Bread of Life, the Most Blessed Sacrament. It is true that no benevolence comes from sin, but goodness can become a fruit of your reaction in combating it. I told you that the worst waste in the world is an unsaid prayer, but the prayer of your manuscript is a wholesome oration against the indifference of nations and peoples regarding the institution of Roman Catholicism. You are prevailing in magnanimous ways. Do not desist in praying for the furtherance of the presence of the Holy Spirit in you by the work of your hands. What do you believe to be the key emphasis in your writing that is having the largest impression? The fact that you mentioned that the world consists of sinners who are reaping unimaginable financial profits by exposing the transgressions of others. This hypocrisy is too obvious to overstate. Your remarkable support for the Sacrament of Confession is having a supernatural impact on the eastern seaboard of the United States, on those who have previously had no comprehension of its power or purpose. I tell you again, the changes that the Lord is seeking in America will not occur in the passing of the next weeks or months, but they will come. My advice is to pursue your goals with the assurance that My words are made manifest, and your eternal reward will be sanctioned by these years as your souls are presented to God for Salvation. I wish for you to have confidence in your submission to the Will of the Father to append the ages as He pleases, and I thank you for your faith and trust.

My Special son, I have come explicitly to tell you how profoundly I love you and to give you spiritual support in your holy offices. I know that life is difficult for you, that your brother is a cross to bear, that your friends do not call upon you as they should, and that you are not seeing the effects of your labors as anyone in your place might anticipate. Such is the life of a messenger and a child of God's Immaculate Mother. I cannot amend these things without the Will of the Father, no more than you or the rest of humanity might do. However, He has yet to deny any request that I have made because it is He who has vested Me with the title of Mediatrix of all Graces as one might overlay an alb with an ecclesial template. Be assured that He hears our petitions for the propagation of your Apostolate. I wish to be still more clear. Anyone who dares to impede your path or attempt to inhibit your success will fail. Accordingly, anyone who would have you believe that your purpose is not Divine or cause you to have thoughts that you are less-than capable of manifesting Heaven's persuasion will be punished to the fullest extent of God's Wrath. This is how seriously the Lord is preparing the way for your service to His Kingdom to succeed. Please remember that the improvements you discover in the conduct of other men are ones that have been engraved in their psyche, and they often have no memory of their previous approach to daily living."

(Is this how people are purged of stain at their Judgement before being allowed entrance into Heaven?)

"People will be purged of any thoughts of pursuing a path that is not in alignment with the Fruits of the Holy Spirit either of their own accord or having it instilled in those whom Jesus deigns to reside with Him in Paradise because of the intercessions of someone else. We have spoken about this before. As to another matter, suppose you are the editor of your hometown newspaper, and you have not mentioned *White Collar Witch Hunt* in your editions. Would you feel any moral obligation to do so?"

(I told Our Lady that the media are arrogant. They will only feel pressured to mention my work if it begins to receive national attention, and they feel they would be criticized by their peers for passing it over, but not before. They will not do anything until they have something to lose.)

"Yes, this is precisely the answer. Your response indicates that the American media do not care whether they tarnish the reputations of 47,000 priests in the United States. I call your attention to the sentence that you wrote in *At the Water's Edge* about the secular media. You will discover the sentiments of God located there."

(In toto, they are the epitome of that rumor-mill.)

"Now, look at the final sentence on the previous page."

(There is not a whisper of doubt in the minds of men who own greater wisdom that when Jesus Christ finally returns to the Earth in Glory, one of His first bold acts of Justice will be to reduce the public media's fallacious empire into a smoldering pile of rubble and ruins in a heap atop the ground.)

"You have just read the prophesied acts of Jesus Christ when He reclaims His Kingdom on Earth to conclude the ages. How can you not be happy about this? I understand that it becomes awfully burdensome enduring their daily mantra of mindless palaver during the interim. The American bishops who are reading your book will weep grateful tears before nightfall. They may not tell you, but I am revealing it to you now. Be happy! Remember that it is the darkest of night just before the dawn. I have told you clearly that your will is in perfect alignment with Jesus."

Sunday, July 14, 2002
11:04 a.m.

"The showering graces that God has deposited upon your souls during the past years are worthy of your response, and He will continue in the expectation that the prayers you offer will be the deliverance of lost sinners to His Holy Arms. My pretty children, these are the hours during which you willfully place your trust in the Cross because the prophecies of the earlier ages are occurring in your day by virtue of the power of the Crucifixion. Although you have understood this for most of your lives, it is imperative that you recollect everything you know about Heaven before the occasion arrives when Jesus takes you there. I call you to also remind anyone who is evaluating the consequences of My weekly messages that God speaks to His disciples everyday through more distinction than the simple thoughts and passages that I offer paranormally. Intimate communication with Jesus is done through the privacy of your prayers, the expanse of your charitable labors in assisting the poor, and offering your compassion to those in sorrow. All of these constitute the linear interaction between Heaven and Earth, not just what I relate to you while we pray together as Mother and children. Will you remind your brothers and sisters who are seeking miracles from God to search for them at the center of their hearts? You are messengers for the Lord, but you are not favored over any other people. Your hearts have been placed beneath the trust and commission of Christ Jesus, but they are no more lauded in Paradise over the littlest ones who hover in darkness and lonely places around the world. You are fortunate children to be open to My intercession, but much is expected from you as a result. I realize that you live responsibly, humbly, and for the Glory of God. Thank you for your submission to the Holy Spirit as Jesus intervenes through the Roman Catholic Church for the conversion, purification, and sanctification of all humankind. As unbelievable as it may seem, there are more benefits to remaining strong in your faith than those that can be seen with the naked eye. I tell you that the entire material world is aided through your pious convictions and the offerings you tender to those who do not know the meaning of life within the Sacred Heart of Jesus. This is why you are messengers. I told you before that by asking Jesus to transfer your love to those you do not know, He does so by responding to your petitions. You give new life and meaning to the Penitential Psalms when you bow before His holiness and ask to bless those who seek Him with the hope of being redeemed into Heaven. Yes, you are participants in this exchange of international goodness as you inhabit separate republics around the globe. This is not only the interfaith mission that you are called to safeguard, it is the unifying of all peoples under the Cross of Christianity. The statements of fact that I offered last Sunday will forever be the goal of God because He has sent only one Messiah to the Earth to die for the sins of everyone. You may be proud and humbled by your personal recognition of this, but never unwilling to share it wherever you go. If you live in accordance with the Holy Scriptures, you know that your faith will not be wholly welcomed in some foreign lands. Rather than impose rejection, despondence, or further persecution upon your friends who are standing beside you, shake the dust from your feet where your Christianity is rejected, and depart from there, for Jesus will sanctify that area with the revelation of His Providence so profusely that these detractors will follow your tracks to learn about the meaning of life. I assure you that this shall be done before the ages have passed away. Indeed, it is transpiring and culminating now.

My Special son, you are receiving letters from many American Prelates and Cardinals of the Catholic Church who have received your book on behalf of their priests. Their acknowledgment of your work is a profound signal that they have accepted what you have composed. Their hearts are aware of your purpose and intentions, and they should heed the suggestions you have inscribed so they will remember the reason for their calling into the priestly vocation. Each and every one of them holds a place in their heart for those who have fallen into sin because they realize the power of the Sacraments to purify humankind. This has been an edifying experience, not only for you and your brother to know more about what God expects from His disciples, but also for those who teach it and represent Him under the vestments they have been accorded by the Church. Henceforth, your reaction to the sins of others shall be productive, ameliorative, and challenging to those who refuse to acknowledge the power of forgiveness. These are the facts of the legitimacy of your response, the same answer that all men must give Jesus when He asks for their contrition at the autumn of their lives. You are living My messages in obedience because you can see from the depths of your love for Jesus that all sinners are purified in the Blood of the Cross, the same Cross which has redeemed your soul for God. Thank you for doing these things so well. We must ensure that you never retreat while being perpetually on guard against the rogue secularists who would try to whitewash the meaning and purpose of your writing. If you proceed in the discreet ways that you have by penning your sentiments onto the written page for history to record, your expressions cannot be distorted. It is important for you to remember that anyone who receives your messages and does not profess their belief in them will never be someone in whom you can place your trust to dispense them accurately. I know that your good judgement will allow you to recognize who they are. I assure you that your intentions will prevail in the dissemination of the work of your Marian Apostolate. It is a beautiful day in the Lord's earthly vineyard, and I know that you are filled with peace because I sense it radiating from your heart. You are aware of the awesome progress that is being made to glorify the Truth through the years you are giving the Almighty Father. Will you pause and consider how victorious you have been in this regard? Let Me be clear. None of your pious works would have grown if you had not accepted My invitation in February of 1991. It seems an awfully long time ago by now, but the greatest is still to come. I offer you My assurance that your life will culminate in a victory that is an integral part of the Triumph of My Immaculate Heart. Your books will achieve the objectives that you seek. It is time for you to remember My call for patience, however. Please do not think your answers to Me, but state them audibly. What does 'fantastic' mean? I ask this because if you appear at an international forum and use such vernacular, foreigners will assume that you have told them that your work is a derivation of fantasy. And, what if you want them to believe that your work is not credible? You would say 'incredible.' You must be careful not to use such American slang and colloquial expressions! Finally, your parents have wished that someone they trust would come forward and write a masterpiece in defense of Catholic priests. What a surprise for them to know that it was you. Do you remember when your mother wrote to the *Catholic Times* newspaper in defense of the clergy? Thank you for showing your forbears that you will not allow your allegiance to them to preempt your love for Jesus."

Sunday, July 21, 2002
2:20 p.m.

"You are My dearly beloved children of the Light of Truth who shine like beacons in the night for the sinful world. Your presence in this age is a sign from God that He has blessed the 21st century with righteous people and simple hearts whose perception, purpose, and destiny are always wholehearted, not of the self, but outward to enhance the lot of humankind. I ask you to remember your station on the globe as one of piety, servitude, and humility because this is how you are seen by My Son in Heaven. Nothing of malevolence can destroy the peacefulness which has brought you to understand what it means to kneel before the Cross and ask Jesus to be the deliverance of the whole of Creation. You know that all power in Heaven and on Earth has been given to Him, and this is the authority by which He is molding and shaping His Mystical Body for transference into the Light of Paradise. He does this from within, much as a physician treats your internal body and heals you of disease. Jesus reaches you by entering the center of your heart and blooming His Divine purposes from that essential core. When you allow Him room to enter, permission to shape your being, avenues to travel into the darkest corridors of your mortal regrets, and plentiful berth to change your approach to daily life, He will succeed in making you the perfect reflection of His Holy Light. It is an intrinsic portion of the Sacred Mysteries of the Salvation of men that you are to participate in the process of your own purification by engaging the Will of God. What exactly does this commission mean? It refers to your becoming one and inseparable with the pristine grandness of the creative Love of the Almighty Father here in your day and through the expanse of the charismatic generations that have only temporarily set you apart from all previous ones. It means that you become as timeless as the mountains and seas, as open in heart and spirit as the broadest canyons, as steeped in love with Heaven as the oceans' deepest fathoms, as sound in peace and Grace as the Heavenly Firmament, and as willing to fight, bleed, agonize, suffer, and die as all the Saints and Martyrs who preceded you in death. I ask you to become the modern participants of an Eternity of Grace! Dear children, the nature of Divine perfection resides in all the things you do so well for God, recognizing His omnipotent power to alter the face of the Earth and the course of human events in a fraction of a second. It resides in the vestiges and legacies of those who taught you to be Christians from whence you were helpless little children, their goodness now rising from their passage, arching across the breadth of your humanity, and into the culmination of the last of your tomorrows. It is your heart, My children, it is your heart! It is your comprehension of aching and regret, of misfortune, resentment, hatred, vengeance, and warring to the point of human annihilation, and knowing that each of these can never be a fruit of the new beginnings about which I have taught you for hundreds of years. Truly, it is your heart, because only from the heart can your fullest understanding of human sanctification be conceived. Therefore, I call you from within the very essence of your reunion with God through the Most Sacred Heart of Jesus, His Divine Mercy and your perfect submission. There are pearly things spoken about all around the continents today; of wealth, respect, rehabilitation, and the redressing of social contemptuousness. However, only through your discreet and noble intentions of becoming one in the Blood of the Cross will you be brought to distinction among the Angels; only by the resilience of your desire to be victorious over the grave will you be allowed to live in the glorious Light of everlasting peace. I have placed the interrogatory before My people all over the world; will you go there with Me? Will you follow Me where the bellows of change are so beautiful that your eyes will well with tears, where your souls will genuflect in ecstasy and thanksgiving, where your pain and sorrows will be entirely expunged, and where God's New Jerusalem will supplant the wreck of this world that will suddenly pass away? Inside your beings lives the exhortations of tassel-bearing orators, principals, kings, laborers and painters admiring their finished masterpieces, and mystics who have seen their prophesies finally come of age. From within your humble hearts springs the compassion for the multitudes who are cast away, the suppliance that will heal the broken of spirit, their reason for living in hope again, and the saturation of all the universes with the Will of Almighty Love.

  I give you peace and grant you the promise that Jesus has remade you into the likeness of Himself. And, toward that purpose, when will humanity respond? When in mortal time and the throes of the awful annals of history will the people who inhabit the Earth come back and regain the dignity that was lost before you were born? There is no question that time is very short, but this is not as of great importance as it is for every soul alive to be transferred into the Passion of Jesus for the whole of every hour, now in this day of means and opportunity. It would make no difference if you were living yet in the first century with nineteen more to go, the time for the conversion of man to the perfection of Paradise has arrived. It is perpetual, eager, urgent, of the highest reward, and the greatest honor of any living species to be born from the Will of God the Father. The Holy Spirit speaks eloquent volumes about the Master of the Ages, the Court of Heaven, the Center of Justice, and the discovery of the lost. All these things are true, but they are still unfinished until every last man, woman, and child is handed over to them for the reasoned elevation of Creation en masse. I beseech you to listen to this Mother to whom you are given, that you will heed the call of the Matriarch who has been deigned to you, that all the madness of the galaxies is purged and destroyed with the simple whimper from the heart, your own proclamation, that love lives there. There is genius and healing in every intonation from your parted lips that you fully understand that God is the Maker and Ruler of the nations, the Earth, the

Heavens, of everything that is more beautiful than gold and crystal chandeliers, and all that is consoling to the touch and made available to those who accept the Dominion of goodness with the contrition of little children. Too many among you bewail their inability to see God because they are blinded by the insolence which has been wrought by their own lack of faith, and by the making of an obstinance so egregious that they refuse to recognize their own error.

When the Son of Man returns to Earth in the Glory of the Second Coming, you will understand what I have said here today, but it is incumbent upon you to be the seeds of righteousness in your time to make it come true. All eyes shall see at the conclusion of time, but not all will accept the Glory in their sight. This, My children, is why I am teaching and praying, imploring, designing, and fashioning My earthly offspring for these latter years. It takes no prophet to detect that the world is in disarray because of the terror of aggressors and the plight of victims. These things have borne their rite of passage centuries before. They are not the matter of making peace out of war or redressing grievances which have stood far too long. They are symptoms of the greater problem that humanity has suffered to this date; the reluctance of man in exile to understand where he is stationed in the universe, why he is there, and how to be rescued both from the imprisonment of mortality and the finality of death. Conflicts have been fought, enemies have been conquered, fields of valorous foot-soldiers slaughtered, leaders vanquished, governments felled, dictators executed, and massive numbers of innocent civilians killed. Does not the world realize by now that this is not the way to win the favor of God who has reigned so quietly above? I am calling for more than the value of the intellect today, but the entire economy of your awareness of Salvation to be the reason for your love, life, awakening, and completion. My Immaculate Heart is pleading for your understanding that God is not found in your warfare, fractured innuendoes, and bloodbaths. He is in your hearts where your love resides, where children are healed, paupers fed, friendships restored, and souls given to the Holy Cross. I will remind you each and everyone until My Son returns again; it is in the heart! Every grand and benevolent intention springs from there, and it is to the heart that you must take the cause of your actions and the truisms by which you practice your beliefs. Why? Because they will be transferred from there to the Kingdom of Divine origin to be perfected, and thereafter sent back to you refined, blessed, and recreated as the best of all possible worlds through your words and deeds to finally—finally make the home of Jesus Christ the Earth for which He pines to be completely open to receive His Messianic Will.

My Special son, I speak to you in loftier terms today because this is such a joyful time for Me. I am elated because I am with you and can communicate in such an open way. Your love and obedience have given Me the venue to teach the entire of humanity what it means to rise deeply in love with Jesus. I am sure that you cannot fully comprehend what this means to Me.

You must realize that some of the things you see are not really as they seem, but that the world is changing everyday to become the Light of Love which will ultimately overcome everything that is standing in your path. Do you remember that the love in your heart blooms around its obstacles? This is what you do very well. And, there are manifestations that you are taught by the Holy Scriptures encountered only through the conditioning of the heart, through the power and Grace of the Sacraments, and by the intervention of the Holy Spirit. It is a mystery that *Thou Shalt Not Kill* eventually led to the Redemption of the entire human race when Jesus' executioners violated this Sacred Commandment. This is the Divine Providence of the New Covenant, and I have taught you about such ironies before. They seem like contradictions at the outset, but are clarified once the full benefit of history is revealed. This is why I so admire the charitable faith of those who believe in Jesus. I see the finest loyalties of God in little people; His power, purpose, creative ingenuity, Love, devotion, plenteous generosity, and the dispensation of life anew. I do not see all the things that you were taught to cower from when you became old enough to learn. There is a sense of providing by the Almighty Father for the physical world, His way of effecting the resurgence of the energy behind His desire for humankind to succeed in inheriting the Earth, making it His final domain, rendering it fit for the Angels to tread with delight, and causing it to be the plateau upon which His chosen people share His regenerative life. I see the anticipation of joy, vindication in the compliance of humanity in resurrecting the dying, communication with the unseen hand of destiny, and the fashioning and finishing of everything God wishes for His people to do in union with His Will for life to proceed. I see these things happening around you when those who exercise their faith do so in the name of Truth. You will someday understand My perception about the wholesome qualities of the Redemption of men, the reason for placing earthly priorities in new perspective, and knowing how the Holy Spirit wells from within your heart to make all creatures on Earth align with the Glory of Heaven. Do you know how this can occur? My child, I am teaching you about Truth by utilizing ways that the world does not understand, indeed that humanity clearly despises. Will you allow Me to teach you about such strength and vision?"

Sunday, July 28, 2002
2:38 p.m.

"The remarkable splendor of Truth resides in your hearts and flourishes in this home amidst the presence of the Angels and the Divine Holy Spirit who has allowed us to speak together again. It is in this joy that I have come to offer you the blessings from God that He placed into being the moment His Creation was finished. Will you not continue to be contented that humanity is so fortunate as to have a God of such high benevolence? We seek together the transformation of the world into the likeness of Jesus because He has reclaimed it for the Almighty Father in the name of Divine Love. We wish for every living soul to become aware of this fresh beginning and of the nourishment of the heart which is found in His Sacrifice on the Cross so mortal time will ultimately close having reaped each and every child of Mine into righteous conversion through our prayers. My children, you have seen that it can be a lonely and desolate Earth absent your faith. Let us pray resolutely that your brothers and sisters will decide to embrace it, for faith is a gift from Heaven. Thereafter, the face of humanity can be gladdened because your souls will be healed. I would be remiss if I failed to thank you every time the opportunity arises for contributing to this great task of Christian evangelization, a mission that shall not end until you have closed your eyes in death and opened them again in the Light of Eternal Life. Today, I ask you to remember the poor, those who are contemplating self-destruction, and the millions of unborn children who are living in their mothers' wombs. Indeed, please ask the Father to continue to bless the papacy of Pope John Paul II as so many hundreds-of-thousands have traveled to pray with him in Canada. It is a bountiful sight to behold while I hover quietly in the midst of a half-million young Christians who decided to honor Jesus in such a profoundly sacrificial way. My Immaculate Heart is filled to overflowing with admiration for all who live in obedience to his Pontificate. This is one of the greatest Popes to have fathered the Roman Catholic Church, and he is sincerely dependent upon My Maternal intercession for the expressions of his service. All dignity and honor of the Lord are alive in his humble heart, and the Love of God presides resoundingly in his presence. Yes, the world shall move forward in time and Grace to reach the pinnacle of piety because of the servitude of all who are praising Jesus in their various apostolic vocations. What a wonderful display of loyalty to have so many cling to their allegiance to Me when the rest of the world seems to be turning away. You are given the sincerest reward from the Hosts of Heaven for remaining steadfast in your trust in Jesus' Plan for the recapturing of the lost inside an umbrella of purity that is unfurling before your eyes. Thank you for living chastely, for remaining pure of heart and of your flesh. Since you are sown to the Spirit, you are more able to comprehend the meaning of holiness and accept the sacrifices that will take you there. Yes! As I urge you to pray for these things, I also pray with you for the Kingdom of God to overwhelm those who still live in doubt. Allow the God of your fathers to give them new reason to enhance their faith by the presence of His sovereign work among them. These are grand and glorious days because so much good is being wrought from beneath the perils of those who witness so courageously on behalf of the Holy Spirit. You know that their enemies have already been foiled, and it is your hope in the springtime of your Resurrection that keeps your spirits high. It is the intention of Jesus to ask you to help Him convert the lost in your company to the kindness of His Sacred Heart and to defeat those who are persecuting His Church with hatred and scorn. You have the spiritual prowess to amend the fate of the world by praying the Holy Rosary in many arenas, fora, and cenacles wherever you should travel at home or abroad. Indeed, a novena to My Most Immaculate Heart has rendered possible the rescue of nine souls who would have otherwise perished in the pit of a mine, one soul for each day. And, while thousands know this to be true, it is important that the rest of America hear that the Mother of God has pronounced this good fortune as a result of your petitions.

My Special son, how swiftly the time is passing now that your work for Me is progressing. In another month, you shall begin to pen another book about little children, and please allow Me to state that it is a work that is of particularly fond favor to Me. You know how I love the little ones and pray earnestly for those who are suffering in the likeness of My Son. I realize that you have said that each new book you write is your favorite, but this time you will truly know what it means to make such an acclamation! *Babes in the Woods* is how Jesus sees all of you. It is because you love Him in return that you are accorded the venues and miracles to produce the awesome writings that touch so many broken hearts. It must be made clear to you that the extraordinary propagation of your books is in the near offing, but Jesus is holding them at bay so you can proceed in a more anonymous vein. I am sure that you understand the meaning for this if you ponder it from the depths of your heart. Do you recall what God told humanity through the Book of Ecclesiastes? The time will soon come when you will be forced to take residence in another place because of the influx of curious people arriving at your front door. I will tell you in advance of that time to make it a smoother transition. Then, as I told you in the spring of 1991, I will deliver them to the Tabernacle to receive My Eucharistic Son. You are now performing the work that I have known all along would lead to the completion of your prayer room downstairs. Someday, we shall enjoy our conversations together again down there. I am furthermore pleased that you find consolation in hindsight from the messages I have offered since March of 1997. Can you discern that I love My little children with every fiber of My Holy Being?"

(I told Our Lady out of thanksgiving that I realized clearly that God has never allowed such a magnitude of Her intercessory guidance in the history of the Church.)

"I offer you the explanation that there has never been a messenger in the history of Creation who has been so obedient as you to offer your complete compliance with My every request! This, and only this, is the reason why I am able to succeed in telling humanity about Jesus as I have through your life. Thank you for giving Me the gift of your years the way you have. As I told you before, it is My hope that you will not have to wait until the end of the ages before you fully understand the reasons why. You are a creature of God whom He has given to Me! You are My gift from the Maker of men, the wonderful design whom He has seen fit to place under My Mantle for the joy that My soul magnifies to the people of the Earth. There are no inanimate depictions that can offer Me the comfort that you do when you are so obediently attuned to the intentions of My Immaculate Heart. And, as you have poured your servitude upon this land, it has caused Creation to leap in jubilation with the power of God so that all He has made can be united to His Will. This, My child, is the way that the flowering Crucifixion of Jesus is discovered by those who are yet blind to the Love which has redeemed them from damnation. You, like many Saints before you, are the reflection of Jesus' Passion and Crucifixion because you extol the definitive Truth of God in a world that is still asking the question, '...why is there life?' You reverberate the conceptions of nobility and Virtue the way that wanderers are finally discovered; you are the source of the elation of the Angels, and you expand the awesome travels of Saint Michael the Archangel whose Sword is striking down the enemies of the Church. As I have said, it may be difficult for you to comprehend these things right now, but all will become clear as the weeks and months expire. You see that your mission is on course, both for Me and the modernization of your home, and that you have every reason to be hopeful about the life you are leading in the Light of My Son's Resurrection. Please know that your progress is in accordance with the way My wishes have been prefigured all along. Thank you for showing Me how your trust in the freedom of the Light of God can be enhanced through the enlistment of your faith on Earth."

Sunday, August 4, 2002
10:42 a.m.

"Indeed, the Lamb of God who takes away the sins of the world dispenses His Divine Mercy upon all who love Him! You must remember that all men are sinners, but it is not inevitable that you should be lured into its trap. By living in accordance with the Sacred Scriptures; and by praying, fasting, performing holy works, and accepting the penitential manifestations that Jesus places before you, your soul will be bound for Heaven without delay. Please remember that you live in a nation where there are many who are indifferent about Christianity, millions who place no value in the Cross. Pagans and atheists are attempting to draw the most from the secular forces that are trying to diminish your faith so as to lead people away from the Grace of spiritualism. They will ultimately fail because they underestimate the tenacity of the Holy Spirit. Those who teach only rationalism and realism are in grave danger as the ages come to a close. What is the definitive proof that this is true? Because Jesus has told the world through every venue that the Father commands that those who reject Him shall be cast into the inferno of Hell. I come seeking the prayers of the faithful so millions more will be converted to Christianity. My children, while theologians of all persuasions speak in your midst about the End Times, about the culmination of human mortality, about a certain period of peace either prior or subsequent to the final battle for souls, they are looking too far into the future because the Plan of Salvation is prevalent today. If only those who spend their time prophesying how God will end the world would do more to make it a better place for the poor, lost and lonely, then perhaps Jesus would arrive before sundown at the summit of such a blessed day and take you all to Paradise. I am asking for your participation in bringing the Kingdom of God to the Earth through an ecclesial engagement here and now, that you will address the problems that are scandalizing the dignity of too many children and elderly citizens. I am urging you to elevate your spiritual debate by actualizing your faith in ways that are worthy of the Saints. America has become filled with selfish glory seekers, and not fighters for the Glory of Paradise. Those who appear on television and speak through various written works are doing only little to effect the Love of God in the world when they do nothing more than sit in their parlours and ponder '...what might be.' I am asking philosophers to become practitioners instead, for they are only hypocrites. Does the Mother of God know precisely who they are? Of course I do! It is easy for them to parse sentences of vitriol and offer warnings about the future, but let these same elitists crawl into the trenches with the true people of Christ Jesus to help heal the broken-hearted, starving, and afflicted. I ask My children to rebuff those who place their haughty fortune-telling between fancy book covers because such authors are only slothful meddlers in a Kingdom that will never belong to them! What a waste of words for lay-theologians to cast aspersions against the Son of Man without ever having walked in His sandals or borne any crosses of their own in the likeness of His! Shame on those who take to the airwaves dressed in silk-laced suits and wearing gaudy neckties, presuming what God will do with Creation tomorrow. Such pious platitudes are more of the chaff that Jesus will toss into His flames of Justice. Christians indeed! Launching false tirades about the destiny of humankind over satellite communications in the name of Christianity is part of the vanity that will be thrown into perdition once the record of human events has been told. Let Me be perfectly clear on behalf of My Sacrificed Son. The simple of life and humble of heart, and those who are the perpetual healers of suffering men are those upon whom Jesus' favor rests. Will you not see, My children, what I am saying to you today? So, let Me remind you about the suffering of the poor who have no access to the greater world to detail the gruesome effects of their agony and pain. There have been countless speakers appearing on television in America, even on Catholic networks, who have hailed and celebrated only their own written works in defiance of the Sacred Beatitudes and in contradiction to the teachings of the Holy Father, Pope John Paul II, in Rome. Such arrogant publicists are waiting for their reward from God by praying in the open to elevate their pride and divining some sort of unwarranted blessing from beyond the Heavenly Firmament. I tell you, they will be counted among the least. There are some who will be called last, if at all. They speak of heresy and apostasy in certain circles of men, but they fail to recognize their own footsteps in departing from the Truth of humble service and sacrificial living. My Special son, please tell them for Me! You are to admonish them that the Immaculate Mother to whom they claim to owe their allegiance is prepared to seek from them sacrifices of unforeseen self-denial. I shall not allow the Savior of the world to see their hypocrisy without their having admitted it among themselves. These are My children, and I love them! Would a mother allow her children to live in darkness when she can take them by the hand and deliver them to the Light? The privilege of knowing Jesus is always abused by someone who claims to know Him better than the poorest of the poor!

I have spoken these words so you might be able when the time is right to advise humanity that prophesies are merely prophesies. I am seeking followers of Jesus who hope for tomorrow in Eternity, but are willing to live in the present by becoming the incarnate Divinity of Jesus through their very mortal existence before it is too late and they die not having given all they had for the advancement of His Kingdom. Thank you for allowing Me to speak with you in such decisive overtones, but I believe that you know that many among you deserve it. Someday, My Special son, the Christian networks will decline to predict what might happen in some futuristic wonderland because they will be too interested in learning from you how you conquered the dangers, inequities, and problems of today. I say to you again, tell them what the meaning of Love is about because they seem to be more interested in prescience than they are the deliverance of a lost humanity to the Sacrifice of the Son of Man. I have spoken to you for eleven and a half years about the Divine nature of God, of the grand possibilities of Creation-renewed, and that millions upon millions are ignoring the restoration of human civility in the Messianic Cross. But, I have also told you that there are factual, practical, and discernable ways to get there. This is the manifestation of Jesus as Human and Divine, and the world must realize that Heaven begins at the center of the heart. As difficult as it may seem for many to accept, it is possible to be so holy that you will not realize your passage from this life into the next. This is what Jesus means when He says 'Be perfect as I am perfect.' There is nothing standing in your way of achieving this goal but pride and obstinance. My Special son, I have given you My message for today. I know that you are becoming more aware as time passes how much greater your life is sown to the Spirit as opposed to the flesh. There is no doubt that Eternity cannot be found in flesh that is destined for the grave. Only your union in our Triune God will matter when time is brought to a conclusion."

Sunday, August 11, 2002
3:33 p.m.

"As contradictory as it seems, there are both grave and meritorious reasons for you to remain headlong in pursuit of the conversion of humanity. I know that the dangers you face are perils that you would rather avoid, but the fruit of new Saints is the goodness that Jesus wishes to behold in your spiritual service to His Kingdom. There are no simple responses to the difficult questions as to why your work for God is so opposed, but time itself will aid in your understanding of the Will of the Almighty Father. My Son is not asking you to decipher the mysteries of evil in the material world, but He is surely calling you to immobilize it wherever you can. This is why we are praying together; it is the purpose in your prayerful existence under the Holy Cross; it is the bastion of hope by which thousands in your midst are living, and it is the centerpiece of the essential beauty that Jesus has given your souls on behalf of our grateful God. I know that My messages are capable of rendering your compliance with His wishes more sweet to the taste of all the faithfully departed. The genius that you are bringing to the Earth by living for your Savior is expelling the ignorance of previously lost people. Indeed, I also realize that you will continue to dignify the lonely and forsaken to alleviate their suffering in the Name of Jesus, and that you will furthermore pray with Me for the transformation of an obstinate humanity into the contrition they require to see Heaven through their acceptance of His Divine Love. My purpose here today is to offer the appreciation from God in that you remain at His side, to grant you the accolades which will precede your entrance into Heaven, and to remind you that the element of time is expiring swiftly before you shall see the Light of Paradise with exacting perfection. Were it not for your spiritual patience, you would not be able to anticipate such joy with the confidence in which you are living. I have also come today to ask the world to remember the cardinal benefit of forgiving the sins of others. Without such mutual absolution, there will never come that final peace for which so many are now praying. I implore and commend My children to beseech Jesus to enter your hearts with kind ferocity and gentle discipline to make this come true. Yes, let everyone pray together for this gift. The Catholic Church is prevailing in a world of unprecedented opposition to its Grace. The Mother of God stands in protection over My children, and I will let no stain of sin linger upon its raiment as the Church is presented in excellence before God at the end of time. Were this not meant to be a difficult process, you would have already surrendered the fight. But, you are strong warriors in the struggle against evil, especially that of your enemies' outright atheistic callousness. Your worship of the Almighty Father is worthy of the blessings He is bestowing upon your land. Please remain steadfast in your righteousness that keeps you open to whatever He asks of you for the future. When Jesus told Creation that '...it is finished' from the purifying heights of the Cross, He was telling you the same principle that He is today, that your love in union with His for God who created all good things is the mainstay and the ratification of human life. The destiny you seek is to regain the Paradise that was lost to you by the sins of Adam and Eve; and Jesus is the Man-God who restored this pristine future. Please embrace Him with all your will, My little children! My Immaculate Heart cries for all who are rejecting the Blood of Jesus to undergo a radical re-examination of their conscience. The acceptance of My Son as your Savior has immortal and irrevocable consequences! Those who are bound for Heaven include many who are still far from His Grace and are only now coming to understand the meaning of sacrificial Redemption. This is why the element of time is so crucial to those who have just begun.

    My children, you endure a lifetime of uncertain spontaneity, a continuum of indecisiveness about your difficulties and the choices you must make to affect the future. This is in many ways the stridence that shrills against your nerves, but it is also to your credit that the mortal Earth will not expire without your having benefitted it in some way. As numbing as the human experience often seems, it can during any moment be lifted out of normalcy into a limelight of sanctity to the surprise of the very same people who are accomplishing it. Christian holiness is not constrained to monumental events; it encompasses even your most mundane hours. Jesus asks everyone at least once during their lives to leap beyond what man's impressions consider to be orthodox and usurp the bonds of practicality. This might consist of carrying a crippled child to the doorstep of a millionaire's mansion, ringing the doorbell, and hiding in the shrubbery to see what they do. If they call someone else to take him away, then you will have your answer. Or, you might approach the Altar on your knees to receive the Holy Eucharist during Mass, and if anyone accuses you of ostentatious piety, then you have yet another answer. What is intrinsic to your Christian evangelization is that you should reach beyond your simple Profession of Faith and force it into motion, to upend your thoughts and actions so that you more clearly comprehend what it was like for Jesus to be spurned. The Scriptures say that He became sin to expunge sin, that He committed by proxy every conceivable crime against humanity to cleanse your souls of guilt. While He was never capable of committing such transgressions, He claimed them so that His Mystical Body could move into Eternity with your baptismal gowns as pure as the wind-driven snow. This begs the question that the Lord asks of His Church. If His Son could attest to being so guilty when His innocence was so unequivocally obvious, why can humanity not reciprocate by claiming your Absolution in the wake of your own indictments? God knew that someone must be blamed, somebody had to bear the cost for the Redemption of the Earth. And, in His indomitable Love for the prodigal human race, He laid it all on Christ Jesus. Hence, you would not suffer the consequences of perdition. This, My children, is Divine Love. It is of such extraordinary intensity that it is a Sacred Mystery, but it is to this elevation of self-sacrifice that you are called; not to death or destruction, or your own crucifixion, but acts of spiritual heroism so profound that they would make Saint Peter weep. What initiates this call to such random acts of virtue? Things like carrying the cripple and bowing in deference before a Blessed Sacrament that more than validates your faith. It is in lunging forward with determination to touch God as though you were cloistered in the dark. As long as He can see your palms waving, He will take you by the hand. You make something of Creation when you give this much to Him. Your identity before Heaven becomes like Jesus' Transfiguration on Mount Tabor, although yours is a spiritual replication of the Glory divulged to Peter, James, and John. Notwithstanding that you were born into the world with the meekness of lambs, Jesus calls you to fight for His Kingdom with the courage of savvy lions, but never surrendering your childlike faith. You have through the power of your prayers the ability to strike-down demons, prepare the Earth with righteousness, purge your brothers' hatred, and lay the groundwork for the purification of man upon which your deliverance to Paradise has already been constructed.

My Special son, it is an honor for Me to be with you again today so as to share the jubilation in your heart with the Hosts of Paradise. It is August 11, 2002, another day in your life when God looks upon you with great favor. He is pleased that you have never allowed your filial emotions to cause you to concede to those who have rejected your work and beg them to forgive your lack of focus upon the tangible world. Quite the contrary, He is elated that you are standing firm in your commitment to uphold the Truth of His spiritual Love which can be seen with the naked eye in the Most Blessed Sacrament. He is glorified that you shun the desire to harbor a collection of worldly goods or engage in behavior that is unbecoming. You and your brother are shining zeniths flanking the Morning Star. You are the right and left guards for the gift of righteousness to bourgeon in your immediate presence. Many around you admire your achievements for Jesus, but do not know how to show it. Let us pray together in hope and peace so that the flourishing of God's Love will be the culmination of the life of joy for those who would otherwise know only sorrow. You are amassing an arsenal of iconography so profound that no one whose soul is bound for Heaven will attempt to rebuke it. I see that you are aware of this. Time is not an issue in this matter. Millions will see it only after they have died."

Saturday, August 17, 2002
7:03 p.m.

"Anticipating that I would find you in good spirits, I have come to speak to you about the Kingdom of Love. Whatever on Earth that people everywhere choose to hitch their proverbial wagon to, I ask that you decide for God and hitch your wagon, your soul, your lot, your future, and your conversion to holiness that makes you infinitely love one another to the Morning Star! My blessings are with you this summer evening. The immensity of the admiration in My Immaculate Heart for you is overwhelming to the Saints and Angels who surround Me now. These are the crucial days that are amending the events of the present and forever changing what will come to be. Your prayers and efforts on behalf of Jesus are of themselves a portion of the Guiding Light of Truth that continues to set burdened people free and incarcerate evil into the dungeons beneath the Earth. I say to you again today, it is not that those who espouse hatred against your work for God are evil in an outright way, but that they are influenced by Satan to remain away from the righteousness that will allow them to fully become one in the Cross of My Son. There are too many distractions and temptations for shallow people to overcome, far too much emphasis on the bleak and material. Their weight is oftentimes so difficult to carry that they become despondent and know not what direction to turn. If only they would give themselves to the Prince of Peace, they would be liberated from their self-imposed imprisonment. This, My children, is what your work is about. And, in this will you find both your reward and their deliverance into freedom. When you ask your enemies where in the world they procure their pretentious premises with which they argue against the Truth, their only response is that they learned it from their faithless predecessors. So, you can see what I mean when I say that your mission is having to destroy more than the indifference which has been generated in your own day. And, this is why My Son's Sorrowful Crucifixion transcends the centuries to eradicate the transgressions of modern sinners from Creation. We pray that more souls will be lifted to dignity in Jesus' Resurrection as they begin to comprehend the power of the Holy Spirit residing in their hearts. I realize that you oftentimes wonder from one week to the next what amazements will transpire as time passes. I do not tell you in advance about these things because I urge you to maintain the instinctiveness of your spiritual strength for the perilous times to come when you are steeped in the darkness of battle and the Hosts of Heaven seem so far away. I will remind you now what I will require of you then; search inside your hearts for peace and strength, and your victories shall be won. Fear and despondence belong to those who place no trust in God. If you carry your fright with you as you profess your oath to Christianity, you will burden yourselves unnecessarily. Your crosses are brought by those who deny your love, by the many who have already rejected the Cross, and millions of others who are envious because they have not chosen wisely the course of Truth. You must direct them to the Table of the Lord, and they will discover themselves what His Holy Will is. And, for sure, they will then realize that it is to heed to My miraculous intercession, for I bear within My Heart the message of Eternal Life. With these high regards and hope-filled wishes, I ask you to relay My words to the whole world, that each and every child of the Father will yearn to see His Face. The time will come sooner, rather than later, when they will be asked to choose the Light of Heaven over the darkness of Hell. How can God's Kingdom thank you for assisting in the transference of humanity to Salvation in Jesus? By seeking your imitation of Him until the day when you join one another before the Holy of Holies at the summit of Paradise. Many are the years and countless the hours when you work tirelessly for a Deific Triumph that you cannot yet see. This is the advantage of true faith that God has given you. Wherever you travel among your peers, your souls exude the purpose of your love because your Light is wholly brilliant. Even in your civil admonishments, you appear to display the ornate and venerable Providence of the Holy Spirit.

    My Special son, could you have imagined prior to this day that the seeds of righteousness that you allowed to be planted in this place nearly twelve years ago would produce such a bountiful harvest? I assure you that you are only seeing the tassels of the gifts your labors have become for humankind. Millions of souls are beginning to savor the fruits of your prayers. While I know that you are humbled by this ongoing blessing to the world, please stay within yourself and carry-on as though no one is watching. This is how your poise is made worthy of the Humble Servant who offers you the Bread of Life. It is imperative that you see in yourself the maturity that for so long has been the hallmark of Jesus in Creation. This, My son, is the origin of your knowledge of human life and the source of the internal joy by which you are living today. I come to you on this night to accompany your prayers with My intercession before God because I have found great Wisdom in knowing Him. He created Me with an Immaculate Soul, and it is this perfection that I am sharing with you now. Whenever you lift high the Cross and the Mother of the Messiah who was Crucified there, you are elevating the Divine Truth before men. Even those who despise you for attempting to persuade them to live by the Holy Gospel will one day make the transformation that took Saul (of Tarsus, Acts 9:1-30, 22:3) to become Saint Paul. If someone approached you and asked you to offer a spiritual review of the past six days, what would you tell them about your life? You know that I often ask your impression of the reflections of those with whom you interact. It is extremely kind that you offered a complimentary book to My humble priests. Thank you, My son, for bearing the message of Good News to My little children everywhere! And, thank you for consoling your brother upon the request that was made of him yesterday. I believe that you recognize by now that it was difficult for him. Your prayers together removed any semblance of pain from his memory. Will you continue to live in the confidence that you have gained by trusting your faith? I know you will."

Sunday, August 25, 2002
1:48 p.m.

"There, there, My little children, I have deigned to beseech the God of your fathers to bless you with the powerful impressions of His Divine Love upon your hearts. Always remain steadfast in your mission to proclaim the Good News of Jesus around the globe because this is what the Son of Man gives as your lifelong pursuit. These are happy days that you will remember as long as you live. Why? Because you are being despised and rejected among men, and you will hereafter be known in Heaven and on Earth as soldiers and warriors against the spiritual poverty and secular indifference that is causing so much pain, agony, grief, and sadness all across the world. The Truth is the freedom that every soul must seek, the Truth of God which has wrapped you in the majesty of His Grace. Thank you for persisting in reaching for Heaven inside your hearts and persuading your brethren to join in your presence there. Today, I come to lift your spirits into the joy that you have been accorded by the Light of My Son's Paschal Resurrection. I am your Mother, and also the Mother of your Teacher. There is a whirlwind of doubt that surrounds the Truth of Christianity by the naysayers in your midst. Do not listen to their pleas for your return to earthly normalcy, for such is not the path to the Kingdom of God. When you glorify the Messiah who died on the Cross to save humanity from eternal perdition, you are telling Creation that you belong to Heaven. In this is your hope, and in this shall you be forever blessed. My

Special son, I come especially to remind you how pleased I am that you are continuing the journey of holiness by directing My messages to humanity through your writings and the series of intercessions you will release in AD 2005. While this may seem a long time from now, think about how far you have come in twelve years. I wish for you to know that you were led yesterday to the passage from My May 18, 1991 message for a specific reason. Do you recall the one? Please refer to the reading from the Sacred Scriptures of Isaiah 22:19. Consider the fall of Adam and Eve from the Garden of Eden. Where did they go? This is extremely important. Do you believe that once they were exiled that they had any recollection of the brilliant Divinity of Heaven? Yes, their souls surely could not lose the vision of the Paradise they lost. However, what of their capacity to explain it to their successors and descendants? They were unable to describe it in mortal terms, as though they had never seen it before. The point is not only what I have previously said, but what it means for all the world as the End Times expire. Every soul created by God saw His beatific vision before they were incarnately placed in their mother's womb. But, what is the wage of sin? What is the effect of the original sin of Adam and Eve? That you would be placed in their shadow until you shall be delivered through the Blood of the Cross to the Mansions of Paradise. In other words, you will recognize the God you have not seen because you will be saintly in His sight. This is a supernatural manifestation for which many Christians have prayed, but only few understand before they die. I am telling you so you can explain it to humanity at a later date, to give masses of sinners new hope in their resurrection from the grave through the power of the Cross and the Mystery of Easter. The concept of time is the factor that divides, separates, and prohibits humanity from seeing this with accuracy. But, with faith, with unifying faith in the Son of Man, all the world can come to this Truth before anyone else should die! This is the gift that has been given to you, the strength of your faith, because you have asked Jesus to grant it. He is the King who loves you beyond any boundaries. I know that you understand this, and I hope with great anticipation that many hundreds-of-thousands will learn it from you. Tell them that I told you about it on this day in the year AD 2002. What can you say to indicate your comprehension? That was a good description, but there will be many who will disagree with your premise. Do you know on what basis? You see the fallacious conclusions about which they will argue until My miraculous sign appears in Medjugorje. It shall not be much longer in coming! I know that this will require your further patience. How long can you be patient? Are you sure? Are you telling Me that I need not ask you to research the meaning of patience in your dictionary? It is a nice Sunday afternoon, and I wish for you and your brother to enjoy it. Thank you for your holy prayers. It will be a happy perpetuity when we sit together in Heaven and recount the miracles that are unfolding before you now. Please pray for the unborn."

Sunday, September 1, 2002
2:33 p.m.

"We wish for every child of God to become acquainted with the sacrifices that are asked of them to better understand the meaning of Beatific Love. Why? Because the Sorrowful Crucifixion of Jesus is the fullness of your comprehension of the perfection you require to be remade into His likeness, a likeness of which you have never before known in your mortal years. This is what God seeks of you while you pursue His pathways of righteousness, to know with the abundance of Light that your homeland is His Kingdom of Love that lives inside your hearts and beyond the Firmament in simultaneous Truth. I have told you that I cannot make you happy in this life, but I can instill your hearts with the expectation that eternal happiness is yours in the Resurrection of My Son. If you will allow Me to take you by the hand and deliver you to Him, He will bathe you in the Blood of His Sacrifice and make you presentable to the Father. We pray that millions will realize that this is a prefigured Absolution portioned through profoundly Sacred Mysteries. When you pray as you have, you know that these things are true. My children, many have been the times when you were lonely or felt neglected and abandoned. This is the adverse ramification of your brothers and sisters failing to embrace you with the blessing of Divine Love. Anyone has the capacity to live in unending peace if only they will allow the Holy Spirit to lead and guide them to their Salvation beyond the parameters of the Earth. Rest assured that there is gladness in this! Those who are despondent must raise their hopes in faith to the Savior of the world, for He is their benefaction of healing and Grace. Those who are huddling in masses around the globe and societies of people who are living beneath the oppression of dictators and savages must come to believe in the gift of life hereafter, and that the purpose of God to set them free will come to pass in their day. While the Americas speak of wars and destruction, the Son of Man is calling them to diplomacy and reconciliation. A weekend has come in the United States when its citizens are honoring the practical aspects of manual labor. What does this mean? Are there any souls left who understand that physical chores are meant for securing the blessings of God and not the accumulation of incalculable new wealth? Have the labors of men's hands been transformed from feeding their children nourishment and sensible morality into performing whatever misdeeds are necessary to subjugate and conquer their neighbors and friends? Indeed, the Earth is in labor from the grief of its unwholesome lack of spirituality. Creation is groaning in pain because of the errors of sinful men. The globe is burdened by injustice, greed, lust, arrogance, and ignorance of the Truth. I urge My children to pray for those who live in such obstinance against the Kingdom of God, and to seek justice in His Sacred Heart. There is no doubt that this requires strength and courage, and they are procured and retained through the power of the Holy Cross. I would like to speak to you for three and four hours at a time, but there is too much to accomplish in between so the Father will know that our deeds are as genuine in purpose as our petitions. I enter this world with the immense desire that My children will take hope in the Wisdom that peace is nigh at hand, and that those who are violating it so recklessly are being brought once and for all before the Mother of God. My admonishments are not a call for retribution against those who have sinned, but that Jesus will have Mercy upon the ones who repent. Every creature beneath the skies has a purpose that is divinely inspired to enhance the goodness of Heaven's Supernal Love. The malfeasances of those who reject Jesus are the reason why there are heated battles still to come.

My Special son, how many times have I told you that I love you, and that you are the living image of Jesus? How much more can I say to explain that your sacrifices are a precise replica of the benisons of Heaven upon the suffering in the world? And, still, I desire to remind you again today. You are becoming more mellow as you mature in years because you know which battles are worth the fight for the advancement of the conversion of humanity. Will you allow Me to tell you how important it is for you to emphasize this course? There are countless ways to prove beyond any refutation that My messages are authentic. But, your heart asks the same question as Mine; why must this be necessary? Why cannot others live the same faith that gives you hope? They are given opportunities aplenty to be obedient to Me, but they have declined on numerous occasions. They may not always realize they are doing it, but time will be their prosecution in the end. I tell you again, they cannot run from My arms quickly enough to prohibit My reaching their souls. I planned to remind you today of the Feast of the Assumption in 1989. As morning broke, you had only hours before been standing on the mountaintop of Medjugorje while I spoke to the seers there. The feeling that overwhelmed you at that moment is the same impassioned Grace that will envelope every soul who encounters your faith before the Earth is through. There is no doubt that many will require intense signs and wonders, and they will receive them because Jesus loves them. Some of the signs will be large in nature, others small, and many will be subtle hints hidden in their hearts. But, the conclusion of their contemplations will be the same, that Jesus' Crucifixion and Resurrection from the Sepulcher are the only things they need to know to be successful in this life and in their storied destiny beyond the grave. Indeed, what was the date when you and your brother crossed the Atlantic to pray in Medjugorje in 1989? December 4. There is a book beneath the cloth beside you. Tell Me what was the number of that day of the year? Day 338. And, what was the number of the day of the Feast about which I have spoken today, that of the Assumption? It is 227. How many days passed from that date until December 4, 1989? Yes, 111. This is a sign of significance that has been celebrated so many times in our messages since February 22, 1991. Do you remember when it appeared through the vision that your brother had in the beginning? You recorded it in your first Diary. Here, you see another reason for this signature. Please do not spend any more time searching for signs because you have much work to do. I will refer to them along the way, and this one is highly significant to you and your brother. I also see that you are mailing your books to those who have shown their support for My priests. This is a noble gesture on your part. Did you know that I was watching your life so closely? This is My house where the origin of the conversion of so many lost sinners has occurred. You will be comfortable here for months to come. I will tell you when it will be necessary to take residence elsewhere, but you will not be required to relinquish possession of this one unless it is something you desire to do."

Sunday, September 8, 2002
2:04 p.m.

"Gracious goodness, what a welcome birthday surprise! How I wish for you to protract your prayers with such love and devotion for God, and in obedience to His Divine Will. In Excelsus! Please recite your most powerful prayers with Me. All the Heavens are shouting Amen! This is the Glory of perfection because your humble supplications to Jesus have taken you to the highest summits of prophetic Truth. My pretty ones, every aspect of your holiness resides in your participation in the goodness that you are sharing with Me. No one has given Me a greater gift on the occasion of the celebration of My Birth. Thank you! We journey together along the paths of God's Justice because you foster the faithful deployment of His timeless Will. Today, therefore, is reason to rejoice in the sustenance of life, the infinity of Grace, the excellency of submission, the Glory of Jesus' Resurrection, and the eloquence of lasting peace. My children, please remember this moment you have afforded Me and the Hosts of Paradise because it will be a measure of strength for others to choose Salvation over the condemnation of their souls. You exist within the favor of the creative Being of Jesus when you offer yourselves in obedience to the Holy Cross. Why? Because He perceives your image of Him as another gift to humanity as has been foretold on numerous occasions throughout the Sacred Scriptures. Should God have reason to celebrate His own Wisdom in deigning My Birth to the nations? The answer is resoundingly affirmative. When we pray together, we ignite flames of righteousness around the globe. We instill a fervor in the Angels and Saints to intercede on behalf of sinners everywhere. We muster the grand marshaling of forces for goodness in places where no Light has ever shined. This, My lambs, is a revelation of the Kingdom you serve when you submit as you have today. Your Christian petitions are benedictions upon the lost and forsaken. Your faith is unimpeachable because you allow it to grow into an indomitable reflection of the presence of God. Thank you! It is true that you do not know the goodness that you are bringing to the Earth. My children, I present the Messiah of earthly domains and dying men.

I AM! I am your Savior and King, the Most High Priest, the Prophet of all Eternal Love, the Light of the World, the Giver and Taker of Life, and the Divine Mercy for which humanity is bleeding! I AM LOVE! To My Special Fathom—My perfect power rests in you forevermore! Amen! The gift you have given to My Mother on this Feast is greater than any priest could afford. You are the depths of obedience and Love! Be satisfied in knowing that I AM your God. We will celebrate together uniquely the Divine Triumph of the Immaculate Heart of our Mother in Heaven very soon! I love you. I love you. Thank you for taking care of My little Chosen one. Be happy! ...your Jesus.

This has been a gift not only for you, but for Me as well. I am happy when My Son speaks to you in such encouraging ways. I know that it strengthens your resolve and keeps your hopes alive that your works in Him are never in vain. I am called Blessed because of the gifts from God that are a fruit of the Nativity of My Son, and all these blessings I forthrightly dispense to you. This is not only a day of celebration, it is a time of rejuvenation for those who come to the Cross because of your untiring labors. This is why I called the priest from India to reach you; we know that you will accept your part of the work that Jesus has given through him. In your service, you have placed a framework into action by which the poor can be nourished, the ignorant brought to understanding of the meaning of life, and those who are far from God's Grace can be delivered to the origin of pardon and peace. Thank you, again!

I wish to take you into My confidence during our messages so that you will embrace My vision of hope for humanity. Trusting and falling deeply in love with God's Kingdom requires bravery in battle, escaping the corrupting gravitation of the Earth, and the moral equivalent of spiritual martyrdom. This is how towering cathedrals are first sighted inside the human heart and built on the community of love that is shared by those who are linked by ingenious faith—elegant, ornate, spiring, and unique; their designers, builders, pastors, and parishioners are all inebriated by God's Grace; their forbears and benefactors struck by divinity and led by the awesome wonder of the Most Blessed Trinity. I urge you to remember them when your thoughts grow weary from the world's insistence, and be strong because they were strong. My children, just because you see indistinctly does not imply that you must see ambiguously. There is nothing vague about the holiness required to usher you to the threshold of Heaven before taking your final earthly bow. The Lord knows that you often struggle with life's militance in abject ways, and that you are presiding over a western civilization whose belief system is on the brink of collapse. You must do everything in your power to keep your faith alive because it is a combustible essence of hope and excitement that renders you over-prepared for the welcome conflagration of the ages. It is entirely legitimate speech to claim that the conversion of the heart to spiritual enlightenment is akin to an internal holocaust whereby everything contradictory to the refinement of the conscience is incinerated and disinherited by irrefutable Truth. And, you emerge from this experience with such face-blushing innocence that it takes the Angels by surprise, giving you an infusion of foreknowledge about the new rendition of the Earth which the Holy Spirit revisits and then moves on, but never departs. It is in this battleground vernacular that you are summoned to fight the good fight in the shadow of Saint Timothy. Anything that is sour, rancid, or putrid evolves from the implicit presence of the world's corruption, the rottening of something previously fresh and well-preserved. This is what has happened to the morality of humankind. What was once considered to be conscientious propriety has again eroded into the heathenism of prehistoric times. This is an unacceptable way for humanity to live, and I have come seeking your aid to manifest a change. There is uncertainty in the future about which the Saints and Angels are praying, and the way it unfolds is contingent upon this and the supplications of Christians around the globe who live in sequestered places, those who are vowing to make the world more holy, not knowing how it will be done. This is the Earth's epilogue that Jesus is waiting to reveal. The Will of the Father shall be sustained! Everything is on course; your lives are playing-out as He ordained. You see omens of this wherever you go. I was amused by your reaction to the human lips on the automobile a few days ago. Jesus wants you to realize that He is with you in ways you cannot imagine."

(I picked Timothy up after work on the way to attend Holy Mass at the Cathedral of the Immaculate Conception in Springfield, Illinois on September 5, 2002. I was being comical as we drove, forming my hand into the shape of a mouth and acting as if it was speaking. Tim saw my ventriloquism and said, 'It doesn't have any lips.' At that moment, I looked into my rear view mirror, and a white Volkswagen Beetle pulled into traffic right behind us with a giant set of red lips painted on the hood. I told him to look out the window. When he did, he nearly fell out of his seat.)

"I have completed My message for today. You have given Me a birthday that I will long remember."

Saturday, September 14, 2002
Feast of the Triumph of the Holy Cross
2:59 p.m.

"A cornucopia of eternal blessings awaits those who tender their hearts and minds to the Divine Mercy of Jesus, and this is the hour of another day when He asks billions to do so. You live on an Earth that is struggling to comprehend the significance of life because too many are defying God's principles of Truth while demanding that He speak in more discernable terms. I assure you that the Holy Spirit is alive and flourishing in the servants of the Church. I wish that in honor of My Immaculate Heart that untold numbers of sinners will humble themselves and come to the Living Water. When we pray together today, My children, let this be our petition to My Son. The question of the revelations which have yet to be reconciled to the universe are of little consequence when one considers that there are only few who have accepted the Virtues previously divulged. Will you join Me in praying that sinners everywhere will see their way clear to bowing in deference to the Holy Cross and live in submission to the Will of the Father? We gather to pray during this instance of joy, the Feast of the Triumph of the Holy Cross. The Cross is the summit of human joy because it is your reunion with God. The Light that is projected from Jesus' Crucifixion illuminates the eyes of every sinner to see their path to sanctification in Him, and it begins with the repentance of the heart. My dear children, I always speak of the heart because it is the source from which all supplications must be lifted, lest they be only tedious strains with no spiritual pursuance. I say to you, the heart contains the power humanity requires to alter the course of history and forestall the errors to come. Without the sentiments of prudent prayer from the center of the heart, your atonement with the Savior of the world is incomplete. My Special son, this is a good day because of the approaches you make to those who despise you. Do not fear for them; do not be offended, and most of all, do not dwell on their frailties because they are consumed by their collective collusion here on Earth. Let us refer to the statement that an individual made to you when you were attempting to console her during a time of mourning. *("I cannot endure any more of your abuse.")* What she implied was that she did not wish to be reminded of how much she loathes you. This is an undue oppression that she has placed upon herself, having nothing to do with anything you might have done to offend her. God is allowing you to see this because He wants you to observe an example of millions of other sinners in her frame of mind. Do you recognize that they blame their hatred on the victims they abhor? This is a unique perspective by which you comprehend the meaning of '...heal thyself.' Such people are embittered souls because they refuse to allow the Holy Spirit to do their bidding. They feel unjustified because Jesus has not destroyed you at their command. What an ironic, disingenuous, and sinful means they have of engaging the tenets of Christianity! These are the same people who castigate My Catholic priests, and who believe that any statement of compassion on their behalf is against the nature of God. They rightly call for the preservation of life in the womb, but then demand that it be taken in the name of penitential vengeance in state-sponsored execution chambers. Do you see these contradictions? This was the vexation that you saw in your estranged friend's face after Holy Mass, one of hypocrisy and exasperation. I remind humanity that this shall not stand! No child of Mine will be allowed to perpetuate behavior such as this. Whatever it takes to humble her heart and millions like her that God chooses to employ shall occur. Please remember that this is not brought in disdain, but by the purifying Mysteries of God's Divine Love.

(The woman to whom the Most Holy Virgin has referred who accosted my sincere attempts to offer her consolation was as of August 2007 in her final agony, suffering from the horrific effects of Alzheimer's disease. God's will is fulfilled. She no longer recalls the hatred she once had for my brother and me. The purification has occurred. We will now one day be in Heaven together playing as little children with no remembrance of any darkness.)

I see that you have been working with expedience to package your recent book for delivery to My priests, and to complete various projects at your home. How prettily you are writing *Babes in the Woods*. The first section of the opening chapter is overwhelmingly profound! And, the second half will be as beautiful because of the literary divineness that you and your brother are praying into being. Why, you might ask? Because when the rest of Creation sees what you have achieved for the Lord on behalf of His priests, children, and the whole economy of Christian Salvation, it will bring Him to the elation that you feel when you pray. I bid you to witness for Him as you have in the past, for *Babes in the Woods* will be another heart-touching book. I know this to be true because I have taught you to become an inspiring author. There are many auspicious things that will occur if you will take life one day at a time. You feel uplifted about what you are accomplishing because you anticipate the result of your labors, your prayers, and your life. Your piety, and that of your brother, is exemplary of the Saints. I do not say this with undue praise because I have no reason to patronize you. I am simply describing your life as God sees it. Please be thankful that He has made you so good because He is grateful that you have tendered your abundant will toward the advancement of His Kingdom. I assure you that the pages of *Babes in the Woods* will be worthy of every hour you invest in them. Could you have guessed that you would be such a prolific writer? You have witnessed the ability of God to make the manifestation you feared in your younger years to be a powerful weapon against evil in these times. Your book is being met with surprise, appreciation, and humility. It makes Me happy to bring you such good news, but this is something that I am not always able to do. Humanity will soon change, and you will see the goodness you have wrought. Please know that the Father places the world's suffering into perspective for the conversion of many to the Sacred Heart of Jesus. All else about the Earth you are writing with the help of the Dominion Angels. How you will enjoy seeing them when you come to Heaven! It is true that you know many of them already. Seeing is an effect of your faith, and you have seen through the power of your love the witness they are bearing for Jesus. Your little nephew is speaking from the heart of a child who will be transformed by the process of aging; he will be healed by the unfolding years, and his memories will be supplanted by new ones. It is obvious that you see Jesus in him. You have a tender and loving heart to identify with the things he is saying and the feelings of his own heart. The Son of Man wishes that people everywhere, regardless of age, would become like this. Please answer your own question for Me."

(Why is there so much difference in the conduct of little boys and girls?)

"It has everything to do with the intrinsic knowledge that young men will become providers in their time. They internalize this by knowing that they will someday work outdoors with their hands, by seeing the stately grace and strength of animals, by recognizing and feeling the affections of their mothers, and being curious enough to ask questions about the Truth. All of these things, along with your prayers to make your nephew a humble child, contributed to the making of the little boy you see today. This proves that no one is born with a propensity to commit sin or choose to behave in any way that is contrary to the wishes of God. Corruption is learned from the environment, even the desires that afflict people who feel provoked to act upon their erroneous perceptions. Prayer from the heart alleviates these problems. Remember always that your work for Jesus is making Creation a much holier place, and that your efforts for the awakening, conversion, and Salvation of the vaulted human family will be triply rewarded by the Father, the Son, and the Holy Spirit."

Sunday, September 22, 2002
2:04 p.m.

"When you cannot conceive the phrases to express your love for Jesus and your desire to serve humanity to the summit of their dreams, please call upon your Mother for help because I can read the impressions of your hearts. I am able to relate to My Son what My infant children are too young to utter in the simplicities of your faithfulness. We pray that more people will come to understand this, to call upon their Mother, Heaven's Lady of Perpetual Help, so that every sorrow can be extinguished from everyone's spirit. I plead with those who know Me to extol your love for Me to every land and upon every boardwalk. I know the Savior of humanity because He is **I AM** to whom I gave birth so that all who follow Him will be commenced to the Light of Paradise. I come to pray with you again today because I know of your needs, and I place the resolution to your problems before the Throne of God as you lay them upon the Altar of Sacrifice. When your prayers invoke the piety that Jesus teaches, no matter what miracles you desire, He will hear you and will respond. I know that there are times during your lives when you feel that prayer is not sufficient. There may be months and years when suffering continues without ease. Wars between nations and peoples regularly endure for decades. All of these are ameliorated in the Sacred Heart of Jesus if only those who are involved and afflicted will turn to Him. My children, My Holy hands are never idle in the works of Christ Jesus. I am listening, teaching, caressing, and nourishing the children of Earth throughout your lives. I bring you comfort and intercession from the Angels and the Communion of Saints to bless you where you uphold those things that elevate the Cross and enhance the Kingdom of God. Yes, I come to speak about the sacrifices you must make to ensure the dignity of your fellows; of helpless children, the lame and maligned, and the incarcerated wherever they may be. You live in an imperfect world, but it is being perfected by the conversion of millions to the Holy Cross and Jesus' Easter Resurrection. There will always be reason for you to pray until the Son of Man returns in Glory because you are participants in the fashioning of the Earth prior to His Dawn. Be assured that the darkness around you is dispelled by the power of the Holy Spirit in your hearts, your compassion for the weak, and in the ways you feed, clothe, shelter, and minister to His flock who are oftentimes downtrodden and broken in spirit. We not only see these things, we ask My Son to address them as in the decades of old through the Love of God in Him who has raised every rolling land that has seen fit to pronounce His Holy Name and implore Him to dispense His fond blessings. This is autumn where you live, My children, a time of harvest and thanksgiving. It is also a season every year for you to pause and realize the true spiritual quality of your faith. Where would you have procured the fruits of your labors had God not answered your prayers? How would your seeds have grown? This is the parable that I urge you to store deep inside your hearts as the Gateway of Eternity opens. When you sow goodness and friendship, they bloom through the splendor of Truth. Someday, all the Earth will be united in the Grace of Jesus' Cross, whereupon He has healed the nations under God. My dear children, He need not yet return for this to occur! You have been handed the tools for this; and they are faith, hope, prayer, unity, decency, and true conviction in the Virtues of Salvation. I assure you that the world as you know it can be transformed into the beauty of Paradise if everyone will extol the Messianic

Gospel. Your transfer to Heaven will be the grand and noble induction into a blissfulness that many of you already foresee. Be generous to the Lord, and He will place you at the center of this exultation when you surrender your souls after your mortal years. My counsel is wise because I am the Lady of Wisdom who has been vested with the Grace to teach you to become like Jesus.

    My loyal sons, I am elated that you are praying with Me today. I thank you for remaining strong in demanding integrity from those in your midst, even the members of your immediate families. Jesus has always taught that His Truth will divide father from son and mother from daughter; and these times are no different from when the Holy Spirit authored these words. Your hearts cannot be broken if you remain steadfast in hope because you will know that your souls are moving through time to their destination of joy in the House of the Lord. These are days of intense happiness for Heaven because we see your way of life. The passing of your birthday on Friday did not find you reveling with carousers like many other people. You met with a Roman Catholic priest from half-a-world away to see how your works can feed starving children and enrich them with a proper education so they can lead self-sustaining lives. Your heart is placed precisely at the center of this Truth. Also, remember to be congenial with your parents when they call upon your spiritual help. There will come such a day. I know that you love them as wholeheartedly as the Saints you have admired. This process has been difficult for them because they have not been privy to the information you have received. They, like several others who have read your books and perused your website, find it difficult to accept the authenticity of the revelations you are claiming. None of this will impede your progress; it will enhance it, just as My Marian apparitions and shrines around the globe have mystically prevailed. All of this is unfolding as it should. I see that your book *Babes in the Woods* is progressing well; it is an epochal manuscript. It is by your love that this is happening, and Jesus is responding by multiplying the expanse of your outreach to people everywhere. My son, you cradle this esteem because you have allowed the Holy Paraclete to light upon your soul in the gentleness of your heart. Do you remember this from your first thirty messages of 1991? The Holy Spirit brings peace and the kindness of the Lord to those who are devoted to Him. He will not barge through any door of opposition to His Grace. By your subservient example, persistence and patience, you will see humanity embrace the piety that you have hailed in your home, your city, this nation, and across the arching hemispheres. Paradise will encompass the Earth when the rest of your brothers and sisters are converted to the perfection of the Love that Jesus manifested when He was born, Crucified, and raised from the Tomb. The deference of the people around you is where the answer to your question resides, and you will not have to wait until your death to hear their collective response."

Sunday, September 29, 2002
9:25 a.m.

"My dear children, it gives Me great joy to pray with you on this day which is given to your devotion to the Angels. Please remember that their love for you is a powerful influence on your journey to Salvation. I delight in speaking about the conversion of humanity through the Holy Cross because My messages are the hinges upon which the future of many lost souls is suspended. Whether they turn to Jesus for Redemption or another way is determined by how well they listen to My call. Thank you for making My intercession so remedial to those who hunger for faith as My Son nourishes them through the unearthly Wisdom that I place in the supernatural context of your messages. My children, please never believe that this is a period of misfortune or assume that My messages, as poignant as some may be, are not comprised of the subsistence of Divine Providence. God chooses whatever venue at His discretion to communicate the Sacred Mysteries of human Salvation to the world, about Truth, repentance, and Eternal Life. I assure you that there are many wanton ways of misguided atheists who try to inhibit our work for Jesus, but none of them will succeed. You are shielded with piety beneath My Holy Mantle, and you should remember this as long as you live. I transfer Jesus' primordial ingenuity to you so that your instruction will be for the benefit of the entire human race. I invite you to never forget the welcoming way that the Holy Spirit enters your conscience. The impassioned letters of Saint Paul were written so that when they are read, they resound as providentially as valedictory speeches delivered before crowds of millions. His mission was not only to evangelize the Gospel, but to issue a warning to everyone who would hear that if you persecute someone's faith or deprive someone of their basic human dignity, there will be little hope for your final Redemption, short of a radical reorientation of your heart. Truly, if anyone knew about this transformation, it was Saint Paul. He learned what it meant to sabotage one's own well-being by failing to recognize the hand and Spirit of the Lord in all beatific works. I ask you not to wait until Heaven's audible voice magnifies Mine to stop you in your tracks and calls you to reverse course, for this has already come through your faith. The punishment that is due humanity because of your reluctance to repent is being extenuated during these present times so that My intercession can be manifested. Jesus realizes that there are multiple layers of insensitivity that the Holy Spirit must penetrate to soften your hardened hearts. While the people of the United States feel dour, glum, and violated because human diversity has permeated deep into your neighborhoods, the Lord expects you to welcome strangers with open arms, for many of them bear allegiance to the Roman Catholic Church and loyalty and affection for the Holy Father, Pope Juan Pablo II. You need them to energize your willingness to accept Jesus and overcome the syndrome of incompleteness by which you exist in exile. Your faith is emboldened by the Lord's Grace, by the mission of the Church, and through the gift-giving blessings of the Holy Spirit residing in you, instilling the redeeming attributes that Jesus prefers in His new disciples. Rather than perceive life as an arduous struggle for meaning, you are beginning to see that it is in many ways like a dramatic pause before the New Jerusalem's Church Triumphant takes over. Remember that God's call is not a forced indoctrination because you have the will to decline, but you stand to perish in that rejection. My lambs, it requires more than lackadaisical intent to effect the riddance of the complicities of your misgivings, errors, and transgressions. Jesus places at your disposal galleries of icons, photographs, statues, Rosaries, chaplets, holy water, and printed books and literature to augment your sanctification through the Holy Sacrifice of the Mass, the Sacred Scriptures, the Crucifix, the Catechism, the Litanies, sound doctrines, dogmas, and prudent theology. You are not weaponless in your fight for holiness. There will come a moment when your strains of language and fashions of tongues will die because they will no longer be relevant; all diction and understanding will be centered in the unspeakable Glory of all the futures combined in one Eternity that will engulf them in Truth.

    My Special son, I come to speak to you specifically because of the gratitude I have for your work, especially Friday evening. If only you knew what good has been done, you would leap for joy in the sight of the Angels to whom the Poor Clare Nuns consecrated you and your brother last year. I wish to address in detail some of the events that occurred with specificity to allow your soul to realize that this is founded in God's Plan. I am going to ask you a series of questions that will at first seem unrelated, and you will thereafter know why. *(The Holy Mother spoke confidentially.)* You can see that the signs have indicated that you were in the proper place at the right time, with the particular people I asked you to encounter. What do you suppose was the overall purpose of that evening? Think about the people you met, what each of their lives had in common, and the reasons they traveled to that location that night. The fact that their lives were torn apart and their hearts devastated is the key. They were attempting to secure some semblance of affection, interaction, and newness. Yes, all of these are correct. You greeted your brother-in-law's former brother-in-law; you consoled a disabled Korean War veteran and a friend from your youth whose life has been a tragedy of errors; and you also comforted the girl to whom you were speaking. Everything you did was of the princely beauty of God's Peace. Thank you for blessing their suffering with the presence of the Holy Spirit in your heart. The demons mentioned in the Scriptures also include interior ones. They are the malefactors that harm insecure people the most. I wish for you to offer your reparative prayers for their healing, reorientation, and well-being; and I am teaching you how. Thank you for allowing Me to be your Mother and teacher."

Sunday, October 6, 2002
3:33 p.m.

"The intentional evangelization of the Holy Gospel of Christ Jesus implies that your heart be open to receive the gift of miracles. I ask you to remember that many are called, but only few are chosen. It is the select among the tormented who stand above the rest and announce their purpose before the nations because, absent the faith of many, these messengers still proclaim the declarations of the Truth of the Salvation of men. When you contemplate that the meaning of human life is to prepare you to receive the prize of Paradise, it becomes ingrained in your consciousness to strive for the holiness that will take you there. Why? Because the mortal world cannot provide the elevation you need to understand the afterlife. No superfluous intellectual discourse can decipher the reasons why God would permit His only begotten Son to be so tortured, scourged, and Crucified in order to absolve an orb of sinners who wish to be disassociated from the Love He came to proclaim. My children, will you not continue stoutly with Me in praying for the conversion of lost societies? We must be prudent in our teachings, persistent in our supplications, and determined that we shall succeed; Me as the Matriarch of Redemption, and you as the humble absolved. I ask only the opportunity to be heard by the masses, to be understood with clarity by parochial theologians, and cherished by the brokenhearted. It has been said in years-past that these are the times that try men's souls. Indeed, this is conversely the moment when many will be lifted to the dignity of Salvation in the Blood of My Son upon the Holy Cross! Wherever you see such men who are searching for the significance of life and the unseen hereafter, it is entirely appropriate to urge them to pray for stronger faith. Believing that Jesus has died for the sins of humanity is of the highest priority in the virtuousness of Love. Knowing that your souls have been bathed in the Blood of the Cross is the reason why God gave you the capacity to render your noblest judgements. When you pray together as pious people belonging to Christ, please never cower to His betrayers. I ask you to elevate one another in His memory, to perceive your neighbors in the way that you wish God to look upon you, and serve them as you wish to be served at the Banquet Table in Heaven. Now that the Son of Man has been Resurrected from the Tomb, you need not be so afraid. You can strike-out with the prevalence of righteousness in His Scepter and pulverize His enemies. Through your Christian love, you can admonish those who are distant from the perfection He requires of His brothers from the days of old. There is no need to feel inferior or any reason to assume that you may appear like weaklings before a counsel of secular tyrants. Your peace lives within you because Jesus is present there. I urge you to wield the domination of His Kingdom from within your hearts! Little ones, as you proceed into the future, know that this has been a period of revelation on the road to your seamless unity in the benignity of God. You might falter and fail once in awhile, but you will not be defeated or rendered void of your vision of the greatness of Heaven. These are the hours of your years when you are discovering the motives of God for placing you on Earth. It has not been solely to banish you from His sacred presence because of the original errors of Adam and Eve. It is that you can become His warriors and messengers among others who have been banned, but who refuse to defer to His Kingship. Be their reason to crave the flavor of the Victory of Salvation. Be their example of what the simplicity of forgiveness is about. There is no need to move mountains in order to retrieve lost souls. When you imitate Jesus' Love in the way He asks, those you have converted will relocate them for you. The fullness of His Light can never be obstructed by the adversaries of your faith. So, pray, pray, pray that all the world will pray, and that this human life in which you discover yourselves will be fuller, holier, and happier for everyone who succeeds you in the dignity and poise of your Roman Catholic beliefs. It is true that there is great profundity in the messages I have offered through the ages, but their essence has always been the same. Be simpler and gentler, and know that Jesus is the Lord on the Earth, the Son of the Creator, and the Man-God whom humanity owes their oathed allegiance. When I gave Him birth in Bethlehem, it was a jubilation more magnificent than women could know because I knew that the Offspring from My Virgin Womb brought the renewal of Creation, the same Creation to whom I am speaking from the confines of this little prayer room in Springfield, Illinois. I herald the American people, the quadrants north, south, east and west, and to every race within the sound of My voice, that Emmanuel will soon return! I ask you to light your lamps with holiness and go out to greet Him in the company of the Angels and Saints. Let your love for Jesus be your vision, and approach Him in the trust that He has reclaimed you for the God of your fathers. This is the reason for your waking in the morning, the words of your mouths, and the meditations in your hearts.

  My Special son, it gives Me the sensation of honor and relief that you and your brother have been chosen to participate in this process because you are so obedient to My Immaculate Heart. You have never failed to accept what I have asked; you have never wavered in your actions on behalf of the suffering, and your intentions have always been in compliance with Mine. You are appreciated for these things in ways much deeper than you know. And, My holiness shines more fluently throughout Creation because you are reflecting the Love of Jesus for Me. I pray with you so our goals remain on course. As you will review during the Holy Sacrifice of the Mass next week, 'many are called, but only few are chosen.' You are among the latter who have never said a discordant word to the calling of the heart that Jesus seeks. Thank you. You have wondered why so many people become infatuated with scandals of the flesh. It is because they decline to adopt sound Christian principles or realize that the body's misuse maligns the dignity of the spiritual purity of the Kingdom of God. Can you see why, given the reason that indulging in the flesh is so inebriating to the senses, that it gives false impressions to the heart? Such is only an illusion, and is why it is important for everyone to be sown to the Spirit instead. There is no fulfillment in sins of the flesh because the mortal frame of humankind is destined for the dust. Only your transparent souls will pass into the boundless Light of Eternity."

Sunday, October 13, 2002
1:11 p.m.

"70,000. That is how many were there. And, to this day, the miraculous impressions of the Sacred Heart of Jesus continue to shower upon the Earth the Truth of His valorous Love. I ask the world of men to remember that no one can recover their vision without having first been blind; no one can be healed unless they have been broken, and only the lost can be found and returned to the Shepherd for guidance, nourishment, and peace. Why will humanity not turn in suppliance and holiness to the God of Dominion for this new opportunity to be regained? Yes, 70,000 were there that day. In the wondrous skies above Fatima, all who were gathered prayed that this would be a fresh beginning for them, and yet not their last, for God was present among them as He is today, bridging the chasm between ignorance and genius, making hay of the best of times for the millions who love Him, bringing Salvation to His people with thankful tears in His eyes, lavishingly reigning over Creation with gifts of power; delivering, purifying, and bestowing great distinction among the nations, and reveling the Kingdom of Everlasting Life to be grasped and owned by those who repent. I watch the grandeur of the unfolding of the universe with glee because I know the prowess of the Sacred Heart who has enveloped His landscapes with Truth. I kneel beside the Altar of Sacrifice knowing that My little children are coming home through the Eucharistic King. I am sorrowful that He died, elated that He was raised from among the dead, and given endless joy that Heaven will be filled with souls whom He sacrificed His Life to Redeem. There is an entire galaxy of persistence that keeps enjoining your hearts, begging those who do not know their Salvation in the Blood of the Cross to be converted to Him. I have asked you to '...be people.' I am today asking you to '...be Divine people.' My children, even as I have been speaking to you for generations, the Earth itself has been expiring too. The time has come for all who will one-day enter Paradise to begin that process headlong. Thank you for asking God through your petitions for the transformation of humanity to the Cross, for still an unwary majority of the population of the Earth does not know who their Savior is. This is why our work for Christianity must proceed unmolested and with great courage from you. What were My signs and requests during the events of Fatima? Has the world answered the call to prayer, piety, sacrifice, selflessness, penance, recitation of the Sacred Mysteries of the Rosary, and regular attendance at the Holy Sacrifice of the Mass? Does the center of the human heart for each and everyone reflect the desire to know Jesus from the unworldly side? Are there wars among men, and rumors of more; and people who are neglected, despised, cast-out, and killed in the womb? Indeed, are there broken spirits in your midst who have no peace inside because they refuse to accept the blessings and Fruits of the Holy Spirit? The essence of My questioning, My children, is centered upon whether the Love of God has been accepted and practiced in the ways which are delineated in the Holy Scriptures. When you see conflicts between materialism and the practice of greed, there will continue to be wars. If a nation of people has been stripped of its homeland, there will be battles aplenty. And, My little ones, none of this will cease until they who are dying on the battlefields of Earth come before the Cross for justification in the Lord. Let us pray for this, that every world conflict will end in the swift resolution of Christianity. Thereafter, the globe will be poised for the Return of the Son of Man in the way that the Dove of Peace lights on a cliff in mid-afternoon. It is still dark in the world because only few will embrace the reflection of Jesus' Heart. We pray, My children. We must pray. We listen with awesome wonder what God will do next. Will He send the stars falling to the ground with brazen power and wipe-out His enemies brigades at a time? Did anything portend such a thing that men can remember? There were 70,000 pilgrims there that day. Will the Lord's Mercy be distended throughout Creation in such plentiful quantity that it will reach every soul who has tread mortal footprints on the Earth? Let us pray that it does, little ones! Let us pray that it does!

So, My Special one, it has come to this. You are My provocative worker of miracles amidst your brothers and sisters because your priorities are with God, and in Christ Jesus, and fully in union with the Holy Spirit. You are helping Him reign! You are opening the doorways of endless opportunities for Him to reach those who will not search for Him in return. In essence, you are the response of Jesus to their hopes for change. You hail His Truth, the excellent fount of perfect contentment that heals the suffering. You are the penetrating kindness in the 21st century that Jesus was for those in the first. And, you are so loved, so appreciated, and so rewarded that you too will be taken aback by the kindness of God to repay you a hundredfold. Why do I weep; why must I persist in trying? Because sooner or later, the entire Earth will realize where true greatness resides. It is seen in the half-open eyes of newborn little children and the wincing frailties of the old. It is found in the elegance of the mountaintops and the prismic colors of the rains that shower upon those who are parched below. Indeed, true greatness resides in what God calls Justice, when those who should be justly recognized are given their due, when former presidents receive the Nobel Prize, when popes are lifted high above the secular void, and when the smallest ounce of dignity remains holy and sacred in the human heart where it belongs. These are the figs of greatness from whence humankind has come, climbing inexorably out of the pit of despair and into the fullness of joy. I tell you and the rest of the world that I harbor these things in My Crown. I hold the answer to every prayer ever lifted in the cradle of My arms. My Special son, I bear Jesus before humanity as the reason for life! I hold Him for you, for every orphan who was ever given to Me, for each and every human being who looked-up at the skies and wished for the purpose of their 'being' to descend from Heaven. The cold darkness around you and the vacuum of the Earth's lack of spiritualism will come to an end. The effects of the secular elitists who control the agenda of the day will close, and they will lay lifeless before Jesus; defeated, expired, converted, and regained. I promise that this is true, and that it will occur in the sight of all creatures. Thank you for allowing Me to speak to you. Your Apostolate has been well planned with perseverance and a great deal of hard work; and it will capture the results you desire. I will remain beside your sister and extend My hands in blessing above her forever. Please do not worry. This is more a moment of thanksgiving than anxiety because you live in a nation where such patients routinely survive. I further remind you that I am praying for your prodigal friends, but they are defying the willingness of the Holy Paraclete to infiltrate their hearts. They know exactly what they are doing. Only few spurn the Kingdom of Salvation without realizing it. And, what do they do next? They complain that their lives are a bed of nails and claim that they lack the strength to get up. It is their burden of sins that holds them down. You stand by purity and Truth, neither of which is popular in America. Many are called, but only few are chosen. 70,000. That is how many were there."

Sunday, October 20, 2002
10:08 a.m.

"Reminding you how hopeful are the Heavens that you will prevail in your obligations to Jesus, I come with His advocacy to acknowledge your struggles as a reminder of the Holy Cross which is glowing throughout time and space. This is a revealing period for all souls because, by your works, you are divulging to the nations the Wisdom that brings counterpoise and stability to your daily lives. My children, your existence has meaning in its every facet when you give its purpose to God. Your actions are in union with His sublimity when you pray from your hearts for the conversion of heathens, atheists, and heretics. Therefore, I hover before you today to pray that these things will come to pass because I love you, Jesus needs you, God commands it, and the Holy Spirit encourages us. When you lift the praises of Jesus in the Eucharistic Celebration, your words and melodies defer to His Kingdom and

His Will to be done on Earth as it is in Heaven. You tender the greatest part of your life to self-denial before the Sacred Altar, and the rest to commending lost sinners to His Divine Mercy. It is true that the liturgical seasons come and go; feast days are a cyclical observation, and these things do not appear to excite you. However, My children, every day is another leap where you are taken through time to sanctify the final ages, replete with the suffering you are asked to endure for the culmination of Creation in the Sacred Heart of My Son. There is wonder and majesty in your wayfaring faith because you are walking by a Light that is seen from within. You are called to comply with the statutes and ordinances of God that emerge from the core of your conscience. Indeed, you are summoned to embrace His Truth from Jesus who is not seen, but known to all by true forgiveness between men and their counterparts. We pray for the everlasting presence of God's Dominion to subdue the Earth and bathe it in a balm of peace. This should be the goal for all Christians, and it is. So, why is there talk about the prosecution of wars, hurling your enemies into the oceans, and threatening global conflicts for generations to come? I call upon My children because you are the offspring of Heaven who have been collected into the fold of the chosen in Jesus' Sacrifice on the Cross. When you elevate His Crucifixion before mankind, all will search for Him; they will anticipate His destiny of good will, and they will see the reason for the Truth that has given meaning to these years. This is a precursor to your Salvation that is dispensed to all whose hearts are open. What service would a reprimand be for a world in which the differences between good and evil are not understood? This is why you must listen and learn. And, it is the purpose of your meditations and contemplations during your Holy Hours before the Most Blessed Sacrament. By all means, it is overwhelmingly more profound than this because such dedication reaches the interior of the soul to provide fresh insight as to what the motivations of your friends and neighbors actually are. When you pray for one another and approach each other in mutual pardoning, you are speaking with the power of God within you, taking all who do not know Him to the mountaintop of Christian Truth. I have told you in times past that I pray with you when you kneel to ask for God's intervention. This will always be true, and you should trust that I magnify your petitions from My station in Paradise. Your Mother knows what rehabilitation you require to be refined in the purity of Divine Love. I understand the meaning of the Messianic parables in the Sacred Scriptures. I have known for endless time the purposes that God holds for every man. If this were not true, He would have told you. I speak to you because His Truth transcends all death and perishing. All Love is immortal! And, it is in this graceful Dominion that I plead for you to begin life anew inside your hearts and among your friends and enemies. Please accept My direction because you will ultimately need it at the end of your lives. If you want to know, the reason is that this is simply what Jesus desires. My Special son, thank you for your prayerfulness. Thank you for showing Satan that he wields no power. God's Eternal Kingdom lives in you with wholesomeness and integrity, and you know which prayers to offer for the advancement of His Word. I assure you that My eyes have shed tears of happiness as a result of your gifts to Him. This is a new beginning for millions of people around the globe because you have shown Jesus that you love and trust Him in ways in which countless others have refrained. I am elated to declare that you are My child, that you have been prayerfully accepting of your sacrifices while gaining more venues to propagate the intensity of your faith. I wish to tell you the most important thing I will say until the end of the Earth. No cause, action, presumption, intention, or implication carries the strength of Providence that you share when you pray as the Almighty Father asks. No matter what else you do for as long as you live, nothing will be as productive as this. And, I ask you to remember that you shall never succeed in any greater excellence than your recitation of the Most Holy Rosary. It is the spiritual suffix to the creation of humankind in the beatific image of Christ. It has been and will always be the source of the miraculous Grace by which you have lived. You glorify God through your prayers, and you have certainly advanced His Kingdom of immortal understanding across the Earth. I am humbled that you are willing to learn this from Me. I know your spirit! Let your passion for the Triumph of My Immaculate Heart proceed without interruption. It is your wish for the success of Jesus in the Kingdom for which you are striving, and He knows this well. All good things will transpire as prescribed and expected. Please know that your preeminent goal is to summon your most powerful prayers when you are called."

Friday, October 25, 2002
1:07 p.m.

"Within this hallowed prayer room come the petitions that cleanse the souls of humanity, and you are the children who are offering them. I hover around you and remain in appreciation to honor the fidelity of your faith, knowing that Jesus responds with His manifest blessing. Thank you for allowing Creation to become more holy by tendering your hearts and offering your lives to the breadth of this goodness. My children, while you do not know the reasons behind every sacrifice you are asked to make, the fruits of their invocation have made your souls like the Divinity of God. We opine and pray together toward the day when all peoples will kneel before the Cross in affection, faith, adoration, and contentment. It is when the human soul reaches tranquility with itself that the Kingdom of God flourishes among men. I appear today to wish you well and to remind you that the Angels and Saints are working for the spiritual reconfiguration of Creation. The thoughts that men are penning in their history books might be sufficient for archivists, but the sentiments that you hold for God contribute the most to your Salvation. When everything is revealed at the end of time, the diaries that I have dispensed to My faithful children will stop Heaven's enemies dead in their tracks. The mightiness of your faith calls the weak to stand undaunted with courage. The essence of your obedience to Me will rescue untold souls from condemnation by leading them to the Blood of the Cross. My children, it is more than simple nobility that you are offering, it is peace and ascendency that only the Holy Spirit can provide. Thank you for surrendering your will so Heaven can prosper through your holiness and humanity. I ask God to bless everyone who is given to the sanctification of the Earth because you are the living remnants of the Saints in this postdiluvian age. My Special son, I come specifically to extend My gratitude for everything you are giving to Jesus, not only your humility as you actualize your faith, but for reaching high and above what you previously believed you could endure. I know that it is a gratifying feeling to realize that you are confirming your love for Jesus the way you have. Thank you on His behalf. I also know that you have spent a great deal of time pondering the issue that I asked you to address last week. Would you like to read it to Me? *(I read the text of my testimony).* You can see precisely why Jesus mandated that His earthly Kingdom be consecrated through the Sacraments by which it is healed, because He is saddened to see hearts that are so dedicated to Him being broken by others' indifference. I urge you to reflect upon the narrative that you have composed. You have described humanity's obstinance against the Holy Spirit, where their desire is to be sown only to the flesh. Your vision of holiness is well taken by the open of heart, and they are those who are most devoted to Me. I am pleased by your testimony because it presents the facts about the brashness of human existence. You can see with distinction how some people do not expect to know the Lord because they will not allow themselves. Indeed, the first section of your writing harkens the opening of a spring flower, one that the persons to whom you present it sometimes trample beneath their feet. This is an appropriate way for you to comprehend how Jesus feels, as you have felt forsaken, used, and rejected. Why is it that humanity always seems to be taking something away and rarely giving the Lord anything in return? This is the question that Heaven asks the lost. After the passing of several years, how do you feel about undergoing the rejection of your piety by irreverent sinners? My son, they represent the epitome of defiance to Jesus. You know how alone He has felt for 2000 years. The 'present' about which you are speaking implies that you wish to see Redemption with your eyes. Millions are seeing it by the hope in their hearts because of the faith of My visionaries, although you may not believe it is happening. Even those to whom I have given My most urgent messages claim that they are unable to see God's Peace on Earth. Why is this so? Because they decline to cite My modern miracles when making their case.

The repercussions of the future will become more obvious by the signs you are given and the Divine Justice that Jesus is orchestrating through the internal aspects of your daily life. Surely you and your brother are aware that the irreducible framework of Christian enlightenment that you are dispensing to Creation is fashioned after My Marian locutions to Father Gobbi. The Triumph of My Immaculate Heart is further choreographed by your messages to the western hemisphere. What does this mean? It is that your holiness, service, resilience, and irreproachable loyalty are a precise reflection of the Sacrifice of Jesus on the Cross; and it pleases God to the point that He shall resurrect, ratify, and resonate your response of spiritual homage before humanity. No one will deny that you have suffered or forget why, and they will understand that your life and gifts to Heaven have been to complement the Sorrowful Passion of My Son. Can you detect that every word I have spoken since 1991 is of this prefigured sequence? The acts that you offer Jesus are given by this Grace alone. I offer signs and wonders to remove your despair. You know clearly how Jesus feels during these times, and you write about it effectively. Can you detect where I have taken your spiritual vision? Your life is woven into the fabric of the Divine Will of God with My messages to the priests through Father Gobbi and the providence of your life because you have said 'yes' to Me. Your existence is intertwined with the impending Salvation of the world. You have completed much of your work for that reason by this hour, and men will seek you out in time. You have borne them across the threshold into My Immaculate Heart by giving them your Diary, and they trust Me and your labors on My behalf because of the actions you are willing to take. Your having directed them to the Lord has succeeded, and many will be healed. Of course, you will see them again to give them the gifts you bear! You should not leave anyone with the impression that they will never see your face again until they die. I have been sent to tell you that it is by your gracious offerings that your mission ensues. You are free to go and relax with your friends for the rest of your days if you wish. This is another sacrifice that you have given to Jesus for the conversion of the wretched and all who are mired in sin. I have made clear that there is nothing in this life that you hope for that you will not receive when you reach the Glory of Heaven. Enduring the interim is another means for you to see how the Divine Romance of the Sacred Heart of Jesus is yearning to know the love of His people in precisely the way you feel about your present experiences. Can you see how you are becoming one in self-denial with Jesus as these lessons occur? And, in this you are growing more holy, loving, sacrificial, and imminently capable of teaching humanity about the awesome benevolence of His Sacrifice on the Cross, His Paschal Resurrection, and how anticipatory He remains about hearing from the Almighty Father when He shall return to the Earth in Glory. He keeps telling God the same thing you told Me at the inception of this message, *Now! Now! I wish to do it now! I want to see it happen now!* And, the Father continues saying to Jesus the same thing I told you today; that it is in due time, a time that is nearly here. Hence, do not allow your pining for the masterpiece of Camelot to stray far from your heartstrings because, thanks to your dedicated love, it is the symphony that will resound when the ages are suppressed into closure. Thank you for being My Special one, and for praying so profoundly to heal this land. The sentiments you write are the essence of transitional power and the making of true goodness in a world that is still struggling to capture the sanctity of its own Eternal Redemption."

Sunday, November 3, 2002
Feast of Saint Martin de Porres (1579-1639)
Companion of Saint Rose of Lima
Canonized in 1962 by Pope John XXIII
2:22 p.m.

"Today, My dear children, it is a high honor which has been bestowed upon Me to speak through the Love and power of the Holy Spirit because I realize that this is part of the Plan of God to heal and sanctify the nations. Your petitions are the delight of Jesus because His desire is to respond to you in many ways that are yet untold. He is the amazement of your hearts and the origin of your fulfillment. Likewise, He also knows that it is you who are breathing the new life of holiness into an otherwise fruitless existence on the Earth for millions of your lost brothers and sisters. Heaven includes the College of Divine Principals who have been with you since time immemorial, your Royal Hosts who have overseen your conversion and the spiritual transformation you require to know God to the highest. Thank you for allowing Me to address your needs with such Motherly care! No one in Creation knows your spirits better than your Immaculate Queen, and no one can console you with the presence of God as I do as Matriarch of the Angels. You are a blessed society of people for these reasons, but most of all because you have accepted the gift of faith to believe in your Eternal Salvation without having seen it in advance. This is your inheritance from God because He loves you with such infinite magnitude. Today, I call upon you to hold fast to the basics of your trust in Jesus as though you were toddlers with a grasp upon His holy palm. You do not understand the consequences of the material world. You do not own a reign over the dimensions that are vying for your holiness and against your Salvation everyday, but you have power over their influence when you take refuge in your Savior. I have been given the Grace to intercede on your behalf, to assist you in becoming Saints of these times, and to take you to the brink of perfection if only you will listen to what I have been telling the Earth for centuries. I afford you the timeliest miracles that Creation has thus far seen not because you are nobler than your predecessors, but because these are the last times, and too many of you are far from being prepared for the Final Judgement of God. We pray because this is the way He listens, and His response is evidence for you to know that He is here. The suffering you see in your midst is your additional call to prayer and personal sacrifice, much in the likeness of Saint Martin de Porres whose life was in service to the lost and for social justice for those considered to be disadvantaged by their Peruvian indigence. Why do I call you to imitate the lives of the Saints more than during any time in history? Because My requests and admonishments are urgent, and the Saints are such pious examples. Soon, the Earth will be moving into its final stages, and the untold billions who have lived will wonder why the voice of their Mother has fallen into silence. I have been appearing in prefigured locations around the globe with messages for many years, but the ones I am giving as this new century opens will be the last; there will be no others before the end of time. This is why it is imperative that we reach as many souls as possible with the Good News of Salvation in the Blood of Jesus on the Cross. My dear children, I am not mortal, and I never was. I did not suffer the ravages of death or the separation of My Immaculate Soul from My Body. However, I witnessed every one of God's creatures who died; all of His people, the animals, the littlest beings on Earth, and the reciprocating seasons of Nature. Humankind is at the pinnacle of the Sacred Heart of Jesus, and it is for your Redemption that He expired and was buried. I ask you to join in supplication for the End Times because many are they whose faith is as indiscernible as the minute creatures who live in the linens on your beds. This is a crisis for modern men of immeasurable proportion. It is urgent that all whom I have summoned dispense the graces that the Almighty Father has given them through every conceivable venue. While there is no reason for panic because God is in control of His Kingdom, this is the most dire time for the transformation of humankind to His Will since the earliest ages you have known.

  My dear children, you must remain open to receive the Wisdom of the Holy Spirit and keep your conscience alive because once you have committed it to the grave, it is never easily exhumed. This is why I have come to speak to you during this opportune moment in your nation's history. Something must be done to end America's deranged addiction to warfare, calamity, fortune, entertainment, materialism, sexualism and pride; and the intent of My messages is to instill in you the desire to comply entirely with the Lord's spiritual edicts for repentance and contrition. When you think about how many times you wanted to go back in history to seek amendment, ratification, renewal and justification, you wished to draw life from your new strength that God has placed inside your hearts. This is the 'if I knew then what I know now' dilemma which causes you to believe that true genius and dignity have not indulged you until today. But, the seeds of this profundity have always been in you, and are now beginning to grow because you remained within reach of God's Providence without straying too far into the darkness for Him to rescue you. Believe it or not, whatever happened back then lent to the growth of the Christian faith that you now possess. You have always been capable of rising from the proverbial ashes of your tragedies and mistakes so the timelessness of Paradise can fly you to Absolution. You must surrender your corporeal instincts in favor of your spiritual ones according to your station in life, and be reminded that Jesus stands beside anyone who espouses the demonstrative expressions of Christian repentance. When the Holy Paraclete graces your conscience with this virtue, you become as near to the origin of spiritual excellence as you will ever be. You begin to take root in Heaven while living on Earth; and the debate ensues as to whether you can be a good Christian without anyone else knowing. Questions need to be addressed as to whether you have conviction in your beliefs. Do they manifest community values and outward affirmation, and is there self-sacrificing honor in what you practice? It is obviously required that you accept Jesus as your Lord and Savior to reach Salvation, but your faith is much larger than any one person. It is focusing on others as the object of your allegiance to Heaven as members of Christ's Mystical Body. And, you must be humble in your awareness that you are conquering the enemies of Truth. While there is no such thing as overdoing your profession, Jesus knew that He needed to heal Creation just enough, being careful not to stoke humanity's pride, not to change a whimpering kitten into a prowling monster. Elevating you to righteousness is not a license for you to embark on a conquest of the universe because your Christian mission originates from within. This is the grand cause by which I speak to you now because I know that we can make a difference in the culmination of the years. I come with compassion for you and to say that Jesus knows your sorrows. He wishes to comfort you because you are children of the Almighty Father who lives and reigns in Heaven in the presence of the Angels and Saints. Jesus and the Holy Spirit are your advocates in your daily lives, and this is why it is important that you continue to call upon them. I leave signs, graces, and wonders in your path because I know clearly that you wish to comprehend the scope and impact of your work. If only you will trust Me, I shall assist your awareness that it is imperative that you remain below the surface of the secular arena during the foreseeable future... I bring this information today to lift your hearts, and to remind you of the increased importance of your good offices. This is the miracle of your life, and God is grateful to you. I also assure you that when the doorway of the universe opens at the hands of Jesus to expose everything that is occurring, humanity will see that the lives of giants among men have been shaped by your humble blessings here at home. Thank you for making your love for your brothers filled with meaningful care. The Lord is glorified. Can you sense this by the gladness inside your hearts? You are writing more pretty pages in *Babes in the Woods*, and many people will embrace the life and purity of little children as a result. Be My happy warriors because you do not know the holiness you are espousing. There are tens-of-thousands of anonymous people, those considered to be insignificant by men's standards, who are poring over your manuscripts, thanking the Lord for you both privately and to their friends, moving closer to My Maternal intercession because you have said 'yes.' Thank you for your servitude! I have enlisted Saint Martin de Porres to be your intercessor all the days of your life!"

Sunday, November 10, 2002
1:59 p.m.

"That humanity will be freed from the stain of sin, I have come to offer the Body, Blood, Soul and Divinity of My Beloved Son, Jesus Christ, whose Sorrowful Crucifixion has taken away the sins of the world. I ask you to pray for each and every one of your brothers and sisters to relinquish the death grip they hold on their transgressions and come to the Everlasting Life that Jesus is offering. My children, in the poetic beauty that your Christian faith procures by the Wisdom of the Holy Spirit, you are capable of seeing the Divine Love of God inside your hearts. I beseech you to discover Him there by allowing Jesus to take residence inside you. It is because of the sacred mission to which you are called that you cast aside the things of Earth and genuflect in humble contrition before the Cross. You do so not solely because your poetry and prose would be otherwise unable to witness to Truth, but because the power of Jesus' Sacrifice allows you to sense the precursors of Paradise without dying in advance. You submit to sonnets, elegies, metaphors, and allegories to instill the happiness in your hearts to those who see and hear, but the power in you to evoke their holiness comes from the Pentecostal Paraclete. Listen with faith and conduct yourselves accordingly! There are too many who are rejecting Jesus outright, those who claim that there is no God, that they have the choice to spurn Him. There are others who recognize the presence of our Creator, but believe that mortals have no relationship with Him. These are people who are prone to say that they have God right where they want Him. My children, the latter of these are in grave danger. We come together praying for the conversion of atheists and agnostics, and to urge Heaven to profoundly touch the consciences of those who believe that Jesus can reveal nothing before them that can make them love Him. When you offer your morning prayers, those you recite at midday, and your vespers before retiring for the night, please call upon Christ Jesus to gently reach-out to the many who have yet to accept Him as their Savior. It is not in mountains and valleys that the most beautiful aspects of Creation can be found, and neither are they limited to lyrics and stanzas. I tell you that none of the arts which you can finesse with the power of the aesthetic imagination can bring you the fullness of unerring Light. You must reach outwardly by sustaining your faith from within. Of all the majesties that ever existed, none is greater than that which is espoused by the Most Blessed Trinity. This is the Truth, My little ones. You are never placated in your deference to it, but evoked into thoughtful reaction on behalf of the Kingdom of God that you cannot see. When you search for this Truth with the vision of the Cross in your hearts, you will find it. There is no greater benefit to ever fall upon the fate of humankind than the Crucifixion of My Son. The moon and stars hail above you and glisten in the broad openness of night. You become enamored by their loftiness, and sometimes even believe that they reveal certain instincts about your existence below. Some foolish people even think that they can predict the future by reading the lay of the constellations above. However, I am the Mother of the God who placed these things over you, and I tell you that nothing that can be seen with the naked eye is more powerful than the love in your hearts in knowing what will be wrought to cease the mortal ages. Through this love, you can smooth the mountain ranges, reverse the course of teeming rivers, turn the night into day, and deter any enemy of your faith from ever tempting you into sin again. Through God's Love, you can rebuild what has been destroyed. You can be victorious over evil legions in ways that have never before been seen. I declare that the Spirit of God in you is of great magnitude in leading you to the Fruits of Divine Truth. We pray and hope for the changes that must come. I understand the anguish you feel because no one else seems to care. For now, My children, let not your hearts be troubled because these things do not matter. The reluctance of societies to give you an indication of their response to your work for Jesus is immaterial to the outcome of the Triumph you shall share in the bounty of My Immaculate Heart.

    My Special son, I have come to offer My assurance to you and to the world that Jesus is in command of His Kingdom. He knows the station of His followers, where they are located in time and space, and how their lives will be utilized in the final battles of Divine Love upon the Earth. You, your brother, and many whom you still believe to be rather worldly will be in the number who shall be the bravest soldiers for peace around the globe and in the universe. Indeed, you already are. You are reviewing My past messages, those of two, three, and four years ago. I am pleased that you have recorded them accurately, that you took the time to pray the Holy Rosary while I was dictating them, and especially that you will deliver these same messages as God had deigned before you and your brother were ever born. As your heart is touched, so shall thousands of others feel equally as loved. If you accept the suggestion given through My Angels this week, you will see that the pages in *Babes in the Woods* will inspire every reader to wish to know more about what I have been saying for nearly twelve years. Can you see how this is true? Indeed, imagine the meeting that you will attend next Saturday occurring in 2003, and all 3000 people present encountering Chapter XVI in *Babes in the Woods*, indicating the profundity of the messages from the Mother of Jesus Christ hidden there. I tell you, all of your work for the past years and that of the next will guide the

'Children of Mary' back to your first Diary. This has been My plan, and I promise that it will occur. It has taken the penning of your other manuscripts to get them there. Can you see by what spiritual genius you are doing this? If you continue to be as patient as you are, this will come earlier than previously thought. I will not let you down. I will not let My Jesus down!

The charismatic attributes of what you are accomplishing is the purpose of placing Chapter XVI in your book. You have learned and participated in the themes through which you can explain what it means to become love, know love, give love, receive love, and most important, to describe the gifts and sacrifices that accompany the multiplex reciprocity of the mortal and Divine. You own the venue to speak on behalf of God about what true fruits come from obedience and giving your soul for the certainty of befriending Jesus in the Upper Room, on the Holy Cross, and as He walked upright and fully resurrected on Easter Sunday. You are given new perspectives because you offer your spiritual complexion to God. These things must be recorded in Chapter XVI of *Babes in the Woods* to complement My messages, and the world of sinners will coalesce around you. However, you must recall the events of the past six weeks with understanding in your heart; how you were elated, how you yearned, that you were fulfilled by the presence of God, that you felt betrayed by the sinfulness of humanity, and how your hopes and vision have been restored by your relationship with the Queen of Heaven. All of this you must do without giving anyone the slightest inkling of how painfully you learnt it. The Holy Spirit is in you!"

Sunday, November 17, 2002
1:14 p.m.

"My sweet little children, where there is charity and love, there is also God. The Heavens are resounding the Glory of His Holy Name on this 33rd Sunday of the Liturgical Year. I trust that your faith is strengthened by the knowledge that you are walking closer with Him than during this time one year ago, and even yesterday. My joy comes in knowing that My miraculous intercession is effecting the conversion of numerous lost souls to My Son for purification and Redemption. Where would you be, My children, without your Blessed Mother? Where would you be? It is in the Wisdom of Truth that you are found, the same Wisdom of the Holy Spirit living in Me. I share the Glory of Paradise because like Jesus, it is My desire for you to be taken there on the occasion of your mortal passing. It is My hope that you will arrive before the sight of God with your souls intact after having been cleansed by Jesus' Crucifixion. While the world is broken and groaning, it is important for you to be healed and singing with the Angels. Therefore, I come again at this ominous moment to remind you that the future belongs to those who hope, to the ones who have been remanded to the depths of despair by the greedy oppressors in their midst. Human sanctification is about new beginnings, the ones about which I have spoken on so many occasions around the globe for many centuries. You are like My children of past generations who looked up in wonder at the skies, trying their best to glean the benefit of Truth from the Creation they could see with their eyes. And, they ultimately discovered as you are also seeing that the Divine Truth of God is already present in the world at the nucleus of your hearts. It is from there that humanity is healed and goodness is rekindled. Please pray with Me that more and more millions will come before the Holy Cross for the consolation that is theirs in the Sacred Heart of Jesus. Pray with Me that those who hold monopoly over the public discourse will employ their judgement wisely, that they will decide for God in preserving innocent life. Material expedience is the antipathy of human life. Please let no one deceive you into believing that their conscience has been deadened by others who refuse to cooperate. There is no excuse for not allowing the Truth to prevail when there are clamoring minorities in their midst whose favor they fear losing in lesser matters. I ask everyone who can hear with the vision of their hearts to reach inside themselves for every sliver of Christian conscience they can muster. These are much more than times that try men's souls. They are times that will ultimately determine the destiny of your souls for Eternity. Decide for God! Choose Divine Love! Fight for righteousness! Sacrifice your happiness on Earth for an everlasting jubilation in the Kingdom of Heaven! These are the things that make men honorable, not whether they have aptitude in discerning the motivations of other faiths. Lead the blind by the Light of Christ Jesus! For all the reasons that you have been baptized into the Church, recall with the agony of the Suffering Christ that your lives will forever serve the Salvation of humankind in the Blood of the Lamb of God who takes away the sins of the world; only Jesus of Nazareth! Only the Son of Abba and the foster-Child of Saint Joseph can bring Redemption to the temporal world. There are no other prophets who have paid the price for the reclamation of the souls of humanity into Heaven. No matter what other avenues to peace are spoken, regardless of other sacrifices and burnt offerings, only the Crucifixion of Jesus on the Cross of Mount Calvary on Good Friday is the satisfaction that God requires for the forgiveness of the sins of man, from Adam all the way to the last person on Earth to ever draw a breath. My children, this will never change. It is nonnegotiable and subject to no adulteration by men. I beseech you to remember that no one on Earth is alive until he allows the Holy Spirit of Jesus to enter his heart, the same Paraclete who descended from Heaven at Pentecost. Non-Christians may claim to know God for whom they believe Him to be, but they are mistaken if they assume that they will see His Holy Face without their souls being preserved by the Divine Mercy of Jesus Christ. His torment, torture, and bloodshed is their Absolution before the Father. There is no other way that a soul can be rescued from the flames of Hell than through the pardoning that is commissioned by Jesus through His Sorrowful Passion, Crucifixion, and Glorious Resurrection from the Sepulcher.

My children, this should be a pleasing revelation for all the world. Now you can search for the same goal with a single-minded unity to be one people in Him. There is no longer any need for factions to be fighting among themselves because the world is one beneath the Glory of the Cross! What happiness! What elation! Now, all humanity can cast-off the cloak of secularism by bowing before the King of kings. Jesus is the finisher of your wishes and the gladness of the Saints. I beg you with pleading in My Heart to believe what I am saying. Where there is trust in the Lord, you are assured to be led to Him by becoming this same Love. There is nothing subliminal in the Gospel because the open nature of human contrition and servitude are made abundantly clear. Every last parable is another means by which you are sown to the Spirit of Truth. Heed the Testament of the Apostles! Answer the call of the ages to enter into the brotherly union of self-sacrifice in the image of Jesus so that every corner of the Earth will be converted to His Love that emanates from the Holy Cross! If only you will open your hearts, you will see this wellspring of Day overcome the darkness in which so many among you are living in grief and desperation. My Special child, I come entreating your brothers and sisters, and I know you will deliver My message. I love you beyond your capacity to understand. I bring the Light and Love of Christ Jesus, the perfection that the world pines to realize. I offer the blessing of the Angels who cantor the strains of conversion that I have hailed for centuries. Every soul searches for them to come to the Earth and console the weary and the forsaken. The grieving yearn for the good will that flows from those to whom the Angels have come. Let Me be clear, the human soul knows when the Angels are in its midst, and those who encounter anyone who is close to the Angels realize that their inner-spirits are nearer to God. This is why your books are touching so many lives; it is the reason why your prose and verse are mentioned in households in America, and it is this presence-of-heart that many are seeing in your brother, asking if they have met him before. He has the spirit of the Angels inside him, and their souls know that God is there. Their consciousness does not understand what it is, but their minds and heart-of-hearts sense the presence of the Angels nearby. You radiate this same proximity of God uniquely by the works you are writing that will be etched into history, revealing the dynasty of the Blessed Trinity long after the expressions on your brother's face are gone. Please allow Me to thank you for participating in the events that are available to you. Your goodness in sharing My intercession will continue to bear fruit for many years beyond the sight of the world. I wish from the depths of My Immaculate Heart that you were capable of discerning even the slightest amount of good you are bringing to the Earth, but it is of such magnitude that it is larger than life. Thank you! I know that you recognize the timelessness of the offerings you are giving Jesus at My behest. Believe that He is pleased, and be comforted that you are making Creation a better place. If this were not so, I would have told you. I also wish to forewarn you that anyone who has suffered grievously in prison who comes to you not only to share their story with humanity, but to profit from it, has motivations that are not entirely noble. This is the reason why the freedom of Jesus' Holy Gospel must be the topic of conversation across the land. Secularism, as you wrote in *When Legends Rise Again,* is among the enemies of Christian holiness. Yes, they will attempt to destroy you because they see you as a threat to their materialism and autonomy. You realize in your heart, however, that they have already lost, and you have won. Knowing the outcome of this battle should give you the greatest hope of all. Time is your ally. You must be patient while God allows the clock to expire. Remember that I have promised to offer you and your brother a special blessing next Sunday, November 24, 2002."

Sunday, November 24, 2002
Feast of Christ the King
1:11 p.m.

And, He Shall Reign Forever and Ever! Hallelujah! Amen!

"So that you will prosper for Eternity in the Glory of Divine Love, Jesus is Christ the King for all ages! It is with happiness, fulfillment, hope, and humility that I join your prayers for the sanctification of the exiled world. Together, we are allowing those who suffer to redress their grief before the Cross of Salvation. And, to what fate is this grief attributed? The awakening of unrepentant sinners. I ask My children to remember the meaning of suffering; it is your alliance with the Dominion of God. It is His Providence for your retrieval from the darkness of the Earth, to be presented by Jesus at the pinnacle of Paradise. Still, My children, we must pray that suffering will cease. Ours is the designation by My Son to implore the societies of Earth to acknowledge Him as Lord and Master of life. Whereby all souls accept Jesus as their Savior, human suffering will become obsolete. The triumphant reports of the Trumpets of the Ages can be heard in the parlours of the hours. When the bells of Salvation peal beyond distant horizons, they are tolling for you. With every sense of victory in your hearts, I call you to embrace this Feast because it has predestined the Advent of the Second Coming of the Son of Man. What praise, dignity, and eloquence He bestows upon those who love Him! What power and Grace are given to the littlest of His flock! Therefore, remember that your King loves you beyond the echoes of immortal telling. Thank you for your loveliness in assuring your friends that you are dedicated to Him, that you have chosen the course of faithful contrition before the Lamb of God. It is in this that you are rediscovered, rescued from amidst the wreck of this world, and positioned for the greatness that all people seek from Him. He desires to bring you upright in Creation, to raise you perpendicular to the ground; not as its polar opposite, but to heighten your vision of everything that is seen and unseen through the majesty of Sovereign Truth. Jesus' Sacrifice is your foundation for this enlightenment that no pillar or monolith can provide. I have previously told you that the rarest, most grotesque event in human history is the Crucifixion of Jesus Christ, and yet it laid the centerpiece for sanctifying the whole framework of Creation. This is why your suffering in His likeness is so redeeming. Again, I implore you, do not be afraid. There is valor and a pastoral commission inherent in all Christians to be carried-out by everyone who is gifted of heart to perceive the Earth as Jesus saw it during His Passion and Death. You must always remember that even though you see the future through mottled eyes, the Lord never supposes anything because He has witnessed the final act of every man. He deposited your trust and faith onto the Earth long before establishing His Mosaic Law, and prior to birthing the Messiah from My Womb, the Second Person of the Most Blessed Trinity. You are enlisted to remain steadfast beside Him despite any gauntlets that are thrown at your feet. Woe be to anyone who hears at the end of time that they should take a seat next to King Herod or Pontius Pilate, not that they have not been cleansed by the same Sacrifice that absolved their own contemporaries. They eventually saw the utility of confession, and that in the context of virtuousness, choosing not to commit bad deeds is as commendable as performing good ones because the absolute value of the heart blooms from the same benevolence. My children, it is not God's desire that the Earth should end like a Greek tragedy, scripted by humanity's ancient reluctance to change, or by your refusal to deny and condemn corruption, or your resistance to embrace His peace. Therefore, please do everything in your power to overcome your unjustified pall of spiritual disobedience. The Lord asks you to see! Look through the lenses of your repatriated dreams and you will regale cities whose streets you have traveled, but have not yet been to. And, do not attempt to barter for God's blessing, for you have it anyway. Avoid things like 'pull prayers' that purport to guarantee a certain outcome by publishing a specified number of random petitions because the Lord's Grace is not for sale. This is little more than America's penchant for demanding your money's worth.

    My Special son, I come to this home to bless you with My sacred presence. This will be a day for giving you tremendous benefit in knowing why I have asked you to do certain things. It will assist your understanding about how your prayers and sacrifices have sufficed the recorded history of created men. My words are a means to recognize that humanity has traveled from foreign reckonings toward spiritual reasoning, away from temptations of the flesh. I will give you plentiful evidence that Jesus is allowing His people to be sown to the Spirit so they can be presented before God as new and regenerated beings. Indeed, you will know why you have been giving your personal life for such Glory as this, and that which is still to come. At the end of this message, I will give you a higher benediction than millions in your country. *(Our Lady spoke to me at length in private.)* You realize that you live in a dangerous world that is in constantly changing turmoil. Conversely, centuries and customs alter the face of humanity, and yours here in America are becoming closer to God than you earlier believed. Do you see that Jesus intends for humankind to learn a great deal more about Him than you ever have before? And, the reason for this is so the world will never forget that God is a Man! Looking back, can you sense the essence of His supernatural Omnipotence suspending the laws of the Earth? Your prayers, labors, and offerings are overflowing with Truth in His sight, and they are a source of holiness toward your perfect submission before the Saints. What does Heaven demand of humankind? Nothing less than purity and discretion, and being tethered to the Holy Spirit. Thank you for your prayers today. I hope you have enjoyed the graces I have given you on this Feast of Christ the King!"

Sunday, December 1, 2002
First Week of Advent
2:12 p.m.

"Dear children, you have broached the final month of a year during which you have prayed like Christian martyrs and worked as slaves in the open fields for the Kingdom of God on the Earth. Yours shall be His Divine Salvation! Thank you for your charity and chastity, and your perseverance and genuine trust in the admonishments of the Holy Spirit. Also, you are entering the bountiful Season of Advent to celebrate the Birth of Jesus. He is of the sublime perpetuity of God, and this is what He wishes of your future in Him. So your love for Jesus will never die, He has been Crucified on the Holy Cross and raised from the dead. I appear today to continue calling you to nurture the Holy Spirit in your hearts so you will inherit this same perpetuity, the amaranth that will take your hopes far past your fondest dreams of a better world. Your hearts shall shine in Him as the perpetual crimson flower *love-lies-bleeding* adorns the majesty of sublime human love that is flourishing in you now. With all the Heavens singing, I assure you that your souls will bless the corridors of supernal Justice like mighty eagles perched atop the cliffs of Creation. As you ponder Advent, I invite you to share in the Church's supplications that are broadcast by the faithful around the continents for helpless human life, especially the unborn. Would it not have pleased God that more of His people on the Earth might have prayed with greater fervor so the scourge of infanticide that was legalized in the United States in 1973 would have ended long before the passing of a gruesome thirty years? I tell you today that His Justice is swifter in coming than the beseeching hearts which had to be cultivated through the expansion of so many decades. This is a Season of peace and joy, and of new beginnings for those who have strayed from the flock of God's righteous lands. I implore My children to be leaders among them, the petitioners who teach the world how to pray, and the givers of His solace to the lonely and afraid. You have been offered a fresh vision of hope that has been known to no other age, save the first century. I wish for you to remember that you are like earthen clay, and Jesus is the potter. Give your lives to Him so He can make of you what He wills. The desire of the Heavenly Father is that you acquiesce to Jesus in contrition, that you will become a possession in His sacred hands. The world is more than fractured, it has been breached by the bands of hatred that have preyed upon My children for centuries. As I told you before, now is the time during which the Triumph of My Immaculate Heart will annihilate the fiendish legions around you. Inside this miraculous Victory is the seed of conquest, the Most Sacred Heart of Jesus. When you recall His Passion, Crucifixion, and Resurrection during your Novena to the Immaculate Conception, remember all who are living outside the holiness that He instills in you. Reach forth from your hearts and hopes for the conversion of every society and sect, for all nations and peoples, and ask God to render them unable to do anything that would impede their nuptials with the Holy Spirit. It is not our Creator who scorns the lost, but the lost themselves who will condemn their own wretchedness at the end of time and succumb to the massacres of perdition. Give them new reason to choose Redemption! Show them the happiness, purity, and love by which you endure! This is the emphatic reflection of the Nativity of Jesus. It is for these reasons that you should be pleased knowing that He continues to guard over you like a star in the night, the beloved Morning Star! I seek in you the transformation from your worldliness to the piety that made Saints of good people in generations past.

I have urged you to acknowledge that no one mortal can unite the nations. Ironically thinking, imagine a world in which no one died. Recklessness would have little consequence; suffering would have no conclusion, justice would have no recourse, death could provide no liberation, and resurrection would have no meaning. There would be no end to festering arguments and lingering grudges; and enmity would have no grave site. It is crucial that you mend everything that is broken in the brevity of your exile. The Lord seeks compliance in the things of fairness, asking you to rear your progeny in Truth and piety, bringing Heaven's incorrigible discipline to bear on your delinquent sons, and leading them to the sanctifying waters of purity, civility, and prudence. Human existence is a mixture of criticism, coventry and pandemonium whose unity is superceded by the sacred encryption that the Holy Spirit places on your souls. This allows the world to see a glimpse of Salvation in your speeches, actions, and everyday ways of life; and it gives you a reprieve from the frenzy of material collusion. The Bible says that you have the capacity to rewrite a history that has not even occurred. This is why I am calling you into an enchantment with the mystical and charismatic attributes of your Christian faith so you will become accustomed to the transcending things in life that link you with the Divine. This is in part what My messages are all about. My intention is to dissuade you from remaining invested and entrenched in the physical intricacies of ordinary existence, and to intensify your interest in your eternal destiny. You should realize that through My intercession, I have brought the Earth the origin of miracles, and you must feed, nurture, and cultivate it into the fullness of your living faith. Please do not let it die! Your souls will prosper in piousness through My Grace and ascend the invisible staircase to the Lord's magnanimity, allowing you to arrive at perfect awareness of His determination to liberate you from the catastrophic snares of your sins. As you prepare to enter AD 2003, I urge you to perform a sacred analysis of the condition of the United States and your collateral friendships. Remember to God in your prayers people whose stories have never been told, the tortured paupers whose lives have been ruptured by violence and neglect, those whose lot is lessened by poverty, racism, prejudice, and deceit. Ask God to heal those whose future has been squandered by someone else's corruption, by short-sightedness, addiction, and the fraudulent workings of the marketplace exchange. My Special son, I have dictated My message for your brothers and sisters to begin this Advent. I pray that My intercession will have unprecedented effects throughout Creation when the opportunity arrives. I will direct you to several passages of Scripture that describe My sentiments today. If you would be so kind as to open your Bible, I will show you. Please turn to Ephesians 1:7 and begin reading there now.

"In Him, we have Redemption, by His Blood, the forgiveness of transgressions, in accord with the riches of His Grace that He lavishes upon us. In all Wisdom and insight, He has made known to us the Mystery of His Will in accord with His favor that He set forth in Him as a plan for the fullness of times; to sum up all things in Christ, in Heaven, and on Earth. In Him, we were also chosen, destined in accord with the purpose of the One who accomplishes all things according to the intention of His Will, so that we might exist for the praise of His Glory, we who first hoped in Christ. In Him, you also who have heard the Word of Truth, the Gospel of your Salvation, and have believed in Him, were sealed with the promised Holy Spirit, which is the first installment of our inheritance toward Redemption as God's possession, to the praise of His Glory....May the eyes of your hearts be enlightened, that you may know what is the hope that belongs to His call, what are the riches of Glory in His inheritance among the holy ones, and what is the surpassing greatness of His power for us who believe, in accord with the exercise of His great might, which He worked in Christ, raising Him from the dead and seating Him at His right hand in the Heavens; far above every principality, authority, power, and dominion, and every name that is named not only in this age, but also in the one to come." Eph. 1:7-14, 18-21

"Please make a special note to include this reading in Chapter Seven of *Babes in the Woods*. I also ask you to refer to the undying flower *love-lies-bleeding* in that same section. I assure you that your new book will have a glorious impact upon the nations. Do you have something prepared for Me? Would you like to tell Me what it is? You are in possession of the workings of the great miracles that will heal America! You have received the Wisdom and continence of Paradise by capturing Divine human love in a most reverent way. Do you realize that Heaven cannot be defined by the rituals of secular men who decline to accept Jesus as the sustenance of Creation? And, the effects of Creation? And, the unfurling future of Creation? I am pleased by what you have written because you know what it means to reflect the perfection of God. Your creativity and penchant for revealing the Truth are not bound by anything mortal. Would you have ever contemplated ordaining such holiness by any of these analogues before? The Lord will join you in reclaiming His Justice, and it shall be done in these and other ways before the Earth is passed. I will speak to you next week upon one of the greatest Feasts in the history of the Church!"

Sunday, December 8, 2002
Feast of the Immaculate Conception
2:43 p.m.

"To you whose hope is built upon Jesus' Blood and righteousness, I offer you the congratulatory benisons of God. When your prayers reflect the Kingship in whose power you have been retrieved from the darkness of the netherworld, you become one in His Royalty. Therefore, on this Feast upon which you observe the Solemnity of the Immaculate Conception, know that the Lord is pleased by your acceptance and glorified by your trust. Countless miraculous healings have been accorded today because so many have offered the specified Hour of Grace in My Name. The intentions of the faithful through Jesus are also the Will of the Father during this time of supernatural intervention. My children, the Second Week of Advent finds you pondering the willingness of God to come into Creation as His own Son, to be born of My Womb, and to be subjected to the trials of the lost. As you know, and as recorded history provides, He taught humanity about Divine Love; He coopted an apostolate of pious followers to stand beside Him, and He bequeathed a legacy of Immortal Sanctification to be your conveyance to Heaven. While there is no other means to human Redemption than through the Holy Cross, know that God is pleased when He sees so many who bear it high above the crest of fallen humanity so that even those who refuse to believe in Him can witness the Truth. I share with you the jubilation that this procession is ongoing, even at the cost of the martyrdom of modern Christians and others who give of themselves to death while witnessing to the goodness of

Christianity. You have seen that people who do not accept your spirituality can be injurious in their language, abusive in conduct, and accomplices with evil against you. For this, the answers are few, except to say that Heaven's Wrath will overwhelm them like a thief in the night. Whomever will prosper in the material world at the expense of those suffering for Christ will undergo a fate far worse than the fires that have already conquered the worst adversaries of God. We pray together for these reasons, that all peoples of every walk will cease treading in the darkness and expose themselves to the Light. My Special son, I arrive with you today upon a high Feast that itself is positioned in the Advent of the celebration of the Birth of Jesus in Bethlehem. I am honored that your humble heart has been open during these years, and to this day that you understand what human love is about. You have discovered that it is the fruitage of the Divine, that the presence of God rests upon you when you love one another in His image, and that all the greatness of mortal men summed into one cannot eclipse the holiness of a single Messiah. Your soul has been assimilated by His Grace because you are distinctly devoted to Him. And, I am joyful to remind you that there is no reversal of this blessing. You are the possession of the Holy Spirit, which is your endowment of the Everlasting Life you shall receive in the Sacrifice of My Son. Yes, this is a time for celebrating, not only because you have secured your place at the Throne of the Father, but because you are willing to lend your labors to the harvest of souls to share in this transference. It is true that you have seen marvels and wonders in your day, and they have been to the enhancement of your trust in His Kingdom. My child, you are equally a miracle for many who have not previously believed. Your works witness to the fact of My intercession; your prayers reap the profits of innumerable conversions, and the conclusion of your life will bring the culmination of one of the greatest acts of daring to ever stand before the backdrop of Creation. You have written about beatific images in your book about little children, and I am pleased to boast of you as My adopted son because you internalize the burdens under which they suffer. The clarity in which you have written about the lost, lonely, and afraid places you in a group of the few who are willing to be patient with them. *Babes in the Woods* will bolster the deposit of faith that will alter the face of the Earth. I have told you about the impact that your Catholic mission is having and will bear upon humanity in the ways I am describing. The Lord is pleased because you and your brother are His faithful followers; you have witnessed what happens when you serve.

    I am not unmindful of the occurrence of the 150th celebration that is being observed in your diocese. I believe this to be an appropriate way to commemorate the faith of the generations before you. This is a time for prayer and perpetual empathy in anticipation of the Return of Jesus in Glory. I ask you to remember that awarding the Magnificat medal to your fellow parishioners reflects a moment not only fixed in history for the abandonment of the self, but a thesis of prophecy and devotion to suffering for the sake of Salvation, for allowing God to bring whatever cultivating experiences He desires to reclaim the innocence of the Earth, and for bearing the Fruits of the Holy Spirit to a world that has previously cast Him out. However, in the future I urge My children to serve to the exclusion of their own accolades in anonymous ways by giving without the expectation of being rewarded. Is this too much to expect of a nation as wealthy as the United States? I am happy to see that you have configured a way to release your newest book that is planned in a matter of weeks. You are being assisted by the Angels in writing Chapter Sixteen, but no one is going to dispute the efforts required by you to pen your prayerful thoughts on your own. Thus far, you have given of yourself in more than adequate ways. I am equally pleased that you visited your friends during the last two nights by engaging them in religious discussions. It is imperative that you remember to be careful when you encounter such situations as these. Can you foresee the fate of those who do not embrace the consolation of Christianity? Many of them rue the Earth's ill fortunes because they deny the benefits of repentance, confession, and absolution. They endure the agonies and anguishes of mortality in trepidation because they do not summon Jesus for help. Can you see that such people do not espouse the Holy Cross? Sometimes, even their desire for Truth is absent because they dismiss the Lord's Providential Decrees. It has been this way for a long period in America, in many of the European nations, and the isolated Northern Provinces. I am the Maiden who is the fulfillment of your dreams in Peace and Grace, and this is the reason why I call on your brothers and sisters to follow Me to Heaven."

Sunday, December 15, 2002
Third Week of Advent
2:22 p.m.

"Indeed, I have sought the intercessional Providence of the Love of God on your behalf because, knowing Him well, it is clear that there are many blessings still residing in Heaven that He will dispense to you upon your prayerful invocations. When I come to you to pray, My children, it is always in thanksgiving because you are more holy than the time before, your petitions are focused more upon the plight of the suffering, and the conversion which is worthy of all humankind stands with much greater clarity. You are walking gently upon the ground because you know that charity begins in your meekness—not in some cowardly way—but in the peaceful intellect that is the Wisdom of the Holy Spirit. I speak to you today during the mid-season of Advent to remind you that your anticipation of the Return of Jesus in Glory to take your souls to Heaven must become the enveloping reason why you bask in the Light of His Birth. There are too many who continue to wonder why the West is so entangled in the materialism that has brought such destruction upon your country. Other nations around the world who espouse Christianity look at the United States of America with shame and horror to know how you have perverted the true meaning of Christmas. At a time when Jesus is asking His disciples to embrace the Spirit and abandon the flesh, Americans everywhere are diving more deeply into corporeal matters, an inexplicable infatuation with material possessions, and a brash reluctance to receive the Sacrament of Reconciliation. Whatever happened to the grand nation whose forefathers would build their freedom upon? Where now is the trust and honesty that were integral parts of the development of a country of peace and justice? You can see now, My little ones, why they are eluding you! Please do not allow anyone else's desire for material things to distract you from the Nativity of the Prince of Peace. Be on guard against those who would offer you tangible goods in exchange for your fond favor toward them during the Solemnity of Christmas. I am asking for your understanding that the Birth of My Son is meant to take your hearts and souls closer to humility, self-denial, chastity, and to the Sacred Beatitudes which will eventually transform your land into the real city on a hill that will draw the lost into the piety of the followers of God.

It is not enough, it would seem, that the horrible events that befall America are cast aside as the hatred and misunderstanding of another human race; but to vengefully use massive forces against them in retribution even makes your country more ugly in the eyes of the Heavenly Father. Let Me assure you on the date which is only ten days away from the celebration of Christmas, if the people of the United States enter their cathedrals, churches, and sanctuaries asking for the peaceful blessing of Jesus Christ on the occasion of the recognition of His Nativity and thereafter set-out to prosecute another war of military aggression against your perceived enemies, the retaliation that will be brought against you from them will be unprecedented in the history of all humankind! It is not My intention to frighten you with these words because they will reach the ears of those for whom they are intended long-past sufficient time to alter the course of modern events. But, know for the record of history that I have given them, so that when God justifies His vengeance against America on any number of future occasions, you will all know why. My Jesus is angered and sorrowful by the way the people of the United States have turned their backs on the unborn, the poor, and the homeless. What nation on Earth would expend billions of dollars in capital wealth to utilize armaments to slaughter tens of thousands of innocent children overseas in the name of political revenge instead of using those monies to keep your own little children from freezing to death in their homes, on the streets, and hidden in abandoned cars and cardboard boxes in alleyways and basements beneath bars and brothels? If the leaders of the United States of America wish to see true justice, then all they need to do is wait for the Son of Man to return and see their actions tossed with justifiable Wrath into the fires of Gehenna. What He shall do with their souls is a matter for His Divine Mercy and the Final Judgment to come.

It is one of the aspects of the world that makes Me a Sorrowful Mother to be required to tell you these things. Imagine how the Hosts of Heaven are looking upon you! What must they be saying about a nation that has proclaimed the Most Blessed Virgin Mary to be its Patroness Saint, and then live in a way that defies almost everything that Her Crucified Son gave His Life for? I will tell you at a later date because, like the faithful of the Church, I am praying with you that certain circumstances will be eliminated and mitigated before I am forced to place such a reprehensible text into discernable words. I do not wish to tell you that there are millions of Americans whose souls are on the pathway to perdition, as true as it would seem to be! I wish I could make it clear to you that all souls are blessed, and that they are equally praising God in the way that He has prescribed in the Sacred Scriptures. It would give Me great elation to describe the United States as the perfect union of freedom and prosperity, but I cannot! These things are obvious to those who know Jesus well, but seem to be a source of great irritation—even a distraction—to the people whose choices are made only by what they can gain. We pray for these people because they are the ones who are now the farthest from Grace. They are the reason why innocent victims are suffering here and around the globe. I tell you again—My Son is not going to allow this callous disregard for His Crucifixion and Resurrection to continue for very much longer.

(Our Lady then made mystical allusions to terrible occurrences that God would allow to come upon us if we did not convert our hearts.)

...and then the entire platform of selfishness upon which the Western capitalist system is built will come crumbling to the Earth. Please understand Me without any confusion about what I am going to tell you now... *(She further described events destined to occur if the United States did not return to the path of righteousness.)* ...but, in the scope of the Eternal Vision of the Justice of God, it will be a good day! For Christianity! For the retrieval of goodness, piety, and prayerfulness in a nation that has chosen to abandon all three! Who would come forth to say that the Mother of God would never speak of such horrific destruction only ten days prior to Christmas? Let that man approach His Holy Mother and justify the silence of the people of Light in a nation where such is lauded by members of the media, corporate executives, and lazy clergy everywhere! Let a man who has an ounce of righteousness in his bones approach the Immaculate Virgin Mary and say that God does not have the right to sanctify all 50 states in the matter of an instant on a bright sunshiny afternoon, and then let the poorest of the poor around the globe pump their fists in the air that the great devourer in the West has finally been slain! I daresay—let any holy man approach Me and say that the United States of America does not deserve to be castigated...for having killed millions upon millions of its own unborn children in their mothers' wombs outright, with malice aforethought and ruthless indifference. If the American people so fear the terrorism of other sinners, they have not seen chastisement on a massive scale until the God of their fathers repays them for embracing the evils of Satanic works with seeming joy and jubilation... When the Holy Fires and Silver Sword of Justice return to the modern world at the Sacred Hands of Jesus Christ to end the element of time, sinners of all stripes who will then see the Truth with perfect clarity will bow at His Holy Feet and beseech Him '...slay me first! Please, slay me first!' They will look back upon the peaceful Nativity of Jesus through a much different set of eyes then! And, they will have nothing of material wealth to protect them from the devastation which will become their daily mantra for the rest of the ages!

My children, I have given you no new revelations today than that which you have already anticipated because you can clearly see the condition of the world. The possessions of other men are immaterial as far as the spiritual Truth is concerned. They are like millstones around their necks, balls and chains that will keep them from running into God's Kingdom as though they had the fleeting swiftness of the Angels. I beg you during the latter portion of this Advent Season to never relent in your pursuit of Justice on behalf of the Cross. I ask you to gain strength in the knowledge that you are living in the age of the Resurrected Christ! Be humble when you know it is fitting, be bold when circumstances warrant, and slay the opposition to your holiness as though you had silver bayonets in your hands. You are the members of My Army of Souls for Jesus. You are the warriors who search for peace by rooting-out those who live in such hypocrisy against the New Covenant Gospel. You are activists in the culture of Life! And, I assure you that what you shall bind on the Earth in the Name of Jesus for the advancement of Divine Human Love shall also be bound by God in Paradise. These are the sacred promises by which you have lived before, the very faith that you have taken to heart in many times past; and it is the precise perfection in which you will also deliver your spirits over to God upon the happy occasion of your deaths so He will receive you in Jesus' Arms for deliverance to your mansions of beauty with and alongside the Angels and Saints. So, why is Christmas such a holy time, one of peace, a period of reflection of the silence in which Jesus Christ was born? Because the Baby who came into the world like a Lamb will terminate the evil in it soon like a roaring Lion!

My Special son, thank you for praying with Me today and receiving these words on behalf of a suffering humanity—those whose lives are left in ruins by the many around them who are taking more than their share. You have been told by the likes of Saint Thomas the Patriot that you should pay your own way, make the world a better place than when you first discovered it, and pray like the 'dickens' that Jesus Christ will take your soul to Heaven when you finally die. These wishes are rather appropriate as the world moves to its conclusion. I wish for you to gain strength in what I have told you, to not care whether anyone approaches you with any hints that you are a dignitary in their midst, and that you can sense with better perception that everything that causes a tint of darkness to form around your heart is being slowly but surely destroyed by the work you are doing for Me here... I wish for you to always remember that the world would be poorer in Spirit and hope if not for your having given your life to Jesus... This is your holy blessing from your Mother, now. + I will speak to you again very soon! I Love you! Goodnight!"

Sunday, December 22, 2002
Fourth Sunday of Advent
3:08 p.m.

"Thus, your prayerful preparation for the anniversary of the Birth of Jesus is nigh complete, and His Deific Nativity will arrive with hope around the globe. My children, I am the Original Christian from whose Womb Eternal Salvation was birthed, and My Assumption into Heaven did not require God's Absolution. I did it for you! My Love and obedience to the Lord could never have Me do otherwise because in the depths of My Immaculate Heart, I knew the origin of My Wisdom and the purpose of My life. Human Redemption is My gift to Creation, not by My blood, but through the Blood of the Christ of My Womb, My Offspring and Life-giving King. Can you see, My lambs, that Christmas is the most important time for releasing poor souls from their purifying agony in Purgatory? This is a fresh beginning for the whole of humanity because of the miraculous realignment of the priorities of men. When you pray fervently during Christmas, the resonance of your intercessory petitions to the Throne of the Father for the entire year reechoes through the chambers of Jesus' Sacred Heart. He has true compassion, Divine Mercy, and plenteous Salvation for those who love Him. He gives this freely because it is in you that He manifests the Holy Gospel on Earth. Be happy in your newness, and rejoice that God is with you. I shall pray deeply for the multitudes who have embraced the Holy Cross and the innumerable millions who have yet to come to the Waters of Baptism. I assure you that I will not desist in My Motherly labors until every last one of My children has heard the Good News of Salvation in Jesus, whether or not they choose to embrace Him. The Season of Christmas is a time during which the message of the Nativity is spread around the world as a matter of course, and you can see that it bears particular meaning in My efforts to convert My children to the Blood of the Holy Cross. This significance is enhanced by the exhortations of the Lord's Vicar, Pope John Paul II, through his homilies about Virtue, Peace and Grace. He lauds the miracle of the Eucharist to rich and poor, near and far, to the vaunted and forsaken, and to the ends of the Earth where most citizens have never been. Whether you are kneeling in the front pew or crowded in the narthex, Jesus the Sacred Host can see your heart during the Holy Sacrifice of the Mass because His presence defies the concept of distance. He knows how fractured humanity has become, how suffering are the poor, and how far His lost sheep must travel to reach their homeland in Him. In too many ways, the Earth is as broken as when My Jewish and Roman Catholic children were slaughtered by Naziism or confined to the ghettos so they could not hail the Judeo-Christian values that would have annihilated their captors. Worldwide abortion is today's killing fields, and genocide and human trafficking are rampant in places whose names most Americans cannot pronounce. You must pray for their freedom and preservation, and never compromise your Christian beliefs. Be charitable to the poor, be gentle with the Earth's environment, and be conservative in criticism and liberal in affection. Confess your sinfulness, never prostitute your conscience, tell your neighbor good morning; cry if you must, laugh when you can, and pray that the Lord helps you make sense of it all. I tell you that He is looking for a spiritual attraction to the Earth that is reminiscent of Jesus' Bethlehem Nativity that drew so many humble men to the seed of righteousness, Incarnate in a newborn Child. He was rejected among them because He bore the message of self-sacrifice and the preservation of Truth. In His lineage, once you present your Christian works before humanity, be prepared to be skewered, impugned, misquoted, ostracized, heckled, ridiculed, and despised. You will begin to wonder how you could not have foreseen that human beings were capable of such hatred. There will be such backlash that you will even question your own capacity to survive. You will be labeled as the dregs of the Earth and endure the appalling betrayal of your friends. Pockets of resistance that you knew you could sustain in stages will instead hit you all at once. You must remember that Satan is against everything that is good, righteous, holy, and salvific. He is anti-Christian, anti-family, anti-American, and stubborn in the pursuit of breaking down anything that is pure and conciliatory. You do not need to summon the services of a Trappist theologian to recognize his gruesome signature. What will you do with your doleful emotions when wicked sinners and their evil works attack you? Come to your Holy Mother! Make your devotion to Me an abiding part of your faith in Jesus with your expectation to see the Father in the company of all the loved-ones you have buried throughout the annals of time. Tell your enemies who doubt the existence of the Lord that you have undeniable evidence that He has come, and they have only vague opinions that He has not. Tear down their resistance with the indomitable strength of the Holy Spirit living in your hearts.

My Special son, I bid you happiness and joy on the Feast of Christmas; and please share these sentiments with your brother. I am aware that the arrival of the 22nd of the month holds special meaning for you, and today is the designation of such a moment. You will presently reach twelve years since you first accepted the awful burden of becoming My messengers, and I promise that Jesus does not take this sacrifice lightly. Indeed, the work you are continuing today to speak of My Maternal advocacy is an example. Can you see why it is so urgent for Christians to call on the intercession of the Angels? It is their duty to seek the responses that will assist your prescience to anticipate the

Glory of Paradise, the beauty of your Savior, and His Imminent Return to His earthly domain. You are reoriented to the intercession of the Holy Spirit by the Angels, and you sense what this means for those who pray. I speak gently to allow the solace of this Season to fall upon the Earth as quietly as it did in Bethlehem. I have appreciation for everything you are doing for Jesus. With His Peace and Joy, I pray that the future will bring that certain visible response to your writings that you have sought for the comfort of your heart. You should realize that there is a certain amount of seclusion in other people's lives where they are reluctant to reveal how they feel. Please do not see this as a sign of indifference or disdain that they are concealing from you. Most Christians are contemplative among themselves, and are extremely grateful that God is visiting them through the prayers, holy works, and servitude of humble souls like you and your brother. Please dedicate your lives to the things I have asked, and you will achieve good results.

Jesus is pleased that you are taking time to allow the Truth to emerge. It is important for you to remember that as a Christian, you are required to make such declarations a part of life without recompense. Again, let time expire, and you will see the Fruits of the Holy Spirit thriving through your works. This has been a productive year for furthering the message of Christianity by apostolates such as yours. There is no doubt that 2002 will enter the annals of history as being one of the most fruit-bearing you have lived. I urge you to pray intensely for the world as 2003 unfolds because it will bring great devastation upon many innocent lives. You will also arrive at the anniversary of the decision by the U.S. Supreme Court allowing the killing of millions of little children in their mothers' wombs at the end of the eleventh year and eleventh month of your messages. I know that you are praying along with everyone with a Christian conscience for this scourge to end, that future victims will be provided a reprieve from murderous hands, and that Jesus will bring to Justice those who are responsible for doing such evil. This is why it is so important that *Babes in the Woods* be laid bare for the public record before the end of May, as it carries the urgent message of spiritual conversion for everyone involved. And, 2003 will also bring many happy things to your days, to the comfort you enjoy here at home, and for all the reasons why God gave you life over 41 years ago. I beseech you to remember to the depths of your heart that His Love has become your gladness, that you will forever live beneath the arbor of His Grace. Do not be afraid! This is the continuous call that Jesus makes to those who yearn to repose in His sacred presence! You realize, therefore, that these are special times for you and your brother. Thank you for consenting to participate in them. Whereupon you have attended the Holy Sacrifice of the Mass on Christmas, you may spend the day together at home eating your prepared meal, relaxing, giving thanks for your lives, and praying for the conversion of the Earth. This does not imply that you cannot continue your writing at your discretion. I will speak to you and your brother once more prior to the conclusion of 2002."

December 29, 2002
Sunday of the Octave of Christmas
Feast of the Holy Family
2:22 p.m.

"My little children, I wish to speak only for a few moments—only for time-sufficient to tell you that My Love for you is as wholly and Holy profound today as it was when we began our intense work for Jesus many years ago. Therefore, I come to you in an appreciative tone to offer you the thanksgiving of the Lord, to assure you that neither time nor circumstance can divide or separate you from Him now. You have been the warriors for a Kingdom of Holiness that is only now growing wider because of your dedication. This will be My final message of 2002, but I assure you there will be as many as the Almighty Father will allow into the future. What can be said of 2002? It would never be improper to tell you that the world is more shapely in Divine Love by your works and prayers. I assure you that your piety and service have borne the fruit of consolation for tens of thousands of agonizing souls, the food of compassion for innocent priests around the world, and the first step for millions more on their pathway back to Grace. You live in a nation that is yet celebrating the Octave of Christmas, but is speaking of war—military aggression against foreign lands such as Afghanistan, Iraq, and North Korea, and this only days past the celebration of Christmas. How ironic it is that your country celebrates the anniversary of the Prince of Peace by coveting warfare as a means of international diplomacy, so much so that your government is now wishing to reshape the steel from the fallen World Trade Center Towers into a brand new warship named the USS New York. All the talk about world peace from the United States is a hollow lie. You only wish to conquer the enemies of your own consumerism, materialism, your assumed right to strip your unborn children of the gift of life, and to placate those who refuse to stand-up to your obstinance against the Commandments of God. This, My children, is the legacy of America for 2002, but your work here for the King of Love, My Jesus, has been the mitigation of many ills. I have been praying with you while you have written your memoirs about your obedience to Me, about the righteousness that needs to come to your land if it is ever to be the likeness of Paradise.

My commendation transcends your physical works on behalf of God to include the meditations of your hearts and the words of your mouths which have been the instruction of sinners in the ways of Wisdom. I beg you with a Motherly pleading to not give-up the fight now. I am with you for all and everything that is of God. I hold you dear to My Immaculate Heart for all the reasons you have been Baptized into the Catholic faith. Indeed, I will be with you through the end of time and upon your entrance into Heaven to live with

Me and all the Saints, cast brilliantly inside and within the Divine Domain of the Holy Trinity. Providence has you doing these things with Me because you are creatures of a Love so omnipotent that you cannot escape the breadth of God's grasp. You belong to Him and He to you in this Love, so that by waking to every new dawn with your mission for Him in your hearts and spread across the expanse of your thoughts, your lives are the living legend of the conversion of the entirety of humankind. Let there be no mistake—the Holy Spirit has done this in you, and I have been your advocate before Jesus to keep your Love aright. There is no weakening in the resolve of the blessed—although there may be dark moments sometimes—your goals and objectives are clearly to the enlightenment of Creation to its Eternal Redemption in the Blood of the Cross. All of this will live well beyond your own mortal days, past the closure of the ages, and into the infinity which is the power of God. You share it now within the parameters of time because you are the contemporary Saints who are expressing the Will of God to the modern mortal world. I tell you again that there are things you cannot comprehend about the actions of other men, but the Sacred Mysteries of the meaning of human life have all become clear to you now. Thank you for rendering your writings about the Kingdom I have tried to describe to you only in words, for your profound expressions have become the way in which untold millions of people are returning to God.

My Special son, I thank you, I thank you, I thank you. I know not what else to say. My Love for you and your brother has no boundaries, and all the adjectives in your language still leave Me speechless as to describe how you are blessed. There are still so many things to do, so many more words and sentences to connect in the process of bringing the knowledge of God to your fellow men. It is all in you now, and it will come out if only you will disregard the seemingly everlasting dailiness of human life. There is only one more mountain that you need to climb, and it is the very sorrow that keeps you from understanding what I am telling you with greater revelation. There is peace in the world, but humanity will not search for it. There also is healing, consolation, international cooperation, and Divine courage. You and your brother are helping My many other messengers around the globe to make clear the good faith of Jesus to deliver His people to the New Jerusalem with their absolved souls intact. We seek for this to occur earlier rather than later, and with their contrition rather than their arrogance. But, you can see wherein lies the fight when things are not this way. You have already won, and you will win. Jesus has already returned, but not yet. Therefore, go into 2003 with the realization that you have lifted your feet onto the next higher step toward the transformation of the Earth into the likeness of Heaven. I shall never remove My protective Mantle from above your souls or your very lives because you belong to Me. You are My living possessions. You, indeed, are My children. And, I am your Immaculate Mother whose Love knows no end; My determination has nothing in Creation to block My success, and the dreams you hold for the future world will all come true in the Triumph of My Immaculate Heart. I do not tell you these things to give you false hope or to somehow get you through the darkness of night without really telling you the Truth. My messages to you for nearly twelve years have been candid and open. I have reprimanded both you and your brother when the occasions were ripe, and I have given you praise over all other things. And, this is the reason I have come to you briefly today, to give you the prime assurance that your God is pleased with you. Thank you, again, for responding to My call. I know you are happy to be in Love with Him... You are the champion caretaker of the greatest nobility. This is now your holy blessing. ✛ I will speak to you again very soon! Thank you! Please remember to pray for the unborn, for the end of poverty and disease, and for all the other petitions we both hold so close to My Son. I Love you! Goodnight!"

The Morning Star of Our Lord, Incorporated
Other Available Titles

In Our Darkest Hour
Morning Star Over America
February 22, 1991 - December 31, 1992
Volume I

In Our Darkest Hour
Morning Star Over America
January 1, 1993 - February 22, 1997
Volume II

At the Water's Edge
Essays in Faith and Morals

When Legends Rise Again
The Convergence of Capitalism and Christianity

White Collar Witch Hunt
The Catholic Priesthood Under Siege

Babes in the Woods
With a Little Child to Guide Them

To Crispen Courage
The Divine Annihilation

Supernal Chambers
A Resurrection Prayer

See copyright page for ordering information.

www.ingramcontent.com/pod-product-compliance
Lightning Source LLC
Chambersburg PA
CBHW070715160426
43192CB00009B/1191